Fodor's

CITYGUIDE
SAN FRANCISCO

(handwritten notes)
Pager 510
389 0521

4/00 510 893 2549

Work 987 9471

Barns Pager
773 251
2360

FODOR'S TRAVEL PUBLICATIONS, INC.

NEW YORK • TORONTO • LONDON • SYDNEY • AUCKLAND

WWW.FODORS.COM/

Handwritten annotations: Sully 740 Cabrillo SF 94118

Handwritten: 415 386 6873

Handwritten: gtone @ pacbell.net

MARIN COUNTY

Brooks Island

Marin City

Richardson Bay

Tiburon

ANGEL ISLAND STATE PARK

GOLDEN GATE NATIONAL RECREATION AREA

Sausalito

Golden Gate Bridge (Toll)

Alcatraz Island

Treasure Island

San Francisco-Oakland Bay Bridge (Toll)

2

Golden

Gate

Bay St.

Van Ness Ave.

California St.

Geary St.

Market

Fulton St.

GOLDEN GATE PARK

Great Hwy.

19th Ave.

SAN FRANCISCO

3rd St.

Hunter's Point

Southern Fwy.

Mission St.

McLAREN PARK

Lake Merced

Bayshore Fwy.

Candlestick Point

SAN BRUNO STATE PARK

Daly City

Hillside Blvd.

Colma

Skyline Blvd.

El Camino Real

Grand Ave.

South San Francisco

Pacifica

GOLDEN GATE NATL. REC. AREA

San Bruno

San Francisco International Airport

Millbrae

Burlingame

San Andreas Lake

Hillsborough

SAN PEDRO VALLEY COUNTY PARK

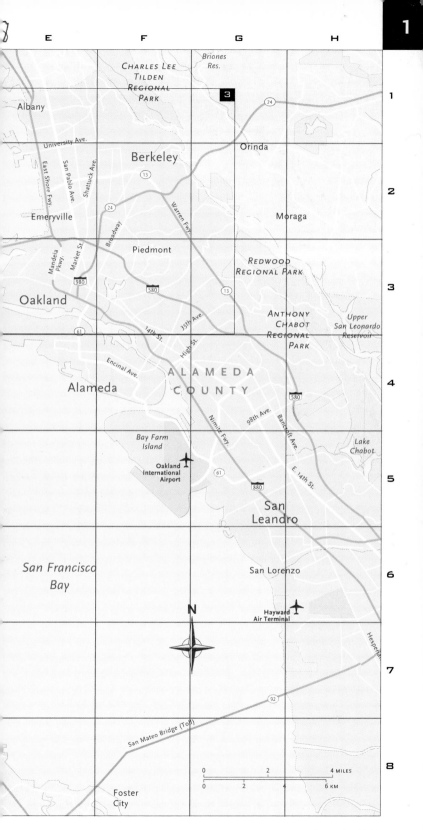

E   F   G   H

1

CHARLES LEE TILDEN REGIONAL PARK

Briones Res.

Albany

3

24

University Ave.

Berkeley

Orinda

13

2

East Shore Fwy.

San Pablo Ave.

Shattuck Ave.

24

Warren Fwy.

Emeryville

Moraga

Mandela Pkwy.

Market St.

Broadway

Piedmont

REDWOOD REGIONAL PARK

980

580

13

3

Oakland

61

14th St.

35th Ave.

ANTHONY CHABOT REGIONAL PARK

Upper San Leonardo Reservoir

High St.

Encinal Ave.

ALAMEDA

580

4

Alameda

COUNTY

98th Ave.

Bancroft Ave.

Lake Chabot

Nimitz Fwy.

Bay Farm Island

Oakland International Airport

61

880

E. 14th St.

5

San Leandro

San Francisco Bay

San Lorenzo

6

N

Hayward Air Terminal

Hesperian

7

92

8

San Mateo Bridge (Toll)

0		2		4 MILES
0	2	4		6 KM

Foster City

THE BAY AREA

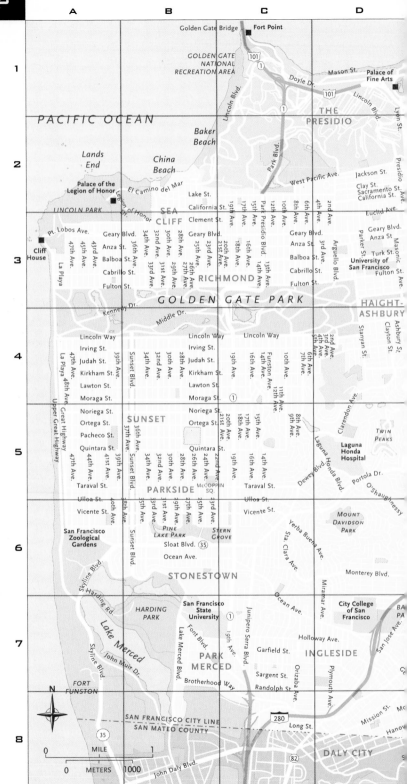

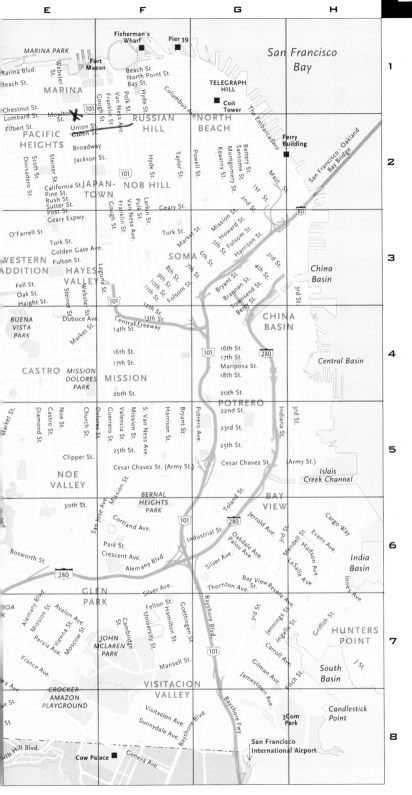

1

MARINA PARK

Marina Blvd.

Beach St.

Fisherman's Wharf

Fort Mason

Pier 39

Beach St.

North Point St.

Bay St.

Columbus Ave.

TELEGRAPH HILL

Coit Tower

San Francisco Bay

Webster St.

MARINA

Chestnut St.

Lombard St.

Filbert St.

PACIFIC HEIGHTS

Broadway

Jackson St.

Moulton St.

Union St.

Green St.

Van Ness Ave.

Franklin St.

Gough St.

Polk St.

Hyde St.

RUSSIAN HILL

NORTH BEACH

Battery St.

Sansome St.

Montgomery St.

Kearny St.

1st St.

2nd St.

Main St.

The Embarcadero

Ferry Building

San Francisco - Oakland Bay Bridge

2

Scott St.

Divisadero St.

Steiner St.

California St.

Pine St.

Bush St.

Sutter St.

Post St.

Geary Expwy.

JAPAN-TOWN

NOB HILL

Hyde St.

Taylor St.

Powell St.

Larkin St.

Polk St.

Van Ness Ave.

Franklin St.

Gough St.

Geary St.

80

3

O'Farrell St.

WESTERN ADDITION

Turk St.

Golden Gate Ave.

Fulton St.

HAYES VALLEY

Fell St.

Oak St.

Haight St.

Steiner St.

Webster St.

Laguna St.

Turk St.

Market St.

SOMA

8th St.

9th St.

10th St.

11th St.

7th St.

6th St.

5th St.

Folsom St.

Mission St.

Howard St.

Folsom St.

Harrison St.

Bryant St.

Brannan St.

Townsend St.

Berry St.

3rd St.

4th St.

3rd St.

China Basin

BUENA VISTA PARK

Duboce Ave.

Market St.

12th St.

13th St.

14th St.

Central Freeway

CHINA BASIN

4

CASTRO

MISSION DOLORES PARK

MISSION

16th St.

17th St.

20th St.

16th St.

17th St.

Mariposa St.

18th St.

20th St.

101

280

Central Basin

Market St.

Castro St.

Diamond St.

Noe St.

Church St.

Dolores St.

Guerrero St.

Valencia St.

Mission St.

S. Van Ness Ave.

Harrison St.

Bryant St.

Potrero Ave.

Indiana St.

3rd St.

POTRERO

22nd St.

23rd St.

25th St.

Cesar Chavez St.

(Army St.)

Islais Creek Channel

5

Clipper St.

NOE VALLEY

Cesar Chavez St. (Army St.)

30th St.

San Jose Ave.

Mission St.

BERNAL HEIGHTS PARK

Cortland Ave.

Park St.

Crescent Ave.

Alemany Blvd.

101

Toland St.

Industrial St.

280

Jerrold Ave.

Oakdale Ave.

Palou Ave.

Silver Ave.

BAY VIEW

Mendell St.

Hudson Ave.

La Salle Ave.

Evans Ave.

Cargo Way

India Basin

Innes Ave.

6

Bosworth St.

280

Silver Ave.

GLEN PARK

Thornton Ave.

Bay View St.

Revere Ave.

Alemany Blvd.

Mission St.

Avalon Ave.

Vienna St.

Moscow St.

Persia Ave.

France Ave.

BOA

Cambridge St.

Felton St.

University St.

Hamilton St.

Coettingen St.

Bayshore Blvd.

JOHN McLAREN PARK

Mansell St.

Jennings St.

Ingalls St.

Carroll Ave.

Gilman Ave.

Jamestown Ave.

3rd St.

Griffith St.

J St.

HUNTERS POINT

South Basin

7

France Ave.

CROCKER-AMAZON PLAYGROUND

VISITACION VALLEY

101

Visitacion Ave.

Sunnydale Ave.

Bayshore Blvd.

Bayshore Fwy.

3Com Park

Candlestick Point

8

uth Hill Blvd.

Cow Palace

Geneva Ave.

San Francisco International Airport

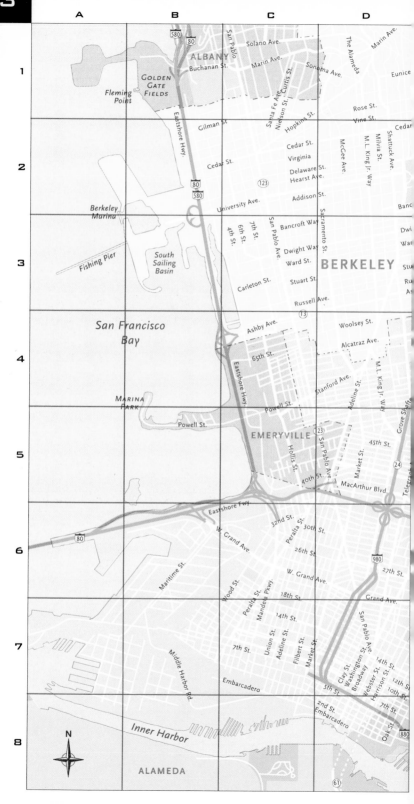

STREETFINDER

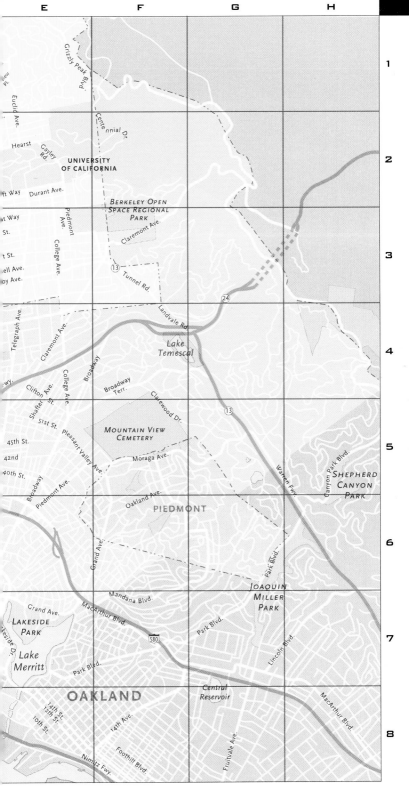

E   F   G   H

1
2
3
4
5
6
7
8

Grizzly Peak Blvd.

Centennial Dr.

Euclid Ave.

Hearst

Cayley Rd.

UNIVERSITY OF CALIFORNIA

ft Way   Durant Ave.

Piedmont Ave.

at Way

St.

Claremont Ave.

BERKELEY OPEN SPACE REGIONAL PARK

t St.

College Ave.

ell Ave.

13

by Ave.

Tunnel Rd.

24

Telegraph Ave.

Claremont Ave.

Landvale Rd.

Lake Temescal

wy.

Clifton Ave.

College Ave.

Broadway

Broadway Terr.

Shafter St.

51st St.

Clarewood Dr.

13

45th St.

Pleasant Valley Ave.

MOUNTAIN VIEW CEMETERY

42nd

Moraga Ave.

40th St.

Broadway

Piedmont Ave.

Oakland Ave.

PIEDMONT

Warren Fwy.

Canyon Park Blvd.

SHEPHERD CANYON PARK

Grand Ave.

Park Blvd.

JOAQUIN MILLER PARK

Mandana Blvd.

MacArthur Blvd.

Grand Ave.

LAKESIDE PARK

Park Blvd.

580

Lincoln Blvd.

es de Dr.

Lake Merritt

Park Blvd.

OAKLAND

14th St.

12th St.

10th St.

14th Ave.

Central Reservoir

Fruitvale Ave.

MacArthur Blvd.

Foothill Blvd.

Nimitz Fwy.

BERKELEY AND OAKLAND

A B C D

1

GOLDEN GATE
RECREATION AREA

Municipal Pier

Pier 45
Pier 47
Fisherman's
Wharf

Pier 43½ Pier 43 Pier 41

East
Harbor

Aquatic Park

FORT
MASON

Mexican
Museum

Maritime
Museum

FISHERMAN'S
WHARF

2

Gashouse
Cove

Marina Blvd.

North Point St.

Bay St.

GHIRARDELLI
SQUARE

RUSSIAN
HILL PARK

San Francisco
Art Institute

Jefferson St.
Beach St.
North Point St.
Bay St.

Jones St.
Taylor St.
Mason St.
Powell St.

Francisco St.
Water St.
Vandewater St.

Chestnut St.

GEORGE R.
MOSCONE
RECREATION
CENTER

Francisco St.
Chestnut St.

Magnolia St.
101
Lombard St.

Moulton St.
Greenwich St.
Harris Pl.
Pixley St.
Filbert St.
Webster St.
Buchanan St.

Gough St.
Jackson St.
Franklin St.
Imperial
Van Ness Ave.

Lombard St.
Polk St.
Larkin St.
Hyde St.
Leavenworth St.

Lombard St.
Greenwich St.
Filbert St.
Union
Green

Filbert St.
Union St.

RUSSIAN
HILL

Mason St.
Taylor St.

COOLBRITH
PARK

Valley

UNION
STREET
X
Union St.

Green St.

Octavia St.

Bonita St.
Vallejo St.

White St.
Waldo Al.
Clover

Green St.

Broadway Tunnel
Bernard St.
Pacific Ave.

Broa

3

4

Broadway

Pacific Ave.

Jackson St.

101
Broadway
Pacific Ave.
Jackson St.

Lynch St.
Wall St.

Jackson St.

Cable Car
Barn

WEBSTER ST.
HISTORIC
DISTRICT

Jackson St.

Washington St.

Washington St.

Clay St.

Pacific
Med. Ctr.

LAFAYETTE
PARK

Washington St.
Clay St.
Sacramento St.
California St.

Troy Al.

Hyde St.

HUNTINGTON
PARK

Clay St.

Jones St.
Taylor St.

NO

5

Buchanan St.
Laguna St.
Webster St.
Orben Pl.

California St.
Gough St.
Franklin St.

Van Ness Ave.

Pine St.
Frank Norris St.
Bush St.

Leavenworth St.

6

Wilmot St.
Cottage Row

Octavia St.

Fern St.
Sutter St.
101
Hemlock St.
Post St.
Cedar St.
Geary St.

Maxfield

Larkin St.
Hyde St.
Leavenworth St.
Jones St.

Cosmo Pl.
Colin Pl.
Stanton St.
Duncan
Derby

O'Farrell St.
Ellis St.
Eddy

Japanese Cultural
& Trade Center

Geary St.
ST. FRANCIS
SQUARE

Cleary Ct.

St. Mary's
Cathedral

Myrtle St.
Olive St.
Ellis St.
Willow St.

Polk St.

Eddy St.

Turk St.

7

Webster St.
Hollis
Ellis St.
Willow St.

Eddy St.
Turk St.
Golden Gate Ave.
McAllister St.

WESTERN
ADDITION

JEFFERSON
SQUARE

Laguna St.
Gough St.
Franklin St.

Larch St.
Turk St.
Elm St.
Golden Gate Ave.
Redwood St.
McAllister St.

Van Ness Ave.

CIVIC
CENTER

CIVIC
CENTER

EAST MARK

Main Post
Office
7th St.

Market St.

8

Fillmore St.

Fulton St.
Grove St.
Hayes St.

HAYES
VALLEY

Western
Addition
Cultural Ctr.

Birch St.
Octavia St.
Linden St.
101
Hickory St.

Ivy St.
Hayes St.
Fell St.
Hickory St.
Oak St.
Lily St.
Page St.
Rose St.

Lech Walesa

Grove St.

9th St.
10th St.
11th St.

Stevenson

Mission St.
Minna St.
Natoma St.
Howard St.
Tehama St.
Clementina St.
Folsom St.
Ringold

8th St.

Steiner St.
Fillmore St.
Fell St.
Oak St.

Hayes St.
Fell St.
Hickory St.
Oak St.
Lily St.

Jessie
Grace St.
Minna St.
Natoma St.
Washburn St.
Dore St.

DOWNTOWN SAN FRANCISCO

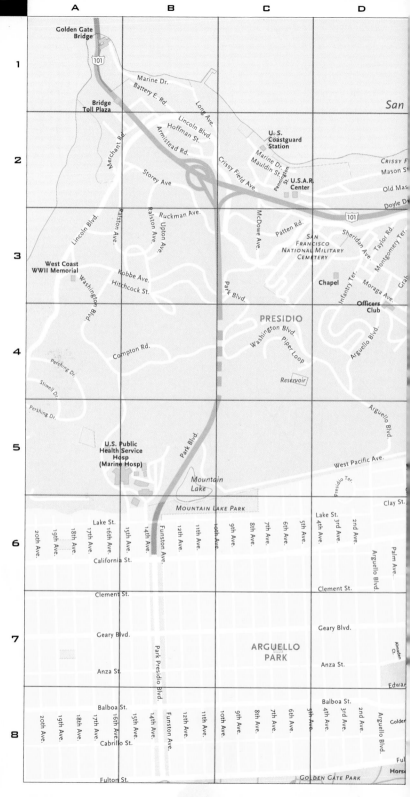

5

A   B   C   D

Golden Gate
Bridge

101

Marine Dr.

Battery E. Rd

Long Ave.

San

Bridge
Toll Plaza

Lincoln Blvd.

Hoffman St.

Armistead Rd.

U. S.
Coastguard
Station

Merchant Rd.

Storey Ave.

Crissy Field Ave.

Marine Dr.
Mauldin St.

Pennington

CRISSY F

Mason St

Old Mas

U.S.A.R.
Center

Lincoln Blvd.

Ralston Ave.

Ralston Ave.

Ruckman Ave.

Upton Ave.

McDowe Ave.

Patten Rd.

Doyle Dr

101

San
Francisco
NATIONAL MILITARY
CEMETERY

Sheridan Ave.

Taylor Rd.

Montgomery Ter.

West Coast
WWII Memorial

Kobbe Ave.

Hitchcock St.

Park Blvd.

Chapel

Infantry Ter.

Moraga Ave.

Gra

Washington Blvd.

Officers
Club

PRESIDIO

Compton Rd.

Washington Blvd

Piper Loop

Arguello Blvd.

Pershing Dr.

Stilwell Dr.

Reservoir

Pershing Dr.

Park Blvd.

Arguello Blvd.

U.S. Public
Health Service
Hosp
(Marine Hosp)

West Pacific Ave.

Presidio Ter.

Clay St.

Mountain
Lake

MOUNTAIN LAKE PARK

Lake St.

California St.

Clement St.

Geary Blvd.

Anza St.

**ARGUELLO
PARK**

20th Ave.

19th Ave.

18th Ave.

17th Ave.

16th Ave.

15th Ave.

14th Ave.

Funston Ave.

12th Ave.

11th Ave.

10th Ave.

9th Ave.

8th Ave.

7th Ave.

6th Ave.

5th Ave.

4th Ave.

3rd Ave.

2nd Ave.

Arguello Blvd

Palm Ave.

Clement St.

Geary Blvd.

Anza St.

Alameda Ct.

Edwar

Park Presidio Blvd.

Balboa St.

Cabrillo St.

Balboa St.

Arguello Blvd.

Golden

Ful

Horse

20th Ave.

19th Ave.

18th Ave.

17th Ave.

16th Ave.

15th Ave.

14th Ave.

Funston Ave.

12th Ave.

11th Ave.

10th Ave.

9th Ave.

8th Ave.

7th Ave.

6th Ave.

5th Ave.

4th Ave.

3rd Ave.

2nd Ave.

Fulton St.

GOLDEN GATE PARK

STREETFINDER

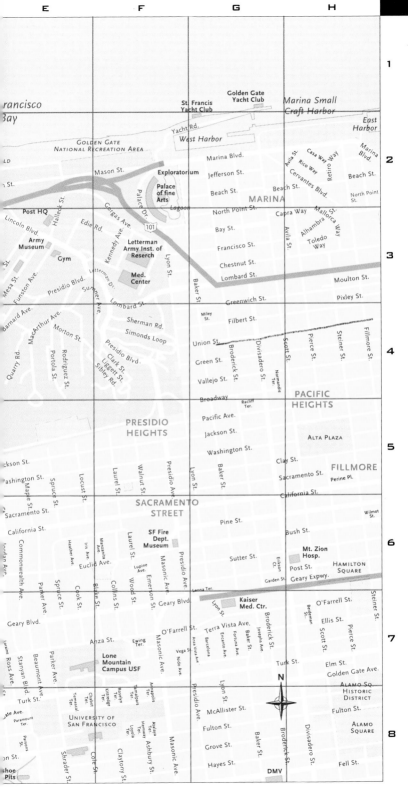

E   **F**   **G**   **H**

1

rancisco
Bay

Golden Gate
Yacht Club

St. Francis
Yacht Club

Marina Small
Craft Harbor

East
Harbor

GOLDEN GATE
NATIONAL RECREATION AREA

Yacht Rd.
West Harbor

Marina
Blvd.

Avila St.
Casa Way Way
Rico Way
Retiro Way

Beach St.

2

LD

Mason St.

Marina Blvd.

Jefferson St.

Cervantes Blvd.

North Point
St.

n St.

Exploratorium

Palace
of fine
Arts

Beach St.

Beach St.

MARINA

Post HQ

Lincoln Blvd

Hallec St.

Gorgas Ave.

Palace Dr.

Lagoon

North Point St.

Capra Way

Mallorca Way

Mallorca St.

Edie Rd.

Kennedy Ave.

101

Bay St.

Avila St.

Alhambra
St.

Toledo
Way

Army
Museum

Gym

Letterman
Army Inst. of
Reserch

Lyon St.

Francisco St.

Chestnut St.

Mesa St.

Presidio Blvd.

Sumner Ave.

Letterman Dr.

Med.
Center

Lombard St.

Lombard St.

Baker St.

Moulton St.

3

barnard Ave.

Funston Ave.

MacArthur Ave.

Morton St.

Sherman Rd.

Simonds Loop

Greenwich St.

Pixley St.

Miley
St.

Filbert St.

Quarry Rd.

Rodriguez St.

Portola St.

Presidio Blvd.

Clark Ave.

Liggett St.

Sibley Rd.

Union St.

Broderick St.

Divisadero St.

Scott St.

Pierce St.

Steiner St.

Fillmore St.

4

Green St.

Vallejo St.

Normande
Ter.

Broadway

Racliff
Ter.

PACIFIC
HEIGHTS

PRESIDIO
HEIGHTS

Pacific Ave.

Jackson St.

Washington St.

ALTA PLAZA

5

ckson St.

ashington St.

Maple St.

Spruce St.

Locust St.

Laurel St.

Walnut St.

Presidio Ave.

Lyon St.

Baker St.

Clay St.

Sacramento St.

FILLMORE

Perine Pl.

Sacramento St.

California St.

Wilmot
St.

Sacramento St.

California St.

SACRAMENTO
STREET

Pine St.

Bush St.

6

California St.

Commonwealth Ave.

Jordan Ave.

Heather Ave.

Iris Ave.

Manzanita Ave.

Laurel St.

SF Fire
Dept.
Museum

Presidio Ave.

Sutter St.

Erickson
Ct.

Mt. Zion
Hosp.

Post St.

Geary Expwy.

HAMILTON
SQUARE

Parker Ave.

Spruce St.

Cook St.

Blake St.

Euclid Ave.

Lupine
Ave.

Emerson St.

Masonic Ave.

Wood St.

Garden St.

Leona Ter.

Kaiser
Med. Ctr.

Bedeman
St.

O'Farrell St.

Steiner St.

Geary Blvd.

Geary Blvd.

Lyon St.

Broderick St.

Ellis St.

Scott St.

Pierce St.

7

Anza St.

Ewing
Ter.

O'Farrell St.

Masonic Ave.

Vega St.

Niño Ave.

Terra Vista Ave.

Anza Vista Ave.

Barcelona

Encanto Ave.

Fortuna Ave.

Baker St.

Josepha Ave.

Turk St.

Elm St.

Golden Gate Ave.

Parker Ave.

Beaumont Ave.

Staryan Ave.

Lorraine Ross Ave.

Lone Mountain
Campus USF

ALAMO SQ.
HISTORIC
DISTRICT

Turk St.

Gate Ave.

Paramount
Ter.

Parsons
St.

Chabot
Ter.

Temescal
Ter.

Kittredge
Ter.

Roselyn
Ter.

Tamalpais
Ter.

Annapolis
Ter.

Hemway
Ter.

Anzalya
Ter.

Loyola
Ter.

Presidio Ave.

McAllister St.

Fulton St.

ALAMO
SQUARE

8

on St.

shoe
Pits

Shrader St.

UNIVERSITY OF
SAN FRANCISCO

Cole St.

Claytony St.

Ashbury St.

Masonic Ave.

Fulton St.

Grove St.

Hayes St.

Baker St.

Broderick St.

Divisadero St.

Fell St.

N

DMV

THE PRESIDIO AND RICHMOND DISTRICT

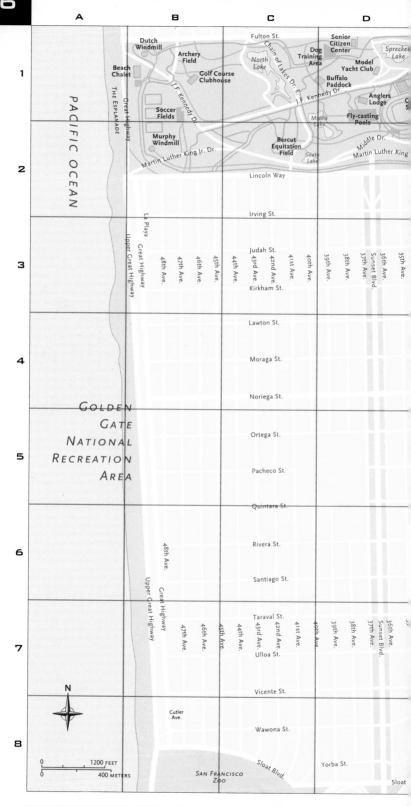

6

PACIFIC OCEAN

THE ESPLANADE

Great Highway

Upper Great Highway

GOLDEN GATE NATIONAL RECREATION AREA

Dutch Windmill
Beach Chalet
Archery Field
Golf Course Clubhouse
J.F. Kennedy Dr.
Soccer Fields
Murphy Windmill
Martin Luther King Jr. Dr.

Fulton St.
Chain of Lakes Dr. E.
North Lake
Dog Training Area
Senior Citizen Center
Spreckels Lake
Model Yacht Club
Buffalo Paddock
J.F. Kennedy Dr.
Anglers Lodge
Middle Lake
Fly-casting Pools
Bercut Equitation Field
South Lake
Middle Dr.
Martin Luther King

Lincoln Way

La Playa
Great Highway
Upper Great Highway

Irving St.

Judah St.
48th Ave.
47th Ave.
46th Ave.
45th Ave.
44th Ave.
43rd Ave.
42nd Ave.
41st Ave.
40th Ave.
39th Ave.
38th Ave.
37th Ave.
Sunset Blvd.
36th Ave.
35th Ave.
Kirkham St.

Lawton St.

Moraga St.

Noriega St.

Ortega St.

Pacheco St.

Quintara St.

48th Ave.
Upper Great Highway
Great Highway

Rivera St.

Santiago St.

Taraval St.
47th Ave.
46th Ave.
45th Ave.
44th Ave.
43rd Ave.
42nd Ave.
41st Ave.
40th Ave.
39th Ave.
38th Ave.
37th Ave.
Sunset Blvd.
36th Ave.
Ulloa St.

Vicente St.

N

Cutler Ave.

Wawona St.

Sloat Blvd.
Yorba St.

| 0 | | 1200 FEET |
| 0 | | 400 METERS |

SAN FRANCISCO ZOO

Sloat

STREETFINDER

E   F   G   H

Spreckels Lake Dr.   Cross Over D

Marx
Meadow

Redwood
Memorial
Grove

J.F. Kennedy Dr.   Lloyd
Lake   Boat
House

Transverse Dr.

Lindley
Meadow

Barbecue
Pits   Pioneer
Log Cabin

1

lden Gate
k Stables

Speedway
Meadow   Cross Over Dr.   Stow Lake Dr.

en Gate Park
um Football
Polo Field   GOLDEN GATE PARK   Strawberry
Hill   Stow Lake

Metson
Lake   El Glen
Lake

Mallard
Lake   Middle Dr.   Martin Luther King Jr. Dr.

Metson Rd.

Lincoln Way   Lincoln Way   2

Irving St.   Irving St.

Judah St.   3

33rd Ave.   32nd Ave.   31st Ave.   30th Ave.   29th Ave.   28th Ave.   27th Ave.   26th Ave.   25th Ave.   24th Ave.   23rd Ave.   22nd Ave.   21st Ave.   20th Ave.   19th Ave.   18th Ave.   17th Ave.   16th Ave.   15th Ave.   14th Ave.

34th Ave.

Kirkham St.   Kirkham St.

Lawton St.   Lawton St.   Lawton St.

Lawton St.

Aloha Ave.

Lomita Ave.   Aloha Ave.

SUNSET
REC.
CENTER   GRAND
VIEW
PARK

Moraga St.   Moraga St.   4

SUNSET

DISTRICT   Noriega St.   Noriega St.

14th Ave.

Ortega St.   Ortega St.

Sunset
Reservoir   Pacheco St.   5

Pacheco St.

19th Ave.   18th Ave.   17th Ave.   16th Ave.   15th Ave.   14th Ave.

Quintara St.   Quintara St.

Rivera St.   Rivera St.   6

Cecilia Ave.

Santiago St.   Santiago St.

McCOPPIN
SQUARE

Taraval St.   Ulloa St.   7

33rd Ave.   32nd Ave.   31st Ave.   30th Ave.   29th Ave.   28th Ave.   27th Ave.   26th Ave.   25th Ave.   24th Ave.   23rd Ave.   22nd Ave.   21st Ave.   20th Ave.   19th Ave.   18th Ave.   17th Ave.   16th Ave.   15th Ave.   14th Ave.

34th Ave.

LARSEN PARK

Vicente St.   Vicente St.

Escolta W   PARKSIDE
SQUARE   Wawona St.   8

Wawona St.   Wawona St.

Laguna
Puerca   PINE LAKE PARK   STERN GROVE   West Portal Ave.

Crestlake Dr.

Yorba St.   Crestlake Dr.   Ardenwood Way   Portola Dr.   San Leandro Way

Crestlake Dr.   Constanso Way   Sloat Blvd.   San Rafael Way

d.

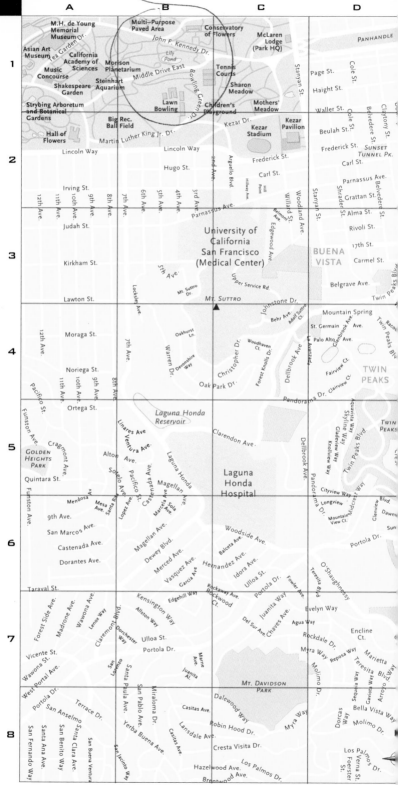

| | A | B | C | D |

M.H. de Young Memorial Museum

Asian Art Museum

California Academy of Sciences

Music Concourse

Morrison Planetarium

Steinhart Aquarium

Shakespeare Garden

Strybing Arboretum and Botanical Gardens

Hall of Flowers

Multi-Purpose Paved Area

Conservatory of Flowers

John F. Kennedy Dr.

Lily Pond

McLaren Lodge (Park HQ)

PANHANDLE

Tea Garden Dr.

Middle Drive East

Bowling Green Dr.

Tennis Courts

Sharon Meadow

Lawn Bowling

Children's Playground

Mothers' Meadow

Big Rec. Ball Field

Kezar Dr.

Kezar Stadium

Kezar Pavilion

Martin Luther King Jr. Dr.

Stanyan St.

Page St.

Cole St.

Haight St.

Waller St.

Cole St.

Beulah St.

Belvedere St.

Clayton St.

Frederick St. SUNSET TUNNEL Pk.

Lincoln Way

Lincoln Way

Hugo St.

2nd Ave.

Arguello Blvd.

Hillway Ave.

Frederick St.

Carl St.

Carl St.

Parnassus Ave.

Stanyan St.

Shrader St.

Grattan St.

Belvedere St.

1

2

Irving St.

12th Ave.

11th Ave.

10th Ave.

9th Ave.

8th Ave.

7th Ave.

6th Ave.

5th Ave.

4th Ave.

3rd Ave.

Parnassus Ave.

Judah St.

Kirkham St.

Lawton St.

5th Ave.

Locksley Ave.

Mt. Suttro Dr.

Upper Service Rd.

Mt. SUTTRO

University of California San Francisco (Medical Center)

Woodland Ave.

Willard St.

Belmont Ave.

Edgewood Ave.

Alma St.

Rivoli St.

17th St.

BUENA VISTA

Carmel St.

Belgrave Ave.

Twin

3

Moraga St.

12th Ave.

11th Ave.

10th Ave.

9th Ave.

8th Ave.

7th Ave.

Warren Dr.

Oakhurst Ln.

Devonshire Way

Christopher Dr.

Oak Park Dr.

Woodhaven Ct.

Forest Knolls Dr.

Johnstone Dr.

Behr Ave.

Adolf Suttro

Avanzada

Dellbrook Ave.

Mountain Spring

St. Germain Ave.

Glenbrook Ave.

Palo Alto Ave.

Fairview Ct.

Clairview Ct.

Pandorama Dr.

Racco

Twin Peaks Blv

Twin Peaks Blvd

TWIN PEAKS

Noriega St.

4

Pacifico St.

Funston Ave.

Cragmont Ave.

GOLDEN HEIGHTS PARK

Quintara St.

Ortega St.

Laguna Honda Reservoir

Linares Ave.

Ventura Ave.

Alton

Sotelo

Pacifico St.

Castenada Ave.

Magellan Ave.

Laguna Honda

Clarendon Ave.

Laguna Honda Hospital

Dellbrook Ave.

Pandorama Dr.

Aquavista Way

Skyline Way

Gladeview Way

Knollview Way

Cityview Way

Longview

Mountain View Ct.

TWIN PEAKS

Midcrest Way

Twin Peaks Blvd

Glenview

Blvd.

Dawn

Sun

5

Funston Ave.

Mendosa Ave.

Mesa Ave.

Santa Blvd.

Lopez Ave.

9th Ave.

San Marcos Ave.

Castenada Ave.

Dorantes Ave.

Taraval St.

Magellan Ave.

Dewey Blvd.

Merced Ave.

Vasquez Ave.

Garcia Ave.

Marcela Ave.

Sola Ave.

Woodside Ave.

Balceta Ave.

Hernandez Ave.

Idora Ave.

Ulloa St.

Portola Dr.

Fowler Ave.

Teresita Blvd

O'Shaughnessy

Portola Dr.

6

Forest Side Ave.

Madrone Ave.

Wawona Ave.

Lenox Way

Vicente St.

Wawona St.

West Portal Ave.

Claremont Blvd.

Dorchester Way

Kensington Way

Alliston Way

Ulloa St.

Portola Dr.

Rockaway Ave.

Edgehill Way

Rockwood Ct.

Del Sur Ave.

Chaves Ave.

Juanita Way

Agua Way

Rockdale Dr.

Myra Way

Evelyn Way

Encline Ct.

Reposa Way

Marietta

Teresita Blvd

Molimo Way

7

Portola Dr.

San Anselmo

Terrace Dr.

San Fernando Way

Santa Ana Ave.

San Benito Way

Santa Clara Ave.

San Buena Ventura Way

San Jacinto Way

Santa Paula Ave.

San Pablo Ave.

Miraloma Dr.

Yerba Buena Ave.

Casitas Ave.

Juanita Al.

Marne Al.

San Lorenzo

Casitas Ave.

Lansdale Ave.

Hazelwood Ave.

Dalewood Way

Robin Hood Dr.

Cresta Visita Dr.

Los Palmos Dr.

Brentwood Ave.

MT. DAVIDSON PARK

Myra Way

Molimo Dr.

Dorcas Way

Bella Vista Way

Molimo Dr.

Los Palmos Dr.

Teresita Blvd

Marietta Dr.

Verna St.

Foerster St.

8

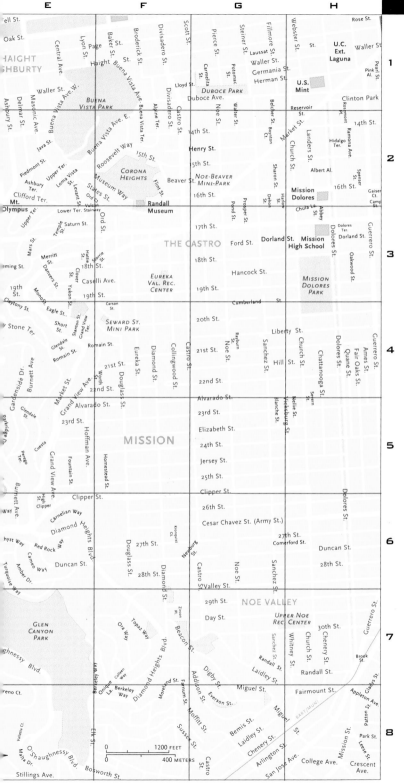

THE CASTRO, NOE VALLEY, AND THE MISSION (WEST)

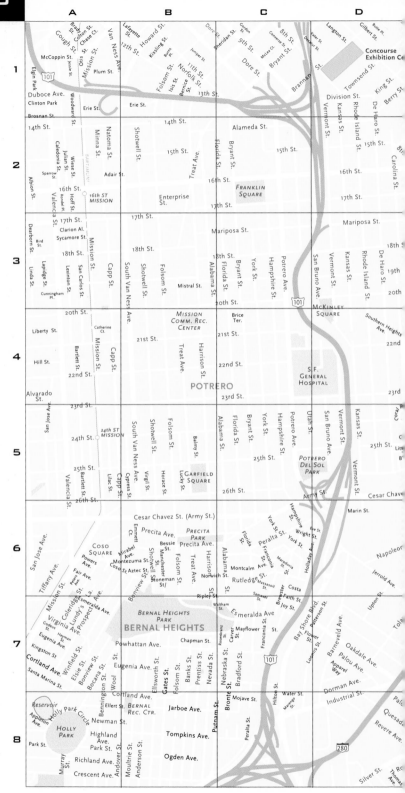

E   F   G   H

1

Channel St.

Mission Creek Marina

Mission Rock St.

3rd St.

7th St.

6th St.

Owens St.

Merrimac St.

Alameda St.

San Francisco Bay

Cooper St.

Irwin St.

Hubbell St.

Daggett St.

El Dorado St.

China Basin St.

2

16th St.

AGUA VISTA PARK

0   1200 FEET
0   400 METERS

Mariposa St.

Central Basin

Arkansas St.

Connecticut St.

Missouri St.

Texas St.

Mississippi St.

Pennsylvania Ave.

Minnesota St.

Tennessee St.

3rd St.

Michigan St.

3

20th St.

Wisconsin St.

Illinois St.

280

Sierra St.

4

POTRERO HILL REC. CENTER

Turner Ter.

Missouri St.

Watchman W.

Iowa St.

Indiana St.

22nd St.

Tubbs St.

N

Madera St.

23rd St.

Dakota St.

Texas St.

Mississippi St.

24th St.

3rd St.

Connecticut St.

5

25th St.

Missouri St.

Indiana St.

Minnesota St.

26th St.

26th St.

Cesar Chavez St. (Army St.)

(Army St.)

Tennessee St.

Illinois St.

Michigan St.

Evans Ave.

Marin st.

Marine St.

6

Toland St.

Tulare

Islais St.

Islais Creek Channel

Galvez Ave.

Hudson Ave.

Innes Ave.

Rankin St.

Custer

Davidson

Quint St.

Ave.

Evans Ave.

Amador St.

3rd St.

Burke Ave.

Cargo Way

HUNTERS POINT

7

PRODUCE DISTRICT

Kirkwood Ave.

Rankin St.

McKinnon Ave.

Newcomb Ave.

Quint St.

Evans Ave.

Fairfax Ave.

Galvez Ave.

Hudson Ave.

Newhall St.

Lane St.

ale Ave.

Drummond Al.

Phelps St.

Jerrold Ave.

Innes Ave.

Newhall St.

Kirkwood Ave.

La Salle Ave.

Keith St.

Jennings St.

8

Newcomb Ave.

Mendell St.

McKinnon Ave.

LEE REC. CTR.

Dukes Ct.

Young Ct.

Ridgards Ct.

Circle

Lindsey Circle

Mabrey Ct.

Hillview Ct.

Hawkins La.

Hudson Ave.

Reuel Ct.

Westbrook Ct.

West Pt. Rd.

Middle Point Rd.

Wills St.

Palou Ave.

St.

BERNAL HEIGHTS, POTRERO, AND THE MISSION (EAST)

A B C D

1

2

BERKELEY

3

4

5

6

7

OAKLAND

8

EMERYVILLE

Francisco St.
Curtis St.
Chestnut St.
Delaware St.
Hearst Ave.
Berkeley Way
Acton St.
Delaware St.
Hearst Ave.
Berkeley Way
University Ave.
Addison St.
Bonita Ave.
Shattuck Ave.
Shattuck Sq.
Oxford St.
Center St.
BERKELE

BOWLING GREENS
Curtis St.
Bonar St.
Browning St.
Allston Way
St.
Bancroft Way
West St.
Valley St.
Acton St.
Edwards St.
Sacramento St.
Spaulding Ave.
Allston Way
California St.
Jefferson St.
McGee St.
Roosevelt St.
Grant St.
McKinley Ave.
Bancroft Way
Channing Way
Martin Luther King Jr. Way
Milvia St.
Kittredge St.
Shattuck Ave.

Channing Way
Dwight Way
Matthews St.
Mabel St.
Blake St.
Acton St.
Parker St.
Carleton St.
Derby St.
Ward St.
10th Ave.
San Pablo Ave.
Wallace St.
Matthews St.
Mabel St.
SAN PABLO PARK
Sojourner Truth Ct.
Oregon St.
Dohr St.
Stanton St.
Park St.
Acton St.
Sacramento St.
California St.
McGee St.
Dwight Way
Blake St.
Parker St.
Carleton St.
Derby St.
Grant St.
Ward St.
Stuart St.
Oregon St.
Russell St.
Julia St.
Martin Luther King Jr. Way
Milvia St.
Adeline St.
Otis St.
Shattuck Ave.
Ashby
Emerson St.

Ashby Ave.
Murray St.
Folger Ave.
Carrison St.
Haskell St.
Mabel St.
67th St.
66th St.
67th St.
66th St.
Herzog St.
Idaho St.
Baker St.
Sacramento St.
Ashby Ave.
Tyler St.
Prince St.
Woolsey St.
Fairview St.
King St.
Ellis St.
Harper St.
65th St.
Alcatraz Ave.
63rd St.
62nd St.
Adeline St.
Essex St.
Prince St.
W
6
F
6
61st St.
60th St.
59th St.

65th St.
Peabody Ln.
Ocean Ave.
64th St.
63rd St.
62nd St.
61st St.
60th St.
59th St.
63rd St.
62nd St.
61st St.
Sacramento St.
Market St.
Loma
Whitmer St.
Maccal St.

62nd St.
61st St.
59th St.
Powell St.
Doyle St.
Beaudry St.
Vallejo St.
Fremont St.
Marshall St.
San Pablo Ave.
6th St.
59th St.
Stanford Ave.
Arlington Ave.
Gaskill St.
57th St.
Aileen St.
Los Angeles Ave.
Grace Ave.
Lowell St.
Occidental St.
56th St.
55th St.
Stanley St.
Genoa St.
58th St.
55th St.
Market St.
Martin Luther King Jr. Way
Dover St.

No. Calif. Center
for African American
History & Life
Hollis St.
Emery Bay Dr.
Doyle St.
Boyer St.
54th St.
53rd St.
48th St.
47th St.
45th St.
53rd St.
Adeline St.
52nd St.
47th St.
46th St.
45th St.
54th St.
53rd St.
West St.
24
OAKLAND

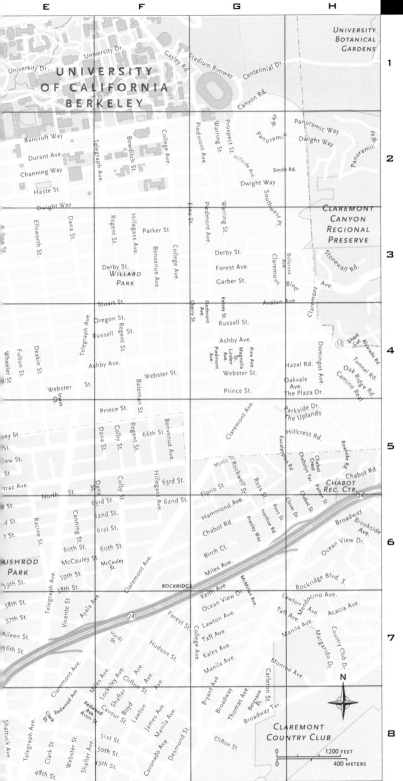

E   F   G   H

UNIVERSITY BOTANICAL GARDENS

University Dr.

UNIVERSITY OF CALIFORNIA BERKELEY

University Dr.

Cayley Rd.

Stadium Rimway

Centennial Dr.

Canyon Rd.

1

Bancroft Way

Durant Ave.

Channing Way

Haste St.

Dwight Way

Telegraph Ave.

Bowditch St.

College Ave.

Piedmont Ave.

Warring St.

Prospect St.

Hillside Ave.

W. Panoramic

Panoramic Way

Dwight Way

Smith Rd.

Dwight Way

Panoramic Way

2

Ellsworth St.

Dana St.

Regent St.

Hillegass Ave.

Parker St.

Benvenue Ave.

College Ave.

Derby St.
WILLARD
PARK

Etna St.

Piedmont Ave.

Warring St.

Derby St.

Forest Ave.

Garber St.

Southwest Pl.

Claremont Blvd.

Bellrose Ave.

Claremont Ave.

CLAREMONT CANYON REGIONAL PRESERVE

Stonewall Rd.

3

St.

Telegraph Ave.

Oregon St.

Russell St.

Regent St.

Ashby Ave.

Stuart St.

Cherry St.

Piedmont Ave.

Kelsey St.

Avalon Ave.

Russell St.

Magnolia St.

Pine Ave.

Linden Ave.

Webster St.

Prince St.

Domingot Ave.

Hazel Rd.

Oakvale Ave.

The Plaza Dr.

13

Alvarado Rd.

Short Cut

Tunnel Rd.

Oak Ridge Rd.

Camino Real

4

Deakin St.

Fulton St.

Wheeler St.

Webster St.

Irwin Ct.

Prince St.

Bateman St.

Benvenue Ave.

Piedmont Ave.

Claremont Ave.

Parkside Dr.
The Uplands

Hillcrest Rd.

Eucalyptus Rd.

5

sey St.

St.

ew St.

St.

traz Ave.

Dana St.

Colby St.

Regent St.

66th St.

Hillegass Ave.

North St.

Colby St.

63rd St.

62nd St.

Florio St.

Mystic St.

Rockwell St.

Ross St.

Chabot Crest

Chabyn Ter.

Chabot St.

Patton St.

Roanoke Rd.

Chabot Rd.

CHABOT REC. CTR.

24

5

d St.

t St.

Racine St.

Canning St.

62nd St.

61st St.

60th St.

60th St.

63rd St.

Hammond Ave.

Chabot Rd.

Birch Ct.

Miles Ave.

Ivanhoe Rd.

Presley Way

Clover Dr.

Ross St.

Broadway

Brookside Ave.

Ocean View Dr.

6

USHROD PARK

59th St.

McCauley St.

58th St.

Telegraph Ave.

59th St.

McCauley St.

Claremont Ave.

ROCKRIDGE

Keith Ave.

Ocean View Dr.

McMillan St.

Rockridge Blvd. S.

7

58th St.

57th St.

Aileen St.

56th St.

Vicente Ave.

Ayala Ave.

24

Hardt St.

Forest St.

College Ave.

Hudson St.

Lawton Ave.

Taft Ave.

Kales Ave.

Manila Ave.

Taft Ave.

Mendocino Ave.

Acacia Ave.

Manila Ave.

Monroe Ave.

Margarido Dr.

Country Club Dr.

7

N

Claremont Ave.

Miles Ave.

Lockeley Ave.

Shafter Ave.

Clark St.

Redwood Ave

Clifton St.

Boyd Ave.

Redwood Ave.

Cavour St.

Avon St.

Lawton

Shattuck Ave.

Telegraph Ave.

Clark St.

Webster St.

Shafter Ave.

51st St.

50th St.

49th St.

48th St.

James Ave.

Manila Ave.

Coronado Ave.

Desmond St.

Bryant Ave.

Broadway

Thomas Ave.

Clifton St.

Carleton St.

Broadway

Belgrave Pl.

Broadway Ter.

CLAREMONT COUNTRY CLUB

0   1200 FEET

0   400 METERS

8

A   B   C   D

1

Hubbard St.
Horton St.
Holden St.
Hollis St.
40th St.
San Pablo Ave.
40th St.
39th St.
Apgar St.
MACARTHUR
MacArthur Blvd.
37th St.
Telegraph

Yerba Buena Ave.
MacArthur Blvd.
MacArthur Fwy.
36th St.
580

2

34th St.
Ettie St.
32nd St.
Hannah St.
Helen St.
Louise St.
Hollis St.
34th St.
San Pablo Ave.
35th St.
580
34th St.
33rd St.
Brockhurst St.
32nd St.
24
Martin Luther King Jr. Way
37t
36th

Mandela Pkwy.
32nd St.
30th St.
31st St.
980
34th St.
Elm St.
28th

3

Campbell St.
Peralta St.
Poplar St.
Union St.
Magnolia St.
Adeline St.
28th St.
Market St.
30th St.
29th St.
West St.
31st St.
Telegraph Ave.
30th St.
McClure St.
Summit St.

Kirkham St.
26th St.
Alice St.
28th St.
29th St.
28th St.
Summit

24th St.
27th St.
Milton St.
Mead Ave.
27th St.
26th St.
Sycamore St.
Grove Shafter Fwy.
28th St.
28th St.

4

20th St.
Grand Ave.
Athens Ave.
25th St.
26th St.

19th St.
21st St.
Isabella St.
24th St.
25th St.
Webster St.

DeFremery Park
Chestnut St.
Linden St.
Filbert St.
Myrtle St.
Market St.
Curtis St.
22nd St.
21st St.
West St.
Brush St.
23rd St.
24th St.
Valley St.
23rd
Grand Ave

18th St.
16th St.
22nd St.

5

14th St.
Lowell Park
Marston Campbell Park
21st St.
20th St.
Williams St.
San Pablo Ave.
19th St.
Paramount Theater
22nd St.
21st St.

12th St.
13th St.
Grove Shafter Fwy.
Castro St.
18th St.
17th St.
16th St.
15th St.
Telegraph St.
20th St.

10th St.
19th STREET
SNOW PARK

6

8th St.
7th St.
11th St.
980
13th St.
Martin Luther King Jr. Way
Lafayette Square
Jefferson St.
Clay St.
Washington St.
OAKLAND CITY CENTER/
12th STREET
Broadway
Franklin St.
Webster St.
14th St.
13th St.
12th St.
11th St.
Harrison St.
Alice St.
Jackson St.
17th
OAKLAN

5th St.
LINCOLN SQUARE

7

Filbert St.
Market St.
Brush St.
Castro St.
Jefferson St.
4th St.
3rd St.
Clay St.
Washington St.
Broadway
Jefferson Square
Webster St.
Harrison St.
10th St.
9th St.
8th St.
7th St.
880
HARRISON SQUARE
Nimitz Fwy.
Oak
Embarcadero W.

N

8

0   1200 FEET
0   400 METERS
Webster Tube
Posey Tube
Jack London Square
Franklin St.
Webster St.
2nd St.
Embarcadero W.
Jack London Village
Fallon St.
4th St.

ALAMEDA
ESTUARY PARK

STREETFINDER

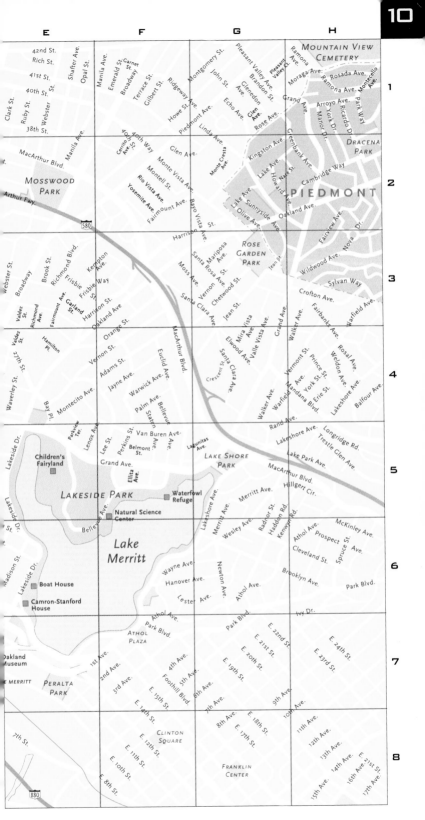

E   F   G   H

MOUNTAIN VIEW CEMETERY

1

2

3

4

5

6

7

8

42nd St.
Rich St.
41st St.
40th St.
38th St.
Clark St.
Ruby St.
Webster
Shafter Ave.
Opal St.
Manila Ave.
Emerald St.
Garnet
Broadway
Terrace St.
Gilbert St.
Ridgeway Ave.
Howe St.
Piedmont Ave.
Montgomery St.
John St.
Echo Ave.
Pleasant Valley Ave.
Brandon St.
Glendon Ave.
Glen Ct.
Rose Ave.
Pleasant Valley Ct.
Ramona Ave.
Moraga Ave.
Rosada Ave.
Ramona Ave.
Montecello Ave.
Grand Ave.
Arroyo Ave.
York Dr.
Ricardo Dr.
Park Way

MacArthur Blvd.
Manila Ave.
MOSSWOOD PARK
Arthur Fwy.
40th St.
40th Way
Genoa St.
Glen Ave.
Monte Vista Ave.
Montell St.
Rio Vista Ave.
Yosemite Ave.
Fairmount Ave.
Linda Ave.
Monte Cresta Ave.
Bayo Vista Ave.
St.
Kingston Ave.
Lake Ave.
Howard Ave.
Greenbank Ave.
Nace St.
Manor Dr.
DRACENA PARK
Cambridge Way
PIEDMONT

Webster St.
Broadway
Richmond Blvd.
Frisbie St.
Kempton Ave.
Frisbie Way
Valdez St.
Richmond Ave.
Fairmount Ave.
Garland St.
Harrison St.
Oakland Ave.
Harrison St.
Moss Ave.
Santa Mariposa St.
Santa Rosa Ave.
Vernon St.
Chetwood St.
Santa Clara Ave.
Jean St.
ROSE GARDEN PARK
Sunnyside Ave.
Olive Ave.
Oakland Ave.
Fairview Ave.
Nova Dr.
Wildwood Ave.
Crofton Ave.
Sylvan Way
Fairfield St.

Valdez St.
11th St.
Hamilton Pl.
Waverley St.
27th St.
Bay Pl.
Montecito Ave.
Orange St.
Vernon St.
Adams St.
Jayne Ave.
Warwick Ave.
Euclid Ave.
Palm Ave.
Staten Ave.
Bellevue
MacArthur Blvd.
Crescent St.
Santa Clara Ave.
Elwood Ave.
Mira Vista Ave.
Valle Vista Ave.
Grand Ave.
Walker Ave.
Vermont St.
Prince St.
York St.
Erie St.
Mandana Blvd.
Warfield Ave.
Rand Ave.
Fairbanks Ave.
Rosal Ave.
Weldon Ave.
Lakeshore Ave.
Balfour Ave.

Lakeside Dr.
Children's Fairyland
LAKESIDE PARK
Lakeside Dr.
Parkview Ter.
Lenox Ave.
Lee St.
Perkins St.
Belmont St.
Van Buren Ave.
Grand Ave.
Ellita Ave.
Bellevue Ave.
Natural Science Center
Waterfowl Refuge
Lagunitas Ave.
LAKE SHORE PARK
MacArthur Blvd.
Hillgert Cir.
Lakeshore Ave.
Lake Park Ave.
Longridge Rd.
Trestle Glen Ave.

Lakeside Dr.
St.
Madison St.
Lakeside Dr.
Boat House
Camron-Stanford House
Lake Merritt
Lakeshore Ave.
Merritt Ave.
Wesley Ave.
Merritt Ave.
Radior St.
Haddon Rd.
Kenyon Rd.
Athol Ave.
Cleveland St.
Prospect St.
Spruce Ave.
McKinley Ave.

Oakland Museum
E MERRITT
PERALTA PARK
Wayne Ave.
Hanover Ave.
Lester Ave.
Newton Ave.
Athol Ave.
Brooklyn Ave.
Park Blvd.

7th St.
Athol Ave.
Park Blvd.
ATHOL PLAZA
1st Ave.
2nd Ave.
3rd Ave.
4th Ave.
Foothill Blvd.
5th Ave.
6th Ave.
7th Ave.
E. 15th St.
E. 14th St.
8th Ave.
Park Blvd.
E. 22nd St.
E. 21st St.
E. 20th St.
E. 19th St.
E. 18th St.
E. 17th St.
Ivy Dr.
9th Ave.
10th Ave.
E. 24th St.
E. 23rd St.
11th Ave.
12th Ave.
13th Ave.
14th Ave.
E. 21st St.
16th Ave.
17th Ave.

E. 12th St.
CLINTON SQUARE
E. 11th St.
E. 10th St.
E. 8th St.
FRANKLIN CENTER
15th Ave.

OAKLAND

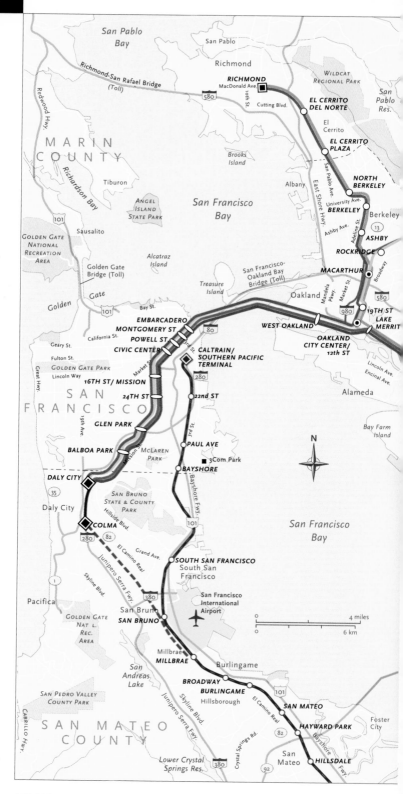

THE BART SYSTEM

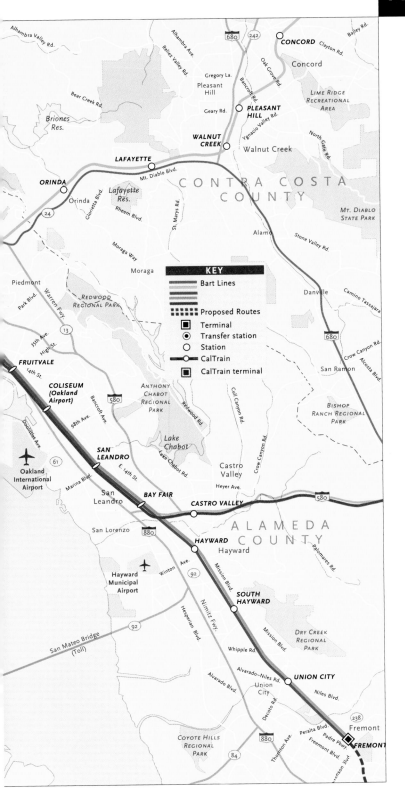

KEY

Bart Lines

Proposed Routes

■ Terminal

◉ Transfer station

○ Station

○— CalTrain

■ CalTrain terminal

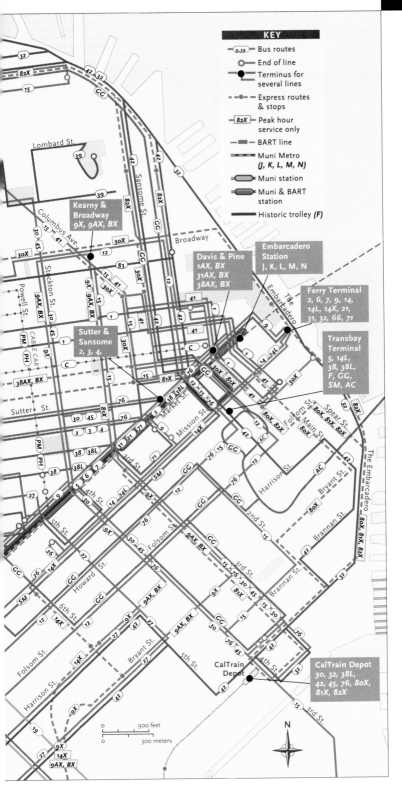

KEY

- 9.39 — Bus routes
- ○ — End of line
- ● — Terminus for several lines
- ●--●-- — Express routes & stops
- 82X — Peak hour service only
- — BART line
- — Muni Metro (J, K, L, M, N)
- — Muni station
- — Muni & BART station
- — Historic trolley (F)

Kearny & Broadway
9X, 9AX, BX

Davis & Pine
1AX, BX
31AX, BX
38AX, BX

Embarcadero Station
J, K, L, M, N

Ferry Terminal
2, 6, 7, 9, 14,
14L, 14X, 21,
31, 32, 66, 71

Sutter & Sansome
2, 3, 4,

Transbay Terminal
5, 14L,
38, 38L,
F, GG,
SM, AC

CalTrain Depot

CalTrain Depot
30, 32, 38L,
42, 45, 76, 80X,
81X, 82X

0 — 900 feet
0 — 300 meters

N

DOWNTOWN SAN FRANCISCO

N

PACIFIC OCEAN

Golden Gate Bridge

GOLDEN GATE
NATIONAL
RECREATION AREA

THE PRESIDIO

Baker
Beach

Lands
End

China
Beach

Point
Lobos

LINCOLN PARK

Pt. Lobos Ave

California St.

Clement St.

Geary Blvd.

Balboa St.

Euclid Ave.

Geary Blvd.

Fulton St.

Fulton St.

GOLDEN GATE
PARK

Stow
Lake

Lincoln Way

Lincoln Way

Sunset Blvd.

Noriega St.

Sunset
Reservoir

Quintara St.

McCoppin
Sq.

TWIN
PEAKS

MT.
DAVIDSON
PARK

Pine
Lake Park

Sloat Blvd.

STERN
GROVE

Monterey Blvd.

Merced Blvd.

HARDING
PARK

Lake Merced

John Muir Dr.

Garfield St.

SAN FRANCISCO
CITY LINE

SAN MATEO COUNTY

MUNI

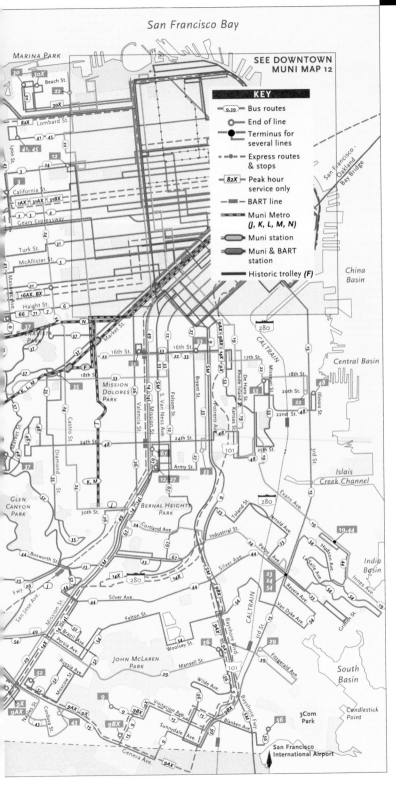

SEE DOWNTOWN
MUNI MAP 12

KEY

- 9.39   Bus routes
- End of line
- Terminus for several lines
- Express routes & stops
- 82X   Peak hour service only
- BART line
- Muni Metro (J, K, L, M, N)
- Muni station
- Muni & BART station
- Historic trolley (F)

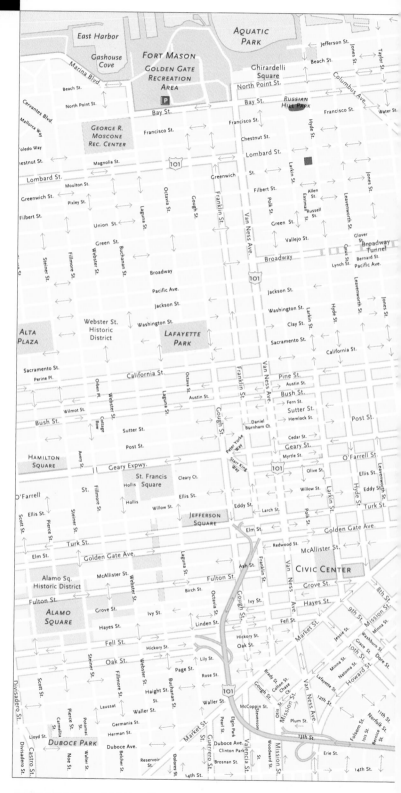

DRIVING AND PARKING

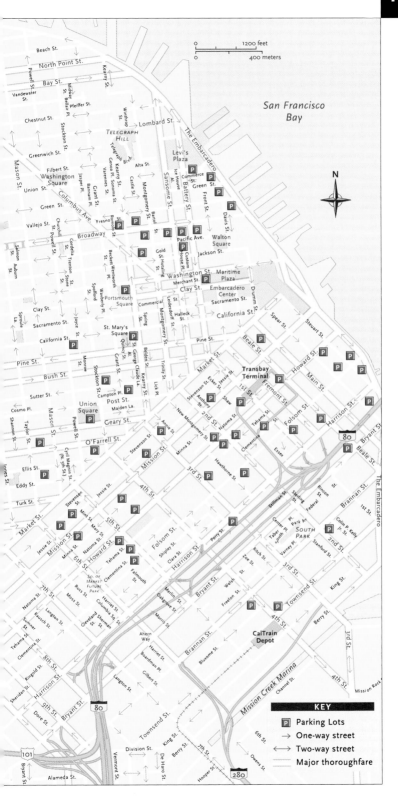

San Francisco
Bay

N

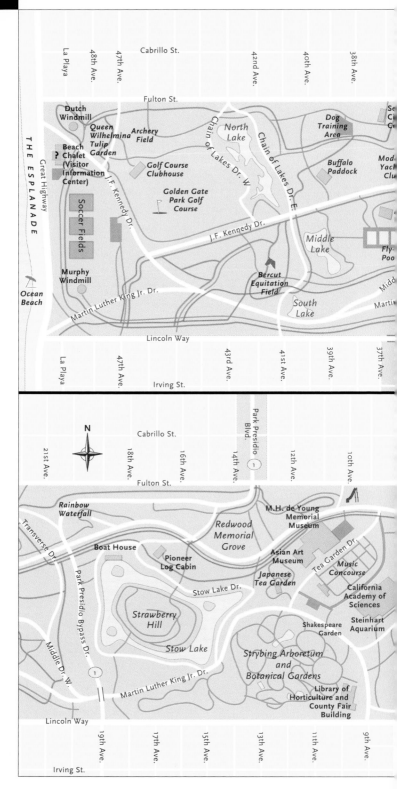

GOLDEN GATE PARK

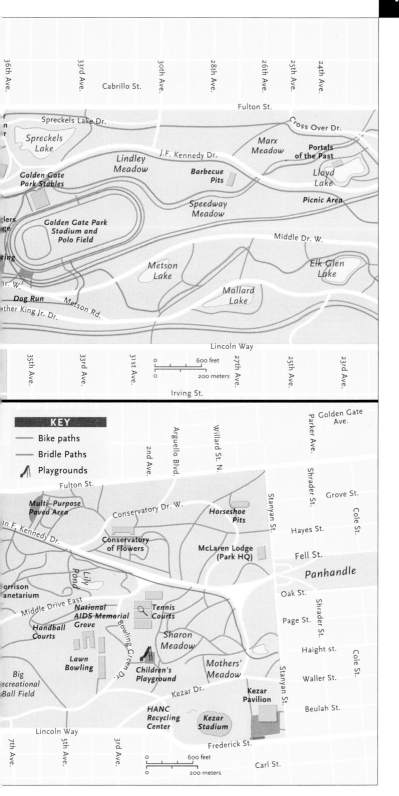

TOP: WEST END, BOTTOM: EAST END

Map labels (top, West End):

36th Ave. · 33rd Ave. · Cabrillo St. · 30th Ave. · 28th Ave. · 26th Ave. · 25th Ave. · 24th Ave.

Fulton St.

Spreckels Lake Dr. · Cross Over Dr.

Spreckels Lake · Marx Meadow · Portals of the Past

Lindley Meadow · J.F. Kennedy Dr. · Lloyd Lake

Golden Gate Park Stables · Barbecue Pits · Picnic Area

Speedway Meadow

Golden Gate Park Stadium and Polo Field · Middle Dr. W.

Metson Lake · Elk Glen Lake

Mallard Lake

Dog Run · Metson Rd. · ...ther King Jr. Dr.

Lincoln Way

35th Ave. · 33rd Ave. · 31st Ave. · 27th Ave. · 25th Ave. · 23rd Ave.

600 feet / 200 meters

Irving St.

Map labels (bottom, East End):

KEY
— Bike paths
— Bridle Paths
⚑ Playgrounds

Parker Ave. · Golden Gate Ave.

Arguello Blvd. · Willard St. N. · Stanyan St. · Shrader St. · Grove St. · Cole St.

2nd Ave.

Fulton St.

Multi–Purpose Paved Area · Conservatory Dr. W. · Horseshoe Pits

...n F. Kennedy Dr. · Hayes St.

Conservatory of Flowers · McLaren Lodge (Park HQ) · Fell St.

Panhandle

...orrison ...anetarium · Middle Drive East · Lily Pond · Oak St. · Shrader St.

National AIDS Memorial Grove · Tennis Courts · Page St. · Cole St.

Handball Courts · Sharon Meadow · Haight st.

Lawn Bowling · Children's Playground · Mothers' Meadow · Waller St. · Stanyan St. · Cole St.

Big ...ecreational Ball Field · Kezar Dr. · Kezar Pavilion · Beulah St.

HANC Recycling Center · Kezar Stadium

7th Ave. · 5th Ave. · 3rd Ave. · Lincoln Way · Frederick St. · Carl St.

600 feet / 200 meters

Your Source in the City

MANY MAPS • WHERE & HOW

FIND IT ALL • NIGHT & DAY

ANTIQUES TO ZIPPERS

BARGAINS • BAUBLES • KITES

ELEGANT EDIBLES • ETHNIC EATS

STEAK HOUSES • FISH HOUSES

BISTROS • TRATTORIAS

CLASSICAL • JAZZ • CABARET

COMEDY • THEATER • DANCE

BARS • CLUBS • BLUES

COOL TOURS

HOUSECLEANING • CATERING

LOST & FOUND • THE CABLE GUY

GET A LAWYER • GET A DENTIST

GET A NEW PET • GET A VET

MUSEUMS • GALLERIES

PARKS • GARDENS • RINKS

AQUARIUMS TO ZOOS

BASEBALL TO ROCK CLIMBING

FESTIVALS • EVENTS

DAY SPAS • DAY TRIPS

HOTELS • HOT LINES

PASSPORT PIX • TRAVEL INFO

HELICOPTER TOURS

DINERS • DELIS • PIZZERIAS

BRASSERIES • CAFÉS

BOOTS • BOOKS • BUTTONS

BICYCLES • SKATES

SUITS • SHOES • HATS

RENT A TUX • RENT A COSTUME

BAKERIES • SPICE SHOPS

SOUP TO NUTS

Fodor's

CITYGUIDE
SAN FRANCISCO

FODOR'S TRAVEL PUBLICATIONS, INC.

NEW YORK • TORONTO • LONDON • SYDNEY • AUCKLAND

WWW.FODORS.COM/

FODOR'S CITYGUIDE SAN FRANCISCO

EDITOR
Amy McConnell

EDITORIAL CONTRIBUTORS
Jennifer Brewer, Glen Helfand, Amy McConnell, Sharon Silva, Sharron Wood

EDITORIAL PRODUCTION
Linda K. Schmidt

MAPS
David Lindroth Inc., *cartographer*; Bob Blake, *map editor*

DESIGN
Fabrizio La Rocca, *creative director*; Allison Saltzman, *text design*;
Tigist Getachew, *cover design*; Jolie Novak, *photo editor*

PRODUCTION/MANUFACTURING
Robert B. Shields

COVER PHOTOGRAPH
Robert Holmes

Series created by Marilyn Appleberg

COPYRIGHT

SPECIAL SALES

CONTENTS

METROPOLITAN LIFE

On a bad day in a big city, the little things that go with living shoulder-to-shoulder with a few million people wear us all down. But the special pleasures of urban life have a way of keeping us out of the suburbs—and thankful, even, for every second of stress. The field of daffodils in the park on a fine spring day. The perfect little black dress that you find for half price. The markets—so fabulously well stocked that you can cook any recipe without resorting to mail-order catalogs. The way you can sometimes turn a corner and discover a whole new world, so foreign you can hardly believe you're less than a mile from home. The never-ending wealth of possibilities and opportunities.

If you know where to find it all, the city cannot defeat you. With knowledge comes power. That's why Fodor's has prepared this book. It will put phone numbers at your fingertips. It'll take you to new places and remind you of those you've forgotten. It's the ultimate urban companion—and, we hope, your **new best friend in the city.**

It's the **citywise shopaholic,** who always knows where to find something, no matter how obscure. We've made a concerted effort to bring hundreds of great shops to your attention, so that you'll never be at a loss, whether you need a special birthday present for a great friend or some obscure craft items to make Halloween costumes for your kids.

It's the **restaurant know-it-all,** who's full of ideas for every occasion—you know, the one who would never send you to Café de la Snub, because he knows it's always overbooked, the food is boring, and the staff is rude. In this book we'll steer you around the corner, to a perfect little place with five tables, a fireplace, and a chef on her way up.

It's a **hip barfly buddy,** who can give you advice when you need a charming nook, not too noisy, to take a friend after work. Among the dozens of bars and nightspots in this book, you're bound to find something that fits your mood.

It's the **sagest arts maven you know,** the one who always has the scoop on what's on that's worthwhile on any given night. In these pages, you'll find dozens of concert venues and arts organizations.

It's also the **city whiz,** who knows how to get you where you're going, wherever you are.

It's the **best map guide** on the shelves, and it puts **all the city in your briefcase** or on your bookshelf.

Stick with us. We lay out all the options for your leisure time—and gently nudge you away from the duds—so that you can truly enjoy metropolitan living.

YOUR GUIDES

No one person can know it all. To help get you on track around the city, we've hand-picked a stellar group of local experts to share their wisdom.

Our expert on shopping, exploring, and outdoors, **Jennifer Brewer,** lives, works, plays, and shops in the City by the Bay. She has written for *Mademoiselle* and *New Woman* magazines and is currently putting the finishing touches on her first screenplay.

Art critic and curator **Glen Helfand,** a San Francisco–based freelance writer who has written for the *San Francisco Bay Guardian, San Francisco Magazine, Wired,* the *Bay Guardian, LA Weekly,* and *Travel & Leisure,* has scoped out the best art galleries in the Bay Area.

Local eating-out guru **Sharon Silva** contributes regularly to *San Francisco Magazine* and *San Francisco Sidewalk,* an on-line cultural guide.

A veteran Fodor's contributor and current managing editor of *On the Road* (a San Francisco–based Web site for business travelers), **Sharron Wood,** leads you to the best late-night hangouts and hotels.

Editor **Amy McConnell** is a native of Marin County, a graduate of the South Peninsula's Stanford University, and a former Berkeley Guides writer who now lives in New York, which she classifies as the second-best city in the U.S.

Marilyn Appleberg, who conceived this series, is a city-lover through and through. She plots her urban forays from an archetypal Greenwich Village brownstone with two fireplaces.

It goes without saying that our contributors have chosen all establishments strictly on their own merits—no establishment has paid to be included in this book.

HOW TO USE THIS BOOK

The first thing you need to know is that everything in this book is **arranged by category and by alphabetical order** within category.

Now, before you go any farther, check out the **city maps** at the front of the book. Each map has a number, in a black box at the top of the page, and grid coordinates along the top and side margins. On the text pages, every listing in the book is keyed to one of these maps. Look for the map number in a small black box preceding each establishment name. The grid code follows in italics. For establishments with more than one location, additional map numbers and grid codes appear at the end of the listing. To locate a museum that's identified in the text as **7** *e-6,* turn to Map 7 and locate the address within the e-6 grid square. To locate restaurants that are nearby, simply skim the text in the restaurant chapter for listings identified as being on Map 7.

Throughout the guide, as applicable, we name the neighborhood in which each sight, restaurant, shop, or other destination is located. We also give you complete opening hours and admission fees for sights; closing information for shops; and credit-card, price, reservation, and closing information for restaurants.

At the end of the book, in addition to an **alphabetical index,** you'll find **directories of shops and restaurants by neighborhood.**

Chapter 1, Basics, lists essential information, such as entertainment hot lines (for those times you can't lay your hands on a newspaper). **Chapter 8, Help!,** covers resources for residents—everything from vet and lawyer-referral services to caterers worth calling.

We've worked hard to make sure that all of the information we give you is accurate at press time. Still, time brings changes, so always confirm information when it matters—especially if you're making a detour.

Feel free to drop us a line. Were the restaurants we recommended as described? Did you find a wonderful shop you'd like to share? If you have complaints, we'll look into them and revise our entries in the next edition when the facts warrant. So send us your feedback. Either e-mail us at editors@fodors.com (specifying *Fodor's CITYGUIDE San Francisco* on the subject line), or write to the *Fodor's CITYGUIDE San Francisco* editor at Fodor's, 201 East 50th Street, New York, New York 10022. We look forward to hearing from you.

Karen Cure

Karen Cure
Editorial Director

chapter 1

BASICS

essential information for visitors

BANKS

The following are all full-service banks, members FDIC. For the address of the nearest ATM accepting Cirrus cards, call the **Cirrus Cash-Machine Locator** (800/424–7787). For help finding an ATM that accepts Plus cards, call the **Plus ATM Locator** (800/843–7587).

Bank of America (415/615–4700 for 24-hour service): More than 60 branches in San Francisco, all with ATMs accepting Plus, Star, and Interlink cards. Most are open Saturday 9–2. Additional free-standing B of A ATMs are located at 3Com Park, the San Francisco airport, San Francisco Shopping Centre, and in many Lucky supermarkets.

Bank of the West (800/488–2265): Six citywide branches with ATMs accepting Cirrus, Star, and Explore cards. Branches are closed on Saturday.

California Federal Bank (800/843–2265): More than 20 branches, most with ATMs accepting Plus, Star, and Explore cards. Several CalFed branches are open Saturday, though hours vary.

Citibank (800/756–7047; main branch at 590 Market St., at 2nd St., Financial District): 12 branches in San Francisco, all with ATMs accepting Cirrus cards. Some branches are open Saturday 9–4.

EurekaBank (800/538–7352, or 800/307–7577 for 24-hour service): Five branches in San Francisco; one is open Saturday 9–2. All have ATMs accepting Plus, Star, and Explore cards.

Home Savings of America (800/933–3000): 9 branches citywide, some open Saturday 9–2. All have ATMs accepting Plus and Star cards.

Wells Fargo (800/869–3557): "Anytime, anywhere banking" at more than 20 branches citywide, all with ATMs accepting Star, Cirrus, Explore, Maestro, and Global Access cards. Additional ATMs are located at many Safeway supermarkets. Select branches are open Saturday 9–4.

CURRENCY EXCHANGE

All of the currency exchange offices listed below buy and sell travelers checks and foreign currency, though it's best to call ahead to check on availability, particularly if you require special denominations or large amounts of currency.

American Express (800/461–8484 for general information; 560 California St., at Kearny St., Financial District, 415/536–2658; 455 Market St., at 1st St., Financial District, 415/536–2600; 124 Geary St., at Grant St., Union Square, 415/398–8578; 333 Jefferson St., at Jones St., Fisherman's Wharf, 415/775–0240) handles currency exchange at all four locations. The office at Fisherman's Wharf is open daily from 10 to 9. The Union Square office is open Saturday mornings.

Bank of America (345 Montgomery St., at California St., Financial District, 415/622–2451): Foreign Currency Services offices are on the main level of the Bank of America building. Open weekdays 9–6.

Bank of America at SFO (415/877–0264): On the departure level of the International Terminal at San Francisco International Airport. Open daily 7 AM–11 PM.

Foreign Exchange, Ltd. (415 Stockton St., at Sutter St., Union Square, 415/677–5100): Convenient downtown location between Chinatown and the shopping district of Union Square. Open weekdays 9–5:30, Sat. 10–4.

Mutual of Omaha/Travelex at SFO (415/266–9420): On the departure level of the International Terminal at San Francisco International Airport. Open daily 6:30 AM–10:30 PM.

Thomas Cook (75 Geary St., 1 block north of Market St., Union Square; 800/287–7362 for general information;): Open weekdays 9–5, Sat. 10–4. Also: Pier 39, next to Eagle Café, Fisherman's Wharf. Open daily 10–6.

ENTERTAINMENT INFORMATION

Many of the city's museums, clubs, and performing arts groups maintain their own telephone hot lines, and should be contacted directly.

BASS Tickets (510/762–2277), for information and tickets to concerts, sports, and other events.

BASS Tickets Performing Arts Line (415/776–1999), for information and tickets to theater, opera, and ballet.

City Line (415/512–5000 or 415/808–5000), for local and national news, weather, sports—even California lottery results. Dial extension 7800 for Bay Area entertainment listings.

Live 105 Concert & Entertainment Line (415/357–9428), for movie, dance club, comedy show, and concert listings.

Moscone Center (415/974–4000), for recorded information on conventions and other monthly events.

Movie Phone (415/777–3456).

SFCVB Information Hotline (415/391–2000 or 415/391–2001), for multilingual information on events, attractions, and weather.

TIX Bay Area (415/433–7827), for tickets and information on Bay Area performing arts, as well as sporting events and clubs.

GEOGRAPHY

San Francisco sits at the tip of a 32-mi-long peninsula surrounded on three sides by the San Francisco Bay and the Pacific Ocean. The city is 46 sq mi, surprisingly small considering its mighty international reputation. Steep hills are San Francisco's most notable geographical feature; there are approximately 40 of them; some—Nob Hill, Russian Hill, Telegraph Hill—are quite famous. The hills cleave the city into distinct areas that are the foundation of its distinctive neighborhoods. They also make for some hair-raising descents. You'll come face-to-face (literally) with several of the city's steepest hills when exploring downtown San Francisco.

Union Square, the downtown shopping district, is at the heart of San Francisco. From there, prime destinations such as Chinatown, North Beach, Fisherman's Wharf, Civic Center, and the Financial District are easy to reach by cable car, by bus, or (for those who don't mind a little climbing) on foot. The city's two beloved parks, Golden Gate Park and the Presidio, lie several miles west of the downtown area, along the Pacific Ocean. The neighborhoods surrounding the parks are primarily residential. San Francisco's famous Golden Gate Bridge extends from the tip of the Presidio north to wealthy Marin County.

Most of San Francisco's neighborhoods are laid out along a neat grid, so it helps to know the nearest cross street when searching for an address. An exception to the city's tidy pattern is **Market Street,** the main downtown thoroughfare, which runs diagonally through the heart of the city. Downtown, on the south side of Market Street (SoMa), a series of **numbered streets** begins with 1st and continues south to 30th. The first 12 streets run southeast–northwest, while the remaining ones run east–west. Far west of downtown are the Richmond and Sunset districts; the **numbered avenues** in these districts run north–south, starting with 2nd and ending near the ocean with 48th. The avenues intersect with a series of alphabetically named east–west streets, which begin with Anza and Balboa and continue south to Wawona and Yorba (there's no X or Z Street) just north of Sloat Boulevard. Be careful not to confuse streets and avenues when reading addresses.

The major east–west streets north of Market Street are **Geary Boulevard** (it's called Geary Street until Van Ness Avenue), which runs to the Pacific Ocean; **Fulton Street,** which begins at the back of the Opera House and continues along the north side of Golden Gate Park to Ocean Beach; and **Fell Street,** whose left two lanes cut through Golden Gate Park and empty into **Lincoln Boulevard.** The latter continues on the park's south side to the ocean.

The longest street in San Francisco, **Mission Street,** heads southwest from the Embarcadero to Van Ness Avenue, then turns due south to Army Street, after which it resumes a southwest course into Daly City.

Among the major north–south streets are **Divisadero Street,** which becomes Castro Street at Duboce Avenue and continues past Army Street; **Van Ness Avenue** (it becomes South Van Ness Avenue a few blocks south of City Hall); and **Park Presidio Boulevard,** which empties into **19th Avenue.**

HOLIDAYS

During the following holidays, all offices of the city and county of San Francisco are closed, as are many other places of business. See the "Events" section of Chapter 2 for information on holiday events and celebrations.

New Year's Day. January 1.

Zip Codes

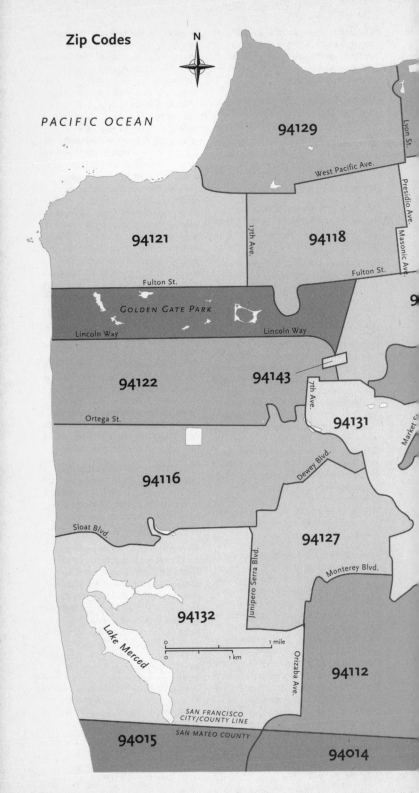

N

PACIFIC OCEAN

94129

West Pacific Ave.

Lyon St.

Presidio Ave.

Masonic Ave.

17th Ave.

94121

94118

Fulton St.

Fulton St.

GOLDEN GATE PARK

Lincoln Way

Lincoln Way

94122

94143

7th Ave.

94131

Market St.

Ortega St.

94116

Dewey Blvd.

Sloat Blvd.

94127

Monterey Blvd.

Junipero Serra Blvd.

94132

Lake Merced

0   1 mile

0   1 km

Orizaba Ave.

94112

SAN FRANCISCO
CITY/COUNTY LINE

SAN MATEO COUNTY

94015

94014

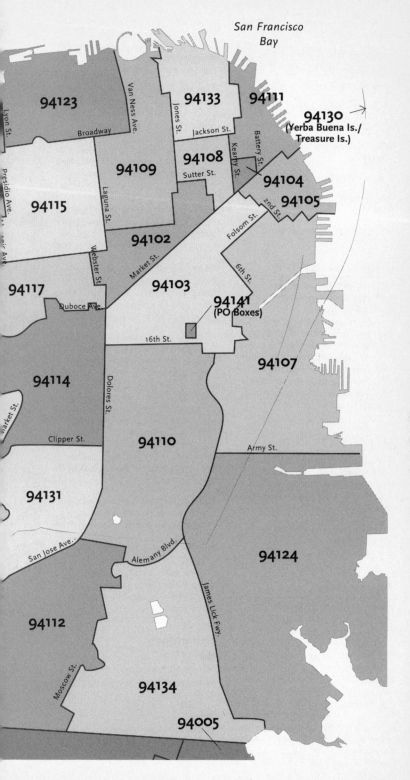

San Francisco
Bay

94123

94133

94111

94130
(Yerba Buena Is./
Treasure Is.)

Van Ness Ave.

Lyon St.

Jones St.

Jackson St.

Battery St.

Broadway

94109

94108

Kearny St.

94104

Sutter St.

94105

2nd St.

Presidio Ave.

94115

Laguna St.

94102

Folsom St.

Webster St.

Market St.

6th St.

94117

94103

94141
(PO Boxes)

Duboce Ave.

16th St.

94107

94114

Dolores St.

Market St.

Clipper St.

94110

Army St.

94131

94124

San Jose Ave.

Alemany Blvd.

94112

James Lick Fwy.

Moscow St.

94134

94005

Martin Luther King, Jr., Day. Third Monday in January.

President's Day. Third Monday in February.

Memorial Day. Last Monday in May.

Independence Day. July 4.

Labor Day. First Monday in September.

Columbus Day. The Monday closest to October 12.

Veteran's Day. November 11.

Thanksgiving Day. Fourth Thursday in November.

Christmas Day. December 25.

LIQUOR LAWS

Packaged alcoholic beverages may be purchased daily from 6 AM to 2 AM at liquor stores, grocery stores, and some drug stores. During the same hours, most San Francisco restaurants, bars, and night clubs are licensed to serve a full line of alcoholic beverages by the glass or bottle. However, some hold permits to sell beer and wine only. The legal age for purchase and/or consumption is 21; proof of age is required.

NO SMOKING

Almost all hotels and motels have no-smoking rooms; in larger establishments entire floors are reserved for nonsmokers. Most bed-and-breakfasts do not allow smoking on the premises.

In accordance with California law, San Francisco restaurants and bars do not permit smoking.

PARKING

The best advice to those visiting San Francisco by car: Park it, and rely on your feet and the city's excellent public transportation system. Downtown, limited metered parking is available, but most meters limit parking to 30 minutes or 1 hour. Additionally, certain streets have designated tow-away zones during rush hours (7 AM–9 AM and 3 PM–6 PM). If your car is towed, take the registration or rental agreement papers to the nearest police station. You'll be required to pay the parking fine plus a $100 towing fee to free your vehicle. In outlying neighborhoods, watch for street-cleaning signs indicating when parking is prohibited. Some areas require resident parking permits, and nonresident parking is severely restricted.

Throughout the city, pay attention to curb colors. The colors painted on the curbs indicate rules: red means no stopping or parking at any time; yellow is for loading and unloading vehicles with commercial plates only; green has a 10-minute parking limit for all vehicles; white, for passenger loading and unloading, has a five-minute limit that is in effect during the adjacent business' hours of operation; blue is for vehicles displaying a California disabled-person plate or placard. In all parts of the city except Fisherman's Wharf, parking regulations are not enforced on New Year's Day, Memorial Day, Independence Day, Labor Day, Thanksgiving Day, and Christmas Day. New Year's Day, Thanksgiving, and Christmas are the only meter-free days at Fisherman's Wharf.

If you insist on parking on one of San Francisco's famous hills, the law requires that you curb your wheels—that is, turn them toward the street if the car is facing uphill, toward the curb if facing downhill. Remember to set the car's emergency brake, and if it's a stick shift, leave the car in gear. Failure to curb a vehicle's wheels on a hill earns a $23 parking ticket. For more information on parking in San Francisco, call the city's **Department of Parking and Traffic** (415/554–7275).

Parking garages are plentiful but expensive. The three best downtown garages—a bargain for shoppers, since they average only $1.50 per hour—are the Fifth and Mission Garage, the Ellis-O'Farrell Garage (across from Macy's), and the Sutter-Stockton Garage. The garages listed below are all near shopping and tourist attractions; call for hours and rates.

chinatown
4 *e-4*

Holiday Inn Parking (750 Kearny St., at Washington St., 415/781–3942). Open 24 hours.

4 *e-4*

Portsmouth Square Garage (733 Kearny St., between Clay and Washington Sts., 415/982–6353). Open 24 hours.

| 4 | *e-5* |

Sutter-Stockton Garage (330 Sutter St., at Stockton St., 415/982–7275). Open 24 hours.

civic center/opera plaza

| 4 | *c-7* |

Civic Center Plaza Garage (Civic Center, McAllister St., between Polk and Larkin Sts., 415/863–1537). Open Mon.–Thurs. 6 AM–midnight, Fri. 6 AM–1 AM, Sat. 8 AM–1 AM, Sun. 8 AM–midnight.

| 4 | *c-7* |

Opera Plaza Garage (601 Van Ness Ave., between Golden Gate Ave. and Turk St., 415/771–4776). Open 24 hours.

downtown

| 4 | *e-6* |

Ellis-O'Farrell Garage (123 O'Farrell St., at Stockton St., Union Square, 415/986–4800). Open daily 8:30 AM–1 AM.

| 4 | *f-4* |

Embarcadero Center Garage (1–4 Embarcadero Center, at Battery St., Embarcadero, 800/733–6318). Open 24 hours.

| 4 | *e-7* |

5th & Mission Garage (833 Mission St., South of Market, 415/982–8522). Open 24 hours.

fisherman's wharf

| 4 | *d-1* |

Pier 39 Garage (2550 Powell St., at The Embarcadero, across from Pier 39, 415/705–5418). Open 24 hours.

| 4 | *d-2* |

The Wharf Garage (350 Beach St., between Taylor and Mason Sts., 415/921–0226). Open daily 7:30 AM–11:30 PM.

ghirardelli square

| 4 | *b-2, b-3* |

Ghirardelli Square Parking Garage (900 North Point St., between Larkin and Polk Sts., 415/929–1665). Open daily 9 AM–2 AM.

PARKS INFORMATION

For information on city parks, call the **San Francisco Recreation and Parks Department** (415/831–2700) or send a SASE to: Recreation and Parks, McLaren Lodge, Golden Gate Park, 501 Stanyan St., San Francisco 94117. The McLaren Lodge visitor center is open weekdays 8–5.

California State Parks in the San Francisco area include Angel Island, Mt. Tamalpais, and Samuel P. Taylor. For more information, contact the California State Parks and Recreation Dept., Bay Area District Office, 250 Executive Park Blvd., Suite 4900, San Francisco 94134, 415/330–6300.

The vast **Golden Gate National Recreation Area,** administered by the U.S. Department of the Interior's National Park Service, encompasses much of the San Francisco and Marin coastline: beaches, redwood groves, historic forts, the Presidio, and more. For information, contact the National Park Service, Western Regional Information Center, Bldg. 201, Fort Mason, San Francisco 94123, 415/556–0561. This office handles all national parks in California, Oregon, and Washington. The Fort Mason Visitors Center is open weekdays 9:30–4:30. A smaller office on the lower level of the Cliff House (1090 Point Lobos Ave., at Great Hwy., Richmond District, 415/556–8642.) is open daily 10–5.

The best places to stock up on pamphlets, books, and maps are **Rand McNally** (595 Market St., at 2nd St., 415/777–3131) and **Sierra Club Bookstore** (85 2nd St., at Mission St., 415/977–5600).

PERSONAL SECURITY

As in any city these days, it's important to use common sense while visiting and touring. Be wary in the Tenderloin, parts of the Mission (around 14th Street, for example), the lower Haight, and SoMa (South of Market) if you aren't in the main thoroughfare, where clubs and nightlife are centered. When going out at night, know your destination, how you are getting there, and most importantly, how you are getting back: Cabs are scarce and therefore difficult to hail on the street, but hotels, restaurants, clubs, and bars will call one for you upon request.

PUBLICATIONS

daily

San Francisco Chronicle. The city's main newspaper is published each morning. The Sunday paper, published jointly with the *Examiner*, contains the must-read "Datebook" (the Pink Section). It's chock-full of reviews and listings for museums, galleries, performing arts, movies, nightlife, restaurants, and festivals.

San Francisco Examiner. The *Examiner* hits newsstands every afternoon except Sunday, when a morning paper is published jointly with the *San Francisco Chronicle*. For extensive listings of city events, pick up Friday's "Weekend" section.

weekly and monthly

Bay Area Reporter. The city's free gay weekly is published each Thursday. It features local and national news, as well as listings of local events.

Bay Guardian. This free, alternative weekly (published Wednesdays) has in-depth cultural listings, and occasional daring investigative pieces. Look for its "Best of the Bay Area" special every August and the "Insider's guide" issue in February.

San Francisco Focus. A monthly publication of KQED (the city's public radio and TV stations), *Focus* covers arts, fine dining, and shopping in the city, as well as engaging features about the City By the Bay.

SF Weekly. This free, alternative weekly, published on Wednesdays, has extensive, beyond-the-mainstream cultural events listings.

RADIO STATIONS

Due to the Bay Area's many hills, not all of the stations listed here will be in range all of the time.

fm radio stations

KZSC (88.1): eclectic

KQED (88.5): NPR news, public affairs

KUSP (88.9): NPR news, variety

KCEA (89.1): Big Band

KLEL (89.3): rock

KOHL (89.3): Top 40

KPOO (89.5): Third World

KFJC (89.7): college radio, eclectic

KZSU (90.1): eclectic

KUSF (90.3): college radio, eclectic

KSJS (90.5): college radio, variety, jazz

KALX (90.7): college radio, variety

KCSM (91.1): NPR news, jazz

KKUP (91.5): eclectic

KALW (91.7): international news, variety

KLOV (91.1): Christian music

KZWC (92.1): Spanish music

KSJO (92.3): album-oriented rock

KZSF (92.7): Spanish music

KRQC (92.7): '70s hits

KYCY (93.3): country

KAXT (93.5): country

KPFA (94.1): eclectic

KUFX (94.5): classic rock

KYLD (94.9): hits, dance

KRTY (95.3): country

KOYT (95.7): adult contemporary

KSQQ (96.1): Portuguese

KOIT (96.5): light rock

KWAV (96.9): adult contemporary

KLLC (97.3): adult contemporary

KBGG (98.1): '60s–'80s classic rock

KOME (98.5): modern rock

KSOL (98.9/99.1): Spanish pop

KFRC (99.7): '60s and '70s rock

KBAY (100.3): adult contemporary, light rock

KTOM (100.7): country

KKHI (100.9): classical

K101 (101.3): adult contemporary

KXDC (101.7): light jazz

KDFC (102.1): classical

KBLX (102.9): jazz

KSCU (103.3): college radio, alternative rock

KKSF (103.7): adult contemporary

KISE (103.9): oldies

KRAY (103.9): Spanish music

KMBY (104.3): alternative rock

KFOG (104.5): album-oriented rock

KBRG (104.9): Spanish music

KOCN (105.1): oldies

KITS (105.3): modern rock

KARA (105.7): oldies

KMEL (106.1): hits, dance

KLUE (106.3): adult contemporary

KEZR (106.5): adult contemporary

KEAR (106.9): Christian talk, music

KVRG (107.1): Spanish talk, music

KPIG (107.5): country, rock

KSAN (107.7): classic rock

am radio stations

KSFO (560): sports, talk

KFRC (610): '60s and '70s rock

KSTE (650): talk

KNBR (680): talk, sports

KVRG (700): Spanish music

KCBS (740): news

KGO (810): news, talk

KNEW (910): country

KABL (960): Big Band

KCTY (980): Spanish music

KATD (990): Christian contemporary

KIQI (1010): Spanish music

KOFY (1050): Spanish music

KSCO (1080): news, talk

KFAX (1100): Christian music, talk

KZSJ (1120): Spanish dance music

KLOK (1170): Spanish music

KDFC (1220): classical

KNRY (1240): news, talk, oldies

KOIT (1260): adult contemporary, light rock

KAZA (1290): Spanish rock

KDIA (1310): soul

KLBS (1330): Portuguese, Spanish

KOMY (1340): news, talk

KKSJ (1370): nostalgic

KTOM (1380): country

KVTO (1400): Asian programming

KRML (1410): Jazz

KNTA (1430): Spanish

KEST (1450): Chinese

KSJX (1500): Vietnamese

KNOB (1510): jazz

KMPG (1520): Spanish music

KPIX (1550): country

KTGE (1570): Spanish music

KLIV (1590): news

SIGHTSEEING INFORMATION

California Office of Tourism (801 K St., Suite 1600, Sacramento 95814, 916/322–2881 or 800/862–2543): Answers questions about travel in the Golden State. Call or write for a free copy of the "California Visitors Guide," which includes a calendar of statewide events.

`4` *e-6*

SFCVB Visitor Information Center (900 Market St., at Powell St., Hallidie Plaza, San Francisco 94102, 415/391–2000 or 415/391–2001 for 24-hour recorded information): In the lower level of Hallidie Plaza, next to the Cable Car Turnaround and Powell Street BART Station. Write or call for a free copy of their complete "Visitor Information Package," which includes tips on city lodging, sightseeing, shopping, dining, entertainment, sports, and arts. Or stop by the center for free maps, brochures, and sightseeing guides, as well as discount public transportation passes, all dispensed by a helpful, multilingual staff. The center is open weekdays 9–5:30, Saturday 9–3, and Sunday 10–2.

`4` *c-2*

Redwood Empire Association (2801 Leavenworth St., 2nd Floor, San Francisco 94133, 415/394–5991 or 888/678–8507): The association's visitor center in the Cannery shopping center is open Tuesday–Saturday 10–6. Its staff provides free information on San Francisco and surrounding areas. Their 48-page *Redwood Empire Visitor's Guide* has useful maps, events listings, and recreation highlights for San Francisco, the wine country, redwood groves, and the north coast. To receive a copy by mail, send $3 (cash, check, or money order). The guide is $1 at the association's visitor center, free at the airport and San Francisco Visitor Information Center. Also worth obtaining is the association's handy free booklet "How to Get There from Union Square," which explains how to reach approximately 50 points of interest in downtown San Francisco by public transportation.

The San Francisco Bay Area encompasses dozens of towns, and many of them have chambers of commerce that are happy to provide you with information. A few of the largest are:

`3` *d-2*

Berkeley Convention and Visitors Bureau (2015 Center St., Berkeley 94704, 510/549–7040 or 510/549–8710 for recorded information).

Marin County Convention and Visitors Bureau (Marin Center, Avenue of the Flags, San Rafael 94903, 415/472–7470).

`3` *d-7*

Oakland Convention and Visitors Authority (550 10th St., Suite 214, Oakland 94607, 510/839–9000).

San Jose Convention and Visitors Bureau (McEnery Convention Center, 150 W. San Carlos St., San Jose 95113, 408/977–0900 or 408/295–2265 for 24-hour recorded entertainment and events listings).

SPORTSPHONE

BASS Tickets (510/762–2277) sells tickets to many Bay Area sporting events.

City Line (415/512–5000 or 415/808–5000, ext. 6000): Up-to-the-minute local and national sports reports, area fishing reports.

TAXES & GRATUITIES

The California State Tax on all purchased items (except food for preparation and items purchased for out-of-state delivery) is 8.5%. Although there is no sales tax on hotel rooms, there is a 14% "transient occupancy tax" added to your bill. The rate quoted will not normally include this tax.

The average tip for good service in a restaurant is 15% of the bill; the same percentage is used for taxis. For those who carry your bags at the airport or hotel, the going rate is $1–$2 a bag.

TELEVISION

KTVU *(Fox/Oakland): 2*

KRON *(NBC/SF): 4*

KPIX *(CBS/SF): 5*

KGO *(ABC/SF): 7*

KQED *(PBS/SF): 9*

KNTV *(ABC/San Jose): 11*

KDTV *(Spanish/SF): 14*

KOFY *(WBN/SF): 20*

KTSF *(Independent/SF): 26*

KMTP *(Independent/SF): 32*

KICU *(Independent/SF): 36*

KCNS (Independent/SF): 38

KBHK (Independent/SF): 44

KPST (Independent/SF): 66

A&E (Arts & Entertainment): 39

AMC (American Movie Classics): 35

BAYTV (Bay TV): 30

BET (Black Entertainment Television): 57

BRAVO (Bravo): 54

CNBC (Consumer News & Business): 27

CNN (Cable News Network): 42

COM (Comedy Central): 79

COURT (Court TV): 75

CSPAN (House of Representatives): 68

DISC (Discovery Channel): 37

DISN (The Disney Channel): 53

E! (The Entertainment Channel): 63

ENC (Encore): 92

ESPN (Entertainment Sports Network): 34

ESPN2 (Entertainment Sports Network 2): 88

FAM (The Family Channel): 47

FX (Fx Channel): 89

HBO (Home Box Office): 33

HIST (History Channel): 77

KNO (Knowledge TV): 82

LIFE (Lifetime): 46

LRN (The Learning Channel): 51

MAX (Cinemax): 45

MSNBC (Microsoft NBC): 84

MTV (Music Television): 48

NASH (The Nashville Network): 49

NICK (Nickelodeon): 38

NOST (Nostalgia): 64

PLAY (The Playboy Channel): 25

SHOW (Showtime): 41

SPT (Sports Channel): 59

STARZ (Starz): 73

TBS (Turner Broadcasting System): 43

TMC (The Movie Channel): 58

TNT (Turner Network Television): 52

TRAV (The Travel Channel): 81

USA (USA Network): 44

VH-1 (Video Hits One): 62

TRANSPORTATION

The **TravInfo Hotline** (415/817–1717, 510/817–1717, 650/817–1717, and 408/817–1717) has up-to-the-minute information on public transit lines, highway traffic conditions, carpooling, parking, and airport transit for all nine Bay Area counties. The *Regional Transit Guide* ($3.95) is an excellent resource listing Bay Area transportation agencies, lines, and frequency. It's available in bookstores as well as the San Francisco Visitor Information Center at Hallidie Plaza.

the muni system

Muni (Municipal Railway) (415/673–6864, 415/923–6336 for 24-hour route assistance, 415/923–6168 for lost and found) is a network of diesel buses, electric trolley buses, Muni Metro streetcars, historic streetcars, and the world-famous cable cars. The 80 Muni routes include 16 express lines, plus special service to 3Com Park on game days. Service operates 24 hours daily, but is limited after midnight; during weekdays buses run approximately 10–15 minutes apart. For a comprehensive map of all Muni routes send $2.50 (check or money order, payable to S.F. Municipal Railway) to: Muni Map, 949 Presidio Ave., Room 238, San Francisco 94115. The map is sold at many stores in San Francisco and throughout the Bay Area.

Adult fare for Muni-system buses and streetcars is $1. For senior citizens and youth 5–17, the fare is 35¢. Exact change is required. **Transfers** are issued free on request at the time the fare is paid for bus or streetcar service, and are valid for 90 minutes to 2 hours for two boardings in any direction. There are a number of discount travel plans: The **Fast Pass** ($35) is an adult monthly pass good for all Muni transport, including cable cars, as well as BART and CalTrain within San Francisco. The Fast Pass for youth and senior citizens costs $8 (proper identification required). The **Weekly Pass** ($9) is valid from Monday through Sunday on all Muni buses and streetcars, and each cable car ride is an additional $1. **Passport** passes allow unlimited access to Muni buses, street-cars, and cable cars for one day ($6), three days ($10), or seven days ($15). Passport passes are the best option for visitors who plan to do plenty of sight-seeing, and they are also good for dis-counts at tourist attractions around San Francisco, including the museums in Golden Gate Park. Purchase passes at the Visitor Information Center at Halli-die Plaza, or at the Muni booth next to the cable-car turnaround at Fisherman's Wharf.

CABLE CARS

San Francisco's charming cable cars have delighted residents and visitors since 1873. Cable car fare for all riders is $2. Senior citizens (65 and older) pay $1 daily between 9 PM and 7 AM (at other times they pay the full fare). Tickets are purchased aboard the car. Exact change is not required, and transfers are neither issued nor accepted. (With a valid Muni Fast Pass or Passport there is no addi-tional charge to ride the cable cars.) Each car has seats for up to 100 passen-gers; standing and straphanging are also allowed. To board a cable car midway along its route, move toward it quickly as it pauses, wedge yourself into any avail-able space and hold on tightly. Cable cars operate daily from 6 AM until 1 AM.

The **Powell–Mason line** (No. 59) runs from downtown (Market and Powell Streets) through Union Square, Nob Hill, Chinatown, and North Beach, end-ing at the east end of Fisherman's Wharf. The **Powell–Hyde line** (No. 60, the most scenic route), which also begins at Powell and Market streets near Union Square, runs through Nob Hill, Chinatown, and Russian Hill, and ends at the west end of Fisherman's Wharf. The wait to board at either Fish-erman's Wharf or the cable-car turn-around at Powell and Market streets can often exceed an hour. The **California Street line** (No. 61) runs from Van Ness Avenue and California Street through Nob Hill, Chinatown, and the Financial District; it ends at the Embarcadero Muni station, at Market and California Streets. Though the views on this line are not as spectacular, there are fewer crowds.

bart

BART (Bay Area Rapid Transit) (415/992–2278 in San Francisco, 510/465–2278 in the East Bay, and 510/464–7090 for lost and found) is a smooth, air-con-ditioned subway and commuter rail sys-tem that operates between San Francisco and the East Bay. It's best for moving from city to city around the San Francisco Bay rather than traveling between points in San Francisco itself. The five colored-coded lines are Rich-mond to Fremont; Richmond to Daly City/Colma via San Francisco; Pitts-burg/Bay Point to Colma via San Fran-cisco; Fremont to Daly City via San Francisco; and Dublin/Pleasanton to Daly City via San Francisco. BART will take you from San Francisco to Oak-land, Berkeley, and Concord, as well as the Oakland Coliseum and Oakland International Airport. Each line operates under a different schedule, but trains generally run every 10 to 20 minutes until midnight, with service starting up again at 4 AM weekdays, 6 AM Saturdays, and 8 AM Sundays. Evenings, Sundays, and holidays only the Richmond–Fre-mont, Pittsburg/Bay Point–Colma, and Dublin/Pleasanton–Daly City lines operate.

Fares run from $1.10 to $4.70, depend-ing on length of journey, though trans-fers between the lines (at designated transfer stations) are free. Ticket vend-ing machines at each station allow you to buy tickets worth $1.10–$60; the newest machines accept ATM cards as well as cash. Insert your ticket into the fare gate, then keep it in a safe place after it pops out the top—you'll need your ticket to exit. The fare is automati-cally deducted from your ticket at the exit gate; any amount left unused can be used on your next ride, as you can add fare to old tickets. If you're plan-ning to take a Muni or AC Transit bus after your BART ride, pick up a bus transfer slip at one of the specially marked white vending machines as you exit the BART station.

Several discount BART fare packages are available. Adults can purchase the **High-Value Ticket**—$48 worth of rides for $45 (a $3 savings); or the **Blue Ticket,** $32 worth of rides for $30. The **Red Ticket,** for children between the ages of 5 and 12, is $16 worth of rides for $4 (a $12 discount). The **Green Ticket,** for senior citizens 65 years and older, is also $16 worth of rides for $4. Appropriate identification is required for purchase of Red or Green tickets. **BART Plus** tickets provide substantial discounts on local bus systems: A $28–$61 ticket (8 different values) entitles you to $15–$50 worth of BART rides plus unlimited rides on any Bay Area bus system for either the first or last two weeks of the month.

ferry

In San Francisco, the main point of departure is the landmark **San Francisco Ferry Building** (on the Embarcadero, at the foot of Market Street). In most cases, you purchase your ticket after you board. All ferries are equipped with snack bars and toilets. Your ferry ticket acts as a free transfer to buses on both sides of the bay.

Alameda–Oakland Ferry Service (510/ 522–3300 for 24-hour FerryFone, or 415/ 705–5555 for group reservations) runs ferries from the SF Ferry Building to Alameda (2990 Main St.) and Oakland's Jack London Square (Clay St., at The Embarcadero). One-way fare is $4, senior citizens $2.50, children 5–12 $1.50. There is no service on Thanksgiving, Christmas, or New Year's Day. Call for a current schedule.

Weekends from May through October the Alameda–Oakland Ferry Service operates ferries from Alameda and Oakland to Angel Island State Park. Round-trip fare (park admission included) is $13; senior citizens and youth 13–18 pay $9, and children 5–12 pay $6. A limited number of bikes is allowed on board at no additional charge, on a first-come, first-served basis. Call for a schedule.

Blue and Gold Fleet (415/773–1188 for 24-hour recorded information or 415/ 705–5555 for ticket purchase) sends ferries to Tiburon, Sausalito, Angel Island State Park, and Alcatraz. The weekday commuter ferry to Tiburon (20 min) departs from the SF Ferry Building. All other departures are from Pier 41 at Fisherman's Wharf, including weekend service to Tiburon (30 min) and daily service to Sausalito (30 min), Angel Island (40 min), and Alcatraz. One-way

fare to Sausalito or Tiburon is $5.50, $2.75 for children 5–11. To Angel Island, round-trip fare (including park admission) is $10, $9 for youth 12–18, $5.50 for children 5–11, free for children under 5. Bikes are allowed on board at no additional charge, though space is limited. To Alcatraz, fare includes a worthwhile audio tour: $11, $9.25 for senior citizens, $5.75 for children 5–11. Without the audio tour the cost is $7.75, $6 for senior citizens, $4.50 for children 5–11, free for children under 5. There is no service on Thanksgiving, Christmas, or New Year's Day. Call for a current schedule.

Golden Gate Ferry Service (415/923–2000, or 415/455–2000 in Marin County) ferries passengers from the SF Ferry Building to Sausalito and Larkspur in Marin County. To Larkspur, one-way fare is $2.50 weekdays, $4.25 weekends and holidays. To Sausalito, one-way fare is $4.25. Senior citizens ride at a 50% discount at all times; children 6–12 receive a 25% discount. There is no service on Thanksgiving, Christmas, or New Year's Day. Call for a current schedule.

Harbor Bay Ferry (510/769–5500, or 415/247–1604 for reservations) shuttles between Harbor Bay Isle in the East Bay, near the Oakland International Airport, and both the San Francisco Ferry Building and Pier 41. Fare is $4, $3 senior citizens, $2 children 6–12. The Harbor Bay Isle ferry to San Francisco operates weekdays year-round and weekends from May to October. The Harbor Bay Ferry also provides round-trip service to **3Com Park** (30 min) for weekend afternoon Giants and 49ers games. For Giants games, round-trip fare is $10, or $7 for senior citizens and children under 12; roundtrip fare with Giants game tickets is $15, $12 for senior citizens and children under 12. For 49er games, round-trip fare is $15, or $12 for senior citizens and children under 12. Call for game dates and for information on 49ers game ticket packages. Reservations are recommended for ferry service to 3Com Park as seating is limited.

Vallejo Baylink Ferry (707/643–3779 for recorded information, or 415/705–5555 for group reservations) provides service between San Francisco, Angel Island, and Vallejo with connecting shuttles to Marine World Africa USA. In San Francisco, ferries leave from the SF Ferry Building and Pier 39. One-way fare from

San Francisco to Vallejo is $7.50, or $3.75 for senior citizens, persons with disabilities, and children 6–12. The **Marine World Africa USA Package,** which includes round-trip ferry transportation between San Francisco and Vallejo, a shuttle bus between the Vallejo Ferry Terminal and Marine World, and park admission, costs $39, $32 for senior citizens, $23.50 for children 6–12. Round-trip fare from Vallejo to Angel Island State Park (park admission included) is $11, $9 for senior citizens, and $6 children 6–12. The Vallejo Baylink Ferries can carry between 25 and 30 bikes each, on a first-come, first-served basis. Call for a current schedule.

bus

AC Transit (Alameda–Contra Costa Transit) (415/817–1717) provides bus service in Alameda and Contra Costa counties, and transbay service between those counties and San Francisco via the Bay Bridge. Use AC Transit buses to reach Berkeley, Oakland, and Treasure Island. Buses depart from San Francisco's Transbay Terminal (Mission St., between 1st and Fremont Sts.). Call for schedules and information.

Golden Gate Transit (415/453–2100) provides bus service in San Francisco, Marin, and Sonoma counties, and connecting service between the counties. Buses depart from the Transbay Terminal (Mission St., between 1st and Fremont Sts.) and several other points in San Francisco. Fares are calculated on a zone system; call for schedules and information.

SamTrans (800/660–4287) buses serve all of San Mateo County, with local and commuter express routes traveling as far south as Palo Alto. Additional buses run to SFO, the Hayward BART Station, and the Transbay Terminal (Mission St., between 1st and Fremont Sts.) in downtown San Francisco.

train

CalTrain (800/660–4287) commuter train service operates between San Francisco and Gilroy, with many stops in San Mateo and Santa Clara counties. On weekdays, Muni express shuttle buses connect the CalTrain station (4th and Townsend Sts.) with San Francisco's Financial District, South of Market, and Levi's Plaza. Call for schedules and

information. A free CalTrain–SFO shuttle operates daily between the Millbrae Station and the airport; call SFO Rides (800/736–2008) for information about this service.

taxi

Taxis charge $1.70 for the first mile, $1.80 for each additional mile, and 30¢ for every minute in stalled traffic. The appropriate tip for good service is 15%. A ride from downtown to San Francisco International airport averages $30 plus tip. Taxis are scarce on San Francisco streets, and particularly difficult to hail during rush hours. Look for the lighted sign on the cab roof, wait for one at the taxi stand or a major hotel, or call for a reservation. It is safest to stick with a city-licensed taxi denoted by the city insignia on the front door. Check the Yellow Pages under taxis for a number of choices. Two reliable companies are **Veteran's Cab** (415/552–1300) and **Yellow Cab** (415/626–2345).

In the East Bay you'll pay a $2 base fee, plus $2 per mile; a ride from Oakland to San Francisco can cost $25 or more. Call **Friendly Cab** (510/536–3000) or **Yellow Cab** (510/841–8294).

bicycle

In 1996, the **S.F. Bicycle Program** (415/585–2453) began marking the most bicycle-friendly of San Francisco's streets with numbered route signs. North–south routes have odd numbers, while east–west routes are even-numbered; the numbers go up as you move west and south. The route map is printed in the San Francisco Yellow Pages. Purchase the *San Francisco Biking/Walking Guide* ($3), an excellent biking map that shows street grades and routes, at select city stores or the **Berkeley TRiP Commute Store** (2033 Center St., one block west of Berkeley BART, Berkeley, 510/644–7665). For personalized route maps, safety information, a list of Bay Area bicycle advocacy groups, commuter information, and updates about the San Francisco Bicycle Program, call the San Francisco Department of Parking and Traffic's **Bicycle Information Hotline** (415/585–BIKE). The grassroots **San Francisco Bicycle Coalition** (1095 Market St., Suite 215, San Francisco 94103, 415/431–BIKE) provides information on activities, advocacy, cycling groups, routes, and public transportation options.

You can take your bicycle on Bay Area transit systems with varying degrees of hassle. **Muni** currently allows bikes only on Bus 76, which travels to the Marin Headlands. Approximately 10 other lines (traversing some of the city's steepest hills) are slated to receive bike racks in 1998; contact Muni for more information. **BART** allows bikes in all but the first car of each train, except during commuter rush hours (6:30 AM–9 AM and 3:30 PM–6:30 PM). During these hours, a bike shuttle ($1) operates every 30–45 minutes between MacArthur BART and the Transbay Terminal (Mission St., between 1st and Fremont Sts.); call **CalTrans** (510/286–0669) for more information. In the future, BART may require a special permit for those who wish to bring their bikes on board; for details call the **BART Office of Passenger Service** (510/464–7127). All **ferries,** except the Blue and Gold Fleet's Bay cruises, accept bicycles on a first-come, first-served basis. For a summer weekend jaunt to Angel Island State Park you'll want to line up well before departure time to secure a spot for your bike.

getting to the airports

SAN FRANCISCO INTERNATIONAL AIRPORT (SFO)

San Francisco International Airport (415/876–7809) lies 15 mi south of downtown San Francisco off Highway 101. For information on transportation options to and from the airport, call **SFO Rides** (800/736–2008).

By Public Transportation. From the Transbay Terminal (Mission St., between 1st and Fremont Sts.), **SamTrans Buses 7B** (1 hr, $1) and **7F** (45 min, $2.50) provide direct service to the airport. Bus 7F is an express bus that does not allow luggage. From the Colma BART Station, SamTrans **Bus 3X** (15 min, $1) also has direct service to SFO. At the **CalTrain** station in Millbrae, a free airport shuttle service (10 min) connects with all arriving and departing trains. For more information on SamTrans and CalTrain services, call 800/660–4287.

By Shuttle Van. For most San Franciscans, the preferred method of travel to SFO is by shuttle van; 12 such companies provide 24-hour, door-to-door service between the airport and addresses in San Francisco, the East Bay, Marin County, and along the Peninsula. Most shuttle services require reservations only three hours in advance. Average cost ranges from $10 to $14 per person one-way. Reliable companies include **Super Shuttle** (415/558–8500), **Bay Shuttle** (415/564–3400), **Quake City** (415/255–4899), and **Yellow Shuttle Service** (415/282–7433). **Airport Connection** (510/841–0150) requires reservations 24 hours in advance. For others, check the San Francisco Yellow Pages under "Airport Transportation Service."

By Express Bus. Three private companies run express bus service between SFO and major San Francisco hotels. The **SFO Airporter** (415/495–8404) stops at points around Union Square and downtown. The **Wharf Airporter** (415/550–0888) travels along Van Ness and through Fisherman's Wharf. The **Pacific Airporter** (415/282–6088) route covers Moscone Center and the Civic Center area. Average cost is $10 per person one-way.

By Taxi and Limousine. Taxi service to SFO costs approximately $30 from downtown San Francisco or $34 from Fisherman's Wharf, plus tip. Taxis may carry a maximum of five people. The city has nine registered limousine services that provide transport to SFO. The minimum charge is $40 for one hour; average cost from downtown is $60. Limousines may carry up to 12 people. For a list of companies, check the San Francisco Yellow Pages under "Airport Transportation Service."

Airport Parking. Long- and short-term parking are available at SFO. **Long-term parking** is located near the San Bruno Avenue East exit off Highway 101; the cost is $11 per day for a maximum of seven days, plus $14 for each additional day. Free shuttles transport passengers between the long-term lot and the airport terminals. This lot tends to fill up during peak travel times, especially on three-day holiday weekends. Call the airport's **Parking Hotline** (415/877–0227) to check on parking availability, rates, directions, and valet parking.

OAKLAND INTERNATIONAL AIRPORT

Oakland International Airport (1 Airport Dr., off Hegenberger Rd., 510/577–

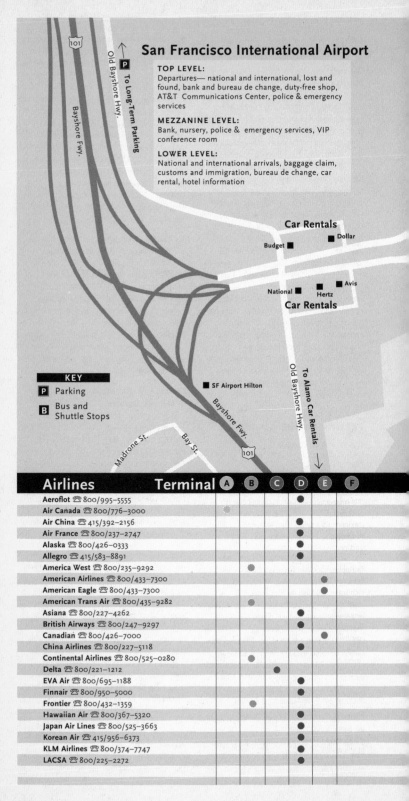

San Francisco International Airport

TOP LEVEL:
Departures— national and international, lost and found, bank and bureau de change, duty-free shop, AT&T Communications Center, police & emergency services

MEZZANINE LEVEL:
Bank, nursery, police & emergency services, VIP conference room

LOWER LEVEL:
National and international arrivals, baggage claim, customs and immigration, bureau de change, car rental, hotel information

KEY

- **P** Parking
- **B** Bus and Shuttle Stops

Airlines	Terminal A	B	C	D	E	F
Aeroflot ☎ 800/995–5555				●		
Air Canada ☎ 800/776–3000	●					
Air China ☎ 415/392–2156				●		
Air France ☎ 800/237–2747				●		
Alaska ☎ 800/426–0333				●		
Allegro ☎ 415/583–8891				●		
America West ☎ 800/235–9292		●				
American Airlines ☎ 800/433–7300					●	
American Eagle ☎ 800/433–7300					●	
American Trans Air ☎ 800/435–9282		●				
Asiana ☎ 800/227–4262				●		
British Airways ☎ 800/247–9297				●		
Canadian ☎ 800/426–7000					●	
China Airlines ☎ 800/227–5118				●		
Continental Airlines ☎ 800/525–0280		●				
Delta ☎ 800/221–1212			●			
EVA Air ☎ 800/695–1188				●		
Finnair ☎ 800/950–5000				●		
Frontier ☎ 800/432–1359		●				
Hawaiian Air ☎ 800/367–5320				●		
Japan Air Lines ☎ 800/525–3663				●		
Korean Air ☎ 415/956–6373				●		
KLM Airlines ☎ 800/374–7747				●		
LACSA ☎ 800/225–2272				●		

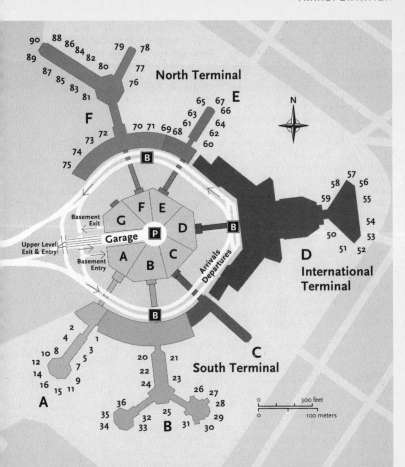

Airlines (cont.) Terminal	A	B	C	D	E	F
LTU International Airways				●		
Lufthansa ☎ 800/645–3880				●		
Mexicana ☎ 800/531–7921				●		
Midwest Express ☎ 800/452–2022		●				
Northwest (Domestic) ☎ 800/225–2525			●			
(International) ☎ 800/447–4747				●		
Philippine Air Lines ☎ 800/435–9725				●		
Reno Air ☎ 800/736–6247			●			
Rich International		●				
Shuttle by United ☎ 800/748–8853						●
Singapore Airlines ☎ 800/742–3333				●		
Skywest/Delta Connection ☎ 800/221–1212			●			
Southwest Airlines ☎ 800/435–9792	●					
TACA ☎ 800/535–8780				●		
Tower Air ☎ 800/221–2500				●		
TWA ☎ (Domestic) ☎ 800/221–2000		●				
(International) ☎ 800/892–4141		●				
United (Domestic) ☎ 800/241–6522						●
(International) ☎ 800/538–2929				●		
United Express ☎ 800/241–6522						●
US Airways ☎ 800/428–4322	●					
US Airways Express ☎ 800/428–4322	●					
Virgin Atlantic ☎ 800/862–8621				●		
Western Pacific ☎ 800/930–3030					●	

4000) is 6 mi south of downtown Oakland, off Highway 880. From San Francisco, take Highway 80 east across the Bay Bridge to Highway 980 south, then continue following signs south on Highway 880.

The **Air-BART Shuttle** (510/562–7700) runs every 15–20 minutes between the airport and the Coliseum BART Station. Buy tickets ($2) at the BART station or airport terminal before you board. **AC Transit Bus 58** ($1.25) follows the same route, continuing on to downtown Oakland. Most of the city's **private shuttle services** operate between San Francisco and the Oakland airport; expect to pay between $20 and $35 per person one-way. A taxi to downtown San Francisco from Oakland International Airport generally ranges from $30 to $35. **Long-term airport parking** (510/633–2571) is $10 for 24 hours or $8 in the economy lot next to Terminal 1. A free shuttle carries passengers between the parking lot and the airport terminal.

WEATHER

San Francisco is blessed with a temperate marine climate and mild weather year-round. It's rarely warmer than 70°F, or colder than 40°F. The warmest months are May, September, and October. In summer, morning and evening fog rolls in over the bay; they bring a chill but dissipate quickly. Visitors will be most comfortable if they bring a light jacket or coat, and leave lightweight summer clothes at home. December through March is the rainy season (annual rainfall averages 19.24″), making an umbrella essential. Note that the weather in San Francisco is known for its changeability and actually varies within the city; the bay side of Twin Peaks and Mt. Davidson are warmer and drier areas than those along the Pacific. It's best to dress in layers.

The rest of the Bay Area is divided into myriad micro-climates, with temperatures in Northern Marin, Napa, the Contra Coast, and the South Bay running between 15 and 20 degrees warmer than the city. In the **East Bay** highs average 72°, lows 43°. **Marin County**'s weather varies from town to town: The coast is usually fogged in, the bayside towns of Tiburon and Sausalito get a cool breeze, and San Rafael checks in at a solid few degrees warmer than most of the Bay Area, with an average summer high of 82°. In the **South Bay,** average summer highs, both on the coast and inland, hover in the 80s. In the winter, things cool down to a medium rare, with lows dipping to 40°.

For updated local weather reports, call the **National Weather Service's Bay Area Forecast office** (415/364–7974). **City Line** (415/512–5000 or 415/808–5000 extension 3000) has local and national weather reports. The **SFCVB Information Hotline** (415/391–2000 or 415/391–2001) provides local weather updates. For ski conditions in Northern California, Tahoe, or the Sierras, call the **California State Automobile Association's Ski Report Hotline** (415/864–6440).

January

Daily mean maximum: 56.1°F

Daily mean minimum: 46.2°F

Rainfall total inches: 4.48″

February

Daily mean maximum: 59.4°F

Daily mean minimum: 48.4°F

Rainfall total inches: 2.83″

March

Daily mean maximum: 60.0°F

Daily mean minimum: 48.6°F

Rainfall total inches: 2.58″

April

Daily mean maximum: 61.1°F

Daily mean minimum: 49.2°F

Rainfall total inches: 1.48″

May

Daily mean maximum: 62.5°F

Daily mean minimum: 50.7°F

Rainfall total inches: 0.35″

June

Daily mean maximum: 64.3°F

Daily mean minimum: 52.5°F

Rainfall total inches: 0.15″

July

Daily mean maximum: 64.0°F

Daily mean minimum: 53.1°F

Rainfall total inches: 0.04"

August

Daily mean maximum: 65.0°F

Daily mean minimum: 54.2°F

Rainfall total inches: 0.08"

September

Daily mean maximum: 68.9°F

Daily mean minimum: 55.8°F

Rainfall total inches: 0.24"

October

Daily mean maximum: 68.3°F

Daily mean minimum: 54.8°F

Rainfall total inches: 1.09"

November

Daily mean maximum: 62.9°F

Daily mean minimum: 51.5°F

Rainfall total inches: 2.40"

December

Daily mean maximum: 56.9°F

Daily mean minimum: 47.2°F

Rainfall total inches: 3.52"

chapter 2

PLACES TO EXPLORE

galleries, gargoyles, museums, and more

For such a small city, San Francisco has a remarkably large international following. Millions all over the world know how to hum a few bars of "I Left My Heart In San Francisco" and can identify the stunning skyline of the City by the Bay from mere glimpses in movies and magazines. Beyond its famous cable cars and majestic Golden Gate Bridge, however, lies much more. Wander the city and you'll discover unique ethnic neighborhoods, provocative art galleries, and unusual museums. Spend time on the waterfront, at Fisherman's Wharf, and you're sure to succumb to the temptation of a ferry boat ride across the bay or out to eerie, foreboding Alcatraz Island. Throughout the city, Victorian mansions—confectionary structures with turrets and gingerbread trim—stand as reminders of the great 1906 earthquake and fire, which destroyed the homes of 250,000 San Franciscans, two-thirds of the population at that time. Even when you think you've seen all of the sights, you still have all of San Francisco's culture to contend with—all at its brilliant best in the many fairs, parades, and festivals that take place year-round in the balmy outdoors.

where to go

ART GALLERIES

4 e-6

ARTISTS FORUM

Four shows (solo and group) per year are augmented with gallery talks, musical performances, workshops, and demonstrations at this gallery-cum-salon. All of these activities help foster the gallery's goal of giving the public greater access to artists and their ideas. *251 Post St., at Stockton St., Union Square, 415/981–6347. Closed Sat.–Mon.*

7 g-2

BELCHER STUDIOS GALLERY

A slickly converted early 20th-century warehouse on a residential street contains this gallery and small outdoor sculpture area. The focus is on up-and-coming local talent working in various media. The building also houses a complex of artists' studios. *69 Belcher St., between 14th St. and Duboce Ave., The Castro, 415/255–8900.*

4 e-6

BOMANI GALLERY

Bomani showcases work with multicultural viewpoints, often by African-American artists. It's a stately place displaying folk art as well as historical and contemporary art in several rooms. You may spot Danny Glover here; he's married to gallery owner Asake Bomani. *251 Post St., at Stockton St., Union Square, 415/ 296–8677. Closed Sun. and Mon.*

4 e-5

BRAUNSTEIN–QUAY GALLERY

Part of the Union Square scene since 1961, this classy gallery features works by contemporary artists such as Richard Shaw and Nell Sinton, including painting, sculpture, assemblage, photography, and ceramics. Works by younger, less well-known artists are displayed in the front of the gallery. *250 Sutter St., between Grant Ave. and Kearny St., Union Square, 415/392–5532. Closed Sun. and Mon.*

4 d-2

CAMPBELL-THIEBAUD GALLERY

In a brown shingled building that previously housed a speakeasy and artists' studios, paintings of the Bay Area Figurative school are displayed on two floors. Artists include Wayne Thiebaud, Christopher Brown, and Manuel Neri. Outside is a lovely, sculpture-filled garden. *645 Chestnut St., between Columbus and Mason Sts., North Beach, 415/441–8680. Closed Sun. and Mon.*

4 g-7

CAPP STREET PROJECT

Taking its name from its initial incarnation on Capp Street in the Mission District, this spacious gallery gives artists the opportunity to create major site-specific installations as part of its renowned artist-in-residence program. While the gallery itself is a rough-hewn warehouse, the solo shows, by internationally known contemporary artists such as Janine Antoni, Glen Seator, and Ilya Kabakov, tend toward slick and state-of-the-art. *525 2nd St., between Bryant and Brannan Sts., South Beach, 415/495–7101. Closed Sun.–Mon.*

4 f-6
CATHARINE CLARK GALLERY

Small but growing steadily, Catharine Clark shows contemporary painting, sculpture, and mixed media with a slightly sinister, surrealistic edge. Most of the work is by Bay Area artists, but the roster has expanded to include some from Canada, southern California, and beyond. *49 Geary St., at Kearny St., Union Square, 415/399–1439. Closed Sun.*

4 f-6
CROWN POINT PRESS

As one of the world's most respected printmaking facilities, Crown Point Press has hosted artists of international repute such as Wayne Thiebaud, Richard Diebenkorn, John Cage, Pat Steir, and Helen Frankenthaler. The sleek, ample gallery puts on group and solo exhibitions. *20 Hawthorne St., off Howard St., between 2nd and 3rd Sts., South of Market, 415/974–6273. Closed Sun. and Mon.*

4 e-5
DOROTHY WEISS GALLERY

Contemporary ceramic and glass works are on display at this well-respected, two-floor gallery. Ceramists Michael Lucero, Annabeth Rosen, and Annette Corcoran, and glass artists Therman Statom, Jay Musler, and Hank Murta

---

SAN FRANCISCO'S TOP DRAWS

You can't see all of San Francisco in a single day, but if you're pressed for time, some sights shouldn't be missed.

Alcatraz (Historic Sites & Architecture)
   The famous island prison, a.k.a. "The Rock."

Cable Cars (Historic Sites & Architecture)
   The San Francisco treat.

Chinatown (Notable Neighborhoods)
   Produce stands and pagoda-topped roofs on crowded, narrow streets.

Cliff House (Historic Sites & Architecture)
   Prime spot for viewing the crashing Pacific waves.

Coit Tower (Historic Sites & Architecture)
   The beacon of Telegraph Hill, with WPA murals inside.

Fisherman's Wharf (Notable Neighborhoods)
   Seagulls, street performers, clam chowder, and crowds.

Golden Gate Bridge (Bridges)
   The city's most majestic landmark.

Haight-Ashbury (Notable Neighborhoods)
   Countercultural mecca of the '60s.

Lombard Street/"Crookedest Street" (Historic Sites & Architecture)
   Eight hairpin turns in a single city block.

Mission Dolores (Historic Buildings and Streets)
   Oldest building in the city, and the sixth of Father Serra's missions.

The Presidio (Notable Neighborhoods)
   Historic military base, now a splendid National Park.

San Francisco Museum of Modern Art (Art Museums)
   A landmark museum with a striking, Florentine–inspired design.

North Beach (Notable Neighborhoods)
   The birthplace of the Beat Generation.

Twin Peaks (Viewpoints)
   360° views of the San Francisco Bay Area.

Adams regularly exhibit their works here, though shows usually include artists from Europe and Asia as well. *256 Sutter St., at Grant Ave., Union Square, 415/397–3611. Closed Sun.–Mon.*

4 *c-2*

DYANSEN GALLERY

Large, colorful water sculptures mark the entrance to this vast art emporium. Inside are more traditional wares, such as original paintings and prints by Peter Max, Charles Bragg, and child prodigy Alexandra Nechita. Dyansen Gallery is one of the original publishers of Érte's graphic works, and also carries his sculptures. *799 Beach St., at Larkin St., Fisherman's Wharf, 415/928–0596.*

4 *f-6*

871 FINE ARTS

This intriguing small space specializes in printed matter—posters, Fluxus artifacts, and more. Its outstanding bookstore stocks hard-to-find art publications and monographs. *49 Geary St., at Kearny St., Union Square, 415/543–5155. Closed Sun.–Mon.*

8 *a-2*

ESP

Painting, photography, collage, and even a collection of nightclub flyers by promising local talent comprises the repertoire at this small, hip gallery. While most of the artists are unknown, they invariably prove interesting. *305 Valencia St., at 14th St., Mission District, 415/252–8191. Closed Sat.–Tues.*

8 *a-2*

FOUR WALLS

Formerly a firehouse, this 1,200 square-foot, light-filled gallery with Victorian accents is a funky backdrop for group and solo shows by emerging Bay Area artists. Hip, lively openings and experimental film screenings round out the program. Four Walls sits above a bar on one of San Francisco's most bohemian blocks. *3160-A 16th St., at Albion St., Mission District, 415/626–8515. Closed Sun.–Tues.*

4 *f-6*

FRAENKEL GALLERY

San Francisco's preeminent photography gallery presents museum-quality exhibitions. Solo and group shows of modern and 19th-century masters are in two main galleries. Selections from the inventory are in the back; William Wegman, Nan Goldin, Hiroshi Sugimoto, Diane Arbus, and Robert Adams are all represented. Its annual summer overview appears under the playful moniker of "Several Exceptionally Good Recently Acquired Pictures." *49 Geary St., at Kearny St., Union Square, 415/981–2661. Closed Sun. and Mon.*

8 *c-5*

GALERÍA DE LA RAZA

The city's premiere forum for art by Chicano and Latino artists is also the sponsor of the popular and spooky Día de los Muertos parade (*see* Events, *below*). The gallery, founded in the early '70s, mounts six to eight exhibitions per year reflecting issues affecting the community: immigration, sexuality, and spirituality. Murals on the building bring the art outdoors. *2857 24th St., at Bryant St., Potrero Hill, 415/826–8009. Closed Sun.–Mon.*

4 *f-6*

GALLERY PAULE ANGLIM

In a skylit main gallery you can see shows by important artists such as Louise Bourgeois, Nayland Blake, Enrique Chagoya, Jess, and Melissa Porkorny. While many of the artists have Bay Area connections, particularly the conceptual school of the 1970s, the gallery's programming is of international caliber. *14 Geary St., at Kearny St., Union Square, 415/433–2710. Closed Sun. and Mon.*

ART AND ACTING, UNDER ONE ROOF

The following art galleries can be counted on as venues for frequent, and often intriguing, performance art events.

New Langton Arts (Art Galleries)
The granddaddy of the city's mixed media centers.

Place Pigalle (Art Galleries)
Combination European café–bar, art gallery, and theater.

SOMAR Gallery (Art Galleries)
Thought-provoking theatrical pieces.

Southern Exposure (Art Galleries)
A former cannery with plenty of space for creative performances.

8 *d-2*

GALLERY 16

Sharing facilities with a digital printing service, this innovative gallery provides artists with technological tools as well as exhibition space. The shows take place in two enormous rooms—double solo exhibitions are common—and artists are free to work in large, installation format: Artist Philip Ross once created a huge sculpture that sprouted live mushrooms. The place has attracted a number of up-and-coming, as well as established, imagemakers. *1616 16th St., 3rd Floor, at Kansas St., Potrero Hill, 415/ 626–8403. Closed Sun.*

4 *e-5*

HACKETT FREEDMAN GALLERY

The best in contemporary realist painting is showcased in this superbly lit, well-appointed gallery. This can mean anything from traditional floral still-lifes to experimental renderings of the human figure—all by various internationally known artists. *250 Sutter St., between Grant Ave. and Kearny St., Union Square, 415/362–7152. Closed Sun.–Mon.*

4 *f-6*

HAINES GALLERY

Gorgeous blond-wood floors distinguish this stately gallery specializing in sleek, high-concept painting and sculpture. Gallery artists include Andy Goldsworthy, Alan Rath, and Baochi Zhang—ask to see Goldsworthy's remarkable cracked-mud wall in the back room. *49 Geary St., at Kearny St., Union Square, 415/397–8114. Closed Sun.–Mon.*

4 *g-7*

HOSFELT GALLERY

On the outskirts of Multimedia Gulch, the small Hosfelt Gallery showcases painting, photography, and installation. The works, by artists such as Shahizia Sikander, Richard Barnes, and Alfredo Jaar, have a conceptual and political bent and international repute. The gallery's exhibitions, receptions, and talks are crowded with the city's top curators, collectors, and art lovers. *95 Federal St., 2nd Floor, at 2nd St., South Beach, 415/495–5454. Closed Sun.–Mon.*

4 *e-5*

JOHN BERGGRUEN GALLERY

This blue-chip showcase for modern art occupies three full floors of galleries and private viewing rooms. The emphasis is on California artists—it's a great place to investigate the Bay Area's Figurative greats—but national and European artists also appear in group and solo exhibitions. Shows range from classic modernism to contemporary mixed media, and a project room on the fourth floor is dedicated to emerging artists. *228 Grant Ave., between Post and Sutter Sts., Union Square, 415/781– 4629. Closed Sun.*

8 *a-2*

THE LAB

Catch talented local imagemakers at this spacious alternative gallery. Group art shows, performance art pieces, and a music series reflect the cultural perspectives of young, mostly Bay Area, artists. In the lobby, a series of murals completed in spring 1997 commemorates San Francisco's history of progressive labor movements. *2948 16th St., at Capp St., Mission District, 415/864–8855. Closed Sun.–Mon.*

4 *g-8*

LIMN GALLERY

Behind the Limn Company (one of San Francisco's most respected furniture stores) is a spiffy space highlighting commercial and fine arts. Past exhibitions have included one devoted to digital art, and another to the sculptural paintings of Frank Stella. Call ahead, as shows are sporadic. *290 Townsend St., at 4th St., South Beach, 415/977–1300 or 415/778–6220.*

4 *e-6*

THE LUGGAGE STORE

This gallery was formerly a luggage store, but now functions handily as an art venue and community center. The exhibitions explore edgy subjects— homelessness, gender issues, drugs— as perceived by emerging artists. Educational, cultural, and social events are held weekly, and sculptural installations are displayed in a storefront across the street. *1000 Market St., at Taylor St., The Tenderloin, 415/255–5971.*

1 *b-2*

MARIN HEADLANDS CENTER FOR THE ARTS

The Headlands Center for the Arts is a sprawling complex of early 20th-century military bunkers converted to studio spaces. The building itself is the biggest draw: Look for David Ireland's evocative, amber-shellac wall treatment; a mess hall designed by Ann Hamilton; and a public latrine remodeled by the Interim Office of Architecture. Artists in residence, both local and international, work in more modest studios closer to the beach. You can see their artwork or witness their performance works at twice-yearly open houses. *944 Ft. Barry Rd., near Field Rd., Sausalito, 415/331–2787; or 415/331–2887 for directions from San Francisco.*

4 *e-5*

MARTIN LAWRENCE GALLERY

The Martin Lawrence Gallery has a slick retail edge. Even from the street, you can see, through the windows, its collection of colorful pop prints of celebrities by Andy Warhol and Steve Kaufman. Inside the clean, well-lit gallery you'll find works by other favorites such as Érte and Keith Haring. *465 Powell St., at Sutter St., Union Square, 415/956–0345.*

4 *e-5*

MAXWELL GALLERIES

An old world flavor fills this established gallery of 19th- and 20th-century European and American painting. Founded in 1940, the gallery has rooms organized by theme, such as early California art; featured artists include Thomas Hill, Maynard Dixon, Edgar Payne, and Albert Bierstadt. Four times a year Maxwell mounts shows organized by theme or artist, including contemporary realist painters from the Bay Area. *551 Sutter St., at Powell St., Union Square, 415/421–5193. Closed Sun.*

4 *e-5*

MERIDIAN GALLERY

A nonprofit gallery founded in 1989 to promote pan-ethnic art, this intimate space is a refreshing contrast to others in this commercial neighborhood. Along with mounting nearly a dozen shows a year, Meridian hosts lecture programs, organizes international exchange shows, and operates an internship program pairing urban teens with local artists. *545 Sutter St., at Powell St., Union Square, 415/398–7229. Closed Sun.–Mon.*

8 *a-5*

MISSION CULTURAL CENTER FOR LATINO ARTS

The Mission Cultural Center's huge second-floor exhibition space is a venue for group shows, while the smaller Salla gallery hosts solo shows, poetry readings, and video screenings. Shows have included works by women, Latino gays, lesbians, and bisexuals. *2868 Mission St., between 24th and 25th Sts., Mission District, 415/821–1155. Closed Sun.–Mon.*

4 *f-6*

MODERNISM

Photo realism and historical works from the Russian avant garde make up the bulk of the contemporary European and American art on display. Two concurrent solos open every six to seven weeks, with the occasional thematic group exhibition thrown in for good measure. *685 Market St., at 3rd St., Union Square, 415/541–0461. Closed Sun.–Mon.*

4 *d-8*

NEW LANGTON ARTS

Founded in 1975, this two-story interdisciplinary gallery is one of the city's most enduring alternative spaces. The main floor hosts five exhibitions annually, including a fall awards show and a holiday fundraising auction. A prominent reading series, new music and jazz concerts, and performance projects take place in New Langton's theater. *1246 Folsom St., between 8th and 9th Sts., South of Market, 415/626–5416. Closed Sun.–Tues.*

4 *b-8*

PLACE PIGALLE

This cozy European-style café and bar also has a respectable art gallery. Funky works by subcultural artists are displayed in thematic group shows; one recent exhibition featured female tattooists; another conveyed millennium malaise through various artists' eyes. At night, the multi-purpose gallery morphs into a venue for readings, musical events, and performance art pieces. *529 Hayes St., at Octavia St., Hayes Valley, 415/552–2671.*

4 *b-8*

POLANCO

Mexican art fills this vibrant space, including fine art, antiques, folk crafts, jewelry, and contemporary art. Polanco mounts group and solo exhibitions of works by contemporary artists from Mexico, as well as thematic shows of folk art, vintage movie posters, Day of the Dead crafts, and other seasonal items. *393 Hayes St., at Gough St., Hayes Valley, 415/252–5753. Closed Mon.*

4 *f-6*

REFUSALON

The adventurous Refusalon gallery—in the same building as Crown Point Press (*see above*)—brings experimental works to downtown audiences. Its solo and group shows of Bay Area and international artists have conceptual, minimalist, or multimedia installation tendencies. A side gallery serves as a showcase for represented artists such as Pip Culbert, Gay Outlaw, and Uri Tzaig. *20 Hawthorne St., near Howard St., between 2nd and 3rd Sts., South of Market, 415/546–0158. Closed Sun. and Mon.*

4 *e-6*

RENA BRANSTEN GALLERY

Exhibitions range from San Francisco landscape painting and figurative works on paper to abstract painting, conceptual art, and ceramic sculpture. It's one of the few commercial galleries that also

---

┌─────────────────────────────────────┐

JUST FOR SHUTTERBUGS

Fans of photography will find some excellent galleries and a museum in San Francisco:

Ansel Adams Center for Photography (Art Museums)
   The largest museum of art photography on the West Coast.

Fraenkel Gallery (Art Galleries)
   San Francisco's preeminent photography gallery.

Robert Koch Gallery (Art Galleries)
   Rare prints from the 19th and early 20th centuries.

SF Camerawork (Art Galleries)
   2,000 sq ft of exhibition space, plus lectures and a library.

Shapiro Gallery (Art Galleries)
   20th-century black-and-white photography.

└─────────────────────────────────────┘

---

presents electronic art and video installation by internationally known artists. There's usually a solo exhibition in each of the two main exhibition spaces. *77 Geary St., at Grant Ave., Union Square, 415/982–3292. Closed Sun. and Mon.*

4 *f-6*

ROBERT KOCH GALLERY

Robert Koch Gallery deals in photography, with a focus on Eastern European work. There are rare prints from the 19th and early 20th centuries, as well as work by more recent artists such as Jan Saudek and Bill Owens. The mostly black and white images stand out against the main room's burnished blond-wood floors. *49 Geary St., at Kearny St., Union Square, 415/421–0122. Closed Sun.–Mon.*

4 *c-7*

SAN FRANCISCO ART COMMISSION GALLERY

The city's official art venue occupies two modest square rooms on the first floor of City Hall. Shows emphasize cultural diversity, and have examined everything from surfing and skateboarding to African-American history. Writing programs and lunchtime art talks take place weekly. *401 Van Ness Ave., at McAllister St., Civic Center, 415/554–6080. Closed Sun.–Tues.*

4 *a-1*

SAN FRANCISCO MUSEUM OF MODERN ART RENTAL GALLERY

In addition to selling and renting an eclectic selection of works by local artists, this waterfront gallery stages group shows featuring three to a dozen artists at a time. The annual spring artists' warehouse sale is extremely popular. *Fort Mason Center, Building A, Marina Blvd. at Laguna St., The Marina, 415/441–4777.*

8 *a-3*

SCENE/ESCENA

This avant-garde gallery is the size of a walk-in closet, but excels at capturing the SF scene. Its two artist-owners throw wild openings once a month, attracting a colorful crowd of artists, gender-benders, and club kids. The art typically has pop culture overtones and a sense of sinister fun; it's viewable by appointment if you miss the party. *44 San Carlos St., off 18th St., between Mis-*

sion and Valencia Sts., Mission District, 415/621–4104.

4 *e-5*

SERGE SORROKKO

In a tastefully furnished, two-story space, Serge Sorrokko shows well-known modern European and American artists. Thematic group shows often look at provocative subjects, such as the "The Last Party: Nightworld in Photographs"—a compilation of martini-swilling celebrities. *231 Grant Ave., at Sutter St., Union Square, 415/421–7770.*

4 *f-6*

SF CAMERAWORK

Devoted to the art of photography since 1979, SF Camerawork is a city institution, with thematic shows by emerging artists from around the world in a 2,000-square-foot exhibition space. There's an excellent lecture program with noted photographers and critics; a small bookstore that stocks hard-to-find periodicals, monographs, and art theory books; and a 3,000-volume reference library. *115 Natoma St., between New Montgomery and 2nd Sts., South of Market, 415/764–1001. Closed Sun.–Mon.*

4 *e-5*

SHAPIRO GALLERY

Shapiro specializes in 20th-century black-and-white photography—particularly works by the f64 Group, which included photo luminaries Ansel Adams, Edward Weston, and Imogene Cunningham. It also represents an international roster of contemporary modernist photographers such as Masao Yamamoto, George Tice, and Kenro Izu. *250 Sutter St., between Grant Ave. and Kearny St., Union Square, 415/398-6655. Closed Sun.–Mon.*

8 *c-1*

SOMAR GALLERY

Nearly the size of an airplane hangar, this community center and arts facility gives artists room to express themselves. It has hosted a show of large paintings from the Beat era, as well as the overview show for the annual citywide Open Studios event (*see* Events, *below*). Exhibitions are sporadic, so call ahead. *934 Brannan St., between 8th and 9th Sts., South of Market, 415/552–2131. Closed Sun.–Mon.*

8 *b-2*

SOUTHERN EXPOSURE

A 20-year-old gallery housed in a former cannery, Southern Exposure is an important venue for emerging West Coast artists, and its annual juried show draws hundreds of submissions from all over northern California. The high ceilings and vast floor space of its main gallery allow for large group exhibitions and dinosaur-size sculptures, while the cozier mezzanine gallery is reserved for smaller works and shows. Provocative panel discussions, musical events, and performance pieces accompany most exhibitions. *401 Alabama St., at 17th St., Potrero Hill, 415/863–2141. Closed Sun.–Mon.*

4 *f-6*

STEPHEN WIRTZ GALLERY

Consistently interesting exhibitions of contemporary painting, sculpture, and photography are mostly by Bay Area artists. A spacious back room is open for viewing selections from the gallery stable: Deborah Oropallo, Lucy Puls, Raymond Saunders, and Jim Goldberg. *49 Geary St., at Kearny St., Union Square, 415/433–6879. Closed Sun.–Mon.*

1 *b-1*

SUSAN CUMMINS GALLERY

The best gallery north of the Golden Gate Bridge is a longtime fixture in Mill Valley's main square. Cummins has a formidable reputation for selecting choice painting, sculpture, and jewelry by Bay Area artists. *12 Miller Ave., at Throckmorton Ave., Mill Valley, 415/383–1512.*

4 *f-6*

TERRAIN

A quirky, compact gallery with a homey feel, Terrain shows contemporary sculpture, photography, and installations by local and international artists. The gallery directors have an interest in theater, so the shows often have theatrical themes. *165 Jessie St., between 3rd and New Montgomery Sts., South of Market, 415/543–0656. Closed Sun., Mon.*

4 *c-2*

WALTER/MCBEAN GALLERY

Part of the San Francisco Art Institute, the Walter/McBean Gallery presents shows on two floors with raw concrete walls. In addition to hosting annual student-award and faculty shows, the gallery introduces young international artists—many working with alternative media—to Bay Area audiences. Past solo shows have exhibited Nicole Eisenman, Sue Williams, and David Ireland. *800 Chestnut St., between Leavenworth and Jones Sts., North Beach, 415/749–4545. Closed Mon.*

ART MUSEUMS

4 *f-7*

ANSEL ADAMS CENTER FOR PHOTOGRAPHY

The largest repository of art photography on the West Coast began its life in Carmel in 1967, established by Adams himself. In 1989 the center moved to SoMa, where it became the first arts organization built at the new Yerba Buena Gardens complex. Now in even larger quarters, the center showcases experimental, contemporary, and historical photography as well as changing exhibitions of Adams's work. The bookstore is outstanding. *250 4th St., between Howard and Folsom Sts., South of Market, 415/495–7000. Admission: $5, $3 students, $2 senior citizens and youth 13–17, children under 13 free. Closed Mon.*

GALLERIES AT 49 GEARY STREET

The building at 49 Geary Street is top to bottom galleries, which means you could easily spend the better part of a day browsing here.

Catharine Clark Gallery (Art Galleries)
Contemporary painting, sculpture, and mixed media.

871 Fine Arts (Art Galleries)
Posters and printed matter.

Fraenkel Gallery (Art Galleries)
The city's preeminent photography gallery.

Haines Gallery (Art Galleries)
High-concept art.

Robert Koch Gallery (Art Galleries)
Eastern European photos and rare prints from the 19th and early 20th centuries.

Stephen Wirtz Gallery (Art Galleries)
Contemporary painting, sculpture, and photography.

---

7 *a-1*

ASIAN ART MUSEUM OF SAN FRANCISCO

In the same building as the M. H. de Young Museum (*see below*), this is the West Coast's largest museum of Asian art and artifacts. Collection highlights include the oldest known dated Chinese Buddha image (AD 338), the largest museum collection in the United States of Japanese *inro* (small, intricate lacquer boxes for carrying personal items), the Leventritt Collection of blue-and-white porcelain, and a superb collection of carved jade. The first floor is devoted to Chinese and Korean art; on the second floor are treasures from Iran, Turkey, Syria, India, Tibet, Nepal, Pakistan, Korea, Japan, Afghanistan, and Southeast Asia. The Avery Brundage Collection of nearly 12,000 sculptures, paintings, and ceramics from 40 Asian countries illustrates the major periods of Asian Art. The museum is scheduled to move to the refurbished Main Library building in the Civic Center in 2001. *John F. Kennedy and Tea Garden Drs., near 10th Ave. and Fulton St., Golden Gate Park, 415/379–8801. Admission: $7, $5 senior citizens, $4 youth 12–17, children under 12 free; $1 discount with Muni transfer; free first Wed. of the month. Closed Mon. and Tues.*

3 *e-2*

BERKELEY ART MUSEUM

Though the low, concrete building may not look like much from the street, this museum houses the largest university-owned art collection in the country. It began with a bequest from the abstractionist Hans Hoffman, who donated 50 of his paintings to the University of California at Berkeley in the 1960s (these paintings now form one of the museum's most impressive permanent installations). Today the museum, which shares a building with the Pacific Film Archive, showcases Asian art and 20th-century Western painting, sculpture, photography, and conceptual art. The permanent collection is spotty and wide-ranging, but it does have some gems by Peter Paul Rubens, Albert Bierstadt, Mark Rothko, and Eva Hesse. A sculpture garden to the rear of the museum is open in summer. *2626 Bancroft Way, at College Ave., Berkeley, 510/642–0808. Admission: $6, $4 senior citizens, students, and youth 12–17; children under 12 free; free Thurs. 11–noon and 5–9. Closed Mon.–Tues.*

`4` *f-6*

CALIFORNIA HISTORICAL SOCIETY

The Historical Society occasionally mounts exhibitions of paintings, drawings, and photographs pertaining to California's history. *See* History Museums, *below.*

`2` *a-2*

CALIFORNIA PALACE OF THE LEGION OF HONOR

A cast of Rodin's "Thinker" ponders in the courtyard of this gorgeous, Beaux-Arts building, a handsome environment for the city's European fine arts. Within are several other works by Rodin, as well as centuries of French, English, Flemish, and Italian painting and sculpture. Period rooms and antiquities are on view, and a new underground gallery complex houses the Achenbach collection of works on paper. The spectacular cliffside setting allows for breathtaking views of the city and the Golden Gate Bridge—best seen from the patio seating at the museum's café. *Lincoln Park, entrance at 34th Ave. and Clement St., Richmond District, 415/750–3600. Admission: $7, $5 senior citizens, $4 youth 12–17, children under 12 free; $2 discount with Muni transfer; free second Wed. of the month. Closed Mon.*

`4` *e-6*

CARTOON ART MUSEUM

Colorful characters like Krazy Kat, Zippy the Pinhead, and Batman greet you as you walk in the door to the Cartoon Art Museum, the only museum on the west coast devoted to "the funnies." The 12,000-piece permanent collection includes everything from political cartoons of the 1700s to "Far Side" and *New Yorker* cartoons of the present day. There's also a 3,000-volume library, a CD-ROM room, a children's gallery, and a gift shop overflowing with comics. Special exhibits in the past have spotlighted underground comics and Hanna Barbera studios. *814 Mission St., at 4th St., South of Market, 415/227–8666. Admission: $4, $3 senior citizens and students, $2 children 6–12, children under 6 free. Closed Mon.–Tues.*

`4` *f-6*

CENTER FOR THE ARTS

This remarkable arts center in the Yerba Buena Gardens complex has two main gallery spaces, a high-tech gallery, and a film and video screening room, all devoted to art with a multicultural bent. Exhibits focus on contemporary works, usually of emerging local and regional artists; a recent hit was its "Art of Star Wars" exhibit. The adjacent Forum, a multipurpose room, is the site of events and performances. *701 Mission St., at 3rd St., South of Market, 415/978–2787. Admission: $5, $3 senior citizens, students, and youth under 17; free first Thurs. of the month 6 PM–8 PM. Closed Mon.*

`4` *g-5*

JEWISH MUSEUM SAN FRANCISCO

This small museum displays the works of Jewish artists, contemporary as well as old masters, and mounts special exhibitions examining Jewish history, culture, and contemporary life. In the year 2000, the Jewish Museum plans to move into a former power station in the Yerba Buena Center. *121 Steuart St., between Mission and Howard Sts., South of Market, 415/543–8880. Admission: $5, $2.50 senior citizens and students, children under 12 free; free first Mon. of the month. Closed Fri.–Sat.*

`4` *a-2*

MEXICAN MUSEUM

The first American showcase to be devoted exclusively to Mexican, Mexican-American, and Chicano art, this museum has an enormous permanent collection with everything from pre-Columbian Indian terra-cotta figures and Spanish Colonial religious images to works by Rodolfo Morales and Diego Rivera. Recently the museum acquired a 500-piece folk-art collection, a gift from the Nelson A. Rockefeller estate. Temporary shows feature contemporary and historical works by Chicano, Central, and South American artists. Limited exhibition space accommodates only a fraction of the permanent collection; the museum plans to relocate to more spacious quarters at Yerba Buena Gardens by the year 2000. *Fort Mason Center, Building D, Marina Blvd. at Laguna St., The Marina, 415/441–0404. Admission: $3, $2 senior citizens and students; free first Wed. of the month. Closed Mon.–Tues.*

`7` *a-1*

M.H. DE YOUNG MEMORIAL MUSEUM

The de Young has the finest collection of American art on the West Coast, including paintings, sculpture, textiles, and decorative arts from the 1670s through the 20th century. More than 200 paintings of American masters such as Copley, Eakins, Bingham, and Sargent comprise the John D. Rockefeller III Collection of American paintings. Frederic Church's moody, almost psychedelic *Rainy Season in the Tropics* dominates the room of landscapes, and the marvelous gallery of American still-lifes includes trompe l'oeil paintings by William Harnett. The de Young also has large collections of art, sculpture, baskets, and ceramics from Africa, Oceania, and the Americas, and textile installations on everything from tribal clothing to couture. In addition to its permanent collections, the museum hosts selected traveling shows—often blockbuster events that involve long lines and additional admission charges. The de Young currently stands adjacent to the Asian Art Museum (*see above*) in a building constructed for the 1894 California Midwinter International Exhibition, but plans to move downtown around 2000. *John F. Kennedy and Tea Garden Drs., near 10th Ave. and Fulton St., Golden Gate Park, 415/863–3330. Admission: $7, $5 senior citizens, $4 youth 12–17, children under 12 free; $2 discount with Muni transfer; free first Wed. of the month. Closed Mon. and Tues.*

4 *a-2*

MUSEO ITALO AMERICANO

This modest West Coast outpost of Italian culture showcases permanent and temporary exhibits of paintings, sculpture, etchings, installations, and photographs by 19th- and 20th-century Italian-American artists. Special exhibits, lectures, and films are presented as well. An important work of the rotating permanent collection is Arnaldo Pomodoro's bronze sculpture *Tavola della Memoria* (1961). *Fort Mason Center, Building C, Marina Blvd. at Laguna St., The Marina, 415/673–2200. Admission: $3, $2 senior citizens and students; free first Wed. of the month. Closed Mon.–Tues.*

3 *e-7*

OAKLAND MUSEUM OF CALIFORNIA

Focusing on environment, history, and art, specifically as they relate to California, the Oakland Museum has a populist feel. It's housed in an innovative, multi-level building near Lake Merritt, and has separate sections devoted to natural history, local history, and visual arts, with excellent collections in each section.

Temporary exhibits almost always have alluring themes such as hot-rod culture, West Coast Surrealism, or objects made with recycled materials. Take time to walk around the museum's terraced gardens and the nearby Sculpture Court (1111 Broadway, at Oakland City Center) for a look at some surprisingly beautiful assemblages. *1000 Oak St., at 10th St., Oakland, 510/238–2200. Admission: $5, $3 senior citizens and students; free Sun. 4 PM–7 PM. Closed Mon.–Tues.*

4 *e-4*

PACIFIC HERITAGE MUSEUM

The museum's rotating displays feature rare art and artifacts from China, Taiwan, Japan, Thailand, and many other Asian nations, all from private collections. Past exhibitions have spotlighted furniture, paintings, vases, ceramics, and calligraphy. Call for the latest exhibition information. The museum is part of the Bank of Canton but has a separate entrance. *608 Commercial St., at Kearny St., Chinatown, 415/399–1124. Admission free. Closed weekends.*

4 *a-2*

SAN FRANCISCO AFRICAN-AMERICAN HISTORICAL AND CULTURAL SOCIETY

Though its collection has primarily a cultural and historical bent (*see History Museums, below*), the society also has an art gallery with works by African and African American artists.

4 *a-2*

SAN FRANCISCO CRAFT AND FOLK ART MUSEUM

Folk art, tribal art, and contemporary crafts from the United States and around the world are on exhibit on two levels at this tiny but elegant space. Thematic shows span everything from traditional Asian arts to whimsical contemporary metalwork. The gift shop has reasonably priced knickknacks. *Fort Mason Center, Building A, Marina Blvd. and Laguna St., The Marina, 415/775–0990. Admission: $3, $1 senior citizens, students, youth 12–17, children under 12 free; free Sat. 10 AM–noon and first Wed. of the month. Closed Mon.*

4 *f-6*

SAN FRANCISCO MUSEUM OF MODERN ART (SFMOMA)

This striking museum, designed by Swiss architect Mario Botta, was a San

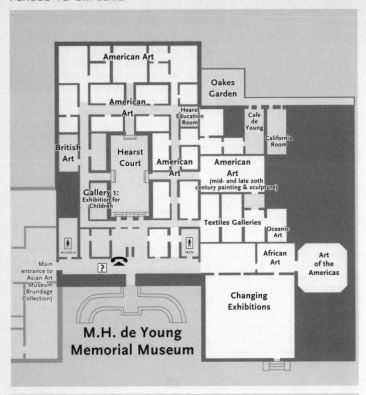

M.H. de Young Memorial Museum

American Art

Oakes Garden

American Art

Hearst Education Room

Cafe de Young

California Room

British Art

Hearst Court

American Art

American Art
(mid- and late 20th century painting & sculpture)

Gallery 1: Exhibition for Children

Textiles Galleries

Oceanic Art

WOMEN

MEN

African Art

Art of the Americas

Main entrance to Asian Art Museum (Brundage Collection)

Changing Exhibitions

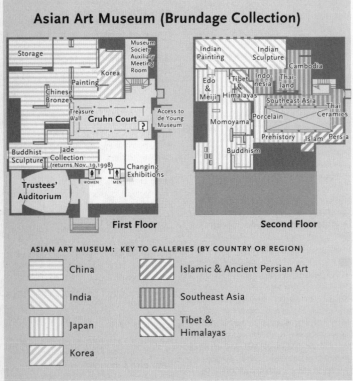

Asian Art Museum (Brundage Collection)

Storage

Museum Society Auxiliary Meeting Room

Indian Painting

Indian Sculpture

Cambodia

Korea

Edo & Meiji

Tibet & Himalayas

Indo-nesia

Thai-land

Painting

Chinese Bronzes

Access to de Young Museum

Southeast Asia

Thai Ceramics

Treasure Wall

Gruhn Court

Momoyama

Porcelain

Prehistory

Islam

Persia

Buddhist Sculpture

Jade Collection
(returns Nov. 19, 1998)

Changing Exhibitions

Buddhism

WOMEN

MEN

Trustees' Auditorium

First Floor

Second Floor

ASIAN ART MUSEUM: KEY TO GALLERIES (BY COUNTRY OR REGION)

China

Islamic & Ancient Persian Art

India

Southeast Asia

Japan

Tibet & Himalayas

Korea

Francisco landmark from the moment it opened in 1995. The building consists of a stepped-back, sienna brick facade and a central tower constructed of alternating bands of black and white stone. Inside, natural light from the tower floods the central atrium and some of the museum's galleries, and a grand stone staircase leads up to four floors of galleries. Traveling exhibits and films are a big part of the museum's adventurous programming agenda. The strong permanent collection includes works by Matisse, Picasso, O'Keeffe, Frida Kahlo, Jackson Pollock, and Andy Warhol, along with respected photography, media arts, and design departments. There is an excellent museum store as well as a comfortable, reasonably priced café. *151 3rd St., between Mission and Howard Sts., South of Market, 415/357-4000. Admission: $8, $5 senior citizens, $4 students; free first Tues. of the month; half-price Thurs. 6 PM–9 PM. Closed Wed.*

SAN JOSE MUSEUM OF ART

Housed in a former post office building, San Jose's excellent art museum has a strong permanent collection of paintings, large-scale multimedia installations, photographs, and sculptures by local and nationally known artists. Until the year 2000, the museum will be exhibiting many modern works from New York's Whitney Museum along with its own modern holdings, in a collaboration effort highlighting the development of 20th-century American art. On Thursdays the museum stays open until 8 PM. *110 S. Market St., at San Fernando St., San Jose, 408/294-2787. Admission: $6, free first Thurs. of the month. Closed Mon.*

BRIDGES

1 *b-3*

GOLDEN GATE BRIDGE

For six decades (since 1937), the Golden Gate Bridge, connecting San Francisco and Marin County, has awed sightseers with its distinctive rust color and simple but powerful Art-Deco design by Joseph Strauss. At 1.7 miles including its approaches, this is one of the longest suspension bridges in the world. It's also one of the strongest, made to withstand winds of more than 100 miles per hour and the onslaught of some 40 million vehicles per year. The best way to experience the bridge and its amazing views is by walking across (about 50

minutes one-way); bundle up as it's often gusty and misty. The two raised sidewalks are open to pedestrians daily from 5 AM until 9 PM and to bicyclists 24 hours daily; follow posted instructions as to which walkway, east or west, to use. You can park near the toll stations on the San Francisco side, or at Vista Point on the Marin side. If you cross by car, note that the $3 toll is paid only on the southbound approach into the city. *U.S. 101 Hwy., 415/921-5858.*

1 *c-3, d-3*

SAN FRANCISCO-OAKLAND BAY BRIDGE

Connecting San Francisco with Oakland and the East Bay, this bridge designed by Charles H. Purcell is less glamorous than the Golden Gate Bridge; however, it opened six months earlier and is much longer: It stretches 8.25 miles, making it one of the longest steel bridges in the world. From the city to Yerba Buena Island, in the middle of the bay, the Bay Bridge is a twin suspension bridge; a tunnel carries vehicles through the island, and cantilever and truss spans complete the bridge to Oakland. A $1 toll is collected from westbound traffic only. *I-80, 510/286-1148.*

4 *h-8*

THIRD STREET BRIDGE

The Third Street Bridge, also known as the Francis "Lefty" O'Doul Bridge, was designed by J. B. Strauss, who also designed the Golden Gate Bridge. It's the city's only drawbridge, and a beauty, too, with the original harbormaster's cottages at either end. The bridge is still raised and lowered so crafts may pass from the Mission Creek Marina into China Basin and the San Francisco Bay. *3rd St., near Berry St., South of Market.*

CEMETERIES

7 *h-2*

MISSION DOLORES CEMETERY

The pretty little mission cemetery was made famous by a scene in Alfred Hitchcock's *Vertigo*. Among the San Francisco notables buried here are Don Francisco de Haro, San Francisco's first mayor, and Don Luis Antonio Arguello, the first governor of Alta California. Kim Novak paid a memorable visit in the 1958 Alfred Hitchcock thriller *Vertigo*.

The $2 admission fee is good for entrance to both the cemetery and the adjacent Mission Dolores (*see* Historic Sites & Architecture, *below*). *Dolores and 16th Sts., Mission District, 415/621–8203.*

5 *e-7*

SAN FRANCISCO COLUMBARIUM

Laid to rest on the four ornately decorated stories of this fine 1898 burial vault are some of San Francisco's most illustrious families: the Magnins, Folgers, Turks, and Eddys. *1 Loraine Ct., off Anza St., between Arguello Blvd. and Stanyan St., Richmond District, 415/752–7891.*

5 *c-3, d-3*

SAN FRANCISCO NATIONAL CEMETERY

Just west of the Main Post in the Presidio is a cypress-shaded 19th-century cemetery that is the final resting place for some 30,000 American servicemen and women. Headstones here predate the Civil War. Contact the Presidio Visitors Center (415/561–4323) for information about occasional docent-led walking tours of the cemetery. *Lincoln Blvd. at Sheridan Ave., The Presidio, 415/561–2008.*

CHURCHES, SYNAGOGUES, & TEMPLES

4 *e-4*

BUDDHA'S UNIVERSAL CHURCH

This five-story temple, completed in 1961, was hand-built using exotic woods. It's decorated with tile mosaics and murals and topped with a roof garden. The church is open to visitors on the second and fourth Sunday of the month, except in February and March, when it presents a bilingual costume play on Saturdays and Sundays to celebrate the Chinese New Year. *720 Washington St., at Kearny St., Chinatown, 415/982–6116.*

4 *d-6*

GLIDE MEMORIAL UNITED METHODIST CHURCH

The dynamic Reverend Cecil Williams has made this the city's most famous church, known for its gospel and rock-and-roll services with a funky band and choir. It's also respected widely for its social programs; among them are a daily free meal program, an HIV/AIDS project, a families in crisis center, recovery programs for men and women, and women's health services. Sunday services at 9 and 11 AM are a joyous experience. *330 Ellis St., at Taylor St., Tenderloin, 415/771–6300.*

4 *d-5*

GRACE CATHEDRAL

It took 53 years to build this grand, Gothic cathedral, the seat of the Episcopal Church in San Francisco, on the site of Charles Crocker's mansion. The east entrance doors were taken from casts of Ghiberti's *Gates of Paradise*, which are on doors to the famed Baptistery in Florence, Italy. The twin towers are 170 feet high, and the north tower contains 44 working bells. The AIDS Memorial Chapel, dedicated in 1995, contains a sculpture by the late artist Keith Haring and rotating panels from the AIDS Memorial Quilt. The church's ⅓-mi-long Labyrinth is a replica of the 13th-century stone labyrinth on the floor of the Chartres Cathedral. Visitors are welcome for the singing of vespers every Sunday at 3:30 PM or Thurday at 5:15 PM. Guided tours of the cathedral are free (donations accepted). *1051 Taylor St., at California St., Nob Hill, 415/749–6310.*

4 *b-4*

HOLY TRINITY ORTHODOX CATHEDRAL

The oldest Eastern Orthodox church in the country was founded in 1857. Tours are available by appointment. *1520 Green St., at Van Ness Ave., Pacific Heights, 415/673–8565.*

4 *e-4*

KONG CHOW TEMPLE

America's oldest Chinese Buddhist temple was established in 1851 and moved to its present location in 1977. Amid the statuary, flowers, richly colored altars (red signifies "virility," green "longevity," and gold "majesty"), and plumes of incense are a pair of plaques announcing that MRS. HARRY S. TRUMAN CAME TO THIS TEMPLE IN JUNE 1948 FOR A PREDICTION ON THE OUTCOME OF THE ELECTION.... THIS FORTUNE CAME TRUE. A $1 donation is requested. *855 Stockton St., 4th Floor, at Clay St., Chinatown, 415/434–2513.*

7 *h-2*

MISSION DOLORES

See Historic Sites & Architecture, *below.*

4 *e-5*

OLD ST. MARY'S CATHEDRAL

Built of granite quarried in China, this structure was dedicated in 1854 and served as the city's first and only Catholic cathedral until 1891. It survived both the 1906 quake and a 1966 fire. Look for classical chamber music concerts on Tuesday and Thursday afternoons, following noontime mass (*see* Concert Halls *in* Chapter 5). *660 California St., at Grant Ave., Chinatown, 415/ 288–3840 for concert information.*

4 *b-6*

ST. MARY'S CATHEDRAL

In 1962 a devastating fire destroyed the 72-year-old mother church of the city's Catholic archdiocese. To replace it an ultramodern Catholic house of worship was designed in the Italian travertine style by a team of local architects and Pierre Nervi of Rome. It was dedicated in 1971 at a cost of $7 million, and was affectionately dubbed by locals "Our Lady of the Maytag" for its resemblance to an old-fashioned washing-machine agitator. The four magnificent 139-foot-long stained-glass windows that cross in the massive dome represent the four elements: the blue north windows, water; the light-color south windows, sun; the red west windows, fire; and the green east windows, earth. Above the altar is a spectacular freestanding sculpture by Robert Lippold made of 7,000 aluminum rods that symbolize ascendant prayer. *1111 Gough St., at Geary St., Japantown, 415/567–2020.*

4 *e-3*

STS. PETER AND PAUL CHURCH

The splendid Romanesque church on Washington Square is also known as the Italian National Cathedral. Completed in 1924, it has a pair of fanciful turreted stone towers that are local landmarks. Sunday masses are said here in English, Italian, and Chinese. On the first Sunday of October a mass followed by a parade to Fisherman's Wharf celebrates the annual Blessing of the Fleet. *666 Filbert St., at Columbus Ave., North Beach, 415/ 421–0809.*

5 *f-5*

SWEDENBORGIAN CHURCH

This beautifully detailed 1894 church is the stunning product of the California Arts and Crafts Movement. Bruce Porter provided the original design and the stained-glass windows, while Bernard Maybeck was responsible for the pegged wooden chairs with seats of woven rushes—said by Gustav Stickley to be the inspiration for his Mission-style furniture. The roof is supported by rough-hewn trunks of madrone trees and shelters a giant brick fireplace. Adjacent to the church is a raised, walled garden full of flowers, shrubs, and trees from every continent. *2107 Lyon St., at Washington St., Pacific Heights, 415/346–6466.*

5 *d-6*

TEMPLE EMANU-EL

Temple Emanu-El's congregation dates to 1850. The current building, a striking Levantine design combining Byzantine, Roman, and Mediterranean influences, was dedicated in 1926. Within the impressive 150-foot domed interior are several stained-glass windows depicting Fire and Water; these were created in 1972–1973 by San Francisco artist Mark Adams. Tours are given on weekdays. *Arguello Blvd. at Lake St., Laurel Heights, 415/751–2535.*

4 *e-4*

TIEN HOU TEMPLE

Though ornate painted balconies and Chinese Buddhist temples are scattered throughout Waverly Place, Tien Hou is one of the most picturesque. Day Ju, one of the first three Chinese immigrants to arrive in San Francisco, dedicated the temple to Tien Hou, the Queen of the Heavens and the Goddess of the Seven Seas, upon his safe arrival in 1852. The small sanctuary, filled with incense, red-and-gold lanterns, and wood carvings of gods at play, is at the top of three flights of stairs. A $1 donation is requested. *125 Waverly Pl., at Clay St., Chinatown, 415/391–4841.*

4 *a-3*

VEDANTA SOCIETY OLD TEMPLE

This 1905 structure, the first Hindu temple in the West, is a pastiche of colonial, Queen Anne, Moorish, and Hindu opulence; its turrets are oddly juxtaposed with onion domes and Victorian detailing. The design is appropriate: Vedanta, the highest of the six Hindu systems of religious philosophy, maintains that all religions are paths to one goal. The interior is closed to visitors. *2963 Webster St., at Filbert St., Cow Hollow.*

HISTORIC SITES & ARCHITECTURE

There are more than 200 designated historical landmarks in San Francisco, plus countless architectural gems. The following are the highlights.

1 *c-2*

ALCATRAZ

The infamous island federal prison, closed in 1963, served for 59 years as the nation's most notorious federal penitentiary for high-risk prisoners: Al Capone, Robert "The Birdman" Stroud, and Machine Gun Kelly were among its more famous inmates. In 1969, a group of Native Americans attempted to reclaim the land, saying that an 1868 federal treaty allowed Native Americans to use all federal territory that the government wasn't actively using. Named by the Spanish, Alcatraz means "pelican," but inmates called it "The Rock." Before it became a prison it was the site of the Pacific Coast's first lighthouse.

The Blue and Gold Fleet provides the only public transportation to Alcatraz, with frequent departures from Pier 41 at Fisherman's Wharf beginning daily at 9:30 AM. Round-trip fare includes the "Cell House Audio Tour," a self-guided audiocassette walking tour of the island prison, featuring former inmates and guards describing their experiences on Alcatraz. (Though you may also buy round-trip fare without the taped tour, the latter is one of the best parts of the experience and is well worth the money.) On the island, the National Park Service gives related talks on subjects such as escape attempts, the island's history as a 19th-century military fort, the Native American occupation, and Alcatraz's unique properties as part of an island chain in San Francisco Bay. Check schedules at the ranger station when you arrive or call the dock office (415/705–1042). Allow about 2½ hours total for the boat ride and self-guided walking tour; note that sections of the tour involve climbing steep hills. Tickets are sold daily at Pier 41 on a first-come, first-served basis starting at 8 AM; advance ticket purchase is strongly advised year-round, and is

essential in summer. *Blue and Gold Fleet: 415/773–1188 for recorded information, 415/705–5555 or 800/426–8687 for advance ticket sales with $2 service charge. National Park Service: 415/556–0560. Admission: Round-trip fare $11, $9.25 senior citizens, $5.75 children 5–11, children under 5 free (without audiocassette tour: $7.75, $6 senior citizens, $4.50 children 5–11).*

4 *f-4*

ALCOA BUILDING

This 25-story "earthquake-proof" office tower designed by Skidmore Owings and Merrill in 1964 was one of the first buildings to incorporate seismic bracing as a design element. The entry lobby is two stories up, surrounded by a sculpture garden; beneath it are three levels of parking. *1 Maritime Plaza, Battery St. between Clay and Washington Sts., Financial District.*

2 *f-2*

ALHAMBRA THEATRE

A bit of the Middle East beckons at this stunning 1920s movie palace built by the important arhictectural firm Miller and Pflueger, known also for their masterpiece Castro Theatre (*see below*). The Alhambra is a Moorish romantic beauty with an elaborate lobby and a regular schedule of first-run films (*see Movie Theaters Worth Noting in Chapter 5*). *2330 Polk St., between Green and Union Sts., Russian Hill.*

4 *f-5*

BANK OF CALIFORNIA

William Chapman Ralston, nicknamed "the man who built California" founded a commercial bank on this spot in the 1800s. By a stroke of luck, the original bank headquarters were torn down just before the 1906 earthquake and fire to make way for this Corinthian temple, completed in 1907 by Bliss & Faville. It was modeled after a bank in New York City designed by the legendary firm of McKim, Mead and White. *400 California St., at Sansome St., Financial District.*

4 *e-4, f-4*

BARBARY COAST TRAIL

In the latter half of the 19th century, San Francisco was home to one of the most infamous red-light districts ever to exist—a hotbed for the gold miners who poured into California looking to make a quick fortune (and sometimes just as quick a loss). Saloon keepers, gamblers, and prostitutes all flocked to the so-called Barbary Coast, now the Jackson Square Historic District (*see* Notable Neighborhoods, *below*) and the Financial District. The strip of Pacific Avenue between Sansome Street and Columbus Avenue, once called "Terrific Pacific," was the heart of the action: Every building along this street once sheltered a dance hall, saloon, gambling hall, or bordello. Many of these buildings survived the 1906 earthquake and fire, though by 1917 the Barbary Coast had been tamed by the Red-Light Abatement Act. In October 1996 the city designated 50 sites as stops along an official, 3.8-mi-long Barbary Coast Trail. Bronze sidewalk plaques have been installed on every street corner, starting at the Old Mint, at 5th and Mission streets, and running north through downtown, Chinatown, Portsmouth Square, Jackson Square, North Beach, and Fisherman's Wharf, ending at Aquatic Park. For information about the sites on the trail, pick up Daniel Bacon's **Walking San Francisco on the Barbary Coast Trail** (Quicksilver Press, $13.95) at the San Francisco Visitors Information Center.

6 *b-1*
BEACH CHALET
The long-shuttered Beach Chalet, in westernmost Golden Gate Park, reopened in 1997 as part of a $6 million renovation of the park. The building's upper level houses the Beach Chalet Brewery and Restaurant (*see* Contemporary *in* Chapter 3) and the lower level a visitor center. The Beach Chalet was designed by noted San Francisco architect Willis Polk, and completed in 1929; sweeping murals by famed French artist Lucien Labaudt were added in the 1930s (*see* Statues, Murals, & Monuments, *below*). The exquisite wooden staircase is carved with mermaids and sea creatures. *1000 Great Hwy., at John F. Kennedy Dr., Golden Gate Park.*

CABLE CARS
San Francisco's famed cable cars have been trundling up and down its steep hills since August 1, 1873, when young engineer Andrew Hallidie demonstrated his first car on Clay Street. In 1964 the tramlike vehicles were designated National Historic landmarks—the only ones that move! Before 1900, 500 cable cars spanned a network of 110 miles. Today there are 45 cars on three lines, and the network covers just 10 mi. Most

of the cars date from the last century, although the entire network had a complete $56 million overhaul in the early 1980s. For more information on fares and routes, *see* Transportation *in* Chapter 1. The Cable Car Museum (*see* History Museums, *below*) is a worthwhile stop for those curious about how exactly these little red cars are able to climb "halfway to the stars."

2 *a-2*
CALIFORNIA PALACE OF THE LEGION OF HONOR
Spectacularly situated in Lincoln Park on cliffs overlooking the Pacific Ocean and Golden Gate Bridge, this landmark building reopened in 1995 after extensive renovations. On display is San Francisco's collection of European fine arts (*see* Art Museums, *above*). Adolph and Alma Spreckels donated the magnificent graystone building—designed by George Applegarth in 1924 in the style of the 18th-century Palais de Legion d'Honneur in Paris—as a memorial to the state's World War I dead. A pyramidal glass skylight in the entrance court illuminates the new lower-level galleries. *Lincoln Park, Legion of Honor Dr., 34th Ave. at Clement St., Richmond District.*

4 *c-2*
THE CANNERY
This three-story brick structure was built in 1894 to house what became the Del Monte Fruit and Vegetable Cannery. Today the Cannery is home to shops, art galleries, restaurants, and the Museum of the City of San Francisco (*see* History Museums, *below*). There's a glass elevator in the open-air courtyard and a constant stream of free performances by mimes, magicians, and jugglers. *2801 Leavenworth St., at Beach St., Fisherman's Wharf, 415/771–3112.*

7 *f-3*
CASTRO THEATRE
This 1920s Spanish Baroque movie palace, now a Castro District landmark, was the flagship of a San Francisco cinema baron who also built theaters in Noe Valley. Miller and Pflueger, one of the city's top architectural firms, designed the Castro Theatre before going on to design six others, including the Alhambra (*see above*). The Castro's 1,500-seat auditorium has an elaborate plaster ceiling cast in the form of a tent, replete with sculpted swags, ropes, and

tassels. This is one of the few 1920s theaters that hasn't been broken up to
accommodate a multiplex (see Movie
Theaters Worth Noting in Chapter 5).
429 Castro St., at Market St., The Castro.

4 e-5

CHINATOWN GATE

A pagoda-topped gate, flanked on either
side of Grant Avenue by stone dragons,
is the official entrance to Chinatown—a
symbolic and literal transition from the
rather generic downtown landscape to
what could easily pass for a section of
old Hong Kong. Note that the dragons
are stamped MADE IN *FREE* CHINA—a not-
so-subdued political statement. Bush St.
and Grant Ave., Chinatown.

4 e-4

CHINATOWN YWCA

A large Chinese lantern welcomes those
who enter through the arched doorway
of this handsome 1932 redbrick building, originally established as a meeting
place and residence for Chinese women
in need of social services. Inside, the
lobby hearkens back to early 20th-cen-
tury Chinatown, with heavy, filigreed
wood furniture and mirrors etched with
delicate calligraphy. The architect, Julia
Morgan, was the first female architect to
be licensed in California; she is remem-
bered mainly as the designer of the
famous Hearst Castle, at San Simeon,
California. The Chinese Historical Society of America (see History Museums,
below) is scheduled to move into the
Chinatown YWCA building in 1998. 965
Clay St., at Powell St., Chinatown.

4 c-7

CITY HALL

San Francisco's monumental City Hall is
modeled after the Capitol in Washington, D.C., though many architectural
critics feel it surpasses the original as
the finest French Renaissance Revival
structure in the United States. The masterpiece of granite and marble, with a
bronze dome taller than that of the
Capitol, was built 1913–1915 after the
destruction of the old city hall in the
1906 earthquake and fire. Its Paris-
trained architects, Bakewell and Brown,
also designed Temple Emanu-El (see
Churches, above). The building has been
witness to interesting times: Joe DiMag-
gio and Marilyn Monroe were married
here on January 15, 1954; civil rights and
freedom of speech protesters were

washed down the central stairway with
fire hoses in 1960; Mayor George
Moscone and Supervisor Harvey Milk
were murdered here on November 27,
1978; and on February 14, 1991, scores
of gay couples were married on the front
steps in celebration of the passage of
San Francisco's Domestic Partners Act.
In front of City Hall are formal gardens
with fountains, walkways, and seasonal
flower beds. The palatial interior, with its
four-story-high rotunda, was scheduled
to reopen in late 1998 after extensive
seismic upgrades. Bordered by Van Ness
Ave., Polk, Grove, and McAllister Sts.;
Civic Center.

4 c-7

CIVIC CENTER

One of the country's great governmental
building complexes, the Civic Center
includes City Hall, the War Memorial
Opera House, the Veterans' Building,
the Bill Graham Civic Auditorium, and
the old San Francisco Main Library. This
Beaux-Arts complex is a product of the
turn-of-the-century "City Beautiful"
movement—the same movement that
produced the Mall in Washington, DC.
As with the nation's capital, there's a
stark juxtaposition of the powerful and
the powerless here: The streets and
plazas of the Civic Center have been
home to many of the city's most desti-
tute residents since the Depression. In
the last decade, efforts have been made
to push the homeless out of the area,
but very little has been accomplished
beyond displacing them to other neighborhoods. East of City Hall is United
Nations Plaza, home to a colorful twice-
weekly farmers' market, on Wednesday
and Sunday mornings. The handsome
new San Francisco Main Library (see
Libraries, below) is just a block west of
the plaza. On the west side of City Hall
are the opera house, the symphony hall,
and several other cultural institutions
that are collectively referred to as the
San Francisco Performing Arts Center.
Bordered by McAllister, Grove, Franklin,
and Hyde Sts.

7 f-3

CLARKE MANSION

Built in 1891, this sprawling off-white
Victorian is a beauty, with huge turrets,
rounded bay windows, and lots of surrounding greenery. It was constructed
on 17 acres for the flamboyant attorney
Alfred "Nobby" Clarke, and earned the

nickname Nobby Clarke's Folly when his wife refused to inhabit it because it was too far from Nob Hill, the fashionable part of town. The Clarkes lived here a total of five years. *250 Douglass St., at Caselli Ave., The Castro.*

2 *a-2*

CLIFF HOUSE

At the westernmost tip of San Francisco, this 1909 Newport-style beach house is one in a succession of ill-fated buildings on the same site. The original building, which dated from 1863, hosted several U.S. presidents and wealthy locals who would drive their carriages out to Ocean Beach; it was destroyed by fire on Christmas Day 1894. The second Cliff House, the most luxurious, was built in 1896; it rose eight stories and had an observation tower 200 feet above sea level. It burned down a year after surviving the 1906 quake. The present building has restaurants, a busy bar, a gift shop, and a visitor center (*see* Sightseeing Information *in* Chapter 1) with a display of fascinating, historic photographs of the many Cliff House incarnations and of the formerly glorious Sutro Baths (*see below*) that lie just below. Across Point Lobos Avenue from the Cliff House is the Musée Mécanique (*see* History Museums, *below*). *1090 Point Lobos Ave., at Great Hwy., Richmond District, 415/556–8642 for visitor center.*

4 *e-3*

COIT TOWER

Built in 1933 to memorialize San Francisco's volunteer firefighters, the 210-foot concrete observation tower atop Telegraph Hill is named for the heiress Lillie Hitchcock Coit (1843–1929), who bequeathed the funds to build it. During the early days of the gold rush, Miss Lil (as she was called) was said to have deserted a wedding party and chased down the street after her favorite engine, Knickerbocker Number 5, while clad in her bridesmaid finery. She was soon made an honorary member of the Knickerbocker Company, and after that always signed her name as "Lillie Coit 5" in honor of her favorite fire engine. The $3 elevator ride to the top of Coit Tower is worthwhile for its spectacular views of the Golden Gate Bridge, the Bay Bridge, and Alcatraz. Inside the tower are 19 WPA-era murals depicting laborers (*see* Statues, Murals, & Monuments, *below*). Parking at the tower is limited, but Bus

39-Coit can shuttle you over from Washington Square. Those who are physically fit may want to hike up to Coit Tower on the charming but steep Filbert Steps or Greenwich Stairs. *Telegraph Hill Blvd., at Greenwich St., Telegraph Hill, 415/362–0808.*

4 *c-8*

DAVIES SYMPHONY HALL

This well-integrated addition to the Beaux-Arts Civic Center complex was designed by Skidmore, Owings and Merrill in 1980. It's a fascinating, futuristic $37.9 million building, with a glass-encased wraparound lobby and a curvy, pop-out balcony high on its southeast corner. Inside, 59 adjustable Plexiglass acoustical disks cascade from the ceiling. Seventy-five minute tours of Davies Symphony Hall, the War Memorial Opera House, and Herbst Theatre are conducted on Mondays, departing from the Grove Street entrance of Davies Symphony Hall. *201 Van Ness Ave., between Hayes and Grove Sts., 415/552–8338.*

7 *h-1, h-7*

DOLORES STREET

Dolores Street was once the beginning of El Camino Real, the road that the Spaniards constructed in the 18th century to connect the 21 missions founded by Father Junípero Serra. Fittingly, it's still a splendid boulevard with a row of stately Canary Island palms lining the median; these trees were planted for the 1915 Panama-Pacific International Exposition by John McLaren, the man who for a half-century supervised the building of Golden Gate Park. The 1906 fires stopped near 20th Street, and many grandiose Victorians remain in the hills above that street. *Between Market St. and Randall St., Mission District.*

6 *b-1, b-2*

DUTCH WINDMILL AND MURPHY WINDMILL

At the very western end of Golden Gate park is the 1902 Dutch Windmill, which once pumped 20,000 gallons of water per hour to the park reservoir on Strawberry Hill. Restored in 1982, with its patina dome and wood-shingle body still intact, the wind overlooks the photogenic Queen Wilhelmina Tulip Garden (*see* Gardens *in* Chapter 6), which blooms in early spring and late summer. South of the Dutch Windmill, the unrenovated Murphy Windmill (Martin Luther King, Jr., Dr., near Great Hwy.) was the world's largest when it was built in 1905. It, too, pumped water to the Strawberry Hill reservoir. *John F. Kennedy Dr., between 47th Ave. and the Great Hwy., Golden Gate Park.*

4 *f-4, g-4*

EMBARCADERO CENTER

Nicknamed "Rockefeller Center West" for its similarity to the famed New York City complex, the Embarcadero Center houses more than 100 shops, 40 restaurants, a five-screen cinema featuring first-run special-interest and foreign films, two hotels, the indoor–outdoor observation area the Skydeck (*see* Viewpoints, *below*), and office space, on what was formerly the site of the city's produce market. A city landmark designed by John Portman and Associates between 1971 and 1982, it consists of a set of four neatly stacked identical concrete buildings with multilevel outdoor gardens and stages connected by walkways and bridges. A fifth tower houses the Hyatt Regency Hotel (*see* Very Expensive Lodgings *in* Chapter 7). Its Portman–designed atrium lobby is 20 stories high and ringed by balconies. *Bordered by Battery, Drumm, Clay, and Washington Sts., The Embarcadero, 800/733–6318.*

4 *g-4*

FERRY BUILDING

The 1898 Ferry Building was the main gateway to the city before the bridges were built; until 1958, some 170 ferries disembarked here every day. It's still a departure point for ferries to Oakland, Sausalito, Larkspur, and Vallejo (*see* Ferry *in* Chapter 1). The building's 230-foot clock tower, modeled on the Giralda tower of the Seville Cathedral, is clearly visible for the first time in 30 years after the freeway blocking it was torn down following the 1989 quake. Illuminated at night, it's one of the city's loveliest sights. Across from the Ferry Building the Ferry Plaza Farmers' Market is held Saturday mornings year-round. *Foot of Market St., The Embarcadero.*

FILOLI

If you love old mansions—especially when they're coupled with acres of formal gardens (*see* Gardens in Chapter 6)—Filoli certainly merits a visit from San Francisco. Willis Polk built the Geor-

gian Revival–style house in 1915–1917 for wealthy San Franciscan William B. Bourn II, who came up with the name Filoli as an acrononym for "fight, love, live." If Filoli's redbrick walls and lovely tile roof look familiar to you, you might have watched too much *Dynasty* in the 1980s. Indeed, this was the setting for that over-the-top show. The house and gardens are open from mid-February through the end of October, Tuesday through Thursday for guided tours (reservations essential), and Friday and Saturday for self-guided tours. *Cañada Rd. near Edgewood Rd., Woodside, 650/364–8300. Admission: $10, $1 children 2–12.*

4 *d-4*

THE FLAG HOUSE

According to local legend, this simple shingled turn-of-the-century house atop Russian Hill was saved from the 1906 earthquake and fire by alert firefighters who spotted an American flag flying from the roof and managed to quench the flames using seltzer water and wet sand. The flag had been hoisted by its owner, a flag collector, who thought his house should go down in a noble fashion, with "all flags flying." *1652–1656 Taylor St., at Vallejo St., Russian Hill.*

4 *e-6*

FLOOD BUILDING

Overlooking the Powell Street cable car turnaround is a bold Classic Revival edifice. This 12-floor, 1904 building was designed by architect Albert Pissis for James Flood, Jr. (heir to the Comstock Lode fortune) to lend grandeur to the downtown area. Though the first two floors were replaced after the 1906 earthquake, the floors above remain essentially as they were constructed. It now houses shops and offices. *870 Market St., at 5th St., Union Square.*

4 *a-2, b-2*

FORT MASON

Spanish explorers called the site of present-day Fort Mason *Punta Medanos* (Black Point). It was named a U.S. military command post in 1850, but remained occupied until the Civil War. From World War I through the Korean War it was used as a depot for the overseas shipment of troops and supplies. In 1977, Fort Mason's imposing military-style warehouses were converted into a cultural center housing a collection of unique museums, galleries, performance spaces, shops, and nonprofit organizations—the Mexican Museum, Museo Italo Americano, San Francisco African-American Historical and Cultural Society, and San Francisco Craft and Folk Art Museum—as well as the famous vegetarian restaurant Greens (*see* Vegetarian in Chapter 3). Most of the museums and shops at Fort Mason Center close by 7 PM, though the restaurant and theaters stay open later. Wide lawns surround the Fort Mason Center buildings, and the San Francisco Bay lies just beyond. *Marina Blvd. at Laguna St., The Marina, 415/979–3010 for event information.*

5 *a-1*

FORT POINT NATIONAL HISTORIC SITE

Fort Point was constructed between 1853 and 1861 by the U.S. Corps of Engineers to protect San Francisco from sea attack during the Civil War; during World War II it was used as a coastal defense fortification post where soldiers stood watch. Ironically, the massive fort, capable of holding 500 soldiers and 126 cannons, was never called upon to fire a single shot. Now a National Historic Landmark in the shadow of the Golden Gate Bridge, the site has been converted to a museum filled with military memorabilia; the building has a melancholy air and is suitably atmospheric. There's a superb view of the bay from the top floor. The National Park Rangers lead guided tours, show history films, and present cannon drills every day; call for times. *Marine Dr., off Long Ave., The Presidio, 415/556–1693. Admission free. Closed Mon.–Tues.*

4 *e-5*

450 SUTTER STREET

One block north of Union Square is this Art Deco masterpiece, a 1929 terra-cotta skyscraper by Miller and Pfleuger. Though terra cotta was chosen because it was cheaper than stone, this is now one of the city's most-admired office buildings, due in part to the handsome Mayan-inspired designs that cover the building both inside and out. Inside are medical and dental offices. *Between Stockton and Powell Sts., Union Square.*

2 *f-1*

GHIRARDELLI SQUARE

Since 1964 Ghirardelli Square shopping center has been a favorite tourist stop with many specialty shops, cafés, and galleries. From 1893 until the early 1960s it housed the Ghirardelli Chocolate Company, Domenico Ghirardelli's legendary candymaking business. The charming complex of 19th-century red-brick factory buildings includes a fairytale 1915 clocktower, inspired by the one at the Château de Blois in France, and the 1859 Pioneer Woolen Mill building, which produced uniforms for the Union Army during the Civil War. **Ghirardelli Fountain and Candy** (415/771–4903) is an old-fashioned emporium that utilizes some of the original chocolate factory vats and ovens in making its delicious concoctions. Ghirardelli Square hosts a chocolate lover's festival every September (*see* Events, *below*). *900 North Point St., at Polk St., Fisherman's Wharf, 415/775–5500.*

4 *e-3*

GRANT AVENUE

Originally called *Calle de la Fundación*, Grant Avenue is the oldest street in San Francisco. Here you'll find dusty bars such as **The Saloon** (1237 Grant Ave., at Columbus Ave., 415/989–7666) and the **Grant & Green Blues Club** (1371 Grant Ave., at Sutter St., 415/693–9565) that evoke the Wild West flavor of the city's Gold Rush years. Below Columbus, the wonderfully atmospheric cafés and authentic Italian delis of North Beach give way to the odd curio shops and unusual import stores of Chinatown. *Between Columbus Ave. and Filbert Sts., North Beach.*

2 *f-2*

HAAS-LILIENTHAL HOUSE

San Francisco is filled with splendid Victorian mansions, but this gabled and turreted beauty is the only one open to the public. The 1886 Queen Anne–style house, built for businessman William Haas at an original cost of $18,500, was considered modest in its day; its original occupant, Alice Lilienthal (daughter of William Haas) and her husband Samuel Lilienthal lived here until Alice's death in 1972. One-hour guided tours ($5) of the fully furnished interior shed light on turn-of-the-century tastes and lifestyles. The house is operated by the Foundation for San Francisco's Architectural Heritage, which has its headquarters here; tours are given on Wednesdays and Sundays. The foundation also leads Sunday walking tours of Pacific Heights (*see* Walking Tours, *below*). *2007 Franklin St., between Washington and Jackson Sts., Pacific Heights, 415/441–3004.*

4 *f-5*
HALLIDIE BUILDING
Regarded by many critics as the city's most important modern building, the Hallidie Building (named for cable car inventor Andrew Hallidie) was designed by Willis Polk and Co. in 1918. Its revolutionary glass-curtain wall—believed to be the world's first such structure—hangs a foot beyond the reinforced concrete of the frame. With its graceful all-glass facade, decorative exterior fire escapes, and Venetian Gothic detailing, this unusual building dominates the block. *130 Sutter St., between Kearny and Montgomery Sts., Financial District.*

7 *f-3*
HARVEY MILK PLAZA
This plaza, in the spiritual and physical heart of the Castro, is named in honor of California's first openly gay elected official. On November 27, 1978, City Supervisor Milk and then-mayor George Moscone were assassinated by Dan White, a disgruntled former supervisor. At his trial White launched the now-famous "Twinkie defense," claiming that the high sugar content of his junk-food diet had altered his mental state. He was convicted of voluntary manslaughter by reason of "diminished capacity." A candlelight vigil is held at the plaza every year on the anniversary of the assassination. *Castro and Market Sts., The Castro.*

5 *h-5*
HILLS PLAZA
In 1991, the 1933 Hills Brothers Coffee Building became Hills Plaza, a block-long apartment complex cum commercial development incorporating the original Romanesque arched-brick facade. The Hills Brothers building itself has taken on a new identity, this time as a producer not of beans, but of hops—with Gordon Biersch Brewery (*see* American/Casual in Chapter 3) as its tenant. On the south end of the plaza, under the tower, there's a pleasant garden with a view of the Bay Bridge. *345 Spear St., at Harrison St., South of Market.*

4 *f-5*
HOBART BUILDING
Market Street, which bisects the city at an angle, has consistently challenged

San Francisco's architects. The 1914 Hobart Building successfully rises to the challenge with a tower that combines a flat facade and heavily ornamented oval sides. It is considered one of architect Willis Polk's best works in the city—and it was built under budget in a record 11 months. Though now dwarfed by surrounding high-rises it's still a majestic sight when viewed from Second Street. *582 Market St., at 2nd St., Financial District.*

4 *a-6*
JAPAN CENTER
Built in 1968 with a design by noted American architect Minoru Yamasaki, this 5-acre, 3-block-long complex was a multimillion-dollar endeavor—yet its static structures fail to capture the spirit and beauty of traditional Japanese architecture. The complex houses shops, teahouses, sushi bars, a public garage, a theater, and an excellent spa, all connected by partially open walkways. Its centerpiece is the five-tiered, 100-foot-tall Peace Pagoda designed by Japanese architect Yoshiro Taniguchi to convey the "friendship and goodwill" of the Japanese people to the people of the United States. (In the 1,000-year-old-tradition of Japanese architecture, miniature round pagodas symbolize eternal peace.) The pagoda overlooks the Peace Plaza, site of several annual festivals. *Post St., between Fillmore and Laguna Sts., Japantown, 415/922–6776.*

8 *a-1*
LEVI STRAUSS & CO. FACTORY
The Levi Strauss World Headquarters lie downtown, in the Financial District. In the Mission District, however, remains the original Levi Strauss factory built in 1906, renovated in 1970, and still turning out thousands of pairs of the world-famous blue jeans annually—making it the oldest jeans-making facility in the west. Free, 1½-hour tours of the cutting and sewing areas are given on Tuesdays and Wednesdays; reservations are required. *250 Valencia St., between 14th St. and Duboce Ave., Mission District, 415/565–9159.*

4 *f-3*
LEVI STRAUSS & CO. WORLD HEADQUARTERS
The makers of America's favorite blue jeans spent nearly $150 million to create

this carefully landscaped complex that looks so collegiate it is affectionately known as LSU (Levi Strauss University). With stepbacks meant to echo the slope of the hill, the 1982 design incorporated two turn-of-the-century warehouse buildings. Grassy knolls and fountains designed by Lawrence Halprin complement the redbrick buildings, a perfect backdrop for brown-bag and picnic lunches. *Levi's Plaza, 1155 Battery St., at Union St., Telegraph Hill.*

4 *c-3*

LOMBARD STREET ("CROOKEDEST STREET")

A must-see for visitors to San Francisco, the "crookedest street in the world" makes eight hairpin turns in a short city block as it descends the east face of Russian Hill to Leavenworth Street. The beautifully landscaped street was designed in the 1920s to mitigate the steepness of the slope. Join the line of cars waiting to drive down it, or walk down the steps on either side of the street. *Lombard St., between Hyde and Leavenworth Sts., Russian Hill.*

4 *e-6*

MAIDEN LANE

Off the east side of Union Square is a 2-block alley that was known as Morton Street in the late 19th century, when it was home to the "cribs" (brothels) that formed the center of a notoriously rowdy red-light district. After the 1906 fire destroyed the bordellos, the street was renamed Maiden Lane—it's now a quaint pedestrian mall lined with chic boutiques and sidewalk cafés, as well as the only Frank Lloyd Wright building (*see* 140 Maiden Lane, *below*) in San Francisco. *Between Stockton and Kearny Sts., Union Square.*

7 *h-2*

MISSION DOLORES

Mission Dolores encompasses two churches standing side by side. The humble adobe building known as Mission San Francisco de Asis was constructed between 1782 and 1791 as the sixth of the 21 California missions founded by Father Junipero Serra. The Spanish nicknamed it Dolores after a nearby stream *Arroyo de Nuestra Señora de los Dolores* (Stream of Our Lady of the Sorrows) that has long since disappeared. The survivor of three major earthquakes, it is now the oldest build-

ing in San Francisco. Architecturally, it's the simplest of all the California missions—it's also one of the most intact. The ceiling depicts traditional Native American basket designs hand-painted with vegetable dyes by local Costanoan Indians. The roof consists of timbers lashed with rawhide; the walls are of 4-foot-thick sun-dried adobe mud. Next door to the original Mission, the handsome multidomed Mission Dolores Basilica dates from 1913. English- and Spanish-language services are held in both the Mission San Francisco de Asis and in the Basilica. There is also a small museum, and outside, a small, pleasant cemetery (*see* Cemeteries, *above*). The Mission audio tour is extremely interesting. *Dolores and 16th Sts., Mission District, 415/621–8203. Admission: $2; $5 with 45-minute audio tour.*

4 *f-6*

MOSCONE CENTER

Named for slain San Francisco mayor George Moscone, the Moscone convention center is part of the Yerba Buena development project and has been a major revitalizing force in the SoMa district. The building, designed in 1981 by Hellmuth, Obata and Kassabaum, contains one of the world's largest column-free exhibition halls, while the Esplanade Ballroom lobby features a giant replica (25 ft by 40 ft) of the first known map of San Francisco. *747 Howard St., at 3rd St., South of Market.*

4 *e-6*

NEIMAN-MARCUS

The department store's crowning glory is an enormous skylight stained-glass dome, a remnant of the old City of Paris dry goods store that occupied the site since the turn of the century. Many San Franciscans rallied unsuccessfully to save the old building, and continue to regard its 1982 replacement by Philip Johnson and John Burgee as inferior. *Stockton and Geary Sts., Union Square.*

4 *e-6*

140 MAIDEN LANE

San Francisco's only Frank Lloyd Wright building stands on charming Maiden Lane. With its circular interior ramp and skylights, this handsome brick structure is said to have been a model for the Guggenheim Museum in New York. It was constructed in 1948 as the Morris Store. At press time it had no tenants and was closed to the public. *140 Maiden Ln., between Stockton and Kearny Sts., Union Square.*

4 *b-4*
OCTAGON HOUSE-MUSEUM

Eight-sided houses were considered lucky in the 1850s and 1860s, and San Francisco once had around a half-dozen. Now only two remain (the other is a private residence at 1067 Green Street). This simple grey-and-white charmer was built by William McElroy in 1861 and was originally across Gough Street. In 1952 it was purchased by the National Society of Colonial Dames of America, who converted it to a museum (*see History Museums, below*). *2645 Gough St., at Union St., The Marina, 415/441–7512. Donation requested. Closed Jan.*

4 *e-4*
OLD CHINESE TELEPHONE EXCHANGE

Now a branch of the Bank of Canton, this was the first building to set the style for the new Chinatown after the original buildings burned down in the 1906 earthquake and fire. The intricate three-tier pagoda, built in 1909, housed the Chinatown phone system's operators, who were famed for their great linguistic skills. (The operators were required to speak English and five Chinese dialects). *743 Washington St., at Grant Ave., Chinatown.*

4 *c-7*
OLD SAN FRANCISCO MAIN LIBRARY BUILDING

Completely refurbished in 1997, this beautiful Beaux Arts building is scheduled to be occupied by the Asian Art Museum in 2001. It was designed by East Coast architect George Kelham in 1915–1916. Just across Fulton Street is the gleaming new San Francisco Public Library. *Fulton and Larkin Sts., Civic Center.*

4 *e-7*
OLD U.S. MINT

The "Granite Lady" is the nickname of this fine 1869 Federal Classic Revival building, the oldest stone building in San Francisco. Though still owned by the U.S. Treasury Department, it is no longer a working mint and is closed to the public. *5th and Mission Sts., South of Market.*

4 *f-5*
PACIFIC COAST STOCK EXCHANGE

This imposing templelike structure dates from 1915, though architects Miller and Pfleuger updated it in 1930. Around the corner, the Stock Exchange Tower (155 Sansome St., at Pine St.) is a 1930 Moderne classic by the same architects, with an Art Deco gold ceiling and a black marble wall entry. *301 Pine St., at Sansome St., Financial District.*

4 *d-5*
PACIFIC UNION CLUB

The 1906 quake and fire knocked down the palatial Nob Hill mansions of railroad barons Leland Stanford, Mark Hopkins, Collis Huntington, and Charles Crocker. The mansion belonging to silver magnate James C. Flood—the first brownstone on the West Coast, and the only one of the Nob Hill mansions that wasn't made of wood—is one of the few that survived. This attractive 45-room structure was built in 1886 by the Comstock silver baron at a reputed cost of $1.5 million. In 1909 the property was purchased by the prestigious Pacific Union Club, a private club of the wealthy and powerful; famous architect Willis Polk redesigned the building at that time. A small park is adjacent to the club. *1000 California St., at Mason St., Nob Hill.*

4 *c-6*
PACKARD AUTO SHOWROOM

The 1927 Maybeck structure was designed to showcase one of the 1920s' premier automobile lines. The frieze just below the roof depicts a bear, California's state animal. *901 Van Ness Ave., at O'Farrell St., Civic Center.*

4 *f-6*
PALACE HOTEL

Now a Sheraton property, this is the oldest hotel in the city and also one of the grandest. The original, opened in 1875 and destroyed in the 1906 quake and fire, was replaced in 1909 with a design by architect George Kelham (who also designed the old San Francisco Main Library). The hotel has a storied past, some of which is recounted in glass cases off the main lobby: President Warren Harding died here while still in office in 1923, and another room is thought to be haunted by the ghost of the last reigning monarch of Hawaii, who spent a night there. In the glass-dome Garden Court restaurant, a four-story skylight contains 25,000 panes, and mosaic floors replicate Oriental rug designs; here, the San Francisco Symphony occasionally performs. Guided tours of the hotel's grand interior take place on Tuesdays, Wednesdays, Thursdays, and Saturdays. *2 New Montgomery St., at Market St., South of Market, 415/392–8600.*

5 *f-2*
PALACE OF FINE ARTS

At the far western edge of the Marina is the Palace of Fine Arts, a stunning colonnaded Roman temple designed by Berkeley architect Bernard Maybeck. The palace is the sole survivor of the 32 plaster buildings erected for the 1915 Panama-Pacific International Exposition, which celebrated the opening of the Panama Canal and the anniversary of the discovery of the Pacific. Despite the public's enthusiasm for this temporary classical city, in the ensuing 50 years it fell into disrepair. Huge private donations and legions of sentimental citizens later, the palace building was recast in concrete at a cost of $7 million, and reopened in 1967. The massive columns, great rotunda (dedicated to the glory of Greek culture), and swan-filled reflecting lagoon have appeared as a backdrop to countless fashion layouts and recent films. It now houses an unusual hands-on science center, the Exploratorium (*see* Science Museums, *below*). *Baker and Beach Sts., The Marina, 415/563–7337 for palace tours.*

4 *d-2*
PIER 39

Natives think the pier is tacky; tourists come in droves. It's certainly the most popular of San Francisco's waterfront attractions. A 1,043-foot former cargo pier, once abandoned and decaying, it now houses more than 100 shops and fast-food stands, 10 full-service restaurants, a 350-berth marina, a double-decked Venetian carousel, and a games arcade. Street performers vie for attention, while California sea lions gambol just offshore. Accessible validated parking and nearby public transportation ensure crowds most days. *The Embarcadero, at Jefferson St., Fisherman's Wharf, 415/981–7437.*

4 *e-4*
PORTSMOUTH SQUARE

This Chinatown square, dotted with pagoda-shaped structures, was once a lowly potato patch before becoming the plaza for Yerba Buena (the Mexican settlement that was later renamed San Francisco). On this spot, Montgomery raised the American flag in 1846, and public hangings took place in the late 1950s. These days, it's a favorite place for morning t'ai chi; in the afternoons elderly Chinese men gather to play chess. *Kearny St., between Washington and Clay Sts., Chinatown.*

2 *d-2*
THE PRESIDIO

The flags of Mexico, the Bear Flag Republic and the U.S. Army have all flown over the Presidio—one of the oldest military installations in the United States. The Presidio was established by the Spanish as a military garrison in 1776—in Spanish, "presidio" means walled fortification—and taken over by newly independent Mexico in 1822. The Americans took possession of the fort during the Mexican-American War of 1846. Since then, the Presidio has been a training ground for Civil War soldiers, a refuge for residents following the 1906 earthquake, and headquarters of the U.S. Sixth Army. In October 1994 its 1,480 acres became a National Park (*see* Parks in Chapter 6). At the Presidio's **Visitors Information Center** (Lincoln Blvd., at Montgomery St., 415/561–4323; map 5, e-3) or the Presidio Museum (*see* History Museums, *below*), pick up the pamphlet titled "The Presidio of San Francisco Main Post Walk: 200 Years of History and Architecture" for a 1-mile self guided walking tour of the Presidio's most important structures. One building of note is the **Officer's Club** (Moraga Ave., between Arguello Blvd. and Funston Ave.; map 5, d-4). It contains one adobe wall reputed to date from 1776, the year the base was founded. *Entrance at Lombard and Lyon Sts., The Presidio.*

RINCON CENTER

The city's old post office, built in 1939 in the Streamline Moderne style, was incorporated into a large shopping and office complex in 1989. In the art deco lobby where the post office's walk-up windows used to be is a controversial 27-panel WPA mural painted by artist Anton Refregier (*see* Statues, Murals, &

Monuments, *below*). A permanent exhibit below the murals contains interesting photographs and artifacts of life in the 1800s. The exhibit and the murals form a fascinating minimuseum and enhance what might otherwise be just another humdrum modern office space. *Spear St., at Mission St., South of Market.*

4 e-5
RITZ-CARLTON HOTEL
This gleaming, 1909 Roman-Renaissance building has seen it all, first as the Metropolitan Life Insurance Company, then as Cogswell College, then as the site of Werner Erhard's EST activities, before it became a luxury hotel (*see* Very Expensive Lodgings *in* Chapter 7). *600 Stockton St., at California St., Nob Hill.*

4 b-6
ST. MARY'S CATHEDRAL
See Churches, *below*.

4 c-3
SAN FRANCISCO ART INSTITUTE
The SFAI's Spanish Colonial Revival building was designed in 1926 by Bakewell and Brown, back when the school was known as the California School of Fine Arts. With its bell tower, red-tiled roofs, and courtyard graced by a Moorish-tiled fountain, it makes a pleasant addition to the neighborhood. Established in 1871, the school inhabited temporary quarters for its first two decades, then operated out of the Mark Hopkins mansion at California and Mason streets from 1893 to 1906, when it was destroyed by the earthquake and subsequent fire. The campus bustles with students during the week, and with those who come to enjoy its Walter/McBean Gallery (*see* Art Galleries, *above*), San Francisco Cinematheque, and Diego Rivera mural—one of only three in San Francisco (*see* Statues, Murals, & Monuments, *below*). *800 Chestnut St., between Leavenworth and Jones Sts., Russian Hill.*

4 f-4
SAN FRANCISCO FIRE DEPARTMENT STATION 13
How did famed hotel architect John Portman come to design a firehouse? It was a tradeoff made when, in clearing the way for Embarcadero Center, an old fire station was removed in 1974: This was the consolation prize. *532 Sansome St., at Washington St., Financial District.*

4 f-6
SAN FRANCISCO MUSEUM OF MODERN ART (SFMOMA)
Italian-Swiss architect Mario Botta, known for his skylights, has created a great slanting ellipse for the roof of the museum—a landmark the instant it opened in 1995. The striking structure consists of a stepped-back, sienna brick facade and a central tower constructed of alternating bands of black and white stone. Inside, an imposing black-and-gray stone staircase leads from the atrium up to four floors of galleries (*see* Art Museums, *above*).

4 e-6
SAVINGS UNION BANK
The former Savings Union Bank of San Francisco, now occupied by Emporio Armani (*see* Clothing for Women & Men/General), is a classical temple inspired by the Roman Pantheon. The granite-clad steel frame has a reinforced-concrete dome, Ionic columns, and a pediment with a bas-relief sculpture by Haig Pattigan. Architects Bliss and Faville apprenticed at the legendary firm of McKim, Mead, and White before designing this 1910 structure. *1 Grant Ave., at Market St., Union Square.*

4 f-5
SHELL BUILDING
This slender, terra-cotta tower, designed in 1929 by George Kelham, is an attractive Art Deco skyscraper in the Financial District. Look for the seashell motif, inside and out. *100 Bush St., between Battery and Sansome Sts., Financial District.*

7 e-1
SPRECKELS MANSION— THE HAIGHT
Not to be confused with the Spreckels Mansion of Pacific Heights, this house was built in 1898 for a member of the wealthy Spreckels family, which made its fortune in the sugar industry. It's a sturdy, putty-color Queen Anne Victorian that stands out for its intricate "wedding-cake" detailing. Later tenants included Jack London and Ambrose Bierce. *737 Buena Vista Ave. W, between Frederick and Waller Sts., The Haight.*

2 *f-2*

SPRECKELS MANSION—PACIFIC HEIGHTS

The most imposing residence overlooking Lafayette Park is the formal French baroque residence built in 1913 for sugar heir Adolph Spreckels and his wife Alma de Bretteville Spreckels; it's sometimes called the Sugar Palace. Mrs. Spreckels also commissioned architect George Applegarth to design the California Palace of the Legion of Honor, which was presented by the Spreckels as a gift to the city. A more recent owner of the Spreckels mansion was author Danielle Steele, who lived here with her husband. Sadly, the Utah limestone of the building's beautiful facade has eroded noticeably. *2080 Washington St., at Octavia St., Pacific Heights.*

2 *e-2*

STANYAN HOUSE

One of the oldest houses in the city, the Stanyan House was built in 1854 and remained in the Stanyan family for 110 years. Only a few of the prefabricated New England houses that were sent around Cape Horn from Boston by boat have been identified with certainty; this is one of them. Compared to the city's ornate Victorians it's a model of austerity that would look more at home on Nantucket. *2006 Bush St., at Buchanan St., Pacific Heights.*

2 *e-3*

STEINER STREET VICTORIANS ("POSTCARD ROW")

These six jewel-colored, beautifully restored Queen Anne Victorians across from Alamo Square on the 700 block of Steiner Street—also known as "The Painted Ladies" and "Postcard Row"—may be the most photographed structures in San Francisco after the Golden Gate Bridge. They've been featured on hundreds of postcards and the opening credits of several TV shows set in San Francisco. Set side by side on a steep street with the towers of the Financial District looming in the background, they make for a stunning vista combining historic and new San Francisco. Numbers 710–20 Steiner Street were developed in 1894 and 1895 by carpenter Matthew Kavanaugh. *Steiner St., between Hayes and Fulton Sts., Western Addition.*

2 *a-3*

SUTRO BATHS

Modeled after ancient Roman baths, the Sutro Baths once consisted of six enormous glass-roofed fresh and saltwater pools, 500 dressing rooms, art galleries, several restaurants, and an amphitheater. The complex, which now resembles a set of Roman ruins, covered 3 acres just north of the Cliff House (*see above*). The baths opened in 1896, were closed in 1952 due to budget problems, and then burned down in 1966. You can explore the ruins on your own or take ranger-led walks on weekends. *Point Lobos Ave., at Great Hwy., Richmond District.*

5 *f-5*

SWEDENBORGIAN CHURCH
See Churches, *above*.

4 *e-3*

TELEGRAPH HILL

The views are enviable from this famed 284-foot hill where goats once grazed. At the east end of Lombard Street, this was the location for the first Morse Code Signal Station in 1853, hence the name. At the crest of Telegraph Hill is Coit Tower (*see above*), a stone-white monument that shines as a beacon, especially at night. Parking on top of the hill is scarce, and the climb to the top is steep. *Lombard, Filbert, Kearny, and Sansome Sts., Telegraph Hill.*

4 *e-3*

1360 MONTGOMERY STREET

Bogart fans may recognize the elegant art deco apartment building at 1360 Montgomery Street—indeed, it appeared in the 1947 film *Dark Passage* starring Humphrey Bogart and Lauren Bacall. It's a 1937 Moderne building with etched-glass gazelles and palms counterpointing a silvered fresco of the heroic bridge worker. The building stands at the corner where the Filbert Steps intersect with the Greenwich Steps. *1360 Montgomery St., at Alta St., Telegraph Hill.*

TRANSAMERICA BUILDING

When the narrow, pyramid-shaped Transamerica Building was erected at the foot of Columbus Avenue in 1972, it was regarded as an architectural blunder with a $34 million price tag. Ironically, the William Pereira and Associates–designed building is now considered a landmark; indeed, it's the most-photographed modern building in San Francisco. At 853 feet tall, it's also one of the city's tallest structures. The viewing area on the 27th floor has been closed to the public for several years but may reopen in the future. *600 Montgomery St., between Clay and Washington Sts., Financial District.*

7 *d-5*

TWIN PEAKS

San Francisco's second- and third-highest hills (922 ft and 904 ft respectively) were named *Los Pechos de la Chola* (the Breasts of the Indian Maiden) by 18th-century Spanish arrivals. They now form a 65-acre park with spectacular 360° views of the San Francisco Bay. *Twin Peaks Blvd., off Portola Dr., Twin Peaks.*

4 *c-7*

WAR MEMORIAL OPERA HOUSE

Renovated in 1997 to the tune of $88.5 million, the War Memorial was built in 1932 and inaugurated on October 15 of that year with a performance of *Tosca.* The last of the city's great Beaux-Arts projects, it has a marble foyer, two balconies, and a vaulted and coffered ceiling with a spectacular Art Deco chandelier that resembles a huge silver sunburst. In its long history it has heard more than just arias: This is where the United Nations was formed in 1945, and where the treaty with Japan was signed in 1951. These days, the opera house hosts the San Francisco Opera from September through December (*see* Opera *in* Chapter 5), and the San Francisco Ballet from February through May (*see* Dance *in* Chapter 5). *301 Van Ness Ave., between Fulton and Grove Sts., Civic Center.*

2 *e-2*

WEDDING HOUSES

Dairy rancher James Cudworth had these two identical, white double-peaked homes built around the late 1870s as wedding gifts for his two daughters, who were married at the same time. These days, the Siamese buildings house upscale shops and a pub. *1980 Union St., at Buchanan St., Pacific Heights.*

8 *a-3*

WOMEN'S BUILDING

Since 1979, the Women's Building has acted as the hub of the female community in the Mission District. It houses offices for women's social, political, and educational organizations, and sponsors talks and readings by such noted figures as Alice Walker and Angela Davis. The Mission Revival–style building was erected in 1910 as Turn Hall, a German exercise club, and later became Dovre Hall, a Norwegian social club, before finally becoming the Women's Building. The building has a striking two-sided exterior mural depicting women's peacekeeping efforts over the centuries (*see* Statues, Murals, & Monuments, *below*). *3543 18th St., between Valencia and Guerrero Sts., Mission District, 415/431–1180. Closed weekends.*

HISTORY MUSEUMS

4 *d-4*

CABLE CAR MUSEUM

Not only is this a museum; it's also the control center for the city's famous cable car system. From the mezzanine gallery you'll see (and hear) the four sets of huge power wheels that drive the entire system. You can also go downstairs for a glimpse of the cables running under the city's streets. A 15-minute video describes how the system works (cables must be replaced every 75 to 250 days!); the design is so simple it seems almost unreal. The museum is full of photographs, scale models, signposts, ticketing machines, diagrams, drawings, and vintage cars—including cable car inventor Andrew Hallidie's prototype car dating from 1873. It's all housed in a tri-level red-brick cable car barn, circa 1907—the last of some 14 cable car barns that once operated around the city. *1201 Mason St., at Washington St., Nob Hill, 415/474–1887. Admission free.*

4 *f-6*

CALIFORNIA HISTORICAL SOCIETY

The state's official historical society, founded in 1871, has amassed an awesome collection of Californiana: some 500,000 photographs; 150,000 manuscripts; thousands of books, periodicals, prints, and paintings; and gold rush paraphernalia. The building itself is an airy, skylit space with a central gallery, two adjacent galleries, the North Baker Research Library, and a storefront bookstore. Exhibitions, all exploring California's history, change every two to three months. Call before visiting, as the galleries close between exhibitions. *678 Mission St., at 3rd St., South of Market, 415/357–1848. Admission: $3, $1 senior citizens and students. Closed Mon.*

4 *f-4*

CHINESE HISTORICAL SOCIETY OF AMERICA

The tiny but fascinating Chinese Historical Society is tough to spot, so keep your eyes open for the sign. Despite the modest surroundings it's well worth a visit. Photos and graphics, accompanied by moving explanations, document the

---

FREEBIES

There's no admission charge at the following history museums:

Cable Car Museum
  Control center for the city's famous cable car system.

Chinese Historical Society of America
  The history of Chinese immigrants and their descendants.

Musée Mécanique
  Antique toys and carnival gadgets (bring quarters to operate them).

Museum of Money of the American West
  A mini-museum at the Union Bank of California.

National Maritime Museum
  Ship models, carved figureheads, maps, and more.

Pacific Heritage Museum
  Rare art and artifacts from Asian nations.

Presidio Museum
  History of the city's military base in the midst of a national park.

Randall Museum
  Children's museum with hands-on nature and science exhibits.

San Francisco Fire Department Museum
  Two centuries of San Francisco firefighting paraphernalia.

San Francisco History Center
  Small history museum at the San Francisco Main Library.

Wells Fargo Museum
  Gold-mining tools and treasures, and an old Concord stagecoach.

---

little-publicized history of Chinese immigrants and their descendants from the early 1800s to the present. Among other artifacts, you'll view an altar built in the 1880s and a parade dragon head from 1909. In 1999 the museum plans to move to the historic Chinatown YWCA building (*see* Historic Sites & Architecture, *above*). *650 Commercial St., between Kearny and Montgomery Sts., 415/391–1188. Admission free (donations requested). Closed Sun. and Mon.*

5 *a-1*

FORT POINT NATIONAL HISTORIC SITE

This historic site has been converted to a museum of military memorabilia (*see* Historic Sites & Architecture, *above*).

4 *c-2*

HYDE STREET PIER

Between The Cannery and Ghirardelli Square is this bustling pier, one of the best bargains at Fisherman's Wharf. The highlight of the pier is its collection of fully restored historic ships, all of which can be boarded. The *Balclutha* is an 1886 full-rigged, three-mast sailing vessel that was built in Scotland and sailed around Cape Horn 17 times; comedian Jonathan Winters was once briefly institutionalized after he climbed its mast and hung from it, shouting "I am the man in the moon!" The newly restored 1890 paddle-wheel ferry *Eureka* once carried passengers around the waters of San Francisco Bay. The 1895 three-master schooner *C.A. Thayer* was used to transport lumber, while the 1891 schooner *Alma* hauled hay. Hyde Street Pier is part of the San Francisco Maritime National Historical Park, which also includes the National Maritime Museum (*see below*). *At the foot of Hyde St., off Jefferson St., Fisherman's Wharf, 415/556–3002. Admission: $4, $2 youth 12–17, senior citizens and children under 11 free, $7 Family Ticket (2 adults and up to 4 youth or children), $19 Combo Family Ticket (2 adults and up to 4 youth or children for both Hyde Street Pier and USS Pampanito).*

2 *a-3*

MUSÉE MÉCANIQUE

This quirky penny arcade museum brims with antique mechanical games and carnival contrivances: player pianos, peep shows, pinball machines, marionettes, nickelodeons, and a mechanical laughing lady. Bring a roll of quarters to play with all the old gadgets, and don't miss the miniature amusement park built out of toothpicks by San Quentin inmates. Step outside to take a peek at the Farallon Islands, 30 miles offshore, through the magical lens of the museum's camera obscura. *1090 Point Lobos Ave., at Great Hwy., Richmond District, 415/386–1170. Admission free.*

4 *f-5*

MUSEUM OF MONEY OF THE AMERICAN WEST
The Union Bank of California operates this mini-museum in their Financial District branch. Exhibits tell the story of banking in the Old West, and include samples of privately minted money used before the U.S. Mint was established. There's also a display of counterfeit coins and detection devices. *400 California St., at Sansome St., Financial District, 415/765–0400. Admission free.*

4 *b-2*

NATIONAL MARITIME MUSEUM
Housed in a sturdy, round Art Deco structure, this museum exhibits painstakingly crafted ship models, photographs, carved figureheads, scrimshaw, diaries, maps, ship's logs, and other artifacts chronicling the development of San Francisco and the West Coast through maritime history. The museum is part of the San Francisco Maritime National Historical Park, which also includes Hyde Street Pier (*see above*). *900 Beach St., at Polk St., Fisherman's Wharf, 415/556–3002. Admission free (donation requested).*

2 *f-2*

OCTAGON HOUSE-MUSEUM
The National Society of Colonial Dames operates a charming little museum inside this unusual eight-sided house (*see Historic Sites & Architecture, above*), with antique American furniture, decorative arts (paintings, silver, rugs), and documents from the Colonial and Federal periods. It's open only on the second Sunday and the second and fourth Thursday of the month. *2645 Gough St., at Union St., Pacific Heights, 415/441–7512. Donation requested. Closed Jan.*

5 *e-3*

PRESIDIO MUSEUM
The Presidio Museum is housed in a circa-1860 former hospital, the oldest building on the base put up by the U.S. Army. Its collection illustrates the role of the military in the development of San Francisco from 1776 to the present. Behind the museum are two "earthquake cottages" that were used to house refugees from the 1906 earthquake and fire—5,000 such structures filled the Presidio and Golden Gate Park following the disaster. *Lincoln Blvd., at Funston Ave., The Presidio, 415/561–4331. Admission free. Closed Mon.–Tues.*

4 *a-2*

SAN FRANCISCO AFRICAN-AMERICAN HISTORICAL AND CULTURAL SOCIETY
The only museum of black culture on the West Coast has a research library (*see Libraries, below*), an art gallery, and permanent exhibits on the history of blacks in California and in the Civil War. An intriguing gift shop sells jewelry and artifacts. *Fort Mason Center, Building C, Marina Blvd. at Laguna St., The Marina, 415/441–0640. Admission: $2, $1 senior citizens and students. Closed Mon.–Tues.*

4 *c-7*

SAN FRANCISCO HISTORY CENTER AT THE SAN FRANCISCO MAIN LIBRARY
The main branch of the San Francisco Public Library maintains a small history museum with frequently changing exhibits on its sixth floor. The focus is usually on book arts, such as calligraphy and illustration, as well as rare books and special editions. *Larkin St., at Grove St., Civic Center, 415/557–4400 for Main Library, or 415/557–4567 for San Francisco History Center. Admission free. Closed Mon.*

4 *c-2*

MUSEUM OF THE CITY OF SAN FRANCISCO
The first independent museum on the history of the city displays historical items, maps, and photographs, including the the 700-pound head of the *Goddess of Progress* statue, which was removed from City Hall in 1909 due to damage from the 1906 earthquake. Other exhibits trace the history of Chinatown, Golden Gate Park, and the Sutro Baths, as well as the earthquakes of

1906 and 1989. *The Cannery, 3rd floor, 2801 Leavenworth St., at Beach St., Fisherman's Wharf, 415/928–0289. Suggested donation: $2. Closed Mon.–Tues.*

4 *h-6*

SS JEREMIAH O'BRIEN (NATIONAL LIBERTY SHIP MEMORIAL)

Of a great fleet used to carry troops and supplies to Normandy, this is the last unaltered World War II Liberty Ship freighter that is still seaworthy. On board, volunteers answer questions and lead tours. To keep the ship in sailing shape, its steam engine is fired up dockside on special "steaming weekends" (the third weekend of the month). Full-day Bay tours depart during Fleet Week and Memorial Day Weekend (*see Boat Tours, below*). *Pier 32, at the foot of Brannan St., South of Market, 415/441–3101. Admission: $5, $3 senior citizens, $2 youth 10–18, $1 children under 10.*

1 *d-2, d-3*

TREASURE ISLAND MUSEUM

The museum on Treasure Island presents highlights of the three sea services—the Navy, the Marines, and the Coast Guard—from 1813 to the present. Other exhibits take a look at the Golden Gate International Exposition of 1939–40, the China Clipper flying boats of the '30s, and the history of Treasure Island, the only manmade island in San Francisco Bay. The superb views of San Francisco and the bridges are reason enough to make the trip. *410 Ave. of Palms, Treasure Island, 415/395–5067. Suggested donation: $3.*

4 *c-1*

USS PAMPANITO WORLD WAR II SUBMARINE

Built in 1943, this 312-foot-long submarine saw plenty of action in the Pacific during World War II. These days it's a floating museum where you can go below deck to explore the crew quarters, galley, and control room. The admission fee includes an excellent self-guided audio tour. *Pier 45, at the foot of Taylor St., Fisherman's Wharf, 415/929–0202. Admission: $5, $3 children ages 6–12 and senior citizens, $15 Family Ticket (2 adults and up to 4 youth under 18), $19 Combo Family Ticket (2 adults and up to 4 youth under 18 for both USS Pampanito and Hyde Street Pier.*

4 *f-4*

WELLS FARGO MUSEUM

For a short course in the history of Wells Fargo, California's oldest bank (it opened its first San Francisco branch in 1852), as well as a look at the picturesque Pony Express and Gold Rush–era banking practices, visit this small museum on the street level of Wells Fargo Bank's headquarters. The showpiece is a century-old Concord stagecoach that in the mid-1850s carried 18 passengers from St. Joseph, Missouri, to San Francisco in three weeks. The museum also displays samples of nuggets and gold dust from mines, a mural-size map of the Mother Lode, mementos of the poet bandit Black Bart ("Po8," as he signed his poems), an old telegraph machine on which you can practice sending codes, and many other artifacts. *420 Montgomery St., between California and Sacramento Sts., Financial District, 415/396–2619. Admission free. Closed weekends.*

LIBRARIES

4 *c-5*

ALLIANCE FRANCAISE

The alliance contains 25,000 volumes in French—mostly literature. *1345 Bush St., at Polk St., Nob Hill, 415/775–7755. Admission free. Closed Sun.*

4 *c-7*

BLIND AND PRINT HANDICAPPED LIBRARY

More than 6,000 four-track cassette tapes are available at the Blind and Print Handicapped Library, part of the Library of Congress. It is housed in the San Francisco Main Library (*see below*). *100 Larkin St., between Fulton and Grove Sts., Civic Center, 415/557–4253. Admission free. Closed weekends.*

4 *g-7*

CALIFORNIA GENEALOGICAL SOCIETY

Here is an extensive collection for those interested in tracing their ancestors. The society charges a $5 daily use fee for nonmembers, or $35 for an annual membership. *300 Brannan St., at 2nd St., Suite 409, South Beach, 415/777–9936. Closed Mon., Tues., Fri., and Sun.*

4 *e-5*

GOETHE INSTITUT

The Goethe Institut's library contains some 12,000 items—books, magazines, newspapers, CDs, videos—of or about Germany. Most of the collection is in German. *530 Bush St., at Grant Ave., Union Square, 415/391–0428. Admission free. Closed Sat.–Mon.*

7 *a-2*

HELEN CROCKER RUSSELL LIBRARY OF HORTICULTURE

The Strybing Arboretum and Botanical Gardens (*see* Gardens, *in* Chapter 6) operates this horticultural library, whose 18,000-plus volumes make it the largest such collection in Northern California. *9th Ave. and Lincoln Way, Golden Gate Park, 415/661–1316. Admission free.*

4 *a-2*

J. PORTER SHAW LIBRARY

The National Maritime Museum operates this library at Fort Mason Center as a reference center and public reading room, with more than 25,000 books, newspapers clippings, and pamphlets relating to naval history. There's also a large collection of ship plans, and some 250,000 photographs. *Fort Mason Center, Building E, Third Floor, Marina Blvd. at Laguna St., The Marina, 415/556–9870. Admission free. Closed Sun.–Tues.*

7 *a-1*

MAILLARD REFERENCE LIBRARY

Within the California Academy of Sciences (*see* Science Museums, *below*) is the Mailliard Reference Library, with 180,000 natural sciences volumes, plus

---

WHEN TO SEE FOR FREE

What better incentive to brush up on your facts about Degas and Descartes than a free day at one of the Bay Area's better art and science museums?

Asian Art Museum of San Francisco (Art Museums)
Free first Wednesday of the month.

Berkeley Art Museum (Art Museums)
Free every Thursday 11–noon and 5–9.

California Academy of Sciences (Science Museums)
Free first Wednesday of the month, except for Morrison Planetarium and Laserium.

California Palace of the Legion of Honor (Art Museums)
Free second Wednesday of the month.

Center for the Arts (Art Museums)
Free first Thursday of the month 6 PM–8 PM.

Exploratorium (Science Museums)
Free first Wednesday of the month.

Jewish Museum San Francisco (Art Museums)
Free first Monday of the month.

Lawrence Hall of Science (Science Museums)
Free on Thursdays, excluding Planetarium shows.

Mexican Museum (Art Museums)
Free first Wednesday of the month.

M.H. de Young Memorial Museum (Art Museums)
Free first Wednesday of the month.

Museo Italo Americano (Art Museums)
Free first Wednesday of the month.

Oakland Museum of California (Art Museums)
Free Sundays 4 PM–7 PM.

San Francisco Craft and Folk Art Museum (Art Museums)
Free Saturdays 10 AM–noon, and all day on the first Wednesday of the month.

San Francisco Museum of Modern Art (SFMOMA) (Art Museums)
Free first Tuesday of the month; half-price Thursdays 6 PM–9 PM.

CD-ROM databases and, in its Special Collections department, more than one million visual and audio items such as slides, photos, magazine articles, and videotapes. There is a small lending library here as well. *Music Concourse, near John F. Kennedy and Tea Garden Drs., Golden Gate Park, 415/750–7102 for Mailliard Library, 415/750–7122 for Special Collections. Admission free. Closed weekends.*

4 *f-6*

NORTH BAKER RESEARCH LIBRARY

The California Historical Society's research library, open by appointment only on Wednesdays, has 35,000 books and pamphlets dating from 1535 to the present; 150,000 manuscript items; a 500,000-piece photographic collection; a collection of *The San Francisco Chronicle* dating to 1906; and maps, posters, periodicals, newspapers, microfilm, and ephemera. The library use fee for non-members is $5 per day, $3 per day for students. *678 Mission St., at 3rd St., South of Market, 415/357–1848.*

4 *a-2*

SAN FRANCISCO AFRICAN AMERICAN HISTORICAL AND CULTURAL SOCIETY

The society maintains a research library and historical archive with books, magazines, computer databases, and rare print material. *Fort Mason Center, Building C, Marina Blvd. at Laguna St., The Marina, 415/441–0640. Admission: $2, $1 senior citizens and students. Closed Mon.–Tues.*

4 *c-7*

SAN FRANCISCO MAIN LIBRARY

The new main library, which opened in April 1996, is one of the most technologically advanced in the country: It has 300 computer terminals, many with free Web access and CD-ROM capability. The building is a striking, modernized version of the old Beaux-Arts library that sits just across Fulton Street (that building is scheduled to become the new site of the Asian Art Museum in 1999). In addition to its collection of books, records, and CDs, the new space also contains several specialty rooms, including the Wallace Stegner Environmental Center, an art gallery, a café, a center for people with hearing and visual impairments (*see above*), a children's library, a gay and lesbian history center, African-

American and Asian centers, and a rooftop garden and terrace. The new San Francisco History Room and Archives is full of historic photographs, maps, and other memorabilia. At the library's center is a five-story atrium with a skylight, a grand staircase, and murals painted by local artists. *Larkin St., between Grove and Fulton Sts., Civic Center, 415/557–4400. Admission free.*

7 *b-8*

SAN FRANCISCO PERFORMING ARTS LIBRARY AND MUSEUM (PALM)

This library and research center is a virtual clearinghouse for information on the performing arts world, particularly the performing arts of the Bay Area. It's the largest collection of its kind on the West Coast, with more than 8,000 books and periodicals and nearly 2,000 radio interviews with performers. A small gallery has fascinating quarterly exhibitions of programs, photographs, manuscripts, costumes, and other memorabilia from the collection. PALM also hosts an excellent lecture series. *399 Grove St., at Gough St., Civic Center, 415/255–4800. Admission free. Closed Sun.–Tues.*

NOTABLE NEIGHBORHOODS

CASTRO DISTRICT

The heart of the city's predominately gay neighborhood is the intersection of Castro and 18th streets, just south of Market Street. The first gay bars opened on Castro Street in the late 1960s, and in the '70s the scene exploded. Lured by national publicity, gay men and lesbian women from all over the country migrated to the Castro and Polk Street and made this their social, cultural, and political center. Today the Castro District remains one of the liveliest and most welcoming neighborhoods in the city. The streets teem with people out shopping, pushing political causes, heading to art films, and lingering in bars and cafés. Cutting-edge clothing boutiques and unique gift shops predominate, as do pairs of pretty young things holding hands.

CHINATOWN

Exotic, exuberant, and aromatic, this 14-block area is one of the largest Chinese communities outside of Asia. Housing discrimination in the past kept residents from moving outside Chinatown, and the tightly packed area has been a magnet for Chinese residents ever since. The main thoroughfare, Grant Avenue from Bush Street to Broadway, is lined with trinket shops, herbal medicine shops, produce stands, fish markets, tiny eateries selling steaming dumplings, and about a hundred restaurants. Within the narrow side streets, good-luck banners of crimson and gold hang beside dragon-entwined lampposts and street signs with Chinese calligraphy, and virtually every roof is topped with a pagoda. Listen for the sound of conversations in Cantonese or Mandarin, and the clink of mah-jongng tiles issuing from the windows of houses along quiet alleys. You needn't be shy about exploring here: Chinatown has been a tourist stop for more than 100 years, and most of its residents welcome guests.

FISHERMAN'S WHARF

Once shunned as the city's working-class commercial fishing center, colorful Fisherman's Wharf is now the first stopping point for tourists. Take a cable car here from downtown to see the fishing boats (the fleet arrives back in port by mid-afternoon) and to stroll through the chaotic streets, past countless seafood restaurants, sidewalk crab pots, and counters selling take-out shrimp and crab cocktails along with crusty sourdough bread. You'll also find dozens of tacky souvenir shops, talented and amusing street performers, and so-called novelty museums such as **Ripley's Believe It or Not** (175 Jefferson St., at Powell St., 415/771–6188; map 4, d-2) and the **Wax Museum** (145 Jefferson St., at Powell St., 415/885–4975; map 4, d-2). Pier 39, the Cannery, and Ghirardelli Square are historic buildings converted to shopping and entertainment complexes, while Hyde Street pier is port for a few historic ships (see Historic Sites & Architecture, above).

HAIGHT-ASHBURY

Despite its growing popularity among upscale residents, "the Haight," the neighborhood east of Golden Gate Park, still wears the spirit of the tie-dyed 1960s on its sleeve. Young people with flowers in their hair and peace and civil rights on their minds began moving here in the early '60s; by 1966 the Haight had become a major destination for rock bands such as the Grateful Dead, whose members moved into a big Victorian at 710 Ashbury Street, and Jefferson Airplane, whose grand mansion was at 2400 Fulton Street. These days, it's still a popular hangout for members of the counter culture. Its shops are full of folk art and funky clothes, and on sunny days even the sidewalks fill with young artists displaying handmade jewelry and crafts for sale. The Haight's cafés are always filled with the young, pierced, and hip (don't these people have day jobs?), who descend on the neighborhood's many clubs and bars come nightfall.

JAPANTOWN

Around 1860 a wave of Japanese immigrants arrived in San Francisco, which they called Soko. Tragically Japantown, which sprang up after the 1906 earthquake and fire left many of the city's Japanese immigrants homeless, was virtually disbanded when many of its residents, including second- and third-generation Americans, were forced into so-called relocation camps during World War II. Today, Japantown doesn't feel much different from other parts of the city, and with the exception of the Peace Pagoda and a few shops on the Japan Center Mall, the architecture in the area is fairly generic.

MISSION DISTRICT

The sunny Mission District is a melting pot of Central Americans, Puerto Ricans, Korean, Chinese, Thai, and other various nationalities. Side-by-side on the streets are Italian restaurants, Irish pubs, and Mexican taquerias, as well as Arabic bookstores, Vietnamese markets, and Filipino eateries. On Mission Street, the heart of the Latino neighborhood, produce stands sell huge Mexican papayas, plantains, and garlands of chiles; this area takes center stage during important festivals such as Cinco de Mayo and Carnaval (see Events, below). In recent years a largely white, young, crowd of political activists, artists, and slackers has flocked to sections of the Mission now known as New Bohemia, centered at the intersection of 16th and Valencia streets. The surrounding streets are filled with cafés, bookstores, secondhand clothing and furniture shops, avant garde art galleries, live-music clubs, and funky, inexpensive restaurants.

NOB HILL

Once known as the Hill of Golden Promise, this neighborhood has the city's most dramatic views of downtown and the San Francisco Bay. The area was officially dubbed Nob Hill during the 1870s, after "the Big Four"—Charles Crocker, Leland Stanford, Mark Hopkins, and Collis Huntington—built their hilltop estates here. The locals below referred to the swells as "nabobs" (originally meaning a provincial governor from India), and the hill itself was called Snob Hill. The 1906 earthquake and fire destroyed most of the grand mansions, many of which were replaced by some of the city's finest hotels.

NOE VALLEY

Noe Valley is a sedate, middle-class residential neighborhood tucked into the hills above the Mission District. Until the early 1980s, the neighborhood was predominately working class (and largely Irish), but a subsequent influx of well-shod liberals has changed the mix. Today Noe Valley feels more like a small (though prosperous) town than any other neighborhood in San Francisco. The storefronts are modest-looking, everyone seems to know each other, and the pace is fairly slow; crowds slump in front of 24th Street's bagel shop and nearby coffee shops, and strollers clog the sidewalks.

NORTH BEACH

Less than a square mile in size but heavily populated, North Beach was at one time an exclusively Italian community, with as many as 125,000 Italian-American residents at one time. Much of the area is now Chinese, but about 2,000 residents of Italian descent remain, most of them elderly. Some still regard this as the best place in the city for cappuccino, biscotti, and pasta; good-smelling authentic Italian restaurants, delicatessens, and bakeries line the streets. North Beach is also the well-known birthplace of the Beat Generation, and homages to Jack Kerouac and Allen Ginsberg appear at every turn. Along Broadway, strip joints carry on the legacy of the city's Barbary Coast days.

PACIFIC HEIGHTS

In the late 1800s, the area now know as Pacific Heights was still the domain of dairy farms—hence the name of one Pacific Heights neighborhood, Cow Hollow. Its tiny lagoon was the city's laundry basin, and until the turn of the century, tanners, slaughterhouses, and sugar factories were located here. With the invention of the cable car, however, came rapid urbanization; many of the city's most beautiful Victorians were built here at that time, and those that survived the 1906 quake and fire can still be seen on the 1700–2900 blocks of Broadway and the 1600–2900 blocks of Vallejo Street. Pacific Heights continues to this day to be one of the most exclusive districts in the city, with mansions and town houses priced at $1 million and up. From almost any point you get a magnificent view of the San Francisco Bay and the Golden Gate Bridge.

RUSSIAN HILL

Russian Hill has long been home to wealthy San Francisco families. During the 1890s, this was the domain of a group of bohemian artists and writers, including Charles Norris, George Sterling, and Maynard Dixon; Jack London, Bret Harte, Dashiell Hammett, Jack Kerouac, and Herbert Gold have also sought and found inspiration here at one time or another. It's a beautifully scenic, highly desirable residential area with sumptuous pieds-à-terre and costly condominiums rubbing shoulders with the few remaining cottages built with $500 Red Cross loans soon after the 1906 earthquake and fire. The neighborhood is home to the renowned San Francisco Art Institute and Lombard Street, "the world's crookedest" (for both, *see* Historic Sites & Architecture, *above*).

SOUTH OF MARKET (SOMA)

Once an industrial area, the 2-square-mile district known as SoMa (an acronym for South of Market) is a burgeoning center for the visual arts. Its heart is the San Francisco Museum of Modern Art, along with the adjoining Yerba Buena Gardens (*see* Art Museums, *above*). With the arrival of *Wired* magazine to offices near South Park, SoMa has also earned the moniker "Multimedia Gulch."

RICHMOND AND SUNSET DISTRICTS

The Richmond district's middle class row houses are home to Eastern Europeans, Russians, Greeks, Chinese, Koreans, Filipinos, and Japanese residents. Interesting shops and international restaurants line Clement Street. In the Sunset, a residential area settled mainly by Chinese and Thai immigrants, ethnic shops and restaurants line Irving Street between 5th and 25th avenues.

SCHOOLS

STANFORD UNIVERSITY

The "Ivy League university of the West Coast," also nicknamed "The Farm," occupies the former 8,180-acre South Bay horse farm of Big Four railroad baron Leland Stanford. Together with his wife Jane, Mr. Stanford founded the school in 1891 in honor of their beloved only son Leland Stanford, Jr., who died at age 15. Frederick Law Olmsted designed the campus, whose yellow Spanish Mission–style sandstone buildings and red-tile roofs give it a distinctly western feel. Stanford currently enrolls 13,811 students at seven nationally top-ranked schools, and proudly claims a 3.6-billion dollar endowment. Daily campus walking tours take in campus attractions such as the stately Romanesque Memorial Church, known for its Venetian mosaic; 285-ft Hoover Tower, with its observation deck; the Rodin Sculpture Garden, known for its awe-inspiring bronze reproduction of the *Gates of Hell*; the Stanford Museum of Art, which is scheduled to reopen in January, 1999; and the Stanford Medical Center, one of the country's finest. Science buffs will want to visit the Stanford Linear Accelerator (SLAC), a research facility with a 2-mile-long electron accelerator used for elementary-particle research. The outdoor Stanford Shopping Center is one of the Bay Area's finest. *University Ave., off Hwy. 101, or Sand Hill Rd., off Hwy. 280, Palo Alto, 650/725–3335.*

3 *d-2, e-2*

UNIVERSITY OF CALIFORNIA AT BERKELEY

Established in 1868 as the first branch of the statewide University of California system, U.C. Berkeley is one of the top public academic institutions in the United States, with 300 degree programs and 31,000 students representing every state and some 100 foreign countries. Its wooded, 1,232-acre campus overlooking San Francisco Bay has seen its share of history: At Sproul Plaza, on the west side of campus, the Free Speech Movement began in 1964. Another campus highlight is Sather Tower (more commonly known as the Campanile), a 307-foot clock tower modeled after the one in Venice's Piazza San Marco. On permanent display in the administrative office of Bancroft Library is a gold nugget purported to have started the California Gold Rush when it was discovered on January 24, 1848, at Sutter's Mill. Free campus tours depart daily from the Visitor Center, on the west side of campus (University Hall, Room 101, 2200 University Ave., at Oxford St., 510/642–5215; map 3, d-2); self-guiding tour maps are also available here. *Bancroft Ave., at Telegraph Ave., Berkeley, 510/642–6000.*

SCIENCE MUSEUMS

7 *a-1*

CALIFORNIA ACADEMY OF SCIENCES

One of the country's top-five natural-history museums, this huge complex is subdivided into several blockbuster sights, including the Morrison Planetarium (*see below*), the excellent Steinhart Aquarium (*see Aquariums in Chapter 6*), and the Natural History Museum. The latter has separate halls devoted to plants, animals, gems, and minerals: The most popular among the natural science exhibits is the Hall of Fossils, with dinosaur bones and a brontosaurus skull. One of the best exhibits is the African Hall, depicting animals (real but stuffed) specific to Africa in their native vegetation; don't miss the sights and sounds of the African watering hole at the end of the room. You can also experience the vibrations of an 8.0-magnitude quake in the "earthquake room" of the Space and Earth Hall; learn the story of evolution from the beginnings of life on earth to the age of mammals in the innovative Life Through Time Hall; or explore the languages, physical features, and learning habits of birds with the Birds of a Feather exhibit. In the Wild California Hall, a 14,000-gallon aquarium tank shows underwater life at the Farallones (islands off the coast of northern California), life-size elephant-seal models, and video information on the wildlife of the state. A cafeteria is open daily until one hour before closing time. *Music Concourse and John F. Kennedy Drs., near 8th Ave. and Fulton St., Golden Gate Park, 415/750–7145. Admission to Natural History Museum and Steinhart Aquarium: $8.50, $5.50 senior citizens and youth 12–17, $2 children 4–11, children under 4 free; $1 discount with Muni transfer; free first*

Wed. of the month. Separate admission fee required for Morrison Planetarium and Laserium (see below).

5 *f-2*

EXPLORATORIUM

A world-famous interactive museum housed in the Palace of Fine Arts (*see Historic Sites & Architecture, above*), the Exploratorium contains more than 650 hands-on exhibits, many computer-assisted, about science and technology. Laser beams, miniature tornados, soap bubbles, holograms, microbes, and other interactive exhibits make it a fun place for both children and adults to explore the world of science. Reservations are required for the museum's enormously popular Tactile Dome (415/560–0362), a series of dark, small rooms in which you walk, crawl, and slither through materials of different textures. *3601 Lyon St., between Marina Blvd. and Lombard St., The Marina, 415/561–0360 for recorded information. Admission: $9, $7 senior citizens, $5 youth 6–17, $2.50 children 3–5, children under 3 free; $12 Tactile Dome; free first Wed. of the month. Closed Labor Day–Memorial Day, Mon.*

7 *f-2*

RANDALL MUSEUM

In Corona Heights Park near Buena Vista Park is this small children's museum with changing hands-on nature and science exhibits, including minerals to handle, dinosaur bones to view, a working seismograph, chemistry and biology labs, exhibits on California Indians, and more. The museum's Animal Room has live owls, snakes, and racoons that kids may view up close. Call for information on Saturday art workshops, hikes, and nature classes. *199 Museum Way, at Roosevelt Way, The Castro, 415/554–9600. Admission free. Closed Sun.–Mon.*

3 *f-1*

LAWRENCE HALL OF SCIENCE

The University of California at Berkeley's Lawrence Hall of Science is a memorial to Ernest O. Lawrence, the university's first Nobel laureate and an inventor of the atomic bomb. Its exhibits are mostly hands-on and geared toward children, with an emphasis on biology, chemistry, and astronomy. On weekends, and daily during summer, you can catch films, lectures, laboratory demonstrations, and

planetarium shows. On the hillside outside the museum's rear patio look for the wind organ, a set of 36 long, slender pipes sticking out of the ground: You'll hear their music if you walk among them when the wind is blowing. You can also play with their tones by turning one of six moveable pipes. On clear Saturday evenings from 8 to 11 PM, employees and amateur local astronomers bring their telescopes here to give interested visitors a free peek at the moon, planets, star clusters, and galaxies; call the Hall's Astronomy and Night Sky Information Line (510/642–5132) for details. *Centennial Dr., near Grizzly Peak Blvd., Berkeley, 510/642–5132. Admission: $6, $4 senior citizens and students, $2 children 3–6; free Thurs.*

7 *a-1*

MORRISON PLANETARIUM/LASERIUM

Part of the California Academy of Sciences complex, the Morrison Planetarium presents one-hour sky shows daily on the 65-foot dome of its Sky Theater, as well as "Startalks," a look at the present night skies, on weekends and holidays at noon. Laserium laser-light shows take place most evenings and some days at Morrison Planetarium. In the laserium shows, light patterns are projected onto the planetarium's dome, accompanied by high-tech music; Pink Floyd's *Dark Side of the Moon* is a favorite. On weekend evenings there is a special 3-D laserium show. *Centennial Dr., near Grizzly Peak Blvd., Berkeley, 415/750–7141 for sky shows, 415/750–7138 for Laserium. Admission: up to $2.50 for Planetarium; $6–$8 for Laserium.*

4 *d-3*

UFO, BIGFOOT, AND LOCH NESS MONSTER MUSEUM

One of San Francisco's most unusual mini-museums is devoted to photographic evidence of UFOs, sea monsters, Bigfoot, crop circles, and faces on Mars. Curator–owner Erik Beckjord calls it "a museum of the unknown, of the tentative, of the unproven." Come here to view photos, news clips, videos, artist's conceptions, authentic testimonials straight out of *The X-Files*, and other signs of the Sasquatch. At press time, the museum was moving to a new location in SoMa; call for the exact address. *2nd St., at Howard St. South of Market, 415/974–4339. Admission: $4, $2 children under 12. Closed Mon.*

STATUES, MURALS, & MONUMENTS

8 *b-5*
BALMY ALLEY
In the tradition of the great Mexican muralist Diego Rivera, Mission District artists have transformed their neighborhood with message–minded paintings on walls, buildings, fences, and alleys. The best example is Balmy Alley—the 1-block alley is filled with a series of murals. A group of local children working with adults started the project in 1971; since then dozens of artists have steadily added to it, with the predominant themes being peace in Central America, community pride, and AIDS awareness. (Be careful in this area; the north end of the street adjoins the back of a somewhat dangerous housing project.) *Bordered by 24th, 25th, and Harrison Sts., and Treat Ave., Mission District.*

6 *b-1*
BEACH CHALET
The Beach Chalet's sweeping murals depicting San Francisco city life were added in the 1930s by famed French artist Lucien Labaudt, with funding from the WPA Federal Art Project. Labaudt covered almost the entire interior of the chalet—a roughly 1,500 sq-ft surface—with frescoes done in nine-foot-high panels. There are scenes of picnickers and swimmers at Ocean Beach, fishermen at the Wharf, and the construction of the Bay Bridge; many of the subjects are famous people of the day, or friends and relations of Labaudt. Sculptor Michael Von Meyer created the whimsical sea-creature-motifs on the carved wood staircase. (*See also Historic Sites & Architecture, above.*) *1000 Great Hwy., at John F. Kennedy Dr., Golden Gate Park.*

7 *h-1*
CALIFORNIA VOLUNTEERS' MEMORIAL
The 1903 California Volunteers' Memorial is a classic equestrian statue of an heroic rider—complete with raised sword—mounted on a charging steed. Douglas Tilden, perhaps the city's most talented outdoor sculptor, was the designer; heavyweight architect Willis Polk is responsible for the base. Behind the statue commences the grand stretch of Dolores Street, with a stately row of palm trees along its median strip. *Dolores St., at Market St., Mission District.*

4 *g-7*
CAPP STREET PROJECT
The highly regarded Capp Street Project sponsors three controversial murals South of Market. *Inner City Home* (6th and Brannan Sts., South of Market; map 4, f-8) comments on homelessness; *One Tree* (10th and Brannan Sts., South of Market, map 8, c-1) provokes thought about deforestation; and *Extinct* (5th and Folsom Sts., South of Market, map 4, f-7) takes on the issue of endangered animal species. *525 2nd St., between Bryant and Brannan Sts., 415/495–7101, South of Market.*

4 *e-3*
COIT TOWER
Standing in front of Coit Tower is **Discoverer of America,** an impressive bronze statue of Christopher Columbus, donated by the local Italian community in 1957. Inside the tower are 19 WPA-era murals painted by 25 artists, depicting California's laborers in a Socialist–Realist style pioneered by Diego Rivera. The U.S. government commissioned the murals as a Public Works of Art project, and the artists were each paid $38 a week. On Saturday mornings you can view the second-floor murals that are normally closed to the public by signing up for a tour of Coit Tower with City Guides (*see* Guided Tours, *below*). An illustrated brochure for sale in the Coit Tower gift shop explains the various murals for those who prefer the self-guided route. *Telegraph Hill Blvd., at Greenwich St., Telegraph Hill, 415/362–0808.*

4 *f-5*
DONAHUE MONUMENT
Holding its own against the skyscrapers that tower over this intersection is the Donahue Monument—an homage to waterfront mechanics. Its creator, Douglas Tilden, was a noted California sculptor who was deaf and mute. The plaque below the monument marks the spot as the location of the San Francisco Bay shoreline in 1848. *Market and Battery Sts., Financial District.*

4 *c-7*
DOUBLE L EXCENTRIC GYRATORY
Outside the main entrance to the San Francisco Main Library, spinning slowly in the breezes, is **Double L Excentric Gyratory,** an 18-foot stainless steel

kinetic sculpture by American artist George Rickey. The 1982 artwork consists of two delicately balanced "L" shaped pieces perched atop a "Y" shaped base. The sculpture was a gift of Carl Djerassi, the Stanford University professor who pioneered the birth control pill. He allegedly placed the sculpture in the Civic Center to symbolize "literature, literacy, law, and liberty." *Larkin and Fulton Sts., Civic Center.*

7 *a-1*

FRANCIS SCOTT KEY MONUMENT

Opposite the bandshell on Golden Gate Park's Music Concourse stands the impressive Francis Scott Key monument, the first monument in the United States to the author of the *Star Spangled Banner*. Sculpted by William Story, the work was commissioned by the city's philanthropist James Lick in 1888, and was moved several times before coming to rest here. The monument's sides are inscribed with phrases from the song such as "long may it wave." *Music Concourse, near John F. Kennedy and Tea Garden Drs., Golden Gate Park.*

2 *b-3*

THE HOLOCAUST

Just north of the California Palace of the Legion of Honor is George Segal's **The Holocaust,** a sobering monument whose white-plaster figures lie sprawled and twisted on the ground, while one lone figure peers out from behind barbed wire. *Lincoln Park, entrance at 34th Ave. and Clement St., 415/750–3600, Richmond District.*

4 *a-6*

JAPAN CENTER FOUNTAINS

At the center of the open-air Japan Center Mall are twin origami-like fountains by local artist Ruth Asawa. They're squat circular structures made of fieldstone, with three levels for sitting and a brick floor that is also a drain. *Buchanan St., between Post and Sutter Sts., Japantown.*

4 *g-4*

JUSTIN HERMAN PLAZA

A favorite with office workers on their lunch breaks, this little plaza is also a worthwhile stop for admirers of art. Here you'll find Armand Vaillancourt's huge building-block fountain where you can walk under, around, and over

streams of falling water. Nearby is Jean Dubuffet's mammoth stainless-steel sculpture, *La Chiffonière. Market and Steuart Sts., South of Market.*

4 *c-8*

LARGE FOUR PIECE RECLINING FIGURE

In front of Davies Symphony Hall is this valuable Henry Moore bronze sculpture, in Moore's trademark abstract style. It is one of only seven editions of this piece completed by the great British artist before his death in 1986. *Van Ness Ave., at Grove St., Civic Center.*

4 *f-6*

LOTTA'S FOUNTAIN

The nondescript Lotta's Fountain has lions' heads spigots that no longer function, and the monument receives little attention from passersby as they rush to and fro on Market Street—though it is on the National Register of Historic Places. It was presented to the city in 1875, on the 25th anniversary of California's statehood, by Lotta Crabtree, a Mae West prototype and the most highly paid American singer of her time. Her "brash music-hall exploits" so enthralled San Francisco's early population of miners that they were known to shower her with gold nuggets and silver dollars after her performances. The buxom Ms. Crabtree is depicted in one of the Anton Refregier murals in Rincon Center (*see below*). *Bordered by 3rd, Market, Kearny, and Geary Sts., Financial District.*

4 *f-6*

MARTIN LUTHER KING, JR. MEMORIAL

The focal point of the Yerba Buena Gardens complex is a Martin Luther King, Jr. Memorial. At the north end of a grassy, spacious esplanade, the memorial consists of 12 glass panels, all behind a shimmering waterfall, engraved with quotes from Dr. King in English and in the languages of each of San Francisco's sister cities. The powerful waterfall is meant to mirror the enduring force of King's words that are carved on the stone walls and on glass blocks behind the waterfall. *Bordered by 3rd, 4th, Mission, and Howard Sts., South of Market.*

7 *f-3*

NAMES PROJECT VISITOR CENTER AND PANELING WORKSHOP

Panels from the **NAMES Quilt**—made as a memorial to those who have died of AIDS—are displayed at the NAMES Project Foundation's Visitor Center and Panelmaking Workshop. The project started in 1987 when gay rights activist Cleve Jones organized a meeting with several others who had lost friends or lovers to AIDS; they decided upon a quilt with each panel made by the loved ones of an individual who has died of AIDS. The gigantic quilt now contains more than 44,000 hand-sewn and -decorated panels, portions of which are displayed in San Francisco and several other cities around the world. Those who are interested may create a panel during one of the center's weekly "quilting bees," or send one by mail. *2362A Market St., at Castro St., The Castro, 415/863–1966.*

4 *f-5*

PACIFIC COAST STOCK EXCHANGE

Flanking the entrance to the Pacific Coast Stock Exchange (*see* Historic Sites & Architecture, *above*) are a pair of 21-foot-tall Art Deco statues, *Earth's Fruitfulness* and *Man's Inventive Genius*, created in 1930. The monumental granite pair are both by Ralph Stackpole. *301 Pine St., at Sansome St., Financial District.*

4 *c-7*

PIONEERS MONUMENT

The city's largest historical monument stands just north of the San Francisco Main Library. The monument was completed in 1894 and stood firm in the 1906 earthquake and fire, even when City Hall was leveled. Historians believe that a time capsule is buried at the base—but nobody knows for sure. The monument's 30-foot-high granite shaft is topped by a bronze figure whose spear, shield, and bear symbolize California. Figures and bas-reliefs at the base depict scenes from early California and important personalities from that time, such as James Fremont, James Lick, Sir Francis Drake, John Sutter, and Junipero Serra. *Fulton St., between Larkin and Hyde Sts., Civic Center.*

4 *e-4*

PORTSMOUTH SQUARE

The focal point of this historic square (*see* Historic Sites & Architecture, *above*) is this bronze galleon atop a 9-foot granite shaft; designed by Bruce Porter, the sculpture was erected in 1919 in memory of Robert Louis Stevenson, who often visited the site during his 1879–80 residence. On the lower level of Portsmouth Square, in the children's play area, is an installation by Mary Fuller of six animal sculptures significant to Chinese astrology: the tiger, ram, serpent, monkey, rabbit, and dragon. *Kearny St., between Washington and Clay Sts., Chinatown.*

8 *b-6*

PRECITA EYES MURAL ARTS CENTER

A nonprofit arts organization begun in 1977, the mural center is the best resource for those interested in exploring and understanding the approximately 80 murals that can be found within an 8-block area in the southeast Mission District. Muralists-in-residence lead bus, bike, and walking tours, along with an introductory slide show (*see* Walking Tours, *below*). The center also sells a handy "Mission Mural Walk" map ($1.50 donation). *348 Precita Ave., between Folsom and Harrison Sts., 415/285–2287, Mission District.*

4 *g-4*

PROMENADE RIBBON

North of the Ferry Building at Pier 5 is the initial section of the 5-foot-wide, 2½-mi-long, glass-and-concrete Promenade Ribbon, billed by the city as the "longest art form in the nation." Except for the middle section, which will be completed by 2000, the ribbon spans the waterfront from the base of Telegraph Hill to South Beach. At various points along the way it curls up to form tabletops and park benches; at night it lights up to insure a safe pathway for pedestrians. *Along the Embarcadero.*

4 *g-5*

RINCON CENTER

Anton Refrigier spent eight years creating the 27-panel mural in the lobby of Rincon Center (*see* Historic Sites & Architecture, *above*). Because it depicts the history of California, including the oppression of Native Americans and the exploitation of workers by capitalist

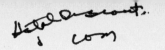
overlords, the mural was criticized by conservative groups, who claimed that Refregier's "radical" approach to the subject matter seemed to espouse Communist principles; to win federal approval, the artist was required to make more than 85 changes to the work. *Spear St., at Mission St., South of Market.*

4 e-5
RUTH ASAWA'S FANTASY FOUNTAIN

On the plaza in front of the Grand Hyatt Hotel, look for this circular fountain 14 feet in diameter. Children and friends helped sculptor Ruth Asawa shape these hundreds of tiny figures from baker's clay; they were then assembled on 41 large panels that were used as molds for the casting of the bronze. See if you can spot all of the city's famous hills, bridges, and unusual buildings within its wonderland of real and mythical creatures. Sculptor Ruth Asawa's work can also be found at the Japan Center Mall (*see above*), and there's a delightful mermaid fountain of hers in Ghirardelli Square. *345 Stockton St., between Sutter and Post Sts., Union Square.*

8 c-5
ST. PETER'S CATHOLIC CHURCH

A stunning mural adorns the rectory building of St. Peter's Catholic Church, made all the more stunning by the irony of its message. The mural, titled "500 Years of Resistance," portrays the struggle of the indigenous people of Central and South America to retain their unique cultures after the arrival of the Spaniards—and, of course, the Spaniards' Catholic church. It was painted in 1993 by master muralist Isaias Mata of El Salvador. *24th and Florida Sts., Mission District.*

4 e-6
SAMUELS CLOCK

The charming 12-foot-tall Samuels Clock appeared on Market Street in front of the Albert S. Samuels Jewelry Company just in time for the opening of the Panama-Pacific International Exposition (which also saw the building of the Palace of Fine Arts). It was built in 1915, and Albert Samuels was one of its principal designers. *865 Market St., between 4th and 5th Sts., Financial District.*

4 c-3
SAN FRANCISCO ART INSTITUTE

Of the three murals painted by Mexican master Diego Rivera in San Francisco, the one at the San Francisco Art Institute is the most accessible and impressive. The seven-section fresco, painted in 1931, is titled *The Making of a Fresco Showing the Building of a City* and features Rivera himself in the foreground, with his back to the viewer and surrounded by his assistants. They are surrounded by construction scenes and laborers, as well as city notables such as sculptor Robert Stackpole and architect Timothy Pfleuger. The gallery is to your left as you enter the institute. *800 Chestnut St., between Leavenworth and Jones Sts., Russian Hill.*

4 h-7
SEA CHANGE

The 10-ton, 70-foot-tall **Sea Change** sculpture soars above South Beach Park, a bright red and steel work with a crown that moves gracefully in the wind. The artist, Mark di Suvero, came to San Francisco as an eight-year-old immigrant from Shanghai, and later worked as a welder on the San Francisco waterfront. *The Embarcadero, between Townsend, 2nd, and King Sts., The Embarcadero.*

4 f-4, g-4
SKY TREE

Embarcadero Center (*see Historic Sites & Architecture*) has a collection of some two dozen pieces of art by nationally renowned artists, and guided art tours are available. Most notable is Louise Nevelson's dramatic 54-ft-high black-steel sculpture, *Sky Tree*, which stands guard over Building 3. *Embarcadero Center, Bldg. 3, bordered by Battery, Drumm, Clay, and Washington Sts., The Embarcadero.*

4 e-5
SUN YAT-SEN STATUE

In tranquil St. Mary's Square, across the street from Old St. Mary's Cathedral, is a 12-ft statue of the founder of the Republic of China, done in stainless steel and rose-color granite by local sculptor Beniamino (Benny) Bufano. The heroic statue of Sun Yat-sen was installed in 1937 on the site of the Chinese leader's favorite reading spot during his years of exile in San Francisco. *Pine, Quincy, and California Sts., Chinatown.*

4 f-4
TRANSAMERICA REDWOOD GROVE

In the Transamerica Redwood Grove is a statue of children playing leapfrog. Named "The Puddlejumpers," this is a work by sculptor Glenna Goodacre, who was also responsible for the new Women's Vietnam War Memorial in Washington, DC. *Columbus Ave., at Montgomery St., Financial District.*

4 e-6
VICTORY MONUMENT

Center stage at Union Square is Robert Ingersoll Aitken's soaring **Victory Monument,** which commemorates Commodore George Dewey's victory over the Spanish fleet at Manila in 1898. The 97-ft Corinthian column, topped by a bronze figure symbolizing naval conquest, was dedicated by Theodore Roosevelt in 1903 and withstood the 1906 earthquake. The city's famous philanthropist and iconoclast Alma Spreckels was the model for the Victory figure at its top. *Bordered by Stockton, Powell, Geary, and Post Sts., Union Square.*

5 g-1
WAVE ORGAN

It's an artwork, but it's also a functioning musical instrument. The sea-powered organ was built by artists with help from the Exploratorium (*see* Science Museums, *above*) and consists of a set of pipes that run along the waterfront and extend into the bay. Take a seat at one of the stone benches, place your ear on a pipe, and listen to the soothing tones created by lapping waves. Acoustics are best at high tide. *At the end of the jetty on Yacht Rd., north of Marina Blvd., The Marina.*

8 a-3
WOMEN'S BUILDING

A striking two-sided mural on the exterior of this community center (*see* Historic Sites & Architecture, *above*) depicts women's peacekeeping efforts over the centuries. *Maestrapeace* was painted by seven principal artists, all Bay Area women; and assisted by 10 guest artists and some 80 volunteers, also all women. All of the images are of women, as well: Look for Audre Lorde, Georgia O'Keeffe, and Rigoberta Menchú among many others. This is the largest of the Mission district mural projects; it was completed in 1994. *3543 18th St.,* between Valencia and Guerrero Sts., 415/431–1180, Mission District.*

VIEWPOINTS

There are so many to chose from! But these are some of the best.

2 b-2
BAKER BEACH

The bridge looms to your right, the ocean extends endlessly to your left, and the mountainous Marin Headlands rise before you. It's one of the city's most beautiful views, and also a popular beach (*see* Beaches *in* Chapter 6).

4 e-5
CALIFORNIA AND POWELL STREETS

The view down the California Street hill from this Nob Hill intersection is simply breathtaking, particularly if you're aboard a cable car.

2 a-3
CLIFF HOUSE

Though natural disasters have wreaked havoc on the buildings on this site (*see* Historic Sites & Architecture, *above*), the splendid views of Ocean Beach, the Pacific Ocean, Seal Rock, and the Marin Headlands remain.

4 e-3
COIT TOWER

For wonderful 360° views of the city, make a pilgrimage to the landmark Coit Tower (*see* also Historic Sites & Architecture), at the summit of Telegraph Hill. For $3, an elevator inside the 210-foot concrete observation tower will take you to the top for a drop-dead, 360° view of Golden Gate Bridge, the Bay Bridge, and Alcatraz.

49-MILE DRIVE

Follow the blue-and-white signs (marked with a seagull) along this scenic drive developed for San Francisco's 1939–1940 Golden Gate International Exposition and inaugurated by President Franklin D. Roosevelt. The drive starts at Civic Center and wends its way through Japantown, Union Square, Chinatown, Nob Hill, North Beach, Telegraph Hill; then, skirting Fisherman's Wharf, it goes past the Marina and the Palace of Fine Arts. The southern approach to the Golden Gate Bridge is one of the best viewpoints; the Presidio and Golden Gate Park also provide sweeping vistas of the Pacific. In the final stretch, the drive climbs Twin Peaks, descends to Mission Dolores, and returns past the Bay Bridge, the Ferry Building, and the Financial District. A free map is available at the San Francisco Visitor Information Center.

2 *b-2*

LINCOLN PARK

Here you can view the Golden Gate Bridge from atop a 200-ft cliff (*see* Parks in Chapter 6).

7 *c-7, c-8*

MT. DAVIDSON

This sylvan summit is 16 feet higher than the much more famous Twin Peaks (*see below*). It's also the site of an ongoing court battle: The largest steel-and-concrete cross in the country, placed on its top in 1934, was lit every evening until 1989, when a multifaith group challenged its constitutionality. Easter Services are still held here, but the cross is now dark. You can hike to the summit by taking the steps between 919 and 925 Rockdale Drive and keeping to the left at every fork, or drive up to the intersection of Myra and Dalewood Ways to get fairly close to the top.

2 *b-2*

SEACLIFF

On sunny days you can catch some of the city's finest views of the San Francisco Bay from in between the houses in the exclusive Seacliff neighborhood. Take the stairway off El Camino del Mar, just west of the end of 32nd Avenue, to a circular viewing deck with wonderful views of the whole Seacliff neighborhood, plus the Golden Gate Bridge and the Marin Headlands. *Bounded by Lake Street and 25th and 33rd Aves., Richmond District.*

4 *f-4*

SKYDECK

This indoor/outdoor observation deck on the 41st floor of Embarcadero Center opened in 1996. Come here for 360° views of the city, plus interactive multimedia presentations of San Francisco history and culture. Buy tickets on the ground floor; the elevator departs from the Mezzanine Level. Call for current hours. *1 Embarcadero Center, Battery and Sacramento Sts., The Embarcadero, 800/733–6318 for Embarcadero Center information, 888/737–5933 for SkyDeck Hotline, 415/772–0591 for SkyDeck ticket booth. Admission: $5, $3.50 senior citizens and students, $3 youth 5–12, children under 5 free.*

2 *a-3*

SUTRO HEIGHTS PARK

This magnificent park—once the grounds of May Adolph Sutro's mansion—overlooks the Cliff House, the Great Highway, and endless Pacific Ocean. Pick up the trail at Balboa Street across from the end of La Playa and head north up the path. *Off Balboa St., near La Playa, Richmond District.*

7 *d-3*

TANK HILL

A footpath leads to a high, craggy overlook where you can gaze at the city to your heart's content. *End of Belgrave Ave., off Stanyan St., Twin Peaks.*

1 *d-2, d-3*

TREASURE ISLAND

See the familiar San Francisco skyline from a slightly different angle by taking the Treasure Island exit from the Bay Bridge, then parking at the water's edge. *Ave. of Palms, Treasure Island.*

7 *d-5*

TWIN PEAKS

The peaks' crest, at the top of winding Twin Peaks Boulevard, is often windy and notoriously chilly, and it can get crowded with tour buses. But the prime panoramic views of the city and Bay are nothing less than breathtaking. *Twin Peaks Blvd., off Portola Dr., Twin Peaks.*

7 *e-6*

UPPER MARKET STREET

A close second to nearby Twin Peaks, this viewing point at the base of Market Street takes in the city and the East Bay. *Portola Dr., at base of Market St., Diamond Heights.*

guided tours

Reservations are recommended, and often required for the following tours.

AIR TOURS

BAY AERO TOURS

Scenic 45-minute San Francisco Bay flights in a Cessna 172 depart from Oakland International Airport and fly over the Bay Bridge, Alcatraz, the Golden Gate Bridge, and the city of San Francisco. Sunset flights are available. 510/632–6763.

SAN FRANCISCO HELICOPTER TOURS

Downtown San Francisco and Alcatraz, the Golden Gate Bridge, the Pacific Coast, Tiburon, and Angel Island are a few of the destinations covered on these scenic helicopter flights. Special Wine Country flights include lunch, and evening flights around San Francisco include dinner or a dinner-and-dancing boat cruise. All flights depart from San Francisco International Airport. 415/635–4500 or 800/400–2404.

SAN FRANCISCO SEAPLANE TOURS, INC.

Seaplane flights take off from the water, departing from either Pier 39 or Sausalito. The Golden Gate Tour from Pier 39 takes in Alcatraz, Angel Island, the Marin Headlands, the Golden Gate Bridge, and the city of San Francisco. The Coast Tour from Sausalito includes all points of interest along the San Francisco Bay as well as Mt. Tamalpais, Stinson Beach, and the Marin County coastline. There's also a sunset champagne flight. 415/332–4843 or 888/732–7526.

SCENIC AIR TOURS

Scenic Air specializes in full-day airplane tours to Yosemite National Park, including private tour bus and guide within the park in addition to the scenic flight (45 minutes each way). The company also offers the only full-day air tour to Grand Canyon National Park, a 2½-hour one-way flight from the Bay Area. 415/922–2386, 800/957–2364.

BICYCLE TOURS

BAY BICYCLE TOURS

Sign up for their 3½-hour tours across the Golden Gate Bridge to Sausalito. Tours depart from the Cannery Shopping Center at Fisherman's Wharf. 415/436–0633 for recorded schedule information or 415/923–6434.

BREAKAWAY

Guided mountain biking tours explore Bay Area state parks, with destinations varying by season. 415/203–9910.

BOAT TOURS

4 e-1

ADVENTURE CAT SAILING CHARTERS

San Francisco's only catamaran sailing vessel used for public excursions departs from Pier 39 for 1½-hour tours of the San Francisco Bay. 415/777–1630.

4 e-1

BLUE AND GOLD FLEET

The Blue and Gold Fleet's 45-minute "Bay Cruise" takes you past the Golden Gate Bridge, Angel Island, Alcatraz, and the San Francisco waterfront. Blue and Gold also provides ferry service to Oakland, Alameda, Sausalito, Tiburon, Vallejo, and Angel Island; the only service to Alcatraz Island (see Historic Sites & Architecture, above); and package tours, including ferry and bus transportation, to the Wine Country and Muir Woods. Between mid-April and mid-December there are 3-hour "Dinner–Dance Cruises" on Friday and Saturday nights. Tours depart from Pier 41 at Fisherman's Wharf. 415/773–1188 for recorded information, 415/705–5555 or 800/426–8687 for advance ticket sales with $2 service charge.

4 f-1

HORNBLOWER DINING YACHTS

Enjoy a weekend brunch cruise or an afternoon or dinner-dance cruise aboard the 183-foot California Hornblower, patterned after the classic steamers of the early 1900s. In summer and occasionally at other times, the same company operates Monte Carlo Cruises, which give you a taste of riverboat gambling (with play money), along with dancing and karaoke singing. Tours depart from Pier 33 at Fisherman's Wharf. 415/394–8900.

4 d-1

MISS FARALLONES

One-hour scenic Bay tours aboard the 38-passenger Miss Farallones take in the San Francisco waterfront, Golden Gate Bridge, and Alcatraz Island, and are narrated in person. The boat is docked at Space 6 (Jefferson Street between Taylor

and Jones streets) at Fisherman's
Wharf. 415/346–2399 or 510/352–5708.

OCEANIC SOCIETY
EXPEDITIONS

The nonprofit Oceanic Society sponsors
excursions to the Farallon Islands
National Wildlife Refuge on an 85-foot
boat that leaves the Yacht Harbor at the
Marina Green from June through
November. You may see dolphins, sea
lions, blue and humpback whales, birds,
and other marine life. From December
through April, the society also organizes
whale-watching trips. 415/474–3385 or
800/326–7491.

4 d-1
RED AND WHITE FLEET

Red and White Fleet's "Round the Rock"
tour is a 45-minute narrated ferry cruise
around Alcatraz Island. As you slowly circle the island you'll hear stories about
famous prisoners, daring escapes, and
other penitentiary lore. Also popular is
the one-hour "Golden Gate Bridge
Cruise," which passes Hyde Street Pier,
Fort Mason, Fort Point, The Presidio,
Alcatraz, Angel Island, and Sausalito,
then crosses under the Golden Gate
Bridge to view the Marin Headlands. The
company also offers discount land and
water tour packages in conjunction with
Gray Line (see Bus Tours, below). Tours
depart from Pier 43½ at Fisherman's
Wharf. 415/447–0597 or 800/229–2784.

4 d-1
RENDEZVOUS CHARTERS/
SPINNAKER SAILING

Join this company for a romantic sail
around the San Francisco Bay aboard the
78-foot, square-rigged Brigantine Rendezvous, built in 1933 in the classic style
of the Tall Ships of the 19th century.
There are three-hour Sunday Brunch
cruises aboard the Rendezvous, as well as
two-hour Sunday afternoon cruises
aboard either the Rendezvous or the
smaller Yukon Jack; all depart from South
Beach Harbor's Pier 40. 415/543–7333.

4 h-6
SS JEREMIAH O'BRIEN
(NATIONAL LIBERTY
SHIP MEMORIAL)

Five days a year, during Fleet Week and
Memorial Day Weekend, this historic
ship (see History Museums, above) goes
out for full-day Bay tours, complete with
gourmet lunch and dance band. Buy
tickets far in advance.

BUS TOURS

CABLE CAR CHARTERS

Here's your chance to ride a motorized
cable car. The one-hour "Heart of San
Francisco" tour takes you to Fisherman's Wharf, Union Square, Chinatown,
and North Beach, while the 2-hour
"Golden Gate Bridge" tour takes in the
bridge, Fisherman's Wharf, The Presidio, and Union Street boutiques. Tours
depart from in front of Sabella's Restaurant (Taylor and Jefferson Sts., Fisherman's Wharf; map 4, d-2). 415/922–2425,
800/562–7383.

GRAY LINE OF
SAN FRANCISCO

Deluxe motor coaches and London dou-
ble-deckers make excursions within San
Francisco and the Bay Area, and also to
Yosemite, Monterey, Carmel, Santa
Cruz, Hearst Castle, and the Wine Coun-
try. The San Francisco Trolley Hop tour,
aboard a motorized cable car, covers
Fisherman's Wharf, Union Street, The
Presidio, Fort Point, and North Beach.
415/558–9400, 800/826–0202.

GREAT PACIFIC
TOUR COMPANY

Twelve-passenger minivans provide an
intimate touring experience, with daily
departures year-round for Muir Woods
and Sausalito in Marin County, as well
as extensive city tours of 13 neighborhoods. Farther-flung tours take you to
the Wine Country as well as Monterey
and Carmel. 415/626–4499.

SUPER SIGHTSEEING
TOURS

Tours of the city, Alcatraz and the San
Francisco Bay, Muir Woods and Sausalito, Monterey and Carmel, the Wine
Country, and Yosemite Valley are on
board deluxe motor coaches. 415/777–
2288 or 888/868–7788.

TOWER TOURS

Tower makes the same excursions as
Super Sightseeing, also aboard deluxe
motor coaches. 415/434–8687.

SPECIALIZED
TOURS

Most specialized tours require advance
reservations.

A DAY IN NATURE
Experienced naturalists lead this company's intimate, customized, half-day tours of Marin County's scenic areas. Group size is limited to four people at most. *415/673–0548.*

ARTICULATE ART: 1930s SAN FRANCISCO
Masha Zakheim, a City College humanities professor for 30 years, leads short, informative tours focusing on artists of the 1930s; destinations include Coit Tower, the Beach Chalet, the murals of Diego Rivera, and other locales. Tours range in length from one hour to half a day. *415/285–0495.*

ESCAPE ARTIST TOURS
Unusual customized adventures cover the Bay Area and beyond. Favorites are the ranch tour of the Gold Country, and the haunted bed-and-breakfast tour. *415/726–7626 or 800/728–1384.*

EXPLORERS' CLUB
The Explorer's Club tours are designed especially for children between the ages of 6 and 12, with or without their parents. The "Mission Salsa" tour takes the children to the Mission Cliffs climbing gym for play time, *panaderías* (bakeries) for snacks, Mission Dolores for a short history lesson and tour, and the Precita Eyes Mural Art Center to create art with help from a professional artist. Other tours go to the Exploratorium, Golden Gate Park, Chinatown, or on a Bay Cruise. Tours range in length from four to seven hours. *415/566–7014, 800/360–7727.*

SHOPPER STOPPER
This 6½-hour tour takes shoppers to warehouses and other outlets normally closed to the public. Prices are lowest in January and February, when all merchandise is marked for clearance. Refreshments are served and drawings for cash and prizes are held throughout the day, giving these tours a party atmosphere. The expert guides willingly give wardrobe–planning advice. *707/829–1597.*

3 BABES AND A BUS NIGHTCLUB TOURS
A wonderful way to sample the city's vibrant nightlife is with 3 Babes and a Bus, run by a stockbroker who started the company in 1990 with two of her friends. The 50-person luxury bus rolls out every Saturday and some Friday nights, and stops at clubs to hear various types of music: '70s disco, Top 40, '80s dance music, urban dance music, blues, R&B, Motown, Brazilian music, and salsa. San Francisco residents celebrating birthdays and bachelorette parties often sign up for these tours. Pickup is at New Joe's Restaurant (347 Geary St., between Powell and Mason Sts., Union Square; map 4, e-6). *415/552–2582.*

WALKING TOURS

For self-guided walking tours, consult *The Bay Area at Your Feet* (Lexikos, $8.95) or *The New San Francisco at Your Feet: Best Walks in a Walkers City* (Grove Weidenfeld, $12.95): The finest of *San Francisco Chronicle* writer Margaret Patterson Doss's "Sunday Punch" columns appear in these two collections. Also recommended is Adah Bakalinsky's *Stairway Walks in San Francisco* (Wilderness Press, $9.95). All three are available in most local bookstores. *Walking San Francisco on the Barbary Coast Trail,* by Daniel Bacon (Quicksilver Press, $13.95), is a guide to the city's official historical walking trail. You can purchase a copy by writing to: Quicksilver Press, 549 Kansas St., San Francisco 94107. Include an additional $3 for shipping and postage.

Almost all of the following guided tours require advance reservations.

ALL ABOUT CHINATOWN!
Longtime Chinatown resident Linda Lee emphasizes history, culture, and traditions on her daily 2½-hour tours. Stops take in Chinese temples, a fortune cookie factory, and a tea shop; a sumptuous dim sum luncheon is the grand finale. *415/982–8839.*

BAY VENTURES
You can't go wrong with Bay Ventures' various specialist-led tours. Standouts: "Movie Hike of San Francisco," which covers famous movie sites; "Herb Caen Way," which explores the haunts of the city's beloved late columnist; and "Stairways to the Gods," which solves the mystery of why streets in Buena Vista are named after deities. Other tours explore downtown landmarks, Victorian Houses, and former gravesites. *510/234–4834.*

THE CITY GUIDES
Friends of the San Francisco Public Library sponsor 25 intriguing tours each

week, covering the history, architecture, and culture of almost every corner of town. Roof Gardens and Open Spaces, the Telegraph Hill Hike, Gold Rush city, Art Deco Marina, History of Haight-Ashbury, and Mission Murals are just a few tour topics. For a list, stop by any San Francisco public library, or send a SASE to City Guides, Main Library, Civic Center, San Francisco 94102. Tours are free, though donations are requested. *415/ 557–4266 for recorded information.*

CRUISIN' THE CASTRO FROM A HISTORICAL PERSPECTIVE

Trevor Hailey's highly recommended tour clues you in on how and why San Francisco became a gay mecca, with stops at various Castro District landmarks, followed by brunch. *415/550–8110.*

FLOWER POWER HAIGHT-ASHBURY WALKING TOUR

It's always the Summer of Love on these 2½-hour tours of the famous hippy District, the Haight-Ashbury. Tours take place Tuesday and Saturday mornings and cover more than just the landmarks

and history of the heady '60s: Under the guidance of longtime Haight residents Pam and Bruce Brennan, a brother-and-sister team, you'll also look at Victorian architecture, and get the scoop on the neighborhood's best bars, restaurants, cafés, and shops. *415/863–1621.*

FRIENDS OF RECREATION AND PARKS

On weekends from May through October, free 1- to 2-hour guided walking tours explore the history, flora, and fauna of glorious Golden Gate Park. Choose from the Japanese Tea Garden tour, Strawberry Hill Walk, Windmill to the Beach Chalet Walk, McLaren's Walk, Grand Concourse Walk, and Lloyd Lake Tour. Less frequent tours explore Stern Grove and McLaren Park. *415/263–0991 for recorded information.*

GLORIOUS FOOD CULINARY WALKTOURS

Retired caterer–chef Ruby Tom, one of the original graduates of the California Culinary Academy, and her husband Ben Tom lead tours of Chinatown (including a dim sum lunch), the Italian neighborhood of North Beach (including cappuccino and biscotti), and, when the Ferry Building Farmer's Market is in full swing, the south Embarcadero waterfront. The emphasis is on culture, history, and, of course, food. *415/441–5637.*

HERITAGE WALKS

On Sundays the expert guides of the Foundation for San Francisco's Architectural Heritage lead two-hour Pacific Heights walking tours of the surrounding blocks' Victorian and Edwardian houses. Also recommended are the one-hour tour of Yerba Buena Gardens, and the hour-long, docent-led tour of the interior of the Haas-Lilienthal House (*see* Historic Sites & Architecture, *above*), the foundation's headquarters. *415/441–3000.*

JAVAWALK

These two-hour tours depart twice weekly from in front of the Mark Rubin Gallery and take in the best of the North Beach coffeehouses, with plenty of time for sipping cappuccinos and discussing history. *415/673–9255.*

ONE DOLLAH STATUEWALKS

Local history buff Peter Garland leads these entertaining weekend tours (the

---

A TASTE OF SAN FRANCISCO—LITERALLY

There's no better way to explore San Francisco than by a walking tour—unless it's a walking tour accompanied by a delicious meal:

All About Chinatown!
Tours end with a dim sum luncheon.

Cruisin' the Castro from an Historical Perspective
Fascinating Castro District tour followed by brunch.

Glorious Food Culinary Walktours
Cruise North Beach, Chinatown, and the Ferry Building Farmer's Market with one of the original graduates of the California Culinary Academy.

Javawalk
A walk through historic San Francisco neighborhoods, latte by latte.

Wok Wiz Chinatown Tours and Cooking Company
The "I Can't Believe I Ate My Way Through Chinatown" tour is a perennial favorite.

suggested price is more than a dollar these days, but still a bargain). The five-hour Saturday tour starts at Civic Center, and the 1½-hour Sunday tour starts at the Ferry Building (at the foot of Market Street, on the Embarcadero). Tours cover important statues, monuments, murals, and city history. 510/834–3617.

PRECITA EYES MURAL ARTS CENTER

Two-hour walking tours every Saturday explore many of the Mission District's 80 or so colorful murals. Less frequent tours range farther afield, by bicycle, BART, or on board the center's "Mexican Bus." All tours are led by one of the center's expert muralists in residence. The center also publishes a "Mission Mural Walk" map for self-guided tours. No reservations are necessary; call for a current schedule. 415/285–2287.

SAN FRANCISCO AFRICAN-AMERICAN HISTORICAL AND CULTURAL SOCIETY

African-American history is the focus of these 45-minute to 2-hour walking tours through downtown San Francisco, with stops at companies owned and run by black businesspeople. 415/441–0640.

A SAN FRANCISCO WALKABOUT WITH GARY HOLLOWAY

These twice-monthly California Historical Society tours are led by guide extraordinaire Gary Holloway, a native Californian who's led more than 1,000 historical and architectural walking tours of San Francisco. His two-hour rambles take in Chinatown, North Beach, and downtown. Tour price includes admission to the California Historical Society museum. 415/357–1848.

SUNSET HIKES

Jeff Morris, a naturalist and Marin County native, leads these small-group nature hikes of Muir Woods, Mt. Tamalpais, and the Marin Headlands. Tours last about 3½ hours and are customized to participants' interests and fitness levels. 415/258–9434 or 800/848–8607.

VICTORIAN HOME WALK

Jay Gifford, an 18-year resident of San Francisco and member of the city's Victorian Alliance, leads daily 2½-hour tours covering Fisherman's Wharf, Union Street, Telegraph Hill, North Beach, and Chinatown, with an emphasis on Victorian-era history and architecture. The leisurely small-group tours include a café break and trolley ride. Tours depart from the lobby of the Westin St. Francis Hotel (Powell St., between Post and Geary Sts., Union Square; map 4, e-6). 415/252–9485.

WOK WIZ CHINATOWN TOURS AND COOKING COMPANY

The enormously popular "I Can't Believe I Ate My Way Through Chinatown" tour, led by chef and cookbook author Shirley Fong-Torres, visits restaurants and markets, ending "when the first person explodes." Wok Wiz also leads several other tours focusing on folklore, history, and food. 415/981–8989.

events

JANUARY

CHINESE NEW YEAR CELEBRATION AND GOLDEN DRAGON PARADE

The city's biggest festival lasts two weeks, usually from late January through early February, with pageantry, outdoor and cultural programs, fireworks, and the spectacular Golden Dragon parade from Market and Second streets to Columbus Avenue. 415/982–3000.

MARTIN LUTHER KING, JR., BIRTHDAY CELEBRATION

Speeches by civic leaders and other events take place on January 15, Dr. King's birth date. 415/771–6300.

SAN FRANCISCO SPORTS AND BOAT SHOW

This nine-day show in mid-January at the Cow Palace is one of the West Coast's biggest expos for boats, fishing tackle, and camping and hunting gear. 415/469–6065.

TET FESTIVAL

On the Saturday closest to the Vietnamese New Year, the Tet Festival features traditional food and performances by Vietnamese, Cambodian, and Laotian singers and dancers in the Tenderloin and Civic Center. 415/391–8050 or 415/554–6710.

WHALE-WATCHING

Between January and April, hundreds of grey whales migrate along the Pacific Coast. Contact the California Office of Tourism for details. *800/862–2543.*

FEBRUARY

CALIFORNIA INTERNATIONAL ANTIQUARIAN BOOK FAIR

For rare and antiquarian books, visit the Concourse Exhibition Center in mid-February, when more than 215 booksellers converge. *888/208–8889.*

CHINESE NEW YEAR

See above.

CHRONICLE GREAT OUTDOORS ADVENTURE FAIR

This three-day adventure fest at the Concourse Exhibition Center includes everything from rollerblading to kayaking to rock climbing, with demo and tryout areas, outfitters, and environmentalists. It takes place in late February and early March. *415/777–7120.*

GOLDEN GATE KENNEL CLUB DOG SHOW

The Cow Palace is a dog lover's heaven during the first weekend in February. *415/469–6065.*

RUSSIAN FESTIVAL

For two days in mid-February, the Russian Center is the site of folk singing, dancing, opera, painting and other crafts, as well as traditional food and flavored vodkas. *415/921–7631.*

SAN FRANCISCO BALLET

In February the ballet starts another season at the War Memorial Opera House. The season runs through May. *415/865–2000.*

SAN FRANCISCO ORCHID SOCIETY'S PACIFIC ORCHID EXPOSITION

Dazzling orchid displays fill Fort Mason for this annual event. *415/546–9608.*

SAN FRANCISCO TRIBAL, FOLK, AND TEXTILE ART SHOW

More than 100 dealers of folk and ethnic art set up shop at Fort Mason to sell North American pottery, basketry, textiles, and jewelry. *310/455–2886.*

WEST COAST CABARET CONVENTION

A new nine-day festival, the Cabaret Convention brings the world's best crooners to venues throughout the Bay Area. *415/547–9633.*

MARCH

BAY AREA MUSIC AWARDS (BAMMIES)

Local musicians gather at Bill Graham Civic Auditorium in mid-March for an evening of awards-giving. *510/762–2277.*

ST. PATRICK'S DAY CELEBRATION

The Irish celebrate their day with religious services at St. Patrick's Church and a gala parade from Civic Center to Spear Street on the Sunday before March 17. The parade begins at 12:30 PM. *415/661–2700.*

SAN FRANCISCO ASIAN AMERICAN FILM FESTIVAL

This film festival at the AMC Kabuki 8 theater in Japantown shows Asian films and videos, including world premieres, documentaries, and experimental films. *415/252–4800.*

TULIPMANIA

More than 40,000 tulips from all over the world bloom at Pier 39 in late February and early March. You can walk around on your own, or join a free guided tour. *415/705–5500.*

APRIL

AMERICAN CONSERVATORY THEATER

One of the country's premier repertory theater companies performs from April through June. *415/749–2228.*

BRITAIN MEETS THE BAY

Anglophiles flock to this citywide celebration of all things British—concerts, art exhibits, and sporting events—from April through early June. *415/274–0373 or 800/915–2682.*

CHERRY BLOSSOM FESTIVAL

Tea ceremonies, martial arts, calligraphy, floral arranging demonstrations, nearly 400 Japanese performers, and numerous exhibits of Japanese art bring the Japantown Center to life over two consecutive weekends in mid-April. Most popular are the taiko drum performance and the parade from Civic Center to Japantown. *415/563–2313.*

EASTER PARADE AND CELEBRATION

The city's annual Easter Parade, held in March or April depending on when Easter falls, brings the Easter bunny and children's activities to Union and Fillmore Streets. *415/775–5703.*

EASTER SUNRISE SERVICE

Since 1923, Mt. Davidson, west of Twin Peaks, has been the setting for this interdenominational sunrise Easter Sunday service, held in March or April, depending on when Easter falls. The service takes place at the base of a controversial 103-foot cross at Dalewood Avenue and Myra Way. *415/564–7535.*

OPENING DAY ON THE BAY

On the first day of Daylight Savings Time the Bay Area celebrates the start of the sailing season with a parade of decorated yachts and local fireboats. *415/381–1128.*

SAN FRANCISCO GIANTS BASEBALL SEASON

In early April the Giants step up to the plate at 3Com Stadium for another season of Major League Baseball. The season runs through September. *800/734–4268.*

SAN FRANCISCO INTERNATIONAL FILM FESTIVAL

Spanning two weeks in April and early May, the nation's oldest film festival (it turned 40 in 1997) features seminars and screenings of 100 films and videos from some 30 countries. Screenings take place at the Kabuki 8 and the Castro Theatre in San Francisco, the Pacific Film Archive in Berkeley, and other locations in the South Bay and Marin. *415/931–3456.*

SAN FRANCISCO SYMPHONY

The Symphony's season begins in April and runs through June, with performances at Davies Symphony Hall. The Symphony celebrates its 85th season in 1998. *415/864–6000.*

WHOLE LIFE EXPO

Nearly 250 booths with healing crystals, energy pyramids, massage tools, and other New Age essentials converge at the city's Fashion Design Center for this three-day New Age festival celebrating personal growth, nutrition, environmental issues, and alternative medicines. A second Whole Life Expo takes place in late October and early November. *415/721–2484.*

MAY

ARTS AND CRAFTS BY THE BAY

Pier 29 puts on this late May festival with live entertainment, food and drink, and around 200 artists and craftspeople selling their wares. *415/956–5316.*

CARNAVAL

This racuous Río-style Mardi Gras festival is held in the Mission District on Memorial Day Weekend, with food, craft booths, a costume contest, and performances by dozens of Latin American musical groups. The parade starts at 10 AM on Sunday at Bryant and 24th streets, travels along Mission Street,

---

NEIGHBORHOOD FESTIVALS

The best way to get a sense of what San Francisco's all about is to drop by one of the many neighborhood festivals:

Blues and Art on Polk (July)
  Groove your way down Polk Street.

Castro Street Fair (October)
  Kick up your heels in the gay Castro district.

Haight Street Fair (June)
  Music and art in the Haight.

Jazz and All That Art on Fillmore (July)
  Jazz and blues in the Fillmore.

North Beach Festival (June)
  Come see the "World's Biggest Salami."

Union Street Spring Festival Arts and Crafts Fair (June)
  Swing dancing and fine wine in Cow Hollow.

and ends at Harrison Street between 16th and 22nd streets, where the party begins. 415/826–1401.

CINCO DE MAYO CELEBRATION

Vibrant mariachi bands and colorful Mexican *folklórico* dancers congregate in the Mission District on the weekend nearest May 5 to celebrate the anniversary of Mexico's defeat of the French at the Battle of Puebla. On Sunday at 11 AM there's a parade through the neighborhood, starting at 24th and Bryant streets and ending on Harrison Street. 415/826–1401.

ETHNIC FESTIVALS

You could easily plan your calendar around San Francisco's many ethnic heritage celebrations.

Cherry Blossom Festival (April)
   Celebrates Japanese culture and customs.

Chinese New Year Celebration/ Golden Dragon Parade (January)
   The city's largest festival.

Cinco de Mayo (May)
   In remembrance of Mexico's defeat of the French on May 5, 1862.

Día de los Muertos (November)
   The Mexican tradition of Day of the Dead.

Festival de las Americas (September)
   Celebrating eight Latin American nations.

Filipino American Fair (August)
   The crescendo is the Perlas ng Silangan (Pearl Parade).

Italian Heritage Day (October)
   Columbus Day festivities in North Beach.

Juneteenth (June)
   June 19, the day Lincoln's Emancipation Proclamation was read in Galveston, Texas.

Polish Spring Festival (May)
   Polka dancing and Polish food.

St. Patrick's Day Celebration (March)
   A gala parade and religious services at St. Patrick's Church.

Tet Festival (January)
   Vietnamese New Year celebrations.

MOTHER'S DAY ROSE SHOW

Treat mom to an afternoon at this annual event at the San Francisco County Fair Building, which features dozens and dozens of lovely roses, as well seminars on buying and growing them. 415/731–3829.

MURAL AWARENESS MONTH

The month of May is dedicated to celebrating the city's splendid murals, on buildings, in lobbies, and at BART stations around the city. Art exhibits, lectures by artists and activists, open houses, and mural tours by bus, bike, and on foot are all on tap. 415/285–2287.

POLISH SPRING FESTIVAL

Look for polka dancing and Polish food and crafts at the San Francisco County Fair Building in mid-May. 415/285–4336.

SAN FRANCISCO EXAMINER BAY TO BREAKERS RACE

The world's largest footrace attracts about 70,000 participants, many of whom don zany costumes to run the 7½-mile course from the Financial District to Ocean Beach. 1998 will mark the 87th race, which takes place on the third Sunday every May. 415/808–5000 ext. 2222.

SAN FRANCISCO SYMPHONY BLACK & WHITE BALL

Proceeds from the city's most elegant affair benefit the San Francisco Symphony. It's a semi-annual black-tie block party on the Embarcadero waterfront with gourmet food, dancing to live music on 15 stages, and 12,000 guests. 415/864–6000 or 510/762–2277 for tickets.

STRYBING ARBORETUM ANNUAL PLANT SALE

Held at the San Francisco County Fair Building, this event in early May is always well attended by the city's green thumbs. Up for sale are plants rare and common, for indoors and out. 415/661–3090.

JUNE

ANIMAL WINGDING

The San Francisco SPCA (Society For the Prevention of Cruelty to Animals) sponsors this one-day festival in early June for furred and feathered folk and their owners. After the games and live music there's a parade in the Mission District. 800/211–7722.

ETHNIC DANCE FESTIVAL

With 900 talented dancers and musicians performing, there's something new every weekend in June at the Palace of Fine Arts Theater. Previews are held on Saturdays in late May and early June at Ghiradelli Square in Fisherman's Wharf. 415/474–3914.

FREE FOLK FESTIVAL

This feel-good festival takes place on a June weekend at the John Adams Campus of City College. Bring your guitar, harmonica, or fiddle to the workshops and impromptu jam sessions that spring up between concerts of folk, blues, and international music. It's a very loosely organized event; check newspaper entertainment listings for details.

GERSHWIN/STRAVINSKY FESTIVAL

The annual festival celebrating these two musical greats is put on by the San Francisco Symphony, at Davies Symphony Hall. It takes place in the latter half of June. 415/864–6000.

HAIGHT STREET FAIR

On a Saturday in mid-June, the fair on Haight Street between Masonic and Stanyan streets features local bands playing rap, jazz, and rock, along with booths by neighborhood merchants, artists, and craftspeople. 415/661–8025.

OAKLAND JUNETEENTH CELEBRATION

Celebrating the day when Lincoln's Emancipation Proclamation was read in Galveston, Texas (June 19, 1865), Oakland's big festival features big-name blues and R&B acts and children's activities at Lake Merritt's Lakeside Park. A smaller festival on Fillmore Street in San Francisco is sponsored by the Supporters of the Western Addition Cultural Center (415/928–8546). 510/238–3866.

KQED INTERNATIONAL BEER AND FOOD FESTIVAL

Join 5,000 San Franciscans at the Concourse Exhibition Center in late June and early July to sample 250 different beers at the largest international beer festival in the nation. There's live music on two stages and international cuisine. Profits support KQED, the city's public TV and radio station. 415/553–2200, or 510/762–2277 for tickets.

LESBIAN, GAY, BISEXUAL, TRANSGENDER PRIDE CELEBRATION

Known as San Francisco Pride for short (and formerly known as the Gay and Lesbian Freedom Day Parade), this celebration on the third or fourth weekend in June features dancing, music, food, speeches, arts and crafts, and the famed Sunday 11 AM parade from Market and 8th Street to Justin Herman Plaza on The Embarcadero. The Annual Dyke March down Castro and Market streets takes place on the preceding Saturday, and draws more than 40,000 women. 415/864–3733.

MIDSUMMER MOZART FESTIVAL

The music of one of the world's best-known and best-loved composers is performed at venues throughout the city from late June through late July. 415/392–4400.

NORTH BEACH FESTIVAL

Come see the "World's Biggest Salami" at the country's oldest urban street fair, held on a weekend in mid-June. Added attractions: arts and crafts, chalk street painting, small-press booksellers, all kinds of live music, and of course plenty of delicious Italian food. 415/403–0666.

SAN FRANCISCO INTERNATIONAL LESBIAN AND GAY FILM FESTIVAL

The second largest film festival in California showcases more than 350 films and videos from all over the world during the week preceding the Lesbian, Gay, Bisexual, Transgender Pride Celebration (see above). Screenings take place at the Castro Theatre and various other venues. 415/703–8663.

SAN FRANCISCO MUSIC DAY

On June 21st, the summer solstice, Market Street and The Embarcadero vibrate with the sounds of more than 200 bands and 1,200 musicians performing free of charge. There's everything from funk to Zydeco to jazz to African indigenous music—plus a huge drum circle at Justin Herman Plaza, followed by a sunset dance party. 415/391–0370.

STERN GROVE MIDSUMMER MUSIC FESTIVAL

A San Francisco tradition since 1937, the Stern Grove Midsummer Music Festival features free live performances of classical, jazz, pop, world music, and more in beautiful Stern Grove. Performances take place from mid-June through August, Sundays at 2PM. *415/252–6252.*

STREET PERFORMERS FESTIVAL

Look for comedians, jugglers, and unicyclists strolling the streets at this weekend-long event at Pier 39 in Fisherman's Wharf. *415/705–5500.*

UNION STREET SPRING FESTIVAL ARTS AND CRAFTS FAIR

In the Marina district's chic Cow Hollow neighborhood on Union Street between Gough and Steiner streets, the spring festival features big bands, a swing dance contest, wine and gourmet food, a garden party, and The San Francisco Waiter's Race. It takes place on the weekend after Memorial Day (usually the first weekend in June). *415/346–9162.*

JULY

BOOKS BY THE BAY

At the Ferry Building on a Saturday in mid-July, this is a reader's delight, with booths representing 40 bookstores, plus readings, book signings, and fun activities for children. *415/927–3937.*

BLUES AND ART ON POLK

In mid-July, groove your way down Polk Street between Jackson and Bush streets during this weekend festival with plenty of blues music, arts, crafts, and food. *415/346–9162.*

FOLK ART TO FUNK

Fort Mason is like one big grandmother's attic on a weekend in mid-July, when it's turned over to vendors of all kinds of folk art, toys, vintage clothing, and more. *310/455–2886.*

FOURTH OF JULY WATERFRONT FESTIVAL

The biggest Independence Day celebration in the Bay Area takes place along the San Francisco waterfront, from Aquatic Park to Pier 39. Live entertainment and a children's program start at 1 PM, and fireworks light the skies at 9:30 PM. *415/777–7120.*

JAZZ AND ALL THAT ART ON FILLMORE

In the 1940s, '50s, and '60s, Fillmore clubs were famous for sizzling jazz and blues. National jazz talents—old-time musicians and young ones too—revive those heady days on the first weekend in July, with outdoor jazz, wine, food, and art on Fillmore Street between Post and Jackson streets. *415/346–9162.*

JEWISH FILM FESTIVAL

The world's largest Jewish film festival runs for two weeks at the Castro Theatre and at Berkeley's UC Theater. *510/548–0556.*

SAN FRANCISCO CABLE CAR BELL RINGING COMPETITION

On the third Thursday every July, the city's cable car operators square off at Union Square to compete for highly coveted prizes. Out-of-towners love this event. *415/6SF–6864.*

SAN FRANCISCO MARATHON

On a Sunday in mid-July some 3,000 hardy spirits race a scenic 26-mi course that starts at the Marin side of the Golden Gate Bridge and ends at Kezar Stadium in Golden Gate Park. *916/983–4622 or 800/722–3466 within Calif.*

SAN FRANCISCO SYMPHONY POPS

Some of the world's greats perform at Davies Symphony Hall from July through early August. *415/431–5400.*

AUGUST

COMEDY CELEBRATION DAY

In this annual rib-tickling event on a Sunday in mid-July, more than a dozen of the nation's top comedians entertain for free at Sharon Meadow in Golden Gate Park. *415/777–8498.*

FILIPINO AMERICAN FAIR

The city's Filipino community throws a joyous outdoor festival at the Center for the Arts at Yerba Buena Gardens on a weekend in mid-July. It concludes with *Perlas ng Silangan* (Pearl Parade) down Market Street on Sunday at noon, starting at The Embarcadero and ending at Yerba Buena Gardens. *415/436–9711.*

SAN FRANCISCO 49ERS FOOTBALL SEASON

The 49ers strap on their helmets and prepare for another winning season of pro football at 3Com Stadium. The season runs through December. *415/468–*

2249 or 415/656–4900 for tickets and game schedule.

NIHONMACHI STREET FAIR

The fall celebration of Japanese culture, at Japantown on a weekend in early August, features lion dancers and taiko drummers in addition to live entertainment, food, and crafts. 415/771–9861.

RENAISSANCE PLEASURE FAIRE

On weekends from mid-August through September at Blackpoint Forest in the city of Novato, the Renaissance fair is a pleasure fest for anyone fascinated by 16th-century Elizabethan England. It's a jousting, dancing, outdoor theater with nearly 1,500 costumed performers. 800/523–2473.

SEPTEMBER

ABSOLUT À LA CARTE, À LA PARK

The annual mouthwatering, stomach-filling food festival with dishes from 50 of the city's top restaurants, plus drinks by California wineries and microbreweries, takes place in Golden Gate Park over Labor Day weekend. 415/383–9378.

A TASTE OF CHOCOLATE

Enter the chocolate-tasting or chocolate-sculpting contests, or just come to eat the chocolate at this sweet-as-can-be festival at Ghiradelli Square in early September. 415/775–5500.

FESTIVAL DE LAS AMERICAS

This mid-month Mission District festival, celebrating the independence of Mexico and seven other Latin American countries, attracts more than 80,000 people to 24th Street between Mission and Hampshire Streets. The alcohol-free, family-oriented, one-day event promotes pride in the Latino community, with Latino musicians, ethnic food, and booths selling original crafts. The El Grito Celebration (415/585–2043) is usually the following day, and marks Mexican Independence Day with mariachi music and folklórico dancers. 415/826–1401.

FESTIVAL OF THE SEA

Sailmaking and rope-making demonstrations, sea-faring music, and a parade of tall ships and yachts along the San Francisco waterfront celebrate San Francisco's maritime tradition. The free festival takes place at San Francisco's Hyde Street Pier on a weekend in mid- or late September. 415/929–0202.

FOLSOM STREET FAIR

One of the city's most popular—and controversial—street fairs features music, comics, dancing, a beer garden, and lots of leather and flesh. People crowd the blocks of Folsom Street between 7th and 12th Streets strutting their latest leatherware, usually on a Sunday in late September. 415/861–3247.

GARDENS GALLERY WALK

On a day in early September the Center for the Arts at Yerba Buena Gardens sponsors an arts mega-tour, with museums, sculptures, and two dozen galleries on the agenda. 415/541–0312.

OPERA IN THE PARK

The San Francisco Opera kicks off the opera season with a free concert in Golden Gate Park's Sharon Meadow on the Sunday after the first performance of the season, usually the week after Labor Day. 415/864–3330.

RINGLING BROTHERS BARNUM & BAILEY CIRCUS

The famed three-ringed circus visits San Francisco's Cow Palace for five days in early September. 415/469–6065.

SANDCASTLE CLASSIC

Sponsored by Leap (Learning Through Education In The Arts Project), this innovative sand-castle building contest at Aquatic Park pairs local architects with teams of school kids. The results, though fleeting, are impressive. Construction starts at noon on a September or October Saturday, depending on when the lowest tide falls. 415/861–1899.

SAN FRANCISCO BLUES FESTIVAL

Local talent as well as big-name musicians like B.B. King and Robert Cray perform at America's oldest blues festival, held on the third weekend in September at Justin Herman Plaza and at Fort Mason's Great Meadow. Advance ticket purchase is advised. 415/979–5588.

SAN FRANCISCO FAIR

The Impossible Parking Space Race, Fog Calling, and the National Skateboard

Championships are some of the more unusual events that take place at Civic Center Plaza in early September. The fair also presents more-predictable exhibits, as well as entertainment and food-and-wine tastings. 415/434–3247.

SAN FRANCISCO FRINGE FESTIVAL

The city's 10-day festival of offbeat and avant garde performing arts is held at various downtown venues. 415/931–1094.

SAN FRANCISCO OPERA SEASON

In 1998 the Opera starts its 76th season, which runs through January. Performances are in the newly renovated War Memorial Opera House. 415/864–3330.

SAUSALITO ART FESTIVAL

This excellent, expansive exhibition of original artworks from all over the world is worth a trip across the Golden Gate Bridge to Sausalito on Labor Day weekend. More than 10,000 works are displayed. 415/332–3555.

OCTOBER

BRIDGE TO BRIDGE RUN

On a Saturday in early October, this is a 12K race/5K fun run from the Golden Gate Bridge to the Bay Bridge. 415/974–6800.

 ### CASTRO STREET FAIR

On the first Sunday of the month, the Castro Street Fair brings crafts vendors; booths run by community, health, and social organizations; and musical entertainment to the city's gay community. 415/467–3354.

FLEET WEEK

During a mid-October week, San Francisco salutes its sailors with activities and booths on Fisherman's Wharf, a parade of ships under the Golden Gate Bridge, and a Blue Angels air show. 415/705–5500.

GRAND NATIONAL RODEO, HORSE, AND STOCK SHOW

San Francisco revisits its western heritage every October at the Cow Palace, in a cowboy and bronco bonanza that runs 10 days. 415/469–6065.

GREAT HALLOWEEN AND PUMPKIN FESTIVAL

This is a fun weekend festival on Polk Street in mid-October, with a pumpkin-carving and pie-eating contest, pony rides, arts and crafts for sale, and a costume parade. 415/346–9162.

HALLOWEEN NIGHT

After nearly two decades in the Castro district, San Francisco's flamboyant Halloween parade and party recently relocated to Civic Center. About 300,000 revelers attend each year, in an event sponsored by the city's lesbian, bisexual, transgender, and gay community. 415/777–5500.

ITALIAN HERITAGE DAY CELEBRATION/ COLUMBUS DAY

The Columbus Day festivities in North Beach, the city's Italian community, include a landing pageant, coronation of Queen Isabella, a 1 PM parade up Columbus Avenue, and the traditional blessing of the fishing fleet at Aquatic Park. 415/434–1492.

PACIFIC HEIGHTS HOME TOURS

This one-day fund-raiser in mid-October gives you a chance to peek inside some of the city's most lavish homes. It's sponsored by the San Francisco Historical Society. 415/775–1111.

SAN FRANCISCO FALL ANTIQUES SHOW

About 60 antiques dealers from all over the world exhibit and sell their wares at Fort Mason for five days in late October. 415/546–6661.

SAN FRANCISCO INTERNATIONAL ACCORDION FESTIVAL

This wacky festival on the third weekend in October features food, dancing, and accordion playing. Look for perennial favorites Zydeco Flames and Those Darn Accordions in the "I'm San Francisco's Main Squeeze" contest, which chooses the accordionist with the wildest costume to be next year's poster child. Events take place at the Anchorage Shopping Center at Fisherman's Wharf. 415/775–6000.

SAN FRANCISCO JAZZ FESTIVAL

Local and national jazz performers sizzle at venues all over the city in this 12-

day jazz festival, one of the country's finest. *415/398–5655 or 800/627–5277.*

SAN FRANCISCO OPEN STUDIOS

Here's a month-long opportunity for the art-loving public to visit and shop the ateliers of more than 500 artists citywide. Most studios are open weekends only. *415/861–9838.*

WHOLE LIFE EXPO

See April, above.

WORLD PUMPKIN WEIGH-OFF

Pumpkins from all over the world vie for the heavyweight title at this one-day festival sponsored by the International Pumpkin Association. The weigh-off takes place on a Saturday at the Ferry Building Farmer's Market. *415/346–4561.*

NOVEMBER

A CHRISTMAS CAROL

A theatrical version of Dickens's holiday classic is performed by the American Conservatory Theatre every November and December. *415/749–2228.*

CHRISTMAS-TREE LIGHTING CEREMONIES

In November and December, tree-lighting ceremonies take place at Ghiradelli Square (*415/775–5500*), Pier 39 (*415/981–8030*), and in Golden Gate Park at Fell and Stanyan streets (*415/831–2700*). Contact each directly for more information.

DÍA DE LOS MUERTOS

The Mexican tradition of Day of the Dead, derived from Aztec rituals and the Catholic All Souls' Day, is celebrated in early November in San Francisco's Mission district with art exhibitions and a parade. *415/826–8009.*

HARVEST FESTIVAL & CHRISTMAS CRAFTS MARKET

On two weekends in mid-November at the Concourse Exhibition Center, this arts and crafts fair lets you get an early start on holiday shopping. *707/778–6300.*

THE NUTCRACKER

A holiday favorite, Tchaikovsky's *Nutcracker* is performed every November and December by the San Francisco Bal-

let at the War Memorial Opera House. *415/703–9400.*

RUN TO THE FAR SIDE

On the Sunday after Thanksgiving, more than 13,000 people dressed as their favorite Gary Larson characters compete in this 10K run/5K walk through Golden Gate Park. The event benefits the California Academy of Sciences' environmental education programs. *415/564–0532.*

SAN FRANCISCO BAY AREA BOOK FESTIVAL

Bibliophiles rejoice at this gargantuan festival held at the Concourse Exhibtion Center on the first weekend in November. More than 300 booths represent small, alternative presses as well as big publishing houses; many sell books at a discount. Nearly 250 authors also show up to sign books, hold readings, or participate in discussions. *415/908–2833.*

SAN FRANCISCO INTERNATIONAL AUTO SHOW

For one week in late November, Moscone Center is the showroom for next year's models and space-aged, futuristic cars. *415/673-2016.*

DECEMBER

A CHRISTMAS CAROL

See November, above.

CELEBRATION OF CRAFTSWOMEN

Glasswork, leather work, and wearable art are displayed at Fort Mason on the first two weekends of December. In addition to crafts demonstrations and sales, child care, entertainment, and refreshments are provided. *415/252–8981.*

CHRISTMAS AT SEA

On a weekend in mid-December, head to Hyde Street Pier for holiday cheer: There's carolling, hot cider, a Santa Claus, and plenty of other surprises for children. *415/929–0202.*

CHRISTMAS-TREE LIGHTING CEREMONIES

See November, above.

FIRST RUN

As an alternative to the usual New Year's Eve bashes, this 2-mi walk and run takes place at midnight on New

Chez Panisse
1517 Shattuck
(510) 548-5525   Café 548-5049

Year's Eve, at Crissy Field in the Marina district. *415/668–2243.*

THE NEW PICKLE CIRCUS

This group, which started as a band of street performers during the early 1970s, performs its acrobatic clowning at Fort Mason and the Palace of Fine Arts during the last three weeks in December. *415/665–6177.*

THE NUTCRACKER

See November, *above.*

SING-IT-YOURSELF MESSIAH

Raise your voice in a chorus of hallelujahs at the Louise M. Davies Hall, in a rousing performance of Handel's *Messiah*. No previous singing experience is required. *415/431–5400.*

day trips from san francisco

ANGEL ISLAND STATE PARK

One of San Francisco Bay's famous islands is a former prison; the other is an exquisite state park. With 750 acres, Angel Island is an oasis of sandy beaches, old military installations, and spectacular views—all just a ferry ride away from San Francisco. Start your tour at the ferry landing in Ayala Cove, where the visitor center (*415/435–1915*) distributes a brochure on the history and geography of the island. Then set out for any of the scenic and historic sites that lie along the 5-mi perimeter road that rings the island; or, better yet, ride your bike along the entire route (*see* Bicycling *in* Chapter 6). A mile north of Ayala Cove is Camp Reynolds, which functioned as an army camp from the Civil War to World War II. On the other side of the island is an immigration station, once known as "The Ellis Island of the West," where immigrants (mostly Asian) were detained when trying to enter the United States between 1910 and 1940. There are plenty of picnic tables and barbecue grills around the island (BYO charcoal, as wood-gathering is not allowed). For information on ferry transportation to and from the island, *see* Chapter 1.

BERKELEY

This vibrant, liberal-minded East Bay town is the storied home of the original University of California, a hotbed of student activism in the tumultuous 1960s. In addition to visiting the beautiful—and now tranquil—campus, make it a point to dine at one of its famous but expensive restaurants, such as Chez Panisse (*see* Contemporary *in* Chapter 2), the founder of California cuisine. The university's Berkeley Art Museum (*see* Art Museums, *above*), Botanical Garden (*see* Gardens *in* Chapter 6), and Lawrence Hall of Science (*see* Science Museums, *above*) are all worthy attractions in town. Berkeley lies 10 miles east of San Francisco and is accessible via the Bay Bridge, BART, or Transbay bus service. *Berkeley Convention and Visitors Bureau, 2015 Center St., Berkeley 94704, 510/549–7040 or 510/549–8710.*

CARMEL

Carmel, once a Spanish mission town, was founded for a second time in 1904 by a group of artists and writers. Its reputation as an arts colony has grown in the decades since, bringing many charming shops and galleries, though strict zoning laws have been enacted to preserve its old-time charm. Drive the cypress-lined "17 Mile Drive" to Monterey for a peek at the lifestyles of the area's rich and famous, as well as views of the famed Pebble Beach and Cypress Point golf courses. The town lies on the Monterey Peninsula just south of Monterey. *Carmel Business Association, Box 4444, Carmel 93921, 408/624–2522.*

MARINE WORLD AFRICA USA

Opened in 1986, this 160-acre oceanarium and wildlife park features performing dolphins and killer whales, sea lions, tigers, elephants, and exotic birds, as well as shows by world-class water skiers. There are camel and elephant rides, an exhibit filled with free-flying tropical butterflies, and a petting zoo where children can talk to the animals. Discount ticket packages are available with purchase of roundtrip fare aboard the Vallejo Baylink Ferry (*see* Ferry *in* Chapter 1) from San Francisco. *Marine World Pkwy. (Rte. 37), off Hwy. 80, Vallejo, 707/643–6722. Closed Mon.–Tues. in winter.*

MONTEREY

The Monterey Peninsula juts out into the Pacific south of Monterey Bay, and the spectacular shoreline with its white sand beaches, craggy rocks, and twisted cypress trees is unsurpassed for scenic beauty. The town of Monterey was the capital of California in 1777 when the area was under Spanish and Mexican rule; today, Monterey State Historic Park preserves several centuries of buildings and inhabitations. Also in Monterey are a colorful Fisherman's Wharf, historic Cannery Row, and the spectacular Monterey Bay Aquarium, one of the world's largest, with more than 500 species of sea creatures. The breathtaking "17 Mile Drive" links Monterey with neighboring Carmel (*see above*). Monterey is approximately 140 mi south of San Francisco via Highway 101. *Monterey Peninsula Chamber of Commerce and Visitors and Convention Bureau, 380 Alvarado St., Monterey 93940, 408/649–1770.*

MUIR WOODS NATIONAL MONUMENT

This stunning 550-acre redwood grove is just 17 mi northwest of the city—a 45-minute drive when traffic isn't heavy. With redwoods nearly 250 ft tall and 1,000 years old, this grove was saved from destruction in 1908 and named for naturalist John Muir. It's a pedestrians-only park with 6 mi of easy trails; no cars are allowed in the redwood grove itself. Crowds (and attendant parking problems) make an early-morning or late-afternoon visit advisable. Muir Woods is off Highway 1. *Muir Woods National Monument, Mill Valley 94941, 415/388–2595.*

OAKLAND

The largest city in the East Bay is Oakland, a major West Coast port whose rich heritage is celebrated in festivals throughout the year, including the Bay Area's largest Juneteenth celebration (*see* Events, *above*). Visit the Oakland Museum (*see* Art Museums, *above*); beautiful Lakeside Park and Lake Merritt; the waterfront Jack London Square for dining, shopping, and nightlife; and the newly refurbished downtown with Art Deco and Victorian buildings. Oakland is 10 mi east of San Francisco, accessible via the Bay Bridge, BART, or Transbay bus service. *Oakland Convention and Visitors Authority, 550 10th St., Suite 214, Oakland 94607, 510/839–9000.*

POINT REYES NATIONAL SEASHORE

The 63,500-acre Point Reyes, the West Coast's only National Seashore, is a favorite for hiking, whale-watching, and solitude-seeking, and also for sea kayaking (*see* Chapter 6) on adjacent Tomales Bay. High rolling grasslands above spectacular cliffs, and miles of sandy beaches and tidepools make this an area of outstanding beauty. The main attraction is the 1870 Point Reyes Lighthouse, a scenic 30- to 40-minute drive from the visitor center. Point Reyes is north of San Francisco in Marin County, accessible via winding Highway 1. *Superintendent, Point Reyes National Seashore, Point Reyes 94956, 415/663–1092.*

SANTA CRUZ

This mellow seaside town has 26 miles of sunny beaches surrounded by ancient redwood forests. At its center is the never-ending carnival of the Santa Cruz Beach Boardwalk, the West Coast's largest seaside amusement park, with its 1924 Giant Dipper wooden roller coaster. Santa Cruz lies 75 mi south of San Francisco (about a two-hour drive), accessible by Highway 1 or 17. *Santa Cruz Area Chamber of Commerce, Box 921, Santa Cruz 95060, 408/423–1111.*

SAUSALITO

Charming Sausalito (Spanish for "little willow") with its winding streets, rustic houses, waterfront shops, and outdoor dining, is the perfect day trip from San Francisco. It's 8 mi north of San Francisco in Marin County, accessible by Blue and Gold Fleet ferries (*see* Ferry *in* Chapter 1), or by Highway 101 across the Golden Gate Bridge. Just offshore in Richardson Bay are some 400 houseboats; these quirky abodes comprise one of the Bay Area's most famous views. An excellent time to visit is Labor Day weekend, during the renowned Sausalito Art Festival (*see* Events, *above*). *Sausalito Visitors Center, 777 Bridgeway, Sausalito 94965, 415/332–0505.*

SILICON VALLEY: SAN JOSE AND SANTA CLARA

Sprawling San Jose, the largest city in the suburban South Bay and fourth-largest city in California, blends in with its neighbor Santa Clara. Together these two cities have earned the nickname Silicon Valley for their plethora of aerospace, technology, and electronics firms. San Jose has become an increasingly recognized cultural center, with excellent performing arts organizations, gardens, the fine San Jose Museum of Art (see Art Museums, above), the Tech Museum of Innovation, and the Winchester Mystery House—a bizarre, 160-room Victorian mansion built over a period of 38 years by Sarah Winchester, the rifle heiress, in an attempt to calm the spirits of those killed with Winchester firearms. Smaller Santa Clara is home to the popular Paramount's Great America theme park, with five giant roller coasters. The two cities lie approximately 50 mi south of San Francisco and can be reached by Highways 101 and 280. The San Jose Convention and Visitors Bureau provides information about both cities as well as the rest of Silicon Valley. *San Jose Convention and Visitors Bureau, McEnery Convention Center, 150 W. San Carlos St., San Jose 95113, 408/977–0900.*

TIBURON

On a peninsula called *Punta de Tiburon* (Shark Point) by Spanish explorers, Tiburon is a beautiful Marin County community with a villagelike atmosphere. San Francisco is directly south, 6 mi across the bay—which makes the views from waterfront restaurants sublime. Like its neighbor Sausalito, Tiburon is connected to San Francisco by Blue and Gold Fleet ferries (see Ferry *in* Chapter 1), and by Highway 101 across the Golden Gate Bridge. Sunday brunch is an institution here, and there are plenty of attractive, upscale shops and galleries to make for an afternoon's browsing. *Tiburon Chamber of Commerce, 96B Main St., Tiburon 94920, 415/435–5633.*

THE WINE COUNTRY

Just 50 miles northeast of San Francisco lies the largest and most prestigious wine-producing region in the United States, with more than 200 wineries concentrated mainly in the Napa and Sonoma valleys. Wine connoisseurs aren't the only ones who've discovered the region's allure; the Wine Country is also famed for its gourmet restaurants, health spas, and charming bed-and-breakfasts, as well as scenic areas for bicycling, horseback riding, hot-air ballooning, and hiking. If wine is your prime interest, search out some of the small wineries off the beaten path; there are hundreds of them and most have free tastings. **The Wine Institute** (425 Market St., Suite 1000, San Francisco 94105, 415/512–0151) publishes dozens of guides to California wineries and wine-growing regions; call or write for a list of titles and prices. Beware of crowds on summer weekends: Traffic often comes to a standstill along Napa's Highway 29. *Napa Valley Conference and Visitors Bureau, 1310 Napa Town Center, Napa 94550, 707/226–7459. Sonoma Valley Visitors Bureau, 453 1st St. E, Sonoma 95476, 707/938–1762.*

YOSEMITE NATIONAL PARK

This 1,169-sq-mi natural wonder is in the Sierra Nevada Mountains, 210 mi southeast of San Francisco—about a 4-hour drive. Elevation within the park ranges from 2,000 ft near the park's west entrance to 13,014 ft at the summit of Mt. Lyell. The main attraction, spectacular Yosemite Valley, was carved by glaciers during the Ice Age and is now filled with cascading waterfalls and the famous El Capitan, Cathedral Spires, and Half Dome mountains. There's fishing, hiking, bicycling, horseback riding, and, in winter, ice skating and cross-country skiing. Accommodations range from tent camping to a luxury hotel. A free bus shuttle service takes you where passenger cars may not. *Superintendent, Box 577, Yosemite National Park 95389, 209/372–0200.*

chapter 3

RESTAURANTS

San Franciscans are regularly accused of acting smug about their burgeoning restaurant community. But they have reason to be. In a city with less than three-quarters of a million people, there are roughly 4,000 licensed eating establishments. About 1,000 of these shut their doors every year, only to be replaced by an equal number of newcomers. In other words, food matters here and the competition for dining-out dollars is serious business.

Trends are serious business, too. For example, by the early '90s, French food had virtually gone the way of hoop skirts, but now smart bistros have opened all over the city. Wrapped meals are the latest trend: You might find anything from Peking duck to paella concealed in an oversized tortilla. At the same time, there's a craze for grazing: Look for tapas, antipasti, and bar snacks at restaurants all over town. Brew pubs have proliferated; so have high-quality neighborhood restaurants and smart dining rooms catering to the new martini crowd.

San Francisco diners remain curious, which means that our legendary ethnic-restaurant mosaic has continued to expand, forming an ever-more-complex culinary landscape. And the city has kept its reputation for imagination, for being a place where chefs are restless if they are not innovating a new dish or sussing out new ingredients.

CATEGORY	COST*
Very Expensive ($$$$)	over $50
Expensive ($$$)	$30–$50
Moderate ($$)	$20–$30
Inexpensive ($)	under $20

*per person for a three-course meal, excluding drinks, service, and 8.5% sales tax

general information

NO SMOKING

Smoking is banned in most Bay Area workplaces, including restaurants, although many lounges for cigar smokers have opened recently. A law went into effect in January 1998 that bans smoking in all bars.

RESERVATIONS

Reservations are hard to come by at many of the hot-ticket restaurants, unless they are booked literally weeks in advance. Recently, in some of these same restaurants, there has been a trend toward leaving up to one third of the seats unreserved for walk-ins. In any case, it is a good idea to call and check the restaurant's policy.

TIPPING

Tipping is about 15% for most restaurants and 20% for classier operations. A good way to figure the gratuity quickly is roughly to double the tax.

restaurants by cuisine

AFGHANI

 4 *e-4*

HELMAND

White table linens, Afghan carpets, and colorful photographs set an elegant scene in this modestly priced Middle Eastern restaurant. For first courses, try the sweetened baked pumpkin with yogurt, or *aushak* (leek-filled ravioli served with yogurt and ground beef). Lamb dishes—kebabs, sliced leg served with sautéed eggplant—are first-rate. There's free nighttime validated parking at Helmand Parking (468 Broadway). *430 Broadway, between Montgomery and Kearny Sts., North Beach, 415/362–0641. AE, MC, V. No lunch weekends. $*

AMERICAN/CASUAL

5 *g-3*

AMERICAN BISTRO AND WINE BAR

Unadorned tile floors and bentwood chairs contribute to the relaxed ambience of this comfortable bilevel space. Garlic roast chicken is served with new potatoes and fiddlehead ferns; salmon rests on a hillock of black and white beans—and there are also simple favorites such as hearty burgers with house-made french fries. A reasonable fixed-price menu gives you a choice of soup, salad, and main course (or two smaller plates). The wine list, however, is surprisingly limited. Brunch is served on weekends. *2372 Chestnut St., between Scott and Divisadero Sts., The Marina, 415/440–2372. MC, V. No lunch. No dinner Sun. $$*

4 *c-7*

BACKFLIP

This bastion of hipness in the Phoenix Hotel has a retro, blue bar area with a tropical theme, and a green dining room that looks out on a real motel swimming pool. Foodwise, it's tough to pigeonhole. The chef has dubbed the fare "cocktail cuisine," though the burger and fries and the house-made vanilla ice cream are arguably the best items. Other hits: crisp-crust pizza topped with lamb and dry jack cheese; mussels cooked with cherry tomatoes and onions and served with grilled bread. Ear-splitting music adds to the happening mood. *Phoenix Hotel, 601 Eddy St., at Larkin St., The Tenderloin, 415/3547. AE, MC, V. $$*

5 *h-3*

BALBOA CAFÉ

In the mid-'90s, the owners of the popular Plumpjack Café (*see* Mediterranean, *below*) pulled this legendary spot into their orbit, spiffed up the surroundings, and redid the menu. The food is satisfyingly straightforward, with steaks, grilled fish, and simple salads. Burgers are the number one draw; pair them with the fine house fries and one of the boutique beers regularly stocked at the bar and you'll understand why. The crowd is casual, corporate, and mostly single. *3199 Fillmore St., at Greenwich St., Cow Hollow, 415/921–3944. AE, D, DC, MC, V. $$*

3 *b-2*

BETTE'S OCEANVIEW DINER

In Berkeley's fashionable 4th Street shopping area, this high-profile '50s-style diner serves what many consider the best buttermilk pancakes on the planet. There are also huevos rancheros for those who like a bit of morning spice, and poached eggs and scrapple for homesick Philadelphians. At noontime, sandwiches, bread pudding, and fruit pie move front and center. The jukebox is loaded with old favorites. Expect long lines or opt for the take-out branch next door. *1807 4th St., between Hearst and Virginia Aves., Berkeley, 510/644–3230. Reservations not accepted. No credit cards. No dinner. $*

7 *h-2*

CHOW

Photographs of film stars decorate this down-to-earth green-and-cream dining room, and an open kitchen with a wood-burning pizza oven stands at the back. There's a little bit of everything on the menu—salads, pastas, pizzas, grills, sandwiches—and the seasonings run the gamut from oregano to ginger. Some of the dishes, such as fire-roasted mussels, Shanghai noodles with peanut sauce, and tomato-topped bruschetta, are decidedly upmarket. Others—Rose's spaghetti and meatballs; meat loaf—are not. *215 Church St., between Market and 15th Sts., The Castro, 415/552–2469. MC, V. $–$$*

5 *f-6*

ELLA'S

On weekends, a line of patient breakfast eaters has already formed before the 9 AM opening of this favorite San Francisco brunch spot with a cozy, flower-filled dining room. In addition to addictive house-made sticky buns, there are buttermilk pancakes, California-inspired omelets, and fresh-squeezed blood-orange juice. On weekdays, lunch and dinner are also served, with grilled fish, chicken pot pie, pot roast in gravy, and big burgers showing up on the regularly changing menu of updated grandmother food. *500 Presidio Ave., at California St., Pacific Heights, 415/441–5669. Reservations not accepted. MC, V. No dinner Sat.–Sun. $$*

4 *f-3*

FOG CITY DINER

Open for more than a decade, this sleek chrome eatery had a lot to do with the renaissance of the American diner. It carries the expected fare—burgers and milk shakes—but there are also such local favorites as chiles rellenos. The service falters on occasion, but a crisp french fry dipped into the house-made ketchup should help you forget the staff's lapses. The shareable "small plates" are a good way to explore the menu. *1300 Battery St., at Greenwich St., The Embarcadero, 415/982–2000. D, DC, MC, V.* $$

4 *h-5*

GORDON BIERSCH BREWERY RESTAURANT

German-style beers made on the premises accompany such classy brew-pub fare as pan-roasted chicken with Tuscan bread salad, garlic lamb with cucumber salad, and tender baby back ribs with garlic fries. There are great views of the bay from the granite- and wrought-iron-filled restaurant, which occupies the historic Hills Brothers Coffee building. Expect to find a gregarious after-work crowd of mostly twentysomethings. *2 Harrison St., at Steuart St., South Beach, 415/243–8246. AE, D, DC, MC, V.* $$

5 *h-3*

HOME PLATE

Loyalists of this postage-stamp-sized neighborhood spot point to the house-baked scones as reason enough to come here for breakfast. The apple-wood-smoked meats, fresh fruit–topped granola, and egg dishes featuring everything from chicken livers to spinach to smoked salmon are additional enticements. Weekends find the line of hungry brunch-goers curling around the corner (you may call ahead and the staff will pen in your name on the waiting list); weekday breakfasts are a calmer affair. *2274 Lombard St., between Steiner and Pierce Sts., The Marina, 415/922–4663. MC, V. No dinner. Closed Mon.* $

2 *f-3*

IT'S TOPS COFFEE SHOP

A few blocks east of Church Street, this retro diner with knotty pine walls and tabletop jukeboxes dates from the mid-'30s, although some of the furnishings go back only to the '50s. You can take a seat at the counter or slide into a booth on the opposite wall. The burgers—hefty and succulent on a tasty grilled bun—and thick milk-shakes are deliciously all-American. The breakfast menu includes pancakes, waffles, and eggs as you like them, while dinners revolve around chops and chicken. In true diner style, It's Tops serves food until 3 AM. *1801 Market St., at Octavia St., The Castro, 415/431–6395. MC, V. No dinner Sun.–Tues.* $

7 *g-1*

KATE'S KITCHEN

It's hard to resist the thick slabs of French toast topped with berries and old-fashioned corned beef at this funky, comfy American-food outpost. Biscuits and gravy, big cornmeal pancakes, and other breakfast items are equally tempting. For lunch, folks munch on meat loaf sandwiches and slurp big bowls of healthy soup. Save room for a slice of homemade pie. *471 Haight St., between Fillmore and Webster Sts., Lower Haight, 415/626–3984. No credit cards.* $

2 *h-3*

MISSION ROCK

A crew of regulars hangs out at this ramshackle wood building, tucked amid piers and dry docks south of the Bay Bridge. Two outdoor decks with prime views of a working marina make a great perch from which to sip cool drinks from the full bar. Sunday brunch and weekend barbecues draw a crowd; the rest of the week it's burgers and batter-fried seafood. *817 China Basin St. near Mission Rock St., China Basin, 415/621–5538. AE, DC, MC, V. No dinner.* $

4 *e-3*

MO'S

Thick, prime chuck patties sit on a fancy grill that rotates above a glowing fire in this regular haunt for burger fans. The choice of toppings goes beyond the traditional—you can opt for blue cheese or Gruyère in addition to good old American cheese. Sandwiches such as grilled lamb burger or grilled chicken breast with Thai curry paste are also on the menu. The black-and-white tile and chrome decor gives Mo's a modern attitude. *1322 Grant Ave., between Vallejo and Green Sts., North Beach, 415/788–3779. MC, V.* $

2 *e-2*

PERRY'S

When Perry Butler arrived in San Francisco from New York in the late '60s, he decided what the city needed was good East Coast saloon food—steak, veal chops, Caesar salad, and the best hamburgers in town. That's precisely what you'll find at his namesake restaurants. The bar at the original Union Street location is a good place to watch whatever major sports event is being broadcasted. The second location, Perry's Downtown, serves the same type food in a more upmarket, mahogany-lined space that attracts Financial District suits midday and after five. *1944 Union St., between Laguna and Buchanan Sts., Cow Hollow, 415/922–9022. AE, MC, V. $$*

4 *f-5*

185 Sutter St., between Montgomery and Kearny Sts., Union Square, 415/989–6895.

8 *c-5*

ST. FRANCIS FOUNTAIN

Welcome to Main Street America—in the heart of the barrio. Since 1918 (its opening year), this place has hardly changed, despite the multi-ethnic history of the neighborhood around it. On one side of the restaurant is the stool-lined counter, where folks make their way through sodas whipped up with ice cream made on the premises, and other nostalgic fare—grilled cheese, tuna salad, and BLT sandwiches. Across from the counter is a display of the homemade candies. *2801 24th St., at York St., Mission District, 415/826–4200. No credit cards. $*

7 *g-1*

SQUAT AND GOBBLE

The name certainly lacks finesse, and the portion sizes do, too. But on sunny days, tables from this mildly grungy Lower Haight mainstay spill out onto the sidewalk and hungry eaters fuel up on crepes stuffed with savory or sweet fillings, billowy omelets paired with pan-fried potatoes, grilled sandwiches, and trencherman salads. Take a number at the counter and wait to hear your order yelled out over the often-cacophonous dining area. *237 Fillmore St., between Haight and Waller Sts., Lower Haight, 415/487–0551. No credit cards. $*

AMERICAN/ CONTEMPORARY

7 *a-2*

AVENUE 9

With the Inner Sunset's new burst of trendy commerce has come a handful of new restaurants, including this cheerful American bistro done in bright yellows and wood. A far-from-classic Caesar salad includes blue cheese, walnuts, and pears; nicely cooked local duck is paired with a chili-laced custard; and a flatiron steak joins forces with a mound of mashed potatoes. The warm gingerbread with vanilla ice cream is a pleasing finale. *1243 9th Ave., between Lincoln Way and Irving St., Sunset District, 415/664–6999. MC, V. No lunch. $$*

6 *b-1*

BEACH CHALET

The Beach Chalet is a great place to watch the sun sink below the horizon while sipping a home-brewed pint, or to relax over Sunday brunch after a walk on the beach. It's housed in a historic colonnaded building overlooking the Pacific; inside, handsome, newly restored Works Project Administration–produced murals portray the City in the mid-1930s. The menu is a mixed bag, with everything from ceviche to buffalo wings to hearty seafood gumbo. The N Judah streetcar will carry you here from downtown in about 40 minutes. *1000 Great Hwy., at John F. Kennedy Dr., Golden Gate Park, 415/386–8439. MC, V. $$*

4 *f-4*

BIX

Occupying a historic building on a charming back alley, this swanky supper club has a bustling bar and dining tables downstairs, and a banquette-filled balcony. Opt for the lower level; the acoustics upstairs are deafening. The menu, which changes with the seasons, lists contemporary renditions of classic American standards such as Waldorf salad and grilled pork chops. A pianist adds to the jazzy mood. *56 Gold St., between Jackson and Pacific Sts. and Montgomery and Sansome Sts., North Beach, 415/433–6300. AE, D, DC, MC, V. No lunch weekends. $$*

4 *g-4*

BOULEVARD

Nationally acclaimed chef Nancy Oakes and design partner Pat Kuleto have

turned the first floor of the 1889 Aud-
iffred Building, a Parisian look-alike and
one of the few structures in the area to
survive the 1906 earthquake and fire,
into an oasis of American seasonal
food. Oakes's menu changes regularly,
but fresh Sonoma foie gras, wood oven–
roasted duck, and wild mushroom
risotto are among the irresistible possibilities. Simpler fare, such as pizza with
braised leeks and pancetta, and crispy
calamari with a Thai vinaigrette, prevails
at midday. *1 Mission St., at the Embarcadero, The Embarcadero, 415/543–6084.
Reservations essential. AE, D, DC, MC, V.
No lunch weekends. $$$*

4 *e-5*
CAMPTON PLACE
In 1984, chef Bradley Ogden put new
American food on the culinary map with
the opening of this elegant dining room,
housed in one of America's premier
small hotels. Although other chefs have
followed, the menu maintains the origi-
nal emphasis established by Ogden: tra-
ditional American dishes with ethnic
influences. Those who wish to sample a
full range of the kitchen staff's culinary
accomplishments can order a six-course
tasting menu, which stretches from
caviar to squab. Power breakfasts are an
institution here. *340 Stockton St.,
between Post and Sutter Sts., Union
Square, 415/955–5555. Reservations essen-
tial. AE, D, DC, MC, V. $$$–$$$$*

 3 *d-1*
CHEZ PANISSE
Alice Waters defined California cuisine
at this more-than-two-decade-old culi-
nary temple, where locally grown ingre-
dients reign supreme. Downstairs,
fixed-course meals are served in an ele-
gantly rustic space. Upstairs in the more
casual café, an à la carte menu is in
force, with pizzas, pastas, salads, and
simple meat and fish on the list. The
ice-cream and fruit desserts (tarts and
cobblers) are legendary. *1517 Shattuck
Ave., between Cedar and Vine Sts., Berke-
ley, 510/548–5525 (dining room), 510/548–
5049 (café). Reservations essential. AE, D,
DC, MC, V. No lunch in café. Closed Sun.
$$–$$$$*

4 *f-4*
CYPRESS CLUB
Bulbous light fixtures, curvy banquettes
with plush velvet upholstery, and imposing pillars give the celebrated Cypress

Club a futuristic look; stone mosaic
floors, hammered copper arches, and
murals depicting northern California
add even more pizzazz. The food is
more down to earth, with sea bass in a
potato crust, venison tenderloin, and
braised sweetbreads among the high-
class selections. *500 Jackson St., between
Montgomery and Kearny Sts., Financial
District, 415/296–8555. Reservations essen-
tial. AE, DC, MC, V. No lunch. $$$*

4 *f-6*
EDDIE RICKENBACKER'S
World War II memorabilia, a vintage air-
plane, and a trio of motorcycles outfit
this gathering place for Financial Dis-
trict suits and young SoMa media
moguls. A menu of hearty, all-American
fare—steaks, burgers, pork chops,
chicken, and sandwiches—comple-
ments the patriotic decor. When the
clock strikes five, it's hard to find a free
barstool at Eddie's, as the regulars
crowd in for after-work camaraderie. *133
2nd St., between Mission and Howard
Sts., South of Market, 415/543–3498. AE,
MC, V. Closed Sun. $$*

4 *g-6*
ELROYS
Southwestern flavors are threaded
through the contemporary American
food served at this SoMa hot spot,
housed in a renovated warehouse: You
might find blue-corn crab cakes with
roasted corn salsa, duck quesadillas
with mango salsa, or fried calamari with
jalapeno ketchup. The food has been
uneven but the crowd doesn't seem to
care—not when there's a tempting
game of billiards upstairs, and a Sunday
brunch that features a 35-foot create-
your-own-Bloody Mary bar with hundreds of hot sauces. *301 Folsom St.,
between Beale and Fremont Sts., South of
Market, 415/882–7989. AE, MC, V. No
lunch Sat. $$*

7 *d-2*
EOS RESTAURANT &
WINE BAR
Chef Arnold Wong churns out intriguing
East-West dishes such as blackened
Asian catfish, steamed mussels in a
broth of coconut milk and green curry,
five-pepper fried calamari, and five-spice
duck confit. Sometimes diners may find
the competing flavors more confusing
than comforting, but Wong's loyal fol-
lowing keeps the place busy. The

attached wine bar, with some 400 vintages, is a good place for friends to meet, and any of the wines on hand can make the trip to your table next door. *901 Cole St., at Carl St., The Haight, 415/566–3063. Reservations essential. AE, MC, V. Closed Sun. No lunch. $$*

2 *h-4*
42 DEGREES
A sophisticated menu, an outdoor patio with a view of the bay, a crowded bar, and a sleek overall design pull in a mostly thirtysomething crowd with a few bucks to spend. Dishes on the Mediterranean-influenced menu range from the classic—marrowbones with toasts, to the contemporary—duck breast with fiddlehead ferns. A selection of little plates is ideal for small appetites or folks looking for something to munch on with their drinks. Live music draws a crowd into the wee hours. *235 16th St., near Illinois St., Potrero Hill, 415/777–5559. MC, V. No dinner Mon. and Tues. Closed Sun. $$—$$$*

4 *f-4*
GLOBE
Although housed in a building dating from 1911, Globe is an up-to-the-minute eatery with an intriguing contemporary menu. In the small, terra-cotta-floored dining room you may find it hard to choose between a starter of grilled sardines and the utterly French *frisée aux lardons* (curly endive with bacon) and a poached egg. Main courses may include T-bone steak with potato gratin or spit-roasted lamb in an artichoke purée. Service is excellent. *290 Pacific Ave., near Battery St., Financial District, 415/391–4132. Reservations essential. MC, V. No lunch Sat. Closed Sun. $$$*

4 *d-6*
GRAND CAFÉ
Eight large, dramatic murals, whimsical sculptures of stylized human figures, striking chandeliers, and big booths outfit this former ballroom inside the trendy Hotel Monaco. The menu is classic California, relying heavily on seasonal local ingredients but freely drawing upon French and Italian culinary traditions. Sandwiches, salads, and pizzas from a wood-burning oven are served in the more casual bar. *Hotel Monaco, 501 Geary St., at Taylor St., Union Square, 415/292–0101. AE, D, DC, MC, V. $$*

4 *g-5*
HARRY DENTON'S
This Barbary Coast–style bar is a favorite of the city's singles, who come for the food every day of the week and the live music and dancing on Thursday, Friday, and Saturday nights. Sometimes Harry himself—the city's best-known barkeep—is on hand to show off his dance steps. At lunchtime the place is quieter, attracting diners with its bay view and rustic menu of pizzas from a wood-burning oven, pot roast with mashed potatoes, and other soothing foods. Breakfast is served daily and extends to brunch on weekends. *161 Steuart St., between Mission and Howard Sts., The Embarcadero, 415/882–1333. AE, DC, MC, V. $$*

4 *f-6*
HAWTHORNE LANE
This celebrated establishment has helped sustain the boom that first hit SoMa in the early '90s. It is the creation of David and Anne Gingrass, one-time chefs at the famed Postrio, and the setting is grand, from the light-flooded dining room to the spacious, table-filled bar. In the latter, you can order a selection of irresistible small plates—Thai-style squid, tempura-battered green beans, and trendy pizzas. Dining-room patrons indulge in more serious fare, such as grilled quail, foie gras with arugula salad and Napa Valley verjus, or seared Maine scallops—all prepared with Mediterranean and Asian touches. *22 Hawthorne st., between 2nd and 3rd Sts., South of Market, 415/777–9779. Reservations essential. D, DC, MC, V. No lunch weekends. $$$*

4 *g-7*
INFUSION BAR & RESTAURANT
What's being "infused" here is vodka: Glass decanters, lined up behind the bar like chess pieces, contain spirits of mango, pepper, coconut, and more. The idea is to taste a few different flavors, all through the course of several small plates of food, such as roasted mussels. Main dishes, some of them infused with the flavored vodkas, consist mostly of meats and pastas. Things pick up after nine, when live music precludes conversation. *555 2nd St., Bryant and Brannan Sts., South of Market, 415/543–2282. AE, DC, MC, V. $$*

4 b-8

JARDINIÈRE

Pricey and elegant, Jardinière is the brainchild of celebrated chef Traci Des Jardins, who built her reputation at Rubicon, and famed restaurant designer Pat Kuleto, creator of such talked-about spaces as Boulevard and Farallon. Jardinière's stunning two-story, black-and-silver interior, complete with gold ceiling, is a suitably flashy setting for Des Jardins's exquisite plates of foie gras, sweetbread salad with haricots verts, seared fish, and bittersweet chocolate–hazelnut torte. Opera and symphony goers crowd the showplace before and after performances. *300 Grove St., at Franklin St., Hayes Valley, 415/861–5555. Reservations essential. AE, D, DC, MC, V. No lunch Sat.–Sun. $$$*

4 e-8

JULIE'S SUPPER CLUB

A crowd of twentysomethings sips martinis and snacks on fried calamari in this throwback-to-the-'50s supper club. The sultry cocktail lounge atmosphere fits the menu of New York steak, grilled chicken with corn soufflé, and house-made pastries. The pink, vinyl-covered bar, with lamps that look as if they were whisked away from a mid-range hotel of yesteryear, contribute to the charm. *1123 Folsom St., between 7th and Rausch Sts., South of Market, 415/861–0707. AE, DC, MC, V. Closed Sun. No lunch. $$*

8 a-7

LIBERTY CAFÉ

Bernal Heights gained its first classy eatery with the opening of this sunny yellow café in the heart of the neighborhood. Regulars know to order the chicken pot pie, which arrives packed with pearl onions and chunks of chicken, potatoes, and carrots, topped with a puff-pastry crust. A memorable Caesar salad, a choice cut of steak, thin-crust pizzas with contemporary toppings, and a banana cream pie that will put your grandmother's to shame round out the menu. Locals come for weekend brunch. *410 Cortland Ave., between Bennington and Andover Sts., Bernal Heights, 415/695–8777. MC, V. No dinner Sun. $$*

4 f-4

MACARTHUR PARK

For more than two decades, San Franciscans have flocked to this renovated pre-earthquake warehouse for baby back ribs, but the oak-wood smoker and mesquite grill turn out other American dishes as well, from Eastern-aged steaks, chicken, and sausages to thick burgers and catfish. The crisp onion rings are worth splurging on. *607 Front St., between Jackson St. and Pacific Ave., Financial District, 415/398–5700. AE, DC, MC, V. No lunch weekends. $$*

2 f-5

MOA ROOM

The chefs here cook what they call "borderless cuisine." That translates into such heady plates as New Mexico grilled salmon with pumpkinseed pesto, soft-shell crab in brown butter with capers and lemon, steak with buttermilk-battered onion rings, and garlic soup with tiny blue cheese–filled pastries floating on the surface. The dining room, with its sky blue walls and soft green banquettes, seats less than four dozen, and regularly fills up with folks who live in the surrounding blocks. *1007 Guerrero St., between 22nd and 23rd Sts., Mission District, 415/282–1007. MC, V. No lunch. $$*

2 f-2

THE MEETINGHOUSE

Modernized American dishes and an inviting dining room of warm yellow walls and Shaker furniture make the Meetinghouse a great place to meet—and eat. The menu is always changing, but rock shrimp–filled johnnycakes with a pepper relish and oyster stew are among the most popular first courses, while hominy-crusted catfish, pan-roasted chicken, and duck breast with cornmeal crisps are satisfying entrées. The old-fashioned hot biscuits and summertime berry shortcakes are addictive. *1701 Octavia St., at Bush St., Pacific Heights, 415/922–6733. AE, MC, V. Closed Mon.–Tues. No lunch. $$*

4 g-4

ONE MARKET

Opened in 1993, this large, lively brasserie across from the Ferry Building is the province of well-known chef Bradley Ogden. The spacious dining room, with its large windows looking out onto Market Street, is smart and comfortable, and a sizable café–bar serves snacks beginning at noon. Although the kitchen suffered from unevenness in its early years, it has since settled down, and the stylish American fare—soft-shell crabs, beef tenderloin, grilled fish—has its loyal partisans. *The Embarcadero, at the foot of Market St., The Embarcadero, 415/777–5577. Reservations essential. AE, DC, MC, V. Closed Sun. No lunch Sat. $$$*

4 *h-6*

PICKLED GINGER

This '90s kitchen, with its self-described Pan Asian–American food, sorts out its mixed identity in such dishes as Caesar salad with pickled ginger and kaffir lime leaves, tea-smoked Chilean sea bass, and Chinese dumplings with ginger-chive sauce. The stylishly casual interior, done in cinnabar red and mustard yellow, includes a lively open kitchen with counter seating where you can watch the sizzling woks. After (or before) dinner, take a walk along the busy Embarcadero. *100 Brannan St., at the Embarcadero, South Beach, 415/977–1230. AE, DC, D, MC, V. $$*

4 *d-6*

POSTRIO

Superchef Wolfgang Puck periodically commutes from his Los Angeles headquarters to check the kitchen in this appealing multilevel bar and dining space, complete with a dramatic staircase for showy entrances. The food has Mediterranean and Asian overtones; roasted Chinese duck and smoked salmon on a giant blini are favorites with many regulars. Good breakfast and bar menus (with great pizza) keep customers happy from dawn until late at night. *545 Post St., between Mason and Taylor Sts., Union Square, 415/776–7825. Reservations essential. AE, D, DC, MC, V. $$$–$$$$*

3 *c-1*

RIVOLI

Chef Wendy Brucker assembles a memorable Californian–Mediterranean menu at this small East Bay restaurant, while her husband, Roscoe Skipper, oversees the dining room. You might start with a beautiful salad of *frisé* (curly lettuce) and arugula with spiced hazelnuts and pears, an order of piping-hot vegetable fritters with lemony aioli, or smoked trout with blood oranges. Entrées are equally notable: Look for braised veal stew with soft polenta and chanterelles, or pepper-coated sirloin steak. *1539 Solano Ave., at Peralta Ave., Berkeley, 510/526–2542. Reservations essential. MC, V. No lunch. $$*

4 *f-4*

RUBICON

With Robin Williams, Robert De Niro, and Francis Ford Coppola among its investors, this sleek, cherrywood-lined restaurant was fated to be a destination. (Both Williams and Coppola live in the city, a fact that dramatically increases the chance for a celebrity sighting.) Set in a handsome, nearly century-old stone building, Rubicon has the dignified air of a men's club. The superb cuisine, primarily sophisticated renditions of seafood and poultry (crab cakes, seared scallops, crisp roast chicken), is served on two floors to Hollywood big shots, Financial District power brokers, and the rest of us. *558 Sacramento St., between Sansome and Montgomery Sts., Financial District, 415/434–4100. AE, MC, V. Reservations essential. Closed Sun. No lunch Sat. $$$*

4 *e-5*

RUMPUS

On an old-time alley in the heart of downtown, this appealing bistro is lively from midday through dinnertime. The Caesar salad has been voted the best in town by devoted Rumpus regulars; a handful of pasta and risotto selections, garlic-laced roast chicken, and apple tart made with puff pastry are among the other stars. A bar menu kicks in midafternoon. *1 Tillman Pl., off Grant Ave. between Sutter and Post Sts., Union Square, 415/421–2300. AE, MC, V. $$*

4 *c-7*

STARS

Jeremiah Tower, the superchef who did much to put California cuisine on the culinary map, opened Stars in the mid-'80s, and it has remained a destination for gourmet out-of-towners ever since. It's also where many local power brokers break bread, and where opera goers dine late at night in a setting reminiscent of a popular brasserie. Food on the daily changing menu may include anything from grilled duck breast to saffron-tinged seafood risotto. Dinners are pricey, but those on a budget can order a hot dog, hamburger, or pizza at the bar and watch the swells dine. *150 Redwood St., between Van Ness Ave. and Polk St., Civic Center, 415/861–7827. Reservations essential. AE, DC, MC, V. No lunch weekends. $$$*

7 *g-2*

2223

Also known as John Cunin's No-Name Restaurant, this upper Market Street establishment was a hit from the day it opened, and the noise level doesn't let you forget it. Cunin, who also owns the celebrated Cypress Club (*see above*), keeps the hip clientele happy with thin-crusted pizzas, earthy seasonal soups such as wild mushroom or puréed winter squash, roast chicken with garlic-mashed potatoes, and pork loin en croute. For Sunday brunch, there's a wonderful rendition of eggs Benedict on an herb-flecked scone. *2223 Market St., between 16th and Sanchez Sts., The Castro, 415/431–0692. MC, V. No lunch Sat. $$*

8 *c-3*

UNIVERSAL CAFÉ

Tucked into an industrial-residential neighborhood that is also home to the local PBS station and the well-known artists' live-work space Project Artaud, the high-style, light-filled Universal serves wonderful midday sandwiches of focaccia filled with roast chicken and aioli or meat loaf and provolone. At night, you might start with sesame-coated grilled tuna, or grilled flatbread topped with sautéed peppers, tomatoes, and goat cheese; then move on to pan-seared filet mignon with Gorgonzola mashed potatoes, or braised rabbit with wild mushroom risotto. *2814 19th St., between Bryant and Florida Sts., South of Market, 415/821–4608. MC, V. Closed Mon. $$*

VIOGNIER

The Peninsula gained high restaurant marks with the opening in June 1997 of this classy new dining room on the second floor of Draeger's Market Place, an equally classy supermarket. Award-winning chef Gary Danko serves breakfast, weekend brunch, lunch, and dinner in the large, light-filled space, with its imposing stone fireplace, exhibition kitchen, and French doors opening onto balconies. Midday, your choices include everything from a half-pound burger on a sesame bun with a side of onion rings to pancetta-wrapped grilled prawns with zucchini and rouille. At dinner, such main courses as duck breast with rhubarb-ginger compote and grilled marinated tuna with leeks join more casual fare. *222 Fourth Ave., San Mateo, 415/685–3727. AE, DC, MC, V. $$–$$$*

4 *d-2*

ZAX

The menu is brief but the delivery is first-rate in this small, flower-decked chef-owned restaurant, where one partner handles the savory end of the menu and the other handles the sweet end. A towering goat cheese soufflé is a delectable way to begin a meal here, although a salad of heirloom tomatoes, feta, and olives in summer or mixed greens with a sherry vinaigrette the rest of the year is also recommended. Lamb stew with grilled polenta and swordfish with peppers and roasted garlic are wonderful mains. Be sure to save room for the apple galettes with homemade ice cream. *2330 Taylor St., near Columbus, North Beach, 415/563–6266. MC, V. No lunch. $$*

BARBECUE

2 *f-4*

BIG NATE'S BAR-B-QUE

The Big Nate here is the famed basketballer Nate Thurman. His barbecue place is pretty stripped down—few seats, lots of linoleum—so most folks come in for takeout. Nate's got smoky ribs, brisket, hot links, and chicken, along with a trio of sauces—hot, mid-range, and mild—and all the standard side dishes. Be ready to do some serious washing up when your meal is done. *1665 Folsom St., between 12th and 13th Sts., South of Market, 415/861–4242. MC, V. $*

2 *g-6*

JAMES & JAMES RIBS 'N' THANGS

The city's barbecue aficionados give thumbs up to James & James, where pork ribs, sausage links, chicken, and beef are liberally coated in a choice of first-rate mild or hot sauce. Side dishes include all the standards—tasty potato salad, coleslaw, brown beans, collard greens, corn bread, corn on the cob—and an old-fashioned sweet potato pie is a wonderful capper. The big barbecue pit stands on a commercial stretch deep in the city's remote southeast corner, but it's worth the trip, especially since unlike many a barbecue spot, this one has a comfortable dining room. *5130 3rd St., between Thornton Ave. and Bay View St., Hunters Point, 415/671–0269. MC, V. Closed Mon. $–$$*

BRAZILIAN

7 *h-3*

CANTO DO BRASIL

Home cooking is what this bright green restaurant serves—both to expat Brazilians and to those of us who dream of the white sands of Ipanema. *Feijoada*, the combination of black beans and meats that is the national dish of the country, is a weekend special. Meat croquettes and fried yuca are tasty first courses; chicken cooked in beer is an interesting main. Brazilian music usually plays in the modest dining room. *3621 18th St. between Guerrero and Dolores Sts., Mission District, 415/626–8727. MC, V. Closed Mon. No lunch. $*

BURMESE

4 *d-6*

BURMA HOUSE

In Myanmar (formerly Burma), many of the restaurateurs are Chinese, so it comes as no surprise that this downtown restaurant serves a combination of Chinese and Burmese specialties. The ginger salad (a tossed mixture of young ginger, fried garlic, yellow peas, chilies, and other ingredients) and the chicken and coconut curry are among the highlights. If you want to stick with Burmese dishes, ask the helpful wait staff to direct you to the national dishes. *720 Post St., between Jones and Leavenworth Sts., Union Square, 415/775–1156. MC, V. $*

5 *c-6*

MANDALAY

At this venerable Richmond District restaurant, the first Burmese eatery in San Francisco, repeat customers especially enjoy the tea salad of dried shrimp, fried garlic, lentils, coconut, sesame seeds, and other ingredients, all tossed together in a savory blend. Follow it with a peppery thick fish soup with noodles, curried prawns, or beef; or *chin mong kyaw*, a sour leafy vegetable prepared with shrimp. Colorful fabric and simple Asian artifacts contribute to the pleasant atmosphere. *4348 California St., between 5th and 6th Aves., Richmond District, 415/386–3895. MC, V. $–$$*

CAJUN/CREOLE

7 *e-1*

CRESCENT CITY CAFÉ

There are no frills here, just red beans and rice, jambalaya, spicy sausages, blackened redfish, and gumbo—plus warm corn-bread that's by no means low-fat. The walls are festooned with New Orleans memorabilia, and from the small counter (with less than a dozen seats), you can keep an eye on the culinary action. There are also half a dozen tables. A blackboard lists the daily special. *1418 Haight St., between Masonic and Ashbury Sts., The Haight, 415/863–1374. MC, V. $*

2 *e-2*

ELITE CAFÉ

The space dates from the 1920s, but the New Orleans–inspired Elite Café is a product of the Cajun–Creole craze of the '80s. The oyster-packed raw bar is a big

---

THE KIDS'LL LOVE IT

Despite its reputation as an adult town, San Francisco has its share of kid-friendly restaurants.

Ella's (American/Casual)
  Sticky buns and pancakes: What more could you ask for?

James & James Ribs 'n Thangs (Barbecue)
  Let 'em make a mess eating ribs.

La Taqueria (Mexican)
  A sure way to break the habit of crisp taco shells.

Mifune (Japanese)
  You're allowed to slurp your noodles here.

Mo's Gourmet Burgers (American Casual)
  Burgers for young but sophisticated palates.

St. Francis Fountain (American Casual
  A soda fountain just like the ones mom and dad used to know.

Tommaso's (Italian)
  Every kid loves pizza, so give 'em a good one.

Ton Kiang (Chinese)
  The wait staff is used to lots of kids and commotion.

draw, as are the blackened meat and fish dishes, crawfish, and crab cakes. The wooden booths are ideal for tête-a-tête evenings, while the long counter along one wall suits folks out for meals on their own. *2049 Fillmore St., between Pine and California Sts., Pacific Heights, 415/346–8668. MC, V. No lunch. $$*

2 *f-3*
JESSIE'S
If you're curious about the taste of alligator, Jessie's may be the ticket for you: Alligator sausage takes on several guises at this combination Cajun, Creole, and Caribbean kitchen. A bowl of hearty gumbo, chock-full of seafood and andouille, or a plate of nicely spiced jambalaya will have you dreaming of the bayou. The tropical-color dining room is cheery and comfortable, and the staff is friendly, albeit sometimes a bit shaky on delivery. *1256 Folsom St., between 8th and 9th Sts., South of Market, 415/437–2481. MC, V. No lunch Sat. Closed Sun. $$*

CARIBBEAN

7 *d-1*
CHA CHA CHA
Be prepared to jockey for a table at this quirky Haight Street institution. The food is updated Caribbean, while the space is a showplace of bright colors and Hispanic shrines and folk art. Many regulars opt for the dozen or so tapas, such as pork quesadillas, steamed mussels, and garlicky shrimp. The menu changes regularly; among the many possibilities are aromatic Cuban roast pork with black beans, or grilled fish with olives and peppers. *1805 Haight St., between Shrader and Stanyan Sts., The Haight, 415/386–5758. Reservations not accepted. No credit cards. $–$$*

8 *b-5*
EL NUEVO FRUTILANDIA
The flavors of Puerto Rico and Cuba are here for the picking. At lunchtime, Cuban sandwiches stuffed with roast pork are filling and tasty, as are the Puerto Rican "dumplings" of shredded pork and olives inside a "skin" made from plantains and yucca. For dinner, you might have chicken in salsa verde or green chilies stuffed with cheese. Plantains, yucca, rice, and beans turn up at every meal. As the name would imply, a tropical fruit shake is the drink of choice. *3077 24th St., between Treat Ave. and Folsom St., Mission District, 415/648–2958. MC, V. $*

CHINESE

2 *d-3*
CHINA FIRST
Here is where you will find the true flavors of Sichuan and Shanghai, from *ma po dofu* (chili-laced bean curd with pork) and salt duck to steamed dumplings and simmered fava beans. Many of the small plates are on view, so you can just point to what you want to try. Otherwise, if you don't read Chinese, consult the waiter, as the best dishes appear on the Chinese-language menu only. *336 Clement St., between 4th and 5th Aves., Richmond District, 415/387–8371. MC, V. $.*

8 *e-3*
ELIZA'S
Although the cooking here is far from authentic Chinese, Ping and Jan Sung have a large, loyal following for their sunflower beef with scallions and enoki mushrooms, slightly sweet shrimp tossed with pine nuts, plump pot stickers, and other California-influenced dishes. The food arrives on colorful Italian plates, and the room is full of lovely Chinese carved-wood antiques and blue-and-white porcelains. A pot of orchids tops each of the tables. *1457 18th St., between Missouri and Connecticut Sts., Potrero Hill, 415/648–9999. Reservations not accepted. MC, V. $–$$*

4 *e-4*
GREAT EASTERN
The busy dining room of this bilevel Cantonese restaurant is home to large tanks of swimming Dungeness crabs, black bass, abalone, catfish, shrimp, rock cod, and other creatures of the sea; a wall menu in both Chinese and English lists the prices of the various choices. Conch stir-fried with yellow chives, crab with vermicelli in a clay pot, and shrimp steamed with garlic are among the chef's many specialties. Late-night appetites favor the tasty noodle dishes. *649 Jackson St., between Kearny St. and Grant Ave., Chinatown, 415/986–2550. AE, MC, V. $–$$*

2 *d-3*

HAPPY FAMILY

Sample the cuisine of China's Shandong Province: boiled dumplings filled with pork or shrimp, and such classic cold dishes as garlic-scented cold seaweed, pig's ear salad, and wine-cooked chicken. Of particular note are the hand-pulled noodles, made without the aid of a knife (a mound of dough is pulled, stretched, and twisted until it forms long, uniform strands); these are served in soup or with various sauces. Kimchi arrives automatically with every order, an acknowledgment of Shandong's border with North Korea. *3809 Geary Blvd., 415/221–5095, between 2nd and 3rd Aves., Richmond District, MC, V. Closed Tues. $*

4 *f-3*

HAPPY VALLEY
SEAFOOD RESTAURANT

The specialty here is the hot pot, a bubbling cauldron of broth into which diners dip meats, seafood, and vegetables. There are four different hot pots, but shrimp, scallops, white fish, mushrooms, pea shoots, and more than half a dozen other items are usually part of the mix. The cost heads upward as the individual ingredients become more pricey, so if you want lobster, bamboo pith (a pricey fungus that grows near bamboo plants), and the like, expect to pay more. *1255 Battery St., between Filbert and Greenwich Sts., The Embarcadero, 415/399–9393. MC, V. $$*

4 *g-4*

HARBOR VILLAGE

Dim sum lunches, fresh seafood from the restaurant's own tanks, and Chinese classics from Peking duck to roast suckling pig are the hallmarks of this deluxe branch of a top-flight Hong Kong–based operation. The dining areas are outfitted with Chinese antiques and teak furnishings, and the main dining room usually hosts a passel of business moguls and various large family groups. A gallery of private rooms is used for weddings, anniversaries, and other special occasions. *4 Embarcadero Center, at Sacramento and Drumm Sts., The Embarcadero, 415/781–8833. AE, DC, MC, V. $$*

4 *e-4*

HING LUNG

A good place for night owls (it's open until 1 AM, Hing Lung is a well-known destination for Chinese comfort food such as *jook* (thick rice porridge laced with various ingredients, from roast duck to preserved egg), stir-fried rice or wheat noodles, bowls of wontons, and plates of crispy roast pork. More substantial meals are available, too: Try steamed catfish in black bean sauce, stir-fried crab with ginger and scallions, or salt-and-pepper squid. The dining room is a sea of bamboo chairs and bare-topped tables, with a small, glass-enclosed kitchen up front. *674 Broadway, between Stockton St. and Columbus Ave., Chinatown, 415/398–8838. MC, V. $*

2 *c-3*

HONG KONG
FLOWER LOUNGE

Whatever is making news in Hong Kong restaurants turns up here in no time, cooked by chefs who are considered masters. The kitchen is known for its seafood—crabs, shrimp, catfish, lobsters, scallops—prepared in classic as well as contemporary variations. (Always check the price before ordering.) Dim sum is available at midday. The signature green roof tiles outside should prevent you from passing this place by. *5322 Geary Blvd., between 17th and 18th Aves., Richmond District, 415/668–8998. AE, D, DC, MC, V. $$*

2 *b-6*

JUST WON TON

This modest, white-walled Sunset storefront specializes in plump, delicate wontons. You can order them in plain broth or partnered with noodles, fish balls, chicken, duck, pork, beef, or assorted innards. If you're still hungry, order up a plate of *chow fun* (rice noodles) or *chow mein* (wheat noodles), stir-fried with meat and vegetables. If you've no time to sit, take out a batch of wontons and cook them at home. *1241 Vicente St., between 23rd and 24th Aves., Sunset District, 415/681–2999. No credit cards. $*

4 *e-4*

NEW ASIA

Hundreds of people can sit down at once in this lively, warehouselike dim sum parlor. Once you take a seat, start flagging down the carts rolling past you: They're stacked with small plates and bamboo baskets holding translucent shrimp dumplings, pork spareribs with black bean sauce, lotus leaves stuffed with glutinous rice, turnip cake, and more. The waiting line for a table is usually lengthy, but the size of the place means your number comes up pretty quickly. At night, a dinner menu takes over and wedding parties are often part of the scene—but dim sum remains their strong suit. *772 Pacific Ave., between Grant Ave. and Stockton St., Chinatown, 415/391–6666. MC, V. $*

4 e-4
R&G LOUNGE
Despite the name, this is not a smoky dive with a bluesy piano player, but a first-rate Cantonese restaurant on two floors. Downstairs (entrance on Kearny Street) is a no-tablecloth dining room that is always packed at lunch and dinner. The more upscale second-floor space (entrance on Commercial Street), complete with shoji-lined private rooms, is a favorite stop for folks on expense accounts. A menu with photographs helps diners decide among the many intriguing dishes, including panfried salted fish with minced pork, drunken scallop soup, and steamed bean curd with shrimp meat. *631 Kearny St., at Commercial St., Chinatown, 415/982–7877 or 415/982–3811. AE, DC, MC, V. $–$$*

4 f-4
TOMMY TOY'S
With its elaborate decor, Tommy Toy's would have made the Empress Dowager feel right at home. The preparations, which meld Eastern and Western influences, sometimes falter, but the roast duck, minced squab, lobster tossed with pine nuts, and seafood bisque in a coconut shell topped with puff pastry are popular with the regulars. The place is usually crowded with suits out to impress their clients; don't expect to show up in a T-shirt and be served. *655 Montgomery St., between Clay and Washington Sts., Financial District, 415/397–4888. Reservations essential for lunch. Jacket required. AE, D, DC, MC, V. $$–$$$*

2 b-3
TON KIANG
Here you will find the rustic Hakka cuisine of southern China, rarely found in this country. Among the regional specialties are salt-baked chicken, braised stuffed bean curd, wine-flavored dishes, and delicate fish and beef balls. Do not overlook the seafood dishes, including salt-and-pepper squid or shrimp and silky bean curd stuffed with shrimp meat,

or the exotic vegetables such as *ong choy* (water spinach). Of the two branches on Geary Boulevard, the newest, at 5821, is more stylish and serves excellent dim sum. *5821 Geary Blvd., between 22nd and 23rd Aves., Richmond District, 415/386–8530. MC, V. $–$$*

5 e-7
3148 Geary Blvd., at Spruce St., Richmond District, 415/752–4440.

4 g-5
WU KONG
The splashy Art Deco Rincon Center is home to this well-known restaurant featuring the food of Shanghai and Canton. The owner, who also operates a restaurant in Hong Kong, attracts a loyal Shanghainese following with his vegetarian "goose," steamed dumplings, and lion's head (large pork meatballs on a bed of greens). At midday there's dim sum. On weekends, large wedding parties regularly sit down to traditional banquets served in the interior courtyard. *101 Spear St., at Mission St., South of Market, 415/957–9300. AE, DC, MC, V. $$*

4 f-4
YANK SING
The oldest teahouse in the city (its original location was in Chinatown), this is still considered by many locals to be the best dim sum kitchen in town; five dozen or so versions of the classic midday Cantonese meal are served on a rotating basis. The handsome Battery Street location seats 300, while the older Stevenson Street site is far smaller, a cozy refuge for nearby office workers who crave plump dumplings at noontime. *427 Battery St., between Clay and Washington Sts., Financial District, 415/362–1640. AE, DC, MC, V. No dinner. $*

4 f-5
49 Stevenson St., between 1st and 2nd Sts., Financial District 415/541–4949. Closed weekends.

DELICATESSENS

4 d-6
DAVID'S DELICATESSEN
San Francisco's best-known deli, in the Theater District, has been serving New York deli food for what seems like forever. Some of the food is not as good as it should be; still, the sinfully rich blintzes are rightfully famous, and the

sandwiches are serious skyscrapers filled with all the traditional fixings: pastrami, corned beef, tongue, chopped liver. Pastry lovers will swoon at the countless caloric choices. Grab a seat at the counter, or settle in to a table or booth. *474 Geary St., between Mason and Taylor Sts., Union Square, 771–1600. AE, DC, MC, V. $–$$*

8 *e-3*

KLEIN'S

At midday, Klein's fills up with Potrero Hill workers and residents who come for hearty, whimsically named sandwiches. The tongue and cheese tucked between slices of pungent dark rye is called the Abzug, while the Minnie Mouse is a trio of cheeses stacked in a Kaiser roll. In addition, pastrami, corned beef, chicken, and turkey sandwiches are all freshly made and filling. Klein's closes in the early evening, so be sure to pick up your deli ration early. *501 Connecticut St., at 20th St., Potrero Hill, 415/821–9149. MC, V. $*

4 *c-7*

MAX'S OPERA CAFÉ

No one will ever accuse Max's of skimpy servings. One corned beef and Swiss on rye will nearly feed a family of four. Dinner plates—brisket, chicken, and the like—are equally generous. The waiters and waitresses take turns at the microphone, singing everything from opera to Broadway show tunes. Max's is packed before and after opera and symphony performances, but there's also a takeout counter for those nights when you don't want to wait. *601 Van Ness Ave., at Golden Gate Ave., Civic Center, 415/771–7301. Reservations not accepted. AE, DC, MC, V. $–$$*

EASTERN EUROPEAN

4 *d-2*

ALBONA RESTAURANT

At this comfortable, well-staffed restaurant you can sample the food of Istria, the peninsula near Trieste that once was Italian but became part of the former Yugoslavia after World War II. *Crafi,* dumplings stuffed with cheese, raisins, and nuts, are served with a meat sauce laced with mildly sweet spices. Puffy fried gnocchi arrive with a similar sauce. Stuffed pork loin, lamb in pome-

granate sauce, and shredded cabbage braised with prosciutto are among the other distinctly Istrian specialties. *545 Francisco St., between Mason and Taylor Sts., North Beach, 415/441–1040. MC, V. Closed Mon. $$*

8 *a-7*

HUNGARIAN SAUSAGE FACTORY

Despite the name, this modest, homey spot is more than a sausage factory, although the pork sausages and pork-liver-and-rice sausages made on the premises are unquestionably first rate. You can easily make a meal of the stuffed cabbage leaves, or opt for *palacsinta,* a paper-thin crepe with a sweet or savory filling. Don't miss the Hungarian sweets, especially the traditional poppy-seed roll. *419 Cortland Ave., between Bennington and Andover Sts., Bernal Heights, 415/648–2847. No credit cards. $*

8 *c-2*

MOXIE BAR AND RESTAURANT

Within throwing distance of Project Artaud, the city's best-known artists' live-work space, Moxie is an outpost of updated Eastern European Ashkenazi Jewish cooking, with a few Sephardic specialties thrown into the mix. Housed in a historic corner building with an exposed-brick interior, the restaurant serves a memorable matzo ball soup, house-cured gravlax and potato latkes, beef brisket with beet-horseradish sauce, and pan-roasted halibut with a potato-filled pastry. *2742 17th St., between Bryant and Florida Sts., Potrero Hill, 415/863–4177. MC, V. No lunch Sat.–Sun. Closed Mon. $$*

ECLECTIC

2 *f-3*

CARTA

The Carta kitchen travels the globe: Each month there's a different menu from a different country or region. The versatile chefs, who have cooked at some of San Francisco best-known restaurants, transport diners to such varied destinations as the American Southwest, Oaxaca, Turkey, Sicily, Morocco, and New England, to name just a few. There are usually about 10 small plates, three main courses, and three or so desserts. A mailing list keeps regulars abreast of the kitchen's itinerary. *1772 Market St., between Gough and Ocatavia Sts., Civic Center, 415/863–3516. AE, MC, V. Closed Mon. No lunch weekends. $$*

2 *e-2*
ORITALIA
The name tips you off as to what you'll find at this stylish eatery: the foods of the Orient—Korea, Japan, China, Thailand, Vietnam—and, of course, Italy. Eastern highlights include Korean beef with sesame seeds, crispy shrimp and pork dumplings with cilantro-mint sauce, and portobello mushrooms topped with plum sauce. From the West, there's chicken with celery root purée and artichokes, and a fine linguine with littleneck clams and tomato broth, among other choices. Small plates make up much of the menu, encouraging diners to share. Textured walls, Japanese art, and handsome pillars contribute to the sleek look of the dining room. *1915 Fillmore St., between Bush and Pine Sts., Pacific Heights, 415/346–1333. AE, DC, MC, V. No lunch. $$*

5 *g-3*
WORLD WRAPPS
What's being wrapped here is a bevy of global burritos: Everything from Peking duck to teriyaki tofu is stuffed inside a plain, spinach, or tomato tortilla. High energy, good-for-you fruit smoothies—papaya, blackberry, banana-date—are paired with the hearty wrapps, which can be eaten on the spot or easily toted away. Not surprisingly, the crowd is mostly young, athletic, and enthusiastic about the food. That enthusiasm has translated into new locations springing up all over the Bay Area. *2257 Chestnut St., between Pierce and Scott Sts., The Marina, 415/563–9727. No credit cards. $*

4 *c-4*

2227 Polk St., between Vallejo and Green Sts., Russian Hill, 415/931–9727.

ENGLISH

7 *g-1*
MAD DOG IN THE FOG
British expats regularly turn up at this soccer-crazy pub as early as 6 AM to catch major matches on cable TV. Later on, they come back for pub grub and pints. Shepherd's pie, bangers and mash, ploughman's lunch, and a few

sandwiches are as fancy as it gets, but the crowd is loyal—thanks especially to the well-used dart board. For those who care, there's a major bar-towel collection. *530 Haight St., between Fillmore and Steiner Sts., Lower Haight, 415/626–7279. No credit cards. $*

ETHIOPIAN

7 *d-1*
MASSAWA
Named for the Eritrean city of Massawa, this Haight Street favorite serves all the traditional Ethiopian fare, from stews to vegetarian dishes to vegetable fritters laced with chili. The dishes—*doro wat* (spicy chicken stew), red and yellow lentils with braised greens, fish and vegetables, and others—are piled on *injera*, a large, round, slightly spongy flat bread that serves as plate and utensil: just tear off a corner, scoop up some lentils, and you've got a mouthful. There's a sidebar of Italian food as well. The dining room is dressed up with basketry and African fabrics. *1538 Haight St., between Ashbury and Clayton Sts., The Haight, 415/621–4129. MC, V. Closed Mon. $*

7 *a-2*
NEW ERITREA RESTAURANT
The best way to enjoy this place is to go with a group and order two combinations, one with meat and one without. The meat selection will include lamb, beef, and chicken, while the nonmeat dishes usually feature squash, okra, and mixed vegetables. Don't pass up the *berberé*, the dynamite chili sauce of East Africa. The simply decorated dining room stands beyond a friendly front-room bar. *907 Irving St., near 10th Ave., Sunset District, 415/681–1288. MC, V. No lunch Mon. $*

5 *g-6*
RASSELAS
Along with some of the best Ethiopian food in the city, you get first-rate jazz at Rasselas. The dining room adjoins a large bar where musicians start playing after 9 PM, so if you want to carry on a dinner conversation easily, eat early. The traditional meat and vegetable stews are served on a round of the Ethiopian bread called injera. Try several different dishes in order to sample the culinary talents of the chef, who was a well-known cook in Ethiopia. *2801 California*

St., at Divisadero St., Pacific Heights, 415/567–5010. AE, MC, V. $$

FRENCH

4 b-8

ABSINTHE

The name is taken from the long-banned, cloudy green liqueur that turn-of-the-century Europeans sipped with abandon. But the menu, which includes such fare as cassis-braised short ribs, squab with risotto, and ricotta dumplings with truffles, is up-to-date French with Mediterranean and Californian touches. A cold seafood bar, a bar menu, and a first-rate selection of imported French cheeses add to the appeal. From the day it opened, in 1998, the sophisticated space of burgundy walls, yards of dark wood, and luxurious banquettes drew the city's social set like politicians to a fundraiser. 398 Hayes St., at Gough St., Civic Center, 415/551–1590. AE, DC, MC, V. Closed Mon. No lunch. $$–$$$

4 e-5

ANJOU

French expats swoon for the sautéed calves' brain seasoned with sage, and the asparagus spears in puff pastry with a morel sauce. Just steps away from the hubbub of Union Square, this comfortable French bistro on two levels is ideal for folks looking for a place to dine before heading to the theater. Duck confit fans should not pass up the kitchen's excellent rendition. 44 Campton Pl., between Post and Sutter Sts. and Grant and Stockton Sts., Union Square, 415/392–5373. AE, D, MC, V. Closed Sun.–Mon. $$

5 g-3

BAKER STREET BISTRO

Not much bigger than a postage stamp, the Baker Street bistro has a four-course menu that's one of the best bargains in town. If you decide to order à la carte, you can choose from such Gallic standards as snails cooked with butter and garlic, rabbit in mustard sauce, and lamb stew with vegetables. On Friday and Saturday nights the dinner crowd spreads into the café space that the owners operate next door. 2953 Baker St., between Greenwich and Lombard Sts., Cow Hollow, 415/931–1475. MC, V. Closed Mon. $–$$

5 h-3

BISTRO AIX

Named for the southern French town of Aix-en-Provence, Bistro Aix is a classic, with banquettes, paper-top tablecloths, and friendly service. On weekdays there's a bargain two-course prix fixe dinner of soup or salad, plus roast chicken, sirloin steak, or seafood pasta. Thin, crisp-crust pizzas, salads of young, tender greens, house-baked breads, and fruit tarts are all worth ordering à la carte. 3340 Steiner St., between Lombard and Chestnut Sts., The Marina, 415/202–0100. MC, V. No lunch. $–$$

4 g-5

BISTRO RÔTI

Reserve a table in the rear of this handsome waterside restaurant, so you can enjoy a view of the San Francisco Bay and the Bay Bridge and avoid the cacophonous bar scene. In the center of the space, a giant wood-burning rotisserie and grill turn out crisp-skinned roast chickens, succulent chops, game, and seafood. A bowl of the Rôti's deeply flavored onion soup will take off the chill of a foggy San Francisco night. 155 Steuart St., between Mission and Howard Sts., The Embarcadero, 415/495–6500. AE, DC, MC, V. No lunch weekends. $$

4 g-8

BIZOU

Award-winning chef Loretta Keller prepares homey bistro fare in this small, sunny dining room. Regulars point to the thin, crisp pizza topped with caramelized onions, featherlight batter-fried green beans, and grilled sardines as evidence of Keller's ability—though first courses tend to outshine the mains. Imaginative yet familiar desserts such as berry pudding (in warmer months only) and crème brûlée are a good way to cap off any meal. *598 4th St., at Brannan St., South of Market, 415/543–2222. AE, MC, V. Closed Sun. No lunch Sat. $$*

4 f-5
CAFÉ BASTILLE

The Bastille has a double life: It's a midday destination for suits who hunger for onion soup or a few slices of pâté; and it's also a nighttime haunt for folks in search of jazz along with their poulet rôti. When weather permits, the outdoor tables are hard-won. Every year on Bastille Day, this simple bistro, along with its French neighbors, celebrates as if this were Paris instead of San Francisco. *22 Belden St., between Bush and Pine Sts. and Kearny and Montgomery Sts., Financial District, 415/986–5673. AE, MC, V. Closed Sun. $–$$*

4 e-5
CAFÉ CLAUDE

A favorite spot of Francophiles, Café Claude is hidden in an alley in the heart of San Francisco's French quarter. A zinc bar, comfy banquettes, and posters that once outfitted a Paris bar create a suitably Gallic scene, and on mild days the tables spill into the alley in true French form. Order a *croque monsieur* (grilled ham-and-cheese sandwich), some pâté, a salade niçoise, or a simple daube and dream of the City of Light. *7 Claude La., off Bush St., Financial District, 415/392–3505. AE, DC, MC, V. Closed Sun. $*

4 e-3
CAFÉ JACQUELINE

This cozy storefront operation is a serious soufflé outpost. The egg-leavened concoctions arrive at the white-cloth-topped tables in fine form: tall and puffy, with a crusty crown and a savory or sweet interior. There are a couple of salads and plenty of French bread to accompany the towering soufflés, which are made with wild mushrooms, broccoli and cheese, or spinach, among other ingredients. Consider dropping by after dinner for one of chef Jacqueline's billowy chocolate creations. *1454 Grant Ave., between Green and Union Sts., North Beach, 415/981–5565. MC, V. Closed Mon.–Tues. No lunch. $$*

4 c-7
CALIFORNIA CULINARY ACADEMY

Housed in a historic theater, this vies with the Culinary Institute of America's Greystone in the Napa Valley for the label of top professional cooking school on the West Coast. In the theaterlike Carême Room, with its showy columns and fancy chandeliers, you can watch the student chefs at work on the double-tier stage while dining on classic French cooking offered as a prix fixe meal or a bountiful buffet; on the prix fixe nights, you may even be treated to tablelike service—order a flambéed dessert for a show. The Academy Grill, an à la carte informal dining room on the lower level, serves casual student-cooked fare such as fried chicken and seafood gumbo. *625 Polk St., at Turk St., The Tenderloin, 415/771–3500. Reservations essential for Fri.-night buffet. AE, DC, MC, V. Closed weekends. $$–$$$*

5 h-3
CASSIS BISTRO

Sit down in this small, sunny yellow bistro and you'll feel as if you've been transported to a town in the south of France. The servers have charming Gallic accents, and the food—warm sausage slices resting in rounds cut from a slice of bread, onion tart, spinach ravioli, veal ragout—has the appeal of good home cooking. If the chef has made tarte Tatin, be sure to sample a wedge. *2120 Greenwich St., between Webster and Fillmore Sts., Cow Hollow, 415/292–0770. No credit cards. Closed Sun.–Mon. No lunch. $–$$*

5 b-7
CHAPEAU!

About a dozen hats hang on the walls of this small, light-filled dining room—thus the name. The food has a contemporary French bistro flair: snails in garlic butter, wilted bitter greens with crisp bits of bacon and a poached egg, sweetbreads on parslied mashed potatoes, and a near-perfect crème brûlée. The lovely wine list is a pleasant surprise in such a small restaurant. *1408 Clement St., near 15th Ave., Richmond District, 415/750–9787. AE, DC, MC, V. Closed Mon. No lunch. $$*

4 d-5
CHARLES NOB HILL

Elegant and pricey, this small, formal restaurant is housed in what was once a private club. It still has a slightly exclusive mood; most of the men in the dining room wouldn't be caught dead without a tie except on the golf course. The food is contemporary French; sautéed scallops served with fennel risotto, parchment-cooked fish with red pepper rouille, and pan-roasted poussin are among the favorites. A five-course tasting menu lets you sample the full range. *1250 Jones St., between Sacramento and Clay Sts., Nob Hill, 415/771–5400. Reservations essential. AE, DC, MC, V. Closed Mon. No lunch. $$$$*

4 *c-2*

CHEZ MICHEL

The sophisticated kitchen and elegant-yet-streamlined look of Chez Michel attract a clientele with high expectations and fat pocketbooks. They sit down to seared foie gras with passion-fruit vinaigrette, accompanied by a salad of greens and pear; or stuffed guinea-hen breast with lemon risotto. Owner Michel Elkaim is usually present in the dining room, watching over the service staff and greeting the diners. *804 North Point St., at Hyde St., Fisherman's Wharf, 415/775–7036. Reservations essential. AE, DC, MC, V. Closed Sun.–Mon. No lunch. $$$$*

4 *e-4*

DES ALPES

This old-fashioned restaurant harkens back to a time when North Beach was home to a handful of boardinghouses catering to Basque residents. Huge, modestly priced dinners are the custom: soup, salad, *two* entrées—panfried sand dabs and roast leg of lamb are a typical pair—ice cream, and coffee. With wood-paneled walls and bright cloths on the tables, it's an unpretentious spot with family-style service and a crowd of all ages. *732 Broadway, between Stockton and Powell Sts., North Beach, 415/788–9900. D, DC, MC, V. Closed Mon. No lunch. $*

4 *d-5*

FLEUR DE LYS

With its elegantly canopied dining room, this romantic, pricey Union Square showplace has long been one of the premier French restaurants in town. Chef-partner Hubert Keller's creative cuisine can be sampled in preset menus, including a vegetarian one, or from an à la carte list. The dishes change constantly, but you can count on finding lobster bisque, salmon with wild mushrooms, and seared venison medallions most of

the time. Desserts are heavenly, and the wine list is impressive. *777 Sutter St., between Taylor and Jones Sts., Union Square, 415/673–7779. Reservations essential. AE, DC, MC, V. Closed Sun. $$$$*

4 *g-8*

FRINGALE

Chef Gerald Hirigoyen has put his dazzling bistro on the regular route of a well-turned-out crowd from the Financial District and beyond, although his reasonable prices draw everyday pocketbooks, too. They come for his French Basque–inspired dishes such as *frisée aux lardons* (curly endive with bacon) steamed mussels, bouillabaisse, and duck confit. Hirigoyen trained as a pastry chef in Paris, so leave room for one of the fine desserts for which this kitchen is known—crème brûlée is a must. The small dining room, with classic bistro wood furniture and paper-topped white cloths, will make you dream of the City of Light. *570 4th St., between Bryant and Brannan Sts., South of Market, 415/543–0573. Reservations essential. AE, MC, V. Closed Sun. No lunch Sat. $$*

4 *c-4*

LA FOLIE

You can explore the elegant food at this pretty storefront restaurant by ordering the five-course set meal or by selecting from the à la carte menu. Chef Roland Passot creates seasonally changing, artful presentations in the form of tasty terrines, tender *galettes* (flat, round cakes), and savory napoleons. The roasted birds—quail, squab—are always excellent; but so is everything else Passot dreams up. *2316 Polk St., between Green and Union Sts., Russian Hill, 415/776–5577. Reservations essential. AE, D, DC, MC, V. Closed Sun. No lunch. $$$–$$$$*

4 *e-5*

LE CENTRAL

Power lunchers have occupied the tables and stood alongside the zinc bar in this quintessential bistro for years. All the classics are served here—leeks vinaigrette, steak with Roquefort sauce, cassoulet, grilled blood sausage with crisp french fries—although not always with the finesse they deserve. The service generally shines, however, especially if you are in the company of regulars. *453 Bush St., between Kearny St. and Grant Ave., Financial District, 415/391–2233. AE, DC, MC, V. Closed Sun. $$*

4 f-7

LE CHARM

In the early '90s, Alain Delangle and Linda Yew, a formidable culinary husband-and-wife team, opened this cozy bistro, complete with outdoor patio, in a plain-Jane strip of SoMa. It was wildly popular almost immediately. The prix fixe dinner is an unqualified bargain, with a choice of sautéed chicken livers on a tangle of greens, or rich onion soup; followed by roast chicken with puréed potatoes, or salmon on a bed of greens. Yew's tarte Tatin is outstanding. *315 5th St., between Folsom and Harrison Sts., South of Market, 415/546–6128. MC, V. Closed Sun. No dinner Mon. No lunch Sat. $*

4 e-5

MASA'S

This legendary flower-filled dining spot, with its burgundy walls and small marble bar, is housed in the Vintage Court Hotel. Chef Julian Serrano carries on the tradition of the late Masa Kobayashi, who put Masa's on the national map. Pricey items such as foie gras and black truffles figure largely on the menu in such intriguing preparations as foie gras sautéed with Madeira truffle sauce. There's also a fine boudin of lobster, shrimp, and scallops, and a fillet of black bass with saffron sauce. Book a table at least two weeks in advance. *648 Bush St., between Stockton and Monroe Sts., Union Square, 415/989–7154. Reservations essential. AE, D, DC, MC, V. Closed Sun.–Mon. and 1st 2 wks of Jan. No lunch. $$$$*

4 f-3

PASTIS

A cement bar, exposed brick walls, and handsome wooden banquettes give Pastis a casual yet upmarket ambience. At lunchtime, well-heeled workers from the surrounding blocks come in for prawns marinated in pastis (anise-flavored French liqueur), and seared scallops with leeks. The evening menu may include foie gras with a verjus sauce, lamb with rosemary, or duck confit. If you're not a fan of oxtails, you may well become one when you try the braised oxtails with *sauce gribiche* (an oil-based sauce of hard-boiled egg yolks, capers, gherkins, and herbs). *1015 Battery St., near Green St., The Embarcadero, 415/391–2555. AE, MC, V. Closed Sun. No lunch Sat. $$*

4 f-5

PLOUF

The catchy name means "splash," a good moniker for this sleek spot with its mussel-heavy menu. There are seven hefty-portioned mussel preparations from which to choose, including *marinière* (garlic and parsley), apple cider, leeks and cream, and crayfish and tomato. Big appetites might want to start with a mixed seafood salad or crab cakes. French vintages are well represented on the carefully selected wine list. *40 Belden St., between Bush and Pine Sts. and Kearny and Montgomery Sts., Financial District, 415/986–6491. MC, V. Closed Sun. No lunch Sat. $$*

4 e-5

RITZ-CARLTON DINING ROOM AND TERRACE

This Nob Hill showplace holds both The Dining Room, a pricey, formal space with urbane French cuisine served in three- to five-course dinners; and The Terrace, which has a garden patio for outdoor dining and hosts a popular Sunday brunch with live jazz. The Dining Room executive chef is Sylvain Portay, previously chef de cuisine at New York's celebrated Le Cirque. *600 Stockton St., at Pine St., Nob Hill, 415/296–7465. AE, D, DC, MC, V. The Dining Room: closed Sun; no lunch. $$$–$$$$*

4 g-7

SOUTH PARK CAFE

Tucked into a pleat of the city's hip Multimedia Gulch, South Park Cafe is an utterly Gallic stop. An order of frisée (curly endive) with baked goat cheese, steak with pommes frites, *boudin noir* (blood sausage) with sautéed apples, or perfectly cooked duck breast is solid evidence of the kitchen's commitment to the Paris culinary tradition. Weekdays, you can grab a simple breakfast of café au lait and a croissant while practicing your French with the wait staff. *108 South Park Ave., between 2nd and 3rd Sts. and Bryant and Brannan Sts., South of Market, 415/495–7275. MC, V. Closed Sun. No lunch Sat. $$*

8 a-2

TI COUZ

When crepes came back into fashion in the mid-'90s, this Breton-style crêperie was leading the pack. Working in an assembly-line setup, cooks wrap the large, thin pancakes around your choice of fillings—ratatouille, salmon, mushrooms, or spinach. The perfect accompaniments are green salad and hard cider, both available here. Cap off the feast with a sweet fruit- or chocolate-filled crepe. *3108 16th St., between Guerrero and Valencia Sts., Mission District, 415/252–7373. MC, V. $*

7 *d-2*
ZAZIE
When San Francisco's bone-chilling winds blow, those seeking comfort head to Zazie for a warming beef daube or some garlicky roast chicken. The staff of this small, brick-walled dining room serves waffles and omelets in the early morning, filling sandwiches midday, and full-scale dinners at night. The Provençal-style fish stew is a good bet, and the desserts, including wonderful fruit crisps, are homey and delicious. *941 Cole St., between Carl and Parnassus Sts., The Haight, 415/564–5332. No credit cards. $–$$*

GERMAN

4 *d-6*
GERMAN COOK
This tiny, no-frills downtown restaurant has a small counter with just a few stools and a wall of cozy wooden booths. The hearty fare is home-style, with such old-fashioned items as stuffed cabbage and meat loaf, ham hocks and bratwurst, sauerbraten, and stuffed pork chops. The small staff does a fine job, and always with a smile. *612 O'Farrell St., between Leavenworth and Hyde Sts., The Tenderloin, 415/776–9022. No credit cards. No lunch Sat.–Tues. $*

7 *h-6*
SPECKMANN'S
In the heart of San Francisco's original German neighborhood, Speckmann's houses both a delicatessen and a restaurant. The dining room, with its photographs of snowy mountain tops and atmospheric Dortmunder beer lanterns, brings to mind a *gasthaus* somewhere in the Black Forest. Among the generous entrées are veal kidneys in mushroom gravy and smoked pork chops with mashed potatoes, all best accompanied by a stein of any of the excellent German beers. *1550 Church St., at Duncan St., Noe Valley, 415/282–0565. MC, V. $$*

4 *b-8*
SUPPENKUCHE
At this hip outpost of German cuisine and brews, bratwurst and red cabbage are standards, along with smoked pork chops, schnitzel with spaetzle, and delicious house-made soups. The place is often crowded and strangers regularly end up seated together at the long, unfinished pine tables—a good way to meet new friends. There's also a bountiful weekend brunch. *601 Hayes St., at Laguna St., Hayes Valley, 415/252–9289. AE, MC, V. No lunch. $–$$*

GREEK

8 *e-3*
ASIMAKOPOULOS CAFÉ
A plate of assorted appetizers at this longstanding neighborhood haunt will allow you to taste everything from dolmas to *tiropetes* (phyllo-wrapped spinach triangles). Various meat kebab dishes are the best main-dish choices. A fortune teller will predict your fate on some nights. *288 Connecticut St., at 18th St., Potrero Hill, 415/552–8789. MC, V. No lunch Sat.–Sun. $$*

DESPERATELY SEEKING CAFFEINE

San Franciscans are fussy about their coffee, which means there's stiff competition among espresso purveyors.

Antica Trattoria (Italian)
The espresso is short and serious.

Café Claude (French)
Where Francophiles take their café express.

Mario's Bohemian Cigar Store Café (Italian)
The cappucino is the neighborhood benchmark.

Pacific Restaurant No. 2 (Vietnamese)
Ultraslow-drip Vietnamese filtered coffee sweetened with condensed milk.

South Park Café (French)
Order a café au lait and pick up yesterday's Le Monde.

Vineria (Italian)
$1.35 for a stellar espresso.

Zuni Café & Grill (Mediterranean)
Icy espresso granita laced with a ribbon of cream.

INDIAN

7 *c-2*

THE GANGES

Strictly vegetarian food—no eggs, no gelatin—is served at this small storefront restaurant. Waitresses in saris deliver delicious curries of potato and cauliflower with black mustard seeds or "meatballs" made with black-eyed peas. The *pakoras* (vegetable fritters) are featherlight and served with two chutneys. On some nights, live Indian music helps set the mood. *775 Frederick St., between Arguello Blvd. and Willard St., The Haight, 415/661–7290. MC, V. Closed Sun., Mon. No lunch. $–$$*

4 *b-2*

GAYLORD'S

A tandoor oven is used to prepare the mildly spiced foods of northern India: delicate salmon, succulent lamb, and other tempting choices. The kitchen falters on occasion, but beautiful bay views help keep diners happy. The elegant dining rooms are full of handsome Indian antiques and fine fabrics in rich browns, greens, and golds. The daily lunch is replaced with brunch on Sundays. *Ghirardelli Sq., 900 North Point St., at Polk St., Fisherman's Wharf, 415/771–8822. AE, D, DC, MC, V. No lunch Sun. $$—$$$*

7 *g-1*

INDIAN OVEN

Tandoori chicken is arguably the best thing to order at this Victorian storefront restaurant. The bird arrives succulent and flavorful, complemented by breads and vegetarian curries. A complete meal, called a *thali* for the metal plate on which it arrives, includes a choice of entrée, plus soup, a curried vegetable, basmati rice, nan, and chutney. *223 Fillmore St., between Haight and Waller Sts., Lower Haight, 415/626–1628. MC, V. No lunch. $$*

4 *e-3*

KAMAL PALACE

Although the specialties of northern India are listed first on the menu here, look for the southern specialties, including *masala dosa*, a large, thin, crisp crepe filled with potatoes, onions, and chilies. The vegetarian dishes are stellar, including *saag paneer*, creamy spinach with cubes of Indian cheese; a flavorful roasted eggplant with onions and toma-

toes; and a tasty yellow dal. Finish your meal with a bowl of the pistachio-coated ice cream known as *kulfi*. The service can be absent-minded, so bring a measure of patience. *641 Vallejo St., near Columbus Ave., North Beach, 415/421–1132. AE, MC, V. $–$$*

2 *e-1*

NORTH INDIA

An old-timer among the city's Indian restaurants, the burgundy-outfitted North India has long seduced a regular clientele with its fine tandoori preparations. The kitchen is visible behind glass walls, so you can easily watch as chickens, shrimp, and lamb speared on long skewers are slipped into the clay oven. The curries are tasty as well, and the breads are addictive. The service is uneven, but the spicy fare is worth the inconvenience. *3131 Webster St., between Moulton and Lombard Sts., Cow Hollow, 415/931–1556. AE, DC, MC, V. No lunch Sat., Sun. $$*

INDONESIAN

5 *c-8*

JAKARTA

Batik, shadow puppets, and masks from Indonesia decorate this handsome representative of Southeast Asian cuisine. Seating is in two dining rooms, both with white walls and dark carpeting. Shrimp cakes, with fruit chutney for dipping, or spicy ground fish cooked in a banana leaf are good ways to start. Follow up with satay dipped in creamy peanut sauce; the long-cooked *gudeg* (curry) of beef and jackfruit; or chili-coated fried chicken. *615 Balboa St., between 7th and 8th Aves., Richmond District, 415/387–5225. AE, D, MC, V. Closed Mon. No lunch Sat., Sun. $$*

IRISH

4 *e-3*

O'REILLY IRISH PUB AND RESTAURANT

If you're looking for corned beef and cabbage, head for this lively pub-cum-restaurant. The dish, which also includes potatoes and turnips, is considerably more sophisticated than what is served in most pubs in Ireland, but the Gaelic spirit is intact. You can also order steak-and-kidney pie, finnan haddie (smoked

haddock), Irish stew (lamb and potatoes), and roast chicken and *champ*
(mashed potatoes with green onions),
all in hearty portions. Chase your meal
with one of the many brews on tap. *622
Green St., between Powell and Stockton
Sts., North Beach, 415/989–6222. AE, MC,
V. $$*

ITALIAN

4 *c-5*
ACQUERELLO
This quiet restaurant, one of the most
romantic spots in town, serves contem-
porary Italian food in an elegant setting
of watercolors and fine table service.
Ingredients of the highest quality are
assembled into memorable plates that,
understandably, don't come cheaply.
The gnocchi and tortellini are always fla-
vorful and refined, and the fish dishes
and stuffed roasted quail are superb.
*1722 Sacramento St., between Polk St.
and Van Ness Ave., Nob Hill, 415/567–
5432. Reservations essential. AE, D, DC,
MC, V. Closed Sun., Mon. No lunch. $$$*

4 *c-3*
ANTICA TRATTORIA
Classy yet straightforward in both food
and atmosphere, this charming neighborhood restaurant has a small but
intriguing menu and a first-rate kitchen.
For a great opener, order the antipasto of
coppa, cured pork-sausage slices topped
with a few fresh fava beans and a thread
of extra-virgin olive oil; or chicken liver–
topped crostini. Rare venison medal-
lions, roasted whole bass, and beef fillet
riding atop polenta are among the main
courses. For dessert, the custard topped
with berries and cream is delectable.
*2400 Polk St., at Union St., Russian Hill,
415/928–5797. AE, DC, MC, V. Closed
Mon. No lunch. $$–$$$*

8 *e-3*
APERTO
Portrero Hill's restaurant community is
centered on the corner of 18th and Connecticut streets, and Aperto is one its
most important members. The food is
generous and rustic, from polenta
topped with gorgonzola to penne tossed
with eggplant. Braised lamb shanks and
roast chicken with olives are among the
main courses. A pair of big picture windows brings light and openness to the
always-bustling dining room. *1434 18th
St., at Connecticut St., Portrero Hill, 415/
252–1625. No reservations. MC, V. $$*

4 *b-8*
CAFFE DELLE STELLE
The food at this cheerful trattoria is
homey and hearty and the portions are
bountiful—the kitchen's faithful fans
love to eat the big bowls of pasta tossed
with sausage, eggplant, tomatoes, and
greens. The brightly dressed dining
room has a familial Italian feel, and
large windows on two sides keep diners
up to date on who's heading to the
nearby opera house. Those in the know
cap off their meals with an order of the
excellent tiramisù. *395 Hayes St., near
Gough St., Hayes Valley, 415/252–1110.
MC, V. Closed Sun. $$*

4 *d-3*
CAPPS'S CORNER
This North Beach favorite is a throwback to the days when family-style Italian dinners were the neighborhood
norm. Hearty meals of minestrone, a

CITY VIEWS

*A number of restaurant views make it
easy to understand why San Francisco is one of the most-photographed
cities in the United States.*

**Beach Chalet (American Contem-
porary)**
*Toward sundown, the Pacific
Ocean seascape turns an inky
black.*

Bistro Roti (French)
*Ferryboats skim along the bay
toward Alameda and beyond.*

Greens (Vegetarian)
*Sailboats bob in nearby slips,
with a backdrop of the Golden
Gate Bridge.*

Julius' Castle (Italian)
*Treasure Island, Alcatraz, the
East Bay hills, and both bridges.*

McCormick & Kuleto's (Seafood)
*Look for hardy swimmers in the
San Francisco Bay.*

Mad Dog in the Fog (English)
A gritty urban sidewalk scene.

Moose's (Mediterranean)
*A bird's-eye view of Washington
Square.*

green salad, pasta (usually with tomato sauce or pesto), a main course (the roast lamb or beef is a good choice), and dessert (spumoni) are served at old-fashioned prices. The tables are covered with red-and-white-checkered cloths, and the bar is a friendly slice of yesteryear. *1600 Powell St., at Green St., North Beach, 415/989–2589. MC, V. No lunch Sat., Sun. $*

4 *d-3*
GIRA POLLI

A large Palermo-built rotisserie capable of holding scores of rotating birds stands near the center of the handsome dining room. The big, succulent, garlic-and-herb-rubbed roast chickens are served with potatoes and crusty bread rolls. There's a good selection of salads to start, and tasty cheesecake to finish. A steady stream of nearby residents stops by for takeout. *659 Union St., between Columbus Ave. and Powell St., North Beach, 415/434–4472. MC, V. No lunch. $*

4 *f-3*
IL FORNAIO

This upscale trattoria, with its hand-painted ceiling and marble counters, has a lovely outdoor seating area as well as a heated patio. The kitchen is known for its pizzas from a wood-burning oven, including one with gorgonzola, onions, and pine nuts. The various pastas are popular too, as are the spit-roasted meats, including rabbit. Special Italian regional menus are available on occasion. *Levi's Plaza, 1265 Battery St., between Filbert and Greenwich Sts., The Embarcadero, 415/986–0100. AE, DC, MC, V. $$*

5 *h-5*
JACKSON FILLMORE TRATTORIA

The atmosphere in this simply decorated Upper Fillmore trattoria is infectiously festive, and the southern Italian food is a hit. Grilled portobello mushrooms served on a tangle of arugula, mammoth-sized artichokes stuffed with herbed crumbs, or tomato-topped bruschetta are good ways to start a meal. The pastas are paired with full-flavored sauces, and the main courses of baked fish and chicken with sausage and mushrooms are satisfying. There's a long counter as well as tables. Reservations are taken only for parties of three or more; otherwise,

expect a wait. *2506 Fillmore St., near Jackson St., Pacific Heights, 415/346–5288, MC, V. No lunch. $$*

4 *e-3*
JULIUS' CASTLE

Arguably, this restaurant claims the best view in the city: both bridges, Treasure Island, Alcatraz, sailboats on the San Francisco Bay, and the curve of the East Bay hills. In the past, the food was no match for the stunning panorama, but in recent years it has improved, with some decent—albeit pricey—pastas and antipasti available. The grilled salmon fillet with fava beans and caramelized onions is a good choice, as is the pheasant with seared polenta. *1541 Montgomery St., between Greenwich and Lombard Sts., Telegraph Hill, 415/392–2222. Reservations essential. AE, DC, MC, V. No lunch. $$$*

4 *e-6*
KULETO'S

The contemporary cooking of Northern Italy, the atmosphere of old San Francisco—imparted in part by the large, beautiful carved bar—and a terrific bar menu showcasing contemporary and traditional antipasti have made Kuleto's a hit since it opened more than a decade ago. Comfortable booths and an open kitchen fill one side of the restaurant; a skylighted room lies beyond. The chefs are not always in top form, but the lively ambience keeps the crowds coming. The adjoining Caffè Kuleto dispenses coffees, morning pastries, and sandwiches. *221 Powell St., at O'Farrell St., Union Square, 415/397–7720. AE, D, DC, MC, V. $$*

4 *e-3*
L'OSTERIA DEL FORNO

A truly low-tech kitchen—everything is done in a little oven or on simple burners—turns out some of the neighborhood's best Italian food: tiny white onions dressed in balsamic vinegar, tuna-and-white-bean salad, polenta with gorgonzola, thin-crust pizzas, pork cooked in milk, sandwiches of house-made focaccia. A handful of tables fills the two front windows, and the staff is always friendly and helpful. *519 Columbus Ave., between Union and Green Sts., North Beach, 415/982–1124. No reservations. No credit cards. Closed Tues. $–$$*

4 e-3

MARIO'S BOHEMIAN CIGAR STORE CAFÉ

There is a wonderful conviviality in this narrow space overlooking Washington Square. Neighborhood denizens ease their way through the crowd to a table or a counter-side stool to down a powerful espresso made with beans from nearby Graffeo's coffee store or to munch on a thick meatball sandwich on focaccia from a nearby bakery. There are sandwiches of chicken or turkey and mozzarella and a wonderful, old-fashioned tuna melt; the cannelloni is another good choice. A slice of ricotta cheesecake is the sentimental finish. The branch on Polk Street between Green and Vallejo lacks the same charm. *566 Columbus Ave., at Union St., North Beach, 415/362–0536. No credit cards. $*

4 c-4

2209 Polk St., between Vallejo and Green Sts., Russian Hill, 415/776–8226.

3 e-4

OLIVETO

Celebrated throughout the Bay Area, this superb Italian restaurant on the corner of a bustling gourmet markeplace shows off the considerable culinary skills of famed chef and co-owner Paul Bertolli. He prepares such classics as chicken cooked under a brick, ravioli stuffed with pumpkin, a salad of grilled quail and greens, house-made sausages, and simply grilled fresh fish. The dining room has an elegant yet comfortable ambience, and the service is attentive without being intrusive. *5655 College Ave., at Shafter St., Oakland, 510/547–5356. Reservations essential. AE, DC, MC, V. No lunch Sat., Sun. $$$*

4 f-5

PALIO D'ASTI

Suits from surrounding offices swarm here at lunchtime for Piedmontese dishes such as fresh ravioli in sage-butter sauce, and thin-crust pizzas topped with prosciutto and arugula. A second branch, called Paninoteca Palio d'Asti, is a hit for its stylish takeout or eat-in lunchtime *panini* (Italian sandwiches) on house-made bread. Both are lunch-only establishments, keeping what the management calls bankers' hours. *640 Sacramento, near Kearny St., Financial District, 415/395–9800. AE, MC, V. Closed Sat.–Sun. No dinner. $$–$$$*

4 f-5

505 Montgomery St., at Sacramento St., Financial District, 415/362–6900. $

5 h-4

PANE E VINO

The Italian-born owner-chef favors the dishes of Tuscany and northern Italy, with roasted whole fish, braised rabbit, *vitello tonnato* (cold veal with a tuna sauce), and comforting risotto among the popular choices. The small, rustic dining room has wooden furniture and bright white walls punctuated with colorful pottery. Expect a long wait for a table if you haven't made reservations. *3011 Steiner St., between Union and Filbert Sts., Cow Hollow, 415/346–2111. Reservations essential. MC, V. No lunch Sun. $$–$$$*

5 h-3

PASTA POMODORO

This is the first location of a homegrown multibranch Italian pasta operation where good-quality pasta, salads, and sandwiches cost less than a first-run-movie ticket. The tiny storefront has counter seating only, and folks queue up to eat noodles tossed with gorgonzola and cream; penne with puttanesca sauce; and spaghetti tossed with scallops, squid, and mussels. The salads range from simple tossed greens to more elaborate concoctions with vegetables, cheeses, and olives. *2027 Chestnut St., near Fillmore St., The Marina, 415/474–3400. No reservations. No credit cards. $*

4 d-3

655 Union St., near Columbus Ave., North Beach, 415/399–0300.

7 g-2

2304 Market St., between 16th and Noe Sts., The Castro, 415/558–8123.

7 a-2

9th Ave. and Irving St., Sunset District, 415/566–0900.

4 e-3

ROSE PISTOLA

Named for one of North Beach's best-known barkeeps, Rose Pistola is a wildly successful outpost of Italian food with a contemporary flair. The menu favors the dishes of Liguria, plus some local favorites such as cioppino, a tomato-laced seafood stew. The assortment of antipasti—roasted peppers, house-cured fish, fava beans and pecorino cheese, baby artichokes—is every bit as interesting as the mains, such as whole roasted fish, and rabbit with polenta. A crowd of regulars fills the dining room and the large and inviting bar area, and often, the sidewalk tables outside. *532 Columbus Ave., between Union and Green Sts., North Beach, 415/399–0499. Reservations essential. AE, DC, MC, V. $$*

4 *e-5*

SCALA'S BISTRO

A smart bilevel dining room and a large, intriguing menu have given this hotel restaurant a sterling reputation. Carpaccio topped with slivers of raw artichoke and Parmesan cheese, grilled portobello mushrooms, and a tower of fried calamari are among the best antipasti, while the pastas and grilled meats and poultry, including a bronzed roast chicken, satisfy most main-course appetites. The kitchen's Bostoni cream pie, a rich custard-and-orange chiffon cake topped with chocolate sauce, is too rich for good health—and very popular. *432 Powell St., between Post and Sutter Sts., Union Square, 415/395–8555. Reservations essential. AE, DC, MC, V. $$*

2 *f-4*

VINERIA

A long, slim space with a brushed-metal bar, track lights, and sleek, colorful chairs, Vineria is a welcome addition to the hip, lively North Mission. Run by the same people who operate L'Osteria del Forno in North Beach (*see above*), Vineria serves many of the same dishes, including flavorful little balsamic-dressed onions, and fine "white pizzas" of mozzarella cheese and porcini. Pumpkin-stuffed ravioli with sage and butter, orecchiette tossed with broccoli rabe, and thin slices of rare roast beef with oven-roasted potatoes are simple and satisfying. *3228 16th St., between Guerrero and Dolores, Mission District, 415/552–3889. MC, V. Closed Mon.-Tues. No lunch. $–$$*

2 *e-2*

VIVANDE PORTA VIA

This pricey combination Italian delicatessen-restaurant draws a crowd at lunch and dinner for both its sit-down and takeout fare (a cold case that runs along one wall holds all kinds of Italian gourmet delicacies). The regularly changing menu lists half a dozen pastas and risottos, including a classic Sicilian pasta *alla Norma* (with eggplant), and northern specialties such as risotto with radicchio, pancetta, and pine nuts. *2125 Fillmore St., between California and Sacramento Sts., Pacific Heights, 415/346–4430. AE, DC, MC, V. $$$*

4 *c-7*

VIVANDE RISTORANTE

Owner-chef Carlo Middione, who also operates the popular Vivande in Pacific Heights (*see above*), oversees this sublime restaurant near the Opera House, a favorite after-hour supper stop. The menu is full of irresistible choices: grilled radicchio, pasta tossed with assorted mushrooms, bass dressed with lemony oil, and risotto laced with shrimp. *670 Golden Gate Ave., between Van Ness Ave. and Franklin St., Civic Center, 415/673–9245. AE, DC, MC, V. $$$*

4 *d-3*

WASHINGTON SQUARE BAR AND GRILL

National journalists, political power brokers, and other celebrities have long flocked to "the Washbag," drawn by its nightly piano music and the no-nonsense ambience of the darkly wainscoted dining room. The food is Italian with some Californian accents. Simply cooked fish, a mound of fried calamari, and a nicely seared veal chop are the best dishes here; the pastas are average at best. *1707 Powell St., at Union St., North Beach, 415/982–8123. AE, DC, MC, V. $$*

5 *g-3*

ZINZINO

The thin, oblong pizza topped with prosciutto and arugula is a favorite at this popular Chestnut Street destination, as is its cousin that comes crowned with chunks of fennel sausage and caramelized onions. Chianti-flavored mashed potatoes are paired with beef tenderloin, while roast chicken arrives with a salad of wiry greens, warm potatoes, and goat cheese. The desserts are good-sized and delectable, including house-made ice creams. The slim dining room ends in a patio for outdoor dining. *2355 Chestnut St., between Scott and Divisadero Sts., The Marina, 415/346–6623. MC, V. No lunch. $$*

JAPANESE

2 c-3
CLEMENT OKAZU YA

The *teishoku* (complete) dinners at this reasonably priced Japanese eatery are a remarkable buy. In fact, the hamachi sashimi dinner with a generous portion of the buttery yellowfin tuna, a bowl of miso soup, rice, pickles, and ice cream, is a downright steal. A large sushi selection is also modestly priced. There are a dozen interesting appetizer-sized dishes and a number of noodle and *donburi* (meat- or chicken-topped rice bowls) selections. *914 Clement St., between 10th and 11th Aves., Richmond District, 415/668–1638. MC, V. Closed Tues. $*

7 g-5
HAMANO SUSHI

Noe Valley residents pack into this small, serene sushi bar and restaurant in search of fresh fish and a masterful sushi hand. The sushi chef is particularly adept at assembling *makizushi*—rolls of vinegared rice and vegetables or fish in a seaweed wrapper. Dinner, served in the rear of the narrow restaurant, ranges from tempura to grilled fish; entrées are served with miso soup, rice, and a saucer of pickled vegetables. *1332 Castro St., between 24th and Jersey Sts., Noe Valley, 415/826–0825. MC, V. No lunch. $*

2 e-3
JUBAN

Yakiniku, or grilled beef, is the specialty at this large, contemporary restaurant. Down-draft grills installed in each table clear the smoke away from diners and keep the beef grilling over perfect heat. In addition to rib-eye, short ribs, and tongue, there are squid, scallops, and other items for cooking over the flames. The house-made pickles are addictive, and a fine selection of sake complements the meal. *Kinokuniya Bldg., 1581 Webster St., between Geary Blvd. and Post St., Japantown, 415/776–5822. AE, DC, MC, V. $$*

2 c-3
KABUTO SUSHI

Master sushi chef Sachio Kojima flashes his knives with the grace of a samurai warrior. Take a seat at the sushi bar and put yourself in his hands: A succession of exquisite sushi is sure to be your reward. In addition to first-rate sushi and sashimi, traditional Japanese dinners are served in the adjoining dining room, where tatami seating is available. *5116 Geary Blvd., between 15th and 16th Aves., Richmond District, 415/752–5652. MC, V. Closed Sun., Mon. No lunch. $$*

2 e-3
KUSHI TSURU

The specialties of this simple Japanese restaurant are deep-fried, skewered vegetables and meats served with a quartet of dips. Other sure-bet orders are the Osaka-style *battera sushi* (preserved fish molded with rice), and the eel and salmon dishes. Start with a small plate of sesame-tossed spinach or boiled soybeans. The long, narrow dining room opens onto one of the busiest passageways in the Japan Center. *Kintetsu Mall, Japan Center, between Webster and Laguna Sts., Japantown, 415/922–9902. AE, DC, MC, V. Closed Tues. $–$$*

4 f-6
KYO-YA

This extraordinarily authentic restaurant, housed in the historic Palace Hotel, serves tempuras, one-pot dishes, deep-fried and grilled meats, and more. The grilled bass is simple and exquisite, and eel on rice in a lacquer box is superb. The sleek, cypress sushi bar is manned by chefs from Japan, and the raw fish prices match their mastery. The lunch menu is more limited and more reasonably priced than the dinner list. *Palace Hotel, 2 New Montgomery St., at Stevenson St., South of Market, 415/546–5000. AE, D, DC, MC, V. Closed Sun. No lunch Mon. and Sat. $$–$$$*

2 e-3
MAKI

The owner, clad in a lovely kimono, watches over her tiny, attractive dining room, where many of the diners order the house special of *wappa meshi*, fish and/or vegetables steamed atop rice in individual bamboo steamers. The kitchen also delivers a fine sukiyaki and *shabu shabu* (raw beef cooked at the table in broth); and other Japanese standards—tempura, teriyaki—are given a respectable turn. Various sakes are available; ask the waitress to describe the selection. *Kinokuniya Building, Japan Center, between Fillmore and Webster Sts., Japantown, 415/921–5215. AE, MC, V. Closed Tues. No lunch. $$*

MIFUNE

You're often faced with a queue at this Japan Center institution—a testament to the quality of Mifune's signature thin, brown *soba* (buckwheat) and thick, white *udon* (wheat) noodles, all made on the premises. Served both hot and cold and with more than a score of toppings, they are well worth the wait. Pass the time by studying the fine plastic food models lined up in the front windows; they are a visual record of the menu. Seating is at rustic wooden tables. There is even a children's noodle dish that arrives aboard a bullet-train lookalike. *Kintetsu Building, Japan Center, between Webster and Laguna Sts., Japantown, 415/922–0337. Reservations not accepted. AE, D, DC, MC, V. $*

2 d-3

MURASAKI

A small sushi bar and four tables are all the seating this homey and comfortable little storefront holds. Sushi buffs come here for the perfectly fresh fish and the camaraderie of the crowd made up mostly of locals and discriminating Japanese. The rest of the menu is given over to tempura, a couple of noodle dishes, and a few appetizers. *211 Clement St., between 2nd and 3rd Aves., Richmond District, 415/668–7317. AE, MC, V. No lunch. $$*

7 h-2

NIPPON SUSHI

This offbeat wedge of a sushi bar has been around for years, and it still lacks an outdoor sign to identify it. The sushi is inexpensive and very good for the price, and the sushi makers are wonderfully eccentric. There's almost always a line, rain or shine, for one of the only two dozen or so seats. The rustic interior has the patina of a well-worn restaurant, which only adds to its charm. *314 Church St., at 15th St., The Castro, no phone. Reservations not accepted. No credit cards. Closed Sun. $*

2 e-2

SANPPO

Although this longtime family-operated restaurant has seen a recent change in management, it still serves an enormous selection of Japanese food—*nabemono* dishes (one-pot meals), grills, *donburi* (poultry- or meat-topped rice bowls), *udon* and *soba* (wheat and buck-wheat noodles, respectively), tempura, and sushi—and does it well. Wood screens and a wood ceiling impart a rustic air, and a good-size list of small dishes provides plenty of grazing possibilities. *Buchanan Mall, 1702 Post St., at Buchanan St., Japantown, 415/346–3486. Reservations not accepted. MC, V. Closed Mon. No lunch Sun. $*

4 d-5

SANRAKU

Here you'll find a two-fer: On one side is a boisterous, inexpensive restaurant with everything from sushi to teriyaki to tempura to *nabeyaki udon* (udon noodles topped with seafood, chicken, and vegetables); on the other side is a serene, 20-seat dining room serving *kaiseki* dinners (traditional seasonal menus that commonly number seven or more courses). The foods are exquisitely prepared and presented, each one made with ingredients at their peak of taste and texture. If you wish to go the formal route, reserve one day in advance. *704 Sutter St., at Taylor St., Union Square, 415/771–0803. AE, D, MC, V. Kaiseki meals dinner only. $–$$*

2 e-2

SUSHI-A

A television set, usually tuned to a ball game, keeps diners entertained. Those who are more interested in food watch the chef, who does magic with raw fish. A menu board lets eaters know which fish are featured that day. In addition to sushi, good choices are the light and crisp tempura; and the seafood *nabemono*, a one-pot dish packed with shellfish, noodles, and vegetables. Several tatami rooms at the rear of the dining room may be reserved for *kaiseki* (seasonal) feasts. *Buchanan Mall, 1737 Buchanan St., between Post and Sutter Sts., Japantown, 415/931–4685. AE, DC, MC, V. Closed Tues., Wed. $$*

KOREAN

2 d-3

BROTHERS RESTAURANT

The local Korean community fills up this smoky spot until the wee hours. They come mainly to sit down at a table-top grill and cook beef and short ribs, although other items such as beef heart and tongue, pork, and chicken are also available. Small bowls filled with everything from kimchi to sesame-doused spinach to tiny dried fish tossed with chilies arrive with your grilling order, along with rice and a clear soup. Be prepared to toss your smoky clothes in the washer when you get home. *4128 Geary Blvd., between 5th and 6th Aves., Richmond District, 415/387–7991. MC, V. $–$$*

2 b-3
KOREAN BUFFET
The drill here is do-it-yourself, meaning you select the food from long counters and carry it back to your table-top lava-rock grill. There are countless spicy pickles, various kimchi, seaweeds, cool bean sprouts tossed with sesame, and a fiery chili sauce for wrapping in lettuce leaves with your grilled meat and a knob of rice. A clear soup and steamed rice will help quell the flames, and orange slices are a nice cap to the meal. *6314 Geary Blvd., between 27th and 28th Aves., Richmond District, 415/221–0685. MC, V. $*

2 e-3
NEW KOREA HOUSE
If you are interested in tracking down an authentic Korean breakfast, this Japantown institution is where you'll find it. (The morning menu is hidden from anyone who doesn't read Korean, but you can usually charm the wait staff into doing a quick translation.) The authentic dishes include Korean sashimi, which combines raw tuna with cooked octopus, clams, julienned vegetables, strips of omelet, and pine nuts—just toss and eat. Standard grilling items are available, along with some tasty soups, noodles, and simmered casseroles. *1620 Post St., between Buchanan Mall and Laguna St., Japantown, 415/931–7834. MC, V. $$*

2 e-3
SEOUL GARDEN
Despite this restaurant's location in the East Wing of the Japan Center, it is strictly Korean. Beyond the handsome doorway, topped by a blue-tiled roof, are a bar and a pair of dining rooms. All the classics are here: skate tossed with fiery cold noodles, large *mandoo* (beef dumplings) in broth, fish and tofu casserole, grilled octopus, Korean-style steak tartare, grilled short ribs, and more. Check the board for the daily Korean specialties. *Japan Center, between Webster and Laguna Sts., Japantown, 415/563–7664. AE, DC, MC, V. $$*

MEDITERRANEAN

8 a-3
BRUNO'S
In the late 1930s, Bruno's was a favorite of local power brokers and fans of Italian-American food. After closing briefly in 1994, it made a comeback within several months, this time as one of the hottest dining and music spots in town. The smart, retro-'50s, giant red-leather booths—the only seating in the dining room—are conducive to intimate conversation. The menu changes regularly but always includes stylishly garnished fresh fish fillets. *2389 Mission St., between 19th and 20th Sts., Mission District, 415/550–7455. Reservations essential. MC, V. Closed Mon. No lunch. $$*

4 f-6
CAFFÈ MUSEO
When San Francisco's classy Museum of Modern Art opened in the mid-'90s, this equally classy eating spot, with its granite floors and leather directors' chairs, started serving throngs of art lovers. Its fare runs the gamut from hearty soups and grilled-vegetable or chicken focaccia sandwiches to saffron rice laced with rock shrimp, or couscous with vegetables. In the mornings, stop by for an espresso and one of their irresistible pastries. Next door to the museum's main entrance, it's primarily a lunch spot, but on Thursdays, when the museum stays open until 9 PM, the café follows suit. *151 3rd St., between Mission and Howard Sts., South of Market, 415/357–4500. MC, V. Closed Wed. No dinner Fri.–Tues. $*

3 c-1
LALIME'S
Berkeley denizens dote on this top-flight kitchen, which has a regular fixed-priced menu in addition to an enticing à la carte list. Both types of menu span the globe: You might find Moroccan couscous, French duck foie gras, Spanish paella, or Italian pasta tossed with springtime vegetables on any given night. The comfortable two-story space is bright and peaceful, and always crowded, so call ahead for reservations. Put your name on the mailing list to keep up on the restaurant's many special dinners. *1329 Gilman St., near Neilson St., Berkeley, 510/527–9838. MC, V. No lunch. $$*

4 *f-7*

LULU

Although founding chef Reed Hearon has left the scene, LuLu remains a magnet on the SoMa scene. The fritto misto of deep-fried artichoke hearts, fennel, and thin lemon slices is dynamite, as are the mussels roasted on an iron platter. Main courses, from spit-roasted rabbit to herb-laced pork roast, are generous and generally first-rate. The atmosphere in the bar is SRO and rather boisterous; a table in the smaller, quieter room off to one side makes dinner conversation easier. The café on the opposite side serves food from morning until late at night. *816 Folsom St., near 4th St., South of Market, 415/495–5775. Reservations essential. AE, DC, MC, V. $$*

7 *h-2*

MECCA

This giant, highly popular space combines late-20th-century industrial—aluminum air ducts, shiny metal bar, sharp corners—with mid-20th-century nightclub—velvet drapes, cut-glass chandeliers, good jazz and blues. The menu is contemporary Mediterranean, with pizzas from a wood-burning oven; thick, rich hummus accompanied by housemade pita; grilled asparagus and greens tossed with blood oranges, toasted nuts, and Roquefort; and crisp-skinned roasted chicken. The cleverly named cocktails—Mecca-Rita, Stellatini, Ima Gimlet—may tempt you to order a drink. *2029 Market St., between Duboce and 14th Sts., The Castro, 415/621–7000. AE, DC, MC, V. $$*

4 *e-3*

MOOSE'S

A top celebrity destination from the moment it opened in 1992, Moose's remains the fueling station of choice for politicians, media types, actors, and those who enjoy supping within throwing distance of fabled Washington Square. Owners Ed and Mary Etta Moose brought in new executive chef Brian Whitmer in mid-1997, but the Mediterranean culinary focus remains. Try to reserve one of the hard-won window seats with a view of the square. Live music keeps you entertained until your first course appears. *1652 Stockton St., between Union and Filbert Sts., North Beach, 415/989–7800. Reservations essential. AE, DC, MC, V. $$–$$$*

5 *h-3*

PLUMPJACK CAFÉ

The name is the title of an opera composed by famed oil tycoon and music lover Gordon Getty, whose sons are two of the partners here. They also run the Balboa Café, just down the street; a nearby respected wine store (making for excellent wine prices here); and a restaurant in Lake Tahoe. But this dinner house is their most stylish operation. Chef Maria Helm oversees a regularly changing menu that spans the Mediterranean, with gravlax and blini, an herbed chicken flanked by polenta, and crispy duck confit among the possibilities. The crowd is generally well-heeled and carefully attired. *3201 Fillmore St., at Greenwich St., Cow Hollow, 415/463–4755. AE, MC, V. Closed Sun. No lunch Sat. $$–$$$*

5 *h-4*

ROSE'S CAFÉ

This airy, trendy self-service café (you order at the counter and the food is brought to your table), housed in what used to be a branch of Il Fornaio Bakery, has sophisticated Mediterranean food with a solid emphasis on Italian. That comes as no surprise, since the brains behind the concept is Reed Hearon, the mastermind of Rose Pistola (*see* Italian, *above*). You can eat here from 7 AM until 10:30 PM on weekdays, starting with berry-studded focaccia, and later moving on to creative sandwiches and pizzas. For dinner you might find parchment-wrapped fusilli tossed with broccoli rabe, chilies, and anchovies. The food delivery can be haphazard, but most folks put up with it. *2298 Union St., at Steiner St., Cow Hollow, 415/775–2200. AE, MC, V. $–$$*

2 *c-3*

SOCCA

Socca is a crisp, flat, savory chickpea cake native to the south of France. It is just one of the specialties at this Mediterranean dinner house, where neighborhood residents go for a salad of quickly cooked rock shrimp, a main of lamb shanks and white beans, and crème brûlée in three flavors: pumpkin, lime, and maple. The bright blue, green, and yellow walls and cool tile floors evoke the sun and the sea, and the attentive service makes you feel right at home. *5800 Geary Blvd., at 22nd Ave., Richmond District, 415/379–6720. MC, V. Closed Mon. No lunch. $$*

4 g-4

SPLENDIDO

A crisp, brick oven–cooked pizza will set you to thinking about Italy, while a warm goat-cheese salad will transport you to France. But the stunning view of San Francisco Bay from the wall of windows will bring you back home. The chefs have come and gone, but for the moment the food is holding up; and the handsome dining room has always been a wonderful place to sit and enjoy the sun-splashed cuisine of the Mediterranean. *Embarcadero 4, at Sacramento and Drumm Sts., The Embarcadero, 415/986–3222. AE, DC, MC, V. $$–$$$*

4 f-4

VERTIGO

The base of what is arguably San Francisco's best-known building houses this sleek restaurant popular with the monied crowd. Since its opening in the mid-'90s, Vertigo has had some trouble holding on to chefs, but the food has settled into a mostly Mediterranean vein, with an occasional Asian touch. The three-tiered space has see-through ceilings, a parklike entrance, and a good-looking wood bar. *600 Montgomery St., at Clay St., Financial District, 415/433–7250. AE, D, DC, MC, V. Closed Sun. No lunch Sat. $$$*

4 c-8

ZUNI CAFÉ & GRILL

Zuni's Mediterranean menu carries a heavy dose of Italian culinary influence. A spacious, window-filled balcony dining area overlooks the large bar, where shellfish, one of the best oyster selections in town, and drinks are dispensed. Perhaps the most popular main course here is a whole roast chicken and Tuscan bread salad for two, but the house-cured anchovies, Caesar salad, shoestring potatoes, and heavenly burgers on focaccia are also the stuff of food myths. The eclectic crowd regularly orders the icy espresso granita with cream to cap off the evening. *1658 Market St., between Franklin and Gough Sts., Hayes Valley, 415/552–2522. Reservations essential. AE, MC, V. Closed Mon. $$–$$$*

MEXICAN

5 g-3

CAFÉ MARIMBA

In the midst of a hip, youthful neighborhood, this colorful Mexican café full of playful folk art serves contemporary yet authentic versions of Mexico's regional fare: tamales with mole *negro* (sauce of chilies and chocolate) from Oaxaca; shrimp with roasted tomatoes in the style of Zihuatanejo; and grilled chicken from Yucatán, packed into a tortilla. Two kinds of house-made salsa, usually one red and one green, come with a mountain of freshly fried chips that always seem to get eaten. Squash-blossom quesadillas, available sometimes, are worth a try. *2317 Chestnut St., near Scott St., The Marina, 415/776–1506. MC, V. No lunch Mon. $$*

8 b-3

CHAVA'S

On Saturdays, *menudo* aficionados head for this barrio favorite, where they sit down to huge portions of the famed Mexican tripe-and-hominy stew cherished as a surefire antidote to a hangover. Regulars also know that weekends are the time to sample the kitchen's fine *birria*, braised goat with onions and cilantro. You can scoop up anything you order with house-made corn tortillas, including excellent huevos rancheros and *huevos con nopales* (eggs with cactus). The brightly painted dining room attracts families, couples, and singles. *3248 18th St., at Shotwell St., Mission District, 415/552–9387. No credit cards. $*

8 a-5

LA TAQUERIA

The operation's logo claims "The Best Tacos & Burritos in the Whole World"— and in fact, it's not far from the truth. Choose from *carne asada* (grilled steak), *carnitas* (braised pork), or hefty chunks of chicken, and watch the staff stuff your request into piping-hot tortillas. The burritos are packed with tasty beans and rice, and the salsas come in varying levels of hotness. Cool down with a glass of agua fresca (fresh juice). It's mostly takeout, though there is limited seating. *2889 Mission St., between 24th and 25th Sts., Mission District, 415/285–7177. No credit cards. $*

8 a-2

PANCHO VILLA

The line here usually snakes out the door, and the women making tacos and burritos behind the counter never have a moment's rest. Carne asada is usually sizzling away on the griddle, alongside green onions. Full-dinner plates include everything from chiles rellenos to grilled tequila-marinated prawns, but most people settle on the tortilla-wrapped specialties. *3071 16th St., between Valencia and Mission Sts., Mission District, 415/ 864–8840. No credit cards. $*

7 *g-3*
POZOLE

This hip Mexican restaurant has Day of the Dead memorabilia cheering up the modest dining room, and a healthy menu including flavorful low-fat, low-salt specialties. Among the good-for-you dishes are two burritos, one of cactus and tomato and the other of chicken and tomatillo. The quesadillas are crisp and filled with sweet peppers and mushrooms or cheese and chicken. The noise level can be tiring, so if conversation is to be part of your meal, rest your vocal cords before you arrive. *2337 Market St., between 16th and 17th Sts., The Castro, 415/626–2666. No credit cards. $*

8 *a-5*
TAQUERIA SAN JOSÉ

This is the real thing. The tacos, served in paper-lined plastic baskets, are classics: soft tortillas wrapped around a choice of meat—carne asada, *al pastor* (barbecued pork), chorizo, *lengua* (tongue), *cabeza* (head), *sesos* (brains)—along with fiery or mild salsa, onions, and cilantro. Everything is perfectly fresh, right down to the bowls of tomatillo salsa on the tables. Bigger appetites can try the burritos filled with the same meats, plus rice and beans. *2830 Mission St., near 24th St., Mission District, 415/282–0203. No credit cards. $*

MIDDLE EASTERN

8 *a-3*
AMIRA

Belly dancers take to the stage, and itinerant mariachis sometimes stop by, but the pan-Arabic Amira is known for more than its music and dance. Big plates of couscous surrounded with chicken, lamb, or sausages, and kebabs on mounds of rice are two popular choices, as are the appetizers, including the chef's signature walnut dip. The fabric-draped ceiling, low benches, and large, round brass trays evoke the feeling of a kasbah transplanted to the trendy North Mission. *590 Valencia St., between 16th and 17th Sts., Mission District, 415/621–6213. MC, V. Closed Mon. No lunch. $–$$*

4 *f-5*
FAZ

Sample food from around the Mediterranean in this second-story ocher dining room. A wonderful meal might include creamy *baba ghannoush* (eggplant spread) or beef-and-rice-filled dolmas; greens tossed with pomegranate seeds and walnuts; a pasta or pizza dish prepared with Italian flair; and a house-smoked fish platter, with salmon, trout, and sturgeon. Midday, suits from the surrounding towers enjoy hearty sandwiches made with rosemary-flecked focaccia. *161 Sutter St., between Montgomery and Kearny Sts., Union Square, 415/362–0404. AE, DC, MC, V. Closed Sun. No lunch Sat. $$*

7 *g-2*
JUST LIKE HOME

At the front of this neighborhood deli–restaurant stands a large glass case holding many of the kitchen's tasty Middle Eastern creations: pizzalike flat breads topped with seasoned ground lamb, tabbouleh, hummus, *baba ghannoush* (garlicky puréed eggplant), *kibbeh* (balls of ground lamb), and stout dolmas filled with rice, pine nuts, and spices. You can order piping-hot falafel stuffed into pocket bread, a plate of *musakhan* (oven-roasted chicken smothered in onions), or, if you're feeling adventurous, spleen stuffed with onions and spinach. The house-made sweets are made with nuts, filo, and honey. *1024 Irving St., between 11th and 12th Aves., Sunset District, 415/681–3337. MC, V. $*

4 *e-3*
MAYKADEH

Teheran-born San Francisco opera director Lotfi Mansouri eats in this handsome Persian restaurant whenever he wants a taste of his homeland. Grilled lamb brains with saffron butter, plump rice-filled dolmas, lamb tongue with sour cream and lime, and tangy feta cheese and fresh herbs are all delicious ways to launch your meal. Kebabs of marinated chicken, lamb, and beef served with fluffy white rice are favorite main courses. Or try the classic Persian *ghorme sabzee*, lamb shanks with red beans, onions, tomatoes, and a mix of Middle Eastern spices. *470 Green St., between Grant Ave. and Kearny St., North Beach, 415/362–8286. MC, V. $$*

7 g-1

YA HALLA, FROM NADIA

The Lower Haight is a magnet for the X Generation, and this long, narrow, nicely decorated eatery is one of their routine stops. Members of the local Palestinian community also turn up here, drawn by the excellent rotisseried lamb or chicken shawermas (wrapped in big rounds of flat bread with tomatoes, cucumbers, onions, and hummus), meat or vegetarian dolmas, falafel, lamb-filled pastries, smoky eggplant purée, kebabs, and other Levantine classics. The name of the restaurant is Arabic for "welcome," and Nadia, the chief cook, is an exuberant greeter. *494 Haight St., between Fillmore and Webster Sts., Lower Haight, 415/522–1509. MC, V. $*

7 f-4

YAYA FROM THE FERTILE CRESCENT

Fans of chef-owner Yahya Salih's Middle Eastern cuisine did not have to mourn long when his original restaurant, Yaya Cuisine, closed late in 1997—now the same food can be enjoyed at a new downtown takeout operation or in an adjoining dining room brightened by green and blue tiles and a mural depicting ancient Mesopotamia. Headlining the takeout menu are tabbouleh; hummus; *baba ghannoush* (smoky eggplant purée); and *leffa* (a Middle Eastern flatbread wrap concealing meats or vegetables, hummus, marinated onions, and other condiments); and *laham bea'ajeen*, a close relative of pizza. In the dining room, Salih serves everything from lamb shanks to chicken kebabs, all with a California touch. *663 Clay St., between Kearny and Montgomery Sts., Financial District, 415/434–3567. MC, V. No lunch Sun.. $–$$*

MOROCCAN

2 e-2

COUSCOUS MOROCCO

The menu at this modest North African eatery is brief: two soups, two salads, and a list of couscous and tagine (stew) offerings. You can start with a bowl of *harira* (lentil-and-chickpea soup), or a salad of roasted peppers, tomatoes, and onions drizzled with olive oil. Couscous comes with highly spicy merguez sausage, lamb shanks, chicken, beef, or vegetables; chicken, beef, and lamb tagines are also available, all of them

loaded with vegetables. The unpretentious dining room holds a handful of tables, and the French-speaking staff is friendly, if slightly unpolished. *2165 Union St., between Webster and Fillmore Sts., Cow Hollow, 415/563–9638. No credit cards. Closed Mon. $–$$*

PAN-ASIAN

4 a-4

BETELNUT

Although the service is too often dismally bad, this fashionable pan-Asian outpost remains popular. The adventurous drinks list—with everything from house-brewed rice beer to martinis—draws a mostly young crowd to the bar area, where lacquered walls, bamboo ceiling fans, and hand-painted posters create a comfortably exotic mood. A plate of tasty stir-fried dried anchovies, chilies, peanuts, garlic, and green onions is arguably the best dish from the kitchen, although many diners also rave about the Vietnamese five-spice grilled chicken, fiery green papaya salad, and sweet, garlicky spareribs. *2030 Union St., between Buchanan and Webster Sts., Cow Hollow, 415/929–8855. D, DC, MC, V. $$*

4 e-5

E & O TRADING COMPANY

The look is turn-of-the-century Asian trading house, complete with bamboo, dragons, flowing fabric, and high ceilings. The menu jumps from Vietnamese salad rolls and soy-ginger grilled quail to chicken satay, Thai green curry, Indian nan with raita and tomato chutney, and Indonesian fried rice. Draft beer, brewed on the third floor, is yet another draw: Try India pale ale, unfiltered wheat beer, or malty brown ale. *314 Sutter St., near Grant Ave., Union Square, 415/693–0303. AE, MC, V. $$*

4 g-5

LONGLIFE NOODLE COMPANY AND JOOK JOINT

This slick, black-gray-and-red pseudo-cafeteria space is the first in what the owners hope will be a string of Asian noodle houses. The noodles are principally adaptations from Thailand, China, Japan, Singapore, Malaysia, and Vietnam. They turn up in broths, stir-fried, and cold, usually with too-cutesy names such as laksa luck (rice noodles in a spicy coconut milk broth), and dragon's breath (garlic noodles tossed with vegetables). Various buns, spring rolls, wontons, and pot stickers round out the menu. The food and service have both been uneven, but still the crowds throng here, especially around midday. *139 Steuart St., between Mission and Howard Sts., The Embarcadero, 415/281–3818. MC, V. No lunch Sat., Sun. $*

2 *d-3*

STRAITS CAFÉ

Although not a true pan-Asian restaurant, this highly popular eatery serves the cuisine of Singapore, a combination of the culinary traditions of China, India, and the Malay archipelago. Chef-owner Chris Yeo serves an exotic list of complex curries, sticks of fragrant satay, and seafood noodle soups. He also adds a contemporary twist to many classic Asian dishes: raw tuna with pickled ginger, shallots, and greens tossed with a ginger-plum dressing; and sea bass fillet baked in parchment with ginger, mushrooms, rice wine, and *longans* (small, perfumy Asian fruit). One wall in the handsome dining room is decorated with partial re-creations of the old pastel-painted shop-house fronts of Singapore. *3300 Geary Blvd., at Parker St., Richmond District, 415/668–1783. AE, MC, V. $$*

PIZZA

4 *e-3*

NORTH BEACH PIZZA

The Italian–Brazilian owners have figured out just what their customers want: American pizza. Their thick crusted pies are blanketed with cheese and loaded with toppings—pepperoni, mushrooms, clams, olives, and more. The pastas and other Italian menu standards on the menu are less worthwhile. If you want to eat your pizza at home, this is the place to call for fast delivery that puts the chains to shame. *1310 Grant Ave. near Vallejo St., North Beach, 415/433–2444. AE, D, DC, MC, V. $*

4 *e-3*

1499 Grant Ave. at Union St., North Beach, 415/433–2444.

8 *a-1*

PAULINE'S PIZZA

Pauline's made its name with its pesto pizza, whose prebaked crust prevents the basil from turning bitter from too much heat. Their crisp crusts also hold a slew of other classic and contemporary toppings: tomatoes and mozzarella; leeks and Kalamata olives; and Cajun *tasso* (smoked pork shoulder) with parsley and lemon zest are a few of the best. Salads are hearty and suitable for sharing. The neighborhood is a little gritty, but Pauline's is a sure beacon. *260 Valencia St., at Brosnan St. off Duboce Ave., Mission District, 415/552–2050, MC, V. $–$$*

4 *f-7*

PAZZIA

Folks who work at the Italian consulate turn up here for thin, crisp pizzas that remind them of home. The margherita, made with mozzarella, tomato, basil, is classic. Other toppings show the same Italian restraint, including one of arugula and prosciutto, and another with gorgonzola. The calzones are substantial enough for two people to share. Order a salad of radicchio and arugula and a glass of Chianti and you'll think you're in Rome. *337 3rd St., between Folsom and Harrison Sts., South of Market, 415/512–1693. MC, V. $–$$*

4 *e-4*

TOMMASO'S

For more than 60 years, both locals and visitors have been lining up to get into this dark, walk-down North Beach institution for one reason: pizza. It comes in more than a dozen-and-a-half guises, with memorable tomato sauce and whole-milk mozzarella playing major roles. The crusts are thin, crisp, and classic, cooked in San Francisco's original wood-burning pizza oven. Accompany the Italian pies with a room-temperature vegetable such as broccoli, green beans, or asparagus, tossed simply with olive oil and lemon juice. No reservations are taken, but your meal will be worth the wait. *1042 Kearny St., between Broadway and Pacific Ave., North Beach, 415/398–9696. Reservations not accepted. MC, V. Closed Mon. No lunch. $–$$*

4 *b-8*

VICOLO

This is the home of gourmet pizza: crisp cornmeal crusts topped with andouille and smoked mozzarella, blue cheese and roasted eggplant, house-made sausage, garden-fresh tomatoes, wild mushrooms, and imported cheeses. The pies come in paper-lined cast-iron pans; a tossed green salad or one of the marinated vegetable salads is a perfect accompaniment. The opera house and symphony hall are just a stone's throw away, making this busy, cathedral-ceilinged spot a nice stop before you head off for a concert. *150 Ivy St., at Franklin St., Hayes Valley, 415/863–2382. MC, V. $*

RUSSIAN

2 *c-3*

CINDERELLA RESTAURANT AND BAKERY

In the evenings, the bakers roll their cooling racks of freshly baked breads to the doorway of this local institution, to enjoy a curbside smoke. During the day, a stream of regulars comes through the doors to buy the sturdy Russian loaves and the more delicate rolls and sweets, or to sit down in the modest dining room for bowls of pelmeni and plates of cabbage rolls, lamb and kasha, or cheese-filled dumplings. *436 Balboa St., between 5th and 6th Aves., Richmond District, 415/751–9690. MC, V. Closed Mon. $*

2 *d-3*

KATIA'S

There are floor-to-ceiling windows, and flowers on every table at this charming corner-storefront restaurant. The delicious borscht arrives with a dollop of sour cream, a perfect opener to your meal. Or you might start with small plates of smoked salmon and blini, marinated mushrooms, and meat- or vegetable-filled piroshki. The *pelmeni* (small meat-filled dumplings in broth) are delicate and satisfying, as is the chicken Pozharski, seasoned minced chicken formed into a cutlet and sautéed. Save room for a meringue drizzled with berry sauce or a flaky, caloric napoleon. *600 5th Ave., at Balboa St., Richmond District, 415/668–9292. AE, DC, MC, V. Closed Mon. $$*

SALVADORAN

8 *c-4*

LA PAZ RESTAURANT

The cooks here are experts at making El Salvador's national snack, the *pupusa.* With a few swift pats of their hands, they seal a filling of cheese, pork, or a combination of the two inside a chewy

cornmeal disk and cook it on a griddle. The tasty morsels are served hot and accompanied by a pile of vinegary shredded cabbage, which is meant to be stuffed inside. An order of fried *platanos* (plantains) and cream is a good accompaniment, or you might try the pork tamales or rice and beans. *1028 Potrero Ave., between 22nd and 23rd Sts., Mission District, 415/550–8313. MC, V. $*

SEAFOOD

4 *f-5*

AQUA

This quietly glamorous spot, with its monumental floral arrangements and stylish lighting, is arguably the city's most important seafood restaurant. It serves contemporary versions of Mediterranean and American classics: Mussel or lobster soufflé; chunks of lobster alongside lobster-stuffed ravioli; and ultrarare ahi tuna paired with foie gras are especially good. Save room for the regularly changing list of desserts, nearly all of them miniature museum pieces. Don't stint on wine, since this food deserves the best. *252 California St., between Front and Battery Sts., Financial District, 415/956–9662. Reservations essential. AE, DC, MC, V. Closed Sun. No lunch Sat. $$$*

4 *e-6*

FARALLON

There was plenty of talk about this $4 million, Pat Kuleto–designed restaurant before it opened in mid-1997. One reason was Kuleto and all that money. The other reason was chef Mark Franz, who spent 10 years guiding the kitchen at the fabled Stars. That seafood is the specialty here comes as no surprise once you see the scallop-shell entryway, jellyfish-shaped chandeliers, and kelp-covered columns. Soft-shell crab resting on a bed of vine-ripened tomatoes, lobster and prawns paired with nugget-sized gnocchi, and braised pike with Yukon Gold mashed potatoes are just a few of Franz's elaborate creations. Desserts are by Emily Luchetti, another Stars' alum; don't miss the warm chocolate cake. *450 Post St., between Powell and Mason Sts., Union Square, 415/956-6969. Reservations essential. AE, DC, MC, V. No lunch Sun. $$$–$$$$*

4 *b-8*

HAYES STREET GRILL

Consult the blackboard for the seafood selections du jour at this Hayes Valley mainstay, with its classic decor of white walls, wood wainscoting, bentwood chairs, and white-cloth-topped tables. The fish is simply grilled, with a choice of sauces ranging from tomato salsa to a spicy Szechuan peanut concoction to beurre blanc or fruity olive oil. Also recommended are the crab cakes and the various salads, including one of grilled quail and another that combines calamari and fennel. The creme brûlée is famous. *320 Hayes St., between Franklin and Gough Sts., Hayes Valley, 415/863–5545. Reservations essential. AE, D, DC, MC, V. No lunch weekends. $$–$$$*

4 *c-2*

MCCORMICK & KULETO'S

Here is a visitor's dream come true: a fabulous view of the Bay from every seat in the house and dozens of varieties of fish and shellfish prepared in scores of globe-circling ways, from tacos and pot stickers to grills and pastas. The kitchen often stumbles, so the best advice is not to challenge it: stick to the simplest preparations—and enjoy that priceless view. *Ghirardelli Sq., at Beach and Larkin Sts., The Embarcadero, 415/929–1730. AE, D, DC, MC, V. $$–$$$*

4 *f-5*

SAM'S GRILL

Fresh seafood draws crowds of local bankers and brokers to this longtime, no-nonsense grill at lunchtime, where regulars are pampered by the veteran wait staff. The retro, wood-lined space, with its seemingly countless coathooks, has curtained booths at the rear that recall the dining room of a stuffy men's club. Charbroiled seafood and sautéed sole are the standard mains, though steaks and chops keep the red-meat eaters happy. The seafood is sometimes too long on the stove; request it rare if you so desire. *374 Bush St., between Montgomery and Kearny Sts., Financial District, 415/421–0594. AE, DC, MC, V. Closed Sat., Sun. $$–$$$*

4 *c-5*

SWAN OYSTER DEPOT

This renowned fish purveyor and seafood bar has remained unchanged for decades, and that's just fine with the legions of San Franciscans who flock here. It's a delightfully atmospheric operation, with sawdust-covered floors, a marble counter and spinning stools, and a steamy kitchen. The convivial countermen serve old-fashioned clam chowder and fresh oysters on the half shelf. The doors close early, so plan on dinner before 5 PM. *1517 Polk St., between California and Sacramento Sts., Nob Hill, 415/673–1101. No credit cards. Closed Sun. $$*

4 *f-5*

TADICH GRILL

Owners and locations have changed many times since this old-timer opened during the gold rush era, but it has kept its 19th-century San Francisco atmosphere. The kitchen is best at simple sautées—petrale and rex sole are favorites—although an order of cioppino during crab season is mandatory. The old-fashioned house-made tartar sauce that accompanies deep-fried items and the smooth, rich rice pudding have kept locals smiling for more decades than anyone cares to count. There is seating at the counter as well as in private booths, but expect long lines for a table at lunchtime. *240 California St., between Front and Battery Sts., Financial District, 415/391–1849. Reservations not accepted. MC, V. Closed Sun. $$–$$$*

4 *c-4*

YABBIES

For those unable to score a table, there are two seafood bars—one a sturdy concrete number fronting a couple of oyster shuckers hard at work, and the other a see-through glass beauty; both are perfect perches for a meal. Crab cocktail with mango and lemongrass; raw tuna with sesame oil, ginger, and avocado; big, scrumptious crab cakes; and porcini-dusted sea bass are among the outstanding choices. *2237 Polk St., between Vallejo and Green Sts., Russian Hill, 415/474–4088. Reservations essential (except for seafood bars). MC, V. No lunch. $$–$$$*

SPANISH

8 *a-4*

ESPERPENTO

With its Dali-derivative art and hand-painted tabletops, the restaurant has a quirky look, but the food is surprisingly straightforward. Three dozen tapas cater to all different tastes: Shrimp arrive flecked with garlic and chilies; squid comes nicely deep-fried; and the blood sausage is outstanding. There are simpler plates, too, of olives, cheeses, and hams. Lines of mostly neighborhood residents sometimes form on the weekends, and local mariachi bands occasionally drop in to jam. *3295 22nd St., near Mission St., Mission District, 415/ 282–8867. No credit cards. Closed Sun. $$*

4 *f-6*

THIRSTYBEAR

This combination brew-pub-and-tapas outpost stands right around the corner from the Museum of Modern Art; its small plates and brews are a welcome treat after serious gallery cruising. The cavernous interior of concrete floors, brick walls, and shiny tanks holding homemade brews is cool and utilitarian, but the small plates of sherry-infused fish cheeks, steamed mussels, *tortilla española* (egg-and-potato omelet), and white beans with house-made sausage will take away the chill. If you prefer ordering in bulk rather than grazing, request the paella. *661 Howard St., between Hawthorne Lane and 3rd St., 415/974–0905. MC, V. No lunch Sat., Sun. $$*

8 *a-3*

TIMO'S

When the ultrahip Timo's first opened in the North Mission a few years back, you couldn't snag a table. Lovers of the small plates kept the tiny kitchen busy creating cakes of salt cod and potato; shrimp with garlic; and skewers of chicken or pork. Now, however, tapas bars are blooming, so the crowds have thankfully eased up. The service can be lackadaisical even with the reduced pressure, but the decor of bright yellows, greens, and purple create a cheerful mood. A second location in Ghirardelli Square has less appeal. *842 Valencia St., between 19th and 20th Sts., Mission District, 415/647–0558. MC, V. No lunch. $$*

4 *b-2*

Ghiradelli Square, 2nd Floor, North Point St. near Polk St., Fisherman's Wharf, 415/ 440–1200.

4 *c-3*

ZARZUELA

The small, crowded storefront with stucco and brick walls serves nearly 40

different hot and cold tapas, plus a dozen or so main courses. There is a tapa to suit every palate, from poached octopus on new potatoes to seared scallops with barely wilted greens; slabs of Manchego cheese with paper-thin slices of serrano ham is one of the best. If you haven't filled up on tapas, order the paella—saffron-scented rice laced with prawns, mussels, and clams. The amiable staff will answer any questions. *2000 Hyde St., at Union St., Russian Hill, 415/346–0800. MC, V. Reservations not accepted. Closed Sun. $$*

STEAK

4 *b-4*

HARRIS'

Regularly dubbed the best steakhouse in San Francisco, Harris' is the creation of Ann Harris, who grew up on a Texas cattle ranch and was married to the late Jack Harris of Harris Ranch fame. In her New York–style restaurant at the bottom

---

OLD-TIMERS

San Francisco may be a youthful city, but some of its restaurants show their years with respectable dignity.

Beach Chalet (American Contemporary)
  Known for its restored WPA murals.

Boulevard (American Contemporary)
  The gorgeous brick building predates the '06 earthquake.

Chez Panisse (American Contemporary)
  The birthplace of Californian cuisine.

It's Tops Coffee Shop (American Casual)
  A burger joint since the '30s.

Sam's Grill (Seafood)
  A favorite of bankers and brokers for more than 50 years.

Swan Oyster Depot (Seafood)
  Serving oysters since 1912.

Tadich Grill (Seafood)
  In 1849, folks were already saying, "meet me at Tadich."

Tommaso's (Pizza)
  Site of the city's first brick pizza oven, installed in the '30s.

of Russian Hill, she serves top-quality dry-aged steaks cooked exactly as you request. Start with a trendy martini and an order of sweetbread pâté, and accompany your slab of meat with a baked potato dressed with sour cream and bits of bacon. Save room for a wedge of pecan pie. 2100 Van Ness Ave., at Pacific Ave., Russian Hill, 415/673–1888. AE, DC, MC, V. No lunch. $$$

5 h-3
IZZY'S STEAK & CHOP HOUSE
Izzy's, named for a legendary San Francisco barkeep, has a wonderful, saloon-like ambience that steakhouse frequenters love. The menu is naturally heavy on steaks, most of which seem large enough to serve two average appetites. There are chops and seafood, too, plus all the trimmings: scalloped potatoes, roasted carrots, and some of the best creamed spinach in town. A blizzard of Izzy memorabilia and antique advertising art covers almost every inch of wall space, and a long shelf shows off an impressive collection of steak sauces and related condiments. 3345 Steiner St., between Lombard and Chestnut Sts., The Marina, 415/563–0487. AE, DC, MC, V. No lunch. $$

THAI

4 d-8
BASIL
Wood floors, a glass-brick wall, and deep blue and rich yellow accents create a stylish setting for Thai food prepared with modern flair. Intriguing dishes include warm duck salad on watercress, paper-thin pork with garlic and pepper, and beef short ribs in mild curry. The kitchen turns out a sublime version of the classic Thai sweet dessert, sliced mango and sticky rice drizzled with coconut milk. 1175 Folsom St., between 7th and 8th Sts., South of Market, 415/552–8999. MC, V. No lunch Sat. Closed Sun. $$

5 d-6
KING OF THAI KITCHEN
Although the surroundings are sparse, the food at this modest operation has the authentic taste of Thailand. At a steam table in the back of the room, curries and other simmered dishes are served with rice for walkaway diners. Particularly tasty is the Suki hang, a

heady mix of shrimp, squid, chicken, vegetables, and cellophane noodles in a spicy bean curd sauce; another standout is the thinly sliced beef mixed with chili, onion, ground roasted rice, and mint. 346 Clement St., between 4th and 5th Aves., Richmond District, 415/831–9953. MC, V. $

8 b-1
MANORA
Not far from the Performing Arts Center, this smart and popular restaurant, with its fresh flowers, good table linens, and an efficient staff, is a natural stop before an evening of Mozart or Verdi. Standout dishes are fried soft-shell crabs with a tamarind dipping sauce; rice paper–wrapped seafood, black fungus, and sausage; and whitefish steamed in banana leaves. Traditional Thai curries featuring meats, poultry, or seafood are also worth a try. SoMa clubbers often fuel up here before heading out on the town. 1600 Folsom St., at 12th St., South of Market, 415/861–6224. MC, V. No lunch weekends. $

2 d-3
THAI CAFÉ
This little café is a bright, light space with a discreet altar niche at the back. The food is generously portioned and modestly priced, which keeps the tables full for most of an evening. The seafood soup with straw mushrooms in a rich coconut milk broth is a treat, as are the tod mun (fried fish cake), squid with garlic and pepper, and deep-fried chicken wings with sweet-hot sauce. 3407 Geary Blvd., near Jordan Ave., Richmond District, 415/386–4200. MC, V. $

7 g-1
THEP PHANOM
Food critics and restaurant goers have been singing the praises of Thep Phanom ever since it opened in 1985. Duck is deliciously prepared in a variety of ways—in a fragrant curry, minced for salad, or resting atop a bed of spinach—and the squid salad nicely balances the coolness of lime with the sizzling heat of chilies. Daily specials supplement the regular menu, many of them based on seafood. A wonderful mango sorbet is sometimes available for dessert. 400 Waller St., at Fillmore St., Lower Haight, 415/431–2526. AE, D, DC, MC, V. No lunch. $

TIBETAN

5 g-3

LHASA MOON

Outside of Tibet, this type of restaurant is few and far between—which is one of the reasons Lhasa Moon is such a treat for San Franciscans. The other reasons are friendly service and the many unusual and delicious dishes served here: *momos*, traditional plump, juicy dumplings filled with meat or vegetables; light beef soup flavored with blue cheese; mild curries; interesting breads; sturdy noodles, and exotic braises. Beautiful photographs of Tibet decorate the walls of the comfortable dining room. *2420 Lombard St., between Scott and Divisadero Sts., The Marina, 415/ 674–9898. MC, V. No lunch Sat., Sun. Closed Mon. $*

VEGETARIAN

4 a-2

GREENS

The Bay Area's Zen Buddhist Center operates this famed vegetarian restaurant, also the site of the Tassajara Bakery outlet, which is known for its outstanding breads and desserts. Even nonvegetarians rave about the meatless cooking at Greens: the black bean soup, crisp-crusted pizzas, enchiladas verdes, and eggplant fritters are all divine. Dinners are à la carte on weeknights, but only a five-course prix fixe dinner is served on Saturday. *Bldg. A, Fort Mason, Marina Blvd. at Lagua St., The Marina, 415/771–6222. MC, V. No lunch Mon., no dinner Sun. $$*

4 c-7

MILLENNIUM

Tucked into the former carriage house of the venerable Abigail Hotel, Millennium, with its black-and-white checkered floors and sponged walls, is a gold mine for anyone who eschews meat and appreciates imagination. The literature describes the food as "organic cuisine"; almost everything on the menu is not only vegetarian, but also low-fat, low-salt, and dairy-free. The Mediterranean is the inspiration for most dishes, with pastas, polenta, risotto, and grilled fresh vegetables among the most popular choices. Dishes made with *seitan*, a whole-wheat meat substitute, convince believers that veal piccata tastes better made without the veal. A list of organic wines rounds out the health-conscious theme. *246 McAllister St., between Hyde and Larkin Sts., Civic Center, 415/487– 9800. MC, V. No lunch. $$*

VIETNAMESE

4 d-6

BA LE

In the Vietnamese community, Ba Le is probably best known for its house-made charcuterie items, including pâté, head cheese, and ham. They form the bulk of the sandwiches, which are built on large French rolls and stuffed to the brim with shredded carrot, onion, tomatoes, fresh coriander, and a "secret sauce." The kitchen also assembles excellent rice and noodle dishes, among them grilled marinated pork chop and pork sausage atop rice, and shredded pork skin dusted with roasted rice powder over vermicelli. A combination plate lets you eat around the menu. *511 Jones St., between O'Farrell and Geary Sts., The Tenderloin, 415/474– 7270. No credit cards. $*

2 b-3

LA VIE

The informative, congenial staff here is always willing to lead you to such traditional fare as *nep chien* (deep-fried balls of sticky rice stuffed with a mixture of finely cut pork, shrimp, and mushrooms) or "shaking beef," cubes of tender beef with a lime-and-pepper dipping sauce. For a starter, order the small shrimp cakes dotted with yellow mung beans: You wrap up the cakes in crisp lettuce leaves and dip them in a spicy fish sauce. Seafood dishes often dominate the list of specials. *5830 Geary Blvd., between 22nd and 23rd Aves., Richmond District, 415/668–8080. AE, MC, V. $*

5 d-6

LE SOLEIL

As its name implies, Le Soleil is full of sunlight and pastel colors. An eye-catching painting of Saigon hangs on one wall, and a large aquarium of tropical fish stands near the door. The kitchen prepares traditional dishes from every part of Vietnam: Try the excellent raw-beef salad; crisp, flavorful spring rolls; a southern-style pancakelike omelet encasing a filling of shrimp, pork, and bean sprouts; or large prawns simmered in a clay pot. *133 Clement St., between 2nd and 3rd Aves., Richmond District, 415/ 668–4848. MC, V. $*

4 *d-6*

PACIFIC RESTAURANT

Although only a simple noodle house, this restaurant is head and shoulders above much of the competition. Their *pho*, beef and rice noodle soup that is the daily meal of Hanoi, is a big, full-flavored bowl fragrant with spices. You can order the bovine soup in any number of ways—with meatballs, rare thin slices, or tendon. A plate of lime wedges, bean sprouts, and fresh herbs arrives with the soup, along with chili sauce. There are also cold noodles and other refreshing dishes. *337 Jones St., between Eddy and Ellis Sts., The Tenderloin, 415/928–4022. No credit cards. No dinner. Closed Tues. $*

4 *c-7*

607 Larkin St. near Eddy St., The Tenderloin, 415/441–6722.

8 *a-2*

SLANTED DOOR

Since opening in early 1996, owner-chef Charles Phan has developed a steady following for his self-described "real Vietnamese home cooking." There are fresh spring rolls packed with rice noodles, pork, shrimp, and pungent mint leaves, and fried imperial rolls concealing shrimp, pork, black fungus, and vegetables. You usually can't go wrong with the deep-fried pompano with ginger dipping sauce; lightly battered soft-shell crab; or lamb chops with lemongrass. The menu changes every two weeks, but popular dishes are never abandoned. This place is no secret, so plan on waiting for a table. *584 Valencia St., between 16th and 17th Sts., Mission District, 415/ 861–8032. Reservations essential. MC, V. Closed Mon. $–$$*

chapter 4

SHOPPING

The bounty available in San Francisco shops is astounding in its range. Downtown, around Union Square, you'll find Italian designer fashions and Louis Vuitton luggage, while in funky neighborhoods such as the Mission and Haight-Ashbury you can pick through rare jazz LPs or Art Deco clocks.

What you won't find are the shopping malls so common throughout much of America. Rather, in San Francisco, your shopping experience will take you hither and yon, to neighborhoods known for a particular good or service: antiques shops in Jackson Square, fine jewelers in Union Square, rare- and secondhand-book shops in the Mission District, and bargains of all kinds in SoMa (South of Market), where many of the city's discount outlets are clustered. To add to the allure, most of the city's shops—particularly clothing shops—have seasonal sales from January through February and July through August.

shopping destinations

DEPARTMENT STORES

4 e-6
GUMP'S
In business since 1861, Gump's is famous for its large selection of high-quality collectibles and its amusing Christmastime window displays. It carries exclusive lines of dinnerware, flatware, and glassware, as well as Asian artifacts, antiques, and furniture; the jewelry department has extensive displays of jade and freshwater pearls. Gump's is one of the city's most popular stores for bridal registries. 135 Post St., at Grant Ave., Union Square, 415/982–1616.

4 e-6
MACY'S
Fantastic for one-stop shopping, the newly remodeled Macy's has designer fashions and an extensive selection of shoes, cosmetics, fragrances, jewelry, housewares, furniture, electronics, and food. Half of San Francisco seems to be wandering aimlessly through its aisles on any given weekend. The Cellar is devoted to cooking gadgets and gourmet goodies, while the men's department (one of the world's largest) occupies its own building across Stockton Street. Stockton and O'Farrell Sts., Union Square, 415/397–3333.

4 e-6
NEIMAN MARCUS
With its Philip Johnson–designed checkerboard facade, gilded atrium, and stained-glass skylight (see Historic Sites & Architecture in Chapter 2), Neiman-Marcus showcases its high-end goods in luxury surroundings. Eclectic and high-fashion women's and men's clothing, top-brand cosmetics, gem-studded jewelry, and fancy household wares are the draws at this outpost of the Texas-based company. Its biannual "Last Call" sales—in January and July—draw quite a crowd. 150 Stockton St., at Geary St., Union Square, 415/362–3900.

4 e-6
NORDSTROM
The Seattle-based Nordstrom company is known worldwide for its exceptional customer service, and its downtown San Francisco store (the world's largest Nordstrom) is no exception. It's housed on the top five levels of the San Francisco Shopping Centre building (see below), with spiral escalators circling a four-story atrium. Designer shoes, accessories, and cosmetics are among its specialties. 865 Market St., at 5th St., Union Square, 415/243–8500.

4 e-6
SAKS FIFTH AVENUE
The West Coast outpost of this New York City institution has opulent jewelry, cosmetics, and accessories departments that are not to be missed. Designer fashions for women range from conservative to trend-setting; there is also a small men's department. The restaurant, on the top floor, overlooks Union Square. 384 Post St., at Powell St., Union Square, 415/986–4300.

SHOPPING CENTERS & MALLS

4 *c-2*

THE ANCHORAGE

Multicolored nautical flags snap in the wind at this open-air complex in Fisherman's Wharf, a block from the Hyde Street cable car turn-around. Dozens of shops sell everything from casual apparel to jewelry, luggage, and shoes. There are also several specialty shops selling great gift items such as music boxes and redwood furniture. A dozen restaurants serve snacks and sit-down meals. In the central courtyard, street artists perform music, magic, and comedy. *2800 Leavenworth St., at Beach St., Fisherman's Wharf, 415/775-6000.*

4 *c-2*

THE CANNERY

The former Del Monte peach cannery (built in 1906) now houses dozens of shops, restaurants, art galleries, and cafés with views of San Francisco Bay. There's a glass elevator that travels up and down the three levels of the red-brick building; in a courtyard filled with 100-year-old olive trees, mimes, magicians, and jugglers perform for free. This is where you'll find Cobb's Comedy Club (*see* Comedy *in* Chapter 5) and the Museum of the City of San Francisco (*see* History Museums *in* Chapter 2). *2801 Leavenworth St., at Beach St., Fisherman's Wharf, 415/771-3112.*

4 *f-5*

CROCKER GALLERIA

With its spectacular glass dome, this beautiful Financial District shopping complex is modeled after the Galleria Vittorio Emmanuelle in Milan, Italy. Some 40 boutiques and restaurants on three levels cater to discerning downtown business types, with accessories, shoes, home furnishings, jewelry, stationery, flowers, gifts, gourmet foods, and more. The two rooftop gardens are perfect for picnicking. *50 Post St., between Montgomery and Kearny Sts., Financial District, 415/393-1505.*

4 *f-4, g-4*

EMBARCADERO CENTER

Four modern towers of shops, restaurants, and offices make up the Embarcadero Center on the waterfront near Market Street. The eight-block, 10-acre complex contains more than 125 chichi shops catering to harried Financial District workers on their lunch breaks; here are nationally known clothing, housewares, and gift stores, as well as the Skydeck (*see* Viewpoints *in* Chapter 2), a five-screen movie theater specializing in art films, and the Hyatt Regency Hotel (*see* Very Expensive Lodgings *in* Chapter 7). There is free validated parking at the center's garage on evenings and weekends; call for details. *Clay and Sacramento Sts., between Battery and Drumm Sts., The Embarcadero, 800/733-6318.*

4 *b-2, c-2*

GHIRARDELLI SQUARE

Although its oldest redbrick building dates to 1864, this beloved manufacturing complex is best known as the site of Domingo Ghirardelli's chocolate factory from 1893 until the early 1960s. Today it's a charming open-air complex with 70 boutiques and restaurants. Visitors can still watch Ghirardelli chocolate being made in some of the original vats and ovens at the old-fashioned soda fountain on the plaza level, or watch street performers gambol on the West Plaza stage. *900 North Point St., at Polk St., Fisherman's Wharf, 415/775-5500.*

4 *a-6*

JAPAN CENTER

Since 1968, this graceful five-acre complex has been a center for San Francisco's Japanese community. Boutiques on Japan Center's three-block-long shopping arcade sell gifts and artifacts from Japan; there are also art galleries, antiques shops, bookstores, restaurants, a Japanese-style spa, and the huge Kabuki movie theater. The center's Japanese architecture includes a magnificent Peace Pagoda. Special events and free entertainment take place on weekends. *Geary Blvd. between Fillmore and Laguna Sts., Japantown, 415/922-6776.*

4 *e-1*

PIER 39

This 1,043-ft former cargo pier, once abandoned and decaying, now has a festive carnival air that makes it a first stop for many tourists to San Francisco. Here are more than 100 unique shops, 10 restaurants with bay views, numerous fast-food stands, a 350-berth marina, a double-decked carousel, an entertainment complex, and the UnderWater

World aquarium (*see* Zoos & Aquariums *in* 6). Street performers show off their antics daily, and the Blue & Gold Fleet departs nearby. Just offshore is a colony of barking California sea lions. *The Embarcadero, at Beach St., Fisherman's Wharf, 415/981–7437.*

4 *g-5*

RINCON CENTER

Rincon Center's glass-roofed atrium has a central free-falling fountain surrounded by cafés, shops, restaurants, business offices, and landscaped terraces with public seating. The net result is an inviting oasis where people can eat and shop in a relaxed atmosphere, just steps away from the frenzied pace of the Financial District. *101 Spear St., at Mission St., South of Market, 415/543–8600.*

4 *e-6*

SAN FRANCISCO SHOPPING CENTRE

The newest of the city's shopping complexes houses a Nordstrom department store (*see above*) and 90 other trend-setting shops, art galleries, restaurants, and cafés, all surrounding a dizzying nine-story atrium with spiral escalators. It's across from the Powell Street cable car turnaround, three blocks from Union Square. Valet parking is available on 5th Street. *865 Market St., between 5th and 6th Sts., Union Square, 415/495–5656.*

2 *c-6*

STONESTOWN GALLERIA

This indoor mall with vaulted glass skylights and Italian marble floors and walls has a rare but essential bonus: ample free parking. The fine collection of fashionable shops and boutiques caters to people of all ages; there are also banks, beauty salons, medical offices, a post office, and a movie theater. National chains such as Eddie Bauer, Imaginarium, and Williams-Sonoma have outlets here. *19th Ave. and Winston Dr., Stonestown, 415/759–2626.*

SHOPPING NEIGHBORHOODS

the castro

Often called the gay capital of the world, the Castro is a premiere shopping and entertainment district for nongays as well. The neighborhood bustles day and night, with much of the activity revolving around the intersection of Castro and 18th streets, where the famous Castro Theatre stands (*see* Historic Sites & Architecture, *in* Chapter 2). Here are cutting-edge clothing boutiques, quirky home-accessory stores, and various specialty shops such as A Different Light (*see* Books, *below*), one of the country's premier gay and lesbian bookstores. *Best shopping: Castro St., between Market and 19th Sts.*

chinatown

The intersection of Grant Avenue and Bush Street marks the gateway to Chinatown, a 24-block neighborhood of shops, restaurants, markets, and nonstop human activity. Almost anything made or grown in any Asian country can be found here: Crates of bok choy, tanks of live crabs, and hanging whole chickens fill the food shops and stalls, while Chinese silks, toy trinkets, inexpensive electronic goods, colorful pottery, baskets, and figurines of ivory and soapstone are displayed in boutique windows. Jewelry shops specializing in jade and pearls are on every block, as are herb pharmacies selling ginseng and roots. *Best shopping: Grant Ave.*

civic center/hayes valley

The only real attraction for shoppers around Civic Center is the small Opera Plaza, where A Clean Well-Lighted Place for Books (*see* Books, *below*) draws a steady stream of browsers. Just southwest of Opera Plaza, Hayes Valley is a small, up-and-coming shopping neighborhood packed with art galleries, furniture stores, and unusual gift boutiques. *Best shopping: Hayes Street.*

financial district

The shops in this area compliment those of nearby Union Square, catering mostly to the needs of high-rolling executives. The Embarcadero Center and Crocker Galleria (*see* Shopping Centers & Malls, *above*) are full of stylish stores and restaurants. Much of this area shuts down on Sundays, though the shopping centers remain open. *Embarcadero Center: Clay and Sacramento Sts., between Battery and Drumm Sts.; Crocker Galleria: 50 Post St., between Montgomery and Kearny Sts.*

fisherman's wharf

Tourists throng to Fisherman's Wharf, with good reason: Pier 39, the Anchorage, Ghirardelli Square, and the Cannery are all here (*see* Shopping Centers & Malls, *above*), giving shoppers a vast selection of restaurants, souvenir shops, and clothing- and gift boutiques; in the outdoor spaces, musicians, mimes, and magicians create a carnival mood. Best of all are the wharf's view of the bay and proximity to the cable car lines, which can take shoppers directly to Union Square. Down at the piers, fishermen still haul in their catch of the day. *Best shopping: Jefferson St., between The Cannery and Pier 39.*

the haight

Haight Street is always an attraction for visitors, if only to see the sign at Haight and Ashbury streets—the geographic center of the hippie movement during the 1960s. These days, shops here abound with vintage clothing (and the rock stars and movie costumers who frequent them), used books and records, and high-quality handmade jewelry and folk art. There are also plenty of bicycle, skateboard, and in-line-skating shops, reflecting the neighborhood's proximity to Golden Gate Park. The less-traveled Lower Haight—around Webster, Pierce, and Fillmore streets, has one of the best video stores in town (*see* Videos, *below*), and many zany boutiques. *Best shopping: Haight St., between Stanyan St. and Masonic Ave.*

jackson square

Just north of the Financial District, tiny Jackson Square was once the center of the raffish Barbary Coast. Now fully gentrified, the area is home to two dozen of San Francisco's finest antiques dealers, most of them occupying two-story, 19th-century, brick town houses on narrow lanes. Every store has a specialty, and all are appointed like small museums.

japantown

Unlike Chinatown, North Beach, or the Mission District, where ethnic shops and restaurants fill block after block, the social and commercial focal point of San Francisco's Japanese community is the 5-acre Japan Center (*see* Shopping Centers & Malls, *above*). The three-block complex includes an 800-car public garage, an excellent cinema, and three shop-filled buildings. In the Kintetsu and Kinokuniya buildings, shops and showrooms sell cameras, CDs and tapes, futons, food items, art, new and old porcelain, and all kinds of antiquities. *Japan Center: Geary Blvd., between Fillmore and Laguna Sts.*

the marina

The Marina District's two main shopping streets are Chestnut Street and Union Street. Chestnut Street, one block north of Lombard Street and stretching from Fillmore Street to Divisadero Street, caters to the whims of Marina District residents with chichi restaurants, cafés, and bars. Union Street, at the heart of the Cow Hollow neighborhood, is nestled just below the hills of Pacific Heights. The restored Victorian buildings that line the street between Steiner and Octavia streets house contemporary fashion, home furnishing, and custom jewelry shops, along with a few antiques shops and art galleries. The Marina District's trendy designer boutiques are especially popular with young professionals, who are also attracted to the area's lively nightlife. *Best shopping: Chestnut St., between Fillmore and Divisadero Sts.; Union St., between Steiner and Octavia Sts.*

mission district

The Mission District is one of the city's most ethnically diverse neighborhoods, with a large Latino population as well as a growing contingent of young artists, musicians, and new bohemians. Bargain shoppers frequent the area's overflowing warehouses for secondhand clothing and furniture. Look for one-of-a-kind music and bookstores, avant garde art galleries, and *botanicas* and other "magic" shops where you can flirt with the occult. *Best shopping: 16th and Valencia Sts.*

noe valley

Many flower children settled in Noe Valley when they grew up and had children of their own, so it figures that kids' clothing, book, and educational toy stores fill the streets. The neighborhood is also full of natural-fiber clothing boutiques, record and art supply stores, ethnic crafts shops, restaurants, health food stores, and gourmet shops. *Best shopping: 24th St., between Castro and Church Sts.*

north beach

Most of the businesses in this Italian neighborhood are small, chic clothing and gift stores; there are art galleries and antiques and vintage shops as well. Once the center of the beat movement, North Beach is also home to the city's most famous bookstore, City Lights (*see below*), where the bohemian spirit lives on. Stop to enjoy an espresso at one of many quaint cafés, or look for gourmet goodies at the plentiful Italian delicatessens, bakeries, and restaurants. *Best shopping: Grant and Columbus Aves.*

pacific heights/ laurel heights

Pacific Heights residents seeking practical services head straight to busy Fillmore Street, whose many boutiques, bars, and upscale restaurants are concentrated mostly between Post Street and Pacific Avenue. The area's other main shopping street, Upper Sacramento, has a country ambience: Private residences alternate with good bookstores, fine clothing and gift shops, thrift stores, and art galleries. *Best shopping: Fillmore St., between Post St. and Pacific Ave.; Sacramento St., between Divisadero and Maple Sts.*

polk gulch

In the "gulch" between the hilly Pacific Heights, Nob Hill, and Russian Hill neighborhoods is the lively strip of Polk Gulch. Inexpensive and fun clothing stores, vintage clothing stores, record shops and bookstores, movie theaters, and gift boutiques make this a favorite meeting spot for young San Franciscans. *Best shopping: Polk St., between Geary Blvd. and Greenwich St.*

richmond district

In the past several decades this old Russian neighborhood has experienced an international blending of cultures. Chinese bakeries, hippie bookstores, Russian tearooms, yuppie athletic gear stores, Irish pubs, Japanese and Korean markets, and Palestinian delis do business side by side on its main shopping thoroughfare, Clement Street. *Best shopping: Clement St., between 14th Ave. and Arguello Blvd.*

south of market

Dozens of discount and factory outlets line SoMa's streets and alleyways. The former warehouse district has recently blossomed with restaurants, nightclubs, art galleries, and designer boutiques as well. For high-class gifts, don't skip the district's excellent museums, such as the San Francisco Museum of Modern Art and the Center for the Arts at Yerba Buena Gardens (*see Art Museums in Chapter 2*); their gift shops sell handmade jewelry and various other artsy gift items. *SFMOMA: 151 3rd St., between Mission and Howard Sts.*

union square

Discriminating shoppers head straight to Union Square, one of the nation's most prestigious downtown shopping districts; it's on par with those of New York and Chicago. Indeed, Union Square could lay claim to being one of the world's biggest outdoor shopping malls. Within a half-mile radius of the square are most of the city's department stores (*see below*), as well as the pricey international boutiques of Hermès of Paris, Gucci, Celine of Paris, Alfred Dunhill, Louis Vuitton, and Cartier. Appealing to other tastes are entertaining megastores such as F.A.O. Schwarz, Virgin Megastore, the Disney Store, and NikeTown. On Post Street alone, between Powell Street and Grant Avenue you'll find Giorgio Armani, Ralph Lauren, Bulgari, Brooks Brothers, Coach, Williams-Sonoma, Versace, and Eddie Bauer. A dedicated shopper could walk from one of the major hotels or city parking garages and spend an entire day browsing. *Best shopping: Union Square; Post St., between Powell St. and Grant Ave.; Maiden Lane.*

specialist shops

ANTIQUES/ AUCTIONS & SHOWS

auction houses

8 *d-2*

BUTTERFIELD & BUTTERFIELD

The city's premier auction house, founded in San Francisco in 1865, is the oldest and largest in western America. Each month brings estate sales and special auctions of fine furniture, rugs, jewelry, art, wine, stamps, entertainment memorabilia, and more. Free appraisal clinics take place on the first and third Monday of every month. Call for the current auction schedule. *220 San Bruno Ave., at 15th St., Potrero Hill, 415/861–7500.*

8 *c-2*

BUTTERFIELD WEST

The low-key annex of San Francisco's premier auction house holds monthly auctions of "intermediate property"—furniture, objects, and art that are not quite top-of-the-line. Call for an auction schedule. *164 Utah St., at 15th St., Potrero Hill, 415/861–7500, ext. 308.*

shows

In addition to the shows that take place in established locations each year, four antiques and collectors' fairs and three doll shows are sponsored in various locations by **Golden Gate Shows** (Box 1208, Ross 94957, 415/662–9500).

8 *d-1*

ART DECO TO '50s SALE

These June and December shows feature Art Deco, Moderne, and Streamline Modern furniture, jewelry, and collectibles. *Concourse Exhibition Center, 8th and Brannan Sts., South of Market, 415/599–3326.*

4 *a-2*

SAN FRANCISCO FALL ANTIQUES SHOW

Some 100 dealers of furniture and decorative antiques showcase their wares at this benefit sale held in late October. *Festival Pavilion, Fort Mason, Laguna St. at Marina Blvd., The Marina, 415/546–6661.*

ANTIQUES/ FURNITURE & ACCESSORIES

american & european

4 *f-8*

ANTONIO'S ANTIQUES

Antonio specializes in 17th-, 18th-, and early 19th-century English, French, and Continental furniture. He has an especially good collection of French chinois-

erie and of Louis XIV, XV, and XVI pieces. His restoration work is world-renowned. *701 Bryant St., at 5th St., South of Market, 415/781–1737. Closed weekends.*

5 *c-6*

THE ANTIQUE TRADERS

This shop specializes in stained- and beveled-glass windows and lamps, with famous names such as Tiffany, Handel, and Pairpoint. Count on finding interesting examples of American and European artisanship. *4300 California St., at 5th Ave., Richmond District, 415/668–4444.*

4 *f-4*

DILLINGHAM & COMPANY

In this Jackson Square shop, 17th- and 18th-century English and Dutch furniture and accessories abound. There are some French and Italian pieces as well, and unusual small items such as snuff boxes. *700 Sansome St., at Jackson St., Jackson Square, 415/989–8777. Closed Sun. No credit cards.*

4 *f-4*

FOSTER-GWIN ANTIQUES

English and Continental country and formal furniture from the 17th to the early 19th centuries are top-quality at this Jackson Square shop. There are also some fine accessories. *38 Hotaling Pl., between Montgomery and Sansome Sts., at Jackson St., Jackson Square, 415/397–4986. Closed Sun.*

4 *f-4*

HUNT ANTIQUES

Hunt Antiques feels like an English town house, with fine 17th- to 19th-century English and Continental furniture, long-case clocks, porcelains, paintings, and some silver. It's in the heart of Jackson Square, surrounded by great antiques shops. *478 Jackson St., at Montgomery St., Jackson Square, 415/989–9531. Closed Sun.*

4 *f-4*

JOHN DOUGHTY ANTIQUES

This Jackson Square dealer carries fine 18th- and 19th-century English furniture and accessories, including an incredible collection of desks from the late 18th century through the Edwardian period. *619 Sansome St., between Washington and Jackson Sts., Jackson Square, 415/398–6849. Closed weekends.*

4 *c-8*

ONE-EYED JACKS

Come here for Western artifacts such as antique cowboy boots and saddles, as well as 19th-century American furniture. The shop also rents out props. *1645 Market St., between Gough and Franklin Sts., Hayes Valley, 415/621–4390.*

4 *f-4*

ROBERT DOMERGUE & CO.

Well stocked with 17th- and 18th-century French and Continental furniture and art objects, Domergue & Co. carries rare and expensive furniture, tapestries, screens, mantels, architectural drawings, and prints. *560 Jackson St., at Columbus Ave., Jackson Square, 415/781–4034. Closed weekends.*

4 *c-4*

RUSSIAN HILL ANTIQUES

This shop has a fine collection of Eastern European furniture, plus antique glassware, pottery, and costume jewelry. Antique cocktail paraphernalia is a specialty. *2200 Polk St., at Vallejo St., Russian Hill, 415/441–5561. Closed Mon.*

8 *d-2*

THERIEN & COMPANY

Therien & Company sells fine 17th- and 18th-century Continental furniture and

---

THE JACKSON SQUARE ANTIQUES DISTRICT

Jackson Square is chock-full of art and antique dealers selling fine English and Continental furniture and accessories. A few shops you won't want to miss:

Dillingham & Company
  English and Dutch furniture and accessories.

Foster-Gwin Antiques
  English country and formal furniture.

Hunt Antiques
  Like an English town house, with paintings and long-case clocks.

John Doughty Antiques
  Fine desks from the late 18th century through the Edwardian period.

Robert Domergue & Co.
  French and Continental furniture and objets d'art.

---

decorations, including Sheffield silver and porcelain as well as museum-quality Chinese, Vietnamese, and Greco-Roman antiquities. Their showroom at the Design Center, viewable by appointment only, carries custom-designed and custom-made period reproductions. *411 Vermont St., at 17th St., Potrero Hill, 415/956–8850. Closed weekends. No credit cards.*

art deco

4 *c-8*

ANOTHER TIME

This shop is a Deco lover's delight, with a good selection of furniture and accessories by Heywood Wakefield and others. It's conveniently close to a whole host of other stores that stock vintage collectibles. *1586 Market St., at Franklin St., Hayes Valley, 415/553–8900. Closed Mon.*

4 *b-8*

JET AGE

Though it looks a little tatty from the outside, inside are some fine Art Deco and '30s and '40s furniture, plus later pieces designed by Eames, Noguchi, and others. *250 Oak St., at Gough St., Hayes Valley, 415/864–1950. Closed Mon.*

asian

4 *a-4*

A TOUCH OF ASIA

Most of the high-end 19th- and 20th-century Asian antiques here are from Japan and Korea. Exquisite elm and cherrywood furniture, curio cabinets, and chests are the main attractions, though the store also carries Asian sculptures, prints and paintings, and antique vases. *1784 Union St., at Octavia St., The Marina, 415/474–3115. Closed Mon.*

4 *a-6*

ASAKICHI JAPANESE ANTIQUES

This shop, in Japantown's Kinokuniya Building, carries antique blue-and-white Imari porcelains and handsome tansu chests. *1730 Geary Blvd., between Fillmore and Webster Sts., Japantown, 415/921–2147.*

4 *e-5*

DRAGON HOUSE

Unlike many other Chinatown stores that peddle cheap reproductions of Chinese art, Dragon House sells genuine antiques and Oriental fine arts. The ivory carvings, ceramics, and jewelry for sale date back 2,000 years and beyond. *455 Grant Ave., between Pine and Bush Sts., Chinatown, 415/781–2351. Closed Sun.*

4 *a-4*

FUMIKI FINE ARTS

Two specialties here are *obis* (sashes worn with kimonos) and Japanese bamboo baskets. Also for sale are fine Asian art and antiques including Japanese tansu chests, Korean chests, Imari porcelains, Chinese silk paintings, and Japanese and Korean furniture. *2001 Union St., at Buchanan St., Cow Hollow, 415/922–0573.*

4 *a-6*

GENJI ANTIQUES INC.

In addition to beautiful antique Japanese tansu chests, Genji Antiques carries Japanese furniture, folk arts, and some 17th-century kimonos. *1617 Post St., between Webster and Laguna Sts., Japantown, 415/931–1616.*

8 *d-1*

ORIGINS ART AND ANTIQUES

In SoMa's Baker Hamilton Square complex, this shop imports unusual collector's items, Chinese furniture, porcelain, silk, and jade. Antiques here are up to 400 years old. *680 8th St., at Townsend St., South of Market, 415/252–7089. Closed Sun.*

4 *a-6*

SHIGE ANTIQUE KIMONOS

On the Webster Street Bridge that spans Geary Boulevard, this small shop has antique hand-painted, silk-embroidered kimonos, and a fine selection of obis. *1730 Geary Blvd., Japantown, 415/346–5567.*

victorian & vintage

4 *c-8*

BEAVER BROS.

The sign over this eclectic shop reads "This is not a museum. This is junk for sale." The owners sell whatever strikes their fancy: Louis XVI furniture, Art Deco clocks and telephones, 19th- and 20th-century armoires, silver, cut glass, and rugs. Movie companies have rented many an item here; *Star Trek IV* used the

entire store in one scene. *1637 Market St., at Franklin St., Hayes Valley, 415/863–4344.*

8 *d-3*

CARNEGIE ANTIQUES

This Potrero Hill shop sells whatever it pleases, including porcelains, jewelry, signed paperweights and other collectibles, and some furniture. It has the largest collection of bronzes in the Bay Area. *601 Kansas St., at 18th St., Potrero Hill, 415/641–4704. Closed Mon. and Tues.*

4 *c-2*

FRANK'S FISHERMAN'S SUPPLY

Everything here has a seafaring theme: Antique marine lamps, clocks, sextants, and ships in bottles are the specialties. *366 Jefferson St., between Jones and Leavenworth Sts., Fisherman's Wharf, 415/775–1165.*

4 *a-3*

GREAT AMERICAN COLLECTIVE

At this antiques minimall you'll find 38 dealers selling all kinds of goodies, from an antique purse to a Federal-era chest of drawers. The overall feel is upscale-garage-sale, with prices that range from reasonable to ridiculous. *1736 Lombard St., at Octavia St., Cow Hollow, 415/922–2650.*

2 *b-3*

OLD STUFF

The gems are mixed in with the merely dated at this shop that resembles a grandmother's attic. The furniture and collectibles date from the Victorian period through the 1920s, with plenty of jewelry, silver, and porcelains. *2325 Clement St., between 24th and 25th Aves., Richmond District, 415/668–2220.*

4 *c-8*

RETROSPECTIVE

Retrospective specializes in vintage 20th-century American wooden furniture and sofas. *1649 Market St., between Gough and Franklin Sts., Hayes Valley, 415/863–7414. Closed Mon.*

7 *d-1*

REVIVAL OF THE FITTEST

This is the place to find funky vintage telephones, dishes, clocks, jewelry, lamps, and vases—as well as excellent reproductions of the same stuff. *1701 Haight St., at Cole St., The Haight, 415/ 751–8857.*

7 *f-3*

THE SCHLEP SISTERS

This intriguing shop has a fine selection of secondhand American dinnerware, art pottery, and glass, as well as home accessories from the 1920s through the '60s, such as cookie jars and salt-and-pepper shakers. The largest selection is from the 1950s. *4327 18th St., between Diamond and Eureka Sts., The Castro, 415/626–0581. Closed Mon. and Tues.*

4 *e-3*

TELEGRAPH HILL ANTIQUES

The diverse objets d'art at this tiny North Beach store include crystal, art glass, china, porcelain, silver, cloisonné, and bronzes. There's also a nice selection of Wedgwood pieces, Victoriana, and paintings. *580 Union St., at Stockton St., North Beach, 415/982–7055. Closed Sun.*

5 *e-6*

WOODCHUCK ANTIQUES

Original American Victorian furniture can be found here, along with other treasures of the Victorian era, such as advertising memorabilia, toys, and a large selection of bronze lamps. *3597 Sacramento St., at Locust St., Laurel Heights, 415/922–6416. Closed Sun.*

4 *b-8*

ZONAL

The sign on the window here reads ALWAYS REPAIR, NEVER RESTORE—a perfect prelude to the Depression-era American country furniture within. Inside is an assortment of forgotten treasures, such as antique gardening equipment, vintage porch gliders, old croquet sets, and vintage-1930s iron bed frames. *568 Hayes St., at Laguna St., Hayes Valley, 415/255–9307. Closed Mon.*

ART SUPPLIES

5 *a-7*

AMSTERDAM ART

A favorite of local artists for years, Amsterdam Art stocks supplies for painting, printmaking, ceramics, and

more. There's also a full selection of do-it-yourself frames, and a helpful staff. *5424 Geary Blvd., at 19th Ave., Richmond District, 415/387–5354.*

3 *c-2*

1013 University Ave., near San Pablo Ave., Berkeley, 510/649–4800.

7 *g-5*

COLORCRANE ARTS AND COPY CENTER

This Noe Valley shop carries a complete line of art, graphics, and office supplies. Fax, binding, and color copying services are also available. *3957 24th St., at Sanchez St., Noe Valley, 415/285–1387.*

4 *f-8*

DOUGLAS & STURGESS

Tools and supplies for the sculptor are the specialties at Douglas & Sturgess— including all kinds of clays and glazes. General art supplies are also available here. *730 Bryant St., between 5th and 6th Sts., South Beach, 415/896–6283. Closed weekends.*

8 *a-1*

FLAX ART & DESIGN

Some 32,000 items are sold at competitive prices at this upscale warehouse for art supplies. There are bargains on decorative papers, stationery, frames, portfolio cases, easels, paints, drafting tables and lamps, and sketch books. *1699 Market St., at Valencia St., Mission District, 415/552–2355. Closed Sun.*

7 *d-1*

MENDEL'S ART AND STATIONERY SUPPLIES/ FAR-OUT FABRICS

A longtime Haight-Ashbury favorite, Mendel's carries art, graphics, and office supplies. *1556 Haight St., between Ashbury and Clayton Sts., The Haight, 415/621–1287.*

4 *c-2*

SAN FRANCISCO ART INSTITUTE ART SUPPLY STORE

The art supply store at the renowned San Francisco Art Institute has bargain prices on all kinds of art, printmaking, photo, and filmmaking supplies. The store is the cheapest in the city for paper, whether it's watercolor board or decorative handmade paper. *800 Chesnut St., between Jones and Leaven-*

worth Sts., Russian Hill, 415/771–7020. Closed Sun.

BASKETS

FANTASTICO

Baskets of all shapes and sizes are here, in more than 50 different styles. Most are made of willow, but there are also unique woven baskets from Africa and Asia. *See* Crafts & Hobbies, *below.*

3 d-1
NINEPATCH

This grandmotherly Berkeley store sells all sorts of quilts—both new and antique—as well as baskets, including picnic baskets, whitewashed hampers, and African woven baskets with sturdy leather handles. *2001 Hopkins St., at El Dorado Ave., Berkeley, 510/527–1700.*

5 e-7
PIER 1 IMPORTS

Part of a national chain, this popular import store is known as one of the best places in the city to shop for baskets. Their enormous basketry department has all types, from giant wicker hampers to woven picnic baskets to miniature baskets made of delicate reeds. *3535 Geary Blvd., at Stanyan St., Richmond District, 415/387–6642.*

BEADS

7 f-3
THE BEAD STORE

Here you'll find a daunting collection of more than a thousand kinds of strung and unstrung beads, including stones such as lapis and carnelian, Czechoslovakian and Venetian glass, African trade beads, Buddhist and Muslim prayer beads, and Catholic rosaries. Premade silver jewelry is another specialty, along with religious masks, figurines, and statues from India and Nepal. *417 Castro St., at Market St., The Castro, 415/861–7332.*

7 e-1
GARGOYLE BEADS

Why buy jewelry when you can make your own from Gargoyle's exotic beads, seeds, and polished stones? Hanks of seed beads, Czech and German glass, African bone, faceted crystal, and a small selection of semiprecious stones are just some of the treasures here. *1324*

Haight St., between Masonic and Central Aves., The Haight, 415/552–4274.*

5 a-7
THE HOBBY COMPANY OF SAN FRANCISCO

In addition to all kinds of miscellania (*see* Hobbies, *below*), this store has a whole room full of exotic beads. *5150 Geary Blvd., at 16th Ave., Richmond District, 415/386–2802.*

4 e-3
YONE

This shop opened in 1965 and now carries so many types of beads that the owner has lost track—somewhere between 5,000 and 10,000, he thinks. The beads—made of glass, wood, plastic, bone, sterling silver, and semi-precious stones—come from Africa, Indonesia, Thailand, China, Sri Lanka, India, and many other far-off lands. *478 Union St., at Grant Ave., North Beach, 415/986–1424. Closed Wed. and Sun.*

BEAUTY PRODUCTS

4 a-5
THE BEAUTY STORE

This San Francisco minichain, founded on Fillmore Street in 1980, carries a full line of traditional and more organic beauty supplies, including cosmetics previously only available to professionals. The staff is very friendly and will explain how to use each product. *2124 Fillmore St., at California St., Pacific Heights, 415/346–2511.*

7 e-1
1560 Haight St., at Ashbury St., The Haight, 415/552–9696.

7 g-2
3600 16th St., at Noe St., Noe Valley, 415/ 861–2019.

5 h-3
2085 Chesnut St., at Steiner St., The Marina, 415/922–2526.

4 g-4
4 Embarcadero Center, The Embarcadero, 415/982–5599.

2 c-6
Stonestown Galleria, Upper Level, 19th Ave. and Winston Dr., Stonestown, 415/ 681–0779.

4 a-4

BODY TIME

This Berkeley-based minichain sells some of the best concoctions around for the face and body: their own line of soaps, lotions, creams, perfumes, and body oils. They also carry domestic and imported hair ornaments, bathrobes and kimonos, hair brushes, and other toiletries. 2072 Union St. at Webster St., The Marina, 415/922–4076.

3 e-2

2509 Telegraph Ave., Berkeley, 510/548–3686.

4 a-6

1932 Fillmore St., at Bush St., Pacific Heights, 415/771–2431.

7 d-1

BREATH OF HEAVEN

This heavenly smelling shop carries bath gels, lotions, and soaps that can be custom-scented. They also carry essential oils, European soaps, candles, potpourri, aromatherapy items, and incense. 1715 Haight St., at Cole St., The Haight, 415/221–1638.

7 g-5

COMMON SCENTS

Most of the bath and skin-care products at this shop are made in the Bay Area. You'll find all kinds of bath oils, gels, and salts, as well as rubber duckies and other bath toys. Massage oils and lotions, perfumes and incense, and exotic skin-care products round out the selection. Many products can be custom-scented. 3920 24th St., near Sanchez St., Noe Valley, 415/826–1019.

4 a-6

FUJIYA COSMETICS

Fujiya has all of your favorite Shiseido-brand cosmetics, plus Shieseido sun and hair-care products and fragrances for men and women. Makeovers are available by appointment. 1662 Post St., at Buchanan St., Japantown, 415/931–3302.

4 e-6

JACQUELINE PERFUMERY

Since 1969, Jacqueline has carried one of the city's largest and finest selections of perfumes and men's toiletries. Once you've picked out a scent, choose a beautiful crystal perfume bottle to put it in. There's also a choice selection of European skin-care products. 156 Geary St., between Stockton St. and Grant Ave., Union Square, 415/981–0858.

7 f-3

SKIN ZONE

At this environmentally aware shop, many of the men's and women's bath- and skin-care products are sold in bulk and in refillable bottles. In addition, the Skin Zone carries popular brands such as Casswell & Massey and Aubrey Organics. 575 Castro St., at 18th St., The Castro, 415/626–7933.

4 g-8

ZIA COSMETICS

The emphasis here is on natural skin-care products that help the skin's ability to regenerate and renew. Customer service is given careful attention, too; Zia's skin-care hot line (800/334–7546) is staffed by licensed aestheticians. 410 Townsend St., at 5th St., South of Market, 415/543–7546. Closed Sun.

BOOKS

general

4 c-7

A CLEAN WELL-LIGHTED PLACE FOR BOOKS

This bookstore, whose main branch is in the Opera Plaza, bills itself as carrying "a large selection of paperbacks and hardbacks in all fields for all ages." Paperback literature and books on opera and San Francisco history are particularly well stocked in the San Francisco branch. Both locations are known for their well-organized, easy-to-browse shelves. 601 Van Ness Ave., at Turk St., Civic Center, 415/441–6670.

1 b-1

2417 Larkspur Landing Cir., at Sir Francis Drake Blvd., Larkspur, 415/461–0171.

8 a-2

THE ABANDONED PLANET BOOKSTORE

This is a cozy little shop, with an old piano in one corner and a pair of pet cats. Music, theater, and art history are particularly well-represented, and they occasionally have publishers' overstock books at bargain prices. 518 Valencia St., near 16th St., Mission District, 415/861–4695.

`4` *f-5*

ALEXANDER BOOK CO.

With three floors of titles, this "old-fashioned, full-service, independent bookstore" is particularly well stocked with literature, art books, and poetry. It also has an excellent children's books section. *50 2nd St., at Market St., Polk Gulch, 415/495–2992. Closed weekends.*

`4` *d-2*

BARNES & NOBLE BOOKSELLERS

Everything you've come to expect from this national book lover's chain is here, including the bountiful magazine racks and tolerant attitude towards browsing. *2552 Taylor St., at North Point St., Fisherman's Wharf, 415/292–6762.*

`3` *d-1*

BLACK OAK BOOKS

This Berkeley shop is well known for its sophisticated literature, classics, and poetry sections; it also carries quite a few imports. Bestselling and critically acclaimed authors hold weekly readings. *1491 Shattuck Ave., at Vine St., Berkeley, 510/486–0698.*

`7` *d-1*

BOOKSMITH

Founded in 1976, this fine neighborhood bookshop is chock-full of current releases, children's titles, and literary treasures. Reflecting the interests of its Haight clientele, it also carries plenty in the areas of science fiction, counterculture, and alternative medicine. *1644 Haight St., between Clayton and Cole Sts., The Haight, 415/863–8688.*

`4` *e-6*

BORDERS BOOKS AND MUSIC

The Union Square outpost of the national chain is always at the top of the list of San Franciscans' favorite bookstores. It has three floors of books on every subject, plus a friendly staff to help navigate the aisles. *400 Post St., at Powell St., Union Square, 415/399–1633.*

`4` *e-4*

CITY LIGHTS

This North Beach establishment—the city's most famous bookstore—has been a literary landmark since 1955, when it was a meeting place for Beat poets like Jack Kerouac, Gregory Corso, and Allen Ginsberg. Lawrence Ferlinghetti still owns the place, and his old friends still stop by—as do subsequent generations of San Francisco literati. City Lights is particularly well stocked with poetry, contemporary literature, small-press publications, literary reviews, and translations of Third World literature. Many titles are published in-house. *261 Columbus Ave., at Broadway, North Beach, 415/362–8193.*

`3` *e-2*

CODY'S BOOKS

This Berkeley institution stocks every imaginable genre, from poetry and philosophy to self-defense and women's studies. It also has an impressive newsstand, a cheery children's room, an extensive selection of foreign-language books, and an information desk with a hardworking staff. Readings by local and nationally known authors are always crowded; arrive early. *2454 Telegraph Ave., at Haste St., Berkeley, 510/845–7852.*

`3` *b-2*

1730 4th St., between Hearst and Virginia Sts., Berkeley, 510/559–9500.

`5` *c-6*

GREEN APPLE BOOKS

This has been a local favorite since 1967 and is voted the Bay Area's best bookstore by *San Francisco Bay Guardian* readers year after year. It has one of the largest used-book departments in the city, as well as new books in every field. The atmosphere is like Grandma's attic, with strange and wonderful books tucked into every dusty corner. The store's strong suits are literature and history, but there's a broad selection in nearly every discipline. Specialties are comic books and a rare-books collection; sale-priced books spill out into bins onto the sidewalk. A new- and used-fiction annex is two doors down, at 520 Clement Street. *506 Clement St., at 6th Ave., Richmond District, 415/387–2272.*

`8` *a-3*

MODERN TIMES BOOKSTORE

Named after Charlie Chaplin's politically subversive film, Modern Times is a large shop that stocks quality literary fiction and nonfiction, much of it with a political bent. Strong subjects include Spanish-language, art, current affairs, gay and lesbian issues, cultural theory, multicultural childrens' books, and underground newspapers and 'zines. Author readings and public forums are held on a regular basis. *888 Valencia St., between 19th and 20th Sts., Mission District, 415/282–9246.*

MOE'S BOOKS
See Secondhand & Discount Books, below.

2 e-2
SOLAR LIGHTS BOOKS
In the heart of the Union Street shopping district, Solar Lights is a fine independent bookstore carrying contemporary literature, travel, mysteries, New Age psychology, and more. Though it's easy to miss—below street level, down a short flight of stairs—inside, it's surprisingly large. *2068 Union St., at Webster St., 415/567–6082.*

4 e-5
TILLMAN PLACE BOOKSHOP
Find this shop tucked away in a tiny alley off Grant Avenue near Union Square. It has a good selection of children's books, and a strong literature department. *8 Tillman Pl., Grant Ave. between Post and Sutter Sts., Union Square, 415/392–4668. Closed Sun.*

4 e-6
VIRGIN MEGASTORE
Best known for its extensive musical offerings, the Virgin Megastore also has great selections of popular culture and travel books. *See Music, below.*

secondhand & antiquarian

4 c-5
ACORN BOOKS
Customers in search of an antiquarian, out-of-print, or used book know that the dedicated staff at this Polk Gulch shop would scour the earth's four corners to find it. Chances are, however, that the well-stocked store probably already has it somewhere on the shelves. *1436 Polk St., between Pine and California Sts., Polk Gulch, 415/563–1736.*

8 a-2
ADOBE BOOK SHOP
Adobe specializes in used and rare books, particularly those about art and modern philosophy. The staff is erudite but affable, and the prices are some of

the lowest in the city. *3166 16th St., between Valencia and Guerrero Sts., Mission District, 415/864–3936.*

4 d-5
ARGONAUT BOOK SHOP
First editions and other rare books fill the shelves here. There is an excellent selection of history books on San Francisco and the American West, in addition to many art books and collector's maps. *786 Sutter St., between Taylor and Jones Sts., Union Square, 415/474–9067. Closed Sun.*

4 f-6
BRICK ROW BOOK SHOP
Since 1915, Brick Row has specialized in first editions and rare books of 18th- and 19th-century English and American literature. The shop is in the same building as many of the city's finest art galleries. *49 Geary St., at Kearny St., Union Square, 415/398–0414. Closed weekends.*

GREEN APPLE
See General, above.

4 f-6
JEFFREY THOMAS
This shop, in the 49 Geary Street building that houses many of the city's finest art galleries, sells rare books, prints and manuscripts in all fields of interest. *49 Geary St., between Kearney St. and Grant Ave., Union Square, 415/956–3272. Closed weekends.*

4 e-7
MCDONALD'S BOOK SHOP
McDonald's is a throwback to the good old days of used-book selling, with haphazardly stacked shelves that encourage browsing. It has the best, if most disorderly, selection of old magazines in the city. *48 Turk St., near Market St., The Tenderloin, 415/673–2235. Closed Sun.*

3 e-2
MOE'S BOOKS
This beloved Berkeley institution has five floors of secondhand and antiquarian books, as well as a good selection of new books, periodicals, and reviews. The foreign language and art book sections are particularly impressive. *2476 Telegraph Ave., near Haste St., Berkeley, 510/849–2087.*

3 *e-3*

SHAKESPEARE & CO. BOOKS

This used-book store has not changed a bit over the years; it's dusty and disorganized, but filled with treasures in the art, literature, classics, and philosophy genres. For those who wish to spend the afternoon book-browsing, Moe's Books (*see above*) is across the street. *2499 Telegraph Ave., at Dwight Way, Berkeley, 510/841–8916.*

6 *g-2*

SUNSET BOOKS

This is a solid general-interest used bookshop with many titles on art, psychology, music, history, literature, and philosophy. *2161 Irving St., at 23rd Ave., Sunset District, 415/664–3644.*

special interest

7 *f-3*

A DIFFERENT LIGHT

Part of a national chain, this is the place for lesbian, gay, and transgender literature and history, as well as everything from sci-fi and fantasy to religion and film criticism. Added attractions: a large magazine section, stacks of free weekly newspapers, and dozens of flyers about community events. Book signings and readings take place weekly. *489 Castro St., near 18th St., The Castro, 415/431–0891.*

4 *b-5*

AUTOMOBILIA

The bookstore at the back of the San Francisco Auto Center is packed tighter than a Volkswagen at a circus, and all of the books it stocks are about cars. Look for fiction, nonfiction, technical manuals, glossy coffee-table books, and a fine selection of miniature car models and automotive art. *1701 Van Ness Ave., at Sacramento St., Polk Gulch, 415/292–2710.*

1 *a-1*

BOOK PASSAGE

This excellent Marin County shop has all kinds of books, including used and remaindered, but travel books are the specialty. There's an entire room devoted to travel literature, and another room full of travel guides to every nook and cranny on the planet. *51 Tamal Vista Blvd., Corte Madera, 415/927–0960.*

7 *e-1*

BOUND TOGETHER ANARCHIST BOOK COLLECTIVE

This is an old-school anarchist entity founded in the 1970s and staffed entirely by volunteers, with profits contributed to anarchist projects. Books and magazines are divided into sections with headings such as Conspiracies, Drugs, Film & Media, Magick & Spirit, and Syndicalist Periodicals. There's also a small Spanish section. *1369 Haight St., at Masonic Ave., The Haight, 415/431–8355.*

4 *b-2*

BUILDERS BOOKSOURCE

Books about architecture, interior design, gardening, crafts, and construction abound in this beautifully layed-out bookstore, along with a some cookbooks and children's books. A mecca for contractors and construction workers, it's a great source of information on building codes and other technical matters. *900 North Point St., at Polk St., Ghirardelli Square, 415/440–5773.*

3 *b-2*

1817 4th St., at Hearst St., Berkeley, 510/845–6874.

7 *d-1*

COMIC RELIEF

Comic Relief is fully stocked with new and used comic books, graphic novels, art, movie, and TV books, and small-press and underground comic booklets. *1597 Haight St., at Clayton St., The Haight, 415/552–9010.*

3 *d-2*

2138 University Ave., at Shattuck Ave., Berkeley, 510/843–5002.

7 *f-1*

COMIX EXPERIENCE

This shop sells all kinds of comics, from the popular to the obscure. It occasionally holds in-store signings. *305 Divisadero St., between Oak and Page Sts., The Haight, 415/863–9258. No credit cards (for purchases of less than $15).*

3 *f-3*

DARK CARNIVAL OF CRIME, MYSTERY, SUSPENSE, AND TRUE CRIME BOOK STORE

Make a trip to Berkeley to browse the Bay Area's largest selection of sci-fi and fantasy. Mysteries and crime fiction are plentiful as well. *3086 Claremont Ave.,* between Alcatraz and Ashby Aves., Berkeley, 510/595–7637.

4 *e-3*

EASTWIND BOOKS AND ARTS

This shop deals exclusively in new books on all aspects of Asian-America and Asia, particularly China. There are both Chinese- and English-language sections. *1435 Stockton St., 2nd Floor, at Columbus Ave., Chinatown, 415/772–5899.*

4 *c-6*

EUROPEAN BOOK COMPANY

Travelers bound for Europe will want to stop here first to stock up on French-, German-, Italian-, and Spanish-language books, magazines, and newspapers, as well as foreign-language dictionaries, learning cassettes, maps, and travel guides. *925 Larkin St., between Post and Geary Sts., The Tenderloin, 415/474–0626. Closed Sun.*

4 *c-6*

FANTASY, ETC.

Fantasy, Etc., is a great source for all kinds of new and used pulp fiction, science fiction, detective stories, and adventure books. Even though it's tiny, you can't miss this shop, right next to a huge adult cinema. *808 Larkin St., at O'Farrell St., The Tenderloin, 415/441–7617.*

3 *d-1*

GAIA BOOKSTORE

This is a longtime Bay Area favorite for New Age books. It also sells New Age music and instruments, tarot cards, and meditation supplies. *1400 Shattuck Ave., at Rose St., Berkeley, 510/548–4172.*

4 *a-6*

KINOKUNIYA BOOKSTORE

This shop has one of the finest selections of English-language books on Japanese subjects in the United States. A major attraction is the collection of beautifully produced graphics and art books; there are also periodicals in Japanese and English. *Japan Center, Kinokuniya Bldg., 2nd floor, 1581 Webster St., at Post St., Japantown, 415/567–7625.*

7 *h-1*

LIMELIGHT FILM AND THEATRE BOOKSTORE

This establishment carries new and used film and theater titles, plus special-

interest periodicals. *1803 Market St., at Octavia St., Civic Center, 415/864–2265.*

3 *e-4*

MAMA BEARS

Mama Bears is more than a bookstore: It's a women's community center, with a coffee house, crafts, music, bulletin boards, and networking opportunities galore. Books are primarily by women and deal mostly with women's issues; there are some books for children as well. *6536 Telegraph Ave., at 66th St., Oakland, 510/428–9684.*

4 *a-6*

MARCUS BOOKS

Books, periodicals, cards, and gifts here celebrate and reflect upon African and African-American reality. *1712 Fillmore St., at Post St., Japantown, 415/346–4222.*

3 *d-5*

3900 Martin Luther King Way, at 39th St., Oakland, 510/652–2344.

4 *c-2*

THE MARITIME BOOKSTORE

Sailors will want to set a course for this Hyde Street Pier shop, where literature of the sea, boat-building books, and maritime histories abound. *Hyde St. Pier, 2905 Hyde St., at Jefferson St., Fisherman's Wharf, 415/775–2665.*

RAND MCNALLY MAP & TRAVEL STORE

See Maps, below.

7 *f-5*

SAN FRANCISCO MYSTERY BOOKSTORE

Shelves of quality new and used detective fiction make this the shop of choice for the armchair Sherlock Holmes. The shop even carries some first editions. *4175 24th St., between Castro and Diamond Sts., Noe Valley, 415/282–7444. Closed Mon. and Tues.*

3 *e-3*

SHAMBHALA BOOKSELLERS

Shambhala sells books on Eastern and Western religious traditions, Jungian psychology, acupuncture, astrology, Wicca, and magic. *2482 Telegraph Ave., near Dwight Way, Berkeley, 510/848–8443.*

4 *f-6*

SIERRA CLUB BOOKSTORE

In addition to Bay Area trail guides, the Sierra Club shop stocks books on environmental issues, nature poetry, wildlife, environmentally themed children's books, practical guides for hiking and camping, and California ecology. There is a large selection of nature calendars, cards, and T-shirts, as well. A bulletin board lists area hikes, meetings, and events. *85 2nd St., at Mission St., South of Market, 415/977–5600. Closed weekends.*

4 *f-5*

STACEY'S BOOKSTORE

Once a solely professional bookstore, with computer, technical, medical, business, travel, and reference titles forming the bulk of its inventory, Stacey's is now one of San Francisco's best bookstores. More than 100,000 titles are displayed on three floors. *581 Market St., between 1st and 2nd Sts., Financial District, 415/421–4687.*

4 *f-4*

THOMAS BROS. MAPS AND BOOKS

See *Maps, below.*

4 *f-4*

WILLIAM STOUT ARCHITECTURAL BOOKS

Architecture and design books and periodicals are the specialty at this Jackson Square bookshop. The majority of the books are new, although there's an impressive out-of-print collection as well. *804 Montgomery St., between Jackson and Pacific Sts., Financial District, 415/391–6757. Closed Sun.*

3 *e-2*

UNIVERSITY PRESS BOOKS

This shop appeals to academics and heavy thinkers with books published by more than 100 university presses, plus academic lines including Penguin, Routledge, Sage, and Beacon. *2430 Bancroft Way, between Dana St. and Telegraph Ave., Berkeley, 510/548–0585.*

5 *h-4*

VEDANTA SOCIETY BOOKSHOP

At the entrance to the Vedanta Society Old Temple (*see* Churches, Synagogues, & Temples *in* Chapter 2), this shop carries books on Hindu philosophy, in Sanskrit and in English, as well as those about other Eastern and Western religions. *2323 Vallejo St., at Fillmore St., Cow Hollow, 415/922–2323. Closed Tues., Sat., and Sun.*

CANDLES

2 *c-6*

THE CANDLEMAN STORE

Wafting from this shop are the scents of gardenia, cinnamon, and mulberry. In addition to scented and potpourri candles, there are clever candles shaped

---

BOOK-SHOPPING IN BERKELEY

Berkeley brims with excellent bookstores, not surprisingly, considering that it's home to a world-class university. Whether you're seeking classical philosophy or a Tom Clancy thriller, these Berkeley shops merit a trip across the Bay:

Cody's Books (General)
Berkeley's best, with every imaginable genre.

Black Oak Books (General)
A discriminating collection of literature, classics, and poetry.

Dark Carnival of Crime, Mystery, Suspense, and True Crime Book Store (Special Interest)
The Bay Area's largest selection of sci-fi and fantasy.

Gaia Bookstore (Special Interest)
A longtime favorite for New Age books.

Moe's Books (Secondhand & Antiquarian)
Five floors of secondhand and antiquarian books.

Shakespeare & Co. Books (Secondhand & Antiquarian)
A small, dusty shop with all kinds of treasures.

Shambhala Booksellers (Special Interest)
Eastern and Western religious traditions, psychology, acupuncture, astrology, Wicca, and magic.

University Press Books (Special Interest)
Books by more than 100 university presses.

like dogs, dragons, and fish, and more than 100 styles of oil candles. *Stonestown Galleria, 19th Ave. at Winston Dr., Stonestown, 415/566–6773.*

4 *e-6*

San Francisco Shopping Centre, 865 Market St. between 4th and 5th Sts., Union Square, 415/974–3600.

1 *b-2*

THE CANDLESTICK

Make the trip across the Golden Gate Bridge to visit this charming candle shop, opened in 1957. In addition to beeswax candles and oil lamps it carries beautiful stained-glass candle holders made by Bay Area artists. *777 Bridgeway, at Princess St., Sausalito, 415/332–2834.*

8 *a-2*

LADY LUCK CANDLE SHOP

The friendly proprietor of this tiny shop can convince even the most bitter cynic to buy a hope candle. There's a wide selection of incense, devotional candles, and love potions. *311 Valencia St., between 14th and 15th Sts., Mission District, 415/621–0358. Closed Sun.*

CHARITABLE CAUSES

7 *g-5*

GLOBAL EXCHANGE FAIR TRADE CRAFT CENTER

The nonprofit Global Exchange organization aims to help world artisans and farmers achieve self-sufficiency through trade. To that end, the shop sells hundreds of handcrafted gift items, plus handmade clothing, jewelry, musical instruments, and food items from 40 countries. *3900 24th St., at Sanchez St., Noe Valley, 415/648–8068.*

7 *e-1*

PLANETWEAVERS TREASURE STORE

San Francisco's official UNICEF store stocks crafts, clothing, masks, drums, music, books, and toys from around the world. *1573 Haight St., at Ashbury St., The Haight, 415/864–4415.*

7 *g-3*

UNDER ONE ROOF

Affiliated with the NAMES Project (*see* Statues, Murals, & Monuments *in* Chap-

ter 2) this shop sells high-quality gift items gathered from 50 AIDS organizations: books, children's toys, stationary, Christmas ornaments, queer pride T-shirts, picture frames, and more. All profits go directly to AIDS service providers and researchers. *2362-B Market St., between Noe and Castro Sts., The Castro, 415/252–9430.*

CLOTHING FOR CHILDREN & INFANTS

5 *d-6*

CITY KIDS BABY NEWS STORE

This is a veritable kiddie department store, selling clothing, nursery furniture, and diapers—plus books, games, and toys. *152 Clement St., at 3rd Ave., Richmond District, 415/752–3837. Closed Sun.*

5 *e-6*

DOTTIE DOOLITTLE

Dottie Doolittle is where Pacific Heights mothers buy Florence Eiseman dresses for their little girls. The shop has a good selection of domestic and imported clothing for boys and girls, from infants to age 14. It also carries baby furniture and accessories. *3680 Sacramento St., at Spruce St., Laurel Heights, 415/563–3244.*

7 *e-1*

KIDS ONLY

There's a little bit of everything here, from sturdy clothing to amusing games and toys. *1608 Haight St., at Masonic Ave., The Haight, 415/552–5445.*

4 *a-4*

MUDPIE

This charming shop overflows with unique children's wear such as velvet dresses and handmade booties. Quilts, toys, books, and overstuffed child-size furniture make this a fun store for browsing. The Chestnut Street branch's line of clothing is for tots two years old and under. *1694 Union St., at Buchanan St., The Marina, 415/771–9262.*

5 *h-3*

2220 Chestnut St., at Pierce St., The Marina, 415/474–8395.

7 g-5

SMALL FRYS

In the heart of family-friendly Noe Valley, Small Frys carries a complete range of colorful cottons, mainly for infants but also for older children—including Oshkosh and Levi's for Kids. They also stock kiddie accessories. *4066 24th St., between Castro and Noe Sts., Noe Valley, 415/648–3954.*

5 h-5

YOUNTVILLE

This upscale shop carries clothing for children up to age eight, with some European fashions and many California designs. *2416 Fillmore St., at Washington St., Pacific Heights, 415/922–5050.*

2 c-6

Stonestown Galleria, 19th Ave. and Winston Dr., Stonestown, 415/681–2202.

CLOTHING FOR MEN/GENERAL

classic

4 e-6

ALFRED DUNHILL NORTH AMERICA LIMITED

The American outpost of posh London-based Alfred Dunhill carries everything for the man who enjoys spending lots of money on himself. Besides clothing with a decidedly British feel, you'll find luggage, toiletries, and fine cigars (*see* Tobacconists, *below*). *250 Post St., at Stockton St., Union Square, 415/781–3368.*

4 e-5

BROOKS BROTHERS

This classic men's store was established in 1818 and still sells the private-label button-down oxford shirts that first made it famous. The store has women's shirts, sweaters, blazers, slacks, and coats as well. *201 Post St., between Stockton St. and Grant Ave., Union Square, 415/397–4500. Closed Sun.*

4 e-6

BULLOCK & JONES

Bullock & Jones has been a favorite among successful businessmen since it was established in San Francisco in 1853. Bestsellers include its pima cotton dress shirts, linen and wool slacks, and private-label silk ties. *340 Post St., at Stockton St., Union Square, 415/392–4243.*

4 f-5

THE HOUND GENTLEMEN'S CLOTHIERS

This shop carries clothing and accessories for the ambitious young Financial District professional. They have a good selection of robes and pajamas, too. *140 Sutter St., between Kearny and Montgomery Sts., Financial District, 415/989–0429.*

4 f-5

275 Battery St., between Sacramento and California Sts., Financial District, 415/982–1578. Closed Sun.

4 f-5

JAY BRIGGS CLOTHIERS

Here is a full range of men's conservative business clothing and accessories, as well as sportswear made in Italy, Germany, and Australia. The merchandise is fine, as the prices would suggest. *61 Post St., at Montgomery St., Financial District, 415/982–1611. Closed Sun.*

4 e-5

WILKES BASHFORD

A legendary San Francisco haberdashery, Wilkes Bashford carries menswear and accessories, both classic and trendy. Mayor Willie Brown has been known to shop here, among other prominent San Franciscans. The shop is famous for its customer service; its tailors will even make house and office calls. *375 Sutter St., at Stockton St., Union Square, 415/986–4380. Closed Sun.*

contemporary

4 d-6

COURTOUÉ

The fine Italian suits here range in style from classic to avant garde. Evening wear, sportswear, shoes, and accessories are also by Italian designers. *459 Geary St., between Taylor and Mason Sts., Union Square, 415/775–2900. Closed Sun.*

4 e-6

D. FINE

Brioni, Canali, and Pal Zileri are some of the Italian designers represented at D. Fine. The store also carries fine leather jackets and accessories. *300 Post St., at Stockton St., Union Square, 415/986–3001.*

4 *f-5*

DAVID STEPHENS CLOTHIERS

David Stephens provides fine Italian menswear for the fashion conscious. Designer lines include Zegna, Canali, Byblos, and the Redaelli line by Freer. *61 Post St., at Kearny St., Union Square, 415/982-1612. Closed Sun.*

4 *f-4*

KENNETH CHARLES

San Francisco's on-the-rise menswear designer, Kenneth Charles, showcases his fashions in an art gallery–like setting. The suits, jackets, shoes, sportswear, and accessories are stylish but affordable. *582 Washington St., between Sansome and Montgomery Sts., Financial District, 415/399–1059. Closed Sun.*

4 *b-8*

NOMADS

A must for artists and rock stars, this shop has cornered the market on upscale grunge fashions. It sells shepherd's vests, cowhide pants, and other clever necessities and accessories. *556 Hayes St., at Laguna St., Hayes Valley, 415/864–5692.*

4 *e-6*

THE TAILORED MAN

The helpful, multilingual staff will help you choose stylish menswear by top American and European designers. *360 Stockton St., at Post St., Union Square, 415/397–6906.*

discount & outlet

4 *e-5*

EUROPEAN MENSWEAR OUTLET

Quality suits, shirts, ties and belts— mostly Italian—are discounted as much as 60%. *393 Sutter St., at Stockton St., Union Square, 415/788–0340.*

4 *f-6*

THE MEN'S WEARHOUSE

Fine men's suits, sportscoats, accessories, and shoes by top designers are sold 20%–30% below retail at this shop, part of a national chain. The sales staff is pleasant and dedicated to customer service. *601 Market St., at 3rd St., Financial District, 415/896–0871.*

4 *g-4*

27 Drumm St., at the Embarcadero, Financial District, 415/788–6363.

4 *e-6*

17 Stockton St., at Market St., Union Square, 415/544–0627.

unusual sizes

4 *e-7*

CALIFORNIA BIG AND TALL CLOTHING MART

This off-price and clearance center is a great place for great values for hard-to-fit men. Shoes by Bally, Capezio, and Zodiac sell for as much as 60% below retail. *822 Mission St., at 5th St., South of Market, 415/495–4484.*

4 *f-6*

ROCHESTER BIG AND TALL

Rochester has a good selection of suits, sport coats, trousers, sportswear, and formalwear in sizes ranging from 46 regular to 60 extra-long. Their shoe department also deals in hard-to-find sizes. *700 Mission St., at 3rd St., South of Market, 415/982–6455.*

CLOTHING FOR MEN/SPECIALTY

formal wear

2 *c-6*

GINGISS FORMALWEAR

The advantage of doing business with this chain, which has more than 200 stores nationwide, is the ability to coordinate services between cities for major events. Designer tuxedos are available for sale or rent, in addition to shoes, ties, and cummerbunds. *Stonestown Galleria, 19th Ave. and Winston Dr., Stonestown, 415/665–1144.*

4 *f-5*

SELIX

Selix has branches all over the Bay Area, all linked by computer to coordinate wedding information. Designer tuxedos are available for sale or rent, and they sell all accessories. *123 Kearny St., at Post St., Financial District, 415/362–1133.*

2 *b-6*

2622 Ocean Ave., at 19th Ave., Stonestown, 415/333–2412.

shoes

`4` *e-6*

BRUNO MAGLI

Bruno Magli's famous, expensive shoes are available at this tony shop in every conceivable kind of leather, in addition to classic styles. All of the shoes are manufactured in Italy. *285 Geary St., at Powell St., Union Square, 415/421–0356.*

`4` *f-5*

CASSERD SHOES

This Financial District shoe store has a good selection of dress and casual men's shoes at reasonable prices. They have narrow and extra-wide sizes, as well as elevator shoes. *310 Kearny St., at Bush St., Financial District, 415/421–5690. Closed Sun.*

`4` *f-5*

CHURCH'S ENGLISH SHOES LTD.

This shop carries the famed high-quality Church's English shoes as well as expensive Italian and American footwear for men. Rounding out the selection: ties, slippers, and small leather goods. *50 Post St., between Montgomery and Kearny Sts., Financial District, 415/433–5100. Closed Sun.*

`4` *f-4*

THE SHOE TREE

This family-run establishment started in Berkeley in 1958 and moved to the Financial District in 1976. It's principally a street- and golf-shoe business, with a nice selection of luggage, briefcases, and small leather goods. *659 Commercial St., at Montgomery St., Financial District, 415/788–9800. Closed Sun.*

ties

`4` *e-6*

THE TAILORED MAN

This shop has one of the largest tie selections in the Bay Area, in addition to stylish menswear (*see Classic, above*). *360 Stockton St., at Post St., Union Square, 415/397–6906.*

CLOTHING FOR WOMEN & MEN/ GENERAL

classic

`4` *e-5*

BOGNER

The classic sports- and businesswear for sale here are the creations of Munich-based designer Bogner. Suits for men and women are manufactured in wool, cotton, and other natural fibers by the Bogner factories in West Germany and Vermont. *400 Sutter St., at Stockton St., Union Square, 415/434–3888. Closed Sun.*

`4` *e-5*

BURBERRY'S LIMITED

Burberry's has been selling its famed plaid-lined trench coats since World War I. The shop also carries distinctive English-country weekend wear: shirts, blouses, jackets, blazers, sweaters, hats, and umbrellas. *225 Post St., at Stockton St., Union Square, 415/392–2200. Closed Sun.*

`4` *e-5*

CABLE CAR CLOTHIERS

A San Francisco tradition since 1939, this clothier carries British and American classics in 100% cotton and pure wool. Their old-fashioned, high-quality pajamas and robes have long been favorites, as have their undergarments, gloves, tweed hats, caps, and scarves. *246 Sutter St., between Stockton and Powell Sts., Union Square, 415/397–4740. Closed Sun.*

`4` *e-6*

COURTOUÉ

Courtoué manufactures business attire for professional men and women. For those who want custom-made suits, there's an excellent fabric selection right on the premises. The shop's tie selection is one of the best in town. *459 Geary St., at Mason St., Union Square, 415/775–2900. Closed Sun.*

`4` *e-5*

SCOTCH HOUSE

Handsome sweaters, hats, caps, scarves, and blankets are manufactured at fine woolen mills in Britain. They're made of cashmere, lambs' wool, and Shetland. *187 Post St., at Grant Ave., Union Square, 415/391–1264. Closed Sun.*

5 h-4

THREE BAGS FULL

Most of the beautiful imported sweaters here are hand-knitted. *2181 Union St., at Fillmore St., Cow Hollow, 415/567–5753.*

4 e-5

500 Sutter St., Powell St., Union Square, 415/398–7987.

5 f-5

3314 Sacramento St., at Presidio Ave., Pacific Heights, 415/923–1454.

contemporary

7 e-1

BEHIND THE POST OFFICE

Here's all the latest and greatest hip-hop gear: T-shirts, skate-girl dresses, and *phat* baggy pants. *1510 Haight St., at Ashbury St., The Haight, 415/861–2507.*

7 d-1

DALJEETS

This store exemplifies San Francisco's "Bagdad by the Bay" reputation. There's all kinds of trendy merchandise, from T-shirts and jeans to jackets and halter tops. *1744 Haight St., at Cole St., The Haight, 415/752–5610.*

4 e-6

THE GAP

Of the many Gap stores in San Francisco, this branch on Market Street is one of the biggest and best-stocked. You'll find all your favorite weekend basics, like T-shirts and jeans, plus shoes, belts, scarves, sleepwear, and handbags. *890 Market St., at Powell St., Union Square, 415/788–5909.*

7 f-3

HEADLINES

The motto here is "retail entertainment." The clothes range from conservative officewear to outrageous outfits perfect for the SoMa night scene. *557 Castro St., at 18th St., The Castro, 415/626–8061.*

5 g-3

2301 Chesnut St., at Divisidero St., The Marina, 415/441–5550.

4 e-6

838 Market St., between 4th and 5th Sts., Union Square, 415/956–4872.

4 e-6

J. CREW

The popular mail-order company sells its nouveau-preppy couture here. *San Francisco Shopping Centre, 865 Market St., at 5th St., Union Square, 415/546–6262 or 415/434–2739.*

4 e-5

MAC (MODERN APPEALING CLOTHING)

MAC merchandise ranges from dressy to casual. Trendy fashions are by designers such as Todd Oldham, Marc Jacobs, and San Franciscan Hank Ford. *5 Claude Lane, between Bush and Sutter Sts., at Kearny St., Financial District, 415/837–0615.*

4 e-3

1543 Grant Ave., between Filbert and Union Sts., North Beach, 415/837–1604.

7 g-2

NANA

The San Francisco branch of this national chain sells clothes and shoes to ultrahip Gen-Xers. The sales rack holds bargains of up to 50% off. *2276 Market St., at Noe St., Noe Valley, 415/861–6262.*

4 e-3

OCEAN FRONT WALKERS

Printed T-shirts, boxer shorts, and pajamas with designs ranging from animal wildlife to 1950s iconography are all available at this friendly neighborhood store. *1458 Grant Ave., between Union and Green Sts., North Beach, 415/291–9727.*

7 g-5

4069 24th St., at Noe St., Noe Valley, 415/550–1980.

4 b-2

THE OUTLAW

Bikers and wannabikers outfit themselves in Outlaw's leather jackets, T-shirts, hats, and other Harley-Davidson fashions. *Ghirardelli Square, 900 North Point St., between Polk and Larkin Sts., Fisherman's Wharf, 415/563–8986.*

4 d-8

ROLO

This SF minichain keeps the club set up to date. Men's and women's designer-brand denim, sportswear, shoes, and accessories reveal a distinct European influence. *1301 Howard St., at 9th St., South of Market, 415/861–1999.*

7 *f-3*

2351 Market St., at Castro St., The Castro, 415/431–4545.

7 *f-3*

450 Castro St., at 18th St., The Castro, 415/626–7171.

5 *h-4*

UKO

Come here for unique fashions by Japanese designers not yet well known in the United States. The clothes are simple, well tailored, and youthful. *2070 Union St., at Fillmore St., Cow Hollow, 415/563–0300.*

7 *e-1*

X-LARGE

This Los Angeles–based franchise is run by the popular rap group the Beastie Boys and carries hip-hop fashions. Kim Gordon of the New York rock group Sonic Youth oversees the women's clothing line, X-Girl. *1415 Haight St., at Masonic Ave., The Haight, 415/626–9573.*

4 *b-8*

WORLDWARE

San Francisco's most ecologically correct store features men's, women's, and children's clothing made from organic hemp, wool, or cotton. It also carries great furniture and gift items (*see* Gifts & Souvenirs, *below*). *336 Hayes St., between Franklin and Gough Sts., Hayes Valley, 415/487–9030.*

designer

4 *a-4*

ARMANI EXCHANGE

The exchange sells Armani's casual lines—jeans, sweaters, jackets, handbags, T-shirts, and socks. *2090 Union St., at Webster St., Cow Hollow, 415/749–0891.*

4 *e-6*

CELINE OF PARIS

In addition to elegant women's clothing by the famous Parisian couture house, the shop carries lovely Celine shoes, handbags, and scarves. There are also Celine ties, wallets, and belts for men. *216 Stockton St., at Geary St., Union Square, 415/397-1140.*

4 *e-6*

EMPORIO ARMANI

The designer's hip San Francisco flagship store has fashionable jackets, pants, and shirts. Accessories, of course, are no mere sideline. Downstairs is the more casual apparel. *1 Grant Ave., at Market St., Union Square, 415/677–9400.*

4 *f-5*

GIANNI VERSACE

Come to Versace for very sophisticated and dramatic high fashions. The service is exceptional. *Crocker Galleria, 50 Post St., at Kearny St., Financial District, 415/616–0604. Closed Sun.*

4 *e-6*

GUCCI

Gucci's three levels are filled with the famous designer's men's and women's apparel, jewelry, and leather goods, including those with the classic "G"s. Gorgeous architecture and artwork make shopping here an experience. *200 Stockton St., at Geary St., Union Square, 415/392–2808.*

4 *f-5*

POLO STORE— RALPH LAUREN

Ralph Lauren's classic American clothing collections for men, women, and children are beautifully displayed. *90 Post St., at Kearny St., Union Square, 415/788–7656. Closed Sun.*

discount & outlet

4 *g-7*

NEW WEST

Big-name seconds and samples of a practical yet stylish nature are sold here at up to 50% off. You may find such brands as Prada and Jil Sander. *426 Brannan St., between 3rd and 4th Sts., South of Market, 415/882–4929.*

4 *g-7*

660 CENTER

The 660 Center houses nearly two dozen outlet stores filled with apparel, accessories, and shoes for men, women, and children. *660 3rd St., at Townsend St., South of Market, 415/227–0464.*

4 *e-7*

YERBA BUENA SQUARE
The square is a collection of 10 shops selling discount apparel, shoes, and toys. Spend a few hours weeding through the racks and you'll find gems by Armani, Calvin Klein, and Dior. *899 Howard St., at 5th St., South of Market, 415/543–1275.*

vintage & secondhand

7 *e-1*

AARDVARK'S ODD ARK
In the neighborhood known for its love affair with the '60s, Aardvark's enthralls thrift-store shoppers with a great selection of vintage fashions. Men's basics, cotton dress shirts, hats, and vintage Levi's are all on the racks. *1501 Haight St., at Ashbury St., The Haight, 415/621–3141.*

4 *c-6*

AMERICAN RAG
The huge selection of new and used men's and women's clothes from the United States and Europe are all in excellent shape. You'll find racks of stylish suits, classy jackets, and black vintage dresses, plus shoes and accessories such as sunglasses, hats, belts, and scarves. *1305 Van Ness Ave., between Sutter and Bush Sts., Pacific Heights, 415/441–0537.*

7 *e-1*

BUFFALO EXCHANGE
Part of a national chain, Buffalo Exchange sells both new and recycled clothing and will also trade or buy items. It has a wide selection of Levi's, leather jackets, vintage dresses, and flannel shirts, as well as sunglasses and other accessories. *1555 Haight St., at Masonic Ave., The Haight, 415/431–7733.*

4 *c-4*

1800 Polk St., between Washington and Jackson Sts., Polk Gulch, 415/346–5726.

4 *a-6*

CROSSROADS TRADING CO.
At this upscale resale clothing emporium, San Francisco hipsters can conjure up the complete retro look. The prices are a little higher than at other local shops, but so is the quality. *1901 Fillmore St. at Bush St., Pacific Heights, 415/775–8885.*

7 *g-2*

2231 Market St., between Sanchez and Noe Sts., Noe Valley, 415/626–8989.

4 *a-6*

1901 Fillmore St., at Bush St., Pacific Heights, 415/775–8885.

4 *a-5*

DEPARTURES FROM THE PAST
Along with vintage clothing, shoes, and hats, you'll find some costumes, formal attire, and casual wear. *2028 Fillmore St., between California and Pine Sts., Pacific Heights, 415/885–3377.*

7 *d-1*

THE WASTELAND
Wasteland brings you trendy and outrageous treasures, as well as vintage gowns, suits, and costume jewelry. It's one of the city's most popular—but priciest—secondhand stores. *1660 Haight St., between Belvedere and Clayton Sts., The Haight, 415/863–3150.*

7 *f-3*

WORN OUT WEST
Budget-conscious cowboys and western wannabes come here for secondhand western wear and leather goods. *582 Castro St., near 19th St., The Castro, 415/431–6020.*

CLOTHING FOR WOMEN & MEN/ SPECIALTY

formal wear

7 *d-1*

LA ROSA FORMAL WEAR
This Haight-Ashbury shop carries tuxedos in contemporary and classic designs, plus vintage formal wear for men and women. The collection of vintage hats, gloves, spats, buttons, and overwear evoke an earlier age of elegance. *1773 Haight St., at Cole St., The Haight, 415/668–3746.*

hats

4 *b-2, c-2*

HEADING WEST
Here is the city's largest selection of hats for men, women, and kids, including bowlers, gauchos, top hats, and more.

Ghirardelli Square, 900 North Point St., at Polk St., Fisherman's Wharf, 415/928–4727.

2 b-3
PAUL'S HAT WORKS
Since 1918 Paul's has specialized in fine Panama straw hats. The owner takes pride in finding and selling the finest hats available—including some types that take more than a year to make. 6128 Geary Blvd., at 25th Ave., Sunset District, 415/221–5332. Closed Sun. and Mon. No credit cards.

leather

4 e-3
EAST/WEST LEATHER
This North Beach shop has been selling fine leather boots, jackets, belts, purses, and backpacks for women and men since the late 1960s. 1400 Grant Ave., at Green St., North Beach, 415/397–2886.

4 e-6
NORTH BEACH LEATHER
This is the city's best source for high-quality leather garments—skirts, jackets, trousers, dresses, accessories. The store, with its wavy wrought-iron banisters, is itself a work of art. 190 Geary St., at Stockton St., Union Square, 415/362–8300.

shoes

7 g-5
ASTRID'S RABAT
Astrid's concentrates on inexpensive, comfortable shoes, clogs, and boots for men and women. 3909 24th St., at Sanchez St., Noe Valley, 415/282–7400.

4 e-5
BALLY OF SWITZERLAND
The Bally store sells high-quality men's and women's dress shoes. 238 Stockton St., at Sutter St., Union Square, 415/398–7463.

CLOTHING FOR WOMEN/GENERAL

contemporary

4 e-5
ANN TAYLOR
This national chain is famous for high-quality yet affordable fashions. There are tailored clothes suitable for work, play,

and formal occasions. Accessories include stockings, scarves, shoes, belts, and bags. 240 Post St., between Stockton St. and Grant Ave., Union Square, 415/989–5381.

4 f-4
Embarcadero Center, The Embarcadero, 415/989–5355.

4 b-2
Ghirardelli Square, Fisherman's Wharf, 415/775–2872.

2 c-6
Stonestown Galleria, Stonestown, 415/564–0229.

4 e-6
San Francisco Shopping Centre, Union Square, 415/543–2487.

4 a-6
AVANT PREMIERE
This store designs and manufactures its own fashionable clothes, using custom-woven fabrics from France and Italy. 1942 Fillmore St., at Pine St., Pacific Heights, 415/673–8875.

4 e-5
266 Sutter St., between Stockton St. and Grant Ave., Union Square, 415/788–5558.

4 e-5
372 Sutter St., between Stockton and Powell Sts., Union Square, 415/788–5588.

4 a-5
BEBE
Contemporary women's suits and dressy evening wear are the specialties at this national chain. The styling is unmistakably European. 2133 Fillmore St., at California St., Pacific Heights, 415/771–2323.

4 e-6
San Francisco Shopping Centre, 865 Market St., Union Square, 415/543–2323.

4 a-4
2095 Union St., at Buchanan St., The Marina, 415/563–2323.

4 b-4
GEORGIOU
Georgiou excels at dressing the contemporary woman. Career and special-occasion fashions are sold under the shop's own label. 1725 Union St., at Gough St., The Marina, 415/776–1844.

4 f-4

Embarcadero Center, The Embarcadero, 415/981–4845.

4 e-6

152 Geary St., between Grant Ave. and Stockton St., Union Square, 415/989–8614.

4 g-4

TREND

Trend's spirited clothing and accessories move beautifully from office to evening. *3 Embarcadero Center, The Embarcadero, 415/362–0799.*

7 e-1

AMBIANCE

At this inviting Haight-Ashbury shop, the mix of sportswear and separates (some under the shop's own label) is eclectic but attractively priced. During the holiday season they have a terrific selection of party dresses. *1458 Haight St., at Masonic Ave., The Haight, 415/552–5095.*

4 a-4

CP SHADES

CP Shades produces an extremely appealing line of California-casual separates and dresses. Everything is made of 100%-natural fibers and is machine washable. *1861 Union St., at Laguna St., The Marina, 415/292–3588.*

4 e-3

DONNA

Donna's unconstructed linens, cottons, and knits are easy to wear. *1424 Grant Ave., at Union St., North Beach, 415/397–4447.*

7 g-5

GLADRAGS

Natural-fiber apparel is the specialty here, from lingerie to special-occasion dresses. The staff is especially friendly. *3985 24th St., at Noe St., Noe Valley, 415/647–7144. Closed Sun.*

7 g-5

JOSHUA SIMON

This Noe Valley shop stocks unusual women's garments: flowing pants, romantic dresses, woven vests, and hand-painted shirts. Many items are by local designers. *3915 24th St., at Sanchez St., Noe Valley, 415/821–1068.*

4 e-3

KNITZ AND LEATHER

Mother-daughter team Anna Martin and Anna Katherina operate this small shop, selling original-design coats, sweaters, scarves, and handbags. *1429 Grant Ave., at Green St., North Beach, 415/391–3480.*

5 h-5

ZOE LTD.

These beautifully styled clothes have a decidely noncorporate look. Natural-fiber separates and gorgeous sweaters range from casual to dressy. *2400 Fillmore St., at Washington St., Pacific Heights, 415/929–0441. Closed Sun.*

designer

4 a-5

BETSEY JOHNSON

Postmodern designer Betsey Johnson brings you outrageous women's fashions in a campy, neon-lit shop. The styling is youthful and fun. *2033 Fillmore St., between Pine and California Sts., Pacific Heights, 415/567–2726.*

4 e-6

160 Geary St., between Stockton St. and Grant Ave., Union Square, 415/398–2516.

4 b-8

BELLA DONNA

The discriminating selection of creations by talented New York and Los Angeles designers sets this store apart. Owner Justine Kaltenbach designs all the hats on display. *539 Hayes St., between Buchanan and Laguna Sts., Hayes Valley, 415/861–7182.*

4 e-6

THE CHANEL BOUTIQUE

Chanel's world-famous couture clothing, accessories, perfumes, cosmetics, and jewelry fill this stylish shop. *152 Maiden Lane, at Stockton St., Union Square, 415/981–1550.*

7 g-5

DESIGNERS TOO

The local and national designers represented here use natural fibers and luxurious fabrics. In addition to clothing, there's a wide selection of hats, handbags, and locally made jewelry. *3899 24th St., at Sanchez St., Noe Valley, 415/648–1057.*

`4` *e-5*

JAEGER INTERNATIONAL SHOP

British workmanship and beautiful fabrics are the hallmarks of Jaeger's classic jackets, sweaters, pants, blouses, skirts, and accessories. *272 Post St., at Stockton St., Union Square, 415/421–3714. Closed Sun.*

`4` *e-6*

JIL SANDER

Come here for the complete line of Jil Sander's beautifully tailored fashions for women. *135 Maiden Lane, at Stockton St., Union Square, 415/273–7070.*

`4` *a-5*

JIM-ELLE

"Clothes for the fashion confident" is the motto here. The interchangeable separates are by designers such as Romeo Gigli, Harriet Selwyn, Peter Cohen, and Matsuda. *2237 Fillmore St., at Sacramento St., Pacific Heights, 415/567–9500.*

`4` *e-5*

JOANIE CHAR

Silk fashions are what first made Joanie Char famous, though now there's a wider variety of fashions in linen, cotton, and wool as well. *285 Sutter St., at Grant Ave., Union Square, 415/399–9867.*

`5` *e-6*

JUSTINE

A favorite of Francophiles, Justine carries women's clothes by French designers such as Dorothée Bis, Georges Rech, and Fabrice Karel. *3600 Sacramento St., at Locust St., Laurel Heights, 415/921–8548.*

`4` *e-5*

MIX

Fashion-forward women shop here. Mix is one of few American stores to carry Chacok, a French designer favoring flamboyant graphics, and it also has stark fashions by young Finnish designers. *309 Sutter St., at Grant Ave., Union Square, 415/392–1742. Closed Sun.*

discount & outlet

`8` *f-2*

ESPRIT FACTORY OUTLET

San Francisco–based Esprit manufactures hip sportswear, shoes, and accessories, primarily for young women and children. In-season clothing from Esprit women's and children's lines, as well as shoes and accessories, are sold at 30%–70% percent discounts. *499 Illinois St., at 16th St., China Basin, 415/957–2550.*

`4` *b-8*

560 HAYES VINTAGE BOUTIQUE

The '70s are in style at 560 Hayes, where the stock of vintage and used clothing includes pants, coats, and dresses. Most of the fashions here are women's. *560 Hayes St., between Laguna and Octavia Sts., Hayes Valley, 415/861–7993.*

`4` *h-7*

JESSICA MCCLINTOCK FACTORY OUTLET STORE

Come here for samples, irregulars, and past-season fashions by local designer Jessica McClintock. These are highly romantic dresses of silk and lace for elegant evenings, weddings, and other very special occasions. *35 Stanford St., off 2nd St., between Brannan and Townsend Sts., South Beach, 415/495–3326.*

`4` *e-5*

LOEHMANN'S

Savvy shoppers will find astounding bargains at Loehmann's, which stocks labels like Karl Lagerfeld, Calvin Klein, and Krizia at drastically reduced prices. It helps to know designers' merchandise, however, as the labels are often removed. *222 Sutter St., between Kearny St. and Grant Ave., Union Square, 415/982–3215.*

unusual sizes

`4` *a-6*

THE COMPANY STORE

Stylish sports and career wear, jewelry, scarves, and other accessories are made for women sizes 14 and up. *1913 Fillmore St., at Bush St., Pacific Heights, 415/921–0365.*

`4` *e-5*

FORGOTTEN WOMAN

Besides designer fashions for women sizes 14 and up, there's a fine selection of coats, accessories, and formal attire. *550 Sutter St., at Powell St., Union Square, 415/788-1452.*

4 g-8

HARPER GREER

Stylish and sophisticated career attire comes in sizes 14 and up, with a full line of scarves, belts, and jewelry to complete the look. Most of the clothing is in natural, easy-care fabrics. *580 4th St., at Brannan St., South of Market, 415/ 543–4066.*

CLOTHING FOR WOMEN/ SPECIALTY

furs

4 e-5

ROBERTS FURS

In addition to fine furs by top designers, this Union Square salon carries leather and shearling coats for men and women. The staff travels the world to buy furs, so they are very knowledgeable about the inventory. Services include storage, cleaning, repairs, and restyling. *272 Post St., at Stockton St., Union Square, 415/362–6608. Closed Sun.*

handbags

4 e-5

THE COACH STORE

Women treasure their Coach handbags for their versatility, classic styling, and high quality. This shop carries only the Coach handbags and women's belts, while a second store up the street carries men's leather goods and luggage, also all by Coach (*see* Leather Goods and Luggage, *below*). *190 Post St., at Grant Ave., Union Square, 415/392–1772.*

4 e-6

HERMÈS OF PARIS

The entire range of elegant, high-status Hermès leather bags, wallets, and accessories is here. So are the famous silk scarves, equestrian items, and sundry other treasures. The Union Square shop, designed by architect Madam Rena Dumas, is a beauty. *212 Stockton St., at Geary St., Union Square, 415/391–7200.*

hats

4 e-6

HATS ON POST

This Union Square boutique is San Francisco's best-known ladies' millinery.

You'll find elegant hats with all the trimmings; rain hats; summer hats made of straw; and extravagant winter fur hats. Custom designs for brides are available. *210 Post St., at Grant Ave., Union Square, 415/392–3737. Closed Sun.*

lingerie & nightwear

4 f-5

ARICIE LINGERIE DE MARQUE

The beautiful lingerie, loungewear, and sleepwear sold here is by top designers such as Valentino, Wacoal, and Jezebel. The shop also has silk pajamas, boxers, and briefs for men. *50 Post St., at Montgomery St., Financial District, 415/ 989-0261.*

4 a-4

CAROL DODA'S CHAMPAGNE AND LACE LINGERIE BOUTIQUE

Let the legendary and alluring Carol Doda—who led the vanguard to legalize topless dancing in the 1960s—help you find just the right bra, teddy, bustier, corset, garter belt, slinky dress, or bikini. *1850 Union St., at Laguna St., The Marina, 415/776–6900.*

4 e-1

MIDSUMMER NIGHTS LINGERIE

The intimate apparel here ranges from slinky to snuggly. Everything is reasonably priced, and there are even choices for petites and larger sizes. *Pier 39, Fisherman's Wharf, 415/788–0992.*

4 a-5

TOUJOURS

This perfumed Presidio Heights boutique specializes in elegant and expensive lingerie of cotton, silk, and other natural fibers. It's a great place to go gift-shopping. *2484 Sacramento St., at Fillmore St., Pacific Heights, 415/346– 3988. Closed Sun.*

4 e-6

VICTORIA'S SECRET

The famed lingerie chain has an especially large and well-stocked shop on Union Square, staffed with friendly and helpful personnel. There's plenty here for her, as well as a small selection of silk boxer shorts, robes, pajamas, and briefs for him. *335 Powell St., at Post St.,*

*Union Square, 415/433–9671. Call for
other locations.*

maternity

7 *g-5*

LITTLE BEAN SPROUTS

Cotton maternity clothing and Japanese
Weekend-brand maternity wear are the
specialties here. *3961 24th St., at Noe
St., Noe Valley, 415/550–1668.*

4 *e-6*

MATERNITÉ

Perfect for the working mother-to-be,
this shop carries sophisticated maternity clothing for the office, as well as
stylish evening wear and comfortable
casual ensembles. *San Francisco Shopping Centre, 865 Market St., at 5th St.,
Union Square, 415/227–0825.*

shoes

4 *e-6*

JOAN & DAVID SHOES

The beautiful shoes, handbags, and
belts are all by the famous Joan & David
designers. *1 Union Square, at Powell St.,
Union Square, 415/397–1958.*

7 *e-1*

SHOE BIZ

Come to this Haight-Ashbury shop for
platform shoes, spiky heels, or whatever
might be the latest rage in Europe. The
emphasis is on fun and style. *1446
Haight St., at Masonic Ave., The Haight,
415/864–0990.*

4 *f-5*

THE SHOE LOFT

A favorite among working women in
search of bargains, The Shoe Loft carries designer shoes by Charles Jordan,
Ferragamo, Bally, and others. *225 Front
St., at California St., Financial District,
415/956–4648. Closed Sun.*

wigs

4 *d-3*

ROSALIE'S NEW LOOK

This shop has a huge selection of wigs
and a full-service salon. The staff is
friendly and happy to let shoppers try on
as many wigs as they please. *782 Columbus Ave., at Greenwich St., North Beach,
415/397–6246. Closed Sun.*

COINS

2 *c-6*

DON'S VILLAGE COINS

Don's buys and sells American coins,
particularly those from the 18th century. The shop also deals in gold coins
from all countries. *2536 Ocean Ave., at
19th Ave., Stonestown, 415/584–2515.
Closed Sun.*

4 *f-5*

WITTER COINS

Established in 1959, this shop in the
Hobart Building of the Financial District
buys, sells, and appraises U.S. and foreign coins. *582 Market St., Suite 1409, at
Montgomery St., Financial District, 415/
781–5690. Closed weekends.*

COMPUTERS &
SOFTWARE

4 *f-7*

CENTRAL COMPUTER
SYSTEMS INC.

A Silicon Valley-based company, Central
Computer Systems has everything for
the PC: drive, modems, monitors, printers, scanners, CDs, and software. *837
Howard St., between 4th and 5th Sts.,
415/495–5888.*

4 *f-6*

COMPUTOWN

The biggest computer store in the city
has all of the latest products—all at
competitive prices (they'll match the
price of any local store). Come here for
computers, printers, software, and supplies, including brands such as IBM,
Hewlett Packard, Compaq, Toshiba, and
Apple. *710 Market St., at 3rd St., Financial District, 415/956–8696.*

4 *f-6*

EGGHEAD COMPUTERS &
SOFTWARE

This shop boasts more than 1,000 different software titles for PC computers,
and a small selection of Mac software.
It also carries a limited amount of
hardware, such as CD-Rom drives, hard
drives, and memory cards. *701 Market
St., at 3rd St., Financial District, 415/
546–7535.*

5 *h-3*

*369 Pine St., at Montgomery St., Finan-
cial District, 415/956–4488. Closed Sun.*

5 *h-3*

2300 Lombard St., at Pierce St., The Marina, 415/921–5643.

4 *e-8*

MACADAM COMPUTERS

Mac users drop by this Mac-only store on a regular basis to check out the latest software and gadgets. There's a full range of hardware, especially monitors, and of software, especially graphics programs. Those who pay by cash or check instead of credit card receive a 3% discount. *1062 Folsom St., between 6th and 7th Sts., South of Market, 415/863–6222.*

4 *a-7*

PERSONAL COMPUTERS FOR LESS

This shop stocks some new computers, and many used computers (mostly PCs). Let owner Don Marshall help you choose the hardware and software that suits you best. *1309 Fillmore St., at Eddy St., Western Addition, 415/346–1692. Closed weekends.*

CRAFTS & HOBBIES

7 *h-5*

CRADLE OF THE SUN

In addition to a fine collection of hand-blown art glass, Tiffany-style lamps, and stained-glass panels, you'll find stained-glass window tools, supplies, and training at this unusual crafts store. Sign up far in advance; there's a six month waiting list for beginners classes. *3848 24th St., between Church and Sanchez Sts., Noe Valley, 415/821–7667. Closed Mon.*

4 *f-8*

FANTASTICO

This SoMa discount warehouse stocks supplies for any and all kinds of crafts. They have an enormous assortment of dried and silk flowers, ribbons, and wire for bouquet-making, as well as hundreds of baskets. *559 6th St., between Brannan and Bryant Sts., South of Market, 415/982–0680. Closed Sun.*

5 *a-7*

THE HOBBY COMPANY OF SAN FRANCISCO

For hobbyists, this is the best shop in San Francisco. It's stocked with all sorts of goodies, including model cars, air-

planes, and boats; dollhouses and miniatures; paints, thread, and yarn; stenciling and stampmaking supplies. *5150 Geary Blvd., at 16th Ave., Richmond District, 415/386–2802.*

4 *a-2*

ORION TELESCOPE CENTER

Everything a stargazer could want is here, at the Bay Area's largest shop devoted to astronomical telescopes. The small refractor telescopes cost around $100, while top models sell for well over $1,000. *3609 Buchanan St., at Bay St., The Marina, 415/931–9966. Closed Mon.*

ELECTRONICS & STEREOS

7 *f-3*

EBER ELECTRONICS

Though Eber specializes in large-screen home-theater equipment, it's also well stocked with TVs, VCRs, camcorders, speakers, telephones, fax machines, and other electronic essentials. The staff is extremely knowledgeable. *2355 Market St., at Castro St., The Castro, 415/621–4332.*

4 *f-5*

THE GOOD GUYS

This full-service audio/video showroom is part of a national chain. Count on The Good Guys for good deals on TVs, VCRs, and stereo components; you can almost always get 10% off the listed price on big-ticket items simply by looking like you mean it when you ask. *1400 Van Ness Ave., at Bush St., Financial District, 415/775–9323.*

3 *c-4*

WHOLE EARTH ACCESS

A Bay Area institution, the Whole Earth Access store has great selections of cameras, video equipment, electronic devices, computers, and small and major appliances. *2990 7th St., at Ashby Ave., Berkeley, 510/845–3000.*

EROTICA

8 *a-5*

GOOD VIBRATIONS

This friendly, woman-owned-and-operated shop describes itself as a "clean, well-lighted place to shop for sex toys, books, and videos." *1210 Valencia St., at 23rd St., Mission District, 415/974–8980.*

3 *c-3*

2504 San Pablo Ave., at Dwight Way, Berkeley, 510/841–8987.

7 *g-2*

ROMANTASY
At this "sensual, erotic shop for loving couples and romantic singles," purchase such essentials *d'amour* as sexy corsets, chocolate body paint, tantra love swings, and chinchilla-lined G-strings. *2191 Market St., at Sanchez St., Noe Valley, 415/487–9909. Closed Mon.*

FABRIC

4 *e-6*

BRITEX FABRICS
A San Francisco institution since 1952, Britex has the West Coast's largest selection of fabrics and notions on four spacious, well-organized floors. Alongside the latest in bridal, couture, menswear, and home decorating fabrics, you'll find trims, tassels, and more than 30,000 buttons. *146 Geary St., between Stockton St. and Grant Ave., Union Square, 415/392–2910. Closed Sun.*

7 *e-1*

DISCOUNT FABRICS
The satin, wool, and cotton fabrics are cheap here, and there is a full range of New Look, Simplicity, and McCall patterns for sale. Buttons are 10 for $1 in the discount button bin, and you can buy zippers by the yard. *1432 Haight St., at Masonic Ave., The Haight, 415/621–5584.*

4 *e-4*

FAR EAST FASHIONS
There are a few fabric stores in Chinatown to browse through, but this shop has one of the neighborhood's better selections of Chinese embossed silks. *953 Grant Ave., between Jackson and Washington Sts., Chinatown, 415/362–8171 or 415/362–0986.*

7 *d-1*

FAR-OUT FABRICS
In the back of Mendel's Art and Stationery Supplies (*see* Art Supplies, *above*) is a collection of "far-out" fabrics, particularly of the wild '60s genre. *1556*

Haight St., between Ashbury and Clayton Sts., The Haight, 415/621–1287.

3 *d-2*

KASURI DYEWORKS
Come here for traditional Japanese fabrics including handwoven and hand-dyed silk, cotton, and wool. Services include custom-made futon covers, clothing, and bedspreads. *1959 Shattuck Ave., at University Ave., Berkeley, 510/841–4509. Closed Sun. and Mon.*

8 *c-1*

SAL BERESSI FABRICS
This fabric wholesaler's warehouse is open to the public on select days—call ahead to confirm. It's an excellent resource for fine upholstery, drapery, and bedspread fabrics priced below wholesale. The best bargains can be found at its two annual sales, which run from mid-April through May and mid-October through November. *1504 Bryant St., Second Floor, near 13th St., South of Market, 415/861–5004.*

4 *c-5*

SAN FRANCISCO FABRICS
You could do your entire house in different swaths of chintz, so great is the selection of home decorating fabrics here. There's also a wide assortment of 100%–cotton quilting fabrics, and great dress fabrics including silks and wools. Quiltmaking, sewing, and dressmaking classes are held in the store. *1715 Polk St., at Clay St., Nob Hill, 415/673–5848. Closed Sun.*

FLEA MARKETS

2 *f-6*

ALEMANY FLEA MARKET
San Francisco's newest flea market has lots of cast-off knicknacks, plus small selections of clothing, household appliances, furniture, and some antiques and collectibles. Prices tend to be lower than at other city flea markets. *100 Alemany Blvd., at Crescent Ave., Bernal Heights, no phone. Sun. only.*

2 *f-8*

GENEVA SWAP MEET
The motto at this flea market is "anything sells." It's held in the parking lot of the Geneva Drive-In Theater, next to the Cow Palace. Near the front you'll

find cheap, new clothing; furniture and collectibles lurk in the stalls at the back. *607 Carter St., at Geneva Ave., Daly City, 415/587–2884. Weekends only.*

4 *f-2*

PIER 29 ANTIQUE AND COLLECTIBLE MARKET

This is the largest weekly indoor antique and collectible market in California. Classier than the city's other flea markets, it has around 100 indoor booths selling antique furniture, rare books, vintage clothing, kitchenware, jewelry, and collectibles. Unlike other San Francisco flea markets, it charges admission: $2, or $10 before 9:30 AM. *Pier 29, The Embarcadero, between Sansome and Battery Sts., no phone. Sun. only.*

8 *a-1*

SAN FRANCISCO FLEA MARKET

Most of the items for sale here are junk: plastic toys, Chinese-made batteries, and used clothes that were never in fashion. However, it's worth a look if you're searching for new or used kitchen appliances, clock radios, and other small electronics. *1651 Mission St., between South Van Ness Ave. and 12th St., South of Market, no phone. Weekends only.*

FLOWERS & PLANTS

5 *h-4*

A BED OF ROSES

This neighborhood florist has a wonderful selection of cut flowers, interesting vases and baskets, and old-fashioned wrought-iron plant stands. *2274 Union St., between Fillmore and Steiner Sts., Cow Hollow, 415/922–5150. Closed Sun.*

4 *a-6*

FLEURTATIONS

Even on Sundays you can buy unusual fresh flowers at this Upper Fillmore shop. They also have one of the city's best selections of silk and dried flowers. *1880 Fillmore St., between Sutter and Bush Sts., Japantown, 415/923–1070. Closed Mon.*

4 *a-3*

HOOGASIAN FLOWERS

This full-service FTD florist will whip up a beautiful floral or balloon bouquet for you in minutes flat. They also have a

handy outdoor flower stand downtown, at 250 Post Street. *1674 Lombard St., at Octavia St., The Marina, 415/885–4321.*

4 *c-5*

THE PLANT WAREHOUSE

All kinds of plants are available at this 5,000-sq-ft shop, from the common to the obscure. The emphasis is on tropical indoor plants; there's also a large selection of orchids. *1355 Bush St., between Polk and Larkin Sts., Polk Gulch, 415/885–1515.*

4 *f-8*

PODESTA BALDOCCHI

This friendly, old-fashioned florist has been in business since 1871, and is one of the largest in the city. In addition to cut flowers and indoor plants, they have balloon bouquets, fruit baskets, and other creative bouquets. *508 4th St., at Bryant St., South of Market, 415/346–1300. Closed Sun.*

4 *c-8*

RED DESERT

Red Desert is worth a visit even if you're not planning to buy: Hundreds of species of cacti are for sale here, tall and small, rare and common, for indoors or out. *1632 Market St., at Franklin St., Hayes Valley, 415/552–2800.*

4 *c-7*

ROSE BOWL FLORIST

Conveniently located in the Opera Plaza, this florist does stunningly beautiful work with exotic flowers and plants. They also assemble impressive gift baskets that include California wines, French champagnes, and gourmet food items. *601 Van Ness Ave., between Turk St. and Golden Gate Ave., Civic Center, 415/474–1114. Closed Sun.*

FOLK ART & HANDICRAFTS

See also Charitable Causes, *above.*

4 *b-8*

AFRICAN OUTLET

This shop carries beautiful handmade goods from all over Africa—masks from Kenya, Berber and Tuareg jewelry, brilliant Senegalese textiles, and authentic Zulu spears, among other things. *524 Octavia St., at Hayes St., Hayes Valley, 415/864–3576.*

4 *a-4*

THE AMERICAS

The treasures of the American continent are sold here; specialties include Pueblo and Navajo pottery, whimsical carved wooden animals from Mexico's Oaxaca coast, and Day of the Dead artifacts. *1977 Union St., at Laguna St., The Marina, 415/921-4600. Closed Mon.*

4 *a-4*

ANOKHI

Clothing, home furnishings, and accessories from the Indian subcontinent are the stock-in-trade here. The small shop is crowded with exotic treasures such as Indian tea caddies, bolts of hand-printed fabrics, hand-tossed pottery, and wooden children's toys. *1864 Union St., at Laguna St., The Marina, 415/922–4441.*

4 *a-6*

ASAKICHI

Drop by this cozy little shop for beautifully crafted Japanese items such as wind chimes, teapots, and handmade chopsticks. The store also carries small pieces of furniture, such as tansu chests. *Japan Center, on the bridge between Kinokuniya and Kintetsu Bldgs., Japantown, 415/921–3821.*

8 *e-3*

COLLAGE GALLERY

The work of more than 50 Bay Area artists is featured at this studio gallery. The selection of handmade crafts tends to vary, but usually includes some mosaic mirrors, handblown glass objects, handmade jewelry, and delicate glazed vases. *1345 18th St., near Arkansas St., Potrero Hill, 415/282–4401. Closed Mon.–Wed.*

4 *c-8*

F. DORIAN

This is one of the city's most popular and best-stocked shops for handicrafts. In addition to jewelry, art, crafts, and antiquities from Mexico, Japan, Italy, Peru, Indonesia, the Philippines, and Sri Lanka, it carries glass and ceramic works by local craftspeople. *388 Hayes St., at Franklin St., Hayes Valley, 415/861-3191.*

4 *b-1*

FOLK ART BORETTI AMBER

On Ghiradelli Square's Plaza Level is this shop with a vast selection of Baltic amber jewelry sure to dazzle the eye. The owner also has a fine collection of Latin American folk art, such as masks, ceramics, religious art, and Oaxacan wood carvings, as well as some crafts from India. *Ghirardelli Sq., 900 North Point St., at Polk St., Fisherman's Wharf, 415/928–3340.*

4 *f-4*

JAPONESQUE

Japonesque's owner travels to Japan once or twice each year to collect items for the shop, and all are of very high quality. Unlike the mass-produced goods for sale in most stores in Japantown, the antique and contemporary stone, wood, glass, ceramic, and lacquer objects here are fine art pieces. There are also sculptures, paintings, and handcrafted wooden boxes. *824 Montgomery St., between Jackson St. and Pacific Ave., Jackson Square, 415/391–8860. Closed Mon.*

4 *a-6*

MA-SHI'-KO FOLKCRAFT

In Japan Center, Ma-Shi'-Ko carries handcrafted pottery from Japan. A specialty is *mashiko*, the style that has been in production longer than any other. There are also masks and other antique and handcrafted goods, all from Japan. *Kinokuniya Building, 2nd Floor, 1581 Webster St., at Post St., Japantown, 415/346–0748.*

4 *b-8*

POLANCO

More like a gallery than a shop, Polcanco showcases the arts and crafts of Mexico—everything from antiques folk crafts to fine contemporary paintings. Its collection of Day of the Dead figures and religious statues is impressive. *393 Hayes St., between Franklin and Gough Sts., Hayes Valley, 415/252–5753. Closed Mon.*

8 *c-5*

STUDIO 24

Part of the acclaimed Galería de la Raza (*see* Art Galleries *in* Chapter 2), Studio 24 is a fabulous spot to shop for Latin American folk art, works by contemporary artists, or kitschy Mexican products like strings of jalepeño Christmas lights. Proceeds support the gallery. *2857 24th St., at Bryant St., Mission District, 415/826–8009. Closed Sun. and Mon.*

5 g-5
V. BREIER
Every piece in this colorful gallery is one-of-a-kind, from jewelry and ceramics to light fixtures and furniture. The bulk of what's sold is contemporary and traditional North American crafts, mostly by emerging artists, with a sprinkling of items from Asian countries such as Japan and India. *3091 Sacramento St., between Baker and Broderick Sts., Pacific Heights, 415/929–7173. Closed Sun.*

4 b-1
XANADU
Here you can sift through artifacts and art from the far-flung corners of Africa, Oceania, Indonesia, and the Americas. The bulk of Xanadu's masks, sculptures, woven baskets, gorgeous tapestries and textiles, tribal jewelry, and ceramics come from west and central Africa. *Ghirardelli Square, Cocoa Bldg., 900 North Point St., at Polk St., Northern Waterfront, 415/441–5211.*

7 g-5
XELA
This wonderful Noe Valley shop (the name is pronounced "shay-la") sells ancient and contemporary art and crafts from Africa, central Asia, Indonesia, Latin America, and elsewhere. Its collection of ethnic jewelry is superb. *3925 24th St. between Sanchez and Noe Sts., Noe Valley, 415/695–1323.*

FOOD

baked goods

8 a-3
ANNA'S DANISH COOKIE CO.
Anna's has been baking Danish cookies—as well as cakes, brownies, and pastries—since 1936. They also have a large assortment of cookie jars and tins for sale. *3560 18th St., between Valencia and Guerrero Sts., Mission District, 415/8630–3882. Closed Sun. and Mon.*

4 c-4
THE BAGELRY
Transplanted New Yorkers recommended this down-to-earth shop for fresh bagels, bialys, lox, whitefish, and cream-cheese spreads. *2134 Polk St., at*

Broadway, Russian Hill, 415/441–3003. No credit cards.

4 a-3
BEPPLES PIES
This San Francisco legend is most famous for mouthwatering fruit pies, but also makes tasty meat- and vegetable-filled pies. Most people get their pies to go, but each shop also has a small café area for salads, soups, and (of course) pies. *1934 Union St., between Laguna and Buchanan Sts., The Marina, 415/931–6225.*

5 h-3
2142 Chestnut St., at Steiner St., The Marina, 415/931–6226. No credit cards.

4 d-8
THE CAKE GALLERY
Some of the cakes on display here would make a sailor blush! The shop specializes in funny and novel custom cakes, and will bake one to look like *anything*—which explains why they're often the cakemaker of choice for bachelor parties. They can copy a photo in full living color on the cake of your choice, and there's no limit to the size of the cake they'll bake. *290 9th St., between Folsom and Howard Sts., South of Market, 415/861–2253. Closed Sun.*

8 c-5
CASA SANCHEZ
Heavenly soft, fresh tortillas are the draw at this small taqueria. Several varieties and sizes are available daily. *2778 24th St., between York and Hampshire Sts., Mission District, 415/282–2400. No credit cards.*

5 c-8
CINDERELLA BAKERY, DELICATESSEN & RESTAURANT
The city's finest Russian pastries, pirozhki, and piroghi are made here fresh daily. The deli sells such mouthwatering delicacies as borscht, blini, and cabbage rolls, while the tearoom is a gathering place for the neighborhood's Russian immigrants. *436 Balboa St., between 5th and 6th Aves., Richmond District, 415/751–9690. Closed Mon.*

4 e-3
DANILO
Baked fresh daily in this North Beach shop: Italian country-style bread loaves, grissini bread sticks, anise-flavored

cookies, Genovese-style panettone, and to-die-for chocolate tortes. *516 Green St., between Stockton St. and Grant Ave., North Beach, 415/989–1806. No credit cards.*

8 *a-5*

DIANDA ITALIAN-AMERICAN PASTRY

Elio Dianda worked as a pastry chef in Lucca, Italy, for four decades before setting up this pair of San Francisco stores. Today his sons carry on the same fine tradition, making fresh biscotti, *torte de mandorle, zuppa inglese* (liquor-soaked sponge cake layered with custard and/or whipped cream) *panforte* (almond torte), St. Honoré cakes, panettone, and other treats. *2883 Mission St., between 24th and 25th Sts., Mission District, 415/647–5469.*

4 *e-3*

565 Green St., at Columbus Ave., North Beach, 415/989–7745. No credit cards.

8 *c-5*

DOMINGUEZ MEXICAN BAKERY

Hot and crispy *churros* (Mexican doughnuts dusted with cinnamon) are the specialty here. The bakery also makes Latin American treats such as eggbread, crescent rolls, and *panes dulces* (pastries), and sells imported groceries and colorful piñatas. *2951 24th St., at Alabama St., Mission District, 415/821–1717. No credit cards.*

4 *g-4*

JUST DESSERTS

This Bay Area favorite carries delectable chocolate velvet mousse cake, almond-flavored chocolate-chip blondies, and other sinful pleasures. *3 Embarcadero Center, The Embarcadero, 415/421–1609. Call for other locations.*

8 *c-5*

LA VICTORIA MEXICAN BAKERY AND GROCERY

The venerable La Victoria is the Mexican cookie capital of the Mission. You'll also find Mexican breads, cakes, and other goodies at this old favorite. *2937 24th St., at Alabama St., Mission District, 415/550–9292. No credit cards.*

4 *e-3*

LIGURIA BAKERY

Delicious focaccia bread is the only product of this North Beach bakery—

and it's baked the Italian way, in an old-fashioned brick oven. *1700 Stockton St., at Filbert St., North Beach, 415/421–3786. No credit cards.*

7 *g-5*

MANHATTAN BAGEL

To find this San Francisco bagelry, just follow the aroma of fresh bagels, bialys, challah, *hamentashen* (triangular pastry with a sweet filling of prune, poppyseed, or apricot), *rugalach* (fruit-, nut-, or jam-filled crescent-shaped cookies), and *mondelbrote* (sweet almond bread). New York–style deli items include pickles, lox, whitefish, and cream-cheese spreads. *3872 24th St., at Sanchez St., Noe Valley, 415/647-3334.*

7 *e-1*

1206 Masonic Ave., at Haight St., The Haight, 415/626–9111.

5 *h-3*

NOAH'S NEW YORK BAGELS

What started as a single shop in Berkeley has grown to become a California bagel empire. The dozen or so San Francisco Noah's are known for fresh, delicious, New York–style Kosher bagels and spreads, and friendly service. On Sunday mornings the line at any given neighborhood Noah's often snakes outside the door. *2075 Chestnut St., at Steiner St., Marina District, 415/775–2910. Call for other locations.*

4 *b-8*

PENDRAGON BAKERY

San Francisco city and county employees flock to this tiny, inconspicuous bakery near the Civic Center. In the mornings they come for blueberry scones, streusel, and strong coffee, and in the afternoons for quiche, pastries, and cakes. *400 Hayes St., at Gough St., Hayes Valley, 415/552–7017. No credit cards.*

7 *g-2*

SWEET INSPIRATION

Muffins, scones, tarts, tortes, cheesecakes, and breads are all part of this popular bakery's repertoire, though they also make beautiful wedding cakes. The indoor table seating provides a tranquil retreat. *2239 Market St., at Sanchez St., Noe Valley, 415/621–8664.*

4 *a-5*

2123 Fillmore St., at California St., Pacific Heights, 415/931–2815. No credit cards.

7 *b-2*

TART TO TART

At this bustling Sunset hangout, many of the tarts, scones, muffins, and other desserts look like works of art. Whatever you fancy, they probably have it—and the emphasis is on natural, wholesome ingredients. *641 Irving St., between 6th and 7th Aves., Sunset District, 415/753–0643.*

7 *d-2*

TASSAJARA BAKERY

The fabled Zen community bakery sells interesting breads such as cottage cheese-and-dill and sourdough-corn-rye, as well as other baked goods such as pastries and focaccia. Everything is made with natural ingredients. *1000 Cole St., at Parnassus Ave., The Haight, 415/664–8947.*

4 *e-4*

VICTORIA PASTRY CO.

This North Beach bakery has been around since the beginning of the century. Its specialties are Italian pastries (try the horseshoes) and St. Honoré cakes. *1362 Stockton St., at Vallejo St., North Beach, 415/781–2015. No credit cards.*

4 *a-6*

YAMADA SEIKA CONFECTIONERY

Come here for traditional Japanese pastries and candies, including the house-made *manju* (steamed bun with a sweet-bean filling), and imported *yokan* (red-bean jelly candies). *1955 Sutter St., between Fillmore and Webster Sts., Japantown, 415/922–3848. Closed Mon. No credit cards.*

candy

4 *e-5*

THE CANDY JAR

The owner, Hungarian-born confectioner Maria Stacho, has her own truffle recipes that can hold their own with the most famous. The store also sells Godiva and other chocolates. *210 Grant Ave., between Post and Sutter Sts., Union Square, 415/391–5508. Closed Sun.*

4 *e-1*

CHOCOLATE HEAVEN

This is the place to get silly treats like milk-chocolate tool kits, golf clubs, champagne bottles, dog bones, playing cards, and bingo games. There are more than 1,000 different chocolate items to choose from. *Pier 39, Fisherman's Wharf, 415/421–1789.*

4 *g-4*

CONFETTI LE CHOCOLATIER

Come here for candy from all over the world: chocolate imported from France and Belgium, licorice and Gummi Bears from Germany, and hard candies from Spain, among many other choices. *4 Embarcadero Center, The Embarcadero, 415/362–1706.*

4 *c-2*

The Cannery, 2801 Leavenworth St., at Beach St., Fisherman's Wharf, 415/474–7377.

4 *b-2*

GHIRARDELLI FOUNTAIN & CANDY

The Ghirardelli company is San Francisco's most famous chocolate maker. At the shop in Ghirardelli Square you can buy bars of Ghirardelli chocolate to take home, or sit down to a triple hot-fudge sundae. *Ghirardelli Square, 900 North Point St., at Polk St., Fisherman's Wharf, 415/771–4903.*

7 *g-2*

JOSEPH SCHMIDT CONFECTIONS

This is the best place to buy gourmet chocolate in San Francisco. Joseph Schmidt, a Swiss-trained candy maker, sculpts chocolates into fanciful shapes, ranging from chocolate windmills to life-size chocolate turkeys. Egg-shape truffles, which come in more than 30 flavors, are another best-seller; they're also sold in specialty boutiques around the city. *3489 16th St., at Sanchez St., Noe Valley, 415/861–8682. Closed Sun.*

8 *c-5*

ST. FRANCIS FOUNTAIN

This family-owned soda fountain has sold homemade candy and other old-fashioned treats since 1918 (*see American/Casual in Chapter 3*). *2801 24th St., at York St., Mission District, 415/826–4200.*

4 *e-5*

TEUSCHER CHOCOLATES OF SWITZERLAND

Teuscher is best known for its dreamy champagne-filled chocolate truffles, sold singly or by the box. These ultimate

Swiss treats are flown in from Geneva once a week. *255 Grant Ave., at Sutter St., Union Square, 415/398–2700.*

cheese

7 *f-3*

CASTRO CHEESERY

In addition to a good selection of domestic and imported cheeses, this Castro shop has the best cheap coffee in town. It sells some fine stuff for as little as half of other gourmet java shops' prices. *427 Castro St., at Market St., The Castro, 415/552–6676.*

4 *h-8*

COUNTRY CHEESE INC.

This shop sells a wide range of imported and domestic cheeses in bulk at good prices, including delicious locally made mozzarella. Dried fruit, beans, grains, nuts, and spices are also sold in bulk. *415 Divisadero St., between Oak and Fell Sts., Western Addition, 415/621–8130. Closed Sun.*

7 *d-6*

CREIGHTON'S CHEESE & FINE FOODS

Creighton's carries wines and baked goods in addition to 300-plus varieties of imported and domestic cheeses. Noncheese goodies include coffee beans, fresh pâtés, salads, sandwiches, and desserts. There's a coffee bar on the premises. *673 Portola Dr., near O'Shaughnessey Blvd., Twin Peaks, 415/753–0750.*

7 *d-2*

SAY CHEESE

This Haight-Ashbury shop routinely wins votes in polls of San Franciscans' favorite food shops. It carries more than 400 kinds of fine cheese from around the world, plus gourmet goodies like fresh pâtés and wonderful house-made spreads. The staff is helpful and quick. *856 Cole St., at Carl St., The Haight, 415/665–5020.*

5 *c-6*

THE 6TH AVENUE CHEESE SHOP

This shop occasionally offers cheese-tasting classes, so you can better appreciate the more than 200 varieties of cheese for sale. There's a good selection of gourmet items such as caviar, wines, infused oils, and coffees, plus gift and picnic baskets. *311 6th Ave., at Clement St., Richmond District, 415/387–1436.*

7 *g-5*

24TH STREET CHEESE COMPANY

This is Noe Valley's cheese center. It's stocked with exotic cheeses and salamis, gourmet crackers, oils, vinegars, mustards, and other delectables. *3893 24th St., at Sanchez St., Noe Valley, 415/821–6658.*

coffee & tea

8 *b-1*

CAPRICORN COFFEES

This very established SoMa business is a favorite of San Franciscans for fresh-roasted beans that can be custom ground and blended; teas, spices, and coffee-making equipment are also available. Capricorn beans are sold to many fine restaurants around town. *353 10th St., at Folsom St., South of Market, 415/621–8500. Closed Sun.*

7 *f-3*

CASTRO CHEESERY

See Cheese, *above.*

7 *d-1*

COFFEE, TEA & SPICE

This place has a good selection of coffee beans, but it's really known for its diverse assortment of teas. It also sells chocolate and spices. Coffee beans are roasted on the premises. *1630 Haight St., between Cole and Clayton Sts., The Haight, 415/861–3953.*

4 *c-5*

FREED TELLER & FREED

This coffee roaster and tea blender has been doing business in San Francisco since 1899. More than 20 fine blends of coffee beans are available, plus 30 varieties of teas. The shop also carries herbs, spices, jams, preserves, and chocolates. *1326 Polk St., at Bush St., Polk Gulch, 415/673–0922. Closed Sun.*

4 *d-3*

GRAFFEO COFFEE ROASTING COMPANY

Since 1938, this North Beach emporium has been supplying San Franciscans with fine Italian-roast coffee beans. The air is thick with the aroma of beans roasting for the special Graffeo blends.

735 Columbus Ave., at Filbert St., North Beach, 415/986–2420. Closed Sun. No credit cards.

6 g-4
HOUSE OF COFFEE

This family-run Sunset District coffee business is now in its third generation. The specialties are finely ground Turkish-style coffee, plus teas, spices, and Middle Eastern deli items. Beans are roasted fresh daily. 1618 Noriega St., at 23rd Ave., Sunset District, 415/681–9363. Closed Sun. and Mon. No credit cards.

5 f-6
PEET'S COFFEE & TEA

Though Dutch coffee buyer Alfred Peet began with a single Berkeley store in 1966, today Peet's shops are all over the Bay Area, and their beans are even used in the national Au Bon Pain chain. Long-running favorites among the traditional and creative blends include Major Dickason's blends, Garuda, and Sulawesi-Kalossie beans. Peet's also has excellent selections of green and black teas, and all kinds of coffee- and tea-making equipment. 3419 California St., at Laurel St., Laurel Heights, 415/221–8506. Call for other locations.

5 h-5
SPINELLI COFFEE COMPANY

The many San Francisco outlets of this coffee beanery are popular for their espresso and coffee bars. Coffee beans are sold whole or custom ground. 2455 Fillmore St., at Jackson St., Pacific Heights, 415/929–8808. Call for other locations.

4 e-4
TEN REN TEA COMPANY OF SAN FRANCISCO

This Chinatown business has one of the largest selections of teas in the Bay Area. The staff is well versed in the healing and/or energizing properties of each blend. 949 Grant Ave., at Jackson St., Chinatown, 415/362–0656.

ethnic foods

8 a-3
BOMBAY BAZAAR

Here's where you'll find everything you need to prepare an Indian meal: Indian flours, spices, chutneys, chiles, pickles, even paper-thin sheets of gold and silver for making special desserts. 548 Valencia St., at 16th St., Mission District, 415/621–1717. No credit cards.

8 c-5
CASA LUCAS MARKET

Spanish, Caribbean, and Latin American fresh produce are sold here, along with wines and cheeses. Regularly in stock are hard-to-find products like dried hominy, palm oil, Andean potatoes, salt cod, tamarind, and cherimoyas. 2934 24th St., at Alabama St., Mission District, 415/826–4334. No credit cards.

4 e-4
GOLDEN GATE FORTUNE COOKIES

If you have always been curious about how the fortune gets into the cookie, take a tour of the Golden Gate Fortune Cookie Company (415/781–3956 for an appointment). Or just drop by for a bag of cookies. 56 Ross Alley, between Washington and Jackson Sts., Chinatown, 415/781–9977. Closed Sun. and Mon.

5 c-6
HAIG'S DELICACIES

Middle Eastern, Indian, Indonesian, Greek, and Armenian groceries are all carried here: feta cheese, phyllo dough, Kalamata olives, soujouk sausage (spicy sausage), and Armenian dried beef. 642 Clement St., at 8th Ave., Richmond District, 415/752–6283. Closed Sun.

5 c-6
HAPPY SUPERMARKET

This is your one-stop shop for Chinese groceries: dried fish, dried mushrooms, pot stickers, every grade of soy sauce, tofu, abalone, Chinese vegetables and pickles, Chinese herbs and medicines, and many varieties of rice. There are supplies for Philippine, Thai, and other Asian cuisines as well. 400 Clement St., at 5th Ave., Richmond District, 415/221–3195.

4 a-6
K. SAKAI UOKI CO.

This beautiful, clean supermarket in the heart of Japantown has great Asian produce and fresh sushi-quality fish. Come here for Japanese fish cakes, barbecued pork, pickled vegetables, and anything else needed for preparing a Japanese meal. 1656 Post St., at Buchanan St., Japantown, 415/921–0514. Closed Sun. No credit cards.

8 *c-5*

LA PALMA MEXICATESSEN

The handmade tortillas from this "Mexican deli" are excellent. It also stocks all kinds of wonderful dried chiles, beans, hot sauces, and corn husks for making tamales, plus prepared Mexican food. *2884 24th St., at Florida St., Mission District, 415/647–1500.*

5 *h-3*

LUCCA DELICATESSEN

Lucca has been serving the Marina community since 1932. It's famous for its handmade ravioli and its huge selection of Italian gourmet goods: imported olive oils and Parmesan cheese, fresh pastas and Italian sausages, Chianti and other Italian wines, polenta and pancetta flour, roast chickens, and prepared salads. *2120 Chestnut St., at Steiner St., The Marina, 415/921–7873.*

4 *e-4*

MAY WAH
TRADING COMPANY

This Chinatown store specializes in Southeast Asian groceries. Fresh produce includes lemon grass, coconuts, chiles, and locally grown herbs. Prepared foods include pâtés, rice noodle dough, fish and chili paste, dried shrimp, rice paper, and nuts. *1230 Stockton St., at Broadway, Chinatown, 415/433–3095. No credit cards.*

4 *e-4*

METRO FOOD CO.

Shanghai-style groceries are the staples of this Chinatown store, including jellyfish, fungi, noodles, and bean curd skins. Also here: Szechuan vegetables, spices, dumplings, and fermented sweet rice pudding. *641 Broadway, at Grant Ave., Chinatown, 415/982–1874. Cash only.*

4 *e-3*

MOLINARI DELICATESSEN

Billing itself as the oldest delicatessen west of the Rockies, Molinari has been making its own salami, sausages, and cold cuts since 1896. Other homemade specialties include meat and cheese ravioli, tortellini with prosciutto filling, homemade tomato sauces, and fresh pastas. Cured meats, cheeses, and Italian wines fill the room with tantalizing sights and smells. *373 Columbus Ave., at Vallejo St., North Beach, 415/421–2337. Closed Sun. No credit cards.*

8 *a-5*

SAMIRAMIS IMPORTS

This import shop is crowded with all sorts of edible goodies from the Middle East. *2990 Mission St., at 26th St., Mission District, 415/824–6555. Closed Sun.*

7 *h-6*

SPECKMANN'S

Adjacent to the restaurant of the same name, Speckmann's is filled to the rafters with German goodies. Bratwurst, Swiss *bundenfleisch* (salt-cured, air-dried beef), liverwurst, Westphalian ham, and the house-made pork and veal loaf known as *leberkase* are just a few of the meats they carry. About 20 varieties of German beer round out the stock quite nicely. *1550 Church St., at Duncan St., Noe Valley, 415/282–6850.*

fish & seafood

4 *d-1*

CRESCI BROS.

If you're visiting Fisherman's Wharf, stop by Cresci Bros. for live and cooked crabs in season, as well as shrimp, prawns, clams, oysters, and lobsters. They'll even pack your seafood for long trips. *Stall No. 2, Fisherman's Wharf, 415/474–8796.*

4 *a-2*

MARINA SAFEWAY

The fish counter at this supermarket outlet has one of the city's largest and best-priced selections of seafood. There are usually more than 25 varieties of shellfish, including live lobster and crab, and more than 30 kinds of fish from around the world, weather and season permitting. Cleaning and scaling are complimentary. Fish arrives fresh Monday through Saturday. *15 Marina Blvd., at Buchanan St., The Marina, 415/563–4946.*

4 *g-4*

SAN FRANCISCO
FARMERS' MARKET

See Produce, *below*.

3 *c-2*

SPENGER'S FISH GROTTO

The famed Berkeley seafood restaurant, founded in 1890, also has an outstanding fish market. There are always plenty of local catches, plus fish and seafood from around the world. *1919 4th St., near University Ave., Berkeley, 510/845–7771.*

4 c-5

SWAN OYSTER DEPOT

The best place in the city to purchase fresh local shellfish, Swan Oyster Depot also has counter seating and delicious chowder to warm the cockles of your heart (*see* Seafood *in* Chapter 3). The oysters, fish, and other seafood vary according to availability. *1517 Polk St., between California and Sacramento Sts., Nob Hill, 415/673–1101. Closed Sun. No credit cards.*

6 g-2

YUM YUM FISH

This Chinese market has fish and seafood, including tanks with live fish. Buy the fish whole or ask them to clean, scale, and fillet it. *2181 Irving St., between 22nd and 23rd Aves., Sunset District, 415/566–6433. Closed Sun. No credit cards.*

gourmet goodies

7 a-2

ANDRONICO'S MARKET

The Sunset District's best full-service grocery is loaded with gourmet specialties: jams, crackers, pickles, olives, vinegar, and prepared foods. *1200 Irving St., at Funston Ave., Sunset District, 415/661–3220.*

4 f-4

BON APPETIT

Exceptional meat and deli departments are a welcome anomaly in this downtown location, near Embarcadero Center. Each department has an extraordinary selection of high-quality gourmet items from all over the world. Everything is artfully displayed and the busy staff is friendly and helpful. *145 Jackson St., at Front St., The Embarcadero, 415/982–3112.*

4 e-6

THE CELLAR AT MACY'S

The Cellar at Macy's department store is a wonderland of cooking gadgets and gourmet goodies. It's got everything: coffee, tea, meats, candy, smoked fish, cheese, packaged foods, and wine. Their selection of international food items is impressive. *Stockton and O'Farrell Sts., Union Square, 415/397–3333.*

7 g-5

THE CHEF

Original and unique items at this cozy gourmet deli include fresh imported and domestic caviar, plus delicacies such as pâté and smoked duck. The shop's gift baskets and party trays are festive and tasty. *3977 24th St., at Noe St., Noe Valley, 415/550–7982.*

5 f-8

FALLETTI'S FOODS

Falletti's is famed for its produce, but its separate deli, meat, fish, poultry, dessert, bread, and liquor boutiques are also full of mouthwatering gourmet delights. *1750 Fulton St., at Masonic Ave., Western Addition, 415/567–0976.*

4 c-7

OPERA PLAZA GROCERY & DELICATESSEN

Though it's small, this place has an amazing selection of quality gourmet foods and spices. Saffron threads and other hard-to-find ingredients are in abundance. *601 Van Ness Ave., at McAllister St., Civic Center, 415/441–2727.*

4 a-5

VIVANDE PORTA VIA

This just might be the best gourmet shop in the city, if also the priciest. Choose from Italian delights such as antipasti, pâtés, terrines, meats, cheeses, sausages, salads, pastry. Especially stunning are the torta Milanese, the rotisserie, and the breads. Or sit down at a table to enjoy a fine Italian feast (*see* Italian *in* Chapter 3). *2125 Fillmore St., at California St., Pacific Heights, 415/346–4430.*

health food

7 g-3

BUFFALO WHOLE FOOD & GRAIN CO.

Everything at this lovely shop is well organized and displayed, prices are good, and the quality is high. In addition to organic produce there's a large selection of bulk grains, flours, pastas, nuts, spices, and dried fruits. *598 Castro St., a 19th St., The Castro, 415/626-7038.*

8 b-1

RAINBOW GROCERY

This vast cooperatively owned-and-run grocery has every food item a vegetarian, vegan, or natural-foods fan could dream of, including organic produce, baked goods, deli items, cheeses, oils, grains, pastas, herbs and spices—and prices are reasonable. It's a great place to shop for vitamins, health books, juicers and cookware, and natural body-care products. *1745 Folsom St., at 13th St., South of Market, 415/863–0620.*

4 *c-3*
REAL FOOD COMPANY
One of the city's most successful health food stores, Real Food has some of the best fresh produce you'll find outside the farmers' markets, as well as a full line of fresh fish, meat, and grains. The Stanyan Street branch has a small delicatessen. Vitamins and other herbal products are carried at all the stores. The prices may not be the best in town, but the variety is certainly the widest. *2164 Polk St., at Filbert St., Russian Hill, 415/775–2805. Call for other locations.*

5 *a-7*
THOM'S NATURAL FOODS
This roomy organic produce and grocery store has bulk herb and grain bins and a deli counter. *5843 Geary Blvd., at 23rd Ave., Richmond District, 415/387–6367.*

herbs & spices

4 *e-4*
ELLISON ENTERPRISES CO. USA
The friendly staff at this Chinatown shop will happily explain the secrets and powers of Chinese herbal medicine. *801 Stockton St., between Clay and Sacramento Sts., Chinatown, 415/982–3912. Closed Sun.*

3 *e-2*
LHASA KARNAK HERB CO.
Berkeley's best herb shop has two branches. *2513 Telegraph Ave., at Dwight Way, Berkeley, 510/548–0380.*

3 *d-2*
1938 Shattuck Ave., at Durant Ave., Berkeley, 510/548–0372.

8 *a-2*
SAN FRANCISCO HERB CO.
In business since 1973, this outlet store is well stocked with herbs, spices, teas, essential and fragrance oils, flavoring extracts, and all kinds of potpourri ingredients and recipes. *250 14th St., at Mission St., Mission District, 415/861–3018. Closed Sun.*

8 *a-4*
SCARLET SAGE HERB CO.
Choose from more than 250 herbs and spices, many of them organic, and all sold in bulk. There are also vitamins, extracts, oils, teas, and herbal body-care products. *3412 22nd St., between Guerrero and Valencia Sts., Mission District, 415/821–0997. Closed Sun.*

meat & poultry

7 *h-7*
DREWES MARKET
Folks come from all over San Francisco to shop here for fresh meat, poultry, and fish. The counters are impeccably clean and the customer service is outstanding. The shop's freezer section is packed with meats that are stuffed with gourmet ingredients and marinated in house sauces. Foolproof cooking instructions are freely given. *1706 Church St., at 29th St., Noe Valley, 415/821–0555. Closed Sun. No credit cards.*

5 *h-6*
HONEYBAKED HAM COMPANY
Delicious hams, backribs, smoked turkey, sauces, hearty soup mixes, cheeses, and salads are sold at this small, tidy store. *2190 Geary Blvd., at Divisadero St., Western Addition, 415/547–8292. Closed Sun.*

5 *a-7*
ISRAEL KOSHER MEAT, POULTRY & DELI
Come here for fresh kosher beef, lamb, and chicken. *5621 Geary Blvd., at 20th Ave., Richmond District, 415/752–3064. Closed Sat. No credit cards.*

4 *f-8*
KWONG JOW SAUSAGE FACTORY
This SoMa business sells dried sausages, barbecued pork, and bacon rind. *753 Bryant St., at 6th St., South of Market, 415/398–4348. No credit cards.*

4 *e-3*
LITTLE CITY MARKET
Range-fed veal, cut any way you like, is this North Beach butcher's specialty. *1400 Stockton St., at Vallejo St., North Beach, 415/986–2601. Closed Sun. No credit cards.*

nuts & seeds

4 e-6

MORROW'S NUT HOUSE

Fresh roasted nuts fill the glass-fronted bins that line the walls here, and still more nuts fill the fancy gift tins stacked on the shelves. Dried fruits are also for sale. *111 Geary St., between Grant Ave. and Stockton St., Union Square, 415/362–7969. Closed Sun.*

8 d-8

SAN FRANCISCO POPCORN WORKS

Pesto, cheddar cajun, sour cream, caramel, and golden macadamia crunch are among the 40-odd wacky flavors of popcorn sold here. Buy the stuff from gift shops around the city, or direct from the factory store. *1028 Revere Ave., near Silver Ave., Bayview, 415/822–4744 or 800/777–2676. Closed weekends.*

pasta & noodles

4 c-4

AUNTIE PASTA

With four stores in the city, Auntie Pasta has every type of pasta you can imagine, plus freshly made sauces and other necessities. Fresh pastas flavored with garlic, beets, roasted peppers, or chiles are made daily. *2139 Polk St., at Vallejo St., Russian Hill, 415/776–9420.*

4 e-4

NEW HONG KONG NOODLE CO.

This Chinatown shop has Hong Kong and Shanghai style noodles, plus won-ton and potsticker skins. Prices are very reasonable. *874 Pacific Ave., at Powell St., Chinatown, 415/982–2715. No credit cards.*

produce

3 d-3

BERKELEY BOWL MARKETPLACE

Housed in a former bowling alley, this vast market is worth the trip across the Bay Bridge. The vegetable and fruit selection (including organic produce) is seemingly endless, the bulk grains well priced, and the adjoining seafood and cheese departments are both superb. Most local bakeries stock their loaves here. *2777 Shattuck Ave., at Stuart St., Berkeley, 510/843–6929. Closed Sun.*

4 g-4

SAN FRANCISCO FARMERS' MARKET/FERRY PLAZA

The outdoor farmer's market next to the Ferry Building is a shade more upscale than the one at United Nations Plaza (*see below*). It has the same fresh, locally grown produce, plus homemade yogurts, cheeses, tortillas, salsas, breads, and desserts. It's also one of the best places in the city for shellfish straight out of Tamales Bay. *Ferry Plaza, Market St. and The Embarcadero, Financial District, 415/981–3004. Tues. and Sat. only.*

4 c-7

SAN FRANCISCO FARMERS' MARKET/ UNITED NATIONS PLAZA

Many of the farmers who sell their produce at this sprawling outdoor market are from Southeast Asia, so the selection ranges from the expected to the exotic. Produce varies by season, but is always cheap. *United Nations Plaza, 415/558–9455. Sun. and Wed. only. No credit cards.*

4 e-4

WO-SOON PRODUCE CO.

At this Asian produce market, purchase delicacies like water chestnuts, mustard and broccoli greens, baby bok choy, and watercress. *1210 Stockton St., at Pacific Ave., Chinatown, tel 415/989–2350. No credit cards.*

FRAMING

6 h-5

AL BERNZWEIG FRAMING

Al has been doing custom framing at his well-stocked shop since 1967. For those in a hurry, there's one-hour service. *1100 Ortega St., at 18th Ave., Sunset District, 415/664–8052. Closed Sun.*

5 a-7

AMSTERDAM ART

See Art Supplies, *above*.

5 b-7

CHEAP PETE'S

At this factory outlet, choose from hundreds of ready-made picture frames in all sizes and styles. Prices run 30%–70% below retail. *4270 Geary Blvd., at 11th Ave., Richmond District, 415/221–4720.*

4 *f-6*

MUSEUM WEST

Across the street from the San Francisco Museum of Modern Art, Museum West does museum-quality framing of fine art. There's an excellent selection of elegant gold-leaf and period frames, and the staff knows how to handle oversized work. *170 Minna St., at 3rd St., South of Market, 415/546–1113. Closed Sun.*

GIFTS & SOUVENIRS

4 *d-5*

AUSTRALIAN FAIR

Everything in this Union Square shop comes from the Land Down Under. This includes lambskin rugs and coats, toy koala bears and duckbill platypuses, rabbit-pelt Acubra hats, Aussie chocolates, and tins of Vegemite. Best sellers include Glenstone boots and stockman's coats. *700 Sutter St., at Taylor St., Union Square, 415/441–5319.*

4 *e-1*

THE CABLE CAR STORE

After you've fallen in love with San Francisco's charming cable cars, take home a miniature! This Pier 39 shop carries cable-car music boxes, memorabilia, and other clever souvenirs. *Pier 39, Fisherman's Wharf, 415/989–2040.*

4 *d-1*

CELL BLOCK 41

You'll find Cell Block 41 next to the dock where ferries depart for Alcatraz. It's filled with souvenirs of the famous former prison—everything from T-shirts to handcuffs. *Pier 41, Fisherman's Wharf, 415/249–4666.*

4 *f-6*

CENTER FOR THE ARTS GIFT SHOP

The Yerba Buena Gardens gift shop carries beautiful handmade jewelry, tableware, and crafts from both regional and national artists. It also has unusual children's books, T-shirts, and greeting cards. *701 Mission St., at 3rd St., South of Market, 415/978–2710.*

4 *a-4*

THE ENCHANTED CRYSTAL

Dozens of crystal candle holders, vases, and art deco sculptures fill this friendly shop. Many of the pieces—including a large selection of handcrafted glass jewelry—are made by Bay Area artists. *1895 Union St., at Laguna St., The Marina, 415/885–1335.*

5 *a-1*

GOLDEN GATE BRIDGE GIFT CENTER

Mementos featuring the world-famous bridge are for sale at the Round House Building, on the south (San Francisco) side of the Golden Gate Bridge. *Golden Gate Bridge, 415/923–2331.*

4 *e-1*

HOLLYWOOD USA

For movie and radio buffs, this place is a delight: It sells unusual (and sometimes silly) Hollywood themed souvenirs. You'll find plates painted with scenes from "Star Trek" and replica Oscars for "Best Shopper." *Pier 39, Fisherman's Wharf, 415/982–3538.*

4 *e-1*

LEFT HAND WORLD

Got a lefty in your life? Buy him or her a fountain pen with instantly drying ink to prevent smearing, a watch with the bezel on the left side, or a deck of playing cards with the numbers in all four corners. *Pier 39, Fisherman's Wharf, 415/433–3547.*

4 *c-2*

LIGHT WAVE GALLERY

This shop showcases *holographs* (3D-like photorealistic images). Works for sale range from cute and cuddly pictures of teddy bears to lifelike portraits of sports heros. *The Cannery, 2801 Leavenworth St., at Beach St., Fisherman's Wharf, 415/474–0133.*

4 *e-1*

MAGNET P.I.

Only at San Francisco's Pier 39 can you find a shop devoted exclusively to refrigerator magnets. Of the hundreds stuck to this shop's walls and ceiling, many have San Francisco motifs. *Pier 39, Fisherman's Wharf, 4159/989–2361.*

7 *e-1*

MASCARA CLUB

For those in search of quirky gift items, this is a fun place to browse and buy. The goods for sale vary, but you're likely to find novelty mouse pads, recycled art objects, and Mexican crafts. *1408 Haight St., at Masonic Ave., The Haight, 415/863-2837.*

7 *e-1*

PIPE DREAMS

Perfect for your favorite Deadhead, this place sells Day-Glo posters, tie-dye T-shirts, incense, candles, and all kinds of exotic pipes. *1372 Haight St., at Masonic Ave., The Haight, 415/431–3553.*

4 *f-6*

SFMOMA STORE

The San Francisco Museum of Modern Art's gift shop is is famous for its exclusive line of watches and jewelry, as well as its artists' monographs, Picasso dishes and other dinnerware, children's art-making sets and books, and extensive collection of art books for adults. *151 3rd St., South of Market, 415/357–4035. Closed Wed.*

4 *f-5*

THE SHARPER IMAGE

This purveyor of high-end gadgetry, now a national chain, was founded in San Francisco. It carries everything from five-language translators and noiseless rowing machines to state-of-the-art speaker systems and Walkman-size computers. *532 Market St., at Sansome St., Financial District, 415/398–6472.*

4 *b-2*

Ghiradelli Square, 900 North Point St., Fisherman's Wharf, 415/776–1443.

4 *f-3*

680 Davis St., at Broadway, The Embarcadero, 415/445–6100.

4 *b-8*

WORLDWARE

At this shop, recycling is art. The picture frames and candlesticks are made from aluminum cans, while purses and wallets are cut from discarded tires. The owner, Shari Sant, designs her own line of clothing made from organic hemp, wool, and cotton (*see* Clothing for Women & Men, *above*). *336 Hayes St., between Franklin and Gough Sts., Hayes Valley, 415/487–9030.*

HARDWARE & HOUSEWARES

2 *c-6*

BROOKSTONE CO.

Every gadget and tool imaginable is found at this shop, whether it's for home repairs, cooking, cleaning fish, barbecuing, figuring your income taxes, or gardening. *Stonestown Galleria, 19th Ave. and Winston Dr., Stonestown, 415/731-8046.*

4 *e-6*

THE CAPTAIN'S WHARF

Brassware is the specialty here: Look for doorknobs, door knockers, hooks, towel bars, lamps, candle holders, and clocks. *125 Powell St., at Ellis St., Union Square, 415/391–2884.*

7 *f-1*

COOKIN': RECYCLED GOURMET APPURTENANCES

Cookin' carries quality used fondue makers, espresso machines, food processors, cookie cutters, Jell-O molds, pots, pans, and other kitchen gadgets, all at excellent values. *339 Divisadero St., between Oak and Page Sts., The Haight, 415/861–1854.*

4 *e-3*

FIGONI HARDWARE CO.

Restaurant-quality glassware and dishes, kitchen gadgets, cookware, and linens are sold in this old-fashioned Italian business. *1351 Grant Ave., at Green St., North Beach, 415/392–4765. Closed Sun. and Wed. No credit cards.*

5 *f-5*

FORREST JONES INC.

This shop has a full range of French and Italian household goods, including dishes, glassware, kitchen tools, cutlery, and complete table settings. *3274 Sacramento St., at Presidio Ave., Laurel Heights, 415/567–2483.*

5 *h-4*

GORDON BENNETT

Housewares and ceramics made by local artists are some of the delights you'll find here. There's a good selection of garden sculptures, garden tools, and wrought-iron outdoor furniture, too. *2102 Union St., between Webster and Fillmore Sts., The Marina, 415/929–1172.*

4 *b-2*

Ghirardelli Square, 900 North Point St., at Polk St., Fisherman's Wharf, 415/351–1172.

5 *e-6*

JUDITH ETS-HOKIN HOMECHEF KITCHEN STORE

Associated with a cooking school of the same name, the Homechef Kitchen Store has just about every low- or high-tech cooking utensil you might need, from egg whisks to Cuisinarts. Sign up for weekday and weekend cooking classes while you're here. *3525 California St., at Locust St., Laurel Heights, 415/668–3191.*

4 *e-4*

TI-SUN CO.

Chinese cookware, knives, and equipment are sold along with other hardware items at this family-run Chinatown business. Service is friendly and helpful. *614 Jackson St., at Grant Ave., Chinatown, 415/982–1958.*

4 *e-1*

WE BE KNIVES

This tiny shop is filled with wicked-looking sharp things: kitchen cutlery, all kinds of pocket and hunting knives, and even a few swords. *Pier 39, Fisherman's Wharf, 415/982–9323.*

4 *e-5*

WILLIAMS-SONOMA

The retail outlet of the famous mail-order catalog house (which began life as a hardware store in Sonoma County) has stylish cooking equipment, tabletop items, and knickknacks, plus dozens of cookbooks and gourmet food items. *150 Post St., at Grant Ave., Union Square, 415/362–6904.*

4 *e-6*

San Francisco Shopping Centre, Union Square, 415/546–0171.

2 *c-6*

Stonestown Galleria, Stonestown, 415/681–5525.

4 *f-4*

2 Embarcadero Center, The Embarcadero, 415/421–2033.

4 *e-4*

THE WOK SHOP

Though the shop specializes in Chinese woks, it stocks other Chinese cookware

as well—plus Chinese baskets, cookbooks, and aprons. *718 Grant Ave., at Clay St., Chinatown, 415/989–3797.*

4 *a-6*

SOKO HARDWARE

Run by the Ashizawa merchant family in Japantown since 1925, Soko Hardware specializes in beautifully crafted Japanese dishware, gardening tools, carpentry instruments, and housewares such as vases and lamps. *1698 Post St., at Buchanan St., Japantown, 415/931–5510. Closed Sun.*

HOME FURNISHINGS

bedroom & bath

8 *c-1*

BED, BATH, & BEYOND

This vast store, part of a nation chain, has seemingly endless household wares, from chic to cheap. There are two floors of bed, bath, and kitchen necessities, plus picture frames, sculptures, and other decorative items. *555 9th St., at Bryant St., South of Market, 415/252–0490.*

4 *c-7*

THE FUTON SHOP

Here's where you'll find the best selection of futons and frames in San Francisco. You can choose your own futon cover from dozens of fabric samples. The outlet store has outstanding bargains. *801 Van Ness Ave., at Eddy St., Civic Center, 415/563–8866.*

8 *c-5*

Outlet: 2150 Cesar Chavez, at Potrero Ave., Mission District, 415/920–6801.

4 *e-6*

KRIS KELLY

Kris Kelly is a San Francisco favorite for imported and domestic handcrafted tablecloths, decorative pillows, bed linens, bath accessories, window treatments, and porcelain lamps. Handmade quilts from China are a specialty. *174 Geary St., at Stockton St., Union Square, 415/986–8822.*

4 *b-6*

O'PLUME

Sleep in luxury with O'Plume's extremely fine silk sheets, down comforters, duvets, and pillows imported from France, Italy, Belgium, Germany, and Switzerland. You'll also find antique pillow shams, and table linens. *1610 Post St., at Gough St., Western Addition, 415/771-6100. Closed Sun.*

4 *e-6*

SCHEUER LINENS

Designers and everyday shoppers flock to Scheuer for its luxurious linens for the bed, bath, and dinner table—by the very best makers from the United States and Europe. Many of the down comforters, duvet covers, and pillows are imported from Europe. There is also a wide variety of gifts, such as candles, hand-embroidered handkerchiefs, and soaps. *340 Sutter St., at Stockton St., Union Square, 415/392–2813. Closed Sun.*

5 *g-5*

SUE FISHER KING

Fine bedroom linens and an aromatic mix of soaps, perfumes, and candles are among the many choice items here (*see Furniture & Accessories, below*). *3067 Sacramento St., between Baker and Broderick Sts., Pacific Heights, 415/922–7276.*

4 *a-6*

TOWNHOUSE LIVING

This Japan Center store sells futons and pillows as well as household accessories (*see Furniture & Accessories, below*). *1825 Post St., at Fillmore St., Japantown, 415/563–1417.*

carpets & rugs

8 *c-8*

CARPET CONNECTION

This store has San Francisco's largest inventory of new name-brand carpeting. Area rugs and remnants, draperies, miniblinds, and vinyl flooring is all sold at warehouse prices. *390 Bay Shore Blvd., at Industrial St., Bayview, 415/550–7125.*

4 *f-4*

CARPETS OF THE INNER CIRCLE

Owner Roger Cavanna was an architect and city planner before going into the antique carpet business. His shop carries a marvelous range of beautiful kilims and carpets. *444 Jackson St., at Montgomery St., Jackson Square, 415/398–2988. Closed Sun.*

8 *d-1*

JALILI INTERNATIONAL, INC.

Jalili carries an extensive collection of dhurries, kilims, and other fine antique Oriental carpets, as well as contemporary handmade rugs. *101 Henry Adams St., at Division St., South of Market, 415/788–3377. Closed weekends. No credit cards.*

8 *c-1*

OMID ORIENTAL RUGS

This large showroom is piled with Persian, Turkish, Pakistani, Indian, Chinese, Nepalese, and other new, used, and antique rugs. The staff is knowledgeable and helpful. *590 9th St., at Brannan St., South of Market, 415/626–3466.*

5 *h-4*

SILKROUTE INTERNATIONAL

Of the many antique and new kilims and carpets here, many are from Afghanistan. The shop also has Afghani imports such as brass and copper works, jewelry, and needlework. *3119 Fillmore St., at Filbert St., The Marina, 415/563–4936.*

ceramic tiles

8 *d-1*

ANN SACKS TILE & STONE

The ceramic, marble, slate, limestone, and terra-cotta tiles here come from around the world. There are handcrafted tiles, antique tiles, and tile mosaics. *2 Henry Adams St., at Division St., South of Market, 415/252–5889. Closed Sun.*

8 *d-2*

TILE VISIONS

Roger Chetrit of Tile Visions designs delightful trompe l'oeil tiles, as well as tile murals. Much of his work is custom, but he also has ready-made designs, some by European designers. *299 Kansas St., between 16th and 17th Sts., Potrero Hill, 415/621–4546. Closed weekends.*

china, glassware, porcelain, pottery, silver

4 *e-3*

BIORDI ITALIAN IMPORTS

This established family business imports gorgeous hand-painted pottery directly from Italy—mainly Tuscany and Umbria—and ships it worldwide. Dishware sets can be ordered in any combination. Prices range from reasonable to quite expensive. *412 Columbus Ave., at Vallejo St., North Beach, 415/392–8096. Closed Sun.*

4 *e-6*

GUMP'S

San Francisco's fabled department store (*see* Department Stores, *above*) stocks a dazzling assortment of fine china, crystal, and silver—including exclusive lines of dinnerware, flatware, and glassware. *135 Post St., at Grant Ave., Union Square, 415/982–1616.*

8 *d-8*

HERITAGE HOUSE TABLEWARE SHOWROOM

Shop here first: There are some 1,500 patterns by more than 100 manufacturers on display, including all the fine brands like Waterford-Wedgewood, Ginori, and Lenox. There's crystal and silverware, too. Prices on many items run 15%–40% below retail. *2190 Palou Ave., at Industrial St., Bayview, 415/285–1331.*

7 *g-2*

SET YOUR TABLE

San Francisco's largest and best selection of Fitz & Floyd fine china is found in this Upper Market shop. Fine crystal and flatware are also available. *2258 Market St., at 15th St., Noe Valley, 415/ 626-7330.*

7 *g-5*

TERRA MIA CERAMIC STUDIOS

This place lets shoppers create ceramic pieces using their own designs and the store's art supplies and kiln. Teapots, mugs, goblets, and tiles are among the items that can be fired and ready to display within a week. *4037 24th St., between Noe and Castro Sts., Noe Valley, 415/642–9911.*

4 *e-6*

TIFFANY & CO.

Very fine china, crystal, and silver are sold in this famed treasure house. Their jewels are famed worldwide (*see* Jewelry, *below*). *350 Post St., between Powell and Stockton Sts., Union Square, 415/781– 7000. Closed Sun.*

furniture & accessories

4 *d-3*

ABITARE

This popular North Beach shop stocks a quirky and eclectic mix of home furnishings: soaps and bath supplies, candleholders, picture frames, lamps, and one-of-a-kind furniture, artwork, and decorations. *522 Columbus Ave., at Union St., North Beach, 415/392–5800. Closed Sun.*

8 *d-3*

AMBIENTE

Dining room sets, dressers, sofas, and chairs are among the mildly trendy and reasonably priced contemporary home furnishings here. *390 Kansas St., at 17th St., Potrero Hill, 415/863–9700.*

4 *a-3*

THE BOMBAY COMPANY

This national chain specializes in affordable reproductions of 18th- and 19th-century American and British furniture and accessories. *2135 Union St., at Webster St., The Marina, 415/441–1591.*

2 *c-6*

Stonestown Galleria, Stonestown, 415/ 753–2955.

4 *e-5*

CRATE & BARREL

The Union Square store was the chain's first in the western U.S., and it is still the largest. It sells affordable but stylish bed linens, kitchen accessories, dishware, glassware, furniture, and other home furnishings. The outlet store, in Berkeley, has irregular or discontinued products priced 30%–50% below retail. *125 Grant Ave., at Post St., Union Square, 415/986–4000.*

3 *c-2*

Outlet: 1785 4th St., at Hearst Ave., Berkeley, 510/528–5500.

4 *d-8*

EVOLUTION

Evolution carries an unusual selection of imported furniture, home accessories, crafts, and housewares, with many pieces from Indonesia. It also has Amish, Shaker, and Arts and Crafts reproduction furnishings such as armoires, loveseats, and hope chests. *271 9th St., between Folsom and Howard Sts., South of Market, 415/861–6665.*

5 h-5

FILLAMENTO

This Pacific Heights favorite has three floors of home furnishings. You'll find everything from dinnerware and bedding to rugs and furniture to bath and baby accessories, in styles ranging from classic to contemporary. *2185 Fillmore St., at Sacramento St., Pacific Heights, 415/931–2224.*

8 c-1

GALISTEO HOME FURNISHINGS

The furniture and accessories here are all in the style of American West and Southwest. Decorative and folk arts, fabrics, pottery, jewelry, antiques, and fine art are all on display. *590 10th St., at Division St., South of Market, 415/861–5900. Closed Sun.*

5 h-4

GORDON BENNETT

See Hardware & Housewares, *above*).

8 a-2

GREENHAVEN

This Mission shop routinely wins praises by *SF Bay Guardian* readers as the city's "Best Vintage Furniture Store," and it's the pick of Valencia Street's many thrift stores. There's a mixture of old and new, all reasonably priced. *560 Valencia St., between 16th and 17th Sts., Mission District, 415/255–4877.*

4 g-8

LIMN COMPANY

This is San Francisco's best outlet for designer furniture, as well as fine lamps and home accessories. You'll find classic and modern designs by international and local talents. *290 Townsend St., at 4th St., South Beach, 415/543–5466.*

4 g-7

MAISON D'ETRE

Eclectic luxury items for the home include gorgeous wrought-iron light fixtures, luxurious pillows, and ornate mirrors. *92 South Park Ave., between 2nd and 3rd Sts., South Beach, 415/357–1747.*

4 a-5

MIKE FURNITURE

The stylish furniture here tends to be conservative and expensive. The shop does custom work as well. *2142 Fillmore St., at Sacramento St., Pacific Heights, 415/567–2700.*

4 c-6

NIGEL IMPORTS

Nigel has a stunning selection of solid rosewood furniture. All pieces are handcrafted in Asia in either traditional or contemporary styling. Accessories such as Chinese standing screens, Japanese wall screens, and lamps round out the selection. *1244 Sutter St., at Van Ness Ave., Polk Gulch, 415/776–5490. Closed Sun.*

7 f-3

ONLY ON CASTRO

The fine furnishings here have an international flair. Armoires, chests, and wrought-iron furniture are from Malaysia and Indonesia as well as from local artisans. *518 Castro St., between 18th and 19th Sts., The Castro, 415/522-0122.*

4 a-5

PASCUAL'S FURNITURE

Choose from a range of fabrics—from conservative to bright and lively—to cover any of the custom sofas, chairs, headboards, and other furniture available here. *2116 Fillmore St., at Sacramento St., Pacific Heights, 415/346–1098.*

4 f-5

POLO STORE– RALPH LAUREN

The genteel look that designer Ralph Lauren has popularized does not come cheap. This shop displays his version of gracious living, with home furnishings, linens, and elegant accessories. *90 Post St., at Kearny St., Union Square, 415/788–7656. Closed Sun.*

5 g-5

SUE FISHER KING

A favorite among designers and neighborhood residents, Sue Fisher King has decorative pillows and luxurious throws, Italian dinnerware, fine linens for the bedroom and kitchen, and books on gardening and home decoration, among other things. A small garden area gives the store a homey mood. *3067 Sacramento St., between Baker and Broderick Sts., Pacific Heights, 415/922–7276.*

4 *a-6*

TOWNHOUSE LIVING

Lamps, frames, Japanese fabrics, tatami mats, vases, and other graceful household accessories are available at this Japan Center outpost. *1825 Post St., at Fillmore St., Japantown, 415/563–1417.*

4 *a-4*

Z GALLERIE

The home furnishings and accessories here—including dinnerware, desks, chairs, and lamps—are sleek, high-tech, and sometimes playful. Pair a black butterfly chair with one of their many posters. *2071 Union St., at Webster St., The Marina, 415/346–9000. Call for other locations.*

lamps & lighting

4 *e-8*

BAY COMMERCIAL LIGHTING CENTER

Here is the largest selection of track and recessed fixtures in town: Everything from European chandeliers to contemporary floor lights is in stock. Lamps come in traditional and high-tech styles. *1140 Folsom St., at 7th St., South of Market, 415/552–4100. Closed Sun.*

8 *b-1*

CITY LIGHTS LIGHTING SHOWROOM

The art deco– and art moderne–style lamps are made of oxidized brass, limed woods, and other unique materials. City Lights also has a good selection of garden-lighting fixtures. *1585 Folsom St., at 12th St., South of Market, 415/863–2020. Closed Sun.*

5 *b-7*

LAMPS PLUS

Lamps by leading manufacturers are available here. *4700 Geary Blvd., at 11th Ave., Richmond District, 415/386–0933.*

paint & wallpaper

5 *f-7*

STANDARD BRANDS PAINT & HOME DECORATING CENTER

This do-it-yourself paint and wallpaper store also offers decorating consultations. *3 Masonic Ave., at Geary Blvd., Laurel Heights, 415/922–4003.*

JEWELRY

antique & collectible

7 *f-3*

BRAND X ANTIQUES

Estate jewelry and other gems from the early 20th century are available here. You'll also find cut and blown glass, and European, American, and Asian *objets d'art. 570 Castro St., at 18th St., The Castro, 415/626–8908.*

4 *e-6*

DILELIO'S

This shop, in the San Francisco Shopping Centre, has a beautiful collection of antique estate gold and silver jewelry, as well as costume jewelry from the 1940s and '50s. *865 Market St., at 5th St., Union Square, 415/243–9784.*

4 *e-5*

LANG ANTIQUES AND ESTATE JEWELRY

Lang has one of the widest selections of vintage jewelry in San Francisco. In addition, they sell objets d'art, silver hollowware and flatware, and vintage timepieces. *323 Sutter St., at Grant Ave., Union Square, 415/982–2213.*

5 *h-4*

OLD AND NEW ESTATES

This shop has antique and estate jewelry, timepieces, crystal, objets d' art, antiques, and silver. They specialize in Art Deco jewelry, including wedding and engagement rings. *2181 Union St., at Fillmore St., The Marina, 415/346–7525. Closed Wed.*

4 *a-4*

PARIS 1925

A small but handsome shop, Paris 1925 specializes in estate jewelry and vintage watches. Its selection of platinum Art Deco and Art Moderne wedding and engagement rings is particularly fine. *1954 Union St., between Buchanan and Laguna Sts., The Marina, 415/567–1925.*

contemporary

4 *e-5*

CARTIER

Treasures of gold, silver, and platinum, often crusted with precious gems, are the trademarks of this world-renowned jeweler. *231 Post St., at Stockton St., Union Square, 415/397–3180. Closed Sun.*

4 e-6

GUMP'S

This Union Square institution (*see Department Stores, above*) has one of the world's finest collections of jade and freshwater pearls. Much of the opulent jewelry is crafted exclusively for Gump's; prices are appropriately high. *135 Post St., at Grant Ave., Union Square, 415/982–1616.*

4 e-4

JADE EMPIRE

One of the many fine jewelry stores in Chinatown, Jade Empire has good selections of jade, diamonds, and other gems, as well as freshwater pearls, beads, porcelain dolls, and lanterns. *832 Grant Ave., at Clay St., Chinatown, 415/982–4498. Closed Sun.*

4 e-6

PEARL EMPIRE

Pearl and jade pieces are the specialties here. There's also a selection of coral jewelry imported from Hong Kong and Japan. *127 Geary St., at Stockton St., Union Square, 415/362–0606. Closed Sun.*

4 e-5

SHREVE & CO.

Founded in 1852, this is one of the city's most elegant jewelers and the oldest retail store in San Francisco. They carry a dazzling selection of fine diamonds, precious stone jewelry, gold, and Mikimoto pearls, plus gift items such as Baccarat crystal and Limoges porcelain. *Post St. and Grant Ave., Union Square, 415/421–2600. Closed Sun.*

4 e-5

SIDNEY MOBELL FINE JEWELRY

This award-winning jeweler is often lauded as San Francisco's most creative and witty. His custom work has included gold toilet seats, diamond mousetraps, and a million-dollar Monopoly set. *200 Post St., at Grant Ave., Union Square, 415/986–4747. Closed Sun.*

4 a-4

ST. ELEGIUS

Gold and precious-stone jewelry are sold at affordable prices here. They'll do custom work with diamonds and other gems. *1748 Union St., at Octavia St., The Marina, 415/771–2282. Closed Sun.*

4 e-6

TIFFANY & CO.

The San Francisco outpost of the famous New York City jewelry store is just as stunning as you'd expect. Exclusive jewelry designs by Paloma Picasso and others are a large part of why Tiffany's remains America's favorite fine jeweler. The store also carries sterling silver, china, and crystal. *350 Post St., between Powell and Stockton Sts., Union Square, 415/781–7000. Closed Sun.*

4 e-5

TOM WING & SONS

Fine jade, in shades from green to lavender, plus diamonds and pearls are specialties of this well-respected dealer. *208 Grant Ave., at Post St., Union Square, 415/391–2500. Closed Sun.*

4 a-3

UNION STREET GOLDSMITH

A local favorite since 1976, Union Street Goldsmith specializes in custom work. Among the wide selection of rare gemstones are golden sapphires, black Tahitian South Seas pearls, and violet tanzanite. Three jewelers work on the premises. *1909 Union St., at Laguna St., The Marina, 415/776–8048.*

4 e-6

WHOLESALE JEWELERS EXCHANGE

This is the place to find gems and finished jewelry at less-than-retail prices. More than 20 independent jewelers display their own merchandise. *121 O'Farrell St., between Powell and Stockton Sts., Union Square, 415/788–2365.*

4 e-5

YOKOO PEARLS

Yookoo deals exclusively in pearls of all colors and lusters. They sell custom designed jewelry as well. *210 Post St., at Grant Ave., 415/982–5441. Closed weekends.*

costume jewelry

7 f-1

COSTUMES ON HAIGHT

See Theatrical Items, below.

7 *e-1*

GALLERY OF JEWELS

Most of the costume jewelry here—in rhinestone, glass, and silver—is crafted by local artisans. The styles are eclectic, and the prices well below Tiffany & Co.'s. *1400 Haight St., at Masonic Ave., The Haight, 415/255–1180.*

4 *a-3*

JEST JEWELS

You'll find wonderfully witty *bijoux* at this Marina District shop, as well as a good selection of contemporary watches. *2049 Union St., at Webster St., The Marina, 415/563–8839.*

4 *g-4*

3 Embarcadero Center, The Embarcadero, 415/986–4494.

KITES

6 *b-8*

AIRTIME SAN FRANCISCO

This shop specializes in stunt kites, and has a large selection of kites and accessories. They also handle hang-gliding and paragliding instruction and equipment (*see* Hang-gliding & Paragliding *in* Chapter 6). *3620 Wawona St., at 47th Ave., Sunset District, 415/759–1177.*

4 *e-1*

KITE FLITE

Kites of all colors, shapes, and sizes festoon this Pier 39 shop. Their basic single-line parafoil kites start at $25, but there are also plenty of two-line stunt kites, and even some 17-, 25-, and 35-ft dragon kites. *Pier 39, Fisherman's Wharf, 415/956–3181.*

LEATHER GOODS & LUGGAGE

4 *e-6*

BOTTEGA VENETA

When your own initials aren't enough, you can always go with the BV monogram. The Italian-made leather goods—luggage, attachés, handbags, wallets, belts, and purses—are designed to last a lifetime. *108 Geary St., between Stockton St. and Grant Ave., Union Square, 415/981–1700. Closed Sun.*

4 *e-5*

THE COACH STORE

This shop carries classically styled Coach luggage, as well as beautiful, distinctive briefcases, wallets, and men's belts. A second, nearby Coach store carries the famous Coach handbags, women's belts, and other accessories (*see* Women's Clothing/Specialty, *above*). *170 Post St., at Grant Ave., Union Square, 415/391–7770.*

4 *f-4*

EDWARDS LUGGAGE

The luggage, briefcases, and portfolios at Edwards appeal to its Financial District clientele. Top brands such as Hartmann, Travelpro, Samsonite, Eagle Creek, Coach, and Ghurka are all represented. *3 Embarcadero Center, The Embarcadero, 415/981–7047.*

4 *e-6*

EL PORTAL LUGGAGE

This is a one-stop travel shop, with luggage, briefcases, shaving kits, and other necessities by Polo/Ralph Lauren, Hartmann, Samsonite, and others. The staff is multilingual and helpful. *San Francisco Shopping Centre, 865 Market St., at 5th St., Union Square, 415/896–5637.*

4 *e-5*

LOUIS VUITTON

A quality French leather goods and luggage maker since 1854, Louis Vuitton produces the ultimate status symbol: LV-embossed bags, briefcases, luggage, and steamer trunks. The classic Monogram line is available, along with the blue, green, red, and yellow pieces of the coloful Epi line. *230 Post St., at Grant Ave., Union Square, 415/391–6200.*

4 *e-6*

THE LUGGAGE CENTER

Convenient to Moscone Convention Center, the Luggage Center sells top-quality luggage, attachés, backpacks, and travel accessories at up to 50% off regular retail prices. Bring your damaged suitcase here and they'll have it expertly repaired. *828 Mission St., between 4th and 5th Sts., South of Market, 415/543–3771.*

4 *e-5*

MALM LUGGAGE

This upscale shop has been supplying San Francisco with fine luggage and leather goods since 1868. The emphasis is on luggage, travel accessories, and gifts for business executives. *222 Grant Ave., between Post and Sutter Sts., Union Square, 415/392–0417.*

4 *f-5*
Crocker Galleria, 50 Post St., at Kearny St., Financial District, 415/391–5222. Closed Sun.

MAPS

4 *e-6*
JOHN SCOPAZZI GALLERY
The gallery sells a marvelous selection of antique maps from the 16th through the 19th centuries, both framed and unframed. *130 Maiden Lane, between Stockton St. and Grant Ave., Union Square, 415/362–5708. Closed Sun.*

4 *f-5*
RAND MCNALLY MAP & TRAVEL STORE
The famous Rand McNally road maps and atlases are available here, together with maps, language tapes, globes, and domestic and international travel guides from all publishers. The shop carries topographical maps for the Bay Area and Sierras, and can order topo maps for any other area in the United States. *595 Market St., at 2nd St., South of Market, 415/777–3131.*

4 *f-6*
SIERRA CLUB BOOKSTORE
The Sierra Club's shop (*see* Bookstores, *above*) specializes in maps and trail guides for the West Coast and California, particularly the Bay Area.

4 *f-4*
THOMAS BROS. MAPS AND BOOKS
This place has a selection similar to Rand McNally's, of domestic and international maps, travel books and CD-Roms, atlases, and globes. *550 Jackson St., at Columbus Ave., Financial District, 415/981–7520. Closed weekends.*

MEMORABILIA

4 *d-6*
CINEMA SHOP
This tiny storefront, opened in 1967, is jammed with more than 250,000 original posters, stills, lobby cards, and rare videotapes of Hollywood classics and schlock films. *606 Geary St., at Jones St., Union Square, 415/885–6785. Closed Sun. Minimum $20 purchase for credit cards.*

6 *e-3*
LET IT BE RECORDS
See Music, *below.*

4 *d-3*
SAN FRANCISCO ROCK POSTERS AND COLLECTIBLES
The huge selection of rock-and-roll memorabilia here includes posters, handbills, and original art, most of it from the 1960s. Also available are posters from more recent shows at the legendary Fillmore Auditorium, with musicians like George Clinton, Porno for Pyros, and Johnny Cash. *1851 Powell St., between Filbert and Greenwich Sts., North Beach, 415/956–6749 or 800/949–1965. Closed Sun. and Mon.*

4 *e-4*
SHOW BIZ
Stock up here on movie, rock-and-roll, jazz, and theater memorabilia from several decades—posters, playbills, and photos, and the like. Some of it is sensibly priced, some not. *1318 Grant Ave., at Vallejo St., North Beach, 415/989–6744.*

MINIATURES

5 *a-7*
THE HOBBY COMPANY OF SAN FRANCISCO
See Crafts & Hobbies, *above.*

4 *e-5*
THE TREASURE HOUSE
See Toys & Games, *below.*

MUSIC

cds, tapes, & vinyl

3 *e-2*
AMOEBA
Amoeba stocks more than 100,000 new and used CDs, LPs, and tapes, and is always at the top of local "best of" lists. If you're looking for a rare or hard to find release, this is where you'll find it.

2455 Telegraph Ave., at Haste St., Berkeley, 510/549–1125.

8 *a-4*

AQUARIUS RECORDS

Aquarius began as *the* punk rock store in the 1970s, but has since diversified to include indie rock, dance music, experimental electronica, and a great selection of imports. The swank space carries mostly vinyl, but there are tapes and CDs—both new and used—as well. *1055 Valencia St., between 21st and 22nd Sts., Mission District, 415/647–2272.*

4 *b-8*

BPM MUSIC FACTORY

Bay Area club DJs shop here for imports and domestic products. The store's 12-inch collection includes house, techno, acid jazz, and progressive. *573 Hayes St., at Laguna St., Hayes Valley, 415/487–8680.*

8 *b-5*

DISCOLANDIA

This Mission District shop is far and away the city's best bet for current and vintage Latin music. *2964 24th St., between Harrison and Alabama Sts., Mission District, 415/826–9446.*

8 *a-2*

THE EPICENTER ZONE

An ideal resource for the new radical in town, this record store/community center has a large selection of new and used punk rock albums, as well as pool tables, bulletin boards, and a small library. *475 Valencia St., at 16th St., Mission District, 415/431–2725.*

7 *g-1*

GROOVE MERCHANT

Groove Merchant's owners run the highly recommended Luv 'n Haight and Ubiquity labels, both of which put the spotlight on the local acid jazz scene. *687 Haight St., between Pierce and Steiner Sts., The Haight, 415/252–5766. Closed Mon.*

3 *b-2*

HEAR MUSIC

The collection here is a mix of grass roots, folk, jazz, hip hop, international music, and rock. But what really makes this place worth the trip to Berkeley are its 60 listening stations where you can hear *any* CD in the store before you buy.

1809-B 4th St. at Hearst St., Berkeley, 510/204–9595.

6 *g-2*

JAZZ QUARTER

This snug Sunset District shop is tops for jazz lovers. It specializes in new and rare jazz LPs, but also carries new and used CDs. *1267 20th Ave., between Irving St. and Lincoln Way, Sunset District, 415/661–2331.*

6 *e-3*

LET IT BE RECORDS

With a name like this, could this Sunset District store specialize in anything but the Beatles? It carries many rare and out-of-print rock-and-roll records from the 1950s through 1980s, as well as rock memorabilia. *2434 Judah St., between 29th and 30th Aves., Sunset District, 415/681–2113. Closed Sun. and Mon.; by appointment only Tues.–Sat.*

7 *e-1*

RECKLESS RECORDS

One of several shops that make Haight Street a must stop for music lovers, Reckless buys and sells rock, hip-hop and indie recordings, with a large section devoted to vinyl. Music-related magazines, posters, T-shirts, and videos are also for sale. *1401 Haight St., at Masonic Ave., The Haight, 415/431–3434.*

7 *g-2*

THE RECORD FINDER

Visit this Upper Market shop for new and used vinyl, cassettes, and CDs—if you can't find it yourself, the staff will help you search for it. They're strongest with rock, soul, R & B, and classical music. *258 Noe St., near Market St., Noe Valley, 415/431–4443.*

7 *e-1*

RECYCLED RECORDS

A Haight Street favorite, Recycled doesn't have anything new. Instead, it buys, sells, and trades a vast collection of rock, jazz, soul, pop, blues, reggae, folk, and hard-to-find imports on CDs, LPs, 45s, and tapes. *1377 Haight St., at Masonic Ave., The Haight, 415/626–4075.*

5 *h-8*

REGGAE RUNNINS VILLAGE STORE

This reggae wonderland carries records, tapes, videos, T-shirts, jewelry, and other paraphernalia in the Rasta colors of red, gold, black, and green. *505 Divisadero St., between Fell and Hayes Sts., Western Addition, 415/922–2442. Closed Sun.*

8 *a-4*

RITMO LATINO
In the heart of the Mission, this colorful Latin-music store sells ranchero, mariachi, salsa, Tex-Mex, merengue, norteño, and more. You can sample CDs at the listening stations before buying. *2401 Mission St., at 20th St., Mission District, 415/824–8556.*

8 *a-5*

SAMIRAMIS IMPORTS
There's a fine selection of Middle Eastern CDs here, in addition to imported gourmet delicacies (*see* Food, *above*).

4 *b-8*

STAR CLASSICS
Star stocks only classical, opera, symphonic, ballet, New Age, and jazz tapes and CDs. The adjoining Star Classics Recital Hall hosts weekly vocal and musical performances. *425 Hayes St., at Gough St., Hayes Valley, 415/552–1110.*

7 *g-5*

STREET LIGHT RECORDS
A San Francisco institution since the 1960s, Street Light buys and sells thousands of used tapes and CDs, with a

---

HAIGHT-ASHBURY HIGH NOTES

The Upper Haight is heaven for music-lovers. Browse for obscure imports, classic punk—whatever you fancy, it's here.

Groove Merchant
Plenty for the collector, DJ, or serious amateur.

Haight Ashbury Music Center
One of the largest sellers of musical instruments on the West Coast.

Reckless Records
Everything from new imports to vintage rock posters.

Recycled Records
A Haight Street favorite for used vinyl, cassettes, and CDs.

---

vast selection of rock, jazz, soul, and R&B, as well as plenty of vinyl. The selection is usually offbeat and always fresh; the Noe Valley store is smaller, but has a better selection of vinyl. *3979 24th St., between Noe and Sanchez Sts., Noe Valley, 415/282–3550.*

7 *f-3*

2350 Market St., at Castro St., The Castro, 415/282–8000.

4 *c-2*

TOWER RECORDS
This international mega-chain is excellent for CDs in every category. Its three huge San Francisco branches—open daily until midnight—carry full selections of all types of music. The North Beach store is the largest. The outlet store has a more limited selection, but its remaindered items are great for bargain-hunters. *Columbus Ave. and Bay St., North Beach, 415/885–0500.*

7 *g-2*

Market and Noe Sts., Noe Valley, 415/621–0588.

2 *c-6*

Stonestown Galleria, Stonestown, 415/681–2001.

4 *g-7*

Outlet: 660 3rd St., between Townsend and Brannan Sts., South Beach, 415/957–9660.

4 *e-6*

VIRGIN MEGASTORE
The towering monolith of Union Square has hundreds of listening stations, a separate classical music room, and an extensive laser disc department, as well as a bookstore and a café. It's the best place in the city for music-shopping, according to annual *Bay Guardian* surveys. *2 Stockton St., at Market St., Union Square, 415/397–4525.*

sheet music

4 *e-6*

MUSIC CENTER OF SAN FRANCISCO
Under one roof you'll find jazz, pop, and classical sheet music, the largest such selection on the West Coast. The shop also sells accessories such as metronomes, harmonics, and books. *207 Powell St., between Geary and O'Farrell Sts., Union Square, 415/781–6023.*

6 g-5

MUSIC RACK

The San Francisco Conservatory of Music runs this shop stocking new and used sheet music and books. *1201 Ortega St., at 19th Ave., Sunset District, 415/759–3440. Closed Sun.*

MUSIC BOXES

4 c-2

CABLE CAR MUSIC BOX CO.

This shop has about 3,000 different music boxes from around the world. Their cable car music boxes range from a basic model for under $10 to a model that spins and lights up for about $150. *Anchorage Shopping Center, 395 Jefferson St., at Leavenworth St., Fisherman's Wharf, 415/771–7402.*

4 e-6

THE SAN FRANCISCO MUSIC BOX COMPANY

Choose from 2,000 different music boxes, costing anywhere from a song to an arm and a leg. The company started here in 1978, and there are now 175 stores across the United States. *San Francisco Shopping Centre, Union Square, 415/546–6343.*

4 e-1

Pier 39, Fisherman's Wharf, 415/433–3696.

MUSICAL INSTRUMENTS

4 e-5

CLARION MUSIC CENTER

This is routinely praised as the best place in the city to "see, hear, and buy" musical instruments of the world: *didjeridus* (a type of Australian wind instrument), sitars, Tibetan singing bowls, African drums, Native American flutes, Chinese stringed instruments, and more. They also have books and CDs, and live performances on Friday nights. *816 Sacramento St., at Grant Ave., Chinatown, 415/391–1317.*

2 e-6

DRUM WORLD

This is easily one of the best-stocked drum stores in the Bay Area, if not the entire country. The shop buys and sells vintage and used drums, and also has a good selection of books and videos. *5016*

Mission St., between Geneva and Ocean Aves., Excelsior, 415/334–7559.

7 d-1

HAIGHT ASHBURY MUSIC CENTER

This is one of the largest sellers of musical instruments on the West Coast, with mixers, mikes, amps, sheet music, magazines, cables, musical instruments, and hundreds of acoustic and electric guitars, all brought to you by pleasant, knowledgeable salespeople. If they don't have what you're looking for, they'll refer you to someone who does. *1540 Haight St., between Clayton and Ashbury Sts., The Haight, 415/863–7327.*

7 g-5

NOE VALLEY MUSIC

The *Bay Guardian* calls this the "Best place to buy musical equipment without being treated like a cretin." They specialize in stringed instruments, many vintage and custom fretted. *3914-A 24th St., between Noe and Sanchez Sts., 415/821–6644.*

NEEDLEWORK & KNITTING

4 f-5

ARTFIBERS GALLERY

Artfibers specializes in high-fashion and exotic fiber yarns for knitting and weaving, including imported yarns custom-made for European fashion designers.

WORLD MUSIC

For those who crave something other than good ole American rock-n-roll, here are a few alternative options:

Discolandia
   Good selections of current and vintage Latin music.

Hear Music
   World music is a specialty here.

Reggae Runnins Village Store
   Reggae records, tapes, and videos.

Ritmo Latino
   Ranchero, mariachi, salsa, and other Latin sounds.

Samiramis Imports
   Middle Eastern music.

124 Sutter St., 2nd Floor, between Montgomery and Kearny Sts., Financial District, 415/956–6319.

5 g-5
ATELIER YARNS

Among this shop's extensive selection of yarns for knitting, weaving, spinning, and crocheting is a wide selection of natural fibers, including silky domestic cashmere. In addition, Atelier has day, evening, and weekend classes for all levels. *1945 Divisadero St., at California St., Pacific Heights, 415/771–1550. Closed Sun. and Mon.*

5 f-5
ELAINE MAGNIN

This appealing shop stocks well over 1,500 designs of handpainted needlepoint canvases, and some 145 different kinds of fibers. They also have expert finishing and custom canvas designs, just in case you can't find what you want in their vast collection. *3310 Sacramento St., at Presidio Ave., Laurel Heights, 415/931–3063.*

4 e-1
FUN STITCH

Needlepoints, cross-stitches, and crewls are the specialties here, and there are also plenty of supplies, how-to books, and wonderful patterns. Best-selling patterns include those of San Francisco's cable cars and of the Golden Gate Bridge. *Pier 39, Fisherman's Wharf, 415/956–3037.*

4 e-6
NEEDLEPOINT, INC.

A staff of seven artists designs and produces unique handpainted needlepoint canvases exclusively for this shop. The house brand of 100% Chinese silk thread comes in 427 different colors. They have every kind of fiber and tool needed for needlepoint. *275 Post St., Second Floor, between Stockton St. and Grant Ave., Union Square, 415/392–1622 or 800/345–1622. Closed Sun.*

NEWSPAPERS & MAGAZINES

3 d-7
DE LAUER SUPER NEWSSTAND

News junkies appreciate that this East Bay stand is open 24 hours. In addition to foreign and domestic newpapers, the newstand also has a huge magazine inventory, as well as maps and paperbacks. *1310 Broadway Ave., between 13th and 14th Sts., Oakland, 510/451–6157.*

4 f-5
EASTERN NEWSSTAND CORP.

This is the biggest newsstand corporation in San Francisco, with several downtown stands stocking many newspaper and magazine titles—including about 20 titles from England, France, Germany, and Italy. *101 California St., at Front St., Financial District, 415/989–8986.*

4 f-5
444 Market St., at Battery St., Financial District, 415/397–1721.

4 f-4
3 Embarcadero Center, The Embarcadero, 415/982–4425.

7 g-5
GOOD NEWS

Noe Valley's favorite newsstand carries out-of-town papers and periodicals. It's open late every Sunday. *3920 24th St., at Sanchez St., Noe Valley, 415/821–3694.*

4 d-6
HAROLDS INTERNATIONAL NEWSSTAND

Just two blocks from Union Square, Harolds carries many out-of-town papers, most major periodicals, and plenty of postcards. *524 Geary St. at Taylor St., Union Square, 415/441–2665.*

NAKED EYE NEWS AND VIDEO

This quirky shop in the Haight can be counted on for an eclectic stock of periodicals and newspapers, and a full array of 'zines. Their video collection is tops (*see Videos, below*). *533 Haight St., between Fillmore and Steiner Sts., 415/864–2985.*

OFFICE SUPPLIES

5 a-7
GABLES OFFICE SUPPLIES AND STATIONERY

Gables has an old-time feel, with serious business supplies in the back and gifts, stationery, writing instruments, and cards as you enter. *5636 Geary Blvd.,* between 20th and 21st Aves., Richmond District, 415/751–8152.

5 f-7
OFFICE DEPOT
The San Francisco outlets of the national chain provide a full range of office supplies, plus furniture and computers. 2675 Geary Blvd., at Masonic Ave., Western Addition, 415/441–3044.

4 f-7
855 Harrison St., at 5th St., South of Market, 415/243–9959.

7 a-2
SUNSET STATIONERS
Stock up here on office products, computer supplies, and rubber stamps, as well as pens and gifts, unusual greeting cards, wedding invitations, fine stationary, legal forms, and artists' materials. Prices are extremely competitive, and service is friendly. 653 Irving St., at 8th Ave., Sunset District, 415/664–0937. Closed Sun.

4 f-4
WALDECK'S OFFICE SUPPLIES
For decades Waldeck's has been supplying the downtown area with fine pens, stationery and invitations, San Francisco postcards, and all kinds of office supplies. 526 Washington St., between Sansome and Montgomery Sts., Financial District, 415/986–2275. Closed weekends.

4 f-4
3 Embarcadero Center, The Embarcadero, 415/986–2275.

PENS

4 e-6
GOLDEN GATE PEN SHOP
This shop has one of the largest selections of fine writing instruments in San Francisco. They carry 20 lines—including Mont Blanc, Schaeffer, Aurora, Cross, Cartier, and Caran d'Ache—with many limited editions. 260 Stockton St., 5th Floor, at Post St., Union Square, 415/781–4809. Closed Sun.

4 e-5
MICHAEL'S FINE PENS AND GIFTS
The vintage pens sold here are all reconditioned and fully working, and include top of the line brands such as Parker, Schaeffer, Waterman, and Swan. The most expensive date back to the early 1900s. Michael's also carries desk accessories and fine stationery. 517 Sutter St., at Powell St., Union Square, 415/399–9700.

PHOTO EQUIPMENT

4 f-6
ADOLPH GASSER
Gasser has the largest inventory of photography and video equipment in Northern California, including good-quality used gear. The shop rents video and still cameras and has an on-site photo lab. 181 2nd St., between Howard and Mission Sts., South of Market, 415/495–3852. Closed Sun.

2 b-3
5733 Geary Blvd., at 22nd Ave., Richmond District, 415/751–0145. Closed Sun.

4 f-6
DISCOUNT CAMERA
Check the prices here before buying elsewhere: Part of a chain, Discount Camera sells major brands of cameras, VCRs, camcorders, telephones, binoculars, and tape recorders. It also buys, sells, and trades used cameras and lenses. 33 Kearny St., between Post and Market Sts., Union Square, 415/392–1100.

3 e-3
LOOKING GLASS
This small store is great for tripods, paper, film, books, and other photographic supplies. They also offer classes and rent darkroom space. 2848 Telegraph Ave., at Oregon St., Berkeley, 510/548–6888.

4 g-6
PHOTOGRAPHER'S SUPPLY
This place has the best prices in San Francisco and is a favorite of Bay Area professional photographers. Novices may find shopping here a bewildering experience, but it's worth the effort of sifting through their huge supply of film, paper, chemicals in bulk, and the lowest priced Kodak film in town. 576 Folsom St., at 2nd St., South of Market, 415/495–8640.

POSTCARDS

4 *e-3*

QUANTITY POSTCARDS
This North Beach shop has about 15,000 postcards—their own designs, vintage cards, and more. Celebrity, geographical, art, and camp are just a few categories. *1441 Grant Ave., at Green St., North Beach, 415/986–8866. Minimum $10 purchase for credit cards.*

4 *e-3*

TILT
Under the same ownership as Quantity Postcards (*see above*), Tilt specializes in postcards with an Americana theme. The whimsical selection includes old snapshots of San Francisco, '50s family scenes, long-forgotten Hollywood stars, and schmaltzy nature scenes, among other things. *507 Columbus Ave., near Stockton St., North Beach, 415/788–1112.*

7 *e-1*

1427 Haight St., near Masonic Ave., The Haight, 415/255–1199. Minimum $10 purchase for credit cards at both locations.

POSTERS

See also Memorabilia, above.

4 *d-8*

ART ROCK GALLERY
This funky shop sells handmade silkscreened posters, many in a clever faux-vintage style. Like an art gallery, it frequently displays rare and vintage posters on its walls. *1155 Mission St., between 7th and 8th Sts., South of Market, 415/255–7390. Closed Sun. and Mon.*

4 *a-4*

THE ARTISANS OF SAN FRANCISCO
Historical posters and photos of San Francisco are the specialty here. Look at images of the city's heady Gold Rush days, Barbary Coast hedonism, the wrath of the 1906 earthquake, and more. *1964 Union St., at Buchanan St., Cow Hollow, 415/921–0456. Closed Mon.*

4 *e-1*

POSTER SOURCE
To pass the time at Pier 39, browse the contemporary art, rock, sports, and celebrity posters. *Pier 39, The Embarcadero, 415/433–1995.*

4 *e-3*

TILT
Though it's best known for postcards (*see above*), Tilt is also the exclusive distributor of silkscreened, limited-edition rock posters by famed local artist Frank Kozik, whose psychedelic art has advertised Green Day and other bands.

SPORTING GOODS & CLOTHING

general

4 *b-6*

FTC SKI & SPORTS
An all-around excellent sporting goods store, FTC has golf, swimming, and tennis equipment, as well as excellent selections of skateboards, snowboards, and wakeboards (*see Skating and Skiing, below*). *1586 Bush St., at Franklin St., Pacific Heights, 415/673–8363.*

4 *b-8*

G & M SALES
The "Great Outdoors Store" has been a local institution since 1948. It has one of the city's best selections of camping gear—with dozens of fully erected tents on display—plus a large selection of outerwear, hiking boots and shoes, ski goods, and an extensive fishing department. *1667 Market St., at Gough St., Civic Center, 415/863–2855.*

4 *f-5*

HIRSCH & PRICE
This tiny sporting-goods store specializes in softball, baseball, basketball, and football equipment: balls, helmets, pads, jerseys, and the like. Prices are low, and the staff is extremely knowledgeable. *41 Sutter St., at Sansome St., Financial District, 415/781–1790. Closed Sun.*

4 *c-4*

LOMBARDI SPORTS
Like G&M, Lombardi has been serving its devoted clientele since 1948. It's a one-stop shop for ski, camping, and golf equipment; it also has the city's best selection of exercise equipment, shoes, apparel, sunglasses, and other accessories. The shop's annual bike and ski sales draw big crowds. *1600 Jackson St., at Polk St., Russian Hill, 415/771–0600.*

4 *e-5*

NIKETOWN

One of the newest and most hyped shops on Union Square, the three-story NikeTown is equal parts theme park, sports museum, and store. High-priced Nike-emblazoned shoes and apparel are displayed next to busy video screens and memorabilia from past and present-day sports heros. *278 Post St., at Stockton St., Union Square, 415/392–6453.*

4 *e-5*

THE NORTH FACE

The Bay Area-based company is famous for its top-of-the-line, expedition-quality tents, sleeping bags, backpacks, skis, and outdoor apparel, including stylish Gore-Tex jackets and pants. The outlet store is the place to find last season's jackets, sleeping bags, and other gear for 20%–70% less. *180 Post St., at Grant Ave., Union Square, 415/433–3223.*

4 *d-8*

Outlet: 1325 Howard St., between 9th and 10th Sts., South of Market, 415/626–6444.

4 *c-2*

PATAGONIA

Along with sportswear and casual clothing, Patagonia carries body wear for backpacking, fly-fishing, kayaking, and the like. The equipment and clothing is for serious outdoors enthusiasts and tends to be expensive. *770 North Point St., at Hyde St., Fisherman's Wharf, 415/771–2050.*

7 *a-7*

PLAY IT AGAIN SPORTS

Here you can trade in your old golf clubs, exercise equipment, in-line skates, or skis. The shop buys, sells, trades, and consigns good-quality sporting equipment of all sorts, but the largest selections are of new and used in-line skates, golf accessories, and exercise gear. *45 West Portal Ave., between Vicente and Ulloa Sts., Sunset District, 415/753–3049.*

3 *c-1*

REI

The popular retail cooperative has a 30,000-sq-ft store in Berkeley, complete with 35-ft-tall climbing wall and gear for most outdoor pursuits. Monthly events include slide shows and equipment demonstrations; the biannual blowout sales are legendary. A rental department outfits weekend backpackers and kayak-ers. *1338 San Pablo Ave., at Gilman St., Berkeley, 510/527–4140.*

SULLIVAN'S SPORT SHOP

Probably the only sports shop in California that carries bridal registry, Sullivan's has equipment and clothing for camping, fishing, hunting, boxing, baseball, backpacking, swimming, snorkeling, tennis, badminton, table tennis, skiing, boccie, croquet, in-line skating, and in-line hockey. Their repair shop handles tennis rackets, camping gear, and skis; the rental department takes care of volleyball, softball, badminton, camping, croquet, and skiing equipment. *5323 Geary Blvd., between 17th and 18th Sts., Richmond District, 415/751–7070 or 415/751–2738.*

3 *c-1*

WILDERNESS EXCHANGE

Most of the mountaineering, rock-climbing, cross-country skiing, backpacking, and camping gear here are closeouts and seconds sold for 30%–50% off. There are smaller selections of used merchandise and new equipment. *1407 San Pablo Ave., near Gilman St., Berkeley, 510/525–1255.*

bicycling

3 *e-4*

THE BENT SPOKE

This friendly shop specializes in second-hand bikes that the owners have purchased from California police auctions and then reconditioned (though they do not fix cosmetic troubles such as dents or chipped paint). You'll find a wide range of bargains (40 to 60 bikes at any given time), including many kid's bikes. *6124 Telegraph Ave., at 62nd St., Oakland, 510/652–3089.*

3 *d-2*

MISSING LINK BICYCLE COOPERATIVE/ MISSING LINK ANNEX

The East Bay's best bike shop carries Trek, Kona, Ibis, and Bianchi bikes, plus clothing and accessories. The Missing Link Annex, across the street from the main store, houses rental bikes, used bikes, and a repair shop. Used bikes are fully reconditioned and range in price from $50 to $1,000; many come with a 90-day warranty. *Missing Link: 1988 Shattuck Ave., at University Ave., Berkeley, 510/843–4763.*

3 d-2

Missing Link Annex: 1961 Shattuck Ave., at Durant Ave., Berkeley, 510/843–4763.

7 c-1

START TO FINISH BICYCLES

One of the Bay Area's largest bike shop chains, Start to Finish has three San Francisco shops with rentals, high-end demos, free lifetime service on sales, and free maintenance classes. Among the other brands for sale are Gary Fisher, Trek, and Marin. For information on any of their nine stores around the Bay Area, call 800/600–BIKE. *672 Stanyan St., between Haight and Page Sts., The Haight, 415/750–4760.*

4 g-7

599 2nd St., at Brannan St., South of Market, 415/243–8812.

5 g-3

2530 Lombard St., at Divisadero St., The Marina, 415/202–9830.

8 a-4

VALENCIA CYCLERY

This low-key shop has the largest selection of new bikes, parts, and accessories in San Francisco, all priced competitively. There are mountain bikes, hybrids, kid's bikes, and even low-rider bicycles. The repair shop handles all makes and models, many done while you wait. *1077 Valencia St., between 21st and 22nd Sts., Mission District, 415/550–6600 for sales, 415/550–6601 for repair shop.*

1 c-7

WINDSURF BICYCLE WAREHOUSE

At this 7,200-sq-ft warehouse in South San Francisco, you'll find exceptional customer service and great deals on mountain, road, hybrid, and BMX bikes. Their low-price guarantee: If within 30 days you find the identical item with a lower price somewhere else, they'll refund you the difference plus 10%. There's also a fine selection of snowboarding, windsurfing, and in-line skating gear. *428 S. Airport Blvd., Airport Blvd. exit from U.S. 101, South San Francisco, 415/588–1714.*

fishing

2 b-3

GUS'S DISCOUNT TACKLE

The devoted clientele of this friendly, familiar shop drop by before a day's fish-ing to see what's on sale. Gus's stocks everything for salmon, trout, freshwater, saltwater, and surf fishing, at prices 10%–80% percent below retail. *3710 Balboa St., between 38th and 39th Aves., Richmond District, 415/752–6197. Closed Sun.*

2 b-3

HI'S TACKLE BOX

This spacious shop stocks everything you need to catch any kind of fish, including fly-fishing equipment as well as deep-sea fishing gear. It also has an excellent repair shop that can build you a custom rod and reel. Hi's Tackle Box arranges 5- to 10-day deep-sea fishing trips departing from San Diego; reservations are necessary at least six months in advance. *3141 Clement St., at 33rd Ave., Richmond District, 415/221–3825. Closed Sun.*

4 e-5

ORVIS SAN FRANCISCO

Orvis is a mail-order outdoor store chain with around 25 stores nationwide; the shop in San Francisco has an especially large and fine fly-fishing department. *300 Grant Ave., between Bush and Sutter Sts., Union Square, 415/392–1600.*

5 a-7

SULLIVAN'S SPORT SHOP

Fishing gear is a specialty at this general sports store: Look for fly-tying tools and materials for fly-fishing, plus rods and reels for freshwater and saltwater fishing. *5323 Geary Blvd., between 17th and 18th Sts., Richmond District, 415/751–7070 or 415/751–2738.*

golf

4 e-5

DON SHERWOOD GOLF AND TENNIS WORLD

Here you'll find the latest in computerized club fitting (*see Tennis, below*).

FRY'S WAREHOUSE GOLF AND TENNIS

The computerized club fitting at Fry's is free (*see Tennis, below*).

1 b-6

THE GOLF MART

The San Francisco branch of this store is next to the Mission Bay Golf Center (*see Golf in Chapter 6*); but the vast, warehouse-style store in Colma is four times as big as the San Francisco branch. Year-round prices on top-of-the-line golf equipment and apparel is discounted 5%–10% at both stores; get on the mailing list for the scoop on seasonal sales. *4937 Junipero Serra Blvd., at Serramonte Blvd., Colma, 415/994–4653.*

8 *e-1*

Mission Bay Golf Center, 1200 6th St., at Channel St., China Basin, 415/703–6190.

4 *f-5*

MCCAFFERY'S GOLF SHOP

What sets this shop apart is that it has two PGA professionals on staff, who assist customers with choosing clubs and improving their swing. The pro golf equipment and apparel is reasonably priced. *80 Sutter St., at Montgomery St., Financial District, 415/989–4653.*

riding

2 *b-2*

TAL-Y-TARA TEA & POLO SHOPPE

Here's a place that serves a proper British tea, complete with crumpets and scones, to the folks who stop by to buy English riding apparel and equipment. The shop sells polo mallets to members of the city's Polo Club, and can special order whatever equestrian equipment is not in stock. *6439 California St., between 26th and 27th Aves., Richmond District, 415/751–9275. Closed Sun.*

skating

4 *h-8*

BLADIUM

The pro shop at the Bladium indoor in-line hockey rink (*see* Hockey *in* Chapter 6) is the city's best source of hockey equipment, including sticks, pucks, blades, and jerseys. *1050 3rd St., near Berry St., South Beach, 415/442–5060.*

7 *h-1*

DLX

The city's coolest skateboard shop draws a regular posse of skaters who kick back and watch skate videos or peruse the boards, accessories, and clothing from designers like Thunder, Spitfire, and Adrenalin. Local skater and artist Kevin Ancell designs one of the long boards for sale here. *1831 Market St., at Guerrero St., Misssion District, 415/626—5588.*

4 *b-6*

FTC SKI & SPORTS

The skate shop within FTC has skateboards, Rollerblades, rollerskates, safety gear, clothing, and rentals. *1586 Bush St., at Franklin St., Pacific Heights, 415/673–8363.*

5 *g-2*

MARINA SKATE AND SNOWBOARD

Super-friendly service is what distinguishes this shop: Show up Saturday at 8 AM for a free in-line skating lesson, which includes free rental for the duration of the lesson. The shop sells and rents three kinds of in-line skates— recreational, hockey, and aggressive— for skaters who enjoy jumping off stairs and performing tricks. They also sell snowboards. *2271 Chestnut St., near Scott St., The Marina, 415/567–8400.*

7 *a-7*

PLAY IT AGAIN SPORTS

Come here for new and used in-line skates (*see* General, *above*).

6 *d-2*

SKATE PRO SPORTS

The staff at Skate Pro can tell you anything you want to know about the city's skating scene, including information on racing and league play. They sell in-line skating and hockey equipment and accessories; with purchase of skates you get a free two-hour lesson. *3401 Irving St., at 35th Ave., Sunset District, 415/752–8776.*

7 *c-1*

SKATES ON HAIGHT

At the Stanyan Street entrance to Golden Gate Park, Skates on Haight is a great place for in-line skate sales and rentals, skateboard sales, and snowboarding sales and rentals. Prices are some of the lowest in town. Free in-line skating lessons are given Sundays at 8:30 AM to those who rent (free lessons are also given with purchase of any pair of in-line skates). *1818 Haight St., at Stanyan St., The Haight, 415/752–8375.*

skiing & snowboarding

4 *e-6*

ANY MOUNTAIN

This outdoor store, part of a local chain, has an excellent selection of skis for beginners; experts will appreciate its super-slick skis by Rossignol, Fischer, K2, Atomic, and Salomon. In summer the store sells camping and in-line skating gear. *737 Market St., between 3rd and 4th Sts., Union Square, 415/284–9990.*

DEMO-SPORTS

This tiny San Rafael shop has skis and snowboards for 10%–20% less than its Bay Area competitors. Its April demo-ski sale is legendary, with skiers signing up for particular models beginning in February. In summer the shop sells waterskis, in-line skates, and wakeboards. *1101 E. Francisco Blvd., at Bellam Blvd., San Rafael, 415/454–3500.*

4 *b-6*

FTC SKI & SPORTS

Let FTC help you with custom boot fitting, or top-of-the-line ski and snowboard equipment. They sell and rent kids' skis and ski car racks, too. *1586 Bush St., at Franklin St., Pacific Heights, 415/673–8363.*

5 *g-2*

MARINA SKATE AND SNOWBOARD

See Skating, above.

3 *d-3*

MARMOT MOUNTAIN WORKS

Berkeley's superb outdoors store is also the Bay Area's cross-country ski center. By mid-October it's usually fully stocked with cross-country skis of all types—skating and diagonal stride, waxless metal edge and nonmetal edge, and telemark skis. Rentals are available. *3049 Adeline St., at Ashby Ave., Berkeley, 510/849–0735.*

7 *d-1*

SFO SNOWBOARDING

For top-of-the-line snowboarding equipment and clothing, SFO can't be beat. They have more than 100 top brands, including a full line of clothing for women snowboarders. Though there are no rentals, for $35 per weekend you can demo most of the boards available for sale in the shop. *618 Shrader St., at Haight St., The Haight, 415/386–1666. Closed Mon. and Tues. in summer.*

4 *g-7*

SOMA SKI & SPORTZ

The skiing and snowboarding equipment here—by Blizzard, Nordica, K2, Nitro,

and Airwalk—is top-notch, and the prices tend to be 10%–20% lower than at other San Francisco stores. They'll also do overnight tuneups on skis. *689 3rd St., at Townsend St., South Beach, 415/ 777–2165. Closed Sun. from Jun.–mid-Oct.*

soccer

6 *e-2*

SUNSET SOCCER SUPPLY

The only specialty soccer shop in the city, this place has brand-name shoes, balls, bags, shorts, and jerseys. Drop by for information on local leagues, or to browse the collection of soccer-team souvenir memorabilia that's also for sale. *3214 Irving St., between 33rd and 34th Aves., Sunset District, 415/753–2666. Closed Tues.*

tennis

5 *f-5*

BAYSPORT

Buy a new racquet, or choose from the stock of high-quality trade-ins. Or don't buy at all; with the demo program you can test as many racquets as you care to try in 25 days, for $25. *3375 Sacramento St., between Presidio Ave. and Walnut St., Laurel Heights, 415/928–2255.*

4 *e-5*

DON SHERWOOD GOLF AND TENNIS WORLD

Their tennis equipment and clothing is top-of-the-line, and they also have an excellent racquet-demo program: $10 for five days. *320 Grant Ave., at Sutter St., Union Square, 415/989–5000.*

1 *c-7*

FRY'S WAREHOUSE GOLF & TENNIS

All of the big name brands like Prince, Dunlop, and Wilson are here, and all at deep discounts. Though the 16,500-sq-ft store feels like a warehouse, the salespeople go out of their way to make it feel like a small shop. Tennis-racquet stringing is among the services offered. *164 Marco Way, at S. Airport Blvd., South San Francisco, 415/583–5034.*

4 *f-4*

JOHN VETTRAINO'S TENNIS AND SQUASH SHOP

This place has served Financial District tennis and squash enthusiasts since

1976, with a full line of racquets, clothing, and shoes. Demo racquets are $5 apiece, for two days. *424 Clay St., at Battery St., Financial District, 415/956–5666. Closed Sun.*

STATIONERY

4 *a-4*

KOZO

The specialty papers at Kozo are made of materials such as bark, papyrus, and bird's nest. The shop imports hand-silk-screened papers directly from Japan and occasionally from Korea and Italy. Also for sale are various objets d'art, such as hand-bound photo albums and journals, and frames artfully wrapped in hand-made paper. *1969-A Union St., between Buchanan and Laguna Sts., The Marina, 415/351–0869.*

4 *a-4*

UNION STREET PAPERY

The Bay Area's largest selection of custom-printed stationery and invitations is Union Street Papery's claim to fame. Calligraphers on staff will lend a special touch to your invitations and announcement cards. *2162 Union St., at Webster St., The Marina, 415/563–0200.*

THEATRICAL ITEMS

AMERICAN CONSERVATORY THEATER (ACT)

ACT (*see* Theaters & Theater Companies *in* Chapter 5) rents out the gorgeous costumes it's collected over three decades of critically acclaimed performances. Unique, meticulously detailed, well-crafted period costumes are what you'll find, with plenty to choose from in the Victorian, Renaissance, and 18th-century periods. *415/439–2379, by appointment only.*

7 *f-1*

COSTUMES ON HAIGHT

This fun Haight-Ashbury shop carries period, character, and seasonal costumes for sale or rent. Also here is a selection of contemporary clothing, formal wear, and interesting inexpensive jewelry. *735 Haight St., near Divisadero St., The Haight, 415/621–1356.*

4 *f-5*

FOOTLIGHT COSTUME SHOP

At San Francisco's best costume shop you can buy or rent clown ruffles, ball gowns, and sinister capes. Choose from masks, wigs, hats, makeup, and other accessories to put together the perfect costume. *187 Sutter St., at Kearny St., Financial District, 415/421–5657.*

5 *h-3*

HOUSE OF MAGIC

Not just for Houdini fans, the House of Magic stocks costumes and professional theatrical make-up. Zany accessories include tiaras, beards, feather boas, and scary masks. *2025 Chestnut St., at Fillmore St., The Marina, 415/346–2218.*

3 *d-3*

STAGECRAFT STUDIOS

Serious costume-shoppers will want to make the trip to Berkeley to hunt through this shop's collection of 13,000 costumes. In business since 1928, Stagecraft has some new and vintage costumes for sale, and a huge selection for rent. Period costumes from the 17th and 18th centuries, the Renaissance, Middle Ages, and ancient Rome and Egypt are particularly well represented. A talented designer on staff does custom-orders and costume repairs. Look here for wigs, makeup, lighting and other theatrical supplies as well. *1854 Alcatraz Ave., between Adeline St. and Shattuck Ave., Berkeley, 510/653–4424. Closed Sun. and Mon.*

TOBACCONISTS

4 *e-6*

ALFRED DUNHILL NORTH AMERICA LTD.

The American outpost of posh, London-based Alfred Dunhill carries the very expensive and high-quality Dunhill tobaccos, cigars, humidors, pipes, lighters, and other smokers' requisites. *250 Post St., at Stockton St., Union Square, 415/781–3368.*

7 *e-1*

ASHBURY TOBACCO CENTER

The heady Haight-Ashbury wouldn't be complete without a well-stocked smoke shop, and the Ashbury Tobacco Center is just that: Alongside premium and imported cigars and fine tobaccos you'll find Middle Eastern hookahs and exotic pipes. *1524 Haight St., at Ashbury St., The Haight, 415/552–5556.*

4 *f-5*

GRANT'S TOBACCONISTS

Discerning Financial District powerbrokers go to Grant's for pipes, cigars, tobaccos, humidors, and accessories of very high quality. High rollers have been purchasing premium cigars here since 1849; the shop currently claims a stock of 100,000 cigars in its walk-in humidor. *562 Market St., between Montgomery and Sansome Sts., Financial District, 415/981–1000. Closed Sun.*

4 *d-6*

JIM MATE'S PIPE AND TOBACCO SHOP

Well known for its international selection of fine pipes, tobacco, and cigars, Jim Mate's is especially sought out for its house tobacco blend—Jim Mate's Famous Blend—priced at $8.50 for half a pound. *575 Geary St., at Jones St., The Tenderloin, 415/775–6634. Closed Sat.*

4 *f-5*

SHERLOCK'S HAVEN

The fictional pipe-smoking British detective Sherlock would surely approve of this smart shop, with its premium cigars, humidors, fine tobaccos, and, of course, handsome pipes. *275 Battery St., between Sacramento and California Sts., Financial District, 415/362–1405.*

TOYS & GAMES

collectibles

7 *h-4*

BINKY'S

Old favorites from the '60s and '70s— the *Charlie's Angels* board game, the Bionic Woman lunch box, and a bazillion Barbies—are for sale at this brightly colored shop. The staff is enthusiastic and very friendly. *1009 Guerrero St., at 22nd St., Mission District, 415/285–4876.*

3 *d-3*

SCOOBY'S TOYS AND COLLECTIBLES

Baby boomers will recognize most of the vintage toys at this Berkeley shop.

Collectible tin toys from the 1940s and 50s are the specialty. *2750 Adeline St., at Stuart St., Berkeley, 510/548–5349. By appointment only.*

7 *g-2*

UNCLE MAME

Like a shrine to American pop culture in the latter part of the 20th century, this shop deals strictly in collectable cereal boxes, lunch pails, action figures, and the like. *2193 Market St., near Sanchez St., The Castro, 415/626–1953.*

new

8 *d-3*

BASIC BROWN BEAR FACTORY

Make your own teddy bear at this unusual store: They provide the pattern, material, stuffing, and instructions, and you (or your children) put a new cuddly friend together. Bears cost $12–$150, depending on the size and complexity of the pattern. The De Haro Street location is the company factory, and gives free, drop-in tours. *444 De Haro St., at Mariposa St., Potrero Hill, 415/626–0781.*

4 *c-2*

The Cannery, 2nd Floor, Fisherman's Wharf, 415/931–6670.

4 *e-6*

THE DISNEY STORE

Books, toys, games, and clothing await you inside this store, part of a national chain. The building itself is amusing, with colorful walls and gargoyle-shape pillars. Beyond toys, there are collectibles such as framed animation cells, as well as Disney-oriented table- and glassware for sale. *400 Post St., at Powell St., Union Square, 415/391–6866.*

4 *e-1*

Pier 39, Fisherman's Wharf, 415/391-4210.

4 *e-6*

F.A.O. SCHWARZ

Every child's dream is fulfilled at the lavish San Francisco branch of the famed New York–based toy emporium. The beautiful collection of toys from around the world includes dollhouses, dancing bears, carousel rocking horses, life-size stuffed animals, and motorized miniature cars—as well as more mundane toys like Barbie and G.I. Joe. On display (but not for sale) is the giant keyboard used by Tom Hanks in the movie *Big*. 48

Stockton St., at O'Farrell St., Union Square, 415/394–8700.

4 f-4
GAME GALLERY
Board games, puzzles, fantasy card games, and chess computers are among the thousands of games for adults and young adults. *1 Embarcadero Center, The Embarcadero, 415/433–4263.*

7 f-1
GAMESCAPE
This is the place to buy "Magic: The Gathering," the hottest card game around. The shop sells new and used board, computer, and role-playing games, as well as puzzles; it's got everything from Monopoly and chess to crazy Nintendo adventures. *333 Divisadero St., between Page and Oak Sts., Lower Haight, 415/621–4263.*

7 f-3
HELLO GORGEOUS!!
Pay homage to Barbra Streisand at Hello Gorgeous!!, a Castro storefront that bills itself as part shop and part museum. Everything from Barbra-centric CDs to playing cards to fanzines is for sale. *549-A Castro St., between 18th and 19th Sts., The Castro, 415/864–2678.*

5 h-3
HOUSE OF MAGIC
Hundreds of gag gifts (backwards clocks, celebrity face masks) and goofy gadgets (hand buzzers, wind-up toys) make pranksters of all ages merry. The shop also sells magic sets, magic tricks, how-to books and videos, costume supplies such as wigs and wax lips, and even used crystal balls and other used magician's supplies and antique apparatuses. *2025 Chestnut St., at Fillmore St., The Marina, 415/346–2218.*

5 f-6
IMAGINARIUM
A California-based chain of stores, Imaginarium manufactures its own learning-oriented games and gadgets and imports European brands rarely found in larger stores. You won't find toy guns or any other war toys in these shops, but there are lots of creative toys—fun, colorful, and educational stuff for all ages. *3535 California St., at Laurel St., Laurel Heights, 415/387–9885.*

4 f-6
JEFFREY'S TOYS
A San Francisco institution since 1968, Jeffrey's brims with games, stuffed animals, comic books, crafts, and a fine selection of educational toys. Best of all, they never seem to sell out of those lovable Beanie Babies. *7 3rd St., at Market St., Union Square, 415/546–6551.*

4 e-1
PUPPETS ON THE PIER
Marionettes dance in this shop's front window; inside there are reasonably priced finger puppets, storytelling puppets, marionettes, and dolls. The shop also sells a few antique Pelham puppets from the 1930s and '40s. *Pier 39, Fisherman's Wharf, 415/781–4435.*

4 e-6
SANRIO
Castles, rainbows, and stars decorate this two-floor shop devoted to pop icon Hello Kitty and all her friends. You'll find a plethora of items ranging from lunch boxes to huge plush toys. *39 Stockton St., at Market St., Union Square, 415/981–5568.*

7 g-3
SCAIRY HAIRY TOY COMPANY
Underground cartoonists Bruce Helvitz and Flower Frankenstein fill their kooky shop with wildly whimsical toys for "people old enough to know better." Choose an Elvis impersonator doll, Miss PMS Fun Action Toy, or the set of Super Cool Fufu Café People finger puppets. Walls are filled with original works of art and prints from local artists. *3804 17th St., at Sanchez St., Noe Valley, 415/864–6543. Closed Mon. and Tues.*

7 g-5
STAR MAGIC SPACE AGE GIFTS
Noe Valley's "space age gift store" started as a cooperative in 1980 and has now expanded to include branches on the East and West coasts. Crystals, kaleidoscopes, tarot cards, spaceship models, solar-system mobiles, star appliqués, and astronomy board games are some of the space(y) gifts you'll find at this cheery store. *4026 24th St., between Noe and Castro Sts., Noe Valley, 415/641–8626.*

8 c-1

TOYS R US

The San Francisco outlet of this well-established national chain has toys, games, puzzles, dolls—everything a child could wish for. *555 9th St., at Bryant St., South of Market, 415/252–0607.*

5 f-7

2675 Geary Blvd. at Masonic Ave., Laurel Heights, 415/931–8896.

4 e-5

THE TREASURE HOUSE

This is a must for anyone who loves dollhouses and miniatures—it has the largest selection in the Bay Area. Basic dollhouse kits start at about $80; higher-priced versions appeal to serious collectors. They'll even custom commission one of the eight palaces of Europe for around $500,000. *563 Sutter St., between Powell and Mason Sts., Union Square, 415/982–6464.*

4 e-1

WOUND ABOUT

Walk into this shop and you'll be greeted by dozens of windup and battery-operated toys yapping, clapping, swinging, and singing. Some are quite lifelike, while others are hilariously cartoony. *Pier 39, Fisherman's Wharf, 415/986–8697.*

UMBRELLAS

4 f-5

ADORNME

The shop's best-sellers are the Sistine Chapel umbrella and the Winnie the Pooh umbrella (in children and adult sizes). There are practical umbrellas, including fine European brands such as Brigg, and fanciful umbrellas; there's even one made of waterproof velvet. *Crocker Galleria, 50 Post St., Financial District, 415/397–4114. Closed Sun.*

VIDEOS

7 g-2

LASER CINEMA

This shop deals exclusively in laser discs, with the largest rental library in the city. They also have some 6,000 laser disc titles for sale, both domestic and imported. *2258 Market St., between*

Sanchez and Noe Sts., Noe Valley, 415/621–8434.

7 a-2

LE VIDEO

Le Video annually wins the *Bay Guardian* reader poll for best video store, possibly because of its exhaustive collection of more than 30,000 titles in all genres. It has the city's widest selection of foreign and independent film titles for sale or rent, and a sizeable stock of Hollywood releases. Le Video Vault, the shop's annex on the ground floor, contains all of the cult, sci-fi, horror, documentary, and independent titles. *1231 9th Ave., between Lincoln Way and Irving St., Sunset District, 415/566–3606.*

8 a-3

LEATHER TONGUE

This Mission District institution sells and rents mainly cult films, film noir, and sci-fi. Its greatest claim to fame is the extensive collection of films by independent filmmakers, conveniently organized by the name of the director. *714 Valencia St., at 18th St., Mission District, 415/552–2900.*

7 g-1

NAKED EYE NEWS AND VIDEO

This place deals in video rentals only. It's noted for its eclectic assortment of odd foreign and cult titles, plus classic and recent Hollywood films. *533 Haight St., between Fillmore and Steiner Sts., 415/864–2985.*

WATCHES & CLOCKS

antique

5 h-4

OLD AND NEW ESTATES

Fully restored vintage watches of all kinds are a specialty here, particularly vintage Grüen, Rolex, and Hamilton watches. Wedding rings, art glass, jewelry, and lamps are also for sale. *2181 Union St., at Fillmore St., The Marina, 415/346–7525. Closed Wed.*

7 d-1

URBAN ANTIQUES

Though this shop looks minuscule from the street, it's actually 125-ft deep and filled with clocks and music boxes from America, Great Britain, France, Germany, Austria, and Switzerland. *1767 Waller St., at Stanyan St., The Haight, 415/221–0194. Closed Mon.–Wed.*

4 *b-8*

ZEITGEIST TIMEPIECES & JEWELRY

The fully apprenticed owners of Zeitgeist—Carsten Marsch, master watchmaker; and Mac Garmen, clockmaker—repair and restore clocks, jewelry, and fine watches. They also sell beautiful vintage wrist- and pocket watches from the likes of Grüen and Bulova. *437B Hayes St., at Gough St., Hayes Valley, 415/864–0185. Closed Sun. and Mon.*

contemporary

6 *e-4*

CALIFORNIA WATCH, CLOCK, AND JEWELRY CO.

This shop has the largest selection of clocks in the city: grandfather clocks, wall clocks, cuckoo clocks, digital clocks, and more. Most are new, though they do have a few antiques. *2436 Noriega St., at 32nd Ave., Sunset District, 415/566–9902. Closed Sun.*

4 *f-5*

CRESALIA JEWELERS

One of the city's top jewelers since 1912, Cresalia carries fine watches such as Movado, Lassale, Concord, Seiko, and Robindino. Their prices are about 25% less than those at shops on Union Square. *1111 Sutter St., between Montgomery and Kearny Sts., Union Square, 415/781–7371. Closed Sun.*

4 *f-5*

RAVITS WATCHES AND CLOCKS

Among the choices of clocks and watches are Omega, Tag Heuer, Movado, Tissot, Swiss Army, Timex, Casio, Seiko, Lassal, Raymond Weil, and many other notable brands. *Crocker Galleria, 50 Post St., at Montgomery St., Union Square, 415/392–1947. Closed Sun.*

4 *e-5*

SHREVE & CO.

Fine watches such as Rolex, Omega, and Baume Mercier fill the elegant cases at Shreve & Co. Since 1852, the company has been famous for diamonds, gold, Mikimoto pearls, and luxury watches. *200 Post St., at Grant Ave., Union Square, 415/421–2600.*

4 *e-1*

THE SWATCH STORE

Brightly colored, plastic Swatch watches with whimsical designs and funny faces fill this Pier 39 shop. The basic models start at $40, and go up to $130. *Pier 39, Fisherman's Wharf, 415/788–4543.*

4 *e-6*

ZWILLINGER & CO.

Owners Mel and Sheilah Wasserman offer excellent service and competitive prices—20%–35% less than the norm—on fine watches, diamonds, and designer jewelry. *760 Market St., Suite 800, at Grant Ave., Union Square, 415/392–4086. Closed Sun. and Mon.*

WINE & SPIRITS

5 *h-3*

CALIFORNIA WINE MERCHANT

Its all-American selection is predictably heavy on California vintages, especially hard-to-find wines from small collections. The staff promises that "anything you want, we'll try to get." You'll also find good Washington and Oregon wines here. *3237 Pierce St., at Chestnut St., The Marina, 415/567–0646. Closed Sun.*

4 *e-3*

COIT LIQUORS

Owner Tony Giovanzana has a wide selection of grappas as well as good values on champagnes, and Italian, French, and California wines. *585 Columbus Ave., at Union St., North Beach, 415/986–4036.*

4 *d-2*

COST PLUS WORLD MARKET

This outlet of the popular import chain sells wines and microbrews from California and Oregon, plus liqueurs and spirits from around the world. The quality is good, prices low, and selection unique. *2552 Taylor St., at North Point St., Fisherman's Wharf, 415/928–6200.*

5 *h-5*

D & M WINE AND LIQUOR CO.

D & M stocks wines from small California boutiques, but San Franciscans come here mainly for the 225 brands of single-malt whiskies; 200 different French champagnes; and the world's largest collection of Armagnacs, dating to 1928. *2200 Fillmore St., at Sacramento St., Pacific Heights, 415/346–1325.*

4 *f-5*

JOHN WALKER & CO.

In business since 1933, John Walker & Co. has a vast selection of California wines, plus French, Italian, South American, and South African wines; cognacs; and champagnes. Come here for rare and older-vintage California and French wines. *175 Sutter St., between Kearny and Montgomery Sts., Financial District, 415/986–2707. Closed Sun.*

4 *f-7*

K&L WINE MERCHANT

At this spacious, well-stocked, and reasonably priced showroom, the friendly staff promises not to sell any wines they haven't tasted themselves. *766 Harrison St., between 3rd and 4th Sts., South of Market, 415/896–1734.*

7 *a-6*

MR. LIQUOR

Despite the silly name, Mr. Liquor is a serious store. Some 1,000 wines are available here, all at warehouse prices; there's also a wine bar with 50¢ tastings. Mr. Liquor takes pride in carrying well-known Bay Area importer Kermit Lynch's line of wines. Free delivery is available with a minimum $75 purchase. *250 Taraval St., at 12th Ave., Sunset District, 415/731–6222.*

4 *d-6*

NAPA VALLEY WINERY EXCHANGE

Stocking only California wines and sparkling wines, the Napa Valley Winery Exchange has a wide selection, knowledgeable staff, and hard-to-find labels from small vineyards such as Solitude (Sonoma County), Schweiger Vineyards (Napa Valley), and Au Bon Climat (Santa Barbara). *415 Taylor St., between Geary and O'Farrell Sts., Union Square, 415/771–2887 or 800/653–9463.*

5 *h-3*

PLUMPJACK WINES

Connected to the popular café of the same name (*see* Mediterranean *in* Chapter 3), this stylish shop has hard-to-find California wines, along with a small selection of Italian wines. Approximately 150 wines are priced under $10. You'll also find gift baskets and other gift items here. *3201 Fillmore St., at Greenwich St., Cow Hollow, 415/346–9870.*

4 *f-8*

THE WINE CLUB

This place makes up for its bare-bones, warehouse feel with a huge selection of high-quality wines at some of the best discount prices in the city. Their largest selection is of French wines, particularly burgundy, Bordeaux, and Alsatian. There's also a wide variety of wine paraphernalia, including glasses, books, openers, and decanters, plus cigars, premium beers, and Russian caviar. Frequent shoppers will want to request the Wine Club's monthly newsletter. *953 Harrison St., between 5th and 6th Sts., South of Market, 415/512–9086.*

4 *g-7*

WINE HOUSE LIMITED

The highly informed and friendly sales staff will help you find the perfect wine for any occasion. Occupying a spacious exposed-brick warehouse, the store has an excellent selection of French wines, and small but well-chosen selections of Italian, Austrian, German, and California wines, all at reasonable prices. They also stock rare vintage California and Italian wines and vintage champagnes and ports. *535 Bryant St., between 3rd and 4th Sts., South Beach, 415/495–8486. Closed Sun.*

5 *f-6*

WINE IMPRESSIONS

For discount prices on thousands of California, French, Italian, Spanish, and Australian wines, try Wine Impressions. This large shop keeps many bottles of wines and champagnes chilled, and also has a good number of rare California and French wines. Their liquor department is well-known for its rare tequilas, as well as good selections of cognac, sherry, port, and dessert wines. On Fridays you can sample 4–12 wines for 10% of the price of each bottle ($1 and up). *3461 California St., at Laurel St., Laurel Heights, 415/221–9463.*

chapter 5

ARTS, ENTERTAINMENT, & NIGHTLIFE

For such a small city, San Francisco has a surprisingly active cultural agenda. The San Francisco Opera, Symphony, and Ballet are among the best in the nation, and many smaller performing arts organizations put on innovative performances throughout the year. Whether you want to dress up for an evening on the town or bundle up against the fog to see Shakespeare performed in Golden Gate Park, your options are wide open.

While theater and music groups are centered around (but by no means limited to) the Civic Center, Union Square, and the theater district, bars and dance clubs abound all around town. South of Market has long been a nightlife hot spot and shows no signs of slowing down, with dozens of dance clubs, live music venues, breweries, and supper clubs—the hottest trend in San Francisco nightlife. The Mission District is another increasingly popular spot for bar hopping, despite its past reputation as a downmarket spot for dive bars and grungy live-music joints; its recent gentrification has also brought a cascade of swanky retro bars. In the Castro virtually every other storefront is a gay bar. The Marina, Pacific Heights, and Russian Hill cater to a well-dressed professional crowd. North Beach is a mix of tourist haunts, local neighborhood bars, and atmospheric old spots that have served San Francisco drinkers for decades. The Tenderloin is possibly San Francisco's seediest neighborhood, but has a number of good live music venues and bars for those with an adventurous streak.

The best guide to arts and entertainment events in San Francisco is the "Datebook" section, printed on pink paper, in the combined Sunday Examiner and Chronicle. The free alternative weeklies, the Bay Guardian and SF Weekly, available at cafés and in boxes all over the city, are stronger for information on bars, dance clubs, and the alternative scene. The free weeklies Bay Times and Bay Area Reporter have extensive listings for gay and lesbian entertainment.

arts

CONCERT HALLS

4 f-6
CENTER FOR THE ARTS THEATER
The 750-seat state-of-the-art facility at Yerba Buena Center for the Arts has superb acoustics and lots of souped-up technological gadgets. The programming is an adventurous mix of dance, theater, performance art, and music, including works by San Francisco Performances (see Davies Symphony Hall, below). Corner of Howard and 3rd Sts., South of Market, 415/978–2787.

4 a-2
COWELL THEATER
With good sight lines and acoustics, the 400-seat Cowell Theater has become increasingly popular with small classical and other ensembles, as well as local dance groups. Fort Mason Center, Pier 2, Laguna St. at Marina Blvd., The Marina, 415/441–5706.

4 c-8
DAVIES SYMPHONY HALL
The home of the San Francisco Symphony also hosts programs by San Francisco Performances (500 Sutter St., Suite 710, 415/398–6449), a company that presents the world's best musicians and dancers, with high-powered events held at various locations from October through May. 201 Van Ness Ave., at Grove St., Civic Center, 415/431–5400.

4 c-7
GREEN ROOM
In the same building as the Herbst Theater, this small room provides an intimate setting for chamber and vocal ensembles. Veterans Building, 401 Van Ness Ave., at McCallister St., Civic Center, 415/621–6600.

4 c-7
HERBST THEATER
World-class soloists, chamber and choral groups, and San Francisco Per-

formances (*see* Davies Symphony Hall, *above*) present their works at the elegant Herbst, in the Veterans Building downtown. Though the theater is plush, the acoustics are mediocre. *Veterans Building, 401 Van Ness Ave., at McCallister St., Civic Center, 415/392–4400.*

4 *d-5*

MASONIC AUDITORIUM

This large hall is used by San Francisco Performances and others for symphonic and other musical events. *1111 California St., at Taylor St., Nob Hill, 415/776–4917.*

7 *g-5*

NOE VALLEY MINISTRY

One of the city's more eclectic venues hosts everything from chamber music to world music to folk tunes. Call ahead for tickets. *1021 Sanchez St., at Elizabeth St., Noe Valley, 415/282–2317.*

8 *c-3*

THEATER ARTAUD

A cavernous converted cannery that still has an industrial air, Artaud is one of the most interesting performance halls in town. The excellent local and traveling shows—often dance, drama, and music all at once, usually have an experimental flavor. *450 Florida St., at 17th St., Potrero Hill, 415/621–7797.*

CONCERTS IN CHURCHES

4 *d-5*

GRACE CATHEDRAL

Free, late-afternoon organ recitals, choral concerts, and other events take place often, usually on Sundays. *1100 California St., at Taylor St., Nob Hill, 415/749–6300.*

7 *h-2*

MISSION DOLORES

The church next to this historic mission has become a popular site for a cappella and other choral recitals, including performances by top groups such as Chanticleer. *16th St. at Dolores St., Mission District, 415/621–8203.*

4 *b-5*

OLD FIRST CHURCH CONCERTS

This well-respected Friday evening and Sunday afternoon series at Old First

Presbyterian Church includes chamber and orchestral music, vocal soloists, and world music and dance. Call for tickets or visit the TIX booth in Union Square (*see* Tickets, *below*). *Van Ness Ave. at Sacramento St., Pacific Heights, 415/474–1608.*

4 *e-5*

OLD ST. MARY'S CATHEDRAL

Stick around after mass for Noontime Concerts, a year-round series of solo and orchestra chamber music on Tuesdays and piano performances on Thursdays at 12:30. A $3 donation is suggested for the concerts. *660 California St., at Grant Ave., Chinatown, 415/288–3840 for concert information.*

4 *b-6*

ST. MARY'S CATHEDRAL

San Franciscans have a love/hate relationship with this unusual modern building, popularly known as "Our Lady of Maytag" (it looks like a washing machine agitator). Organ recitals and choral concerts often occur on Sunday afternoons. *1111 Gough St., at Geary St., Western Addition, 415/567–2020.*

DANCE

8 *a-4*

DANCERS' GROUP STUDIO THEATER

This small space is packed most Friday and Saturday nights with audiences enjoying the creativity of local choreographers. Many performances incorporate text with music and movement to explore personal and political themes. In March, the critically acclaimed Edge Festival showcases an eclectic group of Bay Area artists. *3221 22nd St., at Mission St., Mission District, 415/824–5044.*

MARGARET JENKINS DANCE COMPANY

This experimental troupe has a loyal following. Its namesake has collaborated with a number of internationally recognized talents, including Yoko Ono. *415/826–8399.*

OAKLAND BALLET

Perhaps even more respected than the San Francisco Ballet, this 32-year-old company often performs revivals of early 20th-century classics, as well as new works set to contemporary music. Performances are held in the grand old Paramount Theater (2025 Broadway, at 19th St., Oakland, 510/465–6400; map 3, d-7) in downtown Oakland. *510/452–9288.*

ODC/SAN FRANCISCO
ODC, which stands for Oberlin Dance Collective, presents the works of the collective's choreographers, including Brenda Way. *415/863–6606.*

4 *b-7*

SAN FRANCISCO BALLET
Though the nation's oldest ballet company has never been known for cutting-edge performances, they have recently started attracting more notice for their staging of modern works under the artistic direction of Helgi Tomsson. The season runs from February through

---

May. *Box office: 455 Franklin St., at Grove St., Civic Center, 415/865–2000.*

5 *f-3*

SAN FRANCISCO ETHNIC DANCE FESTIVAL
The city's biggest dance festival, featuring dozens of ethnic dance companies yearly, is held for several days in June at the Palace of Fine Arts Theater. Check the *Bay Guardian* for schedules and dependable recommendations. *Palace of Fine Arts, 3301 Lyon St., at Bay St., The Marina, 415/474–3914.*

FREE ENTERTAINMENT

7 *a-1*

GOLDEN GATE PARK BAND
The band has put on free concerts every Sunday since 1882. Concerts start promptly at 1 PM. *Golden Gate Park Bandshell, at west end of Music Concourse, Golden Gate Park, 415/831–2790.*

6 *g-5*

SAN FRANCISCO CONSERVATORY OF MUSIC
Many of the conservatory's recitals, student-performed and otherwise, are free of charge. Most are held at either of the conservatory's two smallish concert halls. Call for a schedule of upcoming events. *1201 Ortega St., at 19th Ave., Sunset District, 415/759–3477.*

SAN FRANCISCO MIME TROUPE
Scathing musical satires are performed for free in area parks from the weekend of July 4 through September; the first one usually takes place in Dolores Park. When they pass the hat at the end of the performance, remember that audience donations keep this group afloat. Call for their current whereabouts. *415/646–0639.*

7 *b-1*

SAN FRANCISCO SHAKESPEARE FESTIVAL
This popular festival plays at Liberty Tree Meadow in Golden Gate Park, and a few other East Bay and South Bay locations. It usually hits Golden Gate park in September, but watch the papers or call for exact dates. Arrive early for the San Francisco shows and bring warm clothing, as the weather in this part of the

---

CULTURE FOR KIDS

Who says kids don't like opera? Well, maybe that's pushing it, but San Francisco does have plenty of cultural options tailored to those with a short attention span.

Alhambra Theatre (Movie Theaters Worth Noting)
   Kids' movies are screened often at this elaborately decorated theater.

Golden Gate Park Band (Free Entertainment)
   Combine this free concert with an afternoon in the park.

The Marsh (Theater)
   Call for information about special kids' programs.

Oakland Ballet (Dance Groups)
   The December Nutcracker performances tend to sell out.

San Francisco Mime Troupe (Free Entertainment)
   Kids may miss some of the political satire, but they'll still love the show.

San Francisco Symphony (Orchestral Groups)((
   Look for the "Music for Families Series."

Stern Grove Festival (Free Entertainment)
   Family-friendly performances in an outdoor setting.

park is almost invariably cool. *Across Conservatory Dr. from Flower Conservatory, Golden Gate Park, 415/422–2221.*

6 *g-8*

STERN GROVE FESTIVAL

In July and August, the nation's oldest continual free summer music festival hosts Sunday afternoon performances of music and dance in a fabulously atmospheric amphitheater in a eucalyptus grove. Come early to stake out your patch of grass, and bring warm clothing, as the fog is apt to roll in at any moment. *Sloat Blvd. at 19th Ave., Sunset District, 415/252–6252.*

MOVIE THEATERS WORTH NOTING

4 *c-3*

ALHAMBRA THEATRE

This Moorish-style, one-screen theater got a major makeover in the late 1980s. It tends to screen a single movie—often a children's movie—for what seems like ages. *2330 Polk St., between Green and Union Sts., Russian Hill, 415/775–2137.*

4 *f-3*

THE CASTING COUCH MICRO CINEMA

True to its name, this 46-person screening room, used exclusively for independent films, has sofas instead of regular seats—and the staff serves chocolate-chip cookies to boot. Arrive 15 minutes before showtime to secure a seat. *950 Battery St., between Green and Vallejo Sts., The Embarcadero, 415/986–7001.*

7 *g-3*

CASTRO THEATRE

Built in 1922 and still the most beautiful place to see a film in San Francisco, the Castro shows a wide selection of rare, foreign, and unusual films. The man who plays the Wurlitzer organ before performances consistently gets a rousing cheer from the patrons who clap along with his rendition of "San Francisco." The theater's specialties are camp and classics of all genres. *429 Castro St., between Market and 18th Sts., The Castro, 415/621–6120.*

4 *f-6*

CENTER FOR THE ARTS THEATER

Open since 1993, the Center for the Arts shows local and international works, often highly experimental, in its 100-seat film and video screening room. *Corner of Howard and 3rd Sts., South of Market, 415/978–2787.*

7 *d-7*

THE RED VIC

Film buffs either love this cozy coop theater, where you can enjoy herbal tea while watching the movie on one of the couches, or hate it, complaining about the small screen and strange repertoire. Films here are usually artsy, ultrafunky, or rare. *1727 Haight St., between Cole and Shrader Sts., The Haight, 415/668–3994.*

8 *a-2*

THE ROXIE

This slightly run-down Mission theater shows political, cult, and otherwise bent films of widely varying quality. Though some fabulous films pass through here, there's also a fair share of silly old flicks that might just as well be forgotten. *3117 16th St., at Valencia St., Mission District, 415/863–1087.*

5 *d-7*

UNITED ARTISTS CORONET

If you've just got to see a loud action flick, the UA Coronet impresses with its huge capacity, large screen, and Sony Dynamic Digital Sound. *3575 Geary Blvd., at Arguello Blvd., Richmond District, 415/752–4400.*

OPERA

3 *e-3*

BERKELEY OPERA

The opera performs about three fully staged shows each season in the intimate Julia Morgan Theater, a treat for opera-goers used to nosebleed seats at larger opera houses. Many of its lead singers come from the San Francisco Opera Chorus; a few of them have gone on to the Met. *2640 College Ave., at Derby St., Berkeley, 510/841–1903.*

POCKET OPERA

Since 1977, this company has carved a niche for itself by presenting chamber operas in original English translations from February through June. Though performances may lack the polish of those at the San Francisco Opera, they are unfailingly lively and entertaining. Concerts are held at various locations in San Francisco, Marin, the South Bay, and the East Bay. 415/575–1102.

4 c-7

SAN FRANCISCO OPERA

After a season of performing in smaller venues during the renovation of the War Memorial Opera House, the San Francisco Opera returned to its elegant home for its 75th anniversary 97–98 season. One of the most important companies in the United States outside New York, the Opera presents a full season of grand-scale originals and revivals from the first Friday after Labor Day through mid-December. Watch for frequent coproductions with European opera com-

panies. *War Memorial Opera House, 301 Van Ness Ave., at Grove St., Civic Center, 415/864–3330.*

ORCHESTRAL GROUPS

BERKELEY SYMPHONY ORCHESTRA

The Berkeley Symphony Orchestra has managed to hang onto Kent Nagano, a world-famous conductor who spends part of the year with the renowned Lyon Opera in France. The emphasis is on 20th-century composers. Performances take place in Berkeley's Zellerbach Hall (Corner Bancroft and Telegraph Aves., Berkeley; map 3, e-2) and various other East Bay locations. 510/841–2800.

PHILHARMONIA BAROQUE ORCHESTRA

The orchestra performs works by composers of the 17th and 18th centuries at venues throughout the area. Its season lasts from fall through spring. 415/391–5252.

6 g-5

SAN FRANCISCO CONSERVATORY OF MUSIC

The city's major music school has something going on almost nightly, whether it's a performance by students, faculty, or the Conservatory Orchestra. The performances by the Conservatory Opera Theatre are a relatively low-cost introduction to this often pricey art. Most student recitals are free. 1201 Ortega St., at 19th Ave., Sunset District, 415/564–8086.

4 f-6

SAN FRANCISCO CONTEMPORARY MUSIC PLAYERS

The best contemporary company in the area and one of the oldest in the United States stages only about six performances a year at the Yerba Buena Center for the Arts. Concerts generally feature cutting-edge new works by contemporary composers. Ticket prices include a pre-concert discussion with composers and other guests. 701 Mission St., at 3rd St., South of Market, 415/978–2787 or 415/252–6235 for programming information.

HISTORIC SAN FRANCISCO

With bars, movie theaters, and supper clubs opening every other day, it's easy to forget some of San Francisco's beloved older venues that seem to exude a sense of the city's history.

Beach Blanket Babylon (Cabaret)
   Playing since 1974, with topical references to the city.

Castro Theatre (Movie Theaters Worth Noting)
   Built in 1922, it's many San Franciscans' favorite theater.

Eli's Mile High Club (Blues)
   The birthplace of West Coast blues, and still going strong.

The Fillmore (Pop/Rock)
   San Francisco's most famous rock music venue.

Finocchio's (Cabaret)
   Featuring female impersonators since 1936.

Mission Dolores (Concerts in Churches)
   Concerts in a church next to the city's most famous historic mission.

Tosca (Bars)
   Worthwhile for its elegant and historic ambience.

Vesuvio (Bars)
   Popular Beat era hangout.

4 c-8

SAN FRANCISCO SYMPHONY

California-born conductor Michael Tilson Thomas has attracted near-superstar fame since he became music director in September 1995. Innovative programs of 20th-century American works are the symphony's strong suit. Additional programming includes performances by the youth orchestra, a concert series for families, and chamber music. *Davies Symphony Hall, 201 Van Ness Ave., at Grove St., Civic Center, 415/864–6000.*

4 c-7

SAN FRANCISCO WOMEN'S PHILHARMONIC

After a nearly two-year hiatus, this talented group of performers resumed advancing the work of women composers, conductors, and performers in 1997. Their performances, held at Herbst Theater, are often preceded by a discussion with the artists. *Herbst Theater, 401 Van Ness Ave., at McCallister St., Civic Center, 415/437–0123, or 415/392–4400 for reservations.*

THEATERS & THEATER COMPANIES

4 d-6

AMERICAN CONSERVATORY THEATER (ACT)

One of the nation's leading regional theaters, ACT presents about eight plays annually, from October through late spring, in the newly renovated Geary Theater. *415 Geary St., at Mason St., Union Square, 415/749–2228.*

4 d-8

ASIAN AMERICAN THEATER COMPANY

This company presents the works of Asian and Asian-American playwrights. *New Langton Arts, 1246 Folsom St., at 8th St., Mission District, 415/440–5545.*

3 d-2

BERKELEY REPERTORY THEATRE

Across the San Francisco Bay, the Berkeley Rep was awarded the 1997 Tony Award for Best Regional Theater. It performs an adventurous mix of classics and new plays from fall through spring

in a modern, intimate theater near BART's downtown Berkeley station. *2025 Addison St., at Milvia St., Berkeley 510/845–4700.*

8 c-5

BRAVA!

Brava! For Women in the Arts is the full name of this theater company that develops and produces works by women playwrights. They frequently showcase the work of Latina authors. *2789 24th St., at York St., Potrero Hill, 415/826–5773.*

4 d-6

CURRAN THEATRE

At press time *The Phantom of the Opera* was firmly ensconced at the Curran Theatre for years and was showing no signs of budging. *445 Geary St., at Mason St., Union Square, 415/551–2000.*

8 a-5

EL TEATRO DE LA ESPERANZA

The resident company of the Mission Cultural Center produces bilingual work based on the Chicano experience. *2868 Mission St., between 24th and 25th Sts., Mission District, 415/821–1155.*

4 e-6

EXIT THEATRE

Imaginative theater and multimedia productions are the draw at this two-stage café–theater. *156 Eddy St., at Mason St., Union Square, 415/673–3847.*

4 d-7

GOLDEN GATE THEATRE

The program consists primarily of musicals, including "Best of Broadway" shows, at this stylishly refurbished theater. *Golden Gate Ave., at Taylor St., The Tenderloin, 415/474–3800.*

8 a-2

INTERSECTION FOR THE ARTS

Plays, mostly contemporary, poetry readings, and performance art are presented by Intersection in its stark 65-seat space. Unusual sound and visual installations take place in the gallery upstairs. The 30-year-old Intersection is San Francisco's oldest alternative art space, and its shows are consistently good. *446 Valencia St., between 15th and 16th Sts., Mission District, 415/626–2787.*

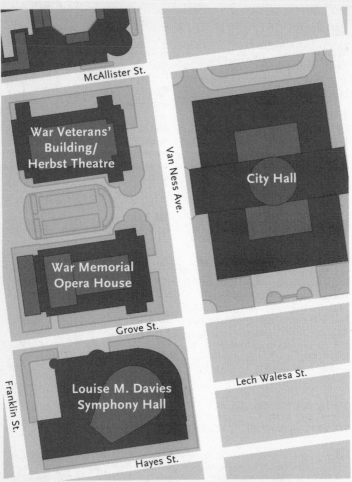

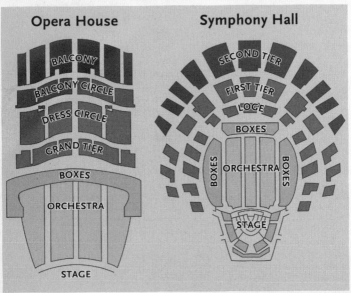

LAMPLIGHTERS MUSIC THEATRE

This group presents lavish productions of Gilbert and Sullivan and other operettas at theaters throughout the Bay Area. Their venues are usually small, the better to appreciate the often whimsical costumes and sets. *415/227–4797 or 415/ 227–0331 (City Box Office) for tickets.*

4 *d-5*

THE LORRAINE HANSBERRY THEATRE

Experimental, musical, and classical works by African Americans and other writers of color are performed at this consistently high-quality theater. *620 Sutter St., at Mason St., Union Square, 415/474–8800.*

8 *b-2*

LUNA SEA

There's an ever-changing lineup of women's projects, including visual arts displays, performance art, and readings, at this smoke- and alcohol-free gallery and theater space. Some events are for women only. *2940 16th St., between Capp St. and South Van Ness Ave., Mission District, 415/863–2989.*

4 *a-2*

MAGIC THEATRE

Once Sam Shepard's favorite showcase, the Magic is now San Francisco's leading showcase for new plays, presenting works by the latest rising American playwrights. *Fort Mason Center, Bldg. D, Laguna St. at Marina Blvd., The Marina, 415/441–8822.*

8 *a-4*

THE MARSH

Alternative theater, performance, comedy, and musical acts come to this "breeding ground for new performances." The 99 house seats include a cozy corner of sofas, and you can purchase freshly baked treats and coffee at intermission. *1062 Valencia St., at 22nd St., Mission District, 415/641–0235.*

MODUS EMSEMBLE

Founded in 1993, Modus Ensemble is dedicated to presenting the works of innovative playwrights, often mixing theater, music, and dance to explore humanistic concerns in a technological age. Their plays are staged at various locations, including the SOMAR Theatre (934 Brannan St., between 8th and 9th

Sts., South of Market, map 8, d-1). *415/ 346–6456.*

4 *d-7*

ORPHEUM

This 2,500-seat theater, a former vaudeville house, is used for the biggest touring shows. *1192 Market St., at Hyde St., Civic Center, 415/551–2000.*

4 *d-8*

PHOENIX THEATRE

The Phoenix presents and produces new plays and original adaptations by Bay Area artists of works by American, British, and European playwrights. *301 8th St., at Folsom St., South of Market, 415/621–4423.*

8 *a-2*

THEATRE RHINOCEROS

The oldest active lesbian and gay theater company in the country, Theatre Rhinoceros stages reliably good plays in its tiny performance space. *2926 16th St., at Capp St., Mission District, 415/861–5079.*

4 *d-6*

THEATRE ON THE SQUARE

Smaller touring dramas and musicals perform here. *450 Post St., at Mason St., Union Square, 415/433–9500.*

TICKETS

The city's charge-by-phone ticket service is **BASS** (510/762–2277), which also operates the separate **BASS Charge Performing Arts Line** (415/776–1999). The latter sells tickets to all but the smallest cultural venues in the Bay Area; its operators are more knowledgeable about arts events than those at the main number. You can purchase tickets in person at the BASS outlets in **Tower Records** and **Wherehouse** stores throughout the Bay Area, as well as at the TIX Bay Area booth (*see below*).

Since BASS adds a per-ticket charge to all purchases, you might want to visit venue box offices in person. By calling the numbers given above for each venue and organization, you can get information about box-office hours or mail-order purchase of tickets, if available. Many venues give discounts for students and senior citizens; perhaps the best deal is with the San Francisco Opera, where $20 and a student ID or senior status can get you excellent seats to many shows. Call ahead for availability.

For same-day, half-price discounts, try the **TIX Bay Area** (251 Stockton St., between Post and Geary Sts., 415/433–7827) booth on Union Square. Open from 11 to 6 Tuesday through Thursday and from 11 to 7 on Friday and Saturday, the booth requires in-person sales; you cannot get information about half-price ticket sales over the phone. Half-price tickets for Sunday and Monday shows are sold on Saturday. TIX is also a full-service ticket agency and BASS outlet selling full-price, advance-purchase tickets for arts, culture, and sports events around the Bay Area.

nightlife

BARS

7 *g-1*

AN BODHRÁN

One of the city's newer Irish bars, this is a good place for a pint and some mellow conversation. Oddly enough, Wednesdays are reggae night (are you transported back to Ireland yet?). On Sundays there's usually more traditional Irish music in the evening, and dancing at night. *668 Haight St., between Pierce and Steiner Sts., Lower Haight, 415/431–4724.*

4 *c-7*

BACKFLIP

From the transvestite doorperson in five-inch platform shoes to the vinyl dresses on the wait staff, everything at Backflip seems designed for maximum visual impact. Open only since spring 1997, the place is outrageously decorated with shag carpet, a preponderance of shiny blue vinyl, and fuzzy-tufted stools in the restrooms. The crowd is mostly young and trendy. *601 Eddy St., at Larkin St., Tenderloin, 415/771–3547.*

5 *h-3*

BALBOA CAFÉ

A young and upwardly mobile crowd mingles over burgers at this lively hangout. It's a great place to find a financially solvent date. *3199 Fillmore St., at Greenwich St., Cow Hollow, 415/921–3944.*

4 *c-2*

BUENA VISTA

Unlike most establishments in the area, this bar near Fisherman's Wharf has a loyal local following. The Buena Vista strenuously claims to have introduced Irish coffee to the New World; whether or not that's true, they do make a mean version, sure to warm you up after your waterfront wanderings. *2765 Hyde St., at Beach St., Northern Waterfront, 415/474–5044.*

7 *g-3*

THE CAFÉ

Formerly the Café San Marco, this large, lively bar with mirrored walls and neon lights used to cater mainly to lesbians, but these days you'll find plenty of gay men as well. Dancing and a quiet chat are equally popular diversions here. If you want to know if the crowd is attractive enough for you, stroll by and check out the patrons drinking out on the balcony. *2367 Market St., at Castro St., The Castro, 415/861–3846.*

8 *d-1*

CAFÉ MARS

An increasingly upscale crowd of Russian Hill and Marina residents comes to this somewhat remote corner of SoMa to have a really good time. Sip Martian Martinis, made with Finlandia Cranberry Vodka and a dried cranberry twist, or order a plate of tapas. You can also shoot pool in the back. *798 Brannan St., at 7th St., South of Market, 415/621–6277.*

4 *f-5*

CARNELIAN ROOM

On the 52nd floor of the Bank of America Building, the Carnelian room has what is perhaps the loftiest view of San Francisco's skyline. Dress up if you don't want the staff to look down their noses at you; dinner patrons are required to wear a jacket. *555 California St., at Kearny St., Financial District, 415/433–7500.*

4 *c-4*

THE CINCH

Except for the music, which is culled from a rather hip collection of CDs behind the bar, this is a Wild West–themed gay men's bar with amazingly cheap drinks. Memorable touches include a cigar store Indian, swinging doors, fake cacti, Navajo rugs, and wagon wheels. *1723 Polk St., between Clay and Washington St., Polk Gulch, 415/776–4162.*

4 *d-5*

CROWN ROOM

This aptly named lounge on the 23rd floor of the Fairmont Hotel is one of the city's more luxurious skyline bars. Those prone to vertigo may want to close their eyes while riding up the glass-enclosed elevator. *Fairmont Hotel, California and Mason Sts., Nob Hill, 415/772–5131.*

7 *d-1*

THE DELUXE

One of the many new, slick retro bars in the city, The Deluxe is unusually free of pretension. Still, patrons enjoy donning their finest '40s duds, sipping martinis, and acting *very* cool. The place is usually booked by swing bands, but sometimes you'll find owner Jay Johnson himself crooning a few tunes. *1511 Haight St., between Ashbury and Clayton Sts., The Haight, 415/552–6949.*

7 *g-3*

THE DETOUR

Minimally decorated with a chain-link fence and pool table, this bar attracts a young, good-looking, somewhat surly crowd of gay men. Urgent techno-house music and Saturday-night go-go dancers set the racy mood, as do the dim blue lights. If you forget the address, listen for the music, since the black-on-black sign is impossible to see at night. *2348 Market St., between Castro and Noe Sts., The Castro, 415/861–6053.*

8 *b-3*

DYLAN'S

Named after Wales's most famous poet, this Potrero Hill pub is plastered with Welsh memorabilia. You may not understand the bartender's thick accent, but he'll understand you when you order a pint. Jazz music on Wednesday nights draws a big crowd. *2301 Folsom St., at 19th St., Mission District, 415/641–1416.*

4 *c-6*

EDINBURGH CASTLE

If you're willing to brave the dicey neighborhood, this British pub with a beautiful bar is an excellent choice. Thick-accented U.K. types, especially Scots, congregate to play darts, eat fish and chips, and drink pints of Guiness.

Local bands make occasional appearances, and Fridays usually bring a kilted bagpipe player. *950 Geary St., between Polk and Larkin Sts., The Tenderloin, 415/885–4074.*

4 *g-6*

EL ROYS

This cavernous new two-story indoor–outdoor restaurant–bar may have replaced Johnny Love's as San Francisco's cruisiest yuppie scene. Packed on weekends and for post-work fêtes on Thursdays and Fridays, El Roys attracts Financial District workers looking for a date: Men are largely in suits, women in clingy little dresses. *300 Beale St., at Folsom St., South of Market, 415/882–7989.*

4 *g-4*

EQUINOX

On the 22nd floor of the Hyatt Regency, this is the city's only revolving skyline bar. You can sightsee, eat, and drink, all without even swiveling your chair. *5 Embarcadero Center, at Market St., The Embarcadero, 415/788–1234.*

SKYLINE BARS

For sightseeing in comfort, nothing beats a skyline bar. You'll find them on the top floor of many of San Francisco's major hotels, as well as in private establishments such as the Carnelian Room.

Carnelian Room, Bank of America Building (Bars)
The best of the best, from the 52nd floor; jackets required.

Crown Room, Fairmont Hotel (Bars)
The crown of the Fairmont, reached by a glass-enclosed elevator.

Equinox, Hyatt Regency (Bars)
A revolving room provides 360-degree views.

Harry Denton's Starlite Room, Sir Francis Drake (Bars)
Live jazz and swing—or taped Frank Sinatra—in swanky, '50s-style digs.

Top of the Mark, Mark-Hopkins Intercontinental (Bars)
A classic.

View Lounge, San Francisco Marriott (Bars)
Live piano or R&B and blues.

7 h-3

THE 500 CLUB

A huge neon martini sign outside attracts neighborhood bar flies to this tiny bar on weekdays; weekends, the crowd is younger, trendier, and more social. Two cramped pool tables and three comfy vinyl booths are just about all there is to this bar, so show up early on weekends, when it's difficult to find a place to stand. 500 Guerrero St., at 17th St., Mission District, 415/861–2500.

4 h-5

GORDON BIERSCH BREWERY AND RESTAURANT

Inside the old Hill Brothers coffee factory, this is a favorite of the twenty- and thirtysomething set. Better-than-average bar food and excellent microbrewed beers make all the other well-dressed patrons look even better. 2 Harrison St., at Embarcadero, The Embarcadero, 415/243–8246.

4 g-5

HARRY DENTON'S

Packed with well-dressed young professionals after work, Harry Denton's was voted "Best Place to Pick Up a High-Powered Executive, or a PR Weasel Who Looks Like a High-Powered Executive" by the Bay Guardian in 1997. Live bands and dancing begin after 10 every night except Sunday. It's also a great place to enjoy stunning views of the bay—especially from the back bar. 161 Steuart St., between Howard and Mission Sts., Embarcadero, 415/882–1333.

4 e-5

HARRY DENTON'S STARLIGHT ROOM

On the 21st floor of the Sir Francis Drake Hotel, this most romantic of rooftop lounges re-creates the 1950s high life with velvet booths and dim lighting. Live combos playing jazz standards and swing are common, as are recorded Sinatra tunes. 450 Powell St., between Post and Sutter Sts., Union Square, 415/395–8595.

4 b-8

HAYES AND VINE

One of the newer bars in a rapidly gentrifying neighborhood, Hayes and Vine has a broad selection of wines by the glass, many of them moderately priced.

After-opera visitors mingle with younger wine aficionados looking for a classy night away from the Lower Haight or the Mission. Although there is no kitchen, you can order plates of cheese, pâté, and caviar. 377 Hayes St., between Franklin and Gough Sts., Hayes Valley, 415/626–5301.

4 e-4

HI-BALL LOUNGE

In the midst of some of North Beach's sleazier sex clubs, this swank bar attracts a retro-dressed crowd with its leopard-skin drapery and red velvet booths. Live swing bands (and accompanying swing dance lessons) are a big draw; unfortunately, the tiny dance floor is too cramped for dancing most weekend nights. 473 Broadway, between Kearny and Montgomery Sts., North Beach, 415/397–9464.

4 g-4

HOLDING COMPANY

Suited-up workers from the Financial District gather here after work. The kitchen and bar are open weekdays. 2 Embarcadero Center, The Embarcadero, 415/986–0797.

4 c-4

JOHNNY LOVE'S

This newly renovated restaurant-cum-singles bar has been a hit ever since it was opened by the popular Mr. Love, a former protégé of Harry Denton's. Whether you want to order from the menu of American club fare, dance to DJ-spun modern rock, listen to live rock, swing, or reggae, or just flirt with the yuppies who look for dates here, you're in luck. 1500 Broadway, at Polk St., Russian Hill, 415/931–8021.

4 e-4

LI PO'S

The dark, cavernous setting and incense-burning altar lend an oddly mystical feel to this bar on the edge of Chinatown. By 1 AM the coveted back booths are filled with boisterous escapees from the crowded bars of North Beach. Extroverts can take part in occasional karaoke. 916 Grant Ave., between Washington and Jackson Sts., Chinatown, 415/982–0072.

7 h-4

THE LONE PALM

Put on some classy duds if you want to feel at home here, where a '40s retro atmosphere, a grand piano in the corner, and skilled cocktail shakers behind the bar set the scene. This is the perfect setting for sipping martinis with that certain someone. *3394 22nd St., at Guerrero St., Mission District, 415/648–0109.*

7 g-2

LUCKY 13

If the young, black-clad crowd at Café du Nord (*see* Jazz, *below*) is a bit too trendy for you, head a few doors down to Lucky 13, where a laid-back, tattooed, and pierced set drinks one of the many beers available on tap. Its location at the crossroads of the Castro, the Mission, and the Lower Haight ensures a diverse but slightly scruffy crowd. *2140 Market St., between Church and Sanchez Sts., The Castro, 415/487–1313.*

7 g-1

MAD DOG IN THE FOG

A crowd of Guiness-drinking Brits frequents this pub in the Lower Haight. On warm summer mornings or afternoons, the beer garden outside is the perfect place for a greasy breakfast like the Greedy Bastard (bacon, sausage, baked beans, scrambled eggs, and tomato). Best of all, dishes of at least $6 include a free pint until 2:30 PM. Team trivia contests on Mondays and Thursdays have become all the rage in the last few years. *530 Haight St., between Fillmore and Steiner Sts., Lower Haight, 415/626–7279.*

8 a-4

THE MAKE OUT ROOM

The dark, quiet street and beckoning marquee may have you convinced that this is a shady strip joint. In fact, it's a perfectly reputable bar, popular with local twentysomethings. The spacious floor means you won't get jostled too unmercilessly on crowded weekend nights. Expect to pay a cover for occasional live band performances. *3225 22nd Ave., at Mission St., Mission District, 415/647–2888.*

7 g-2

THE METRO

More upscale than the nearby Detour and filled with guppies (gay yuppies), The Metro has a balcony that overlooks the intersection of Noe, 16th, and Market streets. The Tuesday night karaoke is bizarrely popular. A line usually forms on weekends. *3600 16th St., at Market St., The Castro, 415/703–9750.*

7 f-3

MIDNIGHT SUN

Two large video screens help alleviate the need for conversation in this crowded gay men's bar, one of the oldest in the Castro. A mix of campy TV shows and music videos play on the giant video screens. The thirtysomething crowd tends toward the clean-cut and upscale. *4067 18th St., at Castro St., The Castro, 415/861–4186.*

7 g-1

MIDTOWN

A grungy group of Lower Haight regulars comes here to release its angst with a beer and game of pool. It's more a place to drink than to see and be seen—perhaps because it's so dark inside you can barely see who's standing next to you. *582 Haight St., between Fillmore and Steiner Sts., Lower Haight, 415/558–8019.*

4 c-6

MOTHERLODE

The city's most popular transvestite haven, Motherlode is *the* place for transvestites, transsexuals, and their admirers. It's sometimes seedy, and always entertaining. Free drag shows draw a crowd on Friday and Saturday nights. *1002 Post St., at Larkin St., The Tenderloin, 415/928–6006.*

7 d-1

MURIO'S TROPHY ROOM

Upper Haight slackers and bikers usually crowd this low-key bar. When the conversation lags, you can always resort to the pool table, jukebox, or TV. *1811 Haight St., between Shrader and Stanyan Sts., The Haight, 415/752–2971.*

7 g-1

NOC NOC

Step inside this Lower Haight institution and you'll find yourself in a postmodern cave complete with chunky Flintstones-style furniture and a very eclectic music repertoire—lots of acid jazz and house. Despite its wild decor and raucous Lower Haight location, it's usually just a mellow place to enjoy a beer or wine (there's no full bar). *557 Haight St., between Fillmore and Steiner Sts., Lower Haight, 415/861–5811.*

4 e-3
O'REILLY'S IRISH BAR AND RESTAURANT

Gleaming brass railings and wooden snugs (booths) set this Irish bar apart from others in the city. Everything about O'Reilly's is classy, from the unusually good Irish breakfasts (no soggy tomatoes here) to the well-dressed crowd and irresistible Irish coffee. *622 Green St., at Columbus Ave., North Beach, 415/989–6222.*

5 d-7
PAT O'SHEA'S MAD HATTER

One of the better sports bars in a city where sports bars get no respect, Pat O'Shea's is a good choice if you just gotta see the game on a big-screen TV. The crowd, enthusiastic about Bay Area teams to say the least, still seems to tolerate the occasional dissenter. *3848 Geary Blvd., at 3rd Ave., Richmond District, 415/752–3148.*

4 a-4
PERRY'S

This upscale singles bar is usually jam-packed with a well-dressed Pacific Heights and Marina crowd. You can dine here on great hamburgers as well as more substantial fare. *1944 Union St., between Laguna and Buchanan Sts., Pacific Heights, 415/922–9022.*

5 h-3
PIERCE STREET ANNEX

Packed with the well-toned, expensively dressed Marina set, this festive bar has a dance floor, pool tables, and nightly drink specials. Entertainment alternates between live music, often acoustic, and DJ dancing, sometimes '70s retro. *3138 Fillmore St., at Greenwich St., Cow Hollow, 415/567–1400.*

4 b-8
PLACE PIGALLE

The vibes are hip and European at this sleek, French-owned wine bar and gallery space in a slightly seedy but up-and-coming neighborhood. Live jazz is performed Thursday through Saturday nights, and occasional spoken-word performances are held during the week. *520 Hayes St., between Octavia and Laguna Sts., Hayes Valley, 415/552–2671.*

7 g-5
THE RAT AND RAVEN

Probably the most popular bar in the relatively bar-free Noe Valley, The Rat and Raven attracts a loyal bunch of neighborhood regulars most nights of the week. Though occasionally it can resemble a frat party, the crowd is friendly and laid back. A patio out back is a plus. *4054 24th St., between Noe and Castro Sts., Noe Valley, 415/285–0674.*

4 d-6
RED ROOM

A hyper-trendy, well-dressed crowd frequents this cocktail bar attached to the Commodore Hotel. Its impressive entrance opens to a curved wall of red bottles stacked to the ceiling, and a shockingly red interior. Dress in black, the better to be seen. *827 Sutter St., at Jones St., The Tenderloin, 415/346–7666.*

8 b-3
THE RITE SPOT

The piano in the corner, candlelit tables, and understated decor all lend a sense of class to this outer Mission bar that's a favorite among locals. The light meals they serve are a cut above most bar fare. *2099 Folsom St., at 17th St., Mission District, 415/552–6066.*

4 e-4
SAN FRANCISCO BREWING COMPANY

A thirtysomething crowd, equal parts jazz lovers and beer connoisseurs, frequents this popular brewery. The frequent mellow jazz ensures that the excellent beers go down smoothly. *155 Columbus Ave., at Pacific St., North Beach, 415/434–3344.*

4 e-3
SAVOY-TIVOLI

A youngish yuppie crowd fills this cavernous North Beach institution. The large, covered front patio opens when the weather's nice, making the Savoy prime territory to drink wine and watch the world go by. If it's raining, you can shoot pool in the back. *1434 Grant Ave., between Union and Green Sts., North Beach, 415/362–7023.*

8 a-2
SKYLARK

A newcomer in the midst of a densely packed cluster of nightspots, Skylark is the classiest of the bunch: This is the place to drink martinis and romance that special someone in the cozy booths next to the front windows. Be sure to look up at the whimsical ceiling mural. *3089 16th St., at Valencia St., Mission District, 415/621–9294.*

4 *e-4*
SPECS'
To call this North Beach bar low key would be an understatement; patrons sometimes seem almost comatose as they quietly nurse their beverages. Still, it's a friendly, no-attitude sort of place where you can gaze for hours at the quirky memorabilia papering the walls. *12 Adler Pl., off Columbus Ave., next to Tosca (see below), North Beach, 415/421–4112.*

4 *d-5*
THE TONGA ROOM
Tropical drinks are served with little paper umbrellas at this absurdly kitschy bar, where quasi-Polynesian decor and an artificial lagoon draw locals and out-of-towners. Every 30 minutes or so, a simulated rainstorm blows through the bamboo-and-palm-filled room, and at 8 PM most nights, an almost comically bad soft-rock band performs from a thatched hut in the middle of the lagoon. *Fairmont Hotel, 950 Mason St., at California St., Nob Hill, 415/772–5278.*

4 *d-5*
TOP OF THE MARK
The bar at the top of the Mark Hopkins hotel was immortalized by a famous magazine photograph as a hot spot for World War II servicemen on leave or about to ship out. Now folks can dance to the sounds of that era on weekends, in a room with a view. Crowds are a bit sedate, and drink prices high, but the views and quality of the swing, jazz, and standards are superb. *Mark Hopkins Inter-Continental, 999 California St., at Mason St., Nob Hill, 415/392–3434.*

7 *g-1*
THE TORONADO
As divey as you would expect from a Lower Haight Bar, The Toronado attracts a leather-clad and slacker set with one of the widest selections of microbrews in the city. The jukebox blares a refreshing mix of kitschy country and western in addition to the standard grunge anthems. *547 Haight St., between Fill-more and Steiner Sts., Lower Haight, 415/863–2276.*

4 *e-4*
TOSCA
Like Spec's and Vesuvio nearby, Tosca holds a special place in San Francisco history. A mostly opera jukebox and a beautiful old espresso machine create an elegant environment—no wonder celebrity patrons (including Francis Ford Coppola, Sam Shepard, and Mikhail Baryshnikov) are occasionally spotted in the enormous red booths. Try one of the excellent liqueur-laced coffee drinks. *242 Columbus Ave., at Broadway, North Beach, 415/391–1244.*

8 *b-1*
20 TANK BREWERY
Serving up a large selection of micro-brews and some hearty bar food such as pizzas and nachos, this former warehouse is a good place to fuel up before heading across the street to the DNA Lounge (*see* Dance Clubs, *below*) or Slim's (*see* Jazz, *below*). A mix of frat boys and Gap-dressed twentysome-things don't seem to mind the cheesy '80s album rock played over the speakers. *316 11th St., at Folsom St., South of Market, 415/255–9455.*

7 *g-3*
TWIN PEAKS
This casual, loungelike gay bar beckons with comfy-looking pillows stacked in the window seats. The Peaks has been around for more than 15 years and proudly claims to have been the first gay bar in the city with clear—as in, not tinted—floor-to-ceiling windows—and this on the busy corner of Castro Street and Market Street. On weekends expect big crowds of mostly older men. *401 Castro St., at Market St., The Castro, 415/864–9470.*

4 *e-4*
VESUVIO
A bohemian hangout during the Beat era (along with City Lights Bookstore next door), Vesuvio is the ideal place to discuss the city's history with the regulars at the bar. The best seats, though, are upstairs all the way in the back, where large windows look out on Columbus Avenue. *255 Columbus Ave., at Broadway, North Beach, 415/362–3370.*

4 *e-6*

VIEW LOUNGE

Enjoy live R&B or blues, or simply some jazz tunes played on piano, on the 39th floor of the San Francisco Marriott. The views through the fan-shaped windows more than compensate for the uninspired corporate-hotel-style decor. *San Francisco Marriott, 55 4th St., at Mission St., South of Market, 415/896–1600.*

2 *f-6*

WILD SIDE WEST

Wild it may not be, but Wild Side West is an excellent place to while away an evening. Though this mellow neighborhood bar out in residential Bernal

---

DRINKING AL FRESCO

With fog rolling in almost every summer evening, it's often too cold to drink outside in San Francisco. This makes it all the more enjoyable to spend that rare balmy evening enjoying a drink outside.

Backflip (Bars)
Sip drinks next to a swimming pool outside the funky Phoenix Hotel.

Bottom of the Hill (Bars)
Escape to the patio when you tire of the alternative rock.

The Cafe (Bars)
A gay and lesbian bar with a balcony facing Market Street.

El Río (Dance Clubs)
Salsa dancing and margaritas are the preferred activities on the patio.

Mad Dog in the Fog (Bars)
Indulge in a tasty Irish breakfast—in the fog?

The Metro (Bars)
The balcony overlooks a busy corner in the Castro.

Mission Rock Resort (Blues)
Two decks have a view of the bay.

The Rat and Raven (Bars)
The back patio is packed on sunny summer evenings.

Sol y Luna (Dining and Dancing)
There's DJ music both inside and out.

Zeitgeist (Bars)
A crowd spills outside in the afternoons.

Heights has a large lesbian contingent, it was voted the "Best Lesbian Bar for Everybody" by the *San Francisco Bay Guardian. 424 Cortland Ave., between Mission and Bayshore Sts., Bernal Heights, 415/647–3099.*

8 *a-1*

ZEITGEIST

Don't be intimidated by the number of motorbikes outside this bar; the crowd is friendly, even if you got here on four wheels. In the afternoon it's popular with bike messengers and neighborhood slacker types; by night the BMW motorbike crowd clogs the outdoor deck, waiting its turn at the pool table. *199 Valencia St., at Duboce St., Mission District, 415/255–7505.*

BLUES

4 *d-6*

BISCUITS AND BLUES

Southern cuisine and southern blues make a great combination at Biscuits and Blues. Unlike at many clubs, all seats have an unobstructed view of the stage. Gospel dinner shows on Sunday are always popular. *401 Mason St., at Geary St., Union Square, 415/292–2583.*

4 *d-6*

THE BLUE LAMP

A friendly downtown hole in the wall, the Blue Lamp books blues, jazz, folk, and rock bands nightly. The crowd is a mix of laid-back regulars and music hounds following their favorite bands. *561 Geary St., at Taylor St., Union Square, 415/885–1464.*

3 *d-5*

ELI'S MILE HIGH CLUB

The reputed birthplace of West Coast blues remains a consistently good bet, continuing to highlight promising local acts, and some more-renowned performers. It's a small club with a pool table, soul food, and music Thursday through Saturday. *3629 Martin Luther King Jr. Way, between 36th and 37th Sts., Oakland, 510/655–6661.*

4 *e-3*

GRANT AND GREEN BLUES CLUB

A welcome contrast to the very civilized cafés and coffeehouses that dominate

North Beach, the dark, smoky Grant and Green Blues Club hosts raucous blues shows from time to time. *1731 Grant Ave., at Green St., North Beach, 415/693–9565.*

5 *c-6*

LAST DAY SALOON

Blues, Cajun, rock, and jazz artists frequent this always-packed club. *406 Clement St., between 5th and 6th Sts., Richmond District, 415/387–6343.*

8 *g-3*

MISSION ROCK RESORT

Unlike any other bar in San Francisco, this old-time spot with two outdoor decks on the waterfront attracts a supremely casual crowd drinking bottles of Bud. The pace picks up on live-music nights, usually Friday through Sunday. Save this one for a sunny day or one of San Francisco's rare warm nights. *817 China Basin, at Mission Rock St., China Basin, 415/621–5538.*

4 *e-4*

THE SALOON

The patrons are sometimes as entertaining as the tip-top performers at this atmospheric blues and R&B hangout in North Beach. Local R&B favorites Johnny Nitro and the Doorslammers play here frequently. *1232 Grant Ave., at Columbus Ave., North Beach, 415/989–7666.*

8 *b-1*

SLIM'S

One of the most popular clubs in town, Slim's specializes in what it labels "American roots music"—blues, jazz, classic rock—with a sprinkling of alternative rock and roll. Co-owner Boz Scaggs helps bring in the crowds and famous headliners. *333 11th St., between Folsom and Harrison Sts., South of Market, 415/255–0333.*

CABARET

4 *e-3*

BEACH BLANKET BABYLON

This zany San Francisco revue has been selling out most nights since 1974, with talented musicians and a wacky script that changes to incorporate topical references and characters. Although the choreography is colorful and the songs

witty, the real stars are the comically exotic costumes and famous ceiling-high headgear. Those under 21 may attend Sunday matinee performances only. *Club Fugazi, 678 Green St., at Powell St., North Beach, 415/421–4222.*

4 *e-4*

FINOCCHIO'S

This world-famous club has been generating confusion with its female impersonators since 1936. The decor hasn't changed much since then. To add to the retro mood, show tunes comprise the bulk of the repertoire. *506 Broadway, at Kearny St., North Beach, 415/982–9388.*

7 *g-2*

JOSIE'S CABARET AND JUICE JOINT

In a predominantly gay neighborhood, Josie's stages everything from serious theatrical pieces to stand-up comedy, drag acts, and cabaret. Drag chanteuse Musty Chiffon and cabaret singer Samantha Samuels have both made appearances here. *3583 16th St., at Market St., The Castro, 415/861–7933.*

SINGLES BARS

If you want to see San Franciscans wearing their best clothes and flirting like mad, check out the scene at the following places.

El Roys (Bars)
A cavernous spot that's hyper-trendy.

Gordon Biersch (Bars)
An old stand-by with good home-made brews.

Harry Denton's (Bars)
Live bands and dancing spice up the scene.

Holding Company (Bars)
The Embarcadero location means it's packed with Financial District workers in the early evening.

Johnny Love's (Bars)
A hit among Russian Hill professionals.

Perry's (Bars)
Pacific Heights and Marina residents mingle here.

`4` *d-6*

PLUSH ROOM

This cabaret space at the York Hotel (a.k.a. the "Empire," one of Kim Novak's hideaways in Alfred Hitchcock's *Vertigo*) has long been a place for torch singers and jazz divas. In recent years small comedies and monologues have been performed here, too. *940 Sutter St., between Leavenworth and Hyde Sts., Tenderloin, 415/885–2800.*

COMEDY

`4` *c-2*

COBB'S COMEDY CLUB

This well-established club books national performers, such as *Jake Johannsen, Rick Overton, and Janeane Garofalo*. Cannery lower courtyard, 2801 Leavenworth St., at Beach St., Northern Waterfront, 415/928–4320.

`4` *f-4*

THE PUNCH LINE

Big-name comics sometimes perform at this club, once a launching pad for the likes of Jay Leno and Whoopi Goldberg. The Sunday-night Comedy Showcase, a bargain at $5, features up-and-coming Bay Area comics. *444-A Battery St., 2nd floor, between Clay and Washington Sts., Financial District, 415/397–7573.*

DANCE CLUBS

`4` *c-8*

BAHIA CABANA

A multigenerational, international crowd dances at this tropical downtown supper club with mural-covered walls. Thursdays and Fridays are salsa nights; other evenings expect Brazilian, Caribbean, Jamaican, and Latin bands. *1600 Market St., at Franklin St., Hayes Valley, 415/626–3306.*

`4` *f-7*

THE BOX

This Thursdays-only, artsy-industrial SoMa club features "Mixtress" Page Hodel, who keeps the dressed-to-sweat crowd in constant motion with house, hip-hop, and funk sounds. For an extra treat, go-go platforms mounted on the walls showcase dancers who gyrate at full throttle. While the club is lesbian-run, the multicultural crowd includes

gay men and straights, too. *715 Harrison St., between 3rd and 4th Sts., South of Market, 415/647–8258.*

`8` *a-6*

CESAR'S LATIN PALACE

Cesar's Latin All-Stars play fiery salsa most nights at this alcohol-free club that attracts serious dancers. Early on you'll find older folks and even families here; things heat up later in the evening when it's mostly young, well-dressed Latinos. Open Friday through Sunday only, the club usually keeps going until 5 AM. *3140 Mission St., at César Chavez (Army) St., Mission District, 415/648–6611.*

`4` *d-6*

CLUB 181

If you're willing to brave an evening in the Tenderloin, Club 181 is a reliable choice on Friday and Saturday, the only nights it's open. Three different rooms, one sometimes closed for private events, feature either DJ dancing or live music. The cavernous front room is best for dancing, while the middle room, painted with swirly psychedelic colors, is where you shoot pool. Both the middle and back rooms have comfy couches. *181 Eddy St., at Taylor St., The Tenderloin, 415/673–8181.*

`4` *h-7*

CLUB TOWNSEND

Local DJs churn out sounds for a largely male crowd at this vast SoMa disco. "Club Universe" on Saturdays is less gender-specific, and the artsy-industrial decor changes to create a stunning new illusion each week. *177 Townsend St., between 2nd and 3rd Sts., South of Market, 415/974–1156.*

`4` *f-7*

COVERED WAGON

Mixed crowds gather here early in the evening before continuing on to other SoMa haunts, but as the night wears on the crowd becomes increasingly lesbian. Live funk, soul, and ska some nights attracts a crowd that's happy to get sweaty; other nights it's DJs dancing under the glow of black lights, against a backdrop of cheesy Western decor. *911 Folsom St., at 5th St., South of Market, 415/974–1585.*

4 *c-7*
DECO
If it weren't for the strains of funk, hip-hop, and acid jazz spilling out from this low-rent downtown club, it might be mistaken for a neighborhood bar. Three floors, each with its own ambience, will amuse you till the wee hours of the morning (when you'll probably want to take a cab home, or stick with a large group as you walk to the car). Look for two-for-one drink coupons in the free weeklies. *510 Larkin St., between Turk and Eddy Sts., The Tenderloin, 415/441–4007.*

8 *b-1*
DNA LOUNGE
Here's a hip but surprisingly low-attitude club, with eclectic acts ranging from rockabilly nights to tattoo and piercing shows. The crowd isn't afraid to break a sweat on the dance floor, but many come just to kick back in dimly lit corners downstairs. On Fridays, dance to the '70s retro-band, Grooveline. DJs usually come on after the live music. *375 11th St., at Harrison St., South of Market, 415/626–1409.*

8 *a-6*
EL RÍO
A healthy mix of men and women, straight and gay, turns up at this casual neighborhood hangout for different dance parties every night of the week. DJs spin a variety of tunes, alternative rock bands play live, and Sunday, you can work off the beer with some salsa dancing on the back patio. *3158 Mission St., at César Chavez (Army) St., Mission District, 415/282–3325.*

4 *e-8*
THE ENDUP
This primarily gay bar has a pool table, a gazebo, and a waterfall, all surrealistically situated almost underneath U.S. 101. Sundays starting at 9 AM, look for the hugely popular "Sunday T-Dance," a gay dance party that lasts until 2 AM Monday morning—a tradition for nearly a quarter of a century. Monday night is "Club Dread," a reggae DJ dance party. *995 Harrison St., at Harrison St., South of Market, 415/357–0827.*

8 *a-2*
ESTA NOCHE
Esta Noche plays a good mix of hard-pumping Latin, house music, and '70s disco to a crowd of mostly Latin gay men plus a handful of drag queens. Women, though few, will feel right at home. *3079 16th St., at Valencia St., Mission District, 415/861–5757.*

8 *d-2*
METRONOME BALLROOM
Turn up any night of the week for lessons in swing, Latin, and almost every other type of ballroom dance. The place is at its most lively on weekend nights, when dancers come to this mellow, smoke-free environment to practice their dance steps. *1830 17th St., at DeHaro St., Potrero Hill, 415/252–9000.*

7 *g-1*
NICKIE'S BBQ
Red-vinyl booths and Christmas lights decorate this unpretentious Lower Haight hole-in-the-wall. DJs spin something different every night—usually jazz and Latin on Thursday, '70s funk on Friday, funk and soul on Saturday, and reggae on Sunday. Patrons have a good time dancing, despite the elbow-to-elbow crush most nights. *460 Haight St., between Webster and Fillmore Sts., Lower Haight, 415/621–6508.*

4 *e-6*
OZ
Far from the industrial warehouses south of Market is this dance club on the top floor of the Westin St. Francis Hotel, accessible via a glass elevator. The weekend cover is outrageous and the music—a mix of oldies, disco, Motown, and a smattering of new (now old) wave—is hardly cutting-edge, but the marble floors, fabulous panorama of the city, and cushy sofas make it a memorable experience for out-of-towners. *Westin St. Francis Hotel, top floor, 335 Powell St., between Post and Geary Sts., Union Square, 415/774–0116.*

4 *e-4*
THE PALLADIUM
A mainstream club popular with bridge-and-tunnel types, the Palladium nevertheless seems to remain packed with a young crowd dancing urgently to house music. Beware of—or look for—men on the make, especially on Thursday nights, when drinks cost $1. *1031 Kearny St., at Broadway, North Beach, 415/434–1308.*

7 *f-3*

THE PHOENIX

For high-energy dance action outside SoMa, gay men have long favored the Phoenix. Great lighting and industrial decor go a long way towards spicing up the tiny dance floor, where the crowd tends to be extremely young. Admission is only $1 on Friday and Saturday nights. *482 Castro St., between 17th and 18th Sts., The Castro, 415/552–6827.*

4 *g-6*

THE SOUND FACTORY

Though tame by city standards, the Sound Factory's Friday-night deep-house dance extravaganza has been embraced by all-nighters as a favorite after-hours hangout. The large SoMa space is a maze of pulsating rooms. Call for upcoming events, which have recently featured a large dose of Latin beats, especially on Saturday nights. *525 Harrison St., at 1st St., South of Market, 415/243–9646.*

8 *c-1*

THE STUD

One of the city's oldest gay bars, with a gender-bending mix of straight, gay, and bisexual patrons, is a reliable choice any night of the week. The club's DJs mix

up-to-the-minute music with carefully chosen hits from the glory days of gay disco. The Tuesday-night club Trannyshack is especially popular, when cross-dressers enjoy "make-up tips and cheap cocktails." *399 9th St., at Harrison St., South of Market, 415/252–7883.*

4 *e-8*

1015 FOLSOM

This mixed gay and straight SoMa spot hosts enough varied music and dancers to make it refreshingly festive and attitude-free. The most crowded nights are Saturday, when the club "Release" features four dance scenes: '70s funk and disco, deep house, hip-hop, and live jazz. Weekdays are more relaxed, and you might actually be able to find a seat in the cozy upstairs lounge that's conveniently shielded from the blare of the speakers. *1015 Folsom St., at 6th St., South of Market, 415/431–1200.*

4 *g-7*

THE TROCADERO

Dancing to DJ industrial and live hard-core are the draws at this loud, minimally decorated SoMa space full of nooks and crannies. Wednesday night there's "Bondage A Go-Go," the oldest fetish dance club in California—it's a light introduction to the real S&M subculture. All ages are welcome to live shows. *520 4th St., between Bryant and Brannan Sts., South of Market, 415/495–6620.*

DINING & DANCING

4 *c-5*

COCONUT GROVE

A great place to display your finest clothes, Coconut Grove has a chic but whimsical ambience, with ceramic and metal palm trees, along with superb cocktails and nouvelle cuisine. Weeknights there's a '40s menu with "'40s prices" (prices climb on weekends). Swing and big band music are the big draws, but R&B and salsa also creep into the schedule. *1415 Van Ness Ave., between Bush and Pine Sts., Western Addition, 415/776–1616.*

4 *f-4*

SOL Y LUNA

An enthusiastic crowd dances to salsa or watches flamenco shows after dinner

---

FREE DANCE LESSONS

If you're looking to pick up a few dance pointers, the following clubs and bars give free lessons (though there's sometimes a cover to get in), usually before the band starts playing. Always call to confirm times and types of lessons; they change frequently.

330 Ritch (Dining and Dancing)
Swing and salsa lessons take place regularly.

Bahia Cabana (Dance Clubs)
Join in salsa classes on Thursday.

Cafe du Nord (Jazz)
Lessons in swing, samba, mambo, or cha-cha.

Cesar's Latin Palace (Dance Clubs)
Friday and Saturday salsa classes.

Hi-Ball Lounge (Bars)
Their swing dancing has a huge following.

Sol y Luna (Dining and Dancing)
Free salsa lessons.

at this popular supper club. Come in your best clothes (women will do well in slinky dresses) and prepare to dance with some of the city's better salsa dancers. DJs spin techno tunes after the flamenco shows some nights. *475 Sacramento St., between Battery and Sansome Sts., Financial District, 415/296–8191.*

4 *g-7*
330 RITCH STREET
Open Wednesday through Sunday, this popular SoMa dinner club attracts a classy crowd with its stylish decor, extensive tapas menu, wooden dance floor, and live jazz, salsa, and swing programming. Recently they've added more modern music to the mix, hosting DJ dance parties many evenings. There's a sizeable following for Thursday's Popscene, with BritPop, mod, and indie rock. *330 Ritch St., between Townsend and Bryant Sts., South of Market, 415/522–9558.*

4 *e-8*
UP AND DOWN CLUB
Sleek deco digs give this multilevel SoMa supper club the feel of a New York lounge. Upstairs you'll find a DJ laying down tracks, but little room to dance. Downstairs, Latin jazz and acid jazz heat up the room. *1151 Folsom St., between 7th and 8th Sts., South of Market, 415/626–2388. Closed Sun.*

JAZZ

2 *b-3*
BAUHAUS
A combination restaurant–jazz club–art gallery, this new supper club has curvy burnished silver furniture fitting the venue's name. In the slick, three-story interior, diners look through floor-to-ceiling windows and listen to mellow jazz—often guitarists—while eating contemporary American food that's pricier than at other city supper clubs. (What do you expect from a place that serves Beluga caviar?) *6139 Geary Blvd., at 25th St., Richmond District, 415/387–1151.*

4 *d-3*
BIMBO'S 365 CLUB
A large, plush room swathed in red draperies, Bimbo's retains a retro ambience apt for the "Cocktail Nation" programming that keeps the dance floor

hopping. Tickets to big-name progressive jazz and alternative rock bands often sell out in advance, but you can usually get tickets to shows by local acts at the door. *1025 Columbus Ave., at Bay St., Russian Hill, 415/474–0365.*

8 *a-3*
BRUNO'S
Restored in 1995 after years of neglect, Bruno's is a slice of retro heaven in a happening neighborhood. In one room diners eat elaborately presented meals at enormous red booths; next door well-dressed hipsters order swanky cocktails at the long bar and listen to the local jazz and swing bands. *2389 Mission St., between 19th and 20th Sts., Mission District, 415/550–7455.*

7 *g-2*
CAFÉ DU NORD
The atmosphere in this basement bar is decidedly casual, but the music, provided mostly by local talent, is strictly top-notch. Saturday nights usually feature the sultry crooning of local faves LaVay Smith & Her Red Hot Skillet Lickers. Those more interested in playing pool or socializing can do so in the front of the bar, while music lovers groove uninterrupted in the back. Dinner is served Wednesday through Saturday nights. *2170 Market St., at Sanchez St., The Castro, 415/861–5016.*

4 *d-8*
COCO CLUB
A variety of acts comes through this narrow, cozy, woman-owned restaurant and performance space south of Market—everything from acoustic rock to avant-garde jazz and blues. The club also hosts a few lesbian events each week, including a few cabarets. The entrance is on Minna Street. *139 8th St., at Minna St., South of Market, 415/626–2337.*

8 *a-3*
THE ELBO ROOM
This popular Mission watering hole becomes unmanageably crowded as the night progresses. Head upstairs for some of the best local live jazz, hip-hop, or occasional DJs and world music acts, or join the locals packed around the pool table. Happy hour stretches from 3 PM until 9 PM. *647 Valencia St., at 17th St., Mission District, 415/552–7788.*

8 *b-1*

ELEVEN

Jazz, funk, and Latin ensembles play from a 15-foot loft while diners enjoy food from the moderately priced Italian menu. A private cigar room rides the wave of one of the nation's hottest obsessions. *374 11th St., between Folsom and Harrison Sts., South of Market, 415/431–3337.*

ENRICO'S

The city's hippest North Beach hangout for a long spell after its 1958 opening, Enrico's is once again all the rage. The indoor–outdoor café has a mellow ambience, a fine menu (tapas and Italian), and mellow nightly jazz combos. *504 Broadway, at Kearny St., North Beach, 415/982–6223.*

4 *e-4*

JAZZ AT PEARL'S

This sedately romantic North Beach joint is one of the few reminders of North Beach's days as a hot spot for cool tunes. The talent level is remarkably high, featuring mostly traditional jazz in a dimly lit setting. During shows there's a two-drink minimum. *256 Columbus Ave., near Broadway, North Beach, 415/291–8255.*

4 *c-2*

LOU'S PIER 47

Though it's in one of the city's most touristed locations, Lou's waterfront bar attracts a laid-back local crowd with cool jazz and hot food. It's a fine place for a break in the middle of the day, as it's open daily from 6 AM until 9 PM. Most days see two bands perform: one in the late afternoon and one in the evening. *300 Jefferson St., at Jones St., Fisherman's Wharf, 415/771–0377.*

4 *f-3*

PIER 23

A waterfront restaurant by day, Pier 23 turns into a packed, unpretentious club at night. Musical arts range from jazz to salsa, Motown to reggae. *Embarcadero and Pier 23, The Embarcadero, 415/362–5125.*

5 *f-8*

STORYVILLE

Storyville switched gears and names in early 1996, going from the rock palace

Brave New World to a dressy, classic jazz club. Both front and back rooms have live music from Tuesday through Saturday. The kitchen serves Cajun cuisine. *1751 Fulton St., at Masonic Ave., Western Addition, 415/441–1751.*

3 *d-8*

YOSHI'S

Serious jazz aficionados make the trip to Oakland to see big names and local favorites perform at Yoshi's. Blues and Latin stars put on shows frequently. *510 Embarcadero St., between Washington and Clay Sts., Oakland, 510/238–9200.*

PIANO BARS

4 *b-7*

ACT IV LOUNGE

In the Inn at the Opera Hotel, Act IV is perhaps the most romantic lounge in the city, with dim lighting, sumptuous Victorian decor, and a crackling fireplace. It's so plush you probably won't even mind the occasionally snooty service. The most popular time to come (and most difficult to get in) is after symphony and opera performances. *333 Fulton St., between Franklin and Gough Sts., Hayes Valley, 415/553–8100.*

4 *e-5*

CLUB 36

On the top floor of the Grand Hyatt, Club 36 has piano music and a view of North Beach and the bay—both draws for out-of-towners. *345 Stockton St., between Post and Sutter Sts., Union Square, 415/398–1234.*

4 *d-6*

REDWOOD ROOM

The Clift Hotel's Art Deco lounge is a classic favorite, especially among martini drinkers. The low-key but sensuous ambience is enhanced by Klimt reproductions, and mellow piano music and jazz standards fill the room. *Clift Hotel, 495 Geary St., at Taylor St., Union Square, 415/775–4700.*

4 *e-5*

RITZ-CARLTON HOTEL

This lobby lounge in the city's most elegant hotel features a harpist during high tea (weekdays 2:30–4:30, weekends 1–4:30). Piano music, with occasional vocal accompaniment, takes over during cocktails—until 11:30 weeknights and 1:30 AM weekends. *600 Stockton St., at California St., Nob Hill, 415/296–7465.*

4 *c-5*
THE SWALLOW

For those who have had it with the young and buffed, this quiet, posh bar at the foot of Nob Hill caters to an older gay male clientele. Pianists play standards nightly from 9 PM to 1 AM, and patrons are often invited to croon along. *1750 Polk St., between Washington and Clay Sts., Nob Hill, 415/775–4152.*

ROCK

8 *e-2*
BOTTOM OF THE HILL

Squeeze into this bar at the bottom of Potrero Hill to hear promising local talent and touring bands. The atmosphere is ultra low-key, although the occasional nationally known act turns up here from time to time. It's one of the city's best bets for quality alternative rock bands. *1233 17th St., at Texas St., Potrero Hill, 415/626–4455.*

8 *a-3*
THE CHAMELEON

A cheap, grungy hold-out in a neighborhood that has recently been overrun by swanky retro bars, The Chameleon is a haven for local, experimental music. When your eardrums start to hurt, head downstairs for Ping-Pong and video games. *853 Valencia St., between 19th and 20th Sts., Mission District, 415/821–1891.*

2 *e-3*
THE FILLMORE

One of San Francisco's most famous rock music halls serves up a varied menu of national and local acts: rock, reggae, grunge, jazz, comedy, folk, acid house—you name it. To avoid paying steep service charges for events here, stop by their box office Sundays between 10 and 4. *1805 Geary Blvd., at Fillore St., Western Addition, 415/346–6000.*

4 *c-6*
GREAT AMERICAN MUSIC HALL

A gorgeous old theater that serves as a midsize concert venue, the Music Hall books an innovative blend of rock, blues, folk, jazz, and world music. The colorful marble-pillared building (constructed in 1907 as a bordello) also accommodates dancing at some shows. A bar menu is available most nights. *859 O'Farrell St., between Polk and Larkin Sts., The Tenderloin, 415/885–0750.*

4 *f-7*
HOTEL UTAH

All manner of local rock, jazz, and acoustic bands perform at this casual SoMa bar. The room in the back where bands play is so small that many patrons end up at the long wooden bar, supposedly shipped from Belgium during the Civil War. The crowd is eclectic and friendly—you'll find lawyers, bikers, and slackers—and a fine view of a U.S. 101 off-ramp is yours through the front windows. *500 4th St., at Bryant St., South of Market, 415/421–8308.*

ROMANTIC RENDEZVOUS

San Francisco is arguably the most romantic city in the United States. If you're not a true believer, try one of the following places.

Act IV (Piano Bars)
A fireplace illuminates the sumptuous Victorian decor.

Harry Denton's Starlite Room (Bars)
The most romantic of the city's rooftop bars.

The Lone Palm (Bars)
A retro atmosphere and excellent cocktails.

Redwood Room (Piano Bars)
A classy art deco lounge with mellow jazz music to set the mood.

Tosca (Bars)
A historic charmer with huge red booths.

8 *a-2*

KILOWATT

Saturdays and Sundays, Kilowatt hosts indie rock bands reaching maximum noise levels. The dark, smoky bar is usually filled with a mix of neighborhood locals. *3160 16th St., between Valencia and Guerrero Sts., Mission District, 415/861–2595.*

8 *b-1*

PARADISE LOUNGE

There are three different stages to choose from here; Sunday-night poetry slams, Tuesday-night open mics, and beyond-the-fringe theatrical performances at the connecting Transmission Theatre are just a small sampling. Although the quality of music varies widely, the broad selection ensures that there's always something worth hearing. *1501 Folsom St., at 11th St., South of Market, 415/861–6906.*

4 *e-4*

THE PURPLE ONION

Indulge in pints of Pabst Blue Ribbon, kick back in one of the oversized red vinyl booths, and enjoy garage-style punk and surf music at this once-famous underground North Beach lounge. *140 Columbus Ave., between Pacific Ave. and Jackson St., North Beach, 415/398–8415. Closed Sun.–Thurs.*

4 *e-7*

WARFIELD

This former movie palace was transformed into one of the city's largest venues for mainstream rock and roll. If you sit downstairs at the tables and chairs there's usually a two-drink minimum. Upstairs is a balcony with theater seating. Performers range from Porno for Pyros to Suzanne Vega to Harry Connick, Jr. *982 Market St., between 5th and 6th Sts., The Tenderloin, 415/775–7722.*

chapter 6

PARKS, GARDENS, & SPORTS

San Francisco is blessed with more than 3,500 acres of parkland and open space. Virtually every day of the year, you're sure to find San Franciscans engaging in all kinds of sporting activities on these large and small patches of green, enjoying everything from tennis to lawn bowling—and plenty of residents choose to use their magnificent parks and gardens simply as places to stroll, picnic, or read a book under a shady tree. Because it's surrounded on three sides by water, San Francisco is also prime territory for water sports: sailing, wind-surfing, sea kayaking, sculling, and "hanging ten" in that quintessential California sport, surfing. For information on races, tournaments, and other sporting events around the city, pick up a copy of the monthly City Sports magazine, available free at sporting-goods stores and many fitness centers.

parks

For the addresses and telephone numbers of city, state, and national parks departments, see Parks Information, in Chapter 1. For information on particular sports in each of the parks, see Sports & Outdoor Activities, below.

5 h-5
ALTA PLAZA PARK
This grassy Pacific Heights park has superb views of the city and beyond. Dog lovers will want to pay their respects at the Dog Park Walk of Fame—two long cement gutters on the north side of the park, in which neighborhood dog owners have carved the names of their four-legged friends. Bordered by Jackson, Steiner, Clay, and Scott Sts., Pacific Heights.

4 b-2, c-2
AQUATIC PARK
Though it's known primarily for its beach, Aquatic Park also has large manicured lawns that are great for picnics and lounging in the sun (or fog). Jefferson St. west of Hyde St., Fisherman's Wharf, 415/556–2904.

7 e-1
BUENA VISTA PARK
Long ago this steeply sloped hillside park was named Buena Vista (Spanish for "good view"), and with good reason: From the cypress- and eucalyptus-covered summit, the views north and west are among the finest in the city. The Golden Gate, the Pacific Ocean, the Bay Bridge, and downtown are all visible. Buena Vista used to be a famous spot for gay trysts; these days it's appreciated by all sorts of San Francisco residents, but—like many parts of the Haight—is best enjoyed during daylight hours. Haight and Lyon Sts., The Haight.

7 c-1
CHILDREN'S PLAYGROUND
The best and biggest playground in the city went up in 1887, but this magical place is continually being refurbished. Kids love the antique carousel. Kezar Dr. near Arguello Blvd., Golden Gate Park.

4 a-2
FORT MASON PARK
The fort itself, once a military command post, is now the headquarters of the Golden Gate National Recreation Area (see below), in the Marina. The Fort Mason Visitors Center (open weekdays 9:30–4:30) dispenses information on the Golden Gate National Recreation Area as well as all national parks in California, Oregon, and Washington. West of the fort, the gently rolling Great Meadow is a pleasant spot for walks, with lovely views of the northern waterfront. North of the Great Meadow is Fort Mason Center (see Historic Structures and Sights in Chapter 2), a series of warehouses built atop three piers, used as a headquarters for various artistic, cultural, recreational, and environmental organizations. The park and center are frequently the sites of fairs and concerts. Pick up the Fort Mason monthly newsletter (available free at any of the museums) for details on classes, lectures, concerts, and special exhibitions, or call the Fort Mason Center hot line (415/979–3010). For more information on the center and the fort itself, see Museums and Historic Buildings in Chapter 2). Marina Blvd. at Laguna St., The Marina.

7 *e-7*

GLEN CANYON PARK

Tucked away in a southwest corner of the city that is rarely visited by tourists, Glen Canyon Park is a complete escape from city life. Explore stands of eucalyptus, grassy hills, a bubbling stream, and even a few climbing boulders—but stay on the marked paths to avoid poison oak. *Between O'Shaughnessy and Diamond Heights Blvds., Diamond Heights.*

GOLDEN GATE PARK

San Francisco's most well-used playground encompasses 1,017 acres, making it one of the world's largest man-made parks. It's 3 mi long and ½ mi wide, stretching from the Pacific Ocean into the geographical heart of the city. In 1870, when William Hall, who became the first supervisor, was retained to prepare a topographic map, the land consisted of sand dunes and scrubby fauna. By 1943, when the fourth supervisor, John McLaren, ended his tenure at the age of 97, it was a shady paradise. A $6 million renovation completed in 1997 has made the park even better. Within its environs are 6,000 varieties of plants, a paddock field with bison, two lakes, vast green lawns for lolling, bridle paths, play areas for every manner of sports activity including golf and tennis, the jogger-filled Panhandle, and Sunday band concerts on the Music Concourse. You'll also find the tranquil Japanese Tea Garden, two Dutch windmills (built in 1902 and used for 20 years to irrigate the park), the beautiful Conservatory of Flowers, the Steinhart Aquarium and the Morrison Planetarium (both components of the California Academy of Sciences; *see* Science Museums *in* Chapter 2), the M. H. de Young Memorial Museum and the Asian Art Museum of San Francisco (*see* Art Museums *in* Chapter 2), and Strybing Arboretum. Free guided walking tours focusing on various aspects of the park depart frequently from the visitors centers; call for a current schedule. Most tours last about two hours. On Sundays, John F. Kennedy Drive, the park's main thoroughfare, is closed to car traffic between Stanyan Street and 19th Avenue, and flocks of bicyclists, in-line skaters, runners, and skateboarders take over. For park information and maps, drop by the **McLaren Lodge** (John F. Kennedy Dr., near Stanyan St., 415/831–2700) weekdays between 8 and 5. A second visitor center is on the western edge of the park in the charming, historic **Beach Chalet** (John F. Kennedy Dr., at Great Hwy.), which also houses a microbrewery and restaurant (*see* Contemporary *in* Chapter 3). *Bordered by Fulton St., Stanyan St., Lincoln Way, and the Great Hwy., Golden Gate Park.*

INSIDE GOLDEN GATE PARK

You could easily spend a day exploring Golden Gate Park's many attractions. The M.H. de Young Memorial Museum and the Asian Art Museum alone deserve several hours (see Art Museums in Chapter 2). In addition, you'll find the following major landmarks as you move through the park, from east to west.

Conservatory of Flowers (Gardens)
Golden Gate Park's oldest structure.

Children's Playground (Parks)
Kids love the antique carousel.

National AIDS Memorial Grove (Gardens)
A moving national monument in the midst of Golden Gate Park.

Steinhart Aquarium (Zoos & Aquariums)
Gaze at the sharks, touch the starfish, and watch the penguins being fed.

Shakespeare Garden (Gardens)
Bring along your Folio edition of Romeo and Juliet.

Japanese Tea Garden (Gardens)
Sip green tea while gazing at the koi fish.

Music Concourse (Gardens)
Site of free summer concerts.

Strybing Arboretum and Botanical Gardens (Gardens)
70 acres of formal gardens.

Golden Gate Park Stadium/Polo Field (Stadiums)
The San Francisco Marathon ends here.

Golden Gate Park Stables (Sports & Outdoor Activities)
San Francisco's only stable.

Queen Wilhelmina Tulip Garden (Gardens)
What could be more Dutch?

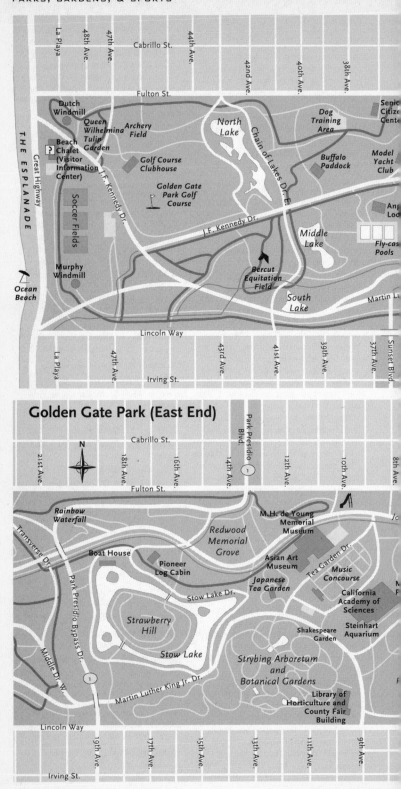

La Playa
48th Ave.
47th Ave.
Cabrillo St.
44th Ave.
4nd Ave.
40th Ave.
38th Ave.

Fulton St.

Dutch
Windmill

Queen
Wilhelmina
Tulip
Garden

Archery
Field

North
Lake

Chain of Lakes Dr. E.

Dog
Training
Area

Senic
Citizen
Cente

Beach
Chalet
(Visitor
Information
Center)

Golf Course
Clubhouse

Golden Gate
Park Golf
Course

Buffalo
Paddock

Model
Yacht
Club

THE ESPLANADE

Great Highway

J.F. Kennedy Dr.

J.F. Kennedy Dr.

Middle
Lake

Ang
Lod

Fly-cas
Pools

Soccer Fields

Murphy
Windmill

Bercut
Equitation
Field

South
Lake

Martin Lu

Ocean
Beach

Lincoln Way

Irving St.

La Playa
47th Ave.
43rd Ave.
41st Ave.
39th Ave.
37th Ave.
Sunset Blvd.

Golden Gate Park (East End)

N

21st Ave.
18th Ave.
16th Ave.
14th Ave.
Cabrillo St.
Park Presidio Blvd.
12th Ave.
10th Ave.
8th Ave.

Fulton St.

Rainbow
Waterfall

M.H. de Young
Memorial
Museum

Jo

Transverse Dr.

Boat House

Redwood
Memorial
Grove

Pioneer
Log Cabin

Asian Art
Museum

Tea Garden Dr.

Music
Concourse

Japanese
Tea Garden

Park Presidio Bypass Dr.

Stow Lake Dr.

California
Academy of
Sciences

M

Strawberry
Hill

Shakespeare
Garden

Steinhart
Aquarium

Middle Dr. W.

Stow Lake

Strybing Arboretum
and
Botanical Gardens

Martin Luther King Jr. Dr.

Library of
Horticulture and
County Fair
Building

Lincoln Way

19th Ave.
17th Ave.
15th Ave.
13th Ave.
11th Ave.
9th Ave.

Irving St.

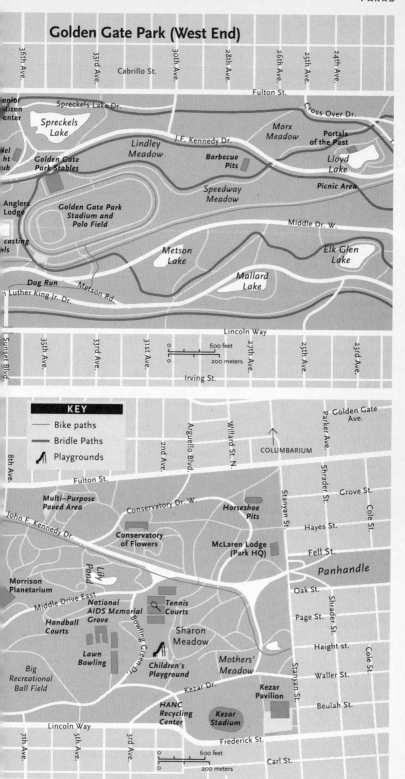

Golden Gate Park (West End)

36th Ave.
33rd Ave.
Cabrillo St.
30th Ave.
28th Ave.
26th Ave.
25th Ave.
24th Ave.
Fulton St.

Senior Citizen Center
Spreckels Lake Dr.
Cross Over Dr.

Spreckels Lake
Marx Meadow
Portals of the Past

Model Yacht Club
Lindley Meadow
J.F. Kennedy Dr.
Barbecue Pits
Lloyd Lake

Golden Gate Park Stables
Speedway Meadow
Picnic Area

Anglers Lodge
Middle Dr. W.

Casting Pools
Golden Gate Park Stadium and Polo Field
Elk Glen Lake

Metson Lake
Mallard Lake

Dog Run
Metson Rd.
Martin Luther King Jr. Dr.

Lincoln Way

Sunset Blvd.
35th Ave.
33rd Ave.
31st Ave.
27th Ave.
25th Ave.
23rd Ave.

| 0 | 600 feet |
| 0 | 200 meters |

Irving St.

KEY
— Bike paths
━ Bridle Paths
𝄃 Playgrounds

Golden Gate Ave.
Parker Ave.

8th Ave.
2nd Ave.
Arguello Blvd.
Willard St. N.
COLUMBARIUM
Shrader St.

Fulton St.

Multi-Purpose Paved Area
Conservatory Dr. W.
Horseshoe Pits
Grove St.
Cole St.

John F. Kennedy Dr.
Stanyan St.
Hayes St.

Conservatory of Flowers
McLaren Lodge (Park HQ)
Fell St.

Morrison Planetarium
Lily Pond
Panhandle

Middle Drive East
Oak St.
Shrader St.

National AIDS Memorial Grove
Tennis Courts
Page St.

Handball Courts
Sharon Meadow
Shrader St.

Lawn Bowling
Children's Playground
Mothers' Meadow
Haight st.
Cole St.

Big Recreational Ball Field
Bowling Green Q
Kezar Dr.
Waller St.

Kezar Pavilion
Stanyan St.

HANC Recycling Center
Kezar Stadium
Beulah St.

Lincoln Way
7th Ave.
5th Ave.
3rd Ave.
Frederick St.
Carl St.

| 0 | 600 feet |
| 0 | 200 meters |

2 *a-7*

HARDING PARK

Within Harding Park are two golf courses, Jack Fleming Golf Course, and Harding Park Municipal Golf Course, as well as Lake Merced, the San Francisco Water Department's emergency reservoir and a popular spot for fishing and boating. A 5-mi jogging path encircles the lake, wending through stands of eucalyptus, cypress, and pine, as well as fields of wildflowers, ferns, and ice plants. *Harding Rd., near Skyline Blvd., Sunset District.*

4 *g-4*

JUSTIN HERMAN PLAZA

In the shadow of the Ferry Building, Justin Herman Plaza is a favorite haunt of brown-bagging office workers. The center of the plaza is dominated by Vaillancourt Fountain, a free-form sculpture made of 101 concrete boxes. Jean Dubuffet's mammoth stainless-steel sculpture, *La Chiffonière*, is also here. During the winter holiday season, Justin Herman Plaza converts to an ice-skating rink. At other times of year it hosts free concerts, usually Wednesdays or Fridays at noon. *Market and Steuart Sts., The Embarcadero.*

4 *a-5, b-5*

LAFAYETTE PARK

Visited by dog walkers, picnickers, and sunbathers, this Pacific Heights park has expansive lawns that slope to a wooded crest—just as those of any well-behaved English-style garden should. On the north side of the park is Spreckels Mansion (2080 Washington Street), an imposing 1913 French baroque structure. Though not as dramatic or expansive as other parks in the neighborhood, it's a pleasant stop. *Bordered by Washington, Gough, Sacramento, and Laguna Sts., Pacific Heights.*

2 *b-2*

LINCOLN PARK

This 270-acre greensward is along the headlands of Point Lobos, in the Richmond District. The 200-ft cliffs add drama to the breathtaking view of the Golden Gate Bridge. At the park's eastern end are the beautiful California Palace of the Legion of Honor and the city's oldest golf course, whose fairways are lined with large Monterey cypresses. *North of Clement St., west of 33rd Ave., Richmond District.*

2 *e-1*

MARINA GREEN

This wide waterfront lawn is a favored spot of joggers (there's a 2½-mi jog and exercise course), in-line skaters, bicyclists, kite-fliers, sunbathers, and those in need of a restful place to gaze out across the water to the Golden Gate Bridge. On weekends, people come here for pickup games, especially soccer and volleyball. Offshore stretches the sailboat-filled Marina Small Craft Harbor. *Marina Blvd. at Fillmore St., The Marina.*

2 *f-7*

MCLAREN PARK

Though McLaren Park is somewhat inconveniently located in a southern corner of the city, it's a gem for those who live near it. Besides wide green lawns and groves of eucalyptus, the park has two small ponds, a playground, boccie courts, tennis courts, and the Gleneagles International Golf Course. *Mansell St., off University St., Visitacion Valley.*

7 *h-3*

MISSION DOLORES PARK

The views of downtown San Francisco, the Bay Bridge, and the East Bay are superb from the north end of Mission Dolores Park, in the midst of a well-to-do residential section of the Mission district. Set on a gently sloping hill, it's a favorite among picnickers and sunbathers on pleasant days; it also has tennis courts, a basketball court, a playground, and a popular dog-run area. Look for the gold fire hydrant at the park's southwest corner. When all the other hydrants went dry during the firestorm that followed the 1906 earthquake, this one kept pumping. *Bordered by 18th, Dolores, 20th, and Church Sts., Mission District.*

5 *f-3*

THE PRESIDIO

The Presidio, a 1,480-acre stretch of prime waterfront land stretching from the western end of the Marina all the way to the Golden Gate Bridge, began its life as a military installation (*see* Historic Sites & Architecture *in* Chapter 2). On October 1, 1994, it became part of the National Park system, though the army will remain here for a while longer in a reduced capacity. By 2010 it will be fully converted for use as a park, with an additional 200 acres of open space restored and more than 100 additional acres replanted with native vegetation—but for now you can still count on finding rolling hills crossed by 11 mi of hiking trails and 14 mi of biking routes; 620 historic buildings; and stunning views of the bay. A few paths lead through a man-made forest of 400,000 pine, cypress and eucalyptus trees; these were planted in the 1880s by schoolchildren and soldiers to make the area look more vast than it actually is. Stop by the **Presidio's Visitors Information Center** (Lincoln Blvd., at Montgomery St., 415/561–4323) to pick up maps or trail guides. On weekends there are free ranger-led walks through the Presidio: These include the 2-mi Ecology Walk, which covers the area's natural history and development; the two-hour Coastal Defense Walk, which includes Fort Point and considers the area's strategic history; and a Tidal Zone Walk along part of the Golden Gate Promenade. Guided hikes range from 45 minutes to three hours.

Stretching along the bay side of the Presidio is Crissy Field, a popular area for pick-up sports, picknicking, kite-flying, and just offshore, windsurfing. Baker Beach (*see below*) is on the Pacific Ocean side of the Presidio. Along the south side of the Presidio are the Presidio Golf Course and Julius Kahn Playground, which has basketball courts. *Entrance at Lombard and Lyon Sts., The Presidio.*

4 d-4
INA COOLBRITH PARK
The funky little staircase at Vallejo and Mason streets will transport you to handkerchief-size Ina Coolbrith Park, which has shady trees and views of Oakland and the Bay Bridge. Continue straight through the intersection of Taylor and Vallejo Streets to a flower-lined path that ends at San Simone Park, where you'll find amazing views of Alcatraz and the East Bay. *Vallejo and Taylor Sts., Russian Hill.*

6 g-8
STERN GROVE
Most San Franciscans think of this 63-acre park as the spot for free Sunday concerts (*see* Events *in* Chapter 2), which have been held here every summer since 1937. During the rest of the year it's an enchanting place for a walk through groves of eucalyptus, redwood, and fir. Besides the natural amphitheater, the park has a playground (just inside the 19th Avenue entrance), picnic and barbecue facilities, croquet lawns,

and a small putting green. *Wawona St. and 19th Ave., Sunset District.*

4 g-7
SOUTH PARK
South Park's proximity to the city's "multimedia gulch" sector of SoMa has earned it the moniker "South Spark." The tree-filled, Parisian-style square is a wel-

---

THE BIGGEST URBAN PARK IN THE WORLD

With 76,500 acres of maritime parks, yacht harbors, ocean beaches, islands, and historic points of interest stretching along 28 mi of coastline in San Francisco and the counties of Marin and San Mateo, the Golden Gate National Recreation Area (GGNRA) maintains more urban parkland than any other city in the world. Congress created the GNNRA in 1972, in part to protect the coastal lands of San Francisco and Marin County from commercial development. In the Marin Headlands, across the Golden Gate Bridge, the GGNRA encompasses wildlife sanctuaries, 100 mi of trails through vast areas of undeveloped lands, and picnic facilities. A few of the highlights:

Aquatic Park (Beaches)
  Barrel-chested swimmers brave the ice-cold water 365 days a year.

Fort Mason (Parks)
  Once a former military command post, now a thriving cultural center.

Marina Green (Parks)
  Look for multicolored kites in the sky and billowing sails in the water.

Baker Beach (Beaches)
  Prime views of the Golden Gate Bridge, Marin Headlands, and the bay.

China Beach (Beaches)
  A swimming beach in the midst of an elegant neighborhood.

Lands End (Beaches)
  Secluded enough for nude sunbathing.

Ocean Beach (Beaches)
  Wild and windy; a prime seal-viewing spot.

Fort Funston(Beaches)
  Hang gliders soar from Funston's cliffs.

come oasis in an area otherwise glutted with warehouses and office buildings; on weekdays its dozens of inviting benches are peopled with graphic artists, writers, architects, attorneys, and computer programmers. Surrounding the park are several cafés and restaurants. For tykes, there's a playground. *South Park Ave., between 2nd and 3rd Sts., South of Market.*

2 *d-4*
SUTRO FOREST
Behind the University of California at San Francisco Medical Center stretches a hilly tract of land thickly forested with eucalyptus and pine trees. While it isn't neatly groomed like nearby Golden Gate Park, it does have some pleasant hiking trails and far fewer crowds. Overlooking the forest is Mt. Sutro (elevation 908 ft), one of the city's tallest hills. *Parnassus Ave. at 2nd Ave., Twin Peaks.*

4 *f-4*
TRANSAMERICA REDWOOD GROVE
This cool pocket-size park is adjacent to the landmark Transamerica Building. It's one of few places in San Francisco outside Golden Gate Park where mighty California Redwood trees grow—a welcome sight for businesspeople on their lunch hour. *Between Washinton and Clay Sts., just west of Montgomery St., Financial District.*

URBAN PARKS WITH HIKING TRAILS

Who said you need to leave San Francisco to hike through the great outdoors?

Glen Canyon Park (Parks)
Follow a bubbling brook through a canyon.

Golden Gate Park (Parks)
Meander past gardens, museums, forests, and even a pair of Dutch windmills and a herd of bison.

Lincoln Park (Parks)
Ends at beautiful Lands End beach.

The Presidio (Parks)
1,480 acres of prime waterfront land.

Sutro Forest (Parks)
Groves full of eucalyptus and pine.

---

4 *e-6*
UNION SQUARE
All day long shoppers charge through and around palm tree–filled Union Square (and underneath it—it covers a subterranean parking lot), toting colorful shopping bags. As the park at the heart of the city's most fashionable shopping district, Union Square hosts many entertainment and civic events—including an ice-skating rink in winter. City planners recently held a contest to redesign the park, and a complete facelift is due in the near future. *Bordered by Post, Stockton, Geary, and Powell Sts., Union Square.*

4 *f-4*
WALTON PARK
Convenient to the Ferry Building, Embarcadero Center, and the Jackson Square Historical District is this attractive downtown park with a soothing fountain as its centerpiece. Plantings of grass, willows, and pine trees create a soothing refuge from the urban jungle. *Bordered by Pacific Ave., Davis St., Jackson St., and Front St., The Embarcadero.*

4 *e-3*
WASHINGTON SQUARE
This small park has a European feel: It's overlooked by the Romanesque church of Sts. Peter and Paul and surrounded by the quaint Italian neighborhood of North Beach. Afternoons, flocks of old men gather to reminisce (in Italian) and chew long-dead cigars; early mornings, Chinese men and women arrive to practice the graceful movements of tai chi. *Bordered by Filbert, Stockton, Union, and Powell Sts., North Beach.*

other green spaces

BEACHES

4 *b-2, c-2*
AQUATIC PARK
Surrounded on three sides by the bustle of Fort Mason, Fisherman's Wharf, and Ghiradelli Square is a quiet cove with large manicured lawns, a quarter-mile stretch of sandy beach, and gentle water. Aquatic Park was created as a WPA project in 1937. Arrive early in the

day and you might spy a curious kind of marine mammal: Members of the city's Dolphin Club swim in its ice-cold waters every morning, with the largest turnout on New Year's Day. Also here: The gleaming white National Maritime Museum Building (originally a bathhouse). *Jefferson St., west of Hyde St., Fisherman's Wharf, 415/556–2904. Restrooms, snack bar, showers.*

2 *b-2*

BAKER BEACH

This 1-mi-long sandy beach is a local favorite, especially among anglers, picnickers, and sunbathers (including nude bathers who gather north of the high-tide sign). Treacherous waves make swimming here dangerous (there are no lifeguards); but you can enjoy stunning views of the Golden Gate Bridge, Marin Headlands, and the bay. On weekends, rangers provide tours of the 95,000-pound cannon at Battery Chamberlin, which overlooks the beach. Though the 1904 cannon is no longer used to defend the San Francisco harbor from seafaring invaders, it can still be manually cranked into firing position. *Gibson Rd., off Bowley St., The Presidio, 415/556–8371. Grills, drinking water, restrooms, picnic tables.*

2 *b-2*

CHINA BEACH

One of the city's safest swimming beaches is also the most convenient, with free changing rooms, showers, and seasonal lifeguards. China Beach was named for the poor Chinese fishermen who camped here in the 1870s (though it's sometimes marked on maps as Phelan Beach). It's comprised of a 600-foot sandy strip just south of The Presidio, surrounded by multi-million dollar homes. *Seacliff Ave., off 26th Ave., Richmond District, 415/556–8371. Drinking water, restrooms, changing rooms, showers.*

2 *a-7*

FORT FUNSTON

The beach at Fort Funston, south of Ocean Beach, is often buffeted by strong winds. That's what makes it so popular with Bay Area hang gliders, who launch from Funston's high cliffs, then soar overhead. Stay clear from takeoff and landing areas; there's a marked viewing area for spectators. A short, gentle paved loop trail provides bird's-

eye views of the Pacific and a few pleasant picnic spots. *Off Skyline Blvd. (Rte. 35), south of Sloat Blvd., Sunset District, 415/556–8371. Phones, restrooms, picnic tables.*

2 *a-2*

LANDS END

The secluded beach at Lands End may be difficult to reach, but it rewards visitors with breathtaking coastal views. To reach it, follow the 1-mi-long Lands End trail from the parking lot near the Sutro Baths. The trail through pine and cypress stands is a magnet for hikers, mountain bikers, and picnickers. The beach itself is largely clothing-optional. Dangerous offshore currents make swimming unsafe. *Trailhead at Merrie Way and Point Lobos Ave., Richmond District, 415/556–8371. Grills, restrooms, picnic tables.*

2 *a-3*

OCEAN BEACH

Stretching along the Great Highway at the western (ocean) edge of the city is this 4-mi-long-wide sand beach. The waves are mighty, the wind is gusty, and it's often shrouded by fog. It's certainly not the city's cleanest beach, but Ocean Beach remains dear to San Franciscans, and for a long walk or jog it's ideal. Lovers gather at sunset and tourists come to peer at Seal Rocks, stony off-

---

PICNIC-PERFECT

When the fog's away, San Franciscans pack a picnic lunch and go out to play. The following places beg to be chosen as your picnic spot.

Baker Beach (Beaches)
Stunning views of the Golden Gate Bridge.

Golden Gate Park (Parks)
The crown jewel in the city's park system.

Lafayette Park (Parks)
A grassy slope surrounded by Pacific Heights mansions.

Mission Dolores Park (Parks)
Look for ice-cream salesmen on summer days.

Stern Grove (Parks)
Site of free evening summertime concerts since 1973.

shore islands so named because seals used to sun themselves here before relocating to Fisherman's Wharf. Extremely dangerous currents make swimming risky, though it's the beach of choice for daredevil surfers. While here, don't miss a visit to the historic Cliff House (see Historic Structures and Sights in Chapter 2). *Great Highway, between Balboa St. and Sloat Blvd., Richmond District, 415/556–8317. Restrooms.*

GARDENS

Golden Gate Park is a bonanza of blooms, with a number of smaller garden plantings in addition to the more major gardens described below. Most gardens in and outside of Golden Gate Park are open daily from dawn until dusk.

3 *e-1*

BERKELEY ROSE GARDEN

Built during the Depression, the terraced rose garden is perched on a Berkeley hilltop, making it an attractive spot to picnic or to watch the sunset. It has more than 3,000 flowering rose-bushes that dazzle the senses. *Euclid Ave., between Bayview Pl. and Eunice St., Berkeley.*

7 *b-1*

CONSERVATORY OF FLOWERS

This magnificent classic Victorian structure, shipped from England and reconstructed on this site in 1879, is the oldest building in Golden Gate Park. It is listed in the National Register of Historic Places as a civil-engineering landmark. The Conservatory is currently closed for renovations and will reopen sometime after the year 2000, when it will once again bloom with rare tropical plants. *John F. Kennedy Dr., at Conservatory Dr. West, Golden Gate Park.*

FILOLI

In addition to its gracious mansion (see Historic Sites & Architecture, in Chapter 2), Filoli is justly known for its 16 acres of lovely formal gardens. These were planned and developed over a period of more than 50 years. Among the designs are a sunken garden, walled garden, woodland garden, yew alley, and a rose garden developed by the last private owner, Mrs. William P. Roth, with more than 50 bushes of all types and colors. There's also a charming Italian Renais-

sance–style teahouse. Spring is the best time to visit, though blooms come up as early as February, and the mild California climate means the gardens are enjoyable through October. The house and gardens are open from mid-February through the end of October, Tuesday through Thursday for guided tours (reservations essential), and Friday and Saturday for self-guided tours. *Cañada Rd. near Edgewood Rd., Woodside, 650/364–8300. Admission: $10, $1 children 2–12.*

7 *b-3*

GARDEN FOR THE ENVIRONMENT

The San Francisco League of Urban Gardeners (SLUG) keeps a greenhouse and garden with drought-tolerant plants. Through workshops, community programs, and tours, the group educates visiting gardeners about benefits of water-wise and pesticide-free gardening and composting. Vegetables are grown on the premises and distributed to homeless people. Though the park is open daily to the public, it is only staffed Wednesdays between 9 and 2, and Saturdays from 10 to 4. Once a month there's a free garden tour (usually on Sunday afternoons); call for a current schedule. *7th Ave. and Lawton St., Sunset District, 415/285–7584.*

7 *a-1*

JAPANESE TEA GARDEN

This beautiful 4-acre garden in Golden Gate Park was created in 1894 as a Japanese village for the California Mid-Winter Exhibit. It is a tranquil oasis of koi-filled pools, streams, bridges, a pagoda, an 18th-century bronze Buddha, torii gates, and, in spring, a dazzling array of pink and white cherry blossoms and azaleas. The Hagiwara family took care of the garden until World War II when they, along with other Japanese Americans, were removed to internment camps. In 1994, on the garden's 100th-year anniversary, a cherry blossom tree was planted in their memory. A Peace Lantern that hangs in the garden was presented to the city by Japanese schoolchildren. The teahouse near the main gates serves green tea and fortune cookies. The garden is in the eastern half of the park, next to the Asian Art Museum. *Tea Garden Dr., between John F. Kennedy Dr. and Martin Luther King Dr., Golden Gate Park, 415/752–4227. Admission: $2.50, $1 children 6–12 and senior citizens.*

7 *a-1*

MUSIC CONCOURSE

This little patch of Golden Gate Park has been the site of free summer Sunday concerts (weather permitting) since 1882. *Near John F. Kennedy and Tea Garden Drs., Golden Gate Park.*

7 *b-1*

NATIONAL AIDS MEMORIAL GROVE

In 1991 hundreds of volunteers labored to create the first living memorial to those lost to AIDS at this 15-acre wooded area (a portion of which was formerly de Laveaga Dell) at the east end of Golden Gate Park. In 1996 Congress and President Clinton signed a bill that granted the Memorial Grove status as a national monument to people with AIDS. *Middle Dr. East, just west of tennis courts, Golden Gate Park, 415/750–8340.*

6 *b-1*

QUEEN WILHELMINA TULIP GARDEN

In the northwest corner of Golden Gate Park adjacent to the historic Dutch Windmill stands this tulip garden some 10,000 tulip plants strong. Bulbs are planted every October and burst into full bloom in February and March. *John F. Kennedy Dr., at Great Hwy., Golden Gate Park, Golden Gate Park.*

7 *a-1*

SHAKESPEARE GARDEN

This is a small garden with more than 200 flowers mentioned in the Bard's works, together with related quotations engraved on bronze plaques. It's in Golden Gate Park, just southwest of the California Academy of Sciences. *Middle Dr. East, near Martin Luther King Jr. Dr., Golden Gate Park.*

7 *a-2*

STRYBING ARBORETUM AND BOTANICAL GARDENS

One of the finest botanical gardens in the country, Strybing is a 70-acre wonderland filled with some 5,000 plant specimens displayed in 17 formal gardens. Arrangements are by country of origin, genus, or even (for the visually impaired) by fragrance. You'll see plants from Australia, South Africa, Chile, and Asia; highlights include the California Native Plants Garden, the Redwood Trail (which winds through a stand of these mighty California trees), the Succulent Garden, and the

Asian Cloud Forest garden. Free guided garden walks take place daily at 1:30 PM with additional tours weekends at 10:30 AM. Free guided theme walks (usually exploring a section of the gardens at its peak blooming period) vary by season; call for a current schedule. Or pick up maps and brochures for a self-guided tour at the Strybing bookstore. The adjacent Helen Crocker Russell Library of Horticulture is an 18,000 volume library that also has rotating exhibits of botanical art. A $1 donation is requested for admission to the arboretum and gardens. *9th Ave. at Lincoln Way, Golden Gate Park, 415/661–1316.*

3 *f-2*

UNIVERSITY OF CALIFORNIA BOTANICAL GARDEN

The university's garden is a valuable research and education center with a diverse collection of plants—more than 10,000 neatly labeled species from around the world. Most of the plants are arranged by region, everything from South African desert to Himalayan forest. There are also specialized plots like the Chinese Medicinal Herb Garden and the Garden of Economic Plants, as well as three indoor exhibits and an extensive rhododendron collection. The location, high in the hills east of Strawberry Canyon, means superb views of the bay. Admission to the garden is $3, free on Thursdays. *200 Centennial Dr., on U.C. Berkeley campus, Berkeley, 510/642–3343. Free tours weekends at 1:30.*

4 *f-6*

YERBA BUENA GARDENS

This $2 billion SoMa arts, performance, garden, and residential complex opened to much fanfare in 1993, after more than 30 years of planning and bureaucratic disputes. The core of the Yerba Buena Gardens complex comprises the Moscone Convention Center, the Center for the Arts and SFMOMA (for both, *see* Art Museums *in* Chapter 2), and two major garden spaces, the Esplanade and the East Garden. The Esplanade, a 5½-acre garden atop the Moscone Center, is a blend of art and plantlife, including an outdoor stage, a grass meadow, two cafés with outdoor terraces, and a city garden full of the native plants of San Francisco's sister cities: carpet bugle (a ground cover) from Haifa, Israel; orchid rockrose (a shrub) from Assisi, Italy; and white and yellow marguerite chrysanthemums from San Francisco. A reflecting pool cascades down a 22-foot high, 50-foot wide waterfall that leads to an etched-glass Martin Luther King, Jr. Memorial. At the northeastern part of the Esplanade meadow is the Cho-En (Butterfly Garden), planted with wildflowers that attract various species of native San Francisco butterflies. At the Third Street entry to the complex, the East Garden mixes eastern and western ideas; for example a group of European sycamores is planted in a triangle (the triangle is the Japanese symbol for Heaven, Earth, and Man). Also in the East Garden are a quiet lawn and a terrace, a cascading fountain, and a small performance area. Both gardens are scattered with interesting sculptures. Under construction is a Children's Center that will have a historic turn-of-the-century carousel, a learning garden, a play stream and fountain, a labyrinth made of hedges, an outdoor amphitheater, and more open lawn areas. *3rd and 4th Sts., between Mission and Howard Sts., South of Market.*

zoos & aquariums

6 *b-8*

CHILDREN'S ZOO

More than 250 mammals, birds, reptiles, and amphibians are housed at the Children's Zoo, on 7 acres adjacent to the San Francisco Zoo. The pint-size pleasures here include a baby animal nursery, nature trail, exhibit of native American animals, nature theater, barnyard petting zoo, and fascinating insect zoo full of creepy-crawlies. During the Petting Zoo "Livestock Stampede" (weekends at 10:45 AM) kids can help feed breakfast to the goats and sheep. *Sloat Blvd. at Great Hwy., Sunset District, 415/753–7080. Admission $1, children under 3 free. Open weekdays 11–4, weekends 10:30–4:30.*

6 *c-8*

SAN FRANCISCO ZOO

Northern California's largest zoological park is home to 220 species of birds and animals, including 15 endangered species such as the snow leopard, orangutan, and black rhino. The zoo's enclosures have been carefully designed to create as natural a setting

as possible for these wild inhabitants: Gorilla World, a $2 million exhibit, is the largest and finest gorilla habitat of any zoo in the world, with three generations of gorillas. Several endangered monkey species live in the Primate Discovery Center. The Feline Conservation Center is a 20,000-sq-ft sanctuary for rare and endangered cats such as the ocelot and jaguar; and the South American Gateway exhibit contains 7 acres of rain forest where tapirs and howler monkeys roam. Other enclosures of note include Koala Crossing, Otter River, the Lion House, and the Australian Walkabout. Don't forget to say hello to popular resident Prince Charles, a rare white tiger (the first of its kind to be exhibited in the West), and the zoo's newest acquisitions, a group of Madagascar aye-ayes, one of the world's rarest primate species. Feeding time is 2 PM Tuesday–Sunday for the big cats, preceded by a "chat with the catkeeper" daily at 1:15 PM. The penguins are fed at 3 PM daily. Additional admission fees apply to the Children's Zoo (*see above*), the circa 1921 carousel ($2 per person), and the Safari Tour Train ($2.50 per person) which winds through the park. *Sloat Blvd., at 45th Ave., Sunset District, 415/753–7080. Admission: $7, $3.50 senior citizens over 64 and children 12–15, $1.50 children 3–11, children 2 and under free; free first Wed. of month. Open daily 10–5.*

7 *a-1*

STEINHART AQUARIUM

Steinhart, part of the California Academy of Sciences complex (*see* Science Museums *in* Chapter 2) in Golden Gate Park, houses a splendid collection of 600 species of fresh and saltwater fish, reptiles and amphibians, and even a flock of adorable black-footed penguins. The piranhas, manatees, jellyfish, sea horses, and other creatures live in 165 tanks designed to approximate natural habitats as closely as possible. The Fish Roundabout is a 100,000-gallon circular tank with saltwater fish such as tuna and salmon swimming in schools. The Touch Tidepool is a collection of sea stars, anemones, hermit crabs, and urchins that visitors can look at and touch. Two of the newest exhibits are the 600,000 gallon Living Coral Reef display, which features dazzling tropical fish and corals, and the Sharks of the Tropics display, with sleek three- to five-foot nurse sharks, black tips, and white tips. The penguins are fed daily at 11:30 AM and 4 PM. The Fish Roundabout feeding time is 2 PM daily. Admission to the aquarium gives you access to the Natural History Museum as well. *California Academy of Sciences, between John F. Kennedy and Martin Luther King Jr. Drs., Golden Gate Park, 415/750–7145. Admission: $8.50; $2 children 4–11; $5.50 students 12–17 and senior citizens 65 and older; free first Wed. of month. Open Memorial Day–Labor Day, daily 9–6; Labor Day–Memorial Day, daily 9–5 (until 8:45 PM first Wed. of the month).*

4 e-1, e-2
UNDERWATER WORLD

At this unique "diver's-eye view" aquarium, visitors listen to a taped 30-minute tour while traveling along a 300-ft-long transparent tunnel surrounded by swimming creatures of the sea. It's a fun experience, like taking a submarine ride to the bottom of the ocean. The two main tanks, which hold a total of 707,000 gallons, are stocked exclusively with fish of San Francisco Bay and offshore waters, including monkey face eels, spiny dogfish, sharks, sturgeons, Northern anchovy, and bat rays. Exhibits on the main floor (sea level) look at creatures of the Sacramento River delta and Sierra Nevada mountain streams. *The Embarcadero at Beach St., just east of Pier 39, 415/623–5300 or 888/732–3483 for tickets. Admission: $12.95, $6.50 children 3–11, $9.95 senior citizens 65 and older. Open June–Sept., daily 9–9; Oct.–May daily 10 AM–dusk.*

stadiums

There are four major sporting venues in the Bay Area, which together host everything from professional baseball, basketball, football, and hockey to circuses and gun shows. Purchase tickets by calling the individual box office, or by phoning BASS (510/762–BASS), which requires an extra surcharge. For information on specific teams mentioned here, *see* the individual listings *in* Sports and Outdoor Activities, *below.*

2 e-8, f-8
COW PALACE

The Cow Palace hosts sporting events such as tournament tennis and professional wrestling, as well as the Grand National Rodeo (*see* Events *in* Chapter 2), with an indoor seating capacity of 10,500–14,500. From downtown San Francisco, drive south on U.S. 101 to the Cow Palace/3rd Street exit; follow signs to Geneva Avenue, then head west 7 blocks. Or take BART to the Balboa Park Station and transfer to Muni Bus 15. *2600 Geneva Ave., at Santos St., Daly City, 415/469–6065 for box office.*

6 d-1, e-1
GOLDEN GATE PARK STADIUM/POLO FIELD

The Polo Field and stadium are used by the public for jogging and other sporting activities, as well as such special events as rock concerts, soccer, and the finish of the San Francisco Marathon. Here in 1967, Allen Ginsberg and hordes of flower children meditated and chanted together at their legendary Be-In, in a mass effort to alter consciousness. *Between John F. Kennedy and Middle Drs., west of 30th Ave., Golden Gate Park.*

1 g-5
OAKLAND-ALAMEDA COUNTY COLISEUM COMPLEX

The Oakland Coliseum Complex includes an indoor arena with a seating capacity of 15,040 and an outdoor stadium seating 39,875. Both received extensive renovations in 1996 and 1997. The Coliseum's newest addition, the West Side Club, is one of the largest sports bars west of the Mississippi. The stadium is home to the American League baseball team the Oakland Athletics (A's) and the NFL football team the Oakland Raiders. The NBA basketball team the Golden State Warriors play their home games in the indoor arena. The arena also occasionally hosts ice skating and other sporting events; contact the box office for a current schedule. From San Francisco, cross the bridge and follow I–880 south to the Coliseum exit. Or take BART to the Coliseum/Oakland Airport Station; the stadium is connected via an elevated walkway with the BART station. *7000 Coliseum Way, off I-880, north of Hegenberger Rd., Oakland, tel. 510/639–7700 for box office.*

SAN JOSE ARENA

In the South Bay, the San Jose Arena is a relatively new indoor stadium that seats

17,190. It's home to the National Hockey League team the San Jose Sharks. From San Francisco, take I–280 south to the Guadalupe Parkway exit, then turn left on Santa Clara Street. *525 W. Santa Clara St., near Autumn St., San Jose, 408/287–9200 for event information or 408/999–5721 for box office.*

2 *h-8*
3COM PARK AT CANDLESTICK POINT

It's windy, but where else can you warm up with a cappuccino or latte while watching a game? 3Com Park (formerly Candlestick Park) is an outdoor stadium in South San Francisco with a seating capacity of 70,000. It's home to the National League baseball team the San Francisco Giants and the NFL football team the San Francisco 49ers. Each team will move to its own new stadium around 2000: the Giants to a stadium to be constructed at China Basin, and the 49ers to a stadium to be constructed in the parking facility of 3Com Park. In the meantime, express city shuttle buses run from numerous bus stops throughout San Francisco on game days; call Muni (415/673–6864) for the stop nearest you. Or take U.S. 101 south to the 3Com Park exit. *Jamestown Ave. and Harney Way, South San Francisco, 415/467–1994.*

sports & outdoor activities

The two best resources for outdoor enthusiasts are **Cal Adventures** (1 Centennial Dr., at Memorial Stadium, Berkeley, 510/642–4000), part of the Outdoor Education Program of the University of California at Berkeley; and **Outdoors Unlimited** (550 Parnassus Ave., at 3rd Ave., 415/476–2078), on the University of California at San Francisco campus. Both have courses that are open to anyone, on everything from fly-fishing to mountaineering. Both rent equipment and organize backpacking and other types of excursions as well.

ARCHERY

Archers practice their sport in Golden Gate Park. The best source for equipment is **The Bow Rack,** in San Pablo

1085 Broadway, San Pablo, 510/236–8303), just off the Richmond–San Rafael Bridge about an hour southeast of San Francisco. In addition to their stock of nearly 400 bows, the store also has a 16-lane indoor range, as well as classes and coaching for all levels, and a "Junior Olympics" for kids on Saturday mornings. The store is closed Sundays.

6 *b-1*
GOLDEN GATE PARK ARCHERY FIELD

At the west end of the park, just north of the municipal golf course, the archery field is open daily from dawn until dusk. One block north of the field is the **San Francisco Archery Shop** (4429 Cabrillo St., 415/751–2776) where, during summer, you can rent an archery package ($15 per day) that includes bow, arrow, arm and finger protection, and target. The store is closed Sundays. *Fulton St., between 45th and 46th Aves., Golden Gate Park.*

BASEBALL & SOFTBALL

teams to watch

For credit-card purchases of either A's or Giants tickets, call the BASS Baseball Line (510/762–BASS). There is a per-call processing charge of $2.50, and per-ticket handling fees may also apply.

OAKLAND A'S

The American League's four-time World Champions ('72, '73, '74, and '89) play home games in the Oakland Coliseum. Bleacher seats cost $4, plaza level $5–$25. Same-day tickets can usually be purchased at the stadium's ticket office. Tickets may also be purchased at any BASS ticket center or through the BASS Baseball Line (*see above*). *510/638–0500 for ticket office, 510/430–8020 ext. 4040 for A's Promotional Hotline, 510/568–5600 for ticket information.*

SAN FRANCISCO GIANTS

The National League's Giants play home games in windy 3Com Park at Candlestick Point—at least until their brand-new stadium is completed at China Basin in 2000. In the meantime, bring an extra layer of clothes. Tickets are $6 for bleachers, $7–$21 for plaza level. Purchase tickets at the stadium; at any BASS ticket center; through the BASS Baseball Line (*see above*); or from the city's three Giants Dugout Stores (4 Embarcadero Center, The Embarcadero, 415/951–8888; 844 Market St., between Stockton and Powell Sts., Union Square, 415/982–9400; 114 Serramonte Center, Daly City, 415/755–7571). Game-day tickets are usually available at the stadium's ticket office. *415/467–8000 or 800/734–4268.*

STANFORD UNIVERSITY CARDINALS

Stanford's home games at the sunny Sunken Diamond often sell out. Tickets cost $3–$5 and may be purchased by telephone or in person at the Stanford Athletic Ticket Office (Gate 2, at the south end of Stanford Stadium, Stanford University campus, Palo Alto). *800/232–8225.*

UNIVERSITY OF CALIFORNIA GOLDEN BEARS

The Bears play ball at Evans Diamond, at Bancroft Way and Oxford Street. Tickets cost $5 and may be purchased by phone or in person at the Cal Athletic Ticket Office (2223 Fulton St., at Bancroft Way, Berkeley). *800/462–3277.*

where to play

Reservations for the city's five regulation baseball fields and approximately 65 softball fields are handled through the **San Francisco Recreation and Parks Department's Athletic Fields Reservations office** (415/753–7024). Reservations may be made up to two weeks in advance; the cost is $20–$25 for 1½ hours of play. Two of the most popular playing fields are in Golden Gate Park: The **Big Rec Ball Field** (near 7th Ave. and Lincoln Way) is for baseball only, while the **Little Rec Ball Field** (Sharon Meadow, north of Children's Playground) is a smaller field for softball.

Softball and baseball in San Francisco aren't pick-up sports; most people who are interested in playing join a league. Contact the office of the **Municipal Softball League** (415/753–7022 or 415/753–7023) for information. There are two seasons: spring (end of March through late June) and summer (end of July through end of October). The cost to join is $375.

BASKETBALL

teams to watch

GOLDEN STATE WARRIORS

The Warriors play NBA basketball at the Oakland Coliseum Arena from November through April. Tickets ($19.50–$60) go on sale in late September or early October and sell out quickly; call BASS Tickets (510/762–2277). *510/986–2200.*

STANFORD UNIVERSITY CARDINAL

The women's team is a consistent NCAA championship contender. Both men's and women's games are played at the Stanford Maples Pavilion. Tickets to men's and women's games cost $15, and may be purchased by telephone or in person at the Stanford Athletic Ticket Office (Gate 2, at the south end of Stanford Stadium, Stanford University campus, Palo Alto). *800/232–8225.*

UNIVERSITY OF CALIFORNIA GOLDEN BEARS

UC Berkeley's basketball games are usually played on campus at Harmon Gym. Men's tickets often sell out the day they go on sale. Tickets to men's basketball games cost $18, to women's games $5–$7, and may be purchased by phone or in person at the Cal Athletic Ticket Office (2223 Fulton St., at Bancroft Way, Berkeley). *800/462–3277.*

where to play

Pick-up basketball games can be found all over the city. The following San Francisco courts usually get going weekday afternoons and weekend mornings between 8 and 11.

7 *f-3*
EUREKA VALLEY RECREATION CENTER

On Monday nights there's full-court play for women. *100 Collingwood St., between 18th and 19th Sts., The Castro, 415/554–9528.*

7 *d-1*
GOLDEN GATE PARK PANHANDLE

The small courts in the Panhandle have highly competitive games going all the time. *Masonic Ave., between Oak and Fell Sts., The Haight.*

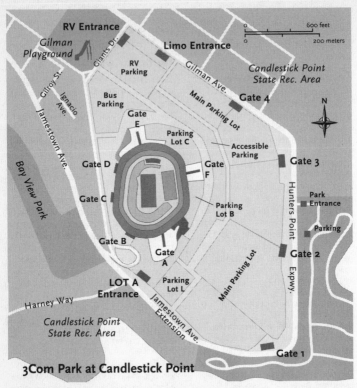

3Com Park at Candlestick Point

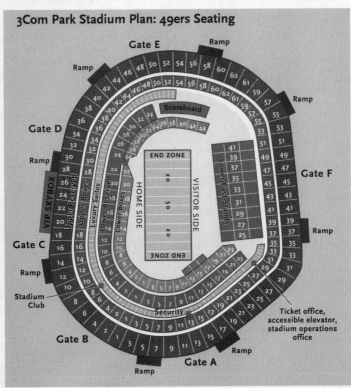

3Com Park Stadium Plan: 49ers Seating

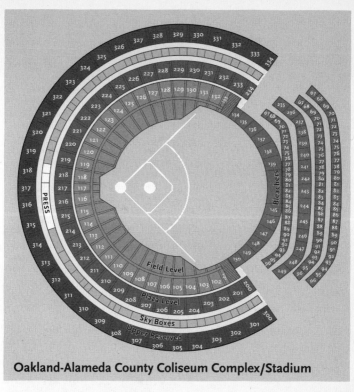

Oakland-Alameda County Coliseum Complex/Stadium

Oakland-Alameda County Coliseum Complex/Arena

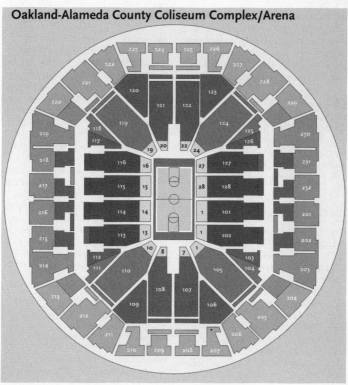

7 *d-2*

GRATTAN PLAYGROUND

The courts at Grattan see casual play weekday afternoons; weekends draw larger crowds and more ferocious competition. *Grattan and Stanyan Sts., The Haight.*

7 *g-5*

JAMES LICK MIDDLE SCHOOL

Relatively low-key four-on-four games begin early on weekends here. The two full-length courts are often taken up with four half-court games by a talented pool of weekend warriors—lawyers, artists, and other professionals in the 20-to-40 category who still enjoy shooting hoops. *Castro St., between Clipper and 25th Sts., Noe Valley.*

4 *a-3*

MOSCONE RECREATION CENTER

These popular courts have night lighting and unforgiving double rims. *1800 Chestnut St. at Buchanan St., The Marina, 415/292–2006.*

7 *g-7, h-7*

UPPER NOE PLAYGROUND

Though the single full outdoor court is unlighted, it's adjacent to a single lighted outdoor tennis court. Low-key pickup games take place almost every weekend. *Day and Sanchez Sts., Noe Valley.*

8 *e-4*

POTRERO HILL RECREATION CENTER

Games here are highly competitive, especially on Monday and Thursday nights. *Arkansas and 22nd Sts., Potrero Hill, 415/695–5009.*

BICYCLING

Two handy publications for San Francisco cyclists are: The *San Francisco Biking/Walking Guide* ($3), which indicates street grades and delineates biking routes that avoid major hills and heavy traffic; and *City Sports* magazine, which lists local and regional biking activities in the Calendar section. The *Biking/Walking Guide* is sold in select city bookstores; *City Sports* is free at fitness centers and athletic supply stores. For additional information about bicycling in San Francisco, *see* Transportation *in* Chapter 1.

where to ride

San Francisco's legendary hills hold countless challenges for cyclists, but there are plenty of scenic routes that traverse level ground. An enormous number of bike shops provide rentals as well as sales and service. One surefire place to find them is along so-called "Bike Row"—Stanyan Street adjacent to Golden Gate Park. The Great Highway along Ocean Beach (at the end of Golden Gate Park near Lincoln Way) has still more vendors renting mountain bikes, tandem bikes, and bikes with child trailers that hook onto the back. One of the largest local chains is **Start to Finish Bicycles** (672 Stanyan St., between Haight and Page Sts., The Haight, 415/750–4760; 599 2nd St., at Brannan St., South of Market, 415/243–8812; 2530 Lombard St., at Divisadero St., The Marina, 415/202–9830; or 800/600–2453 for information on store locations).

1 *c-2*

ANGEL ISLAND STATE PARK

Angel Island is possibly the best spot in the Bay Area for a scenic, low-key cycling excursion. Start by taking the ferry (*see* Transportation, *in* Chapter 1) to the island (bikes are allowed on the ferry). The bike path begins behind the Visitors Center (where you can pick up a map of the island's roads and trails); it's a fairly steep climb uphill to the bike path, but once there you can cruise the 5-mi road that meanders around the perimeter of the island. For the most part the bike path is paved, with only one difficult hill. You'll discover secluded picnic spots, attractive beaches, a few historic points of interest, and spectacular views of the city, the Golden Gate Bridge, and the rest of the bay. If you don't want to bring your own bike you can rent one on the island, at the **Angel Island Company** (415/897–0715), near the Ayala Cove Visitors Center. Rentals are available from April through October.

6 *a-1*

BAY TRAIL (GOLDEN GATE PARK– THE PRESIDIO– GOLDEN GATE BRIDGE– MARIN COUNTY)

For a full day's cycling adventure, start at the west end of Golden Gate Park, where John F. Kennedy Drive meets the Great Highway. Follow JFK Drive through the park (the road is at a slight incline), turn left on Conservatory Drive, left again on Arguello Boulevard, exit the park, and head through residential neighborhoods and onto the curvy, downhill roads of the Presidio. Make a right onto Moraga Avenue, then take another right onto Presidio Boulevard for a quick tour of the historic former military base. Make a hard left onto Lincoln Boulevard almost immediately; it leads to the Golden Gate Bridge toll plaza, where posted signs will instruct you on which lanes to use for crossing (depending on time and day of the week). From Golden Gate Park to the Golden Gate Bridge Vista Point in Marin County, it's about 8 mi one-way. You can add some additional miles by following signs to the town of Sausalito (a 1½ mi downhill coast one-way), from which you can catch a ferry back to San Francisco (see Ferry in Chapter 1). If you plan to return to San Francisco on bike via Golden Gate Bridge, follow Lincoln Boulevard west; it turns into El Camino del Mar and runs through the beautiful, grand Sea Cliff neighborhood. At the Palace of Legion of Honor, the road veers right and becomes Legion of Honor Drive before dropping you back onto Clement Street. Turn right on Clement, and when it dead-ends, take Point Lobos Avenue past the historic Cliff House. From here it's easy to follow the Great Highway south to your starting point at Golden Gate Park.

2 g-1
THE EMBARCADERO

A completely flat route along the waterfront at the heart of downtown San Francisco, the Embarcadero runs a spectacular 3-mi course between the San Francisco Bay on one side and sleek high-rises on the other. The wide waterfront promenade extends from Townsend Street in SoMa north to Fisherman's Wharf, passing the historic Ferry Building (at the foot of Market Street) and Pier 39.

2 c-3
GOLDEN GATE PARK

For cycling, Golden Gate Park is tops: More than 7 mi of paved trails wind past rose gardens, lakes, waterfalls, and forests, and ultimately they all end at the Pacific Ocean. Additionally, the park's main road, John F. Kennedy Drive, is closed to motor vehicles between Stanyan Street and 19th Avenue on Sundays. Best of all, the roads and paths in the park are on level ground or over only moderate hills. Get maps and information at one of two visitors centers in the park: McLaren Lodge, at the park's east end; or the Beach Chalet, near the Pacific Ocean at the park's west end. From end to end, the park is about 3 mi long and just over ½ mi wide. Once you reach the ocean, you can opt to continue your ride along the Sunset Bike Path (see below) which follows the Great Highway. For bike rentals, try **Surrey Bikes & Blades** at Stow Lake (415/668–6699), in the northwest corner of the park near 19th Avenue; or, for mountain bikes, **Park Cyclery** (1749 Waller St., at Stanyan St., The Haight, 415/751–7368), just outside the park.

2 e-1
MARINA GREEN

The Marina Green's ¾-mi flat, paved promenade is a popular place to cycle; most extend their ride by continuing along the Golden Gate Promenade in The Presidio (see below). The Marina Green is also the starting point of a route to the Golden Gate Bridge and beyond: Follow Lombard Street west into the Presidio to Lincoln Boulevard. From here, you can cycle onto the Golden Gate Bridge following the Bay Trail directions (see above).

MT. TAMALPAIS STATE PARK

Mt. Tam, as locals call it, is known for spectacular mountain-biking over rugged but scenic terrain—in fact, this is where the mountain bike was first invented, by Bay Area bicycle racer Gary Fisher in 1974. Pick up one of several topo maps ($1–$6) at the park's Pantoll Ranger Station (Panoramic Hwy. at Pantoll Rd., Mt. Tamalpais, 415/388–2070), and take care to distinguish fire trails, where biking is allowed, from walking trails, where biking may net you a fine up to $120.

5 f-3
THE PRESIDIO

Within the Presidio, 14 mi of meandering bicycle routes wind past coastal bluffs, forested hills, and historic military buildings. One popular ride follows Presidio Avenue into the park, where it becomes first Presidio Boulevard and then Lincoln Boulevard. Lincoln Boulevard loops and dips through The Presidio and eventually reaches Baker Beach (see Beaches, above). If you want a less hilly ride, follow Lincoln Boulevard to Long Avenue (at the "Y" in the road after Lincoln passes under U.S. 101) and then turn left onto Marine Drive, which ends at historic Fort Point. From Long Avenue you may also turn left onto the Golden Gate Promenade Bike Path, which runs east along the water and eventually links up with the Marina Green. The first 1/10 mi of the promenade is often wet from the crashing waves, so it's best to walk your bike to the corner where Long and Marine separate. For more information and a map of Presidio routes, stop by the park visitors center (Lincoln Blvd., at Montgomery St., The Presidio, 415/561–4323).

6 a-2, a-8

SUNSET & LAKE MERCED BIKE PATHS

On a fogless day, the Sunset Bike Path along the Pacific Ocean (1 block east of the Great Highway) can be breathtaking. The 2-mi raised bike path extends south from Lincoln Way (the southern border of Golden Gate Park) to Sloat Boulevard (the northern border of the San Francisco Zoo). From Sloat Boulevard, you can pick up the Lake Merced Bike Path, which loops around the lake and the golf course, to extend your ride by another 5 mi. Both bike paths are moderate.

BILLIARDS

4 e-4

AMUSEMENT CENTER

This no-frills billiard parlor and arcade has 15 pool tables and three snooker tables with the best prices in town: $4 per hour for one player, $6 per hour for two players. 447 Broadway, between Kearny and Montgomery Sts., Chinatown, 415/398–8858.

4 g-5

CHALKERS BILLIARD CLUB

With 30 custom-made and antique tables on the floor and Brie on the menu at the café, this elegant billiard hall caters to discerning players. Children over eight are welcome (with their parents) on weekend afternoons. Rincon Center, 101 Spear St. at Mission St., South of Market, 415/512–0450.

2 g-3

GREAT ENTERTAINER

The Bay Area's largest billiards club has 42 pool and snooker tables, plus shuffleboards, table-tennis, darts, fooseball, a video arcade, and a full bar and restaurant. There's a "pool school" for beginners and a pro shop for experts. 975 Bryant St. at 8th St., South Beach, 415/861–8833.

4 d-7

HOLLYWOOD BILLIARDS

The late local columnist Herb Caen once described this place as "a pool player's dream of paradise." The city's oldest pool room has 37 custom-made and antique tables, low cue prices, and reportedly the longest bar in San Francisco. 61 Golden Gate Ave., between Taylor and Jones Sts., The Tenderloin, 415/252–9643.

4 h-7

SOUTH BEACH BILLIARDS

A hipster's haven, South Beach has 40 pool tables, a snooker table, a boccie court, darts, a café, and a full bar. 270 Brannan St., between 1st and 2nd Sts., South of Market, 415/495–5939.

BIRD-WATCHING

The Bay Area is home to more than 200 species of birds, many of which can be spotted in the region's parks. For guided bird -watching tours, contact the **Audubon Society Golden Gate** (2530 San Pablo Ave., Suite G, Berkeley, 510/843–2222), which leads half-day forays to Bay Area Parks. **Oceanic Society Expeditions** (Fort Mason Center E-230, 415/474–3385 or 800/326–7491) has naturalist-led boat tours of the Farallon Islands National Wildlife Refuge, 27 mi west of the Golden Gate, where tufted puffins, pigeon guillemots, rhinoceros auklets, cormorants, and oystercatchers may be spotted. Trips depart from June through November from Fort Mason.

BOATING

Weekend boaters and picknickers choose Stow Lake in Golden Gate Park, while more serious crew teams and fisherfolk head to the much larger Lake Merced. Children (and adults) sail their toy boats on Golden Gate Park's Spreckels Lake.

2   *a-7, b-7*
LAKE MERCED

Lake Merced is a large lake that's great for fishing and rowing. The city's rowing clubs maintain boathouses at Merced, so there are always boats out on the lake—but it's never too crowded. You can rent rowboats and canoes at **Lake Merced Boating & Fishing Company** (1 Harding Rd., off Skyline Blvd., 415/753–1101. *Between Skyline and Lake Merced Blvds., Sunset District.*

6   *h-1*
STOW LAKE

At Golden Gate Park's largest lake you can row, paddle, or motor the day away. Picnickers head for Strawberry Hill, an island in the middle of the lake. Rent boats at the **Stow Lake Boathouse** (Lake Dr., off John F. Kennedy Dr., 415/752–0347), in the northwest corner of Stow Lake, near 19th Avenue. The lake is open daily year-round, weather permitting; call for seasonal hours.

BOCCIE

4   *b-2, c-2*
AQUATIC PARK

The boccie court at Aquatic Park is enormously popular with elderly Italian men. *Jefferson St., west of Hyde St., Northern Waterfront.*

2   *e-8*
CROCKER-AMAZON PLAYGROUND

The Crocker-Amazon boccie court is adjacent to McLaren Park, in the southeast section of San Francisco. *Moscow St., at Italy Ave., Visitacion Valley.*

4   *d-3*
NORTH BEACH PLAYGROUND

In the heart of a lively neighborhood, this boccie court has recently been repainted and the playing surface refinished. *Columbus Ave. and Lombard St., North Beach.*

4   *h-7*
SOUTH BEACH BILLIARDS

The hip SoMa billiards parlor has a boccie court. *270 Brannan St., between 1st and 2nd Sts., South of Market, 415/495–5939.*

BOWLING

San Francisco has only one bowling lane, and it's seen a return to popularity with the introduction of "Cyber Bowl" nights. A 12-lane bowling center is scheduled to open at the new, $56 million Children's Center at Yerba Buena Gardens (*see* Gardens, *above*) in mid-1998.

4   *a-6*
JAPANTOWN BOWL

The city's only bowling alley at press time, Japantown Bowl has 40 lanes with automatic scorekeepers, plus an on-site coffee shop and 3 hours of free parking across the street at the Japan Center Garage. On Tuesday, Thursday, Saturday, and Sunday nights this is the home of Cyber Bowl, a bowling extravaganza with black lights, fog machines, and the latest dance music. Reservations are required for Cyber Bowl; call 415/739–0724. On Friday and Saturday the bowling alley is open all night long. All other nights it closes at 1 AM. *1790 Post St. at Webster St., Japantown, 415/921–6200.*

BOXING

5   *g-6*
GORILLA SPORTS

In addition to boxing and kick boxing, you can try out spinning, free weights, aerobics, and yoga at these two San Francisco locations. A day pass ($10) is good for any classes. *2450 Sutter St., at Divisadero, Pacific Heights, 415/474–2699.*

4   *g-7*
501 2nd St., at Bryant St., South Beach, 415/777–4653.

CROQUET

Croquet reservations are handled by the **San Francisco Croquet Club** (415/928–5525). The SFCC gives free introductory courses at 10 AM on the first Saturday of every month; reservations are required and participants must wear flat-soled shoes. The club also hosts free open play for senior citizens on the first and third Wednesday of each month from 1 PM to 4 PM; reservations are required for groups of four or more.

6 *g-8*

STERN GROVE

Tournament croquet in San Francisco is played on two 10,000-sq-ft croquet lawns at Stern Grove. *Wawona St. and 19th Ave., Sunset District.*

DARTS

About 35 bars and pubs in San Francisco are affiliated with dart leagues, offering eight levels of play, from beginners to serious competitors. To join a league you'll need to pay seasonal dues ($20). During the two seasons, January–May and July–December, game time is typically Wednesday at 8 PM. For a comprehensive listing of pubs with teams and competitions, send a SASE to the **San Francisco Dart Association** (Box 192085, San Francisco 94119–2085, 415/781–7332).

6 *g-4*

EAGLE'S DRIFT-IN LOUNGE

The crowd here is mellow, except when it comes to darts. Expect intense competition on its seven boards. *1232 Noriega St. at 19th Ave., Sunset District, 415/661–0166.*

4 *f-8*

THE GAVEL PUB

The work-hard, play-hard ethic of "Silicon Gulch's" best and brightest is demonstrated at this pub's four boards. *15 Boardman Pl., between Bryant and Brannan Sts. and 6th and 7th Sts., South Beach, 415/863–5787.*

7 *g-1*

MAD DOG IN THE FOG

Guinness-drinking Brits put the two boards here to good use. *530 Haight St., between Fillmore and Steiner Sts., The Haight, 415/626–7279.*

8 *a-5*

SCHOONER TAVERN

It's an older crowd here, and the games are casual. The Tavern has three boards. *1498 Valencia St. at 26th St., Mission District, 415/285–4169.*

8 *b-1*

TWENTY TANK BREWERY

On the weekends, Twenty Tank takes on the air of a frat house. There are plenty of microbrews on tap, and two boards

for playing darts. *316 11th St. at Folsom St., South of Market, 415/255–9455.*

4 *a-4*

UNION ALE HOUSE

The Ale House is clubby and collegiate, and on weekend nights there's usually a line to use the two boards. *1980 Union St. at Buchanan St., The Marina, 415/921–0300.*

FISHING

Sporting goods stores sell the state fishing license ($25.25) that is required for seasonal ocean and freshwater fishing. One-day licenses, good for ocean fishing only, are available for $7 on the charter boats.

charters

Charter boats leave from San Francisco and other cities around the bay, including Sausalito, Berkeley, and Emeryville. They go for salmon and halibut outside the bay or striped bass and giant sturgeon within the bay (though heavy pollution in the bay may lower the quality of your catch). Most charter boats depart daily from Fisherman's Wharf during the salmon-fishing season, from March through October. Reservations are advised.

1 *b-2*

BAY AND DELTA CHARTERS

Departures are from Sausalito, the Berkeley Marina, Jack London Square in Oakland, and Pier 40 in San Francisco. *85 Liberty Ship Way, Suite 112, Schoonmaker Point Marina, Sausalito, 415/381–9503.*

CAPTAIN JOHN'S

Captain John leads salmon and rock-cod fishing excursions and whale-watching trips in scenic Half Moon Bay. *Pillar Point Harbor, off Hwy. 1, Half Moon Bay, 415/726–2913, 415/728–3377, or 800/391–8787 for reservations.*

3 *b-5*

EMERYVILLE SPORT FISHING

The friendly staff leads all kinds of fishing excursions. "You name the fish, we'll go catch it" is the unofficial motto. *Emeryville Marina, foot of Powell St., off I-80, Emeryville, 510/654–6040.*

4 *c-1*

HOT PURSUIT SPORT FISHING

Captain Ray Crawford specializes in salmon and rock-cod fishing aboard a super-fast, 25-knot boat that departs from a slip to the east of Castagnola's Restaurant, on Fisherman's Wharf. Fishing lessons are free. Whale watching trips are also available. *Jefferson and Jones Sts., Fisherman's Wharf, 415/965–3474.*

4 *c-1*

LOVELY MARTHA'S SPORTFISHING

Captain Frank Rescino has been leading salmon-fishing excursions and bay cruises since 1965. *Berth 3, Fisherman's Wharf, 415/871–1691. No credit cards.*

4 *c-1*

WACKY JACKY

Jacky Douglas, a.k.a. Wacky Jacky, is one of the Bay Area's few female skippers. Since 1973 she's been leading salmon fishing excursions in a sleek, fast, and comfortable 50-ft boat. Whale-watching and bird-watching trips are available, too. *Pier 45, Fisherman's Wharf, 415/586–9800.*

where to fish

4 *b-2*

4 *c-2*

AQUATIC PARK

Bring a crab net to Aquatic Park and you might be able to catch some red rock crabs. Depending on the season, perch and king fish are catchable anywhere along the beach.

2 *b-2*

BAKER BEACH

Anglers come to Baker Beah to catch surf perch and striped bass, whenever the surf isn't too rough.

3 *b-3*

BERKELEY MARINA PIER

This is the place to catch tiny sharks and, once in a while, bass. *University Ave. and Marina Blvd., Berkeley.*

5 *a-1*

FORT POINT

The fishing areas at Fort Point (see Historic Structures and Sights *in* Chapter 2) are along the seawall and the pier. *Marine Dr., off Long Ave., The Presidio.*

2 *a-7*

2 *b-7*

LAKE MERCED

Rent boats to fish at Lake Merced for trout, catfish, and bass. The North Lake contains the trophy-sized fish; fish in the South Lake are smaller. You must bring your own fishing gear as it is not available for rent. *Between Skyline and Lake Merced Blvds., Sunset District.*

WATER SPORTS

Though San Francisco can't live up to Southern California in terms of sunny swimming beaches, there are enough stretches of sandy shoreline—plus lakes, ponds, and water holes—to satisfy any landlocked mammal. The following spots are great for boating, fishing, swimming, surfing, and more.

Aquatic Park (Beaches)
  Serious open-water swimming.

Baker Beach (Beaches)
  Angle here, or kick back in repose, just gazing out at the view.

Candlestick Point State Recreation Area (Windsurfing)
  Smooth water, strong winds.

China Beach (Beaches)
  One of the city's best swimming beaches.

Crissy Field (Windsurfing)
  Windsurfing strictly for experts.

Fort Point (Fishing)
  Surf's up and the fish are bitin.'

Golden Gate Park Fly Casting Pools (Fishing)
  Cast your rods just a stone's throw away from the Buffalo Paddock in Golden Gate Park.

Lake Merced (Parks, Boating)
  Rent a rowboat or a canoe and try your luck at trout fishing.

Ocean Beach (Beaches)
  Daredevil surfers ride the big waves.

San Francisco Municipal Pier (Fishing)
  Rent a rod, buy a bucket of bait, and try your luck.

Stow Lake (Boating)
  Pack a picnic and paddle to Strawberry Hill.

2 *a-3*

OCEAN BEACH

Anglers catch perch and stripers here. For general information about the beach, *see* Beaches, *above*.

4 *b-1*

SAN FRANCISCO MUNICIPAL PIER

One the city's best fishing spots, this area is loaded with flounder, sand dabs, cod, bass, and perch, as well as crabs for netting. *North extension of Van Ness Ave., just west of Aquatic Park, Fisherman's Wharf.*

FLY-FISHING

Purchase equipment from **San Francisco Flyfishers' Supply** (2526 Clement St., between 26th and 27th Aves., Richmond District, 415/668–3597) or **Fly Fishing Outfitters** (463 Bush St., between Grant Ave. and Kearny St., Financial District, 415/781–3474). For instruction, contact the **Mel Krieger School of Flyfishing** (415/752–1013).

6 *d-1*

GOLDEN GATE PARK FLY-CASTING POOLS

These fly-casting ponds in the middle of Golden Gate Park are among the best in the country. The Anglers Lodge beside them was built during the Great Depression as a WPA project. Both pools and lodge are managed by the Golden Gate Angling and Casting Club; visitors are welcome to drop by the lodge on Tuesday, Thursday, Saturday, or Sunday. Regular club events include tying seminars and casting clinics; some are free and open to the public. *Across John F. Kennedy Dr. from Buffalo Paddock, just west of 36th Ave., Golden Gate Park, 415/386–2630.*

FLYING

Those who have or hope to earn their pilot's license in San Francisco will get a bird's-eye view of some of the most beautiful coastline in California. For flying instruction, try any of the following Bay Area companies: **Cal-Pacific Associates** (510/489–3585); **North Bay Aviation** (415/899–1677); **Sierra Academy of Aeronautics** (510/568–6100; **Stanford Flying Club** (415/858–2200).

FOOTBALL

When San Franciscans gather to play a game on a weekend afternoon, they prefer soccer to touch football—but when it comes to cheering the pros they are fanatical about their home team, the 49ers. Tickets to home games sell out in a nanosecond. Football season runs from August into December.

pro and college teams to watch

OAKLAND RAIDERS

In 1995 the Raiders returned to the Bay Area after a 15-year sojourn in Los Angeles, and so far local residents have given the "L.A. Traitors" a warm reception. Their AFC West Conference home games are played at the newly renovated Oakland Coliseum (*see* Stadiums, *above*). Tickets are usually available. 510/516–1875 or 800/949–2626.

SAN FRANCISCO 49ERS

The 49ers play their NFC West Conference home games at 3Com Park (*see* Stadiums, *above*), at least until their brand-new stadium (in the parking lot of the old facility) is completed in 2000. Tickets are difficult to obtain as most seats are taken by season-ticket holders; when remaining seats go on sale in July, they usually sell out within the hour. Sadly, the ticket crunch won't ease up in the future—the new football-only stadium is to be 20,000 seats smaller. 415/468–2249 or 415/656–4900.

STANFORD UNIVERSITY CARDINAL

The Bay Area's two big universities—Stanford University in Palo Alto and the University of California at Berkeley—have been arch rivals for almost a century, and their Pac-10 football teams duke it out every year during the Big Game (usually the fourth Saturday in November). The Cardinal plays all its home games on campus at Stanford Stadium, near the town of Palo Alto, 33 mi from downtown San Francisco. Tickets cost $10–$25 ($50 for the Big Game) and may be purchase by telephone or in person at the Stanford Athletic Ticket Office (Gate 2, at the south end of Stanford Stadium, Stanford University campus, Palo Alto). 800/232–8225.

UNIVERSITY OF CALIFORNIA GOLDEN BEARS

All of the Bears' football home games are played in U.C. Berkeley's Memorial Stadium, on Piedmont Avenue near Bancroft Way. Tickets cost $14–$22 ($45 for the Big Game) and may be purchased by phone or in person at the Cal Athletic Ticket Office (2223 Fulton St., at Bancroft Way, Berkeley). *800/462–3277.*

where to play

6 *d-1, e-1*

POLO FIELD

To reserve the Polo Field, contact the San Francisco Recreation and Parks Department (415/831–2700). *Between John F. Kennedy and Middle Drs. west of 30th Ave., Golden Gate Park.*

4 *a-3*

MOSCONE RECREATION CENTER

The flag football league of the Golden Gate Sport & Social Club (415/921–1233) holds games at this rec center. *1800 Chestnut St., at Buchanan St., The Marina, 415/292–2006.*

GOLF

To brush up on your stroke, visit **Driving Obsession** (310 Grant Ave., between Sutter and Bush Sts., Financial District, 415/397–4653), where PGA instructors are on staff; or **Pro Active Golf Therapy** (1489 Webster St., at Geary St., Japantown, 415/346–8373), open weekdays by appointment only.

courses

All of the courses listed below are open to the public. The city-run golf courses are Golden Gate Park, Harding Park, Jack Fleming, Lincoln Park, and Sharp Park. To make reservations for tee times at any of these (for a $1 per player surcharge) call the **San Francisco automated tee time reservation system and information line** (415/750–4653). The hot line also provides information about greens fees, golf cart and club rentals, and hours of operation for each municipal course.

The **San Francisco Recreation and Parks Department Golf Division** (415/831–2737) maintains practice putting greens at Moscone Recreation Center (1800 Chestnut St., at Buchanan St., The Marina) and at Stern Grove (19th Ave. and Wawona St.).

2 *f-8*

GLENEAGLES INTERNATIONAL GOLF COURSE

In McLaren Park at the south end of the city, Gleneagles is a full-size, challenging nine-holer, par 36. *2100 Sunnydale Ave., at Brookdale Ave., Visitacion Valley, 415/587–2425.*

6 *b-1, c-1*

GOLDEN GATE PARK GOLF COURSE

Just above Ocean Beach at the west end of Golden Gate Park is this small but tricky "pitch and putt" nine-holer. All of the holes are par three, and all are tightly set and well-wrapped with small greens. Nearby are a practice putting green and a cafeteria. *47th Ave., between John F. Kennedy Dr. and Fulton St., Golden Gate Park, 415/751–8987.*

2 *a-7, b-7*

HARDING PARK GOLF COURSE

This 18-hole, par 72 course adjacent to attractive Lake Merced is heavily forested with Monterey cypress and pine trees. In addition to a well-wrapped course, facilities include a practice putting green, driving range (with practice balls available for rent), and full-service restaurant. Several professional tournaments have taken place here. *Harding Rd., near Skyline Blvd., Sunset District, 415/664–4690.*

2 *b-7*

JACK FLEMING GOLF COURSE

Inside the second nine of the Harding Park Golf Course (*see above*) is the par-32 Fleming course, with all the characteristics of the famed championship course—except that it's shorter, flatter, and less difficult. *Harding Rd., near Skyline Blvd., Sunset District, 415/664–4690.*

2 *a-2, b-2*

LINCOLN PARK GOLF COURSE

This 18-hole, par-68 course is the oldest in San Francisco. Short and hilly though it may be, Lincoln Park has magical views of the city skyline and the Golden Gate Bridge. The rugged course has small greens and strategically located traps. Facilities include a practice putting green and a full-service restaurant. *34th Ave. and Clement St., Richmond District, 415/221–9911.*

5 *c-5*

PRESIDIO GOLF COURSE
This magnificent 18-hole, par-72 course, managed by Arnold Palmer's company, opened to the public in 1995 and has been a hit ever since. On the grounds are a driving range, café, and pro shop. *300 Finley Rd., at Arguello Blvd., The Presidio, 415/561–4653 or 415/561–4664.*

1 *b-7*

SHARP GOLF COURSE
A flat, par-72 oceanside course with numerous traps, this 18-holer is south of the city in the community of Pacifica. You'll find a practice putting green and a full-service restaurant here. *Hwy. 1, at Fairway Dr. exit, Pacifica, 415/359–3380.*

driving ranges
The driving ranges listed below rent golf clubs and buckets of balls on the premises. Call for prices and hours of operation. Additionally, you'll find a driving range at Harding Park Golf Course (*see above*).

8 *e-1*

MISSION BAY GOLF CENTER
There are 66 stalls on this 300-yard two-tiered range, plus a putting green, pro shop, and full-service restaurant with an outdoor deck. Professional instruction is available. *1200 6th St., at Channel St., China Basin, 415/431–7888.*

HANDBALL

7 *a-1, c-1*

GOLDEN GATE PARK
There are two outdoor and two indoor handball courts in the park, across the street from the rear of Steinhart Aquarium. Reservations are not required. *Middle Dr. East, between Martin Luther King Jr. and Bowling Green Drs., Golden Gate Park.*

8 *b-4*

MISSION RECREATION CENTER
Handball players are allowed to use the two squash courts at Mission Rec,

though they're too small for true handball. Reservations may be made up to 1½ hours in advance (in person only), and use of the courts is free. *2450 Harrison St., between 20th and 21st Sts., Mission District, 415/695–5012.*

HANG-GLIDING & PARAGLIDING

For instruction, try **Airtime San Francisco** (3620 Wawona St., at 47th Ave., Sunset District, 415/759–1177). **Chandelle San Francisco Inc.** (1595 E. Francisco Blvd., off Hwy. 580, San Rafael, 415/454–3464) is one of the oldest hang-gliding and paragliding shops in the country, and also has instruction programs. The **San Francisco Hang Gliding Center** (510/528–2300) specializes in tandem hang-gliding flights; no experience is necessary to fly in their two-person gliders with an experienced pilot.

2 *a-7*

FORT FUNSTON
On sunny weekends you can watch brightly colored hang gliders swooping along the cliffs at Fort Funston, a site for experienced pilots only. Call the Fort Funston Weather Hotline (415/333–0100) for recorded up-to-the minute information on temperature and wind conditions. *Off Skyline Blvd. (Rte. 35), south of Sloat Blvd., Sunset District, 415/556–8371.*

HOCKEY

teams to watch

SAN JOSE SHARKS
This popular National Hockey League team plays home games at the San Jose Arena (*see Stadiums, above*), where they have been swatting pucks since the 1993–94 season. The team has been a wild success; in fact, they recently boasted the longest-running sellout in NHL history. Purchase tickets at the box office or from BASS (510/762–BASS). The season runs from October through April. *408/287–4275.*

where to play
The city lacks a year-round ice skating rink, so hockey fans get their fix by strapping on their in-line skates. Contact **Skate Pro Sports** (415/752–8776) for

information on local in-line hockey leagues.

4 *h-8*

BLADIUM

An indoor rink devoted exclusively to in-line hockey, Bladium has adult and youth leagues, clinics, and camps. In addition, you can always find pick-up games here. Reservations are required three days in advance; the cost ($8–$12) varies by time of day and length of game. Free beginners' clinics are held once monthly. There's also a sports bar with satellite TV on the premises. Equipment is available for rental ($3–$10), and the **Pro Shop at Bladium** (415/882–7294) sells sticks, pucks, blades, jerseys. *1050 3rd St., near Berry St., South Beach, 415/442–5060.*

7 *b-1, c-1*

GOLDEN GATE PARK

Pickup roller-hockey is played near the park's tennis courts. *John F. Kennedy Dr., near Bowling Green Dr., Golden Gate Park.*

7 *g-5*

JAMES LICK MIDDLE SCHOOL

The playground at James Lick is a popular spot for pickup rollerblade hockey games. *Castro St., between Clipper and 25th Sts., Noe Valley.*

ROLLADIUM ROLLER RINK

This San Mateo rink sponsors in-line hockey league games and sells a full line of hockey and in-line skating equipment. The rink is open Tuesday–Thursday and Sunday 1–4, Friday 7:30PM–11PM, and Saturday 1–4, 5–7, and 7:30–11. *363 N. Amphlett Blvd., Poplar Ave. exit from U.S. 101, San Mateo, 415/342–2711 or 415/342–2713. Admission: $4; skate rentals $1 per person.*

HORSEBACK RIDING

6 *d-1*

GOLDEN GATE STABLES

San Francisco's only stable offers instruction in English and Western riding, as well as dressage and jumping. Group lessons start at $24 per hour, private lessons start at $45 per hour. Daily scenic trail rides along the 12 mi of equestrian trails in Golden Gate Park

(the Saturday ride also goes to the beach) cost $25 per hour. For kids, there's a summer camp. All trail rides and lessons are by reservation only; call at least two days in advance. *John F. Kennedy Dr. at 36th Ave., Golden Gate Park, 415/668-7360.*

HORSE RACING

BAY MEADOWS RACECOURSE

Thoroughbred racing at Bay Meadows takes place from August through November. In August, racing is part of the San Mateo County Fair, with post time at 1:15 PM Monday, Wednesday, Saturday, and Sunday, and 5:15 PM Thursday and Friday. During September, post time is 1:45 Monday, Wednesday, Thursday, Saturday, and Sunday, and 6:45 Friday. October and November, post time is 12:45 Monday, Wednesday, Thursday, Saturday, and Sunday, and 6:45 Friday. General admission is $3 general, free ages 17 and under. *2600 S. Delaware St., San Mateo, off U.S. 101, 20 mi south of San Francisco, 415/574-7223.*

3 *b-1*

GOLDEN GATE FIELDS

At Golden Gate Fields, the thoroughbred racing season is mid-November through December and late March through mid-June. Post time from Wednesday through Sunday is 12:45, with additional twilight racing Fridays at 6 PM. General admission is $3, free ages 17 and under. *1100 Eastshore Hwy., off Hwy. 80, Albany, 510/559-7300.*

ICE SKATING

The $56 million Children's Center scheduled to open at Yerba Buena Gardens in mid-1998 (*see Gardens, above*) will include a 32,000-sq-ft ice skating rink with an NHL-regulation-size surface for hockey play and practice, figure skating, and recreational skating.

3 *d-3*

BERKELEY ICELAND

Ice skating rinks are few and far between in sunny California, but Berkeley Iceland has been giving skaters a place to twirl since 1944. Daytime admission is $5.50 ($4.50 ages 18 and under); evening admission is $5.50 for all ages. A full range of skating classes ($51 for six lessons) is geared towards everyone from tiny tots to adults only; there's also private instruction. During Wednesday "Family Night," from 6:30 PM until 7:45 PM, admission ($6, $5 ages 18 and under) buys the whole family a half-hour lesson and free skating time following the lesson. At all times, skate rentals are $2 per person. The rink is closed on Monday. *2727 Milvia St., between Ward and Derby Sts., Berkeley, 510/843–8800.*

4 *g-4*
JUSTIN HERMAN PLAZA HOLIDAY ICE CENTER

Winter visitors can enjoy a twirl on the ice from mid-November until President's weekend in February at this outdoor ice-skating rink adjacent to Embarcadero Center. Skating hours are daily from 10 until 10, holidays included. Call for information about special discounts. *Market and Steuart Sts., The Embarcadero, 800/733–6318. Admission: $6, $3 children 8 and under; skate rentals $3 per person.*

4 *e-6*
WESTIN ST. FRANCIS ICE RINK AT UNION SQUARE

The skating season at Union Square is from Thanksgiving through mid-January. The twinkling holiday lights of surrounding shops and buildings make this outdoor rink nearly as magical as Manhattan's Rockefeller Center. Skating hours are daily from 9 AM until 10 PM. *Union Square, 415/752–8464. Admission: $6; $3 children 12 and under; skate rentals $2.50 per person.*

IN-LINE SKATING & ROLLER SKATING

Skaters of all levels are welcome to take part in Friday Night Skate, an evening ramble around town: Depending on the weather, anywhere from several dozen to more than 500 skaters may attend. The group meets Fridays at 8 PM at the Ferry Building (at the foot of Market Street in the Financial District) to depart at 8:30 PM. The route varies weekly. Drop by **Skate Pro Sports** (3401 Irving St., at 35th Ave., Sunset District, 415/752–8776) for the scoop on other local skating activities.

4 *h-8*
BLADIUM

This indoor rink is devoted exclusively to in-line hockey (*see* Hockey, *above*). *1050 3rd St., near Berry St., South Beach, 415/442–5060.*

2 *c-3, d-3*
GOLDEN GATE PARK

There are more than 7 mi of paved trails in and around the park. On Sundays, John F. Kennedy Drive, the park's main thoroughfare, is closed to motor traffic between Stanyan Street and 19th Avenue, making it a paved paradise for in-line skaters of all levels. Beginners practice stopping, and artistic skaters perform their newest moves to music in the large, flat area between the Conservatory and the de Young Museum. There's often a slalom course set up near the Conservatory. **Skates on Haight** (1818 Haight St., at Stanyan St., The Haight, 415/752–8375), conveniently located at the Stanyan Street entrance to the park, includes a free lesson with in-line skate rentals. You can also rent skates at **Surrey Bikes & Blades at Stow Lake** (*see* Bicycling, *above*).

2 *e-1*
THE MARINA

For beginners, the paved path along the Marina is an easy 1½-mi (round-trip) route on a flat, well-paved surface, with glorious views of San Francisco Bay. Rentals are available at **Marina Skate and Snowboard** (2271 Chestnut St., near Scott St., The Marina, 415/567–8400).

ROLLADIUM ROLLER RINK

The closest indoor roller rink is south of San Francisco in San Mateo, where in-line hockey league games often take place. There's a full line of hockey and in-line skating equipment for sale here, though rentals are mostly of roller skates. The rink is open from Tuesday through Thursday and Sunday from 1 PM to 4 PM, Friday from 7:30 PM to 11 PM, and Saturday from 1 PM to 4 PM, 5 PM to 7 PM, and 7:30 PM to 11 PM. To get here, take the Poplar Avenue exit from U.S. 101. *363 N. Amphlett Blvd., Poplar Ave. exit from U.S. 101, San Mateo, 415/342–2711 or 415/342–2713. Admission: $4; skate rentals $1 per person.*

1 *f-1*

TILDEN REGIONAL PARK

Advanced skaters head to Berkeley's Tilden Park for challenging routes and brilliant views. Follow signs to the parking lot at Inspiration Point. There you'll find the trailhead for Nimitz Way, a nicely paved 8-mi (round-trip) recreational path that stretches along a ridge overlooking San Francisco Bay, the East Bay Mudlands, and Mt. Diablo. *Berkeley.*

LAWN BOWLING

7 *b-1*

GOLDEN GATE PARK

The three lawn-bowling greens at Golden Gate Park are managed by the **San Francisco Lawn Bowling Club** (415/ 753–9298), which you must contact for reservations. Look for the lawns at the east end of the park between the tennis courts and Children's Playground, on Bowling Green Drive between Middle Drive East and Martin Luther King Jr. Drive.

RACQUETBALL & SQUASH

4 *g-5*

EMBARCADERO YMCA

A day pass ($12) gives you access to either of the two racquetball courts at the Embarcadero Y. Make reservations on arrival at the club. *169 Steuart St., between Mission and Howard Sts., South of Market, 415/957–9622.*

8 *b-4*

MISSION RECREATION CENTER

At the Mission Rec you'll find two squash courts available for squash or racquetball play. You may reserve the courts up to 1½ hours in advance (reservations must be made in person). Use of the courts is free. *2450 Harrison St., between 20th and 21st Sts., Mission District, 415/695–5012.*

4 *d-2*

NORTHPOINT HEALTH CLUB

The single racquetball court at Northpoint is regulation size (though the ceiling is lower than regulation) and is open to drop-in guests with the purchase of a day pass ($5). *2310 Powell St., at Bay St., Fisherman's Wharf, 415/989–1449.*

4 *a-7*

SAN FRANCISCO ATHLETIC CLUB

The club has one squash and one racquetball court, and reservations are required (drop-in guests may make reservations up to two days in advance). The drop-in fee is $8 off-peak (weekdays 6 AM–4:30 PM and 7–10 PM, weekends all day), $12 peak (weekdays 4:30–7 PM). *The Fillmore Center, 1755 O'Farrell St., at Fillmore St., Japantown, 415/776–2260.*

4 *f-3*

SAN FRANCISCO BAY CLUB

One of the city's best private health clubs has 7 squash courts and 1 racquetball court. Drop-in guests pay $15 and must be accompanied by a member. *150 Greenwich St., between Sansome and Battery Sts., Telegraph Hill, 415/433–2550.*

ROCK CLIMBING

The Bay Area's two outstanding climbing gyms are the place to take classes, find a climbing partner, or get the lowdown on climbing in surrounding parks.

3 *d-5*

CITY ROCK

The East Bay's premiere climbing center—affiliated with Mission Cliffs in San Francisco—has a 45-ft-high wall, 20 top ropes, and approximately 8,000 sq ft of climbing terrain. Classes are available daily for beginners, no advance registration required. Experienced climbers must pass a safety test before climbing. There are also private lessons for all skill levels, monthly clinics, and one- or two-day outdoor climbing programs. To use the center's climbing facilities nonmembers pay $14 for a day pass ($9 for ages 14 and under), with special discount days for women, families, and students. Shoe and harness rental is $6. On the premises are a complete weight room, locker rooms, and showers. The facility is open Monday, Wednesday, and Friday from 6:30 AM until 10 PM, Tuesday and Thursday from 11 to 10, and weekends from 10 to 6. *1250 45th St., Suite 400, at Doyle St., Emeryville, 510/654–2510.*

4 *f-5*

CLUB ONE CITICORP

The outdoor climbing wall here is part of a full-service gym (*see* Fitness Centers and Health Clubs, *below*), and walk-ins must purchase a $15 day pass. The wall is 24-foot-high, with 800 sq feet of climbing terrain; it is closed during inclement weather, so call ahead. On Tuesdays and Thursdays from 5 PM to 7 PM, ropes are set up along 15 of its 35 routes and the wall is open for supervised climbing. At all other times it is open for bouldering only. Private lessons cost $50 per lesson for club members and $55 per lesson for non-members, with discounts for small groups (up to three persons) and for those who purchase a 3-, 5-, or 10-lesson package. *1 Sansome St., at Sutter St., Financial District, 415/399–1010.*

8 *b-3*

MISSION CLIFFS ROCK CLIMBING CENTER

Mission Cliffs, affiliated with City Rock in the East Bay (*see above*), is one of the largest indoor climbing facilities in the country. Its 14,000 sq-ft climbing area has a 50-ft-high wall and more than 40 top and lead ropes, plus 2,000 sq ft of bouldering terrain. Day passes for non-members cost $14 and include use of a weight room, locker rooms and showers, and sauna; special discount days for women, families, and students are available (call for details). Beginners classes are held daily; no advance reservation is required. The center also has a full range of outdoor programs, monthly clinics, private lessons, and kids' activities. You can rent shoes and harness for $6. *2295 Harrison St., at 19th St., Mission District, 415/550–0515.*

ROWING

Early mornings, when the water is still calm, scullers and kayakers take to Aquatic Park and Lake Merced. A few intrepid souls even commute by kayak from San Francisco to the East Bay. Unless otherwise stated, the following private clubs have annual membership dues and require new members to take rowing lessons.

4 *c-2*

DOLPHIN SWIM & BOAT CLUB

The Dolphin Club has a quarterly (not annual) membership fee. A two-day rowing class (included in the membership package) is required of all new members. The main boathouse is at Aquatic Park, and a second boathouse is at Lake Merced. The club keeps singles, doubles, fours, and six-person boats for members' use. *502 Jefferson St., at Hyde St., Fisherman's Wharf, 415/441–9329.*

4 *c-2*

SOUTH END ROWING CLUB

The private South End Rowing club requires new members to take lessons (for no additional fee). The main boathouse, at Aquatic Park, has open-water singles, doubles, and a six-person boat. There is a smaller boathouse at Lake Merced. *500 Jefferson St., at Hyde St., Fisherman's Wharf, 415/776–7372.*

2 *a-6*

UCSF ROWING CLUB

The UCSF Rowing Club, though not affiliated with the university, nevertheless gives discounts for UCSF students and faculty. The club has 10 boats (nine singles and one double) at its Lake Merced boathouse. Sculling lessons are required for new members unless they show proof of prior training. Beginners lessons cost $45 for the first lesson and $25 for each additional one; make reservations at least one day in advance. *1 Harding Rd., off Skyline Blvd., Sunset District, 415/675–9744.*

RUNNING, JOGGING, & WALKING

A handful of running clubs in the city provide a forum for group training and racing. Among the pre-eminent clubs are **Pamakid Runners** (415/333–4780), which emphasizes competitive track work, and **San Francisco FrontRunners** (415/978–2429), a mostly gay and lesbian club that sponsors weekend runs followed by brunch as well as competitive weekday runs. In addition, the **South End Rowing Club** (500 Jefferson St., at Hyde St., Fisherman's Wharf, 415/776–7372) and the **Dolphin Swim & Boat Club** (502 Jefferson St., at Hyde St., Fisherman's Wharf, 415/441–9329) both sponsor running clubs.

The city hosts two major races: The colorful, rollicking Bay to Breakers 12K (May) and the City of San Francisco Marathon (July). For more information, *see* Events *in* Chapter 2.

In Golden Gate Park you'll find a parcourse at the Polo Field and a senior citizens' course behind the Senior Citizens Center (36th Ave. and Fulton St.). Here are a few favorite routes for runners, joggers, and walkers:

2 *b-2*
BAKER BEACH
For a short but spectacular oceanside run, start on Baker Beach near 25th Avenue and run toward the Golden Gate Bridge until you come to the rocks. Turn around and run to the other end, next to the stairs up to Seacliff's houses. Run back to your starting point, and you'll have covered about 1½ mi.

6 *b-2*
GOLDEN GATE PARK LOOP
Paved trails in and around Golden Gate Park total more than 7 mi, but for a pleasant 5-mi run try this route: Start south of the Polo Field and run east on Middle Drive, with the Polo Field on your left. Veer left on Overlook Drive, and when it ends take two lefts to reach Kennedy Drive. After you pass the golf course, turn left onto Martin Luther King Jr. Drive (you'll be heading east again). On the home stretch you'll run into another fork: the left one will put you back on Middle Drive a short distance from the Polo Field.

2 *e-1*
MARINA GREEN
The paved path along the Marina runs a 1½-mi (round-trip) course along a flat, well-paved surface, with glorious views of San Francisco Bay. Extend your run by continuing along the Golden Gate Promenade (*see* The Presidio, *in* Bicycling, *above*).

6 *h-1*
STOW LAKE RUN
Circle Golden Gate Park's Stow Lake, then cross the bridge and run up the path to the top of Strawberry Hill, to run a total distance of 2½ mi.

2 *a-4*
SUNSET & LAKE MERCED BIKE PATHS
The 2-mi raised bike bath from Lincoln Way (the southern border of Golden Gate Park) to Sloat Boulevard (the northern border of the San Francisco Zoo) is enormously popular for jogging as well as biking. From Sloat Boulevard, you can pick up the Lake Merced Bike Path, which loops around the lake and the golf course, to extend your run by another 5 mi.

SAILING

On sunny, breezy days, sailing is enormously popular from the San Francisco Marina, Berkeley Marina, and Sausalito. Choose whichever starting point suits your day's plans, as all provide easy access to superb sailing on the open waters of the San Francisco Bay. Weather permits sailing year-round, but inexperienced sailors should beware of tricky currents and strong winds. Drop by the **Eagle Café** (Pier 39, 415/433–3689) for tips on local sailing conditions. For information on guided sailing trips, *see* Boat Tours *in* Chapter 2.

2 *e-1*
A DAY ON THE BAY
Ideally located in the San Francisco Marina's Small Craft Harbor, A Day On the Bay provides sailing lessons, charters, and rentals. From the harbor you have easy access to the Golden Gate Bridge and open waters. *Off Marina Blvd., between Scott and Webster Sts., The Marina, 415/922–0227.*

3 *b-3*
CAL ADVENTURES
Cal Adventures (*see* Sports & Outdoor Activities, *above*) has several levels of reasonably priced sailing classes and a racing program at the Berkeley Marina's South Sailing Basin. Beginners classes take place year-round. Once you're certified you can rent their 15-foot Coronados. *University Ave. and Marina Blvd., Berkeley, 510/642–4000.*

3 *b-3*
CAL SAILING CLUB
The Cal Sailing Club, not affiliated with Cal Adventures, has operated an affordable sailing school at the Berkeley Marina since the late 1930s. Youths

and adults can learn how to operate 20-ft sloops. Members, once certified, can use the club's boats. On the first Saturday and Sunday of each month the club hosts an Open House where prospective students are invited aboard a free sailboat ride on the bay. *University Ave. and Marina Blvd., Berkeley, 510/287–5905.*

1 *b-2*

CASS' CHARTERS AND SAILING SCHOOL

Cass' has 22- to 75-ft sailboats and cruising yachts and a licensed skipper to navigate them—unless you prefer to do so yourself. To rent sailboats you must have a qualified sailor in your group. Cass' also has a sailing school and a junior sailing camp. *1702 Bridgeway, at Napa St., Sausalito, 415/332–6789 or 800/472–4595.*

3 *b-3*

OLYMPIC CIRCLE SAILING CLUB (OCSC)

This Berkeley Marina sailing school and yacht charter service specializes in group sailing excursions lasting from one hour to several days. Forty 20- to 50-ft sailboats comprise their fleet. *University Ave. and Marina Blvd., 510/843–4200 or 800/223–2984.*

4 *h-7*

SPINNAKER SAILING

Spinnaker Sailing has more than 40 skippered or bare-boat rentals, ranging from 22 to 80 ft. You can take lessons here, sign up for excursions such as their sunset sail tours (*see* Boat Tours *in* Chapter 2), or join their sailing club. *Pier 40, The Embarcadero at Townsend St., South Beach, 415/543–7333.*

SCUBA DIVING

Scuba divers on the California coast face a unique set of rewards and challenges. The beauty of the coast's kelp beds rank them among the world's top diving experiences—and there's always the chance encounter with a migrating humpback whale. Reefs and wrecks are also plentiful. Strong currents and frigid water temperatures are the only drawbacks.

4 *g-8*

BAMBOO REEF ENTERPRISES

This dive shop offers lessons, sales, rentals, and air tank refills. A basic PADI or NAUI certification course (weekend and evening classes available) costs $149.50. The shop has its own heated pool on the premises for diving classes. There's a second branch in the divers' mecca of Monterey (614 Lighthouse Ave., 408/372–1685). The shop is closed Sundays. *584 4th St., at Brannan St., South Beach, 415/362–6694.*

4 *f-6*

SCUBA UNLIMITED

Day, evening, or weekend classes for basic PADI certification cost $138. A full range of diving excursions includes weekend trips aboard the shop's own Monterey-based charter service. Rentals, repairs, and sales are also available here. The store is closed Sundays. *651 Howard St., at New Montgomery St., South of Market, 415/777–3483.*

SEA KAYAKING

Though you can kayak from many points on the bay, it's hard to beat Sausalito, which gives you easy access to Angel Island and lots of undeveloped coastline areas. Farther outside San Francisco, Point Reyes National Seashore and Tomales Bay are spectacular kayaking areas; many of the companies below lead excursions there. Full-moon paddles are another enormously popular way to explore Bay Area waterways. In most cases, previous kayaking experience is not required.

BLUE WATERS KAYAKING

This Inverness-based company leads guided paddling trips in Marin County and the East Bay. They also provide classes and rentals. *Box 983, Inverness 94937, 415/669–2600, 415/669–2600.*

3 *b-3*

CAL ADVENTURES

Cal Adventures (*see* Sports & Outdoor Activities, *above*) offers private sea kayaking lessons year-round at the Berkeley Marina. In addition, there are guided excursions throughout the Bay Area and weekly "group paddle" sessions for all skill levels. Rentals are available. *University Ave. and Marina Blvd., Berkeley, 510/642–4000.*

1 e-3

CALIFORNIA CANOE AND KAYAK

Since 1971, this has been the East Bay's center for kayaking, providing sales, rentals, classes, and guided trips. The company is based at Jack London Square in Oakland. *Jack London Sq., Water St. and Broadway, Oakland, 510/893–7833 or 800/366–9804 for information on classes and trips.*

7 b-3

OUTDOORS UNLIMITED

This UCSF cooperative (*see* Sports & Outdoor Activities, *above*) offers low-cost classes, rentals, and guided excursions to points around San Francisco Bay.

1 b-2

SEA TREK OCEAN KAYAKING CENTER

Based at the Schoonmaker Point Marina in Sausalito, Sea Trek leads trips to Angel Island and other San Francisco Bay destinations, as well as tours of Point Reyes National Seashore. Rentals and classes are available. *Liberty Ship Way, Schoonmaker Point Marina, Sausalito, 415/332–4465 (weekends), 415/488–1000 (weekdays).*

SOCCER

teams to watch

SAN JOSE CLASH

The Clash brought major-league soccer to the Bay Area in 1996. Look for the team from April through September in San Jose's Spartan Stadium (take the Story Road exit from U.S. 101). Buy tickets ($12–$35) through BASS or the San Jose State University box office. *1257 S. 10th St., at Alma Dr., San Jose, 408/985–4625 for tickets.*

where to play

Call the San Francisco Recreation and Parks Department (415/831–2700) for information about the city's soccer leagues, or to reserve one of the city's soccer fields.

2 e-1

MARINA GREEN

Wednesdays after work, folks gather on the Marina Green for brisk pickup soc-

cer games. *Marina Blvd. at Fillmore St., The Marina.*

6 d-1, e-1

POLO FIELD

Sunday mornings year-round, a crowd gathers at two soccer fields at the Polo Field in Golden Gate Park for pickup soccer games. The almost exclusively male players represent many skill levels. Additionally, there are three soccer fields in Golden Gate Park, behind the Beach Chalet at the far west end of the park, opposite 48th Avenue. *Middle Dr., near Martin Luther King Jr. Dr., Golden Gate Park.*

SURFING

Surfing is a quintessential California sport, and daredevil San Franciscans are quick to strap their surfboards to the roofs of their cars when a good south swell hits the coastline. Throughout the Bay Area, waves are best during fall and winter, when storms far out at sea send ripples across the Pacific. Some words to the wise: Many northern California surf spots are for experts only, and along this stretch of the coastline great white sharks roam. When in doubt, check with a local

THE PROS

The Bay Area is proud of its top-notch professional sports teams.

Golden State Warriors (Basketball)
Look for them at the Oakland Coliseum Arena.

Oakland A's (Baseball)
Four-time World Champions.

Oakland Raiders (Football)
Nicknamed the "L.A. Traitors" after they spent 15 years playing in Los Angeles.

San Francisco 49ers (Football)
A football-only stadium is being built for them.

San Francisco Giants (Baseball)
Their brand new stadium is underway.

San Jose Clash (Soccer)
The Bay Area's first major-league soccer team.

San Jose Sharks (Hockey)
Tickets to Sharks games are often sold out.

surf shop about conditions. In addition to Outdoors Unlimited (*see* Sports & Outdoors Activities, *above*), the following are great sources for information, rentals, and lessons: **Livewater** (3450 Hwy. 1, Stinson Beach, 415/868–0333); **Nor-Cal** (5460 Cabrillo Hwy., Pacifica, 415/738–9283); **O'Neil Surf Shop** (1149 41st Ave., Santa Cruz, 408/475–4151 or 408/475–2275 for surf hot line); **Wise Surfboards** (3149 Vicente St., at 43rd Ave., Sunset District, 415/665–7745; 415/665–9473 for surf hot line). In addition, champion surfer Richard Schmidt (408/423–0928) teaches beginners classes through the **Santa Cruz Parks and Recreation Department** (408/429–3663).

5 *a-1*
FORT POINT
One of two popular surf spots in San Francisco, Fort Point has cleaner waves than Ocean Beach, though the strong current and rocky shoreline may deter beginners. On the other hand, you can't beat the views of the Golden Gate Bridge. *Marine Dr., off Long Ave., The Presidio.*

HALF MOON BAY
The beaches along Half Moon Bay are famous hot spots for top-notch surfers, particularly because of a monster wave that occurs every winter in a place known as Maverick's, about ½ mi off Pillar Point Beach at the north edge of Half Moon Bay (near the radar tower). Surfers trek out here from all over the globe, especially in winter. To reach Half Moon Bay from San Francisco, drive 1½ hours south of San Francisco on Highway 1.

2 *a-3*
OCEAN BEACH
Winter waves here can reach up to 25 ft ("triple overhead," to use the current surf lingo). Even when the swells are manageable, the current is extremely strong. Riptides and undertow make it suitable for experienced surfers only. *Great Hwy., between Balboa St. and Sloat Blvd., Richmond District, 415/556–8317.*

1 *a-7*
PACIFICA STATE BEACH
Pacifica breaks best at high tide, with smaller waves for beginners at the southern end of the beach, near San Pedro Point. This is sometimes also known as Linda Mar Beach. Just north of the rocky promontory, on a stretch also known as Rockaway Beach, you'll

find bigger waves—but it's more crowded and competitive. To reach Pacifica, drive 45 minutes south of San Francisco along Highway 1. *Hwy. 1, Pacifica.*

SWIMMING
Though San Francisco Bay is a bracing 55°F, open-water swimming is a local institution. If you'd like to brave the chill, you can minimize the dangers of boat traffic and strong tides by hooking up with members of the two local swimming clubs: the **Dolphin Swim & Boat Club** (415/441-9329), and the **South End Rowing Club** (415/776-7372), both at Aquatic Park (500 and 502 Jefferson St., west of Hyde St., Fisherman's Wharf). Sundays at 7 AM, look for these hardy souls, who usually wear nothing more than bathing suits, headgear, and earplugs. When there's an official swim—usually on a Sunday morning as well—participants may number in the hundreds. Both clubs have been around since the 1870s, and both sponsor biannual swims to Alcatraz Island.

For lap swimmers, the **San Francisco Recreation and Park Department** (415/8831–2700) manages one outdoor swimming pool and seven indoor pools throughout the city. Admission fees at all public pools are $3 adults, 50¢ children ages 17 and under, with discount packages for five, 12, or 15 visits. All public pools have swimming lessons (for children and adults) and water aerobics classes; contact the individual pools for current schedules. A few pools also host workouts for various groups of United States Masters Swimmers, a national swim league.

4 *g-5*
EMBARCADERO YMCA
The Y has has a 25-meter pool, a gym, and spa facilities. A day pass costs $12. *169 Steuart St., between Mission and Howard Sts., South of Market, 415/957–9622.*

5 *h-6*
HAMILTON RECREATION CENTER
The indoor, city-run Hamilton pool is a favorite among Masters swimmers. *Steiner St. at Geary Expressway, Japantown.*

5 *e-8*

KORET HEALTH AND RECREATION CENTER

The well-maintained Olympic-size pool at Koret, part of the University of San Francisco, is open to the public before 2 PM daily with purchase of an $8 day pass. *Parker Ave., at Turk St., Richmond District, 415/666–6820.*

8 *a-3*

MISSION POOL

This is one of the three best city pools. It's outdoors, open from June through September only. *19th and Linda Sts., Mission District, 415/695–5002.*

4 *d-3*

NORTH BEACH POOL

This indoor pool is used by young professionals for lap swimming: It opens as early as 5:45 AM on Mondays, Wednesdays, and Fridays. *Lombard and Mason Sts., North Beach, 415/274–0200.*

5 *d-7*

ROSSI POOL

The six lanes at this excellent indoor pool are open to lap swimmers as early as 5:30 AM on some mornings; call for the current schedule. The pool is rarely crowded. *Arguello Blvd. and Anza St., Richmond District, 415/666–7014.*

6 *g-8*

SAVA POOL

This is one of the more popular (and crowded) indoor city pools. It's 33⅓ yards long, with a total of six lanes. Call for the lap-swimming schedule; the most serious swimmers come to the late-night and early-morning sessions. *19th Ave. and Wawona St., Sunset District, 415/753–7000.*

4 *e-5*

SHEEHAN HOTEL

This hotel allows nonguests to use its four-lane lap pool for a $4 entry fee. *620 Sutter St., at Mason St., Union Square, 415/775–6500.*

TENNIS

The Bay Area hosts the Volvo San Francisco Tennis Tournament (February) in San Francisco, the Cybase Open (February) in San Jose, and the Bank of the West women's tennis tour (October) in Oakland (*see* Events, *in* Chapter 2).

The San Francisco Recreation and Parks Department maintains more than 100 tennis courts around the city. With the exception of courts at Golden Gate Park, all are free and available on a first-come, first-served basis. For information on public tennis courts and a handy map of court locations, contact the San Francisco Recreation and Parks Department (415/831–2700). A few noteworthy private clubs are also listed below.

4 *c-3*

ALICE MARBLE COURTS

These three free courts are unlighted, but still attract a fairly good turn-out of young, tennis-playing professionals year-round. Saturday and Sunday mornings there's usually a wait. *Greenwich and Hyde Sts., Russian Hill.*

7 *b-1, c-1*

GOLDEN GATE PARK

You may make reservations to use the 21 courts at the eastern end of Golden Gate Park on weekends or holidays (reservations are not accepted for weekday use) by calling the Tennis Reservation Line (415/753–7101). Reservations are accepted Wednesdays from 7 PM to 9 PM, Thursdays from 9:15 AM to 5 PM, and Fridays from 9:15 AM to 11:30 AM. Court fees range from $5 to $10. Check the bulletin board at the clubhouse for postings about neighborhood clubs. *John F. Kennedy Dr. at Middle Dr. East, Golden Gate Park.*

5 *h-6*

HAMILTON RECREATION CENTER

Tennis players from all over the city come here to use the two free, lighted courts—even on winter weeknights. *Steiner St. at Geary Expressway, Japantown.*

5 *e-5*

JULIUS KAHN PLAYGROUND

There are four free courts at the southeast corner of The Presidio. *W. Pacific Ave., between Spruce and Locust Sts., The Presidio.*

2 *f-7*

MCLAREN PARK

These six free courts are in the southern section of the city. *Mansell St. near University St., Visitacion Valley.*

7 *h-3*

MISSION DOLORES PARK

These six free courts comprise the largest set of lighted courts in the city. *18th and Dolores Sts., Mission District.*

4 *a-3*

MOSCONE RECREATION CENTER

There are four free, lighted courts and a practice wall here. *1800 Chestnut St., at Buchanan St., The Marina, 415/292–2006.*

4 *d-3*

NORTH BEACH PLAYGROUND

Three free, lighted courts and a practice wall lie within this neighborhood playground. *Lombard and Mason Sts., North Beach.*

8 *e-4*

POTRERO HILL RECREATION CENTER

Find two free lighted courts and a practice wall here. *22nd and Arkansas Sts., Potrero Hill.*

4 *f-3*

SAN FRANCISCO BAY CLUB

One of the city's premiere health clubs, the private Bay Club has two outdoor tennis courts. Drop-in guests must be accompanied by a member, and pay a $15 fee. *150 Greenwich St., between Sansome and Battery Sts., Telegraph Hill, 415/433–2550.*

ULTIMATE FRISBEE

Call the **San Francisco Recreation and Parks Department** (415/831–2700) for information about the local ultimate frisbee league.

7 *c-1*

SHARON MEADOW

To join a free-wheeling game of frisbee, try Sharon Meadow, at the eastern end of Golden Gate Park. On Tuesday and Thursday evenings and weekend mornings, the coed pickup games here sometimes draw up to 40 people. *North of Kezar Dr., Golden Gate Park.*

5 *e-5*

JULIUS KAHN PLAYGROUND

The playground, near the southeast corner of the Presidio, hosts pickup games Wednesday evenings and Saturday mornings. *W. Pacific Ave., between Spruce and Locust Sts., The Presidio.*

VOLLEYBALL

You can rent volleyball nets at **Outdoors Unlimited** (*see* Outdoor Activities & Sports, *above*). The **San Francisco Recreation and Parks Department Division of Athletics** (415/753–7032) runs a women's adult volleyball league; call for information.

7 *e-8*

GLEN PARK RECREATION CENTER

Just south of Glen Canyon Park, you'll find coed adult volleyball on an indoor court twice weekly: Mondays from 7 PM to 9:30 PM for advance players and Tuesdays from 10:30 AM until 1 PM for intermediates. The courts are free of charge and open to all. *70 Elk St., at O'Shaughnessy Blvd., Diamond Heights, 415/337–4705.*

4 *g-4*

JUSTIN HERMAN PLAZA

At the foot of Market Street, in the shadow of the Ferry Building, Justin Herman Plaza has volleyball nets rigged up during summer. *Market and Steuart Sts., The Embarcadero.*

2 *e-1*

MARINA GREEN

Volleyball enthusiasts bring their own nets to the Marina Green on weekends, when dozens of open games take place. *Marina Blvd. at Fillmore St., The Marina.*

4 *a-3*

MOSCONE RECREATION CENTER

The Moscone Rec Center has five unlighted grass courts. High-skill two-on-two games are the norm here. They're first-come, first-served, and you must supply your own nets. *1800 Chestnut St., at Buchanan St., The Marina, 415/292–2006.*

4 *e-7, e-8*

SOUTH OF MARKET RECREATION CENTER

Coed adult volleyball is played on two indoor courts Thursdays from 7 PM until 9:45 PM. The level of play varies between intermediate and advanced. The courts are free of charge. *270 6th St., between Howard and Folsom Sts., South of Market, 415/554–9532.*

WHALE-WATCHING

Several fishing-charter boat services also lead whale-watching trips in season, typically from November through April. **Oceanic Society Expeditions** (*see* Bird-Watching, *above*) leads extended excursions around the Bay Area and shorter trips to the Farallon Islands. Pick up a copy of the *Oceanic Society Field Guide to the Gray Whale*, which includes maps and directions to the best whale-watching sites in California, or call the OSE's Whale Hotline (415/474–0488) for recorded updates on marine-life sightings. In addition, **Dolphin Charters** (Berkeley Marina, University Ave. and Marina Blvd., Berkeley, 510/527–9622), an adventure cruising company, has full-day trips to the Farallon Islands and half-day trips closer to the coastline.

WINDSURFING

The San Francisco Bay is the third-ranked windsurfing spot in the United States, behind Hawaii's Maui island and Oregon's Royal Gorge. The westerly winds that blow from April through August provide optimal conditions; at other times of year, the winds are sporadic and blow either north or south. To tackle this sport in winter, you'll need a 3/2- or 4/3-mm-thick wet suit.

Many of the area's sailing schools also teach windsurfing and rent equipment (*see* Sailing, *above*). In addition, **City Front Sailboards** (2936 Lyon St., at Lombard St., The Presidio, 415/929–7873), just blocks away from Crissy Field, has a beginner's instruction package as well as a full line of equipment, while the **San Francisco School of Windsurfing** (1 Harding Rd., Lake Merced, 415/753–3235) has lessons for beginners on mild Lake Merced, and for advanced surfers at Candlestick Point.

2 *h-8*

CANDLESTICK POINT STATE RECREATION AREA

Windsurfers who crave speed launch from the beach adjacent to 3Com stadium, where the winds average between 19 and 25 mi per hour but occasionally reach a brisk 55 mi per hour. This area is not for beginners; the winds can be fickle, and can leave inexperience surfers stranded out in the bay. Parking at 3Com stadium costs a hefty $20 on game days during football season, $6 during baseball season, and is closed on non-game days. Instead, most windsurfers park within the state recreation area at the "windsurf circle" lot; from U.S. 101, take the 3Com exit, continue halfway around the stadium, then turn right at the first set of yellow gates. Parking at windsurf circle is $6 on game days, free on all other days. For more information on Candlestick Point State Recreation Area, call the ranger office (415/671–0145). The park is open daily from 8 to 8, with shorter hours in winter. *Jamestown Ave. and Harney Way, South San Francisco.*

1 *d-8*

1 *e-8*

COYOTE POINT

South of San Francisco International Airport is another challenging windsurfing spot. The waves are choppy here, but close to shore the wind remains moderate. Follow U.S. 101 south 4½ mi past the airport exit and follow signs to the city of San Mateo's Coyote Point Park (415/573–2592). The park entry fee is $4. There are restrooms and hot showers. *Coyote Point Dr., off Hwy. 101, San Mateo.*

5 *d-2*

CRISSY FIELD

The waters off Crissy Field, in the Presidio, are strictly for expert windsurfers. While beach access makes launching easy, strong tides and currents can easily sweep a novice under the Golden Gate into the Pacific or across the bay to Treasure Island. Add heavy boat and ship traffic and you'll see why more rescues are required here than in all other Bay Area sites combined. *Hwy. 101 and Presidio Ave., The Presidio.*

WRESTLING

2 *e-8, f-8*

COW PALACE

In addition to rodeos and various sporting events, the Cow Palace hosts professional wrestling matches twice each year, usually in February and September. Call for ticket prices and show dates. *2600 Geneva Ave., at Santos St., Daly City, 415/469–6065 for box office.*

YOGA

The city's yoga institutes tailor weekend and evening classes to suit even the busiest schedule. Most welcome participants on a drop-in, pay-per-class basis, with no advance registration required.

7 *h-4*

INTEGRAL YOGA INSTITUTE

The Institute, founded by the Reverend Sri Swami Satchidananda, has daily classes in three levels of Hatha yoga (which emphasize breathing, posture, and meditation) and one gentle yoga class. All of the 1½-hour classes operate on a drop-in basis. Cost is $7, first-time participants and senior citizens $4. Retreats, stress management programs, and meditation workshops are held occasionally throughout the year. *770 Dolores St., at 21st St., Mission District, 415/821–1117; or 415/824–9600 for recorded schedule of classes.*

6 *f-7*

IYENGAR YOGA INSTITUTE OF SAN FRANCISCO

The institute offers more than 30 classes of Iyengar yoga (a type of Hatha yoga) for all levels each week; call for a current schedule. Most classes are 1½ hours and cost $12 per session (drop-ins welcome), or $40 for four. *2404 27th Ave., at Taraval St., Sunset District, 415/753–0909.*

5 *d-6*

MAGANA & WALT BAPTISTE YOGA CENTER

The oldest established yoga school in San Francisco has classes in Baptiste yoga (a type of Hatha yoga) on Wednesday evenings and Saturday mornings. Cost is $12 for a single session, $45 for four sessions, or $110 for 12 sessions. The center also hosts several meditation programs throughout the year; these

cost between $15 and $20 per session. *730 Euclid Ave., between Palm and Jordan Sts., Richmond District, 415/387–6833.*

8 *b-5*

YOGA SOCIETY OF SAN FRANCISCO

At this nonprofit community center, Hatha yoga classes cost $10 per session or $40 for five. Drop-ins are welcome. There are two classes daily, open to all levels; each class is 1½ hours. Daily at 7 AM there is a free 45-minute meditation class. Weekdays from 7:30 PM to 9 PM the center hosts a fire ceremony (meditation and chanting) that's free and open to all. Special events include workshops on spirituality and meditation; call for more information. *2872 Folsom St., at 25th St., Mission District, 415/285–5537.*

fitness centers & health clubs

Most of San Francisco's dozens of fitness centers and health clubs sell day passes for $10–$20, though some of the most luxurious remain "members only." Check the Yellow Pages under "Health Clubs" for a complete listing.

Many of the large downtown hotels have arrangements with neighborhood health clubs, and a number of hotels have health facilities of their own. Nonguests are welcome to use the facilities at the **Fairmont Hotel** (950 Mason St., at California St., Nob Hill, 415/772–5000), where a day pass costs $15; and the **Hotel Nikko** (222 Mason St., betweeen Ellis and O'Farrell Sts., Union Square, 415/394–1153), where a weekly pass costs $35.

4 *c-6*

24-HOUR NAUTILUS FITNESS CENTERS

The four branches of Nautilus are open to the public for a $15 drop-in fee. Facilities and services vary, but most of the clubs have saunas, Jacuzzis, and steam rooms as well as aerobics classes and a complete line of fitness equipment. *1200 Van Ness Ave., at Sutter St., Polk Gulch, 415/776–2200.*

4 d-2

350 Bay St., Fisherman's Wharf, 415/395–9595.

4 g-5

100 California St., Suite 200, Financial District, 415/434–5080.

4 g-6

2nd St. at Folsom St., South of Market, 415/543–7808.

4 f-4
CLUB ONE

A $15 day pass gives non-members access to Club One Embarcadero Center, Club One Citicorp Center, Club One Yerba Buena, and Club One Nob Hill. Like Nautilus, most of these clubs have saunas, Jacuzzis, and steam rooms as well as aerobics classes and a complete line of fitness equipment. The Club One at Citicorp Center has a rock-climbing wall (*see* Rock Climbing, *above*). *2 Embarcadero Center, at Clay St., The Embarcadero, 415/788–1010 or 800/258–2663. Also: 1 Sansome St., at Sutter St., Financial District (map 4, f-5), 415/399–1010; 350 Third St., at Folsom St., South of Market (map 4, f-6), 415/512–1010 ; 950 California St., at Mason St., Nob Hill (map 4, d-5), 415/834–1010.*

4 g-5
EMBARCADERO YMCA

Of the five YMCA fitness centers in San Francisco, this is the best. In fact, it ranks among San Francisco's finest health clubs, YMCA or no. There are two racquetball courts, a 25-meter swimming pool, a basketball court, a small running track, weights and cardiovascular equipment, and aerobics classes. The $12 drop-in fee includes use of the sauna, steam room, and whirlpool—plus magnificent views of the bay. *169 Steuart St., between Mission and Howard Sts., South of Market, 415/957–9622.*

5 e-8
KORET HEALTH AND RECREATION CENTER

On the University of San Francisco campus, Koret is open to the general public before 2 PM daily with purchase of an $8 day pass. Facilities include an Olympic-size swimming pool, basketball courts, cardiovascular and weight equipment, and aerobics classes. The pass also gives you access to showers, lockers, a Jacuzzi, and saunas. *Parker Ave., at Turk St., Richmond District, 415/666–6820.*

WOMEN'S TRAINING CENTER

Those who prefer a women-only atmosphere can work out here for a $10 day fee, which includes use of the sauna. They also have cardiovascular equipment, exercise bikes, StairMasters, treadmills, free weights, and Cybex resistance training equipment, as well as lockers and showers. *2164 Market St., between Church and Sanchez Sts., Mission District, 415/864–6835.*

chapter 7

HOTELS

Not surprisingly, San Francisco, the tourist capital of the United States, has hotel rooms of every size, style, and swankiness: small bed-and-breakfasts with the bath down the hall, opulent luxury hotels on Nob Hill, and everything in between. The bad news is that rooms don't come cheap. First-time visitors are often surprised to find that except for a few rare bargains, even relatively bland hotel rooms in central neighborhoods can go for $150 a night or more.

The largest concentration of accommodations is around Union Square, where mostly ritzy hotels are near the city's best shopping, most of its theaters, and public transportation. A few blocks uphill from Union Square, some of the city's most prestigious hotels look down on the city from Nob Hill. Another cluster of hotels, all held down to four stories or fewer due to city ordinances, is found around Fisherman's Wharf; rooms here are a bit more bland, though prices are high because of the location. The other main hotel area is along Lombard Street, the main corridor leading to the Golden Gate bridge. Though Lombard Street is close to the waterfront and gives you easy access to Marin County, it's not one of the city's more attractive areas, and traffic noise can be a problem.

Don't overlook San Francisco's more residential neighborhoods. Atmospheric North Beach is packed with Italian restaurants and cafés but has surprisingly few hotels; still, a few small B&Bs hide on the neighborhood's side streets. The Castro, the most prominent gay neighborhood in the United States, is full of accommodations catering to gay and lesbian travelers. Haight-Ashbury, with its flower power history, attracts those hoping to recapture the '60s. The upscale residential Marina District and neighboring Pacific Heights draw visitors looking for a quiet neighborhood and views of the bay and the Golden Gate Bridge.

Whenever you come, make reservations as far in advance as possible for the best possible selection. This is especially important in late summer and early fall. And when calculating your expenses, don't forget to figure in the 14% hotel tax that will take an extra bite out of your wallet. Most San Francisco hotels, especially those around Union Square, the Financial District, and Nob Hill charge hefty rates for parking—often around $25 a night. The price categories used below refer to a standard room for two people. At most of these places you can find suites or deluxe rooms for considerably more, and occasionally you can score a smaller room for somewhat less.

Except for some tiny B&Bs, most hotels in San Francisco have at least a few rooms, and often several entire floors, where smoking is prohibited.

price categories

CATEGORY	COST*
Very Expensive Lodgings	over $175
Expensive Lodgings	$120–$175
Moderately Priced Lodgings	$80–$120
Budget Accommodations	under $80

*All prices are for a standard double room, excluding 14% tax.

VERY EXPENSIVE LODGINGS

7 f-1

BELLA VISTA INN

Formerly called Anna's Three Bears, the Bella Vista is on a quiet street in the residential Buena Vista Heights between the Castro and the Haight. Each of the three suites has two or three bedrooms, a spacious living room, a fully stocked kitchen, wood-burning fireplaces, and private decks (the only place where smoking is allowed). Eclectic furnishings and views of downtown San Francisco and the bay make for a gracious yet relaxed environment. 114 Divisadero, at Duboce St., The Haight, 94117, 415/255–3167 or 800/428–

8559, fax 415/552–2959. 3 suites. Parking (fee). AE, D, MC, V.

4 e-5

CAMPTON PLACE

Highly attentive service is the hallmark of this small, top-tier hotel behind a simple brownstone facade. Though many rooms are small, all are supremely elegant, with Asian touches in subtle earth tones, and all have luxurious marble baths. The Campton Place Restaurant is famed for its breakfasts, and Wednesday martini nights (5:30–8:30) in the lounge have become a favorite midweek cruising ground for the downtown crowd. 340 Stockton St., between Post and Sutter Sts., Union Square, 94108, 415/781–5555 or 800/235–4300, fax 415/955–5536. 117 rooms. Restaurant, bar, in-room safes, minibars, room service, laundry service and dry cleaning, concierge, business services, meeting rooms, parking (fee). AE, DC, MC, V.

3 f-3

THE CLAREMONT

About 30 minutes from downtown San Francisco on the Oakland–Berkeley border, this luxurious European–style resort has provided refuge from the urban fray since 1915. Treat yourself to an herbal bath or therapeutic massage in the spa, then dine poolside at the Bayview Café. Rooms, with either hillside or bay views, vary from quite small to elegantly spacious, but all have a refined look that reflects the hotel's respectable age. 41 Tunnel Rd., near Ashby and Claremont Aves. Berkeley, 94705, 510/843–3000 or 800/551–7266, fax 510/848–6208. 279 rooms. 2 restaurants, bar, café, in-room modem lines, minibars, room service, outdoor pool, beauty salon, massage, sauna, steam room, health club, jogging, 10 tennis courts, shops, nightclub, laundry service and dry cleaning, concierge, business services, meeting rooms, parking (fee). AE, D, DC, MC, V.

4 d-6

THE CLIFT

The lobby's dark paneling and enormous chandeliers lend a note of grandeur to this quiet, handsome hotel with a well-deserved reputation for superior service. Rooms, some rich with dark woods and burgundies, others refreshingly pastel, have large writing desks, plants, and flowers. The French Room is the place for power breakfasts and dinners, and the art deco Redwood Room draws an upscale crowd at the end of the working day. 495 Geary St., at Taylor St., Union Square, 94102, 415/775–4700 or 800/652–5438, fax 415/441–4621. 329 rooms. Restaurant, bar, in-room modem lines, minibars, room service, exercise room, laundry service and dry cleaning, concierge, business services, meeting rooms, parking (fee). AE, DC, MC, V.

5 g-5

EL DRISCO

This historic little Pacific Heights hotel (Eisenhower once stayed here), unheard of by most San Franciscans, is known for unfailingly attentive service and a genteel ambience. Wonderful views of the bay from the upper floors are another perk. Eleven of the rooms are rented on a monthly basis. 2901 Pacific Ave., at Broderick St., Pacific Heights, 94115, 415/346–2880, fax 415/567–5537. 54 rooms. Laundry service. AE, D, DC, MC, V.

ROMANTIC GETAWAYS

If you're in the right frame of mind, many of the hotels reviewed here will do very well for a romantic rendezvous. But for that honeymoon trip or anniversary weekend, try one of the following.

The Archbishop's Mansion (Expensive)
   Hold your honey under the chandelier used in Gone With the Wind.

Hotel Bohème (Expensive)
   Near many romantic Italian restaurants.

Hotel Majestic (Expensive)
   Straight out of a storybook, with gas fireplaces and claw-foot tubs.

Inn at the Opera (Expensive)
   Curl up by the fireplace for afternoon tea or evening wine.

Sherman House (Very Expensive)
   The city's most romantic hotel, bar none.

Union Street Inn (Expensive)
   Soak in your own private whirlpool tub.

4 d-5

THE FAIRMONT

Commanding the top of Nob Hill, the Fairmont, which served as the model for the St. Gregory in the TV series *Hotel*, has the most awe-inspiring lobby in the city, with a soaring vaulted ceiling and a grand wraparound staircase. The tower rooms, which have spectacular city and bay views, reflect a more modern style than their smaller Victorian counterparts in the older building. Service isn't always as attentive here as it is at some of San Francisco's other top hotels. *950 Mason St., at California St., Nob Hill, 94108, 415/772–5000 or 800/527–4727, fax 415/837–0587. 596 rooms. 4 restaurants, 5 bars, room service, spa, barber shop, beauty salon, health club, concierge, business services, laundry service and dry cleaning, car rental. AE, D, DC, MC, V.*

4 d-6

HOTEL MONACO

866 622 284

Unquestionably the hippest hotel in town, the Hotel Monaco surprises guests with a dramatic lobby, where a fireplace climbs almost two stories toward the three huge domes of a whimsically painted vaulted ceiling. Though small, the rooms are comfortable and inviting, with a riot of stripes and vivid colors. *501 Geary St., at Taylor St., Union Square, 94102, 415/292–0100 or 800/214–4220, fax 415/292–0111. 201 rooms. Restaurant, bar, in-room modem lines, room service, massage, sauna, exercise room, laundry service and dry cleaning, business services, parking (fee). AE, D, DC, MC, V.*

4 e-6

HOTEL NIKKO
SAN FRANCISCO

A piano player provides live nightly entertainment in the Fountain Lounge of the Nikko Hotel—a nod to the civilized atmosphere of Union Square. Rooms are warmly decorated, largely with elegant diamond-patterned wallpaper, teak desks, and terra-cotta colored furniture. The excellent fifth-floor fitness facility has dry saunas, traditional *ofuros* (Japanese soaking tubs), a *kamaburo* (Japanese sauna), and the city's only glass-enclosed swimming pool and whirlpool. *222 Mason St., between Ellis and O'Farrell Sts., Union Square, 94102, 415/394–1111 or 800/645–5687, fax 415/394–1106. 522 rooms. Restaurant, in-room modem lines, minibars, beauty salon,*

massage, exercise room, laundry service and dry cleaning, concierge, business services, meeting rooms, parking (fee). No pets. AE, D, DC, MC, V.*

8 315

4 d-5

THE HUNTINGTON

Across from Grace Cathedral and the small but captivating Huntington Park, the redbrick Huntington provides a quiet alternative to the larger, flashier Nob Hill hotels. The highly attentive staff is known for attentive personal service and protecting the privacy of its celebrity guests. Individually decorated rooms are relatively large and reflect the Huntington's traditional style, with opulent materials such as raw silks and velvets in deep shades of cocoa, gold, and burgundy. *1075 California St., between Taylor and Mason Sts., Nob Hill, 94108, 415/474–5400 or 800/227–4683; 800/652–1539 in CA; fax 415/474–6227. 140 rooms. Restaurant, bar, in-room modem lines, in-room safes, room service, laundry service and dry cleaning, concierge, meeting rooms, parking (fee). No pets. AE, D, DC, MC, V.*

4 g-4

HYATT REGENCY

The 20-story Hyatt at the foot of Market Street is the focal point of the multimillion-dollar Embarcadero Center, where more than 100 shops and restaurants cater to Financial District workers and visitors. The spectacular 17-story atrium lobby is a wonder of full-size trees, a running stream, and enough greenery to landscape a small park. Rooms, some with bay-view balconies, are decorated in two styles: One strikes a more masculine tone with a black-and-brown color scheme, while the other has soft rose-and-plum combinations. *5 Embarcadero Center, at Market St., Embarcadero, 94111, 415/788–1234 or 800/233–1234, fax 415/398–2567. 805 rooms. 2 restaurants, bar, lobby lounge, room service, exercise room, concierge, concierge floor, parking (fee). No pets. AE, D, DC, MC, V.*

4 f-5

MANDARIN ORIENTAL

In the heart of the city's Financial District, the Mandarin Oriental occupies the top 11 floors of a 48-story building, with two towers connected by a dramatic glass sky bridge. Rooms are sedately decorated with off-white textured wallpaper, walnut armoires, and large writing desks. All have spectacular views, but the real showstoppers are the 22 Mandarin rooms, where enormous marble bathrooms have floor-to-ceiling windows next to extra-deep soaking tubs. A pianist performs in the first-floor lounge every evening from 4:30 to 8:30. *222 Sansome St., between California and Pine Sts., Financial District, 94104, 415/885–0999 or 800/622–0404, fax 415/433–0289. 158 rooms. Restaurant, lobby lounge, in-room modem lines, minibars, room service, exercise room, laundry service and dry cleaning, concierge, business services, meeting rooms, parking (fee). No pets. AE, DC, MC, V.*

4 *d-5*

MARK HOPKINS INTER-CONTINENTAL

An elegant marble-floored lobby is your introduction to this 20-story San Francisco landmark. The dramatic, neoclassical rooms glow with subtle shades of gray, silver, and khaki; bedspreads feature bold leaf prints; and bathrooms are lined with Italian marble. Rooms on the upper floors have views of either the Golden Gate Bridge or the downtown cityscape, and the newly renovated rooftop lounge, the Top of the Mark, provides an almost 360-degree view of the city. *999 California St., at Mason St., Nob Hill, 94108, 415/392–3434 or 800/662–4455, fax 415/421–3302. 392 rooms. 2 restaurants, 2 bars, room service, exercise room, laundry service and dry cleaning, concierge, business services, car rental. No pets. AE, D, DC, MC, V.*

4 *e-5*

NOB HILL LAMBOURNE

Though this urban retreat is designed with the traveling executive in mind— rooms have computers, fax machines, and spacious desks—it's also a great choice for anyone eager to unwind. The on-site spa lends out "wellness" videos on topics such as yoga and tai chi, and exercise equipment may be brought to your room on request. Rooms have queen-size beds with hand-sewn mattresses, luxurious silk damask bedding, and contemporary furnishings in muted colors. A deluxe Continental breakfast and evening wine service are complimentary. *725 Pine St., at Stockton St., Nob Hill, 94108, 415/433–2287 or 800/274–8466, fax 415/433–0975. 20 rooms. Breakfast room, in-room modem lines, kitchenettes, in-room VCRs, spa, laundry*

service and dry cleaning, business services, parking (fee). No pets. AE, D, DC, MC, V.

4 *f-6*

THE PALACE HOTEL

A landmark hotel since its opening in 1875, the Palace, now owned by Sheraton, wows first-time visitors with its stunning entryway and the belle epoque–style Garden Court restaurant, which has graceful chandeliers and a lead-glass ceiling. Among the lavish public spaces is the Pied Piper Bar, named for its Maxfield Parrish mural. Rooms are less exciting, though perfectly functional. The hotels' Kyo-ya restaurant is widely considered the city's best Japanese restaurant. *2 New Montgomery St., at Market St., South of Market, 94105, 415/392–8600 or 800/325–3535, fax 415/543–0671. 550 rooms. 3 restaurants, bar, lobby lounge, in-room modem lines, in-room safes, minibars, room service, indoor lap pool, sauna, exercise room, laundry service, concierge, business services, meeting rooms, parking (fee). No pets. AE, D, DC, MC, V.*

4 *d-6*

PAN PACIFIC HOTEL

Exotic flower arrangements fill all the hushed common areas of this supremeley elegant, business-oriented hotel— including the atrium, which rises 21 stories above a sculpted bronze fountain. Bathrooms lined with Portuguese marble are the highlight of the guest rooms, which are which have pale-green or mauve-and-beige color schemes. The hotel's restaurant, Pacific, is well regarded for its contemporary cuisine. *500 Post St., at Mason St., Union Square, 94102, 415/771–8600 or 800/327–8585, fax 415/398–0267. 330 rooms. Restaurant, bar, lobby lounge, in-room modem lines, minibars, room service, exercise room, piano, laundry service and dry cleaning, concierge, business services, meeting rooms, parking (fee). No pets. AE, D, DC, MC, V.*

4 *d-6*

PRESCOTT HOTEL

Though not as famous as many hotels in the area, the Prescott has several advantages: The relatively small size means personalized service, and its relationship with Postrio, the Wolfgang Puck restaurant attached to its lobby, means you get preferred reservations. Rooms traditional, with a rich hunter-green theme. The fireplace in the hunting lodge–style living room is a perfect setting for the complimentary coffee service and evening wine and cheese receptions. *545 Post St., between Taylor and Mason Sts., Union Square, 94102, 415/ 563–0303 or 800/283–7322, fax 415/563– 6831. 165 rooms. Restaurant, bar, in-room modem lines, minibars, room service, concierge, business services, meeting rooms, parking (fee). No pets. AE, D, DC, MC, V.*

4 *e-5*

RENAISSANCE STANFORD COURT

Built in 1912, this Nob Hill landmark has a reputation as one of the city's most exclusive hotels. The lobby is dominated by a stained-glass dome, a dramatic mural depicting scenes of early San Francisco, and high-quality arts and antiques—it's the perfect setting for an elegant afternoon tea. Rooms invariably achieve understated elegance with a mix of English country manor–style furnishings accented with Asian artwork and accessories. *905 California St., at Powell St., Nob Hill, 94108, 415/989–3500 or 800/227–4736; 800/622–0957 in CA; fax 415/391–0513. 402 rooms. Restaurant, bar, in-room modem lines, room service, exercise room, piano, laundry service and dry cleaning, concierge, business services, meeting rooms, parking (fee). No pets. AE, D, DC, MC, V.*

4 *e-5*

RITZ-CARLTON, SAN FRANCISCO

Recently rated the top hotel in San Francisco for the third year in row by *Condé Nast Traveler* magazine, the Ritz-Carlton defines opulence and attentive service: As you enter the grand lobby, white-gloved staff members present themselves, at the ready. Rich cream colors and top-quality contemporary and antique reproduction furnishings give the spacious guest rooms a luxurious feel, and baths are of Italian marble. The hotel's newly renovated fitness center, complete with swimming pool and saunas, is a destination in its own right, as is the renowned Dining Room (*see* French *in* Dining). *600 Stockton St., at California St., Nob Hill, 94108, 415/296– 7465 or 800/241–3333, fax 415/291–0288. 336 rooms. 2 restaurants, 2 bars, lobby lounge, in-room modem lines, in-room safes, minibars, room service, laundry service and dry cleaning, concierge, business services, meeting rooms, car rental, parking (fee). AE, D, DC, MC, V.*

4 *e-6*

SAN FRANCISCO MARRIOTT

When this 40-story hotel opened in 1989, critics alternately raved about and condemned its distinctive design— modern art deco, with large fanlike windows across the top (it's been compared to a parking meter and a jukebox). The pastel rooms are small but functional. Conventioneers often stay here; it's also a good choice for art buffs, as it's across the street from the San Francisco Museum of Modern Art and the Yerba Buena Gardens complex. *55 Fourth St., at Mission St., South of Market, 94103, 415/896–1600 or 800/ 228–9290, fax 415/896–6177. 1,500 rooms. 3 restaurants, bar, piano bar, in-room modem lines, minibars, room service, indoor pool, sauna, exercise room, laundry service and dry cleaning, concierge, business services, meeting rooms, car rental, parking (fee). No pets. AE, D, DC, MC, V.*

5 *h-4*

SHERMAN HOUSE

This magnificent 1876 Italianate mansion at the foot of residential Pacific Heights is San Francisco's most luxurious small hotel. Decadence is the reigning mood, from the canopied four-poster featherbeds to the wood-burning fireplaces and sumptuous bathrooms, some with whirlpool baths. Every room is different, but all are a tasteful mix of Biedermeier, English Jacobean, or French Second Empire antiques. Though one of the priciest properties in San Francisco, it's also the single most romantic place to stay in the city. *2160 Green St., between Fillmore and Webster Sts., Pacific Heights, 94123, 415/563–3600 or 800/424–5777, fax 415/ 563–1882. 14 rooms. Dining room, room service, in-room VCRs, piano, concierge, airport shuttle. No pets. AE, DC, MC, V.*

4 *e-6*

WESTIN ST. FRANCIS

This grande dame of San Francisco hotels is the preferred destination of visiting royalty and world leaders (all the U.S. presidents since Taft have stayed here), as well as convention and tour groups. The original 1904 building, with its beautiful marble-columned lobby, has been augmented with a 32-floor tower addition. Many rooms in the original building are small by modern standards, but all retain their original

Victorian-style moldings; rooms in the modern tower are larger, with an Oriental motif. *335 Powell St., between Post and Geary Sts., Union Square, 94102, 415/397–7000 or 800/228–3000, fax 415/774–0124. 1,192 rooms. 3 restaurants, 2 bars, in-room modem lines, in-room safes, mini-bars, room service, exercise room, nightclub, concierge, business services, meeting rooms, travel services, car rental, parking (fee). No pets. AE, D, DC, MC, V.*

EXPENSIVE LODGINGS

5 h-8

THE ARCHBISHOP'S MANSION

This Second Empire–style mansion, built in 1904 for Archbishop Patrick Riordan, faces Alamo Square and its brightly painted Victorian homes. In the cavernous sitting room hangs a chandelier used in the movie *Gone With the Wind*. Individually decorated guest rooms are full of ornate antiques; some have whirlpool tubs or fireplaces. Enjoy complimentary Continental breakfast in the dining room or in your room; there's also an afternoon wine service. *1000 Fulton St., at Steiner St., Western Addition, 94117, 415/563–7872 or 800/543–5820, fax 415/885–3193. 15 rooms. Breakfast room, in-room VCRs, piano, free parking. No pets. AE, MC, V.*

5 h-7

CHÂTEAU TIVOLI

Though there are a lot of bright "painted ladies" on Alamo Square, perhaps none is as conspicuous as this late 19th-century château, painted in no fewer than 22 colors. The dramatic rooms vary in style but are large, comfortable, and loaded with antiques and knickknacks; a few have fireplaces, and one of the suites has a kitchenette. Guests are treated to Continental breakfast on weekdays and champagne brunch on weekends. *1057 Steiner St., at Golden Gate Ave., Western Addition, 94115, 415/776–5462 or 800/228–1647, fax 415/776–0505. 5 rooms, 4 with shared bath, 4 suites. Dining room. No pets. AE, MC, V.*

4 f-5

GALLERIA PARK

The black marble facade of Galleria Park is a few blocks east of Union Square, convenient to the Financial District, the Chinatown Gate, and the Crocker Galleria—one of San Francisco's most elegant shopping areas. The comfortable rooms all have floral bedspreads and stylish striped wallpaper. The hotel has the city's only rooftop garden. *191 Sutter St., at Kearny St., Financial District, 94104, 415/781–3060 or 800/792–9639, fax 415/433–4409. 177 rooms. 2 restaurants, in-room modem lines, minibars, room service, exercise room, jogging, concierge, business services, meeting rooms. No pets. AE, D, DC, MC, V.*

4 g-5

HARBOR COURT

Within shouting distance of the Bay Bridge and the many nightclubs and restaurants of SoMa, this cozy hotel is noted for exemplary service. Some guest rooms overlook the bay; others face a garden courtyard. In the evening complimentary wine is served in the cozy, earth-tone lounge, sometimes accompanied by live guitar. Guests have free access to the excellent YMCA facilities next door. *165 Steuart St., between Howard and Mission Sts., The Embar-*

HOTEL ORIGINALS

A new breed of boutique theme hotels is burgeoning in San Francisco. Much more than mere places to sleep, these hotels distinguish themselves with unique styles and attitudes that often conjure up escapist fantasylands, from the tropics to the Far East.

Hotel Monaco (Very Expensive)
   A chic, 1940s theme.

Hotel Triton (Expensive)
   A mecca for the avant-garde.

Mandarin Oriental (Very Expensive)
   Bathing has never been so luxurious!

The Mansions (Expensive)
   A pig collection and a campy magic show.

Nob Hill Lambourne (Very Expensive)
   An urban retreat geared toward health and wellness.

Phoenix Hotel (Moderately Priced)
   Kitschy tropical decor and a celebrity clientele.

Radisson Miyako Hotel (Expensive)
   Some rooms have tatami mats and futon beds.

The Red Victorian (Moderately Priced)
   Request the Summer of Love room.

cadero, 94105, 415/882–1300 or 800/346–0555, fax 415/882–1313. 131 rooms. Restaurant, in-room modem lines, minibars, room service, business services, parking (fee). No pets. AE, D, DC, MC, V.

4 e-3

HOTEL BOHÈME

In the middle of historic North Beach, this little bargain, formerly the Millefiori Inn, gives guests a taste of the past with coral-color walls, bistro tables, and memorabilia recalling the beat generation. Enjoy complimentary sherry in the lobby while you deliberate over the many nearby Italian restaurants and cafés. Rooms in the rear are quieter. 444 Columbus Ave., at Vallejo St., North Beach, 94133, 415/433–9111, fax 415/362–6292. 15 rooms. Parking (fee). No pets. AE, D, DC, MC, V.

4 e-6

HOTEL DIVA

A gray awning and burnished silver facade give this reasonably priced hotel a high-tech look. The lobby is very plain by San Francisco standards, but the rooms pick up the futuristic decor theme with angular velvet sofas, wire-frame chairs, and black-lacquer furniture. Although the Diva's proximity to the city's theaters attracts those with an artistic bent, the hotel is also popular with families, who entertain themselves with the in-room Nintendo and VCRs. 440 Geary St., at Mason St., Union Square, 94102, 415/885–0200 or 800/553–1900, fax 415/346–6613. 110 rooms. Restaurant, in-room modem lines, in-room safes, exercise room, business services, meeting room. AE, D, DC, MC, V.

4 g-5

HOTEL GRIFFON

Occupying a stately 1906 building, the Hotel Griffon attracts business travelers with its proximity to the Financial District, and pleasure travelers with its view of the Bay Bridge. Rooms are quietly elegant, with beige tones and cherry or mahogany pieces. In-room CD players are a nice touch. 155 Steuart St., between Mission and Howard Sts., The Embarcadero, 94105, 415/495-2100 or 800/321–2201, fax 415/495–3522. 62 rooms. Restaurant, in-room modem lines, minibars, room service, laundry service and dry cleaning, business services, meeting room, parking (fee). No pets. AE, D, DC, MC, V.

4 b-6

HOTEL MAJESTIC

One of San Francisco's original grand hotels, this five-story yellow-and-white 1902 Edwardian is extremely romantic. Most of the guest rooms have gas fireplaces, a mix of French and English antiques, and canopied beds; some have original claw-foot bathtubs. In the afternoons, guests enjoy complimentary sherry and homemade biscotti in the lobby, where black-marble stairs, antique chandeliers, and a white-marble fireplace make a statement. 1500 Sutter St., at Gough St., Western Addition, 94109, 415/441–1100 or 800/869–8966, 415/673–7331. 57 rooms. Restaurant, bar, in-room modem lines, minibars, room service, laundry and dry cleaning, concierge, business services, meeting rooms, parking (fee). AE, DC, MC, V.

4 e-5

HOTEL REX

Literary and artistic creativity are the causes célèbres at the stylish Hotel Rex, where thousands of books line the clubby, 1920s-style lobby—the site of frequent book readings and roundtable discussions. Upstairs, quotations from works by California writers are painted on the terra-cotta-color walls of the generously sized rooms, which are outfitted with boldly striped bedspreads and whimsically hand-painted lampshades. 562 Sutter St., between Powell and Mason Sts., Union Square, 94102, 415/433–4434, fax 415/433–3695. 94 rooms. Bar, lobby lounge, in-room modem lines, minibars, laundry service and dry cleaning, concierge, parking (fee). AE, D, DC, MC, V.

4 e-5

HOTEL TRITON

A whimsical lobby of three-legged furniture, star-patterned carpeting, and inverted gilt pillars give you a hint of the zaniness to come: Rooms are decked out with pink and gold paint, S-curved chairs, and oddball light fixtures. The fashion, entertainment, music, and film-industry types who frequent this place don't seem to mind the uncommonly small rooms or the uneven service. 342 Grant Ave., at Bush St., Financial District, 94108, 415/394–0500 or 800/433–6611, fax 415/394–0555. 140 rooms. In-room modem lines, exercise room, laundry service, business services, meeting room, parking (fee). AE, D, DC, MC, V.

4 *e-5*

HOTEL VINTAGE COURT

This bit of the Napa Valley 2 blocks from Union Square has quiet, cheery rooms—some with sunny window seats—decorated with jade and rose floral fabrics. Complimentary wine served every evening in front of the lobby fireplace and a deluxe Continental breakfast have created a congenial atmosphere without driving prices up. Guests get preferred reservations at adjoining Masa's, the city's most celebrated French restaurant. *650 Bush St., between Powell and Stockton Sts., Union Square, 94108, 415/392–4666 or 800/654–1100, fax 415/433–4065. 107 rooms. Restaurant, bar, minibars, refrigerators, laundry service, meeting rooms, parking (fee). No pets. AE, D, DC, MC, V.*

4 *b-7*

INN AT THE OPERA

Highly recommended for its tranquil, intimate setting, this European-style hotel a block or so from Davies Hall and the War Memorial Opera House hosts the music and dance greats that perform at these venues. Creamy pastels and dark-wood furnishings give the rooms an air of warmth, compounded by terry-cloth robes, fresh flowers, and a basket of apples. Each room has a microwave oven and a minibar, should you decide to enjoy a simple supper in privacy. A major attraction is the sumptuously romantic, dimly lighted Act IV Restaurant and Lounge, where a free buffet breakfast is served. *333 Fulton St., between Franklin and Gough Sts., Hayes Valley, 94102, 415/863–8400 or 800/325–2708; 800/423–9610 in CA; fax 415/861–0821. 48 rooms. Restaurant, kitchenettes, room service, piano bar, laundry service and dry cleaning, concierge, valet parking. No pets. AE, DC, MC, V.*

4 *e-6*

INN AT UNION SQUARE

With its tiny lobby, where trompe l'oeil bookshelves are painted on the walls, this inn is a more personal alternative to the neighborhood's larger hotels. Comfortable rooms with sumptuous goose-down pillows and canopied beds promote indolence. Guests like to lounge in front of the fireplaces found in each floor's tiny sitting area, and with good reason: By the time the staff clears away the afternoon tea and pastries, they're already setting out complimentary evening wine and hors d'oeuvres. Continental breakfast is also included. *440 Post St., between Powell and Mason Sts., Union Square, 94102, 415/397–3510 or 800/288–4346, fax 415/989–0529. 30 rooms. Laundry service, parking (fee). No pets. AE, DC, MC, V.*

4 *a-5*

JACKSON COURT

Housed in a three-story 19th-century brownstone, the Jackson Court combines antique and contemporary furnishings in one of the city's more elegant B&Bs. All rooms have have fresh flowers; a standout is the Garden Court room, with handcrafted wood paneling and a picture window overlooking the garden patio. Continental breakfast is served in the sunny little kitchen. *2198 Jackson St., at Buchanan St., Pacific Heights, 94115, 415/929–7670. 10 rooms. No pets. AE, MC, V.*

4 *e-6*

KING GEORGE HOTEL

Built in 1914 for the Panama Pacific Exposition, The King George has a reputation among its loyal European guests for warm hospitality. The small, classic English–style rooms have walnut furniture and a muted rose color scheme. A proper English high tea is served in the hotel's Bread & Honey Tea Room. *334 Mason St., between Geary and O'Farrell Sts., Union Square, 94102, 415/781–5050 or 800/288–6005, fax 415/391–6976. 143 rooms. Room service, laundry service, meeting rooms, parking (fee). No pets. AE, D, DC, MC, V.*

4 *a-5*

THE MANSIONS

Housed in a twin-turreted 1887 Queen Anne, The Mansions blends elegance—witness the sitting rooms with Victorian antiques and the tiny, overgrown flower garden—and eccentricity—there's a pig museum full of the owner's "porkabilia." The cost of a comfortable room includes breakfast and a campy magic show featuring the resident ghost, Claudia. You can eat dinner in a dining room of stunning stained glass, where desserts come with a dusting of 24-karat gold. *2220 Sacramento St., at Laguna St., Pacific Heights, 94115, 415/929–9444 or 800/826–9398, fax 415/567–9391. 21 rooms. Breakfast room, dining room, billiards, laundry service, parking (fee). No pets. AE, D, DC, MC, V.*

4 *d-5*

NOB HILL INN

Guests regularly return to the Nob Hill Inn for its simple, stately style and surprisingly reasonable prices. The elegant 1907 Edwardian has smallish rooms, but each has attractive, mostly 19th-century furnishings. Continental breakfast and afternoon tea service give guests a chance to mingle in the hotel's own wine cellar. *1000 Pine St., at Taylor St., Nob Hill, 94109, 415/673–6080, fax 415/673–6098. 21 rooms. No pets. AE, MC, V.*

4 *b-6*

THE QUEEN ANNE

This four-story Victorian is one of the city's beautiful Painted Ladies. In the spacious lobby, guests gather in front of the fire to drink sherry or eat home-baked goods for breakfast. Rooms come in all shapes and sizes: There's a tiny top floor room with slanted ceilings, a two-bedroom town house with private deck, and everything in between. Most have English antiques, and some have fireplaces. *1590 Sutter St., at Octavia St., Japantown, 94109, 415/441–2828 or 800/227–3970, fax 415/775–5212. 48 rooms. Laundry service, meeting room, parking (fee). No pets. AE, D, DC, MC, V.*

4 *a-6*

RADISSON MIYAKO HOTEL

East meets West at this pagoda-style hotel near the Japantown complex, where guests may choose a Western-style room or a Japanese-style room with tatami mats, futon beds, and deep tubs. Some guest rooms are in the tower building; others are in the garden wing, which has traditional seasonal gardens. The hotel's award-winning Yoyo Bistro specializes in a Franco-Japanese version of Spanish tapas. *1625 Post St., at Laguna St., Japantown, 94115, 415/922–3200 or 800/533–4567, fax 415/921–0417. 218 rooms. Restaurant, bar, in-room modem lines, room service, exercise room, laundry service and dry cleaning, business services, meeting rooms, parking (fee). No pets. AE, D, DC, MC, V.*

4 *d-6*

SAVOY HOTEL

Visitors interested in staying near Union Square (about 4 blocks away), but not interested in spending $250 a night, will appreciate this good-value European-style hotel. The French country–style rooms are simple but unusually comfortable, with featherbeds and down pillows. The attached restaurant, Brasserie Savoy, is well regarded for its seafood and basic brasserie fare. *580 Geary St., at Jones St., Union Square, 94102, 415/441–2700 or 800/227–4223, fax 415/441–2700. 83 rooms. Restaurant, minibars, room service, laundry service, concierge, meeting room, parking (fee). No pets. AE, D, DC, MC, V.*

4 *e-5*

SIR FRANCIS DRAKE

Beefeater-costumed doormen welcome you into the regal lobby of this 1928 landmark, with wrought-iron balustrades, chandeliers, and Italian marble. The haphazarly designed guest rooms don't quite manage the same opulence. On the top floor, Harry Denton's Starlight Room is one of the city's plushest skyline bars, and the hotel's affordable restaurant, Scala's Bistro, serves excellent Italian food in its dramatic, bilevel dining room. *450 Powell St., between Post and Sutter Sts., Union Square, 94102, 415/392–7755 or 800/227–5480, fax 415/395–8599. 417 rooms. Restaurant, café, in-room modem lines, minibars, exercise room, nightclub, laundry service and dry cleaning, concierge, business services, meeting rooms, parking (fee). No pets. AE, D, DC, MC, V.*

4 *d-2*

TUSCAN INN

The plain exterior of the inn gives little indication of the charm of the small, Italian-influenced guest rooms, which are much more inviting than those found at many of the neighboring chain hotels. Room service is provided by Café Pescatore, the Italian seafood restaurant off the lobby. Morning coffee, tea, and biscotti are complimentary, and wine is served in the early evening. *425 N. Point St., at Mason St., Fisherman's Wharf, 94133, 415/561–1100 or 800/648–4626, fax 415/561–1199. 220 rooms. Restaurant, room service, meeting rooms. AE, D, DC, MC, V.*

5 *h-4*

UNION STREET INN

A retired schoolteacher transformed this ivy-draped Edwardian 1902 home into a delightful B&B. Though some of the rooms in the main house share a bath, the very private Carriage House, separated from the main house by an overgrown garden, has its own whirlpool tub. Other thoughtful touches such as fruit baskets and fresh flowers make this a great choice for honeymooners and other romantics. An elaborate complimentary breakfast is served to guests in the parlor, in the garden, or in their rooms. *2229 Union St., between Fillmore and Steiner Sts., Cow Hollow, 94123, 415/346–0424, fax 415/922–8046. 6 rooms. Breakfast room, parking (fee). No pets. AE, MC, V.*

4 *e-3*

WASHINGTON SQUARE INN

This little charmer in the heart of North Beach in perfect for those who want to try out the many Italian restaurants and cafés in this convivial neighborhood. Rooms, though small, are tastefully decorated with antiques. Continental breakfast and afternoon tea are complimentary. *1660 Stockton St., at Filbert St., North Beach, 94133, 415/981–4220 or 800/388–0220, fax 415/397–7242. 15 rooms. Breakfast room, parking (fee). No pets. AE, MC, V.*

4 *d-5*

WHITE SWAN INN

Each of the good-size rooms in this wonderfully warm and inviting inn has a fireplace, private bath, refrigerator, and reproduction Edwardian furniture. Home-baked snacks and afternoon tea are served in the lounge, where comfortable chairs and sofas invite lingering. A library with book-lined walls and a crackling fire is the heartbeat of the hotel. *845 Bush St., at Taylor St., Union Square, 94108, 415/775–1755 or 800/999–9570, fax 415/775–5717. 26 rooms. Breakfast room, library, laundry service, parking (fee). No pets. AE, DC, MC, V.*

4 *d-6*

YORK HOTEL

Hitchcock fans may recognize the exterior of this reasonably priced hotel—it's the building where Kim Novak as Judy Barton stayed in *Vertigo.* Its other claim to fame is the popular cabaret on the premises, The Plush Room—a favorite among the gay travelers and Europeans who frequent the hotel. Inside, moderate-size rooms are a tasteful mix of Mediterranean styles. Although this is not the worst part of the Tenderloin, walking around the surrounding blocks at night is discouraged. *940 Sutter St., at Leavenworth St., Tenderloin, 94109,*

415/885–6800 or 800/808–9675, fax 415/885–2115. 96 rooms. Bar, exercise room, nightclub, laundry service, concierge, parking (fee). AE, D, DC, MC, V.

MODERATELY PRICED LODGINGS

4 *c-7*

THE ABIGAIL HOTEL

Built in 1926, this relatively unknown charmer has an eclectic mix of faux-stone walls, a faux-marble front desk, and an old-fashioned telephone booth in the lobby. Rooms have English lithographs, down comforters, and antiques. The popular Millennium Restaurant, right off the lobby, serves food so delicious it's hard to believe it's vegan (made without meat or dairy). *246 McAllister St., between Larkin and Hyde Sts., Civic Center, 94102, 415/861–9728 or 800/243–6510, fax 415/861–5848. 61 rooms. Restaurant, laundry service. AE, D, DC, MC, V.*

2 *e-3*

ALAMO SQUARE INN

Three buildings encircle a flower-filled patio at this B&B on picturesque Alamo Square. Two of the buildings date from the late 19th century, but rooms have a decidedly modern style. Excellent breakfasts and afternoon refreshments tempt guests to linger. *719 Scott St., at Fulton St., Western Addition, 94117, 415/922–2055 or 800/345–9888, fax 415/931–1304. 13 rooms. Free parking. No pets. AE, DC, MC, V.*

4 *d-6*

THE ANDREWS HOTEL

Two blocks west of Union Square, this Queen Anne–style abode began its life as the Sultan Turkish Baths in 1905. Pastel hues, down comforters, lace curtains, and fresh flowers make up for the smallness of the rooms, which have equally tiny bathrooms (many have showers but no tub). A buffet-style Continental breakfast is served each morning, and there's complimentary wine in the hotel restaurant in the evenings. *624 Post St., at Jones St., Union Square, 94109, 415/563–6877 or 800/926–3739, fax 415/928–6919. 48 rooms. Restaurant, concierge, parking (fee). AE, DC, MC, V.*

4 *a-8*

AUBERGE DES ARTISTES

This elegant 1901 Victorian on a shady stretch of Fillmore Street is not in the city's best neighborhood, but it is just a few blocks from the attractive Alamo Square park, and during the day it's perfectly safe. Enjoy the sunny garden and the hotel's extensive collection of art books, or just curl up by the fireplace in one of the luxurious doubles. One room has a whirlpool tub. *829 Fillmore St., at Grove St., Western Addition, 94117, 415/776–2530 or 415/775–7334, fax 415/441–8242. 5 rooms. Free parking. No pets. AE, D, MC, V.*

4 *a-4*

BED AND BREAKFAST INN

Hidden in an alleyway off the trendiest part of Union Street is this ivy-covered Victorian, which opened in 1976 as San Francisco's first B&B. Victorian-style rooms are full of antiques, plants, and floral paintings. Though the rooms with shared bath are quite small, the two apartments have ample space; the large Garden Suite, with a delightful country kitchen and whirlpool bath, easily accommodates four. *4 Charlton Ct., off Union St. between Buchanan and Laguna Sts., Cow Hollow, 94123, 415/921–9784. 6 rooms, 1 with bath, 2 apartments. Breakfast room, parking (fee). No credit cards.*

4 *d-6*

BRADY ACRES

Near the Theater District, this place is fully equipped: Each room has a microwave, toaster, coffee maker, and mini-refrigerator, plus answering machine, TV, radio–cassette player, and VCR. And don't forget the free coffee and tea. At this rate you would never need to leave your room—though it's a little small for all-day lounging. Service is very friendly. *649 Jones St., between Post and Geary Sts., Union Square, 94102, 415/929–8033 or 800/627–2396, fax 415/441–8033. 25 rooms. Coin laundry, kitchenettes, in-room safes. Parking (fee). No pets. MC, V.*

4 *d-5*

COMMODORE INTERNATIONAL

Billing itself as an "urban adventure," the Commodore provides a giddy alternative to its more stately neighbors: Neo Deco chairs in the lobby strike an outlandish note, and the hotel's Red Room is a startlingly scarlet nightclub filled with well-dressed hipsters. In the fairly large rooms, all painted in soft yellows and golds, framed photographs of San Francisco landmarks add character. *825 Sutter St., at Taylor St., Union Square, 94109, 415/923–6800 or 800/338–6848, fax 415/923–6804. 113 rooms. Restaurant, nightclub, laundry service and dry cleaning, parking (fee). AE, D, MC, V.*

4 *e-5*

CORNELL

This small, French country–style hotel is a bargain, especially considering its convenient location a few blocks above Union Square and the Theater District. Reproduction French paintings hang in the plain but comfortable rooms. The owners also operate a small restaurant in the atmospheric cellar with medieval accoutrements on the walls. *715 Bush St., between Powell and Mason Sts., Union Square, 94108, 415/421–3154 or 800/232–9698, fax 415/399–1442. 58 rooms, 48 with bath. Restaurant, in-room safes, parking (fee). No pets. AE, D, DC, MC, V.*

7 *h-3*

DOLORES PARK INN

On a sedate street not far from Dolores Park, near the border of the Mission District and the Castro, this 1874 Italianate Victorian is consistently rated one of the city's best B&Bs. Rooms vary from quite small to practically palatial; all are comfortable and attractive, with a smattering of antiques. Service is excellent, and breakfast and evening wine are complimentary. *3641 17th St., at Dolores St., Mission District, 94114, 415/621–0482 or 415/861–9335. 4 rooms. Breakfast room. No pets. No credit cards.*

4 *b-5*

HOLIDAY LODGE AND GARDEN HOTEL

Rooms either overlook or open onto the nicely landscaped grounds and heated swimming pool at this hotel within walking distance of Union Street's shopping and restaurants. Though it looks like any other motel from the exterior, the ultra-clean rooms with beige wood paneling and floral bedspreads are a good value. *1901 Van Ness Ave., at Washington St., Pacific Heights, 94109, 415/776–4469 or 800/367–8504, fax 415/474–7046. 77 rooms. Kitchenettes, room service, laundry service, meeting rooms, free parking. AE, D, DC, MC, V.*

4 *d-6*

HOTEL DAVID

Though the rooms are somewhat bland, this hotel is ideally located in the middle of the Theater District, a few blocks from Union Square. It's attached to Davids's Delicatessen, San Francisco's most famous New York–style noshery, where patrons have been coming for knishes for more than 40 years. Breakfast is included in the room rates, as is a 15% discount on lunch and dinner at the deli. The hotel provides free pick-up from San Francisco International Airport for guests who stay two nights or more. *480 Geary St., at Taylor St., Union Square, 94102, 415/771–1600 or 800/524–1888, fax 415/931–5442. 54 rooms. Restaurant, parking (fee). No pets. AE, D, MC, V.*

7 *f-3*

INN ON CASTRO

Pop art brings a cheery look to this beautiful B&B in an 1896 Edwardian. Complimentary brandy, served around the fireplace when weather warrants, and an excellent full breakfast give guests the chance to socialize. Its location in the busiest part of the Castro insures a largely gay and lesbian clientele. *321 Castro St., at Market St., The Castro, 415/861–0321. 8 rooms, 7 with bath. No pets. MC, V.*

8 *b-4*

INN SAN FRANCISCO

On the outskirts of the city's lively Mission District, this B&B is housed in a strikingly pink 1872 Italianate Victorian. Antiques, featherbeds, and a hot tub out back make it a particularly inviting spot for romantics. Fresh flowers and gourmet chocolates in each room are a welcoming touch, as are the complimentary breakfast and tea and sherry service. *943 South Van Ness Ave., between 20th and 21st Sts., Mission District, 94110, 415/641–0188 or 800/359–0913, fax 415/641–1701. 21 rooms, 19 with bath. Breakfast room. Parking (fee). AE, D, DC, MC, V.*

4 *e-6*

THE MAXWELL

Formerly The Raphael, The Maxwell was completely refurbished in 1997 and is now a stylish hotel just a few blocks from Union Square. Behind the dramatic black and red curtains, the Victorian-style lobby welcomes you with a green velvet sofa and boldly patterned chairs; rooms have a clubby, art-deco feel. Next door is the new Gracie's Restaurant, where live jazz bands play on weekends. *386 Geary St., at Mason St., Union Square, 94102, 415/986–2000 or 888/734–6299, fax 415/397–2447. 153 rooms. Restaurant, bar, in-room modem lines, room service, laundry service, concierge, parking (fee). No pets. AE, D, DC, MC, V.*

4 *d-5*

PETITE AUBERGE

The dozens of teddy bears in the reception area may seem a bit precious, but the rooms in this re-creation of a French country inn never stray past the mark. Rooms are small, but each has a teddy bear, bright flowered wallpaper, an old-fashioned writing desk, and an armoire; larger rooms have wingback chairs in front of a gas fireplace. A copious homemade breakfast buffet invites you to linger in the lounge—or in bed. *863 Bush St., at Taylor St., Union Square, 94108, 415/928–6000 or 800/365–3004, fax 415/775–5717. 26 rooms. Breakfast room, parking (fee). No pets. AE, DC, MC, V.*

4 *c-7*

PHOENIX HOTEL

This lively hotel is a kitschy tropical paradise on the edge of the Tenderloin; its rooms open onto a courtyard pool with a mural by Francis Forlenza on its bottom. Rooms are simple, with bamboo furniture, tropical-print bedspreads, and original art by local artists. Although its location in the seedy Tenderloin District tends to scare off visitors, adventurous travelers come here hoping to spot one of the hotel's famed rock-star celebrity guests. *601 Eddy St., at Larkin St., The Tenderloin, 94109, 415/776–1380 or 800/248–9466, fax 415/885–3109. 44 rooms. Restaurant, bar, room service, pool, massage, nightclub, laundry service, free parking. AE, D, DC, MC, V.*

7 *d-1*

THE RED VICTORIAN

An immensely popular Haight Street landmark originally built as a resort hotel in 1904, the Red Vic evokes San Francisco of the '60s: Request the Summer of Love Room, decked out with a tie-dyed canopy and '60s concert posters. Rooms are more quirky than classy, but all are clean, and the staff takes good care of the guests. *1665 Haight St., between Belvedere and Cole Sts., The Haight, 94117, 415/864–1978, fax*

415/863–3293. 18 rooms, 4 with bath. No pets. AE, DC, MC, V.

7 d-2

STANYAN PARK HOTEL

This three-story hotel built in 1905 is a welcome respite from the Haight's usual hippie hoopla; it's also just across from Golden Gate Park. Americana touches such as quilts give the Victorian–style rooms a homey mood; many also have fireplaces. The large suites, with two bedrooms and full kitchens, are perfect for families. *750 Stanyan St., between Waller and Beulah Sts., The*

LOUNGING IN STYLE

In this city of high real-estate properties and tiny hotel rooms, an inviting hotel lobby can be a real boon for visitors who want to meet friends before dinner. The following hotels have some of the city's most elaborate lobbies.

The Archbishop's Mansion (Expensive)
Wildly ornate antiques and chandeliers.

The Fairmont (Expensive)
A soaring vaulted ceiling and a grand staircase.

Hotel Monaco (Very Expensive)
A fireplace climbs almost two stories toward the domed ceiling.

Hotel Rex (Expensive)
Antiquarian books and a clubby, 1920s mood.

Hotel Triton (Expensive)
Brightly colored velvet couches and three-legged furniture.

Hyatt Regency (Very Expensive)
A 17-story garden atrium, with full-size trees and a running stream.

Pan Pacific Hotel (Very Expensive)
A 21-story atrium with an elegant bronze fountain.

Renaissance Stanford Court (Very Expensive)
A stained-glass dome and dramatic paintings.

Sheraton Palace Hotel (Very Expensive)
A stained-glass ceiling, towering Ionic columns, and crystal chandeliers.

Haight, 94117, 415/751–1000, fax 415/668–5454. 36 rooms. Dining room, parking (fee). No pets. AE, D, DC, MC, V.

4 d-2

TRAVELODGE HOTEL AT FISHERMAN'S WHARF

Reasonable rates and a bayfront location at Fisherman's Wharf are the drawing cards here. The higher-priced rooms on the upper floors overlook a courtyard and pool and have balconies with unobstructed views of Alcatraz. Rooms are simple and bright, with blond-wood furniture and rose-color drapes and bedspreads. *250 Beach St., at Powell St., Fisherman's Wharf, 94133, 415/392–6700 or 800/578–7878, fax 415/986–7853. 250 rooms. 3 restaurants, pool, free parking. No pets. AE, D, DC, MC, V.*

5 g-8

VICTORIAN INN ON THE PARK

This fancifully ornamented 1897 Queen Anne Victorian is one of the more elegant B&Bs in the city. Pass through the grand entrance with oak parquet floors, into the formal parlor (where wine is served each evening), and you'll think you've gone back in time. Guest rooms have Eastlake antiques and distinctive wall treatments. Though the location overlooking Golden Gate Park is scenic, it can be dangerous at night, as a very large homeless population lives nearby at the base of the park's panhandle. *301 Lyon St., at Fell St., Western Addition, 94117, 415/931–1830 or 800/435–1967, fax 415/931–1830. 12 rooms. Meeting room, parking (fee). No pets. AE, D, DC, MC, V.*

7 h-2

WILLOWS

Willow furnishings give the name to this quiet B&B where antiques and floral fabrics set the soothing tone. Rooms have wash basins and kimonos for guest use (showers and toilets are down the hall). Sherry and chocolates at turndown ensure that you'll end your day nicely. The location at the edge of the Castro means its extremely popular with gay men and, to a lesser extent, lesbians. *710 14th St., at Market St., The Castro, 94114, 415/431–4770, fax 415/431–5295. 11 rooms, all with shared bath. Parking (fee). No pets. AE, D, MC, V.*

BUDGET ACCOMMODATIONS

7 g-2, d-6
ADELAIDE INN

The bedspreads at this quiet retreat may not match the drapes or carpets, but visitors are nevertheless attracted to the clean rooms and remarkably reasonable rates. Tucked away in an alley just minutes from Union Square, the funky European-style pension hosts many guests from Germany, France, and Italy, some of whom congregate in the common area to do their own cooking. *5 Isadora Duncan Ct., at Taylor St. between Geary and Post Sts., Union Square, 94102, 415/441–2474 or 415/441–2261, fax 415/441–0161. 18 rooms, none with bath. Breakfast room, parking (fee). No pets. AE, MC, V.*

4 d-7
AIDA HOTEL

The low-grade motel decor is by no means impressive, but the rooms are clean, large, and, on the top floor, quite sunny. Guests are attracted by the low prices and the central (if not terribly scenic) location near the Civic Center BART station, not too far from downtown or the clubs south of Market. It's a good choice for serious budget travelers who forgot to reserve in advance, as rooms are often available at the last minute. *1087 Market St., at 7th St., Civic Center, 94102, 415/863–4141 or 800/863–2432, fax 415/863–5151. 174 rooms, 100 with bath. No pets. AE, D, MC, V.*

7 c-2
BOCK'S BED AND BREAKFAST

If peace and quiet are more important to you than a central location, consider this B&B in Parnassus Heights, near Golden Gate Park just a few blocks north of Haight Street. The 1906 Edwardian is simple but comfortable, with redwood paneling and hardwood floors. *1448 Willard St., at Parnassus Ave., The Haight, 94117, 415/664–6842, fax 415/664–1109. 3 rooms, 1 with bath. No pets. No credit cards.*

4 e-5
GOLDEN GATE HOTEL

One of the least expensive options in the Union Square area (it's 3 blocks away), this small, family-run hotel is a good budget choice. Though the 1913 Edwardian has seen slightly better days, the proprietors nonetheless keep the rooms clean and cheerful with a mix of contemporary and 19th-century furnishings. Complimentary Continental breakfast and afternoon tea and cookies add a homey touch. *775 Bush St., between Mason and Powell Sts., Union Square, 94108, 415/392–3702 or 800/835–1118, fax 415/392–6202. 23 rooms, 14 with bath. Parking (fee). No pets. AE, DC, MC, V.*

4 e-5
GRANT PLAZA

One of the best hotel values in San Francisco and popular with visiting families, Grant Plaza is on one of Chinatown's liveliest streets, near the Financial District. The small rooms each have private bath, TV, and phone; bathrooms are tiny, basic, and immaculate. Rooms on the top floor are newer, slightly brighter, and a bit more expensive; for a quieter stay ask for one in the back. *465 Grant Ave., between Bush and Pine Sts., Chinatown, 94108, 415/434–3883 or 800/472–6899, fax 415/434–3886. 72 rooms. Laundry service, parking (fee). No pets. AE, MC, V.*

4 a-3
MARINA INN

Five blocks from the Marina, this place feels like a B&B but is priced like a motel. (It's especially reasonable between November and March.) English country–style rooms are sparsely appointed but have queen-size two-poster beds. Complimentary Continental breakfast and afternoon sherry are served in the sitting room. *3110 Octavia St., at Lombard St., The Marina, 94123, 415/928–1000 or 800/274–1420, fax 415/928–5909. 40 rooms. Barbershop, beauty salon. No pets. AE, MC, V.*

5 g-3
MARINA MOTEL

This quiet, family-owned motel is one of the best of the many hotels along congested Lombard Street. Most rooms have fully-equipped kitchens, and free garage parking makes it an even better deal. The courtyard garden is bright with pink bougainvillea and colorful murals by local artists. *2576 Lombard St., at Divisadero St., The Marina, 94129, 415/921–9406 or 800/346–6118, fax 415/921–0364. 38 rooms. Kitchenettes, free parking. No pets. MC, V.*

7 *f-1*

METRO HOTEL

Though the large, clean, high-ceilinged rooms are some of the nicest for the money in the city, many visitors never make their way to the Metro Hotel, due to its location in the somewhat sketchy Western Addition. (It does have a sizable following among the European crowd, however.) A café downstairs serves breakfast and lunch on a sunny outdoor patio. *319 Divisadero St., between Oak and Page Sts., Western Addition, 94117, 415/861–5364, fax 415/863–1970. 24 rooms. Café. No pets. AE, D, DC, MC, V.*

4 *c-6*

NOB HILL PENSIONE

This European-style inn, built in 1907, has spacious, sunny rooms, most with shared baths. The staff is unfailingly friendly, and amenities include phones with voice mail, satellite TV, and basic business services. Despite the name, it's not on Nob Hill, but rather in a slightly shady neighborhood in the Tenderloin. Still, you won't find many better deals in the city. *835 Hyde St., at Sutter St., The Tenderloin, 94102, 415/885–2987, fax 415/921–1648. 50 rooms, 8 with bath. Restaurant, bar, in-room safes, coin laundry, parking (fee). No pets. AE, D, MC, V.*

4 *e-5*

SAN FRANCISCO RESIDENCE CLUB

A little-known bargain at the top of Nob Hill, the San Francisco Residence club not only has unusually inexpensive rooms, but also throws in breakfast and dinner in the hotel's dining room every day except Sunday. Everything about this place is cheery, from the staff to the sunny garden. Many of the plain but spacious, Victorian-style rooms have views of the bay. Long-term visitors take advantage of weekly rates. *851 California St., at Powell St., Nob Hill, 94108, 415/421–2220, fax 415/421–2335. 84 rooms, 6 with bath. Dining room, piano, coin laundry. No pets. No credit cards.*

4 *d-2*

SAN REMO

A three-story, blue-and-white Italianate Victorian between Fisherman's Wharf and North Beach, the San Remo has smallish, reasonably priced rooms and a slightly tatty elegance reminiscent of a European hotel. Guests share the scrupulously clean bathrooms. Honeymooners often request the "apartment," which has a 360-degree view of the city and a private bath. *2237 Mason St., between Francisco and Chestnut Sts., North Beach, 94133, 415/776–8688 or 800/352–7366, fax 415/776–2811. 62 rooms. Restaurant, parking (fee). No pets. AE, D, DC, MC, V.*

4 *e-6*

STRATFORD INN

Location is what it's all about at this budget find halfway between Union Square and the bustling corner of Powell and Market streets. The rooms are Spartan and a bit dark, but the prices can't be beat for such a well-located hotel, especially if you opt for a room with shared bath. Guests have free access to an indoor pool and fitness center at the nearby Sheehan Hotel. *242 Powell St., between O'Farrell and Geary Sts., Union Square, 94102, 415/397–7080 or 888/504–6835, fax 415/397–7087. 98 rooms, 70 with bath. Coin laundry. No pets. MC, V.*

4 *a-3*

TOWN HOUSE MOTEL

What this recently renovated, family-oriented motel lacks in luxury and ambience, it makes up for in value: The simple rooms have a southwestern pastel color scheme and plenty of lacquered wood. Continental breakfast is complimentary. *1650 Lombard St., between Gough and Octavia Sts., The Marina, 94123, 415/885–5163 or 800/255–1516, fax 415/771–9889. 24 rooms. Airport transport, free parking. AE, D, DC, MC, V.*

7 *g-2*

24 HENRY

Rooms are colorful and cozy at this friendly, gay- and lesbian-oriented hotel. The apartment suite with a full kitchen is an especially good deal for those who want to do their own cooking. Complimentary breakfast is served in the Victorian-style parlor. *24 Henry St., between Noe and Sanchez Sts., Castro, 94114, 415/864–5686 or 800/900–5686, fax 415/864–0406. 5 rooms, 1 with bath. No pets. AE, MC, V.*

HOSTELS

4 e-6

AYH HOSTEL AT UNION SQUARE

A crowd of international students fills this huge hostel, perhaps San Francisco's best-equipped—and certainly its best located, for those who want to be near Union Square. Most rooms have two or three bunk beds; a few suites are reserved for families. Facilities include a TV room, smoking room, library, and kitchen. *312 Mason St., between O'Farrell and Geary Sts., Union Square, 94102, 415/788–5604 or 800/909–4776, ext. 02. 230 beds. No pets. MC, V.*

4 d-8

EUROPEAN GUEST HOUSE

Its South of Market location, near many of the city's best nightspots, is a draw for many wide-eyed club kids amazed at nightlife in the big city. The common rooms, including a kitchen and sun deck, are comfortable if not always immaculately maintained. Rooms have two or four beds. *761 Minna St., near Mission St. between 8th and 9th Sts., South of Market, 94103, 415/861–6634, fax 415/621–4428. 24 beds. Coin laundry. No pets. AE, MC, V.*

4 b-2

FORT MASON INTERNATIONAL HOSTEL

If it weren't for its spectacular views of the Golden Gate Bridge, you might forget you're in San Francisco when you stay at this Fort Mason hostel, smack in the middle of an expanse of bayfront warehouses and lawns that feels removed from the rest of the city. Make reservations in advance or show up early on the day you want to stay. Facilities include a pool table, kitchen, coin-op washers, and that rare commodity—free parking. *Fort Mason, Bldg. 240, Box A, Marina Blvd. at Laguna St., The Marina, 94123, 415/771–7277 or 800/444–6111, fax 415/771–1468. 160 beds. Café, coin laundry, free parking. No pets. MC, V.*

4 d-6

GLOBETROTTER'S INN

This hostel's small size makes it more personable than many of the others. The building is a bit old and creaky but generally well maintained. Common areas include a fully equipped kitchen, TV room, and smoking rooms. Guest rooms have one to four beds. *225 Ellis St., between Mason and Taylor Sts., Union Square, 94102, 415/346–5786. 48 beds. Coin laundry. No pets. No credit cards.*

4 e-4

GREEN TORTOISE GUEST HOUSE

The only hostel at the edge of North Beach, Green Tortoise is so popular with European backpackers it's often tough to get a bed, so call ahead. Perks include unusually clean rooms, a nice kitchen, a friendly staff, and, best of all,

---

HOTELS WITH GREAT RESTAURANTS

Each of the following hotels has (or is attached to) a restaurant that merits a visit in its own right.

The Abigail Hotel (Moderately Priced)
Innovative vegan concoctions at the Millennium.

Campton Place (Very Expensive)
The pre-eminent place for power breakfasts.

The Clift (Very Expensive)
Close that deal in the sedate French Room.

Hotel David (Moderately Priced)
Guests get a discount at the 40-year-old David's Deli downstairs.

Hotel Vintage Court (Expensive)
Affiliated with Masa's, the city's most acclaimed French restaurant.

Inn at the Opera (Expensive)
The Act IV Restaurant is sumptuously romantic.

Mandarin Oriental (Very Expensive)
Silks restaurant has innovative California–Asian cuisine.

Pan Pacific Hotel (Very Expensive)
California cuisine at its best.

Prescott Hotel (Very Expensive)
Attached to Postrio, the famed Wolfgang Puck restaurant.

Ritz-Carlton, San Francisco (Very Expensive)
Consistent thumbs up for the Dining Room.

Sheraton Palace Hotel (Very Expensive)
Kyo-ya, for top-notch Japanese.

no curfew or lockout. Singles and doubles are also available, and rates include breakfast. *494 Broadway, between Montgomery and Kearny Sts., North Beach, 94113, 415/834–1000, fax 415/956–4900. 110 beds. Coin laundry. No pets. No credit cards.*

4 e-8

INTERCLUB GLOBE HOSTEL

Though this hostel is intended for international travelers, U.S. residents can get in by flashing a passport and a smile. A relaxed atmosphere, a South of Market location, and the international clientele make it a lively place to socialize, especially on the pleasant sun deck. Rooms have four or five beds and an adjoining bath. *10 Hallam St., near Folsom St. btw 7th and 8th Sts., South of Market, 94103, 415/431–0540, fax 415/431–3286. 120 beds. Coin laundry. No pets. No credit cards.*

1 b-2

MARIN HEADLANDS HOSTEL

If you have a car and don't mind a bit of a commute, this hostel in the Marin Headlands is ideal for a mellow, relaxing stay. In addition to endless hiking trails and breathtaking scenery just steps outside the door, guests enjoy a communal kitchen, laundry room, tennis court, Ping-Pong table, pool table, and a common room with a fireplace. Private rooms are often available. *Ft. Barry, Bldg. 941, just up hill from visitor center, Sausalito, 94965, 415/331–2777. 103 beds. Coin laundry, free parking. No pets. D, MC, V.*

4 e-5

PACIFIC TRADEWINDS

The smallest of San Francisco's hostels, this homey spot in Chinatown is near some of the city's best restaurants, budget and otherwise. Guests have access to a kitchen and common room. Ask for a key (deposit required) if you want to stay out past midnight. *680 Sacramento St., at Kearny St., Chinatown, 415/433–7970, fax 415/291–8801, 94111. 32 beds. Laundry service. No pets. MC, V.*

8 b-4

SAN FRANCISCO INTERNATIONAL GUEST HOUSE

On the outskirts of the Mission District, this hostel has an unusual five-day minimum stay requirement: This and its

location in one of the city's more popular nightlife districts ensure a youngish, bar-hopping crowd. Common areas include two kitchens, a TV room, and a reading room. International travelers are preferred, but U.S. residents can usually get in with a passport. *2976 23rd St., at Harrison St., Mission District, 94110, 415/641–1411. 28 beds. No pets.*

HOTELS NEAR THE AIRPORT

very expensive lodgings

1 c-8

THE CLARION

This busy hotel, a mile south of San Francisco International Airport, is a favorite of business travelers who pop into town for quick meetings. In the lovely garden area, wrought-iron benches, a heated pool, and a whirlpool tub are set among pine trees. The hotel is locally famous for the quirky messages posted on the sign outside—a nice pick-me-up for weary commuters passing by. *401 E. Millbrae Ave., off U.S. 101 Millbrae 94030, 650/692–6363 or 800/223–7111, fax 650/697–8735. 440 rooms. 2 restaurants, room service, pool, outdoor hot tub, spa, laundry service, meeting rooms, airport shuttle, free parking. No pets. AE, D, DC, MC, V.*

1 d-8

EMBASSY SUITES SAN FRANCISCO AIRPORT— BURLINGAME

One of the most lavish hotels in the airport area, this one set on the bay has up-close views of planes taking off and landing (though rooms are remarkably quiet). All guest rooms are suites that open onto an atrium and tropical garden; each has a work area, sleeper sofa, wet bar, television, microwave, and refrigerator. *150 Anza Blvd., at Airport Blvd., Burlingame, 94010, 650/342–4600 or 800/362–2779, fax 650/343–8137. 339 suites. Restaurant, bar, room service, indoor pool, sauna, steam room, laundry service and dry cleaning, concierge, business services, aiport shuttle, free parking. No pets. AE, DC, MC, V.*

HOTEL SOFITEL— SAN FRANCISCO BAY

Parisian lampposts and a kiosk covered with French posters bring a bit of Paris to this hotel 7 mi south of the airport.

The French-theme public spaces—the Gigi Brasserie, Baccarat restaurant, and La Terrasse bar—have an open, airy feeling that extends to the rooms. A small sitting area in each room is a welcome perk in this city of tiny hotel rooms, as is the Sandra Caron Institut de Beauté, where spa treatments are available. *223 Twin Dolphin Dr., at Ralston Ave., Redwood City 94065, 650/ 598–9000 or 800/221–4542, fax 650/ 598–0459. 324 rooms. 2 restaurants, bar, lobby lounge, pool, spa, health club, laundry service, concierge, meeting rooms, airport shuttle, free parking. No pets. AE, DC, MC, V.*

1 *c-7*

SAN FRANCISCO AIRPORT HILTON

The only hotel actually on airport property, the Hilton has excellent business facilities. Many rooms overlook the heated Olympic-size pool or the garden courtyard, and some have patios opening onto the pool area. *San Francisco International Airport exit off Hwy. 101, Box 8355, 94128, 650/589–0770 or 800/445– 8667, fax 650/589–4696. 527 rooms. 2 restaurants, lobby lounge, in-room modem lines, minibars, pool, outdoor hot tub, exercise room, laundry service and dry cleaning, business services, meeting rooms, airport shuttle, free parking. No pets. AE, D, DC, MC, V.*

1 *d-8*

SAN FRANCISCO AIRPORT MARRIOTT

Five minutes south of the airport, the Marriott has a recreation area with an indoor pool, sauna, and whirlpool. Good-size guest rooms are outfitted with floral prints. *1800 Old Bayshore Highway, Burlingame, 94010, 650/692– 9100 or 800/228–9290, fax 650/692– 8016. 684 rooms. 2 restaurants, bar, in-room modem lines, room service, exercise room, piano, laundry and dry cleaning, business services, meeting rooms, car rental, airport shuttle, free parking. No pets. AE, DC, D, MC, V.*

1 *d-7*

THE WESTIN HOTEL— SAN FRANCISCO AIRPORT

Though geared toward business travelers, the Westin has an atrium-enclosed swimming pool and bayfront location that make it a fine choice for anyone who wants to be near the airport. The medium-size guest rooms have Asian accents in gold, green, and rose. *1 Old Bayshore Hwy., at Millbrae Ave., Millbrae, 94030, 650/692–3500 or 800/228– 3000, fax 650/872–8111. 390 rooms. Restaurant, coffee shop, lobby lounge, in- room modem lines, minibars, room service, sauna, exercise room, business services, airport shuttle, free parking. No pets. AE, DC, MC, V.*

GAY-POPULAR HOTELS

Gay couples can count on a warm welcome from almost any San Francisco hotel, but the following are particularly popular with gay and lesbian visitors.

The Archbishop's Mansion (Expensive)
Popular for weddings, both gay and straight.

Bella Vista Inn (Very Expensive)
A small luxury inn in the hills above the Castro.

Bock's Bed and Breakfast (Budget)
A quiet inn in a quiet neighborhood, frequented by lesbians.

Hotel Diva (Expensive)
Big among those in the arts.

Hotel Monaco (Very Expensive)
A hip hotel with outré decor.

Hotel Rex (Expensive)
Clubby decor and a warm service.

Hotel Triton (Expensive)
Avant-garde decor and a trendy crowd.

Inn on Castro (Moderately Priced)
On Castro Street.

Phoenix Hotel (Moderately Priced)
Home away from home for celebs and pop icons.

24 Henry (Budget)
Cozy rooms in the Castro.

Willows (Moderately Priced)
A serene hotel with willow furnishings.

York Hotel (Expensive)
There's a cabaret on the premises.

moderately priced lodgings

1 c-6

LA QUINTA MOTOR INN

Right off Highway 101, this is a good budget choice for travelers who just staggered off a late flight. Recently renovated rooms with floral decor are well-insulated from the freeway noise. Continental breakfast is complimentary. *20 Airport Blvd., off U.S. 101, South San Francisco 94080, 650/583–2223 or 800/531–5900, fax 650/589–6770. 174 rooms. Restaurant, pool, hot tub, exercise room, coin laundry, free parking. No pets. AE, D, DC, MC, V.*

budget accommodations

1 d-8

RED ROOF INN

Rooms at this popular budget hotel are plain but extremely clean, with light-wood furnishings. The pool makes it popular with families. *777 Airport Blvd., at Anza Blvd., Burlingame, 94010, 650/342–7772 or 800/843–7663, fax 650/342–2635. 212 rooms. Restaurant, pool, free parking. No pets. AE, DC, MC, V.*

B&B RESERVATION SERVICES

If you're looking for a more personal (and sometimes significantly cheaper) overnight experience in a more residential neighborhood, try one of the hundreds of bed-and-breakfasts found in San Francisco. Beware, however, that although you often pay less than $100 per night, accommodations, amenities, service, and privacy may fall short of what you get in hotels. Many B&Bs also enforce a two-night minimum, especially on weekends and holidays. Ask your B&B booking agency for details on breakfast and other food service such as afternoon tea service before you book. Some B&Bs provide sumptuous spreads, while others don't even serve breakfast, despite the name.

B&Bs booked through either of the following services may either be hosted (you are the guest in someone's occupied apartment) or unhosted (you have full use of someone's vacated apartment, including kitchen privileges). Needless to say, the latter option is the more expensive. As for hotels, make reservations as far in advance as possible; the best rooms book up quickly, especially in late summer and fall.

Bed and Breakfast California (Box 282910, 94128, 415/696–1690, 800/872–4500, fax 415/696–1699).

Bed and Breakfast San Francisco (Box 420009, 94142, 415/479–1913 or 800/452–8249, fax 415/921–2273).

chapter 8

HELP

resources for residents

educational resources

ACTING SCHOOLS

American Conservatory Theater *30 Grant Ave., 415/834–3200.*

Bay Area Theatresports School of Improvisation *Fort Mason Center, Building B, 415/474–8935.*

Rob Reece Actors Workshop *466 Geary St., 415/928–8929.*

ADULT EDUCATION PROGRAMS

City College of San Francisco *Public Information Office, 50 Phelan Ave. E200, 415/241–2300.*

Extension Center, University of California *1995 University Ave., 510/642–4111. Also: 55 Laguna St., same phone.*

San Francisco State University, College of Extended Learning *425 Market St., 415/904–7700.*

ART SCHOOLS

Academy of Art College *New Montgomery St., 415/274–2222.*

San Francisco Art Institute *800 Chestnut St., 415/771–7020.*

San Francisco School of Art *667 Mission St., 415/543–9300.*

UC Berkeley Extension Art and Design Programs *55 Laguna St., 510/642–4111.*

CHILDREN'S EDUCATION PROGRAMS

St. John's Educational Center Tutoring for children grades four through nine. *415/864–5205.*

San Francisco Public Library's Fisher Children's Center *Larkin and Grove Sts., 415/557–4554.*

San Francisco Public Schools General Information *415/241–6000 (general school district information).*

CPR & FIRST AID CERTIFICATION

American Red Cross Bay Area Chapter *800/520–5433.*

City Aid First Aid and Safety *415/474–2551.*

LANGUAGE SCHOOLS

Aisea Japanese Language Services *110 Sutter St., 415/296–9295.*

Alliance Française *1345 Bush St., 415/775–7755.*

Berlitz Language Centers *180 Montgomery St., 415/986–6464.*

Casa Hispana *110 Gough St., 415/861–1223.*

Goethe Institut *530 Bush St., 415/391–5194.*

MUSIC SCHOOLS

Blue Bear School of American Music *Fort Mason, 415/673–3600.*

San Francisco Conservatory of Music *1201 Ortega St., 415/564–8086.*

resources

AIDS

AIDS/HIV Nightlife Answered from 5 PM until 5 AM. *415/434–AIDS.*

AIDS Legal Referral Panel *415/291–5454.*

Project Open Hand Two meals a day are delivered to those who are ill with AIDS. *415/558–0600.*

San Francisco AIDS Foundation An umbrella organization that can direct people to the appropriate AIDS-related group. *10 United Nations Plaza, 415/487–8000, or 415/863-2437 for hot line.*

San Francisco Department of Public Health, AIDS Health Project Free, anonymous HIV testing. *415/502–8378.*

ALCOHOLISM

Alcoholics Anonymous 415/621–1326.

Haight Ashbury Free Clinic Alcohol Treatment Services 425 Divisadero St., 415/487–5634.

National Council on Alcoholism and Other Drug Addictions (NCADA) Their 24-hour hot line provides information, assessment, and referral. 944 Market St., 3rd Floor, 415/296–9900.

BABYSITTING

Aunt Ann's Agency 731 Market St., 415/974–3530.

Bay Area Child Care 415/991–7474.

Sunshine Sitters Agency 415/342–2224.

CATERING

Beyond Expectations 3613 Sacramento St., 415/567–8696.

MacArthur Park Catering 607 Front St., 415/398–5703.

Work of Art 1226 Folsom St., 415/552–1000.

CHILD CRISIS

Family Service Agency of San Francisco Twenty-four-hour child-abuse prevention hot line. 415/441–5437.

San Francisco Child Abuse Council Education services and referrals to counselors. 415/668–0494.

San Francisco Department of Human Services, Child Protective Services Emergency Hotline 415/558–2650.

COAST GUARD

United States Coast Guard 510/437–3700 (general information) or 415/556-2103 (emergencies only).

CONSUMER PROTECTION

Better Business Bureau Provides information about business reliability and other consumer issues; files consumer complaints. 415/243–9999.

Consumer Credit Counseling Money management counseling for people with credit problems. 415/788–0288.

Consumer Information Center, Department of Consumer Affairs Receives and investigates complaints against businesses. 800/952–5210.

San Francisco District Attorney, Consumer Protection Unit Receives, investigates, and mediates consumer complaints. 415/553–1814.

CRIME VICTIMS

Center for Domestic Violence Prevention Crisis intervention counseling, support groups, legal assistance, and a shelter program. 415/311–8515.

Critical Incident Response Team Emotional support for families of young people who have been killed or injured in violent acts. 415/671–1010.

Victims of Crime Resource Center Legal information and referrals to local organizations. 800/842–8467.

DOCTOR & DENTIST REFERRALS

California State Medical Board Complaints 800/633–2322.

California State Medical Board, Verification of Licenses 916/263–2635.

Davies Medical Center Physician Referral Service 415/565–6333.

1-800-DENTIST 800/336–8478.

Physician Referral Service, CHW West Bay, Saint Francis, St. Mary's, and Seton Medical Centers 800/333–1355.

St. Luke's Hospital Physician Referral Service 415/821–3627.

San Francisco Dental Society Referral Service 415/421–1435.

San Francisco Dentist 415/433–0265.

UCSF and UCSF/Mount Zion Physician Referral Service 415/885–7777.

DRUG ABUSE

Cocaine Anonymous *415/821–6155.*

Haight Ashbury Free Clinic Drug Detox Program *588 Clayton St., 415/487–5632.*

National Council on Alcoholism and Other Drug Addictions (NCADA) *944 Market St., 3rd Floor, 415/296–9900): 24-hour hot line for information, assessment, and referral.*

San Francisco Health Department 24-hour Drug Line and Information *415/362–3400.*

FAMILY PLANNING

Crisis Pregnancy Center of San Francisco *415/753–8000.*

Planned Parenthood of San Francisco *415/441–5454.*

San Francisco General Hospital Family Planning Clinic *415/206–3410.*

San Francisco Health Department Family Planning Information *415/554–9611.*

GAY & LESBIAN CONCERNS

Communities United Against Violence *973 Market St., Suite 500, 415/777–5500, hot line 415/333–HELP.*

Gay, Lesbian, Bisexual, & Transgender Career Center *760 Market St., 415/296–8024.*

Gay/Lesbian Legal Referral Services *415/621–3900.*

Lavender Youth Recreation and Information Center Peer support group for people 23 and under. *127 Collingwood St., 415/703–6150, hot line 415/863–3636 or 800/246–7743.*

HOUSECLEANING HELP

Cinderella's Housekeeping *45 Franklin St., Suite 301, 415/864–8900.*

New Dimensions Housekeeping Agency *415/731–4900.*

Rainbow Home Cleaning *415/565–0383.*

LANDLORD/TENANT INTERVENTION

California Department of Fair Employment and Housing Handles housing discrimination complaints. *800/884–1684.*

Housing Rights Committee of San Francisco A tenant rights counseling and advocacy organization. *115 Jones St., 415/398–6200.*

San Francisco Tenant's Union Tenants' rights counseling services. Members receive phone counseling; nonmembers attend a drop-in clinic. *558 Capp St., 415/282–6622.*

U.S. Department of Housing and Urban Development Housing Discrimination Hot Line Provides information on housing rights and accepts discrimination complaints. *800/669–9777.*

LEGAL SERVICES

American Civil Liberties Union *415/621-2493.*

La Raza Centro Legal Legal information and referrals in both English and Spanish. *474 Valencia St., 415/575–3500.*

Lawyer Referral Service of the Bar Association of San Francisco Provides referrals to attorneys and attorney mediators. *415/764–1616.*

Legal Aid Society of San Francisco Gives legal referrals and information, especially for low-income families. *415/986–7511.*

State Bar of California, Attorney Complaint Hot Line Provides information about common attorney–client problems and accepts complaints against attorneys. *800/843–9053.*

LOST & FOUND

lost animals

Look in the local papers, including the *San Francisco Chronicle, SF Weekly,* and *Bay Guardian,* for notices regarding lost and found animals.

San Francisco Animal Care and Control Center Call to locate your lost pet. *415/554–6364.*

San Francisco Society for the Prevention of Cruelty to Animals Call if you've found a cat with an SPCA tag on it. For all other animals and cats without SPCA tags, call the San Francisco Animal Care and Control Center (*see above*). *415/554-3084.*

transportation

BART *510/464-7090.*

Muni *415/923-6168.*

Oakland Airport *510/577-4095.*

San Francisco Airport *415/876-2261.*

San Jose Airport *408/277-4759.*

MENTAL HEALTH INFORMATION & REFERRAL

Patient Rights Advocacy Program Advocacy services for people receiving mental health care. *415/552-8100.*

San Francisco Department of Public Health, Psychiatric Emergency Services *415/206-8125.*

San Francisco Health Department Mental Health Programs Information and Referral Answered 24 hours. *415/981-4700.*

Therapist Network Gives referrals to mental health care providers. *800/843-7274.*

ON-LINE SERVICES

Activa.Net *415/863-6965.*

Nautica Communications *415/421-4241.*

Slip.Net *415/536-6111.*

PETS

adoptions

Pets Unlimited Cat Adoption Center *2343 Fillmore St., 415/563-6700.*

San Francisco SPCA *2500 16th St., 415/554-3000 (general information) or 415/554-3080 (recorded information about adoptions).*

grooming

The Barking Lot *209A Sanchez St., 415/431-0969.*

Bill's Doggie Bath-O-Mat *3928 Irving St., 415/661-6950): You can do it yourself here; tub, shampoo, towels, and dryer are provided.*

Pets Unlimited *2343 Fillmore St., 415/563-6700.*

Pet Wash *1840 Polk St., 415/928-8788.*

training

Dog Gone Good *415/437-0848.*

Top Quality Obedience School *1427 Clement St., 415/566-4141.*

veterinary hospitals

Irving Street Veterinary Hospital *1434 Irving St., 415/664-0191.*

Pets Unlimited *2343 Fillmore St., 415/563-6700.*

Vet on Wheels *415/333-4673.*

PHARMACIES OPEN 24 HOURS

Walgreens Drugstore *3201 Divisadero St., 415/931-6415. Also: 498 Castro Street, 415/861-6276.*

PHONE COMPANY

repair service

Pacific Bell *800/310-2355 for residence customer service; 800/214-8433 for 24-hour recorded information; 611 for repair calls.*

long-distance access

AT&T *10288.*

MCI *10222.*

Sprint *10333.*

POSTAL SERVICES

Civic Center Post Office *101 Hyde Street, 94142, 800/275-8777.*

U.S. Postal Service Answer Line Twenty-four-hour automated information line for post office hours, postal rates, zip codes, and more. *800/725-2161*

RAPE CRISIS

San Francisco Health Department Rape Treatment Services *415/206–3222.*

San Francisco General Hospital 24-Hour Rape Treatment Center *415/206–3222.*

SF Women Against Rape *415/647–7273.*

SENIOR-CITIZEN SERVICES

Department of Human Services, Elder Abuse Reporting *415/557–5230.*

Friendship Line for the Elderly Answered 24 hours a day. *415/752–3778.*

Gray Panthers of San Francisco Senior citizen advocacy group. *415/552–8800.*

Senior Citizen Information Line Provides referrals to organizations for senior citizens throughout the Bay Area. *415/626–1033.*

SUICIDE PREVENTION

San Francisco Health Department Suicide and Crisis Line *415/781–0500.*

San Francisco Suicide Prevention Hot Line *415/781–0500.*

TELEVISION— CABLE COMPANIES

TCI Cablevision *800/436–1999 to order, 415/863–9600 for repairs.*

UTILITIES

Pacific Gas and Electric Company *800/ 743–5000 (24-hr emergency and customer service) or 800/743–5002 (24-hr information on electric outages).*

Public Utilities Commission, Inquiries and Complaints *415/703–1170.*

ZONING & PLANNING

San Francisco Planning and Zoning Information Planning and zoning information, planning application status. *415/558–6377.*

travel & vacation information

AIRLINES

Air Canada *800/776–3000.*

Air France *800/237–2747.*

Alaska Airlines *800/426–0333.*

American *800/433–7300.*

America West *800/235–9292.*

British Airways *800/247–9297.*

China Airlines *800/227–5118.*

Continental *800/525–0280.*

Delta *800/221–1212.*

Frontier Airlines *800/432–1359.*

Japan Airlines *800/525–3663.*

Mexicana Airlines *800/531–7921.*

Northwest *800/225–2525.*

Southwest *800/435–9792.*

TWA *800/221–2000.*

United *800/241–6522.*

USAirways *800/428–4322.*

AIRPORTS

San Francisco International Airport Major gateway to San Francisco, about ½ hour south of the city off U.S. 101. *415/761–0800.*

Oakland Airport Serviced by several domestic airlines. It's the same distance from San Francisco as SFO (across the bay via I–880 and I–80), though traffic on the Bay Bridge may add to travel time. *415/577–4000.*

San Jose International Airport About an hour north of San Jose, near Santa Clara, sandwiched between I–880 and U.S. 101; allow much more time during commute hours. The bulk of its flights are to domestic destinations, though it does have some international flights. *408/277–4759.*

CAR RENTAL

All of the following car rental companies have offices at the San Francisco and Oakland airports, as well as at least one location near downtown San Francisco.

Alamo 800/327–9633.

Avis 800/331–1212.

Budget 800/527–0700.

Dollar 800/800–4000.

Enterprise 800/325–8007.

Hertz 800/654–3131.

National 800/227–7368.

Thrifty 800/367–2277.

EMBASSIES & CONSULATES

Australia 1 Bush St., Suite 700, 415/362–6160.

Austria 41 Sutter St., 415/951–8911.

Bolivia 870 Market St., 415/495–513

Brazil 300 Montgomery St., Suite 1160, 415/981–8170.

Chile 870 Market Street, Suite 1058, 415/982–7662.

Colombia 595 Market St., Suite 588, 415/495–7195.

Costa Rica 870 Market St., Suite 660, 415/392–8488.

Dominican Republic 870 Market St., Suite 982, 415/982–5144.

Ecuador 455 Market St., 415/957–5921.

Egypt 3001 Pacific Ave., 415/346–9700.

El Salvador 870 Market St., Suite 721, 415/781–7924.

Finland 333 Bush St., 415/772–6649.

France 540 Bush St., 415/397–4330.

Germany 1960 Jackson St., 415/775–1061.

Great Britain 1 Sansome St., 415/981–3030.

Greece 2441 Gough St., 415/775–2102.

Guatemala 870 Market St., Suite 1057, 415/788–5651.

Honduras 870 Market St, Suite 451, 415/392–0076.

Indonesia 1111 Columbus Ave., 415/474–9571.

Ireland 44 Montgomery St., Suite 3830, 415/392–4214.

Israel 456 Montgomery St., 21st floor, 415/398–8885.

Italy 2590 Webster St., 415/931–4924.

Japan 50 Fremont St., 23rd floor, 415/777–3533.

Republic of Korea 3500 Clay St., 415/921–2251.

Luxembourg 1 Sansome St., Suite 830, 415/788–0816.

Malta 2562 San Bruno Ave., 415/468–4321.

Mexico 870 Market St., Suite 528, 415/392–5554.

Monaco 100 Pine St., Suite 2540, 415/749–1663.

Netherlands 1 Maritime Plaza, Suite 1106, 415/981–6454.

Norway 20 California St., 415/986–0766.

Panama 870 Market St., Suite 551, 415/391–4268.

Peru 870 Market St., Suite 579, 415/362–5185.

Philippines 447 Sutter St., 6th Floor, 415/433–6666.

Portugal 3298 Washington St., 415/346–3400.

Russia 2790 Green St., 415/202–9800.

Singapore 1670 Pine St., 2nd Floor, 415/928–8508.

Spain 1405 Sutter St., 415/922–2995.

Sweden 120 Montgomery St., Suite 2175, 415/788–2631.

Switzerland 456 Montgomery St., Suite 1500, 415/788–2272.

Sweden 120 Montgomery St., Suite 2175, 415/788–2631.

Venezuela 455 Market St., Suite 220, 415/512–8340.

INOCULATIONS & VACCINATIONS

Centers for Disease Control's International Travelers' Hotline Provides health warnings and inoculation information for locations around the world. *404/332–4559.*

San Francisco International Airport Traveler's Clinic *International Terminal, ground floor, 415/877–0444.*

UC San Francisco Traveler's Clinic *UCSF Medical Center, 400 Parnassus Ave., 415/476–5787.*

PASSPORT PHOTOS

Fotek *3499 Sacramento St., 415/563–3896.*

Leetone *615 Sansome St., 415/391–9890.*

PASSPORTS

San Francisco Passport Agency First-time applicants must have proof of U.S. citizenship, a valid driver's license (or employee or military ID), and two identical passport photos taken within the last six months. Payment ($65 for new passport, $55 for renewals, $40 for children) may be made with cash (exact change required), personal check, or money order. Passports routinely take three to four weeks to process. *95 Hawthorne St., 5th floor, 415/744–4444.*

TOURIST OFFICES

San Francisco Convention and Visitors Bureau *201 3rd St., Suite 900, 415/974–6900.*

Visitor Information Center *Hallidie Plaza, next to Powell Street BART at Powell and Market Sts., 415/391–2000, or 415/391–2001 for recorded information.*

U.S. CUSTOMS

U.S. Customs Service, San Francisco Port Office *33 New Montgomery St., 415/782–9210.*

VISA INFORMATION & TRAVEL ADVISORIES

American Express Global Assist Provides travel advisory information and emergency doctor and lawyer referrals to American Express cardholders traveling abroad. *800/554–2639, or 301/214–8228 collect outside U.S.*

Department of State's Office of Citizens Overseas Services Provides travel warnings for dangerous destinations, and alerts on current conditions and visa requirements. Helps citizens in distress abroad. *202/647–5225.*

DIRECTORIES

alphabetical listing of resources & topics

restaurants by neighborhood

shops by neighborhood

resources & topics

restaurants by neighborhood

shops by neighborhood

Restaurants

Berkeley
Chez PANISSE 1517 Shattuck 548-5525

CITY NOTES

CITY NOTES

CITY NOTES

Get away from it all

Fodor's Travel Publications has guidebooks to fit the needs of all kinds of travelers from families to adventure seekers, from nature enthusiasts to urban weekenders. With the range of coverage and the quality of information, it is easy to understand why smart travelers go with **Fodor's**.

At bookstores everywhere.
http://fodors.previewtravel.com/